CONSUMERISM AND CONSUMER PROTECTION IN INDIA

Law and Practice

Dr. P.K. Dutta

M.Com., Ph.D., D.Sc.,

First Edition : 2013

Himalaya Publishing House

MUMBAI • NEW DELHI • NAGPUR • BENGALURU • HYDERABAD • CHENNAI • PUNE • LUCKNOW • AHMEDABAD • ERNAKULAM • BHUBANESWAR • INDORE • KOLKATA • GUWAHATI

First Edition : 2013

Published by : Mrs. Meena Pandey for **Himalaya Publishing House Pvt. Ltd.,**
"Ramdoot", Dr. Bhalerao Marg, Girgaon, **Mumbai - 400 004.**
Phone: 022-23860170/23863863, Fax: 022-23877178
E-mail: himpub@vsnl.com; Website: www.himpub.com

Branch Offices :

New Delhi : "Pooja Apartments", 4-B, Murari Lal Street, Ansari Road, Darya Ganj, New Delhi - 110 002. Phone: 011-23270392, 23278631; Fax: 011-23256286

Nagpur : Kundanlal Chandak Industrial Estate, Ghat Road, Nagpur - 440 018. Phone: 0712-2738731, 3296733; Telefax: 0712-2721215

Bengaluru : No. 16/1 (Old 12/1), 1st Floor, Next to Hotel Highlands, Madhava Nagar, Race Course Road, Bengaluru - 560 001. Phone: 080-32919385; Telefax: 080-22286611

Hyderabad : No. 3-4-184, Lingampally, Besides Raghavendra Swamy Matham, Kachiguda, Hyderabad - 500 027. Phone: 040-27560041, 27550139; Mobile: 09390905282

Chennai : No. 8/2, 2nd Madley Street, Ground Floor, T. Nagar, Chennai - 600 017. Mobile: 09345345055

Pune : First Floor, "Laksha" Apartment, No. 527, Mehunpura, Shaniwarpeth (Near Prabhat Theatre), Pune - 411 030. Phone: 020-24496323/24496333; Mobile: 09370579333

Lucknow : House No 731, Shekhupura Colony, Near B.D. Convent School, Aliganj, Lucknow - 226 022. Mobile: 09307501549

Ahmedabad : 114, "SHAIL", 1st Floor, Opp. Madhu Sudan House, C.G. Road, Navrang Pura, Ahmedabad - 380 009. Phone: 079-26560126; Mobile: 09377088847

Ernakulam : 39/176 (New No: 60/251) 1st Floor, Karikkamuri Road, Ernakulam, Kochi - 682011, Phone: 0484-2378012, 2378016; Mobile: 09344199799

Bhubaneswar : 5 Station Square, Bhubaneswar - 751 001 (Odisha). Phone: 0674-2532129, Mobile: 09338746007

Indore : Kesardeep Avenue Extension, 73, Narayan Bagh, Flat No. 302, IIIrd Floor, Near Humpty Dumpty School, Indore - 452 007 (M.P.). Mobile: 09301386468

Kolkata : 108/4, Beliaghata Main Road, Near ID Hospital, Opp. SBI Bank, Kolkata - 700 010, Phone: 033-32449649, Mobile: 09883055590, 07439040301

Guwahati : House No. 15, Behind Pragjyotish College, Near Sharma Printing Press, P.O. Bharalumukh, Guwahati - 781009, (Assam). Mobile: 09883055590, 09883055536

DTP by : HPH, Editorial Office, Bhandup (Rajani Tambe)

Printed at : Geetanjali Press Pvt. Ltd., Kundanlal Chandak Industrial Estate, Ghat Road, Nagpur - 440 018.

Indian households are spending more on consumer goods like consumer durables, clothing, beverages and services as compared to their expenses on such things five years ago.

Dedication

I learnt my lessons from the consumers during my visits to Rural/Urban markets of India at the beginning of my career.
So, I dedicate the Book to the consumers of India, as customer is the 'King'.

Prof.(Dr.) P.K.Dutta

Dr. P.K. Agrawal I.A.S.
Addi. Chief Secretary
Phone: 2252 0624; Fax: 2252 0053
email: sec-cons@wb.nic.in
Website : http://wbconsumers.gou.in

Consumer Affairs Department
Government of West Bengal
11A, Mirza Ghalib Street
Kolkata – 700 087

FOREWORD

It gives me great pleasure to learn that Dr. P. K. Dutta has taken the decision to publish a book for promoting consumer awareness in India. In his book, *"Consumerism and Consumer Protection in India,"* he has highlighted the following issues:

1. Acts, Rules, Regulations, Orders, Notifications, etc.
2. Standards of quality, quantity and salient features of consumer protection laws in India
3. Outline of landmark judgments, setting standards of fair trade practices and procedures etc.

I congratulate the writer for having found some of the following gems in his research work:

I. The Indian consumers should be more vigilant while purchasing a product.

II. They should buy as far as possible, branded products by reputed manufacturers or products with ISI mark, AGMARK, FPO, ISO, etc., even if the cost may be higher.

III. Consumers should also actively involve themselves in the consumer movement by becoming members of the various consumer groups in order to carry on effectively their own battle against unfair services.

IV. The terms and conditions of the guarantee/warranties should be carefully read and products usage should be done as per instructions by the manufacturers.

V. The clauses given in the guarantee/warranty card should be accurate and in simple language so as to avoid any confusion in the minds of the consumers/users.

VI. The advertisements concerning the products should be informative, free from misleading or false or tall claims.

VII. The manufacturers should provide prompt after sales service. Supply of spares should be ensured through dealers/distributors.

VIII. Government must set up Testing Laboratories and can also give financial aid to voluntary organizations for helping them in setting up such facilities.

IX. Quick and simple legal procedures should be introduced for settlement of disputes arising in all government organizations/undertakings/service departments.

I hope this book will fulfil a long felt need to increase the level of consumer awareness. I have pleasure in extending my best wishes to him for his earnest efforts. The Book will be useful to all concerned, i.e., consumers, research scholars, academicians, students, voluntary consumer organizations (VCOs), NGOs and other persons and institutions like trade and business bodies connected with the consumer movement. The book will be of immense help for general public and will add momentum to ongoing consumer movement in the country.

(Dr. P.K. Agrawal)

PREFACE TO FIRST EDITION

The question arises why people, are so bothered of protecting the interest of consumers only. Having common socioeconomics, the consumers are the largest economic group in a country's economy, affecting and affected by almost every public and private economic decisions. But they are also the only important group whose view are not cared about. The reason is that consumers are the most scattered and unorganized set of people. In an open market economy, the government has minimum interference in economic activities. The producers and suppliers decide the quantity, quality, distribution and price of the goods and services produced, especially, the consumer goods. As a result some profit seeking entrepreneur may adopt such policies and practices that are against the interest of consumers. The producers may produce or offer adulterated, fake or low quality products and sell it at the highest possible price or discriminating price. They may provide the consumer with misleading advertisement or wrong information about the company, deceptive package, exaggeration of claims and false quantity of products. The producers may also show a negligence of services and provide unsatisfactory services/product performances or cause environmental pollution. A wide range of consumer pay their hard earned money to buy several products; but in case they do not get the right value for their money in terms of right quality or quantity of goods and services both or if they are made wrong promises they are supposed to stand against deceit. Quite often, they are unaware of their rights or unable to raise their voice against exploitation. So it is imperative that steps are taken to protect the right of the largest economic entity that is known as consumer. He should surely be saved from any sort of exploitation.

Thanks to the Consumer Protection Act, 1986, our country has a vibrant consumer movement today due to the efforts of Government, consumer organizations and the establishment of consumer courts. India is the only country in the world which has exclusive courts for redressal. This has been internationally praised including the developed countries. The Consumer Protection Act has succeeded in bringing about fair play in the supply of goods and services to a large extent. However, the rapid changes in the consumption pattern of the modern day consumer is bringing new challenges in the consumer movement in the country. The Book focus on the consumer movement in India, Copra(CPA). Its problems and the government's efforts to promote it. It also suggests some steps to be taken for the overcoming lacunae, if any. This is my humble effort for enlighten of consumers and serving the need for awareness as also consumer education.

Supreme Court has given many illuminating judgements interpreting not only the scope and ambit of the Act but also the meaning of different expressions used in the Act. I have interpreted different provisions of the Act in the light of the decisions of the apex court, as far as possible.

Legal environment constitutes an important aspect of business and therefore forms an indispensable part of commerce/ management curriculum. The presentation of the subject matter has been kept simple and logical keeping in view the 'no-legal' background of most of the candidates. Reader's valuable suggestions can be incorporated in the next edition. It is hoped that the book in its present form will meet the needs of the readers. In case the book is found wanting in any manner, I shall feel grateful in being informed about the same.

My labours will be amply rewarded if this edition is found useful by my readers.

Finally I thank Mr. Niraj Pandey & Mr. Anuj Pandey Directors of Himalaya Publishing House (Pvt.) Ltd. in taking active interest in publication of the book for the benefit of the Indian Consumers, also Rajani Tambe (DTP) for doing a good job.

Prof. (Dr.) P.K. Dutta
Dutta Niwas, P.C. Roy Road(Station Road)
PO+Vill: Duillya. Via ANDUL MOURI
Distt. Howrah-711302(WB), India,
Email: askpkd@yahoo.co.in

ACKNOWLEDGEMENTS

I express my deep sense of gratitude to Dr. Raghbir Singh, Professor and Head, Department of Business and Commerce, Guru Nanak Dev University, Amritsar, under whose supervision and guidance, I could accomplish the research work. But for his care, scholarly guidance and encouragement, this task would not have become possible. He had always given a patient hearing to me, whenever I approached him. All chapters of the thesis bear the stamp of his scholarly guidance.

I am indebted to Shri S.K. Roy, Managing Director (Padmashree) and Professor Shyamal Banerjee, Chief Executive (Finance) of The Peerless General Finance and Investment Company Ltd., for their encouragement, kind assistance and cooperation extended to me to complete this research work and publication of the material.

I am grateful to various officials of the Ministry of Civil Supplies (consumer protection cell) New Delhi, the Monopolies and Restrictive Trade Practices Commission, New Delhi for providing their library facilities and giving me necessary literature and other information related to the subject of research, also Consumer Affairs Dept. Govt. of West Bengal for preparation of the Book.

I duly acknowledge the services of Indian Council of Social Science Research Library, New Delhi: Ratan Tata Library, Delhi and Library of Guru Nanak Dev University, Amritsar.

I express my sincere thanks to Dr. D. Roy, ex-scientist E, Defence Research and Development Organisation, New Delhi for going through the whole manuscript critically and giving valuable suggestions.

Mr. A. Singh had carefully typed the thesis, so that I could complete this book.

I owe special thanks to my family members, relatives, official colleagues, well-wishers and others who motivated and helped me in completing this book.

Last but not the least I am grateful to the Indian Council of Social Science Research, New Delhi for granting me special assistance to pursue the Research Work.

This book will be useful to all Professionals related to Law, Commerce, Business Management and Company Affairs including Consumers NGO's (Voluntary Organisations) and Marketing Departments of various organizations also students as well as Research Scholars.

I owe a debt of gratitude to all those, whose ideas I have used inside and therefore my thanks.

Prof. Dr. P.K. Dutta.

M.Com., M.D., Ph.D., Dsc.ND, FCMI., FFA., FIMM., FRAMI, FRGS.,

FABPP., FCQI-CQP., RODP., CAHRI., MCIM., MIAM., MHSM., AIHE., ACI.

drpkd05@gmail.com

Phone 033-25462852

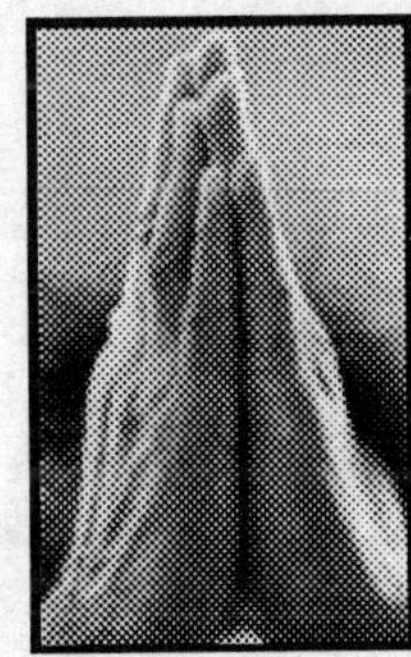

CONTENTS

Part I

CONSUMER PROTECTION ACT

Part II

Part III

ILLUMINATING JUDGEMENTS/DECISIONS(CPA)

PART I

Consumer Protection Acts

Chapter 1

The Consumer Protection Act, 1986

THE CONSUMER PROTECTION ACT, 1986

(Amended upto 18.12.2002)

[Act No. 68 of 1986 as amended by Act 62 of 2002]

24th December, 1986

An Act to provide for better protection of the intests of consumers and for that purpose to make provision for the establishment of consumer councils and other authorities for the settlement of consumers' disputes and for matters connected therewith.

Be it enacted by Parliament in the Thirty-seventh Year of the Republic of India as follows:

CHAPTER I

PRELIMINARY

1. Short title, extent, commencement and application.

(1) This Act may be called the Consumer Protection Act, 1986.

(2) It extends to the whole of India except the State of Jammu and Kashmir.

(3) It shall come into force on such date as the Central Government may, by notification appoint and different dates may be appointed for different States and for different provisions of this Act.

(4) Save as otherwise expressly provided by the Central Government by notification, this Act shall apply to all goods and services.

2. Definitions – (1) In this Act, unless the context otherwise requires,

(a) **"appropriate laboratory"** means a laboratory or organisation –

(i) Recognised by the Central Government;

(ii) Recognised by a State Government, subject to such guidelines as may be prescribed by the Central Government in this behalf; or

(iii) Any such laboratory or organisation established by or under any law for the time being in force, which is maintained, financed or aided by the Central Government or a State Government for carrying out analysis or test of any goods with a view to determining whether such goods suffer from any defect;

(aa) **"branch office"** means –

(i) Any establishment described as a branch by the opposite party; or

(ii) Any establishment carrying or either the same or substantially the same activity as that carried on by the head office of the establishment;

(b) **"complainant"** means –

(i) A consumer; or

(ii) Any voluntary consumer association registered under the Companies Act, 1956 (1 of 1956) or under any other law for the time being in force; or

(iii) The Central Government or any State Government,

(iv) One or more consumers, where there are numerous consumers having the same interest;

(v) In case of death of a consumer, his legal heir or representative; who or which makes a complaint;

(c) **"complaint:** means any allegation in writing made by a complainant that –

(i) An unfair trade practice or a restrictive trade practice has been adopted by any trader or service provider;

(ii) The goods bought by him or agreed to be bought by him; suffer from one or more defects;

(iii) The services hired or availed of or agreed to be hired or availed of by him suffer from deficiency in any respect.

(iv) A trader or service provider, as the case may be, has charged for the goods or for the service mentioned in the complaint a price in excess of the price –

(a) fixed by or under any law for the time being in force

(b) displayed on the goods or any package containing such goods;

(c) displayed on the price list exhibited by him or under any law for the time being in force;

(d) agreed between the parties;

(v) Goods which will be hazardous to life and safety when used, are being offered for sale to the public –

(a) in contravention of any standards relating to safety of such goods as required to be complied with, by or under any law for the time being in force;

(b) if the trader could have known with due diligence that the goods so offered are unsafe to the public;

(vi) Services which are hazardous or likely to be hazardous to life and safety of the public when used, are being offered by the service provider which such person could have known with due diligence to be injurious to life and safety;

(d) **"consumer"** means any person who –

(i) Buys any goods for a consideration which has been paid or promised, for partly paid and partly promised, or under any system of deferred payment and includes any user of such goods other than the person who buys such goods for consideration paid or promised or partly paid or partly promised, or under any system of deferred payment when such use is made with the approval of such person, but does not include a person who obtains such goods for resale or for any commercial purpose; or

(ii) Hires or avails of any services for a consideration which has been paid or promised, or partly paid and partly promised, or under any system of deferred payment and includes any beneficiary of such services other than the person who hires or avails of the services for consideration paid or promised, or partly paid and partly promised, or under any system of deferred payment, when such services are availed of with the approval of the first mentioned person but does not have the approval of the first mentioned person but does not include a person who avails of such services for any commercial purpose:

Explanation – For the purposes of this clause, "commercial purpose" does not include use by a person of goods bought and used by him and services availed by him exclusively for the purposes of earning his livelihood by means of self-employment;

(e) **"consumer dispute"** – means a dispute where the person against whom a complaint has been made, denies or disputes the allegations contained in the complaint.

(f) **"defect"** means any fault, imperfection or shortcoming in the quality, quantity, potency, purity or standard which is required to be maintained by or under any law for the time being in force under any contract, express or implied or as is claimed by the trader in any manner whatsoever in relation to any goods;

(g) **"deficiency"** means any fault, imperfection, shortcoming or inadequacy in the quality, nature and manner or performance which is required to be maintained by or under any law for the time being in force or has been undertaken to be performed by a person in pursuance of a contract or otherwise in relation to any service;

(h) **"District Forum"** means a Consumer Disputes Redressal Forum established under clause (a) of section 9;

(i) (i) **"goods"** means goods a defined in the Sale of Goods Act, 1930; (3 of 1930)

(j) **"manufacturer"** means a person who –

(a) makes or manufactures any goods or part thereof; or

(b) does not make or manufacture any goods but assembles parts thereof made or manufactured by others; or

(c) puts or causes to put his own mark on any goods made or manufactured by any other manufacturer;

Explanation – Where a manufacturer despatches any goods or part thereof to any branch office maintained by him, such branch office shall not be deemed to be the manufacturer even though the parts so despatched to it are assembled at such branch office and are sold or distributed from such branch office.

(jj) **"member"** includes the President and a member of the National Commission or a State Commission or a District Forum, as the case may be;

(k) **"National Commission"** means the National Consumer Disputes Redressal Commission established under clause (c) of section 9;

(l) **"person'** includes –

(a) a firm whether registered or not;

(b) a Hindu undivided family;

(c) a co-operative society;

(d) every other association of persons whether registered under the Society Registration Act 1860 (21 of 1860) or not;

(m) **"prescribed"** means prescribed by rules made by the State Government, or as the case may be, by the Central Government under this Act;

(nn) **"regulation"** means the regulation made by the National Commission under this Act;

(nnn) **"restrictive trade practice**" means a trade practice which tends to bring about manipulation of price or conditions of delivery or to effect flow of supplies in the market relating to goods or services in such a manner as to impose on the consumers unjustified costs or restrictions and shall include –

(a) delay beyond the period agreed to by a trader in supply of such goods or in providing the services which has led or is likely to lead to rise in the price;

(b) any trade practice which requires a consumer to buy, hire or avail of any goods or, as the case may be, services as condition precedent to buying, hiring or availing of other goods or services;

(o) **"service"** means of any description which is made available to potential users and includes, but not limited to, the provision of facilities in connection with banking, financing insurance, transport, processing, supply of electrical or other energy, board or loading or both, housing construction, entertainment, amusement or the purveying of new or other information, but does not include the rendering of any service free of charge or under a contract of personal service;

(oo) **"spurious goods and services"** mean such goods and services which are claimed to be genuine but they are actually not so;

(p) **"State Commission"** means a Consumer Disputes Redressal Commission established in a State under clause (b) of section 9;

(q) **"trader"** in relation to any goods means a person who sells or distributes any goods for sale and includes the manufacturer thereof, and where such goods are sold or distributed in packages form, includes the packer thereof;

(r) **"unfair trade practice"** means a trade practice which, for the purpose of promoting the sale, use or supply of any goods or for the provision of any service, adopts any unfair method or unfair or deceptive practice including any of the following practices, namely;

(1) the practice of making any statement, whether orally or in writing or by visible representation which, -

(i) falsely represents that the goods are of a particular standard, quality, quantity, grade, composition, style or model;

(ii) falsely represents that the services are of a particular standard, quality or grade;

(iii) falsely represents any re-built, second-hand, renovated, reconditioned or old goods as new goods;

(iv) represents that the goods or services have sponsorship, approval, performance, characteristics, accessories, uses or benefits which such goods or services do not have;

(v) represents that the seller or the supplier has a sponsorship or approval or affiliation which such seller or supplier does not have;

(vi) makes a false or misleading representation concerning the need for, or the usefulness of, any goods or services;

(vii) gives to the public any warranty or guarantee of the performance, efficacy or length of life of a product or of any goods that is not based on an adequate or proper test thereof;

Provided that where a defence is raised to the effect that such warranty or guarantee is based on adequate or proper test, the burden of proof of such defence shall lie on the person raising such defence;

(viii) makes to the public a representation in a form that purports to be –

(i) a warranty or guarantee of a product or of any goods or services; or

(ii) a promise to replace, maintain or repair an article or any part thereof or to repeat or continue a service until it has achieved a specified result, if such purported warranty or guarantee or promise is materially misleading or if there is no reasonable prospect that such warranty, guarantee or promise will be carried out;

(ix) materially misleads the public concerning the price at which a product or like products or goods or services, have been or are, ordinarily sold or provided, and, for this purpose, a representation as to price shall be deemed to refer to the price at which the product or goods or services has or have been sold by sellers or provided by suppliers generally in the relevant market unless it is clearly specified to be the price at which the product has been sold or services have been provided by the person by whom or on whose behalf the representation is made;

(x) give false or misleading facts disparaging the goods, services or trade of another person.

Explanation – For the purposes of clause

(1) a statement that is –

(a) expressed on an article offered or displayed for sale, or on its wrapper or container; or

(b) expressed on anything attached to, inserted in, or accompanying, an article offered or displayed for sale, or on anything on which the article is mounted for display or sale; or

(c) contained in or on anything that is sold, sent, delivered, transmitted or in any other manner whatsoever made available to a member of the public, shall be deemed to be a statement made to the public by, and only by, the person who had caused the statement to be so expressed, made of contained;

(2) permits the publication of any advertisement whether in any newspaper or otherwise, for the sale or supply at a bargain price, of goods or services that are not intended to be offered for sale or supply at the bargain price, or for a period that is, and in quantities that are, reasonable, having regard to the nature of the market in which the business is carried on, the nature and size of business, and the nature of the advertisement.

Explanation – For the purposes of clause (2), "bargaining price"

Means –

(a) a price that is stated in any advertisement to be a bargain price, by reference to an ordinary price or otherwise, or

(b) a price that a person who reads, hears or sees the advertisement, would reasonably understand to be a bargain price having regard to the prices at which the product advertised or like products are ordinarily sold;

(3) **permits** –

(a) the offering of gifts, prizes or other items with the intention of not providing them as offered or creating impression that something is being given or offered free of charge when it is fully or partly covered by the amount charged in the transaction as a whole;

(b) the conduct of any contest, lottery, game of chance or skill, for the purpose of promoting, directly or indirectly, the sale, use or supply of any product or any business interest;

(3A) withholding from the participants of any scheme offering gifts, prizes or other items free of charge, on its closure the information about final results of the scheme.

Explanation – For the purpose of this sub-clause, the participants of a scheme shall be deemed to have been informed of the final results of the scheme where such results are within a reasonable time, published prominently in the same newspapers in which the scheme was originally advertised;

(4) permits the sale or supply of goods intended to be used, or are of a kind likely to be used, by consumers, knowing or having reason to believe that the goods do no comply with the standards prescribed by competent authority relating to performance, composition, contents, design, constructions, finishing or packaging as are necessary to prevent or reduce the risk of injury to the person using the goods;

(5) permits the hoarding or destruction of goods, or refuses to sell the goods or to make them available for sale or to provide any service, if such hoarding or destruction or refusal raises or tends to raise or is intended to raise, the cost of those or other similar goods or services.

(6) manufacture of spurious goods or offering such goods for sale or adopts deceptive practices in the provision of services.

3. Any reference in this Act to any other Act or provision thereof which is not in force in any area to which this Act applies shall be construed to have a reference to the corresponding Act or provision thereof in force in such area.

4. Act not in derogation of any other law. The provisions of this Act shall be in addition to and not in derogation of the provisions of any other law for the time being in force.

CONSUMER PROTECTION COUNCILS

5. The Central Consumer Protection Council. –

(1) The Central Government shall, by notification, establish with effect from such date as it may specify in such notification, a Council to be known as the Central Consumer Protection Council (hereinafter referred to as the Central Council).

(2) The Central Council shall consist of the following members namely –

(i) the Minister In Charge of the consumer affairs in the Central Government, who shall be its Chairman, and

(ii) such number of other official or non-official members representing such interests as may be prescribed.

6. Procedure for meetings of the Central Council. –

(1) The Central Council shall meet as and when necessary, but at least one meeting of the Council shall be held every year.

(2) The Central Council shall meet at such time and place as the Chairman may think fit and shall observe such procedure in regard to the transaction of its business as may be prescribed.

7. Objects of the Central Council. – The objects of the Central Council shall be to promote and protect the rights of the consumers such as –

(a) the right to be protected against the marketing of goods and services which are hazardous to life and property;

(b) the right to be informed about the quality, quantity, potency, purity, standard and price of goods or services, as the case may be so as to protect the consumer against unfair trade practices;

(c) the right to be assured, wherever possible, access to a variety of goods and services at competitive prices;

(d) the right to be heard and to be assured that consumers' interests will receive due consideration at appropriate forums;

(e) the right to seek redressal against unfair trade practices or restrictive trade practices or unscrupulous exploitation of consumers; and

(f) the right to consumer education.

8. The State Consumer Protection Councils. –

(1) The State Government shall, by notification, establish with effect from such date as it may specify in such notification, a Council to be known as the Consumer Protection Council for ……(hereinafter referred to as the State Council).

(2) The State Council shall consist of the following members, namely:

(a) the Minister In Charge of consumer affairs in the State Government who shall be its Chairman;

(b) such number of other official or non-official members representing such interests as may be prescribed by the State Government.

(c) Such number of other official or non-official members, not exceeding ten, as may be nominated by the Central Government.

(3) The State Council shall meet as and when necessary but not less than two meetings shall be held every year.

(4) The State Council shall meet at such time and place as the Chairman may think fit and shall observe such procedure in regard to the transaction of its business as may be prescribed by the State Government.

9. Objects of the State Council. – The objects of every State Council shall be to promote and protect within the Sate the rights of the consumers laid down in clause (a) to (f) of section 6.

9A.

(1) The State Government shall establish for every district, by notification, a council to be known as the **District Consumer Protection Council** with effect from such date as it may specify in such notification.

(2) **The District Consumer Protection Council** (hereinafter referred to as the **District Council**) shall consist of the following members, namely:

(a) the **Collector** of the district (by whatever name called), who shall be its **Chairman**; and such number of other official and non-official members representing such interests as may be prescribed by the State Government.

(3) The District Council shall meet as and when necessary but not less than two meetings shall be held every year.

(4) The District Council shall meet at such time and place within the district as the Chairman may think fit and shall observe such procedure in regard to the transaction of its business as may be prescribed by the State Government.

9 B. The objects of every District Council shall be to promote and protect within the district the rights of the consumers laid down in the clauses (a) to (f) of section 6.

CONSUMER DISPUTES REDRESSAL AGENCIES

10. Establishment **of Consumer Disputes Redressal Agencies** – There shall be established for the purposes of this Act, the following agencies, namely :

(a) a Consumer Disputes Redressal Forum to be known as the **"District Forum"** established by the State Government in each district of the State by notification.

Provided that the State Government may, if it deems fit, establish more than one District Forum in a district.

(b) Disputes Redressal Commission to be known as the **"State Commission"** established by the State Government in the State by notification; and

(i) National Consumer Disputes Redressal Commission established by the Central Government by notification.

11. Composition of the District Forum -

(1) Each District Forum shall consist of –

(a) a person who is, or has been, or is qualified to be a District Judge, who shall be its President;

(b) two other members, one of whom shall be a woman, who shall have the following qualifications, namely :

(i) be not less than thirty-five years of age,

(ii) possess a bachelor's degree from a recognised university,

(iii) be persons of ability, integrity and standing, and have adequate knowledge and experience of at least ten years in dealing with problems relating to economics, law, commerce, accountancy, industry, public affairs or administration;

Provided that a person shall be disqualified for appointment as a member if he –

(i) has been convicted and sentenced to imprisonment for an offence, which, in the opinion of the State Government involves moral turpitude; or

(ii) is an undischarged insolvent; or

(iii) is of unsound mind and stands so declared by a competent court; or

(iv) has been removed or dismissed from the service of the Government or a body corporate owned or controlled by the Government; or

(v) has, in the opinion of State Government, such financial or other interest as is likely to affect prejudicially the discharge by him of his functions as a member; or

(vi) has such other disqualifications as may be prescribed by the State Government;

1(A) Every appointment under sub-section (1) shall be made by the State Government on the recommendation of a selection committee consisting of the following, namely :

(i) The President of the State Commission – Chairman

(ii) Secretary, Law Department of the State – member.

(iii) Secretary, Incharge of the Department dealing with consumer affairs in the state – Member.

Provided that where the President of the State Commission is, by reason of absence or otherwise, unable to act as Chairman of the Selection Committee, the State Government may refer the matter to the Chief Justice of the High Court for nominating a sitting Judge of that High Court to act as Chairman.

2. Every member of the district forum shall hold office for a term of five years or upto the age of sixty-five years, whichever is earlier:

Provided that a member shall be eligible for re-appointment for another term of five years or up to the age of sixty-five years, whichever is earlier, subject to the condition that he fulfils the qualifications and other conditions for appointment mentioned in clause (b) of sub-section (1) and such re-appointment is also made on the basis of the recommendation of the Selection committee.

Provided further that a member may resign his office in writing under his hand addressed to the State Governme4nt and on such resignation being accepted, his office shall become vacant and may be filled by appointment of a person possessing any of the qualifications mentioned in sub-section (1) in relation to the category of the member who is required to be appointed under the provisions of sub-section (1A) in place of the person who has resigned:

Provided also that a person appointed as the President or as a member, before the commencement of the Consumer Protection (Amendment) Act, 2002, shall continue to hold such office as President or member, as the case may be, till the completion of his term.

3. The salary or honorarium and other allowances payable to, and the other terms and conditions of service of the members of the District Forum shall be such as may be prescribed by the State Government.

Provided that the appointment of a member on whole-time basis shall be made by the State Government on the recommendation of the President of the State Commission taking into consideration such factors as may be prescribed including the work load of the District Forum.

12. Jurisdiction of the District Forum –

(1) Subject to the other provisions of this Act, the District Forum shall have jurisdiction to entertain complaints where the value of the goods or services and the compensation, if any, claimed "does not exceed rupees twenty lakhs."

(2) A complaint shall be instituted in a District Forum within the local limits of whose jurisdiction -

(a) the opposite party or each of the opposite parties, where there are more than one, at the time of the institution of the complaint, actually and voluntarily resides or carries on business or has a branch office or personally works for gain; or

(b) any of the opposite parties, where there are more than one at the time of the institution of the complaint, actually and voluntarily resides, or carries on business or has a branch office, or personally works for gain, provided that in such case either the permission of the District Forum is given, or the opposite parties who do not reside, or carry on business or have a branch office, or personally work for gain, as the case may be acquiesce in such institution; or

(c) the cause of action, wholly or in part, arises.

13. Manner in which complaint shall be made –

(1) A complaint in relation to any goods sold or delivered or agreed to be sold or delivered or any service provided or agreed to be provided may be filed with a District Forum by –

(a) the consumer to whom such goods are sold or delivered or agreed to be sold or delivered or such service provided or agreed to be provided;

(b) any recognised consumer association whether the consumer to whom the goods sold or delivered or agreed to be sold or delivered or service provided or agreed to be provided is a member of such association or not;

(c) one or more consumers, where there are numerous consumers having the same interest, with the permission of the District Forum, on behalf of, or for the benefit of, all consumers so interested; or

(d) the Central Government or the State Government, as the case may be, either in its individual capacity or as a representative of interests of the consumers in general.

(2) Every complaint filed under sub-section (1) shall be accompanied with such amount of fee and payable in such manner as may be prescribed.

(3) On receipt of a complaint made under sub-section (1), the District forum may, by order, allow the complaint to be proceeded with or rejected:

Provided that a complaint shall not be rejected under this section unless an opportunity of being heard has been given to the complainant:

Provided further that the admissibility of the complaint shall ordinarily be decided within twenty-one days from the date on which the complaint was received.

(4) Where a complaint is allowed to be proceeded with under subsection (3), the District Forum may proceed with the complaint in the manner provided under this Act:

Provided that where a complaint has been admitted by the District Forum, it shall not be transferred to any other court or tribunal or any authority set up by or under any other law for the time being in force.

Explanation - For the purpose of this section "recognised consumer association" means any voluntary consumer association registered under the Companies Act, 1956 (1 of 1956) or any other law for the time being in force.

14. Procedure on admission of complaint –

(1) The District Forum shall, on admission of a complaint, if it relates to any goods –

(a) refer a copy of the admitted complaint, within twenty-one days from the date of its admission to the opposite party mentioned in the complaint directing him to give his version of the case within a period of thirty days or such extended period not exceeding fifteen days as may be granted by the District Forum;

(b) where the opposite party on receipt of a complaint referred to him under clause (a) denies or disputes the allegations contained in the complaint or omits or fails to take any action to represent his case within the time given by the District Forum District Forum shall proceed to settle the consumer dispute in the manner specified in clauses (c) to (g);

(c) where the complaint alleges a defect in the goods which cannot be determined without proper analysis or test of the goods, the District Forum shall obtain a sample of the goods from the complainant, seal it and authenticate it in the manner prescribed and refer the sample so sealed to the appropriate laboratory along with a direction that such laboratory make an analysis or test, whichever may be necessary, with a view to finding out whether such goods suffer from any defect alleged in the complaint or from any other defect and to report its findings thereon to the District Forum within a period of forty-five days of the receipt of the reference or within such extended period as may be granted by the District Forum;

(d) before any sample of the goods is referred to any appropriate laboratory under clause (c), the District Forum, may require the complainant to deposit to the credit of the Forum such fees as may be specified, for payment to the appropriate laboratory for carrying out the necessary analysis or test in relation to the goods in question;

(e) the District Forum shall remit the amount deposited to its credit under clause (d) to the appropriate laboratory to enable to carry out the analysis or test mentioned in clause (c) and on receipt of the report from the appropriate laboratory, the District Forum shall forward a copy of the report along with such remarks as the District Forum may feel appropriate to the opposite party;

(f) if any of the parties disputes the correctness of the findings of the appropriate laboratory, or disputes the correctness of the methods of analysis or test adopted by the appropriate laboratory, the District Forum shall require the opposite party or the complainant to submit in writing his objections in regard to the report made by the appropriate laboratory,

(g) the District Forum shall thereafter give a reasonable opportunity to the complainant as well as the opposite party of being heard as to the correctness or otherwise of the report made by the appropriate laboratory and also as to the objection made in relation thereto under clause (f) and issue an appropriate order under section 14.

(2) The District Forum shall, it the complaint admitted by if under section 12 relates to goods in respect of which the procedure specified in sub-section (1) cannot be followed, or if the complaint relates to any services –

(a) refer a copy of such complaint to the opposite party directing him to give his version of the case within a period of thirty days or such extended period not exceeding fifteen days as may be granted by the District Forum;

(b) where the opposite party, on receipt of a copy of the complaint, referred to him under clause (a) denies or disputes the allegations contained in the complaint, or omits or fails to take any action to represent his case within the time given by the District Forum, the District Forum shall proceed to settle the consumer dispute, –

(i) on the basis of evidence brought to its notice by the complainant and the opposite party, where the opposite party denies or disputes the allegations contained in the complaint, or

(ii) *ex parte* on the basis of evidence brought to its notice by the complainant where the opposite party omits or fails to take any action to represent his case within the time given by the Forum.

(c) where the complainant fails to appear on the date of hearing before the District Forum, the District Forum may either dismiss the complaint for default or decide it on merits.

(3) No proceedings complying with the procedure laid down in sub-sections (1) and (2) shall be called in question in any court on the ground that the principles of natural justice have not been complied with.

(3A) Every complaint shall be heard as expeditiously as possible and endeavour shall be made to decide the complaint within a period of three months from the date of receipt of notice by opposite party where the complaint does not require analysis or testing of commodities and within five months if it requires analysis or testing of commodities:

Provided that no adjournment shall be ordinarily granted by the District Forum unless sufficient cause is shown and the reasons for grant of adjournment have been recorded in writing by the Forum:

Provided further that the District Forum shall make such orders as to the costs occasioned by the adjournment as may be provided in the regulations made under this Act.

Provided also that in the event of a complaint being disposed of after period so specified, the District Forum shall record in writing, the reasons for the same at the time of disposing of the said complaint.

(3B) Where during the pendency of any proceeding before the District Forum, it appears to it necessary, it may pass such interim order as is just and proper in the facts and circumstances of the case.

(4) For the purposes of this section, the District Forum shall have the same powers as are vested in a civil court under the Code of Civil Procedure, 1908 (5 of 1908) while trying a suit in respect of the following matters, namely:

(i) the summoning and enforcing the attendance of any defendant or witness and examining the witness on oath;

(ii) the discovery and production of any document or other material object producible as evidence,

(iii) the reception of evidence on affidavits;

(iv) the requisitioning of the report of the concerned analysis or test from the appropriate laboratory or from any other relevant source;

(v) issuing of any commission for the examination of any witness; and

(vi) any other matter which may be prescribed.

(5) Every proceeding before the District Forum shall be deemed to be a judicial proceeding within the meaning of **sections 193 and 228 of the Indian Penal Code (45 of 1860),** and the District Forum shall be deemed to be a civil court for the purposes of **section 195, and Chapter XXVI of the Code of Criminal Procedure, 1973 (2 of 1974).**

(6) Where the complainant is a consumer referred to in sub-clause (iv) of clause (b) of sub-section (1) of section 2, **the provisions of rule 8 of Order 1 of the First Schedule to the Code of Civil Procedure, 1908 (5 of 1908)** shall apply subject to a suit or decree shall be construed as a reference to a complaint or the order of the District Forum thereon.

(7) In the event of death of a complainant who is a consumer or of the opposite party against whom the complaint has been filed, **the provisions of Order XXII of the first schedule to the Code of Civil Procedure, 1908 (5 of 1908)** shall apply subject to the modification that every reference therein to the plaintiff and the defendant shall be construed as reference to a complainant or the opposite party, as the case may be.

15. Finding of the District forum –

(1) If, after the proceeding conducted under section 13, the District Forum is satisfied that the goods, complained against suffer from any of the defects specified in the complaint or that any of the allegations contained in the complaint about the services are proved, it shall issue an order to the opposite party directing him to do one or more of the following things, namely:

(a) to remove the defect pointed out by the appropriate laboratory from the goods in question;

(b) to replace the goods with new goods or similar description which shall be free from any defect;

(c) to return to the complainant the price, or, as the case may be, the charges paid by the complainant;

(d) to pay such amount as may be awarded by it as compensation to the consumer for any loss or injury suffered by the consumer due to the negligence of the opposite party.

Provided that the District Forum shall have the power to grant punitive damages in such circumstances as it deems fit;

(e) to remove the defects in goods or deficiencies in the services in question;

(f) to discontinue the unfair trade practice or the restrictive trade practice or not to repeat them;

(g) not to offer the hazardous goods for sale;

(h) to withdraw the hazardous goods from being offered for sale;

(ha) to cease manufacture of hazardous goods and to desist from offering services which are hazardous in nature;

(hb) to pay such sum as may be determined by it if it is of the opinion that loss or injury has been suffered by a large number of consumers who are not identifiable conveniently:

Provided that the minimum amount of sum so payable shall not be less than five per cent of the value of such defective goods sold or service provided, as the case may be, to such consumers:

Provided further that the amount so obtained shall be credited in favour of such person and utilized in such manner as may be prescribed;

(hc) to issue corrective advertisement to neutralize the effect of misleading advertisement at the cost of the opposite party responsible for issuing such misleading advertisement;

(i) to provide for adequate costs to parties.

(2) Every proceeding referred to in sub-section (1) shall be conducted by the President of the District Forum and at least one member thereof sitting together:

Provided that where a member, for any reason, is unable to conduct a proceeding till it is completed, the President and the other member shall continue the proceeding from the stage at which it was last heard by the previous member.

(2A) Every order made by the District Forum under sub-section (1) shall be signed by its President and the member or members who conducted the proceeding:

Provided that where the proceeding is conducted by the President and one member and they differ on any point or points, they shall state the point or points on which they differ and refer the same to the other member for hearing on such point or points and the opinion of the majority shall be the order of the District Forum.

(3) Subject to the foregoing provisions, the procedure relating to the conduct of the meetings of the District Forum, its sittings and other matters shall be such as may be prescribed by the State Government.

15A. Appeal - Any person aggrieved by an order made by the District Forum may prefer and appeal against such order to the State Commission within a period of thirty days from the date of the order, in such form and manner as may be prescribed :

Provided that the State Commission may entertain an appeal after the expiry of the said period of thirty days if it is satisfied that there was sufficient cause for not finding it within that period.

Provided further that no appeal by a person, who is required to pay any amount in terms of an order to the District Forum shall be entertained by the State Commission unless the appellant has deposited in the prescribed manner fifty per cent of that amount or twenty-five thousand rupees, whichever is less:

16. Composition of the State Commission –

(1) Each State Commission shall consist of –

(a) a person who is or has been a judge of a High Court, appointed by the State Government, who shall be its President:

Provided that no appointment under this clause shall be made except after consultation with the Chief Justice of the High court;

(b) not less than two, and not more than such number of members, as may be prescribed, one of whom shall be a woman, who shall have the following qualifications, namely:

1. be not less than thirty-five years of age;
2. possess a bachelor's degree from a recognised university; and
3. be persons of ability, integrity and standing, and have adequate knowledge and experience of at least ten years in dealing with problems relating to economics, law commerce, accountancy, industry, public affairs or administration:

Provided that not more than fifty per cent of the members shall be from amongst persons having a judicial background.

Explanation – For the purposes of this clause, the expression "persons having judicial background" shall mean persons having knowledge and experience for at least a period of ten years as a presiding officer at the direct level court or any tribunal at equivalent level:

Provided further that a person shall be disqualified for appointment as a member if he –

(a) has been convicted and sentenced to imprisonment for an offence which, in the opinion of the State Government involves moral turpitude; or

(b) is an undischarged insolvent; or

(c) is of unsound mind and stands so declared by a competent court; or

(d) has been removed or dismissed from the service of the Government or a body corporate owned or controlled by the Government; or

(e) has in the opinion of the State Government, such financial or other interest, as is likely to affect prejudicially the discharge by him of his functions as a member; or

(f) has such other disqualification as may be prescribed by the State Government.

(1A) Every appointment under sub-section (1) shall be made by the State Government on the recommendation of a Selection Committee consisting of the following members, namely:

(i) President of the State Commission .... Chairman;

(ii) Secretary of the Law Department of the State ...... Member,

(iii) Secretary Incharge of the Department dealing with Consumer Affairs in the State ...... Member.

Provided that where the President of the State Commission is, by reason of absence or otherwise, unable to act as Chairman of the Selection Committee, the State Government may refer the matter to the Chief Justice of the High Court for nominating a sitting Judge of that High Court to act as Chairman.

(1B)

(i) The jurisdiction, powers and authority of the State Commission may be exercised by Benches thereof.

(ii) A Bench may be constituted by the President with one or more members as the President may deem fit.

(iii) If the members of a Bench differ in opinion on any point, the points shall be decided according to the opinion of the majority, if there is a majority, but if the Members are equally divided, they shall state the point or points on which they differ, and make a reference to the President who shall either hear the point or points himself or refer the case for hearing on such point or points by one or more or the other members and such point or points shall be decided according to the opinion of the majority of the members who have heard the case, including those who first heard it.

2. The salary or honorarium and other allowances payable to, and the other terms and conditions of service of, the members of the State Commission shall be such as may be prescribed by the State Government.

Provided that the appointment of a member on whole-time basis shall be made by the State Government on the recommendation of the President of the State Commission taking into consideration such factors as may be prescribed including the work load of the State Commission.

3. Every member of the State Commission shall hold office for a term of five years or up to the age of sixty-seven years, whichever is earlier.

Provided that a member shall be eligible for re-appointment for another term of five years or upto the age of sixty-seven years whichever is earlier, subject to the condition that he fulfils the qualifications and other conditions for appointment mentioned in clause (b) of sub-section (1) and such re-appointment is made on the basis of the recommendation of the Selection Committee.

Provided further that a person appointed as a President of the State Commission shall also be eligible for re-appointment in the manner provided in clause (a) of sub-section (1) of the section :

Provided also that a member may resign his office in writing under his hand addressed to the State Government and on such resignation being accepted, his office shall become vacant and may be filled by appointment of a person possessing any of the qualifications mentioned in sub-section (1) in relation to the category of the member who is required to be appointed under the provisions of sub-section (1A) in place of the person who has resigned.

4. Notwithstanding anything contained in sub-section (3), a person appointed as the President or as a member, before the commencement of the Consumer Protection (Amendment) Act, 2002, shall continue to hold such office as President or member, as the case may be, till the completion of his term.

17. Jurisdiction of the State Commission –

(1) Subject to the other provisions of this Act, the State Commission shall have jurisdiction –

(a) to entertain –

(i) complaints where the value of the goods or services and compensation, if any, claimed exceeds rupees twenty lakhs but does not exceed rupees one crore; and

(ii) appeals against the orders of any District Forum within the State; and

(b) To call for the records and pass appropriate orders in any Consumer dispute which is pending before or has been or has been decided by any District Forum within the State, where it appears to the State Commission that such District Forum has exercised a jurisdiction not vested in it by law, or has failed to exercise a jurisdiction so vested or has acted in exercise of its jurisdiction illegally or with material irregularity.

(2) A complaint shall be instituted in a State Commission within the limits of whose jurisdiction, –

(a) the opposite party or each of the opposite parties, where there are more than one, at the time of the institution of the complaint, actually and voluntarily resides or carries on business or has a branch office or personally works for gain; or

(b) any of the opposite parties, where there are more than one, at the time of the Institution of the complaint, actually and voluntarily resides, or carries on business or has abranch office or personally works for gain, provided that in such case either the permission of the State Commission is given or the opposite parties who do not reside or carry on business or have a branch office or personally work for gain, as the case may be, acquiesce in such institution; or

(c) the cause of action, wholly or in part, arises.

17A. On the application of the complainant or of its own motion the State Commission may, at any stage of the proceeding, transfer any complaint pending before the District Forum to another District Forum within the State if the interest of justice so requires.

17B. The State Commission shall ordinarily function in the State Capital but may perform its functions at such other place as the State Government, in consultation with the Statession, notify in the Official Gazette, from time to time.

18. Procedure applicable to State Commission – The provisions of Section 12, 13, and 14 and the rules made thereunder for the disposal of complaints by the District Forum shall, with such modifications as may be necessary, be applicable to the disposal of disputes by the State Commission.

19. Appeals – Any person aggrieved by an order made by the State Commission in exercise of its powers conferred by sub-clause (i) of clause (a) of section 17 may prefer an appeal against such order to the National Commission within a period of thirty days from the date of the order in such form and manner as may be prescribed :

Provided that the National Commission may entertain an appeal after expiry of the said period of thirty days if it is satisfied that there was sufficient cause for not filing it within that period.

Provided further that no appeal by a person, who is required to pay any amount in terms of an order of the State Commission, shall be entertained by the National Commission unless the appellant has deposited in the prescribed manner fifty percent of the amount or rupees thirty-five thousand, whichever is less:

19A. An appeal filed before the State Commission or the National Commission shall be heard as expeditiously as possible and an endeavour shall be made to finally dispose of the appeal within a period of ninety days from the date of its admission:

Provided that no adjournment shall be ordinarily granted by the State commission or the National Commission, as the case may be, unless sufficient cause is shown and the reasons for grant of adjournment have been recorded in writing by such Commission:

Provided further the State Commission or the National Commission, as the case may be, shall make such orders as to the costs occasioned by the adjournment as may be provided in the regulations made under this Act.

Provided also that in the event of an appeal being disposed of after the period so specified, the State Commission or the National Commission, as the case may be, shall record in writing the reasons for the same at the time of disposing of the said appeal.

20. Composition of the National Commission. –

(1) The National Commission shall consist of –

(a) a person who is or has been a Judge of the Supreme Court, to be appointed by the Central Government, who shall be its President;

Provided that no appointment under this clause shall be made except after consultation with the Chief Justice of India;

(b) not less than four, and not more than such number of members, as may be prescribed, and one of whom shall be a woman, who shall have the following qualifications, namely:

1. be not less than thirty-five years of age;
2. possess a bachelor's degree from a recognised university; and
3. be persons of ability, integrity and standing, and have adequate knowledge and experience of at least ten years in dealing with problems relating to economics, law commerce, accountancy, industry, public affairs or administration:

Provided that not more than fifty per cent of the members shall be from amongst the persons having judicial background.

Explanation – For the purposes of this clause, the expression "persons having judicial background" shall mean persons having knowledge and experience for at least a period of ten years as a presiding officer at the district level court or any tribunal at equivalent level:

Provided further that a person shall be disqualified for appointment if he –

(a) has been convicted and sentenced to imprisonment for an offence, which, in the opinion of the Central Government involves moral turpitude; or

(b) is an undischarged insolvent; or

(c) is of unsound mind and stands so declared by a competent court; or

(d) has been removed or dismissed from the service of the Government or a body corporate owned or controlled by the Government; or

(e) has in the opinion of the Central Government such financial or other interest as is likely to affect prejudicially the discharge by him of his functions as a member; or

(f) has such other disqualifications as may be prescribed by the Central Government :

Provided also that every appointment under this clause shall be made by the Central Government on the recommendation of a selection committee consisting of the following, namely:

(i) a person who is a judge of the Supreme court - Chairman;

(ii) the Secretary in the Department of Legal Affairs in the Government of India – Member;

(iii) Secretary of the Department dealing with consumer affairs in the Government of India – Member.

(1A)

(i) The Jurisdiction, powers and authority of the National Commission may be exercised by Benches thereof.

(ii) A Bench may be constituted by the President with one or more members as the President may deem fit.

(iii) If the Members of a Bench differ in opinion on any point, the points shall be decided according to the opinion of the majority, if there is a majority, but if the members are equally divided, they shall state the point or points on which they differ, and make a reference to the President who shall either hear the point or points himself or refer the case for hearing on such point or points by one or more or the other Members and such point or points shall be decided according to the opinion of the majority of the Members who have heard the case, including those who first heard it.

(2) The salary or honorarium and other allowances payable to and the other terms and conditions of service of the members of the National Commission shall be such as may be prescribed by the Central Government.

(3) Every member of the National Commission shall hold office for a term of five years or upto the age of seventy years, whichever is earlier:

Provided that a member shall be eligible for re-appointment for another term of five years or upto the age of seventy years whichever is earlier, subject to the condition that he fulfils the qualifications and other conditions for appointment mentioned in clause (b) of sub-section (1) and such re-appointment is made on the basis of the recommendation of the Selection Committee.

Provided further that a person appointed as a President of the National Commission shall also be eligible for re-appointment in the manner provided in clause (a) of sub-section (1):

Provided also that a member may resign his office in writing under his hand addressed to the Central Government and on such resignation being accepted, his office shall become vacant and may be filled by appointment of a person possessing any of the qualifications mentioned in sub-section (1) in relation to the category of the member who is required to be appointed under the provisions of sub-section (1A) in place of the person who has resigned.

(4) Nothwithstanding anything contained in sub-section (3), a person appointed as a President or as a membe4r before the commencement of the Consumer Protection (Amendment) Act, 2002 shall continue to hold such office as President or member, as the case may be, till the completion of his term.

21. Jurisdiction of the National Commission – Subject to the other provisions of this Act, the National Commission shall have jurisdiction –

(a) to entertain –

(i) complaints where the value of the goods or services and compensation, if any, claimed exceeds rupees one crore; and

(ii) appeals against the orders of any State Commission; and

(b) to call for the records and pass appropriate orders in any Consumer dispute which is pending before or has been decided by any State Commission has exercised a jurisdiction not vested in it by law, or has failed to exercise a jurisdiction so vested, or has acted in the exercise of its jurisdiction illegally or with material irregularity.

22. Power of and procedure applicable to the National Commission –

(1) The provisions of sections 12, 13 and 14 and the rules made thereunder for the disposal of complaints by the District Forum shall, with such modifications as may be considered necessary by the Commission, be applicable to the disposal of disputes by the National Commission.

(2) Without prejudice to the provisions contained in sub-section (1), the National Commission shall have the power to review any order made by it, when there is an error apparent on the face of record.

22 A. Where an order is passed by the National Commission *ex parte* against the opposite party or a complainant, as the case may be, the aggrieved party may apply to the Commission to set aside the said order in the interest of justice.

22B. On the application of the complainant or of its own motion, the National Commission may, at any stage of the proceeding, in the interest of justice, transfer any complaint pending before the District Forum of one State to a District Forum of another State or before one State Commission to another State Commission.

22C. The National commission shall ordinarily function at New Delhi and perform its functions at such other place as the Central Government in consultation with the National commission may notify in the Official Gazette, from time to time.

22D. When the office of President of a District Forum, State commission, or of the National Commission, as the case may be, is vacant or a person occupying such office is, by reason of absence or otherwise, unable to perform the duties of his office, these shall be performed by the senior most member of the District forum, the State Commission or of the National commission, as the case may be:

Provided that where a retired Judge of a High court is a member of the National Commission, such member or where the number of such members is more than one, the senior most person among such members, shall preside over the national commission in the absence of President of that Commission.

23. Appeal: Any person aggrieved by an order made by the National Commission in exercise of its power conferred by sub clause (i) of clause (a) section 21, may prefer an appeal against such order to the Supreme court within a period of thirty days from the date of the order:

Provided the then Supreme Court may entertain an appeal after the expiry of the said period of thirty days if it is satisfied that there was sufficient cause for not filing that within that period.

Provided that no further appeal by a person who is required to pay any amount in terms of an order of the National Commission shall be entertained by the Supreme Court unless that person has deposited in the prescribed manner fifty percent of that amount or rupees fifty thousand, whichever is less.

24. Finality of Orders: Every order of a District Forum, the State Commission or the National Commission shall, if no appeal has been preferred against such order under the provisions of this Act be final.

24A. Limitation Period :

(1) The District Forum, the State Commission or the National Commission shall not admit a complaint unless it is filed within two years from the date on which the cause of action has arisen.

(2) Notwithstanding anything contained in sub-section (1), a complaint may be entertained after the period specified in sub-section (1), if the complaint satisfies the District Forum, the State Commission or the National Commission, as the case may be, that he had sufficient cause for not filing the complaint within such period.

Provided that no such complaint shall be entertained unless the National Commission, the State Commission or the District Forum, as the case may be, records its reasons for condoning such delay.

24 B. Administrative Control:

(1) The National Commission shall have administrative control over all the state Commission in the following matters, namely:

(i) calling for periodical return regarding institutions, disposal, pendency of cases.

(ii) issuance of instructions regarding adoption of uniform procedure in the hearing of matters, prior service of copies of documents produced by one party to the opposite parties, furnishing of English translation of judgements written in any language, speedy grant of copies of documents.

(iii) generally overseeing the functioning of the State Commission or the District Fora to ensure that the objects and purposes of the Act are best served without in any way interfering with their quasi-judicial freedom.

(2) The State Commission shall have administrative control over all the District Fora within its jurisdiction in all matters referred to in sub-section (1).

25. Enforcement of orders by the Forum, the State Commission or the National Commission –

(1) Where an add interim order made under this Act, is not complied with the District Forum or the State Commission or the National Commission, as the case may be, may order the property of the person, not complying with such order to be attached.

(2) No attachment made under sub-section (1) shall remain in force for more than three months at the end of which, if the non-compliance continues, the property attached may be sold and the proceeds thereof, the District Forum or the State Commission or the National Commission may award such damages as it thinks fit to the complainant and shall pay the balance, if any, to the party entitled thereto.

(3) Where any amount is due from any person under an order made by a District Forum, State Commission or the National Commission, as the case may be, the person entitled to the amount may make an application to the District Forum, the State Commission or the National Commission, as the case may be, and such District Forum or the State Commission or the National Commission may issue a certificate for the said amount to the Collector of the district (by whatever name called) and the Collector shall proceed to recover the amount in the same manner as arrears of land revenue.

26. Dismissal of frivolous or vexatious complaints – Where a complaint instituted before the District Forum, the State Commission or the National Commission, as the case may be, is found to be frivolous or vexatious, it shall, for reasons to be recorded in writing, dismiss the complaint and make and order that the complainant shall pay to the opposite party such cost, not exceeding ten thousand rupees, as may be specified in the order.

27. Penalties –

(1) Where a trader or a person against whom a complaint is made or the complainant fails or omits to comply with any order made by the District Forum, the State Commission or the National Commission, as the case may be – such trader or person or complainant shall be punishable with imprisonment for a term which shall not be less than one month but which may extend to three years, or with fine which shall not be less than two thousand rupees but which may extend to ten thousand rupees, or with both:

(2) Notwithstanding anything contained in the code of Criminal Procedure, 1973, the District Forum or the State Commission or the National Commission, as the case may be, shall have the power of a Judicial Magistrate of the first class for the trial of offences under this Act, and on such conferment of powers, the District Forum or the State Commission or the National Commission, as the case may be, on whom the powers are so conferred, shall be deemed to be a Judicial Magistrate of the first class for the purpose of the Code of Criminal Procedure, 1973.

(3) All offences under this Act may be tried summarily by the District Forum or the State Commission or the National Commission, as the case may be.

27 A.

(1) Notwithstanding anything contained in the Code of Criminal Procedure, 1973, an appeal under section 27, both on facts and law, shall lie from –

1. the order made by the District Forum to the State Commission;
2. the order made by the State Commission to the National Commission; and
3. the order made by the National Commission to the Supreme Court.

(2) Except as aforesaid, no appeal shall lie to any court from any order of a District Forum or a State Commission or the National Commission.

(3) Every appeal under this section shall be preferred within a period of thirty days from the date of an order of a District Forum or a State Commission or, as the case may be, the National Commission:

Provided that the State Commission or the National commission or the Supreme Court, as the case may be, may entertain an appeal after the expiry of the said period of thirty days, if, it is satisfied that the appellant had sufficient cause for not preferring the appeal within the period of thirty days.

MISCELLANEOUS

28. Protection of action taken in good faith – No suit, prosecution or other legal proceedings shall lie against the members of the District Forum, the State Commission or the National Commission or any Officer or person acting under the direction of the District Forum, the State Commission or the National Commission for executing any order made by it or in respect of anything which is in good faith done or intended to be by such member, officer or person under this Act or under any rule or order made thereunder.

28.A

(1) All notices required by this Act to be served shall be served in the manner hereinafter mentioned in sub-section (2).

(2) The service of notices may be made by delivering or transmitting a copy thereof by registered post acknowledgement duly addressed to opposite party against whom complaint is made or to the complainant by speed post or by such courier service as are approved by the District Forum, the State Commission or the National Commission, as the case may be, or by any other means of transmission of documents (inclding FAX message).

(3) When an acknowledgement or any other receipt purporting to be signed by the opposite party or his agent or by the complainant is received by the District Forum, the State Commission or the National Commission, as the case may be, or postal article contraining the notice is received back by such District Forum, State Commission or the National Commission, with an endorsement purporting to have been made by a postal employee or by any person authorised by the courier service to the effect that the opposite party or his agent or complainant had refused to take delivery of the postal article containing the notice or had refused to accept the notice by any other means specified in sub-section (2) when tendered or transmitted to him, the District Forum or the State Commission or the National Commission, as the case may be, shall declare that the notice had been duly served on the opposite party or to the complainant:

Provided that where the notice was properly addressed, pre-paid and duly sent by registered post acknowledgement due, a declaration referred to in this sub-section shall be made notwithstanding the fact that the acknowledgement has been lost or mislaid, or for any other reason, has not been received by the District Forum, the State Commission or the National Commission, as the case may be, within thirty days from the date of issue of notice.

(4) All notices required to be served on an opposite party or to complainant shall be deemed to be sufficiently served, if addressed in the case of the opposite party to the place where business or profession is carried and in case of complainant the place where such person actually and voluntarily resides.

29. Power to remove difficulties –

(1) If any difficulty arises in giving effect to the provisions of the Act the Central Government may, by order in the Official Gazette, make such provisions not inconsistent with the provisions of this Act as it appears to it to be necessary or expedient for removing the difficulty.

Provided that no such order shall be made after the expiry of a period of two years from the commencement of this Act.

(2) Every order made under this section shall, as soon as may be after it is made, be laid before each House of Parliament.

(3) If any difficulty arises in giving effect to the provisions of the Consumer Protection (Amendment) Act, 2002, the Central Government may, by order, do anything not inconsistent with such provisions for the purpose of removing the difficulty:

Provided that no such order shall be made after the expiry of a period of two years from the commencement of the Consumer Protection (Amendment) Act, 2002.

(4) Every order made under sub-section (3) shall be laid before each House of Parliament.

29A. Vacancies or defects in appointment not to invalidate orders –

No act or proceeding of the District Forum, the State Commission or the National Commission shall be invalid by reason only of the existence of any vacancy amongst its member or any defect in the constitution thereof.

30. Power to make rules –

(1) **The Central Government** may, by notification, made rules for carrying out the provisions contained in clause (a) of sub-section (1) of section 2, clause (b) of sub-section 4, sub-section (2) of section 5, sub-section (2) of section 12, clause (vi) of sub-section (4) of section 13, clause (hb) of sub-section (1) of section 14, section 19, clause (b) of sub-section (1) and sub-section (2) of section 20, section 22 and section 23 of this Act.

(2) **The State Government** may, by notification make rules for carrying out the provisions contained in clause (b) of sub-section (2) and sub-section (4) of section 7, clause (b) of sub-section (2) and sub-section (4) of section 8A, clause (b) of sub-section (1) and sub-section (3) of section 10, clause (c) of sub-section (1) of section 13, clause (hb) of sub-section (1) and sub-section (3) of section 14, section 15 and clause (b) of sub-section (1) and sub-section (2) of section 16 of this Act.

30A.

(1) **The National Commission** may, with the previous approval of the **Central Government**, by notification, make regulations not inconsistent with this Act to provide for all matters for which provision is necessary or expedient for the purpose of which provision is necessary or expedient for the purpose of giving effect to the provisions of this Act.

(2) In particular and without prejudice to the generality of the foregoing power, such regulations may make provisions for the cost of adjournment of any proceeding before the District Forum, the State Commission or the National Commission, as the case may be, which a party may be ordered to pay.

31. Laying of rules –

(1) Every rule and every regulation made under this Act shall be laid, as soon as may be after it is made, before each House of Parliament, while it is in session, for a total period of thirty days which may be comprised in one session or in two or more successive sessions and if before the expiry of the session immediately following the session or the successive sessions and if before the expiry of the session immediately following the session or the successive sessions aforesaid, both Houses agree in making any modification in the rule or regulation or both Houses agree that the rule or regulation should not be made, the rule or regulation shall thereafter have effect only in such modified form or be of no effect, as the case may be; so, however, that any such modification or annulment shall be without prejudice to the validity of anything previously done under that rule or regulation.

(2) Every rule made by a State Government under this Act shall be laid as soon as may be after it is made, before the State Legislature.

THE CONSUMER PROTECTION RULES (AMENDED UP TO 10.2.2005)

In exercise of the powers conferred by sub-section (1) of section 30 of the Consumer Protection Act, 1986 (68 of 1986), Central Government hereby makes the following rules, namely:

1. Short title, extent and commencement –

(1) These rules may be called **the Consumer Protection Rules, 1987** (as amended utp 2005)

(2) They shall come into force on the date of their publication in the Official Gazette.

2. Definitions. – In these rules, unless the context otherwise require –

(a) **"Act"** means the Consumer Protection Act, 1986 (68 of 1986).

(b) **"agent"** means a person duly authorised by a party to present any complaint, appeal or reply on its behalf before the National Commission;

(c) **"appellant"** means a party which makes an appeal against the order ot the State Commission;

(d) **"chairman"** means a chairman of the Central Consumer Protection Council established under sub-section (1) of the section 4 of the Act;

(e) **"memorandum"** means any memorandum of appeal filed by the appellant;

(f) **"opposite party"** means a persons who answers complaint or claim;

(g) **"president"** means the President of the National Commission;

(h) **"respondent"** means the person who answers any memorandum of appeal;

(i) **"section"** means section of the Act;

(j) **"state"** includes Union Territories also;

(k) **works and expressions** used in the rules and not defined but defined in the Act shall have the meanings respectively assigned to them in the Act.

2A. State Government to recognise a laboratory as an appropriate laboratory –

(1) For the purpose of obtaining recognition as an appropriate laboratory, the applicant shall send application, in triplicate, in the proforma prescribed by the Bureau of Indian Standards with the relevant details to the Department concerned with the consumer protection work of the State Government.

(2) The State Government on receiving the application from the applicant, shall forward its two copies to the Bureau of Indian Standards assess the suitability of the laboratory from the standards prescribed by them (Bureau of Indian Standards). The fee charged by the Bureau of Indian Standards, for this purpose, shall be paid by the applicant.

(3) The State Government on receiving the recommendations and approval of the Bureau of Indian Standards, shall notify that laboratory as an "appropriate laboratory" for the purpose of Consumer Protection Act., 1986, for a period of three years.

3. The Constitution of the Central Consumer Protection Council and the Working Groups –

(1) The Central Government shall, by notification in the Official Gazette constitute the Central Consumer Protection Council (hereinafter referred to as the Central Council) which shall consist of the following members, not exceeding 150, namely;

(a) the Minister In-Charge of Consumer Affairs in the Central Government who shall be the Chairman of the Central Council;

(b) the Minister of State (where he is not holding independent charge) or Deputy Minister-in-charge of Consumer Affairs in the Central Government who shall be the Vice-Chairman of the Central Council;

(c) the Minister In-Charge of Consumer Affairs in States;

(d) eight Members of Parliament – five from the Lok Sabha and three from the Rajya Sabha;

(e) the Secretary of the National Commissioner for Scheduled Castes and Scheduled Tribes;

(f) representatives of the Central Government Departments and Autonomous Organisations concerned with consumer interests – not exceeding twenty;

(a) The Registrar, National Consumer Disputes Redressal Commission, New Delhi.

(g) representatives of the Consumer Organisations or consumers – not less than thirty-five;

(h) representatives of women – not less than ten;

(i) representatives of farmers, trade and industries – not exceeding twenty;

(j) persons capable of representing consumer interest not specified above – not exceeding fifteen;

(k) the Secretary In-Charge of Consumer Affairs in the Central Government shall be the member-secretary of the Central Council.

(2) The term of the Council shall be three years.

(3) Any member may, by writing under his hand to the Chairman of the Central Council, resign from the Council. The vacancies so caused or otherwise, shall be filled from the same category by the Central Government and such person shall hold office so long as the member whose place he fills would have been entitled to hold office, if the vacancy had not occurred.

(4) For the purpose of monitoring the implementation of the recommendations of the Central Council and to suggest the working of the Council, the Central Government may constitute from amongst the members of the Council, a Standing Working Group, under the chairmanship of the Member Secretary of the Council. The Standing Working Group shall consist of not exceeding 30 members and shall meet as and when considered necessary by the Central Government.

4. Procedure of the Central Council. – Under sub-section (2) of section 5, the Central Council shall observe the following procedure in regard to the transaction of its business,

(1) The meeting of the Central Council shall be presided over by the Chairman. In the absence of the Chairman, the Vice Chairman shall preside over the meeting of the Central Council. In the absence of the Chairman and the Vice Chairman, the Central Council shall elect a member to preside over that meeting of the Council.

(2) Each meeting of the Central Council shall be called by giving not less than ten days from the date of issue, notice in writing to every member.

(3) Every notice of a meeting of the Central Council shall specify the place and the day and hour of the meeting and shall contain statement of business to be transacted thereat.

(4) No proceedings of the Central Council shall be invalid merely by reasons of existence of any vacancy in or any defect in the constitution of the Council.

(5) For the purpose of performing its functions under the Act, the Central Council may constitute from amongst its members, such working groups as it may deem necessary and every working group so constituted shall perform such functions as are assigned to it by the Central Council. The findings of such working groups shall be placed before the Central Council for its consideration.

(6) In connection with the journey undertaken to and fro by the non-official members for attending the meeting of the Central Consumer Protection Council or its working group, they shall be entitled to avail first class or two-tier air-conditioned class of railway accommodation by all trains (including Rajdhani Express) and claim such fare or cost of actual mode of travel, whichever is less. The non-official members from Island territories shall be entitled to, to and fro air journey (economy class) in domestic airlines from the Islands to the nearest mainland airport and thereafter rail fare by entitled class. The non-official members who are senior citizens shall be entitled to, to and fro air-journey (economy class) in domestic airlines on availing senior citizen concessional air fare for their journeys provided the distance being travelled is 1000 kms. or above. The non-official members shall be entitled to a sum of ₹ 1,000/- per each day of the meeting as incidental charges to cover the expenditure towards their daily allowance, lodging, local conveyance from residence to the station/airport and from station/airport to the venue of meeting and *vice-versa*. **Every claim made under this sub-rule shall be subject to certifying that the member will not claim any benefit from any other Central Government Ministry, Department or Organization during his visit for attending the meeting of the Central Consumer Protection Council or any of its Working Group. Local non-official members residing at the place of the venue of the meeting, shall be paid consolidated conveyance and hire charges to the tune of ₹ 200 per diem irrespective of the classification of the city. Members of Parliament attending meetings of the Councill or its Working Group shall be entitled to travelling and daily allowances at such rates as are admissible to such member."**

(7) The resolution passed by the Central Council shall be recommendatory in nature.

5. Place of the National Commission – The office of the National Commission shall be located in the Union Territory of Delhi.

6. Working days and office hours of the National Commission – The working days and office hours of the National Commission shall be the same as that of the Central Government.

7. Seal and emblem – The official seal and emblem of the National Commission shall be such as the Central Government may specify.

8. Sitting of the National Commission – The sitting of the National Commission as and when necessary, shall be convened by the President.

9. Staff of the National Commission – The Central Government shall appoint such staff as may be necessary to assist the National Commission in its day to day work and to perform such other functions as are provided under the Act and these rules or assigned to it by the President. The salary payable to such staff shall be defrayed out of the consolidated Fund of India.

9A. Fee for making complaints before District Forum –

(1) Every complaint filed under sub-section (1) of section 12, under sub-section (1) of section 17 and clause (a) of section 21 with a District Forum shall be accompanied by a fee, as specified in the table given below in the form of crossed **Demand Draft drawn on a nationalised bank or through a crossed Indian Postal Order drawn in favour of the President of the District Forum, Registrar of the State Commission or the Registrar of the National Commission**, as the case may be, and payable at the respective place where the District Forum, State Commission or the National Commission is situated.

(2) The concerned authority referred to in sub-rule (1) shall credit the amount of fee received by it into the Consumer Welfare Fund of the respective State and where such fund is not established into the Receipt Account of the State Government and in the case of National Commission, to the Consumer Welfare Fund of the Central Government.

Table 1

Sr. No.	*Value of goods or services and the compensation claimed*	*Amount of fee payable*
1.	Upto one lakh Rupees – for Complainants who are under the Below Poverty Line holding Antyodaya Anna Yojana cards.	Nil
2.	Upto one lakh Rupees – For complainants other than Antyodaya Anna Yojana cardholders	₹ 100
3.	Above one lakh and upto five lakh Rupees	₹ 200
4.	Above five lakh and upto ten lakh Rupees	₹ 400
5.	Above ten lakh and upto twenty lakh Rupees	₹ 500
	State Commission	
6.	Above twenty lakh and upto fifty lakh Rupees	₹ 2,000
7.	Above fifty lakh and upto one crore Rupees	₹ 4,000
	National Commission	
8.	Above one crore Rupees	₹ 6,000

(3) The complainants who are under Below Poverty Line shall be entitled for the exemption of payment of fee only on production of an attested copy of Antyodaya Anna Yojana cards.

10. Additional powers of the National Commission, State Commission and District forum –

(1) The National Commission, the State Commission and the District Forum shall have power to require any person,

(a) to produce before, and allow to be examined and kept by an officer of the National Commission, the State Commission or the District Forum, as the case may be, specified in this behalf, such books, accounts, documents or commodities in the custody or under the control of the person so required as may be specified or described in the requisition, if the examination of such books, accounts documents or commodities are required for the purpose of this Act;

(b) to furnish to an officer so specified, such information as may be required for the purpose of this Act.

(2)

(a) Where during any proceedings under this Act, the National Commission, the State Commission or the District Forum, as the case may be, has any ground to believe that any book, paper, commodity or document which may be required to be produced in such proceedings, are being or may be, destroyed, mutilated, altered, falsified or secreted, it may, by written order, authorise any officer to exercise the power of entry and search of any premises. Such authorised officer may also seize such books, papers, documents or commodities as are required fror the purpose of this Act:

Provided that such seizure shall be communicated to the National Commission, the State Commission or the District Forum, as the case may be, as soon as it is made or within a period not exceeding 72 hours of making such seizure after specifying the reasons in writing for making such seizure.

(b) The National Commission, the State Commission or the District Forum, as the case may be, on examination of such seized documents or commodities, as the case may be, may order the retention thereof or may return it to the party concerned.

10A. Credit of the fine into the Consumer Welfare Fund when consumers are not identified conveniently.

(1) Where an order is passed by the National Commission in exercise of the powers vested under clause (hb) of sub-section (1) of section 14 directing the opposite party to pay such amount as determined by it on account of loss or injury suffered due to defects in goods complained-gains-or alleged deficiency of service to a large number of consumers, who are not identifiable conveniently;

Such sum shall be credited by the National Commission in the Consumer Welfare Fund established by the Central Government under section 12 (c) of the Central Excise Act, 1944 (1 of 1944).

(2) Any amount credited to the said Fund shall be utilized in accordance with the provisions of the Consumer Welfare Fund Rules, 1992.

10B. Number of Members in the National Commission :- The Natioonal Commission shall consist of not less than four members and not more than nine members and at least one of them shall be a woman.

11. Salaries, honorarium and other allowances of the President and Members of the National Commission –

(1) The President of the National Commission shall be entitled to salary, allowances and other perquisites as are available to a sitting judge of the supreme Court and other members, if sitting on whole-time basis, shall receive a consolidated honorarium of ten thousand rupees per month or if sitting on part-time basis, a consolidated honorarium of five hundred rupees per day of sitting.

(2) The President and the members shall be entitled to travelling and daily allowances on official tours at the same rates as are admissible to group 'A' Officers of the Central Government.

(2A) The President and the members of the National Commission shall be entitled to conveyance allowance of one hundred fifty rupees per day of its sitting or a sum of one thousand and five hundred rupees per month, as may be opted by them.

(3) The honorarium or the salary, as the cause may be, and other allowances shall be defrayed out of the Consolidated Fund of India.

12. Terms and conditions of service of the President and members of the National Commission –

(1) Before appointment, the President and a member of the National Commission shall have to take an undertaking that he does not and will not have any such financial or other interest as is likely to affect prejudicially his functions as such member.

(2) Every member of the National Commission shall hold office for a term of five years or upto the age of seventy years, whichever is earlier and shall not be eligible for re-appointment.

(3) Notwithstanding anything contained in sub-rule (2) the President or a member may. –

(a) by writing under his hand and addressed to the Central Government resign his office at any time but his office shall become vacant only when such resignation is accepted by the Central Government,

(b) be removed from his office in accordance with the provisions of rule 13.

(4) The terms and conditions of service of the President and the members shall not be varied to their disadvantage during their tenure of office.

(5) A casual vacancy caused by resignation or removal of the President or any other member of the National Commission under sub-rule (3) or otherwise shall be filled by fresh appointment.

(6) When the office of the President of the National Commission is vacant or a person occupying such office is by reason of absence or otherwise, unable to perform the duties of his office, the same shall, save as otherwise provided in the proviso to section 22D be performed by the senior most member of the National Commission.

(7) The President or any member ceasing to hold office as such shall not hold any appointment in or be connected with the management or administrations of an organisation which have been the subject of any proceeding under the Act during his tenure for a period of 5 years from the date on which he ceases to hold such office.

13. Removal of president or members from office in certain circumstances –

(1) The Central Government may remove from office, the President or any member, who,

(a) has been adjudged as an insolvent; or

(b) has been convicted of an offence which, in the opinion of the Central Government, involves moral turpitude; or

(c) has become physically or mentally incapable of acting as the President or the Member; or

(d) has acquired such financial or other interest as is likely to affect prejudicially his functions as the President or a Member; or

(e) has so abused his position as to render his continuance in office prejudicial to the public interest; or

(f) remain absent in three consecutive sittings except for reasons beyond his control.

(2) Notwithstanding anything contained in sub rule (1), the President or any Member of the National Commission shall not be removed from his office except by an order made by the Central Government on the grounds specified in clauses (d), (e) and (f) of that sub-rule and after an inquiry held by a Sitting Judge of the Supreme Court

nominated by the Chief Justice of India in which the President or Member of the National Commission, as the case may be, has been informed of the charges against him and given a reasonable opportunity of being heard in respect of those charges and found guilty.

14. Procedure to be followed by the National Commission –

(1) A complaint containing the following particulars shall be presented by the complainant in person or by his agent to the National Commission or be sent by registered post, addressed to the National Commission:

(a) the name, description and the address of the complainant:

(b) the name description and address of the opposite party or parties, as the case may be, so far as they can be ascertained;

(c) the facts relating to the complaint and when and where it arose;

(d) documents in support of the allegations contained in the complaint;

(e) the relief which the complainant claims:

(1A) Every complaint under sub-rule (1) shall be filed in quadruplicate or with such number of copies as may be required by the National Commission and accompanied by the relevant fee as is specified in rule 9A.

(2) The National Commission shall, in disposal of any complaint before it, as far as possible, follow the procedure and conditions including the provisions governing adjournments as laid down in section 12 and 13 in relation to the complaints received by the District Forum, with such modification as may be considered necessary by the commission.

(3) On the date of hearing or any other date to which hearing could be adjourned, it shall be obligatory on the parties or their agents to appear before the National Commission. Where the complainant or agent fails to appear before the National Commission on such days, the National Commission may in its dicretion either dismiss the complaint for default or decide it on merits. Where the opposite party or its agent fails to appear on the date of hearing the National commission may decide the complaint *ex parte*.

(4) The National Commission may, on such terms as it deems fit and at any stage of the proceedings, adjourn the hearing of the complaint but the complaint shall be decided as far as possible within a period of three months from the date of notice received by opposite party where complaint does not require analysis or testing of commodities and within five months if it requires analysis or testing of commodities.

(4A) In the event of a complaint being disposed of after the period specified in sub-rule (4), the National Commission shall record in writing, the reasons for the delay in such disposal.

(5) If after the proceedings conducted under sub-rule (3), the National Commission is satisfied with the allegations contained in the complaint, it shall issue orders to the opposite party or parties, as the case may be, directing him or them to take one or more of the things as mentioned in sub-section (1) of section 14. The National Commission shall also have the power to direct that any order passed by it, where no appeal has been preferred under section 2 or where the order of the National Commission has been affirmed by the Supreme Court under the section, be published in the Official Gazette or through any other media and no legal proceedings shall lie against the National Commission or any media for such publication.

14A. Appeal before National Commission – Every appeal filed in terms of section 19 shall be accompanied by such amount as specified in the second proviso to the said section and such amount may be remitted in the form of a crossed Demand Draft drawn on a nationalized bank in favour of the Registrar, National Commission, payable at Delhi. The National Commission dealing with the appeals filed before them shall follow the provisions of section 19 and 19A as may be required to hear the appeals filed before the Commission.

Explanation – In this rule, "nationalized bank" means a corresponding new bank specified in the First Schedule to the Banking Companies (Acquisition and Transfer of Undertakings) Act, 1970 (5 of 1970) or a corresponding new bank specified in the First Schedule to the Banking Companies (Acquisition and Transfer of Undertakings) Act, 1980 (40 of 1980).

15. Procedure for hearing the appeal –

(1) Memorandum shall be presented by the appellant or his agent to the National Commission in person or be sent by registered post addressed to the commission.

(2) Every memorandum filed under sub-rule (1) shall be in legible handwriting preferable typed and shall set forth concisely under distinct heads, the grounds of appeal without any argument or narrative and such grounds shall be numbered consecutively.

(3) Each memorandum shall be accompanied by a crossed demand draft as referred to in rule 14A and by a certified copy of the order of the State Commission appealed against and such of the documents as may be required to support grounds of objection mentioned in the memorandum.

(4) When the appeal is presented after the expiry of the period of limitation as specified in the Act, the memorandum shall be accompanined by an application supported by an affidavit setting forth the facts on which the appellant relies to satisfy the National Commission that he has sufficient cause for not preferring the appeal within the period of limitation.

(5) The appellant shall submit four copies or such number of copies of the memorandum to the Commission for official purpose.

(6) On the date of hearing or on any other day to which hearing may be adjourned, it shall be obligatory for the parties or their agents to appear before National Commission. If appellant or his agent fails to appear on such date, the National Commission may in its discretion either dismiss the appeal or decide *ex parte* on merits. If the respondent or his agent fails to appear on such date, the National Commission shall proceed *ex parte* and shall decide the appeal on merits of the case.

(7) The appellant shall not, except by leave of the National Commission, urge or be heard in support of any ground of objection not set forth in the memorandum but the National Commission, in deciding the appeal, may not confine to the grounds of objection set forth in the memorandum:

Provided that the Commission shall not rest its decision on any other ground other than those specified in the memorandum unless the party who may be affected thereby, has been given, an opportunity of being heard by the National Commission.

(8) No adjournment shall ordinarily be granted by the National Commission, unless sufficient cause is shown and the reasons for grant of adjournment have been recorded in writing by the Commission. The National Commission may also adjourn the hearing of the appeal su motu, on such terms as it may think fit and at any stage of the proceedings for reasons to be recorded in writing. The appeal shall be decided, as far as possible, within ninety days from the date of its admission. In the event of an appeal being disposed of after the period so specified, the National Commission shall record in writing the reasons of the same at the time of disposal of the said appeal.

(9) The order of the National Commission shall be communicated to the parties concerned free of cost.

15A. Sitting of the National Commission and signing of order –

(1) Every proceeding of the National Commission shall be conducted by the President or the seniormost member and at least two members thereof sitting together except when a bench is constituted by the President of the National Commission with one or more members as he may deem fit. Provided that one member or members for any reason are unable to conduct the proceeding till it is completed, the President or the seniormost member, as provided under section 22D of the Act, shall conduct such proceeding from the stage at which it was last heard by the previous member.

(2) Every order made by the National Commission shall be signed by the President or the seniormost member as provided under section 22D and at least two members who conducted the proceeding and if there is any difference of opinion among themselves, the opinion of majority shall be the order of the National Commission.

Provided that where the proceeding is conducted by the President or the seniormost member as provided under section 22D and three members thereof and they differ on any point or points, they shall state the point or points on which they differ and refer the same to the other member for hearing on such point and such point or points shall be decided accordingly to the opinion of the majority of the National Commission.

16. Manner of deposit of amount in appeals before Supreme Court –

Every appeal filed before the Supreme Court in terms of section 23 shall be accompanied by an amount as provided in the second proviso to that section and such amount may be remitted in the form of a crossed Demand Draft drawn on a nationalized bank in favour of Registrar, Supreme Court, payable at Delhi.

Explanation – In this rule, "nationalized bank" means a corresponding new bank specified in the First Schedule to the Banking Companies (Acquisition and Transfer of Undertakings) Act, 1970 (5 of 1970) or a corresponding new bank specified in the First Schedule to the Banking Companies (Acquisition and Transfer of Undertakings) Act, 1980 (40 of 1980).

With the passage of time development of modern economic systems, consumer protection in all its forms has required even more complex regulations and controls on marketing activities.

In today's growing and changing market place there is an important role of the following in protecting the interest of the consumers.

- The manufactures/trading institutions
- The Government
- The voluntary organizations
- The consumer themselves

With the tremendous growth of our industrial society during the twentieth century, a need arose for government to act as a protector of consumers against exploitation by manufacturers. Initially the primary concern was the health and safety of consumers. But as industrialization developed and merchandising and marketing practices grew more complex, the consumer needed to become more and better informed and protected.

PRESENT STATE OF CONSUMER AFFAIRS IN INDIA

In the olden days, the mothers milked the cows; the daughters set it out in pans to separate the cream, one of the sons sold it in the market. Today the agricultural department is mobilized, the milk is homogenized, the supplies are motorized, and the dairies are organized. The result is that the Indian consumer is victimized (Hidayatullah, 1984).

It is estimated that due to unhealthy trade practices restored to by the businessman, the consumers in India are cheated to the extent of ₹ 1,600 crores every year (Rayudu, 1983, p. 23).

In an environment of limited choice, inadequate supplies, incomplete information, gullible customers, and unlimited demand, it is inevitable that the Indian consumer gets cheated. Some glaring examples of how he is affected are given below in the following categories: Black Marketing, Inflation, Public distribution system, Adulteration, Weights and Measures, Environmental Pollution and Advertisement.

1. Black Marketing, Hoarding and Profiteering

In a black market economy the ruling price is not necessarily the consequence of the market stabilizer as is the case with conditions of competition. Generally, the black market is operated by some group of people and not by a single individual. Therefore, we generally find a fluctuating price level with an upward slant. In order to attain maximum profits, artificial manipulation of either demand or supply or both is common in a Black market. The Black Market operators do not care for productivity, growth and equal distribution but aim at maximization of profits only.

Presently in India, wholesalers and particularly retailers are in the habit of hoarding, profiteering and black marketing. Almost all goods are subject to price control are invariably available in black market in all big cities. Today, it is the seller's market for consumer goods and not the buyer's market. Many items of consumer goods like edible oil, sugar, kerosene and cooking gas are in short supply through quiet often artificial and manipulated. When goods are not available and the customer has to stand in queues to get what he wants there is little scope for complaint by him of quality and measure and has to pay excess amount to get the goods and services.

2. Inflation

It is noted that a moderate rise in the prices of goods is in the interests of the economy as it serves as an incentive for producers to produce more.

However, most developing countries, including India are facing undue rise in the price of goods, particularly essential goods. Though inflation not only reduces the real income of the poor but creates problems to the government and the economy as a whole.

A developing country like India is compelled to incur heavy expenditures on various items under a programme of planned development. However, there are serious limitations to raising the output of essential goods. We are facing shortages in respect of crucial inputs like capital. Our villages do not even have the minimum infrastructural facilities. Naturally, there is always a mismatch between supply of money and the availability of goods. While money supply is increasing by about 10 percent per anum, real national income is increasing at around 2 per cent per anum. To this extent, inflation is a mandatory phenomenon.

However, inflation in the Indian context is not really a monetary phenomenon. It is multi-dimensional as price rise is due to social, cultural, political and psychological factors. India is having a mixed economy

With both public and private sector functioning side by side. The private sector is still predominant; its activities are governed by profit motive. Our economy suffers from inequalities in income and wealth. No wonder, our production pattern turns to be preposterous in the market, there are enough comfort and luxuries, but shortages of essential goods! It is difficult to control inflation so long as this situation continues.

Scarcity of resources and goods on one hand and inflationary trends partly inherent in increased state expenditure on the other, make situation in the developing countries unfavorable for the common people (Yogender, 1980, p.17). Basically, inflation rises because there is more income to spend, and less goods to spend it on. Measures like price control, taxation and rationing only relive the symptoms. A lasting solution lies in increasing production on a broader basis and to utilize the market where possible, within the framework of social goals (Narayanan, 1979).

3. Functioning of Public Distribution System — Fair Price Shops

The existing infrastructure of the Public Distribution System not only in Delhi but in other parts of the country has undoubtedly helped in the proper distribution of foodgrains including pulses, kerosene, soft coke, soap, cycle tyres and tubes, sugar, vegetable oil. Most of these items are at present, being sold through retail outlets, co-operative societies or the super bazaars.

During the sixth plan period, the public distribution system admittedly helped in checking the social menace of rising prices particularly of essential commodities. The system also helped in containing the inflation. The seventh plan strategy has also recognized the public distribution system as a permanent feature for controlling the price rise and also for reducing the fluctuations in the distribution of essential goods. Even the 20- point programme as envisaged by our Late Prime Minister Mrs. Indira Gandhi has given due recognition to this system for ensuring adequate and equitable distribution of essential commodities to the poor and needy sections of the society.

According to Government records, the public distribution system had been functioning in the country for many decades and since then a large number of commodities besides food grains, had been coming under its ambit. The public commodities system operates on a national level with the sole objective of making available all essential goods to the consumers, especially those belonging to the weaker sections of our society at fair prices (Wig, 1986).

The very purpose of public distribution system through a chain of fair price shops is defeated if ration commodities are either not available to those in need or are of so poor a quality that it leaves consumers disgusted. For example, a report on public distribution system in West Bengal By CAG (1987) revealed that –

(a) Quality of rice was bad, broken and full of dust and no parboiled rice was allocated. There was an instance of superior quality Basmati rice getting spoilt as it was left in the warehouse for 3 years, the officers being unable to decide its price. In comparison to rice, quality of wheat was found to be generally better.

(b) People were obliged to buy rice from open market, Because the rice supplies through ration shops was largely unfit for human consumption. Oil not being supplied regularly, the consumers could not comment on the quality of oil. Sugar was often given on due slips but there was no provision for due slips for oil or rice. Edible cooking oil was found to be very much in short supply.

(c) Consumers believe that the good quality goods are lifted against fictitious ration cards, by unscrupulous persons with the connivance of the shopkeepers and sold in the open market.

(d) There is no system of checking weights' at ration shops.

(e) There is no co-ordination between ration shops and rationing officers.

The PDS thus needs to be strengthened, recognized and revitalized properly for the attainment of objectives for which it was started in every part of the country (Trivedi, 1979). The Sixth Plan declared: An efficient public distribution system requires annexus between production, procurement, transportation, storage and distribution of the selected commodities (Planning Commission, 1981).

The PDS cannot be effective unless it is backed up by scientific mode of classification to identify the consumers. The down-trodden class consumers are generally found indulging in black marketing of sugar. They take their respective quota from the shop and sell at higher rates elsewhere and then purchase wheat and rice. This flaw in distribution system can be eliminated if only the actual requirement of a consumer is classified and identified to supply the required quantities of commodities (Roy and Srivastava, 1982, p.30).

At present, the system suffers from regular supplies and innumerable bogus ration cards (Shankaraiah, Ojha and Sadanndam, 1982, p.17).

The voluntary consumer organizations should ensure effective functioning of the PDS and provide more effective consumer protection. It rightly declared that "there is need for strengthening the intelligence, early warning and demand-supply management information system". (Planning Commission, 1981, p.81). Thus, the sixth plan laid stress not only on increasing the output of essential goods but efficient management of the supply of those goods in order to safeguard the interest of the customers, particularly the vulnerable section. Our present Prime Minister Mr. P.V.Narashima Rao has also time and again reiterated to reach out the Fair Price Shops (FPS) facility to the remotest villages which needs their attention

4. Adulteration

Adulteration of food articles is rampant in the country and has become a grave menace to the health and well-being of the community. It makes a heavy dent in the already low nutritional standards and the benefits of many are spent are insidiously undermined. A major offensive against this evil is overdue (Govt. of India Gazette, 1976).

A survey conducted by the Consumer Council on India reveals that as much as 774 and 1063 deaths took place in the year 1972 and 1973 respectively due to adulteration of food articles. Sixty-five percent of deaths were attributed to liquor poisoning (Consumer Bulletin, 1974, pp.18-19).

Adulteration is not confined to food articles alone. 'Surma' an eye cosmetic, when recently tested, has indicated the presence of one to five per cent of lead in the samples which can damage the eyes. In view of the high price of petrol, it is being adulterated. It is difficult to detect adulteration of petrol as long as the kerosene content does not exceed 10 per cent.

5. Weights and Measures – Deceiving of Consumers by Traders

Usage of wrong weights and measures is illegal, but the practice is widely prevalent. But most consumers are blissfully ignorant. The enormous loss incurred by consumers by this method would surprise most consumers.

The traders are benefited in more than one way; they charge exorbitant prices, keep the quality below the prescribed standard and use wrong weights and measures. The weights and measures (Law revision) committee, popularly known as the Maitra committee, came to a sad conclusion, "even one per cent error in commercial transactions carried out in the country by inaccurate weights and measures cause the consumers a loss of over ₹ 170 crores in cities; the farmers stand to lose about ₹ 150 crores by a mal practice". Normally, the error and short weight is about 5 per cent and there the loss to the urban consumers and farmers will be about five times as much. A report later released in January 1977, has disclosed that under-weighing alone cheated the consumers to the tune of ₹ 3,000 crores annually (Sundaram, 1985, pp.55-56).

Almost the entire consumer trade revolves round weights and measures. While buying or selling one blindly depends on the genuineness of the weights and measures being used. The implications of these weights and measures themselves being fake can be mind-boggling.

What is of serious concern to the consumer is not only that a number of weights and measures are truly tampered with, but with one cannot depend even on packaged and tinned commodities where the net weight given in some cases is less than the actual weight.

The Standard Weights and Measures Enforcement Act, 1985, puts certain obligations on the manufacturer and seller of packaged commodities. All packed items must have the name and address of the manufacturer, name of the item packed, quantity of item, month and year of manufacture, maximum retail price. The manufacturer, distributor and retailer are liable to be prosecuted if any of the items are missing.

6. Environmental Pollution

With the tremendous technological advances, our environment is being polluted constantly by various sources endangering the lives of human and other living beings.

The pollution in the air is due to smoke and gasses emitted by automobiles, factories, power plants, etc. The water is contaminated by the effluents released by the factories in the rivers, lakes and ponds. The pesticides used by the farmers have caused widespread contamination in agricultural products like vegetables, fruits, cereals and pulses. In fact, a sample survey has revealed that 50 per cent of vegetables consumed by us are contaminated with pesticides (Financial Express, 1985). Besides this, animal foods like meat, milk, eggs and fish have invariably been found to contain levels of pesticides higher than the safe limits. To control the environmental pollution, Government has from time to time enacted various Acts. The Water (Prevention and Control of Pollution) Act, 1974. The Air (Prevention and control of pollution) Act, 1981 and The Environment Protection Act, 1986. Since protection of our environment is a must for our survival, every one of us should work for its success. This can be achieved by creating awareness among the masses about the seriousness of the problem along with the stricter enforcement of various Acts.

7. Advertisement

The advertising policy in India is based mostly on the commercial expediency rather than ethical principle. Spurious toiletries and cosmetics products, medicines and food items are a common feature in the market. Most of these spurious goods are sold under false advertisement, promising wild reliefs while in fact creating the opposite. In the cloth trade, for example, tall promises of fast color and durability are common, while often they do not stand few washes. Similarly, advertisement of some tooth pastes, cosmetics and figure-improving and body building apparatus make claims for the products without explaining how the claimed qualities produce the benefits suggested. Most of the mail order companies indulge in false and deceptive advertisement (Verma, 1978, p.5).

It may be pointed out that in India alone, mail order frauds run into several hundred crores of rupees (Garg, 1981, p.5).

In addition, many such advertisements are not only false in their content and promises but also a disgrace to public decency and morality.

In India, a number of measures to safeguard the consumer interest through legislative protection have been taken. For example, Essential Commodities Act, governs the production, procurement and distribution of all essential commodities. This Act has been amended in 1974, give more protection to consumers by ensuring quicker and more effective actions against the in social activities of the profiteers and blackmarketeers and hoarders.

Dishonest, deceptive and otherwise unprincipled business practices victimize Indian consumers in many ways. Consumers are hurt in the pocket by overcharging, by the purchase of inferior merchandise and by exortionate credit policies. Their health is endangered by impure foods and drugs or by the valueless medical devices. They or their children are often injured by poorly made appliances, unsafe articles and other defective items.

There are various Acts introduced in India from time to time which protects the interests of the consumers. Chief of them are:

1. Agricultural Produce Act, 1937
2. Fruits Products Order, 1955
3. Essential Commodities Act, 1955
4. Maharashtra Scheduled Articles Order, 1969
5. Weights and Measures Act, 1976
6. Prevention of Food Adulteration Act,1954
7. Prevention of Food Rules,1955
8. The Drug and Cosmetics Act,1940
9. Drug and Magic Remedies, 1954
10. The Dangerous Drug Act
11. Poisons Act
12. Bureau of Standards Act
13. Standards and Weights Measures (Packaged Commodities Rules, 1977)
14. Household Electrical Appliances Act, 1976
15. Indian Sales of Goods Act, 1930
16. M.R.T.P Act, 1969
17. Consumer Protection Act, 1986

Legislation is not a total answer to consumer complaints about business. What is needed is vigilant and united consumer organizations in various parts of the country.

Several consumer associations are doing useful work in this field. To name a few following societies deserve mention:

1. Karnataka Consumer Services Society, Bengaluru.
2. Consumer Guidance Centre, Cochin
3. Southern Consumers Union, Chennai
4. Citizen Action Group
5. Consumer Education and Research Centre, Ahmedabad
6. Consumer Guidance Bureau, Bhilai
7. Consumer Guidance Society of India, Mumbai
8. Consumer Action Forum, Kolkata
9. Consumer's Association, Bhimavaram (West Godavari Dist.), Andhra Pradesh
10. Consumer Protection Association, Agartala (Tripura)

These voluntary organisations in India are creating consumer awareness by imparting consumer education. Some are conducting research work while others are imparting training to the consumers.

President John F Kennedy, in his 1962 declaration of rights for the consumers (Engel, Kollet and Blackwell, 1973, p.614) stated that consumers have:

1. The right to safety
2. The right to be informed
3. The right to choose
4. The right to be heard

Lately in India, the Consumer Protection Act,1986, was enacted to include the following two additional rights.

1. Right to seek redressal
2. Right to Consumer Education

Major U.S. legislation Affecting Marketing

Legislation	Purpose
Sherman Antitrust Act(1890)	Prohibits monopolies and activities (price fixing, predatory pricing) that restrain trade or competition in interstate commerce.
Federal Food and Drug Act (1906)	Forbids the manufacture or sale of adulterated or fraudulently labeled foods and drugs. Created the Food and Drug Administration.
Clayton Act (1914)	Supplements the Sherman Act by prohibiting certain types of price discrimination, exclusive dealing, and tying clauses (which require a dealer to take additional products in a seller's line).
Federal Trade Commission Act (1914)	Establishes a commission to monitor and remedy unfair trade methods.
Robinson-Patman Act (1936)	Amends Clayton Act to define price discrimination as unlawful. Empowers FTC to establish limits on quantity discounts, forbid some brokerage allowances, and prohibit promotional allowances except when made available on proportionately equal terms.
Wheeler-Lea Act (1938)	Makes deceptive, misleading, and unfair practices illegal regardless of injury to competition. Places advertising of food and drugs under FTC jurisdiction.
Landam Trademark Act (1946)	Protects and regulates distinctive brand names and trademarks.
National Traffic and Safety Act (1958)	Provides for the creation of compulsory safety standards for automobiles and tires.
Fair Packaging and Labelling Act (1966)	Provides for the regulation of packaging and labeling of consumer goods, Requires that manufactures state what the package contains, who made it, and how much it contains.
Child Protection Act (1966)	Bans sale of hazardous toys and articles. Sets standards for child-resistant packaging.
Federal Cigarette Labelling and Advertising Act (1967)	Requires that cigarette packages contain the following statement: "Warning: The Surgeon General Has Determined That Cigarette Smoking is Dangerous to Your Health."
National Environment Policy Act (1969)	Establishes a national policy on the environment. The 1970 Recorganization Plan established the Environment Protection Agency.
Consumer Product Safety Act (1972)	Establishes a national policy on the environment. The 1970 Recognization Plan established the Environmental Protection Agency.
Consumer Product Safety Act (1972)	Authorizes the FTC to determine rules and regulations for consumer warranties and provides consumer access to redress, such as the class-action suit.
Children's Television Act (1990)	Limits number of commercials aired during children's programs.
Nutrition Labelling and Education Act (1990)	Requires that food product labels provide detailed nutritional information.
Telephone Consumer Protection Act (1991)	Establishes procedures to avoid unwanted telephone solicitations. Limits marketers' use of automatic telephone dialing systems and artificial or prerecorded voices.
Americans with Disabilities Act (1991)	Makes discrimination against people with disabilities illegal in public accommodations, transportation, and telecommunications.
Children's Online Privacy Protection Act (2000)	Prohibits Web sites or online services operators from collecting personal information from children without obtaining consent from a parent and allowing parents to review information collected from their children.

Chapter 1 A

Consumer Protection Rules, 1987

[GSR 398 (E), Dated 15-4-1987]

In exercise of the powers conferred by sub-section (1) of section 30 of the Consumer Protection Act, 1986 (68 of 1986), the Central Government hereby makes the following rules, namely :—

SHORT TITLE AND COMMENCEMENT

1.

(1) These rules may be called the Consumer Protection Rules, 1987.

(2) They shall come into force on the date of their publication in the Official Gazette.

Definitions

2. In these rules, unless the context otherwise requires,—

(a) "Act" means the Consumer Protection Act, 1986 (68 of 1986);

(b) "agent" means a person duly authorised by a party to present any complaint, appeal or reply on its behalf before the National Commission;

(c) "appellant" means a party which makes an appeal against the order of the State Commission;

(d) "chairman" means a chairman of the Central Consumer Protection Council established under sub-section (1) of section 4 of the Act;

(e) "memorandum" means any memorandum of appeal filed by the appellant;

(f) "opposite party" means a person who answers complaint or claim;

(g) "President" means the President of the National Commission;

(h) "respondent" means the person who answers any memorandum of appeal;

(i) "section" means section of the Act;

(j) "State" includes Union Territories also;

(k) words and expressions used in the rules and not defined but defined in the Act shall have the meanings respectively assigned to them in the Act.

State Governments, to recognise a laboratory as an appropriate laboratory —

2A.

(1) For the purpose of obtaining recognition as an appropriate laboratory, the applicant shall send application, in triplicate, in the proforma prescribed by the Bureau of Indian Standards with the relevant details to the Department concerned with the consumer protection work in the State Government.

Consumers be Alert Stay Safe

(2) The State Government on receiving the application from the applicant, shall forward its two copies to the Bureau of Indian Standards to assess the suitability of the laboratory from the standards prescribed by them (Bureau of Indian Standards). The fee charged by the Bureau of Indian Standards, for this purpose, shall be paid by the applicant.

(3) The State Government on receiving the recommendations and approval of the Bureau of Indian Standards, shall notify that laboratory as an 'appropriate laboratory' for the purpose of Consumer Protection AcL, 1986 for a period of three years.

The Constitution of the Central Consumer Protection Council and the Working Groups.

3.

(1) The Central Government shall, by notification in the Official Gazette, constitute the Central Consumer Protection Council (hereinafter referred to as the Central Council) which shall consist of '[the following members, not exceeding [1a][35], namely—]

(a) [the Minister in-chargc of Consumer Affairs in the Central Government], who shall be the Chairman of the Central Council;

(b) the Minister of State (where he is not holding independent charge) or Deputy Minister in-charge of Consumer Affairs in the Central Government who shall be the Vice-Chairman of the Central Council;

(c) the Minister in-charge of Consumer Affairs of two of the States from each region as mentioned in Schedule I to be changed by rotation on expiration of the term of the Council on each occasion;

(ca) an administrator (whether designated as administrator or Lieutenant Governor), of a Union Territory, to represent a Union Territory, as mentioned in Schedule II, to be changed by rotation on expiration of the term of the Council on each occasion;

(d) [two] Members of Parliament — [one] from the Lok Sabha and [one] from the Rajya Sabha;

(e) representatives of the Central Government Departments and autonomous organisations concerned with consumer interests - not exceeding the Registrar, National Consumer Disputes Redressal Commission, New Delhi;]

representatives of consumer organisations from amongst the Indian members of the International Organisation, namely, Consumer International — not exceeding six, to be nominated by the Central Government;

representatives with proven expertise and experience who are capable of representing consumer interests, drawn from amongst consumer organisations, consumer activists, women, farmers, trade and industry not exceeding five, one from each of the regions specified in Schedule annexed to these rules);

(f) the Secretaries in-charge of Consumer Affairs in the States to be nominated by the Central Government—not exceeding three;

(g) [the Secretary in-charge of Consumer Affairs in the Central Government] shall be the Member-Secretary of the Central Council.

(2) The term of the Council shall be three years.

(3) Any member may, by writing under his hand to the Chairman of the Central Council, resign from the Council. The vacancies, so caused or otherwise, shall be filled from the same category by the Central Government and such person shall hold office so long as the member whose place he fills, would have been entitled to hold office, if the vacancy had not occurred.

(4) Procedure of the Central Council.

4. Under sub-section (2) of section 5, the Central Council shall observe the following procedure in regard to the transaction of its business:—

(1) The meeting of the Central Council shall be presided over by the Chairman of the absence of the Chairman, the Vice-Chairman shall preside over the meeting of the Central Council. In the absence of the Chairman and the Vice-Chairman, the Central Council shall elect a member to preside over that meeting of the Council.

(2) Each meeting of the Central Council shall be called by giving not less than ten days from the date of issue, notice in writing to every member.

(3) Every notice of a meeting of the Central Council shall specify the place and the day and hour of the meeting and shall contain statement of business to be transacted thereat.

(4) No proceedings of the Central Council shall be invalid merely by reason of existence of any vacancy in or any defect in the constitution of the Council.

(5) For the purpose of performing its functions under the Act, the Central Council may constitute from amongst its members, such working groups as it may deem necessary and every working group so constituted shall perform such functions as are assigned to it by the Central Council. The findings of such working groups shall be placed before the Central Council for its consideration.

(6) The Selection Committee shall, subject to the provisions of sub-rule (6A), assess the suitability of the candidates for the post of Member:

Provided that the Selection Committee may, if it considers necessary, depending on the number of candidates, short list them on the basis of comparative merit and experience of such candidates for selection (6-4). The Selection Committee shall assess the suitability of the candidates and where short-listing is done, from among the short-listed candidates, for the post of Member in the following manner, namely :—

(a) in the case of candidates having judicial background, by assessing them on the basis of the judgments and other judicial orders passed by such candidates;

(b) in the case of candidates having experience of working under the Central Government or any State Government or an undertaking under the Central Government or a State Government, by assessing such candidates on the basis of their Annual Confidential Reports and their experience relevant to the post applied for;

(c) in other cases, the suitability of the short-listed candidates shall be assessed by the Selection Committee on the basis of personal interview conducted by it:

Provided that notwithstanding anything contained in this sub-rule, the Selection Committee may, for assessing the suitability of a class or category or candidates, if it considers necessary, call such class or category of candidates for interview for assessing their suitability for the post of Member.]

(7) The resolutions passed by the Central Council shall be recommendatory in nature place of the **National Commission.** The office of the National Commission shall be located in the Union Territory of Delhi. Working **days and** office hours of the National Commission.

6. The working days and office hours of the National Commission shall be the same as that of the Central Government. **Seal and Emblem.**

7. The official seal and emblem of the National Commission shall be such as the Central Government may specify. Sittings of **the National Commission.**

8. The sitting of the National Commission as and when necessary shall be convened by the President Staff of the **National Commission.**

9. The Central Government shall appoint such staff as may be necessary to assist the National Commission in its day-to-day work and to perform such other functions as are **Provided** under the Act and these Rules are assigned to it by the President. The salary payable to such staff shall be defrayed out of the Consolidated Fund of India. Fee for **making complaints** before **District Forum.**

9A. [(l)Every complaint filed under sub-section (1) of section 12, sub-section (1) of section 17 and clause *(a)* in sub-clause *(f)* of section 21 of the Act shall be accompanied by a fee as specified in the table given below in the form of crossed Demand Draft drawn on a nationalized bank or through a crossed Indian Postal Order in favour of the President of the District Forum, Registrar of the State Commission or the Registrar of the National Commission as the case may be, and payable at the respective place where the District Forum State Commission or the National Commission is situated, (1) The concerned authority referred to in sub-rule (2) shall credit the amount of fee received by it into the Consumer Welfare Fund of the respective State and where such Fund is not established into the Receipt Account of the State Government and in the case of the National Commission, to the Consumer Welfare Fund of the Central Government,

Sr. No. (1)	*Value of goods or services and the compensation claimed* (2)	*Amount of fee payable* (3)
	District Forum	
(1)	Upto one lakh rupees ₹ 100	
(2)	One lakh rupees and above but less than five lakh rupees	₹ 200
(3)	Five lakh rupees and above but less than ₹ 10 lakh	₹ 400
(4)	Ten lakh rupees and above but not exceeding twenty	₹ 500

Table

Sr. No. (1)	*Total value of goods or services and the compensation claimed* (2)	*Amount of fee payable* (3)
	District Forum	
1.	Up to one lakh rupees - For complainants who are	Nil
2.	under the Below Poverty Line holding Anlyodaya	₹ 100
3.	Anna Yojana cards Up to one lakh rupees -	₹ 200 ₹ 400
4.	For complainants other than Antyodaya Anna Yojana	₹ 500
5.	card holders Above one lakh and up to five lakh rupees Above five lakh and up to ten lakh rupees above ten lakh and up to twenty lakh rupees	
	State Commission	J
6.	Above twenty lakh and up to fifty lakh rupees Above	₹ 2,000 ₹ 4,000
7.	fifty lakh and up to one crore rupees	
	National Commission	
8.	Above one crore rupees	₹ 5,000

(3) The complainant who are under the Below Poverty Line shall be entitled for the exemption of payment of fee only on production of an attested copy of the Antyodaya Anna Yojana cards. Additional powers of the National Commission, State Commission and District Forum.

10.

(1) The National Commission, the State Commission and the District Forum shall have power to require any person,—

(a) to produce before, and allow to be examined and kept by an officer of thi National Commission, the State Commission or the District Forum, as the case may be, specified in this behalf, such books of account, documents or commodities in the custody or under the control of the person so required as may be specified or described in the requisition, if the examination of such books of account, documents or commodities are required for the purposes of this Act; to furnish to an officer so specified, such information as may be required for the purpose of this Act.

(2) Where during any proceedings under this Act the National Commission, i.e., State Commission or the District Forum, as the case may be, has any ground believe that any book, paper, commodity or document which may be required to be produced in such proceeding is being, or may be, destroyed, utilated, altered, falsified or secreted, it may, by written order, authorise any officer to exercise the power of entry and search of any premises. Such authorised officer may also seize such books, papers, documents or commodities as are required for the purpose of this Act:

Provided that such seizure shall be communicated to the National Commission, the State Commission or the District Forum, as the case may be, as soon as it made or within a period not exceeding 72 hours of making such seizure after specifying the reasons in writing for making such seizure. The National Commission, the State Commission or the District Forum, as ecase may be, on examination of such seized documents or commodities, as the case may be, may order the retention thereof or may return it to the party named. Credit of the fine into the Consumer Welfare Fund when consumers are not identified conveniently.

10A.

(1) Where an order is passed by the National Commission in exercise of the powers vested under clause *(hb)* of sub-section (1) of section 14 directing the opposite party to pay such amount as determined by it on account of loss or injury suffered due to defects in goods complained against or alleged deficiency of service to a large number of consumers, who are not identifiable conveniently, such sum shall be credited by the National Commission in the consumer Welfare Fund established by the Central Government under section 12C of the Central Excise Act, 1944 (1 of 1944).

(2) Any amount credited to the said Fund shall be utilized in accordance with p provisions of the Consumer Welfare Fund Rules, 1992.

Number of Members in the National Commission.

10B. The National Commission shall consist of not less than four members and not more than [nine] members and at least one of them shall be a Plan.

1. Inserted by the Consumer Protection (Amendment) Rules, 2004, *w.e.f.* 5-3-2004.
2. Substituted for "six" by the Consumer Protection (Second Amendment) Rules, 2005, *w.e.f.* 10-2-2005.

(3) An advertisement of a vacancy inviting applications from eligible candidates may be published in leading newspapers in India or by vacancy circulars or both, as may be decided by the Central Government.

(4) After scrutiny of the applications received till the last date specified for receipt of applications, a list of eligible candidates along with their applications shall be placed before the Selection Committee constituted under the third proviso to sub-section (1) of section 20.

(5) The Selection Committee shall consider all the applications of eligible applicants referred to it.

(6) The Selection Committee may, if it considers necessary, depending on the number of candidates, short list them on the basis of merit and call such short-listed candidates for personal interview to consider their suitability for the post of Member.

(7) The Selection Committee may, on the basis of its assessment made by it, recommend a panel of names of candidates for appointment as Members from amongst the applicants referred to in sub-rule (5) in order of merit for the consideration of the Central Government.

(8) The Central Government shall, before seeking approval of the Appointments Committee of the Cabinet, verify or cause to be verified the credentials and antecedents of the candidates selected by the Central Government from the panel recommended by the Selection Committee and satisfy the suitability of such candidates for appointment as Members.

(9) Every appointment of a Member shall be subject to his medical fitness.

Removal of President or members from office in certain circumstances.

13.

(1) The Central Government may remove from office, the President or any member who,—

(*a*) has been adjudged an insolvent; or

(*b*) has been convicted of an offence which, in the opinion of the Central Government, involves moral turpitude; or

(*c*) has become physically or mentally incapable of acting as the President or the member; or

(*d*) has acquired such financial or other interest as is likely to affect prejudicially his functions as the President or a member; or

(*e*) has so abused his position as to render his continuance in office prejudicial to the public interest; or

(*f*) remains absent in three consecutive sittings except for reasons beyond his control.

(2) Notwithstanding anything contained in sub-rule (1), the President or any member of the National Commission shall not be removed from his office except by an order made by the Central Government on the grounds specified in clauses *(d), (e)* and *(f)* of that sub-rule and after an inquiry held by a sitting Judge of the Supreme Court nominated by the Chief Justice of India in which the President or member of the National Commission, as the case may be, has been informed of the charges against him and given a reasonable opportunity of being heard in respect of those charges and found guilty procedure to be followed by **the National Commission.**

14.

(1) A complaint containing the following particulars shall be presented by the complainant in person or by his agent to the National Commission or be sent by registered post addressed to the National Commission :—

(*a*) the name, description and the address of the complainant;

(*b*) the name, description and address of the opposite party or parties, as the case may be, so far as they can be ascertained;

(*c*) the facts relating to the complaint and when and where it arose;

(*d*) documents in support of the allegations contained in the complaint;

(*e*) the relief which the complainant claims.

(1A) Every complaint under sub-rule (1) shall be filed in quadruplicate or with such number of copies as may be required by the National Commission.

(2) The National Commission shall, in disposal of any complaint before it, as far as possible, follow the procedure and conditions including the provisions governing adjournments as laid down in sections 12 and 13 in relation to the complaints received by the District Forum, with such modification as may be considered necessary by the Commission.

(3) On the date of hearing or any other date to which hearing could be adjourned, it shall be obligatory on the parties or their agents to appear before the National Commission. Where the complainant or his agent fails to appear belore the National Commission on such days, the National Commission may in its discretion either dismiss the complaint for default or decide it on merits. Where the opposite party or its agent fails to appear on the date of hearing, the National Commission may decide the complaint *ex pane.*

(4) The National Commission may, on such terms as it deems fit and at any stage of the proceedings, adjourn the hearing of the complaint but the complaint shall be decided, as far as possible, within a period of three months from the date of notice received by opposite party where complaint docs not require analysis or testing of commodities and within five months if it requires analysis or testing of commodities.

(4A) In the event of a complaint being disposed of after the period specified in sub-rule (4), the National Commission shall record in writing, the reasons for the delay in such disposal.

(5) If after the proceedings conducted under sub-rule (3) the National Commission is satisfied with the allegations contained in the complaint, it shall issue orders to the opposite party or parties, as the case may be, directing him or them to take one or more of the things as mentioned in sub-section (1) of section.

14. The National Commission shall also have the power to direct that any order passed by it, where no appeal has been preferred under section 23 or where the order of the National Commission has been affirmed by the Supreme Court under that section, be published in the Official Gazette or through any other media and no legal proceedings shall lie against the National Commission or any other media for such publication.

Appeals before National Commission

14A. Every appeal filed in tcrms of section 19 shall be accompanied by such amount as specified in the second proviso to the said section and such amount may be remitted in the form of a crossed Demand Draft drawn on a nationalized bank in favour of the Registrar, National Commission, payable at Delhi. The National Commission dealing with the appeals filed before them shall follow the provisions of sections 19 and 19A as may be required to hear the appeals filed before the Commission.

Explanation – In this rule, "nationalized bank" means a corresponding new bank specified in the First Schedule to the Banking Companies (Acquisition and Transfer of Undertakings) Act, 1970 (5 of 1970) or a corresponding new bank specified in the First Schedule to the Banking Companies (Acquisition and Transfer of Undertakings) Act, 1980 (40 of 1980).]

Procedure for hearing the appeal

15.

(1) Memorandum shall be presented by the appellant or his agent to the National Commission in person or be sent by registered post addressed to the Commission.

(2) Every memorandum filed under sub-rule (1) shall be in legible handwriting preferably typed and shall set forth concisely under distinct heads, the grounds of appeal without any argument or narrative and such grounds shall be numbered consecutively.

(3) Each memorandum shall be accompanied by a [crossed Demand Draft as referred to in rule 14A and by a] certified copy of the order of the State Commission appealed against and such of the documents as may be required to support grounds of objection mentioned in the memorandum.

(4) When the appeal is presented after the expiry of the period of limitation as specified in the Act, the memorandum shall be accompanied by the application supported by an affidavit setting forth the facts on which the appellant relies Lo satisfy the National Commission that he has sufficient cause for not preferring the appeal within the period of limitation.

(5) The appellant shall submit [four copies or such number of copies] of the memorandum to the Commission for official purpose,

(6) On the date of hearing or on any other day to which hearing may be adjourned, it shall be obligatory for the parties or their agents to appear before the National Commission. If the appellant or his agent fails to appear on such date, the National Commission may in its discretion either dismiss the appeal tore decide it *ex-parte* on merits. If the respondent or his agent fails to appear on Riich date, the National Commission shall proceed *ex parte* and shall decide the appeal on the merits of the case.

(7) The appellant shall not, except by leave of the National Commission, urge or be heard in support of any ground of objection not set forth in the memorandum but the National Commission, in deciding the appeal, may not ! confine to the grounds of objection set forth in the memorandum; **Provided** that the Commission shall not rest its decision on any other ground other than those specified in the memorandum unless the party who may be affected thereby, has been given an opportunity of being heard by the National Commission.

(8) No adjournment shall ordinarily be granted by the National Commission, unless sufficient cause is shown and the reasons for grant of adjournment have been recorded in writing by the Commission. The National Commission may also adjourn the hearing of the appeal *suo moto,* on such terms as it may think fit and at any stage of the proceedings for reasons to be recorded in writing. The appeal shall be decided, as far as possible, within ninety days from the date of its admission. In the event of an appeal being disposed of after the period so specified, the National Commission shall record in writing the reasons of the same at the time of disposal of the said appeal.

(9) The order of the National Commission shall be communicated to the parties concerned free of cost. Sitting of the National Commission and signing of orders.

15A.

(1) Every proceeding of the National Commission shall be conducted by the President or the senior most member and at least two members thereof sitting together [except when a bench is constituted by the President of the National Commission with one or more members as he may deem fit]:

[**Provided** that one member or members for any reason are unable to conduct proceedings till it is completed, the President or the senior most member, as **Provided** in section 22D of the Act shall conduct such proceedings from the stage at which it was last heard by the previous member.]

(2) Every order made by the National Commission shall be signed by the President 'for the seniorrnost member [2][as **Provided** under section 22D] and at least two members who conducted the proceeding and if there is any difference of opinion among themselves, the opinion of the majority shall be the order of the National Commission:

Provided that where the proceeding is conducted by the President for the seniorrnost member [as **Provided** under section 22D] and three members thereof and they differ on any point or points, they shall state the point or points on which they differ and refer the same to the other member for hearing on such point or points and such point or points shall be decided accordingly to the opinion of the majority of the National Commission. **Manner** of deposit **of** amount **in** appeals **before** Supreme Court.

16. Every appeal filed before the Supreme Court in terms of section 23 shall be accompanied by an amount as **Provided** in the second proviso to that section and such amount may be remitted in the form of a crossed Demand Draft drawn on a nationalized bank in favour of Registrar, Supreme Court, payable at Delhi.

Explanation – In this rule, "nationalized bank" means a corresponding new bank specified in the First Schedule to the Banking Companies (Acquisition and Transfer of Undertakings) Act, 1970 (5 of 1970) or a corresponding new bank specified in the First Schedule to the Banking Companies (Acquisition and Transfer of Undertakings) Act, 1980 (40 of 1980).

Schedule I

[*See* rule 3(l)(c)]

1. *Eastern Region* – to consist of the States of Bihar, Chhattisgarh, Jharkhand, Orissa and West Bengal.
2. *Western Region* – to consist of the States of Goa, Gujarat, Maharashtra, Madhya Pradesh and Rajasthan.
3. *Northern Region* – to consist of the States of Haryana, Himachal Pradesh, Jammu & Kashmir, Punjab, Uttar Pradesh and Uttaraiichal.
4. *Southern Region* – to consist of the States of Andhra Pradesh, Karnataka, Kerala arid Tamil Nadu.
5. *North Eastern Region* – to consist of the States of Arunachal Pradesh, Assam, Manipur, Meghalaya, Mizoram, Nagaland, Tripura and Sikkim.

Schedule II

[*See* rule 3(l)(ca)]

The Union Territories of the Andaman and Nicobar Islands, Chandigarh, Dadra and Nagar Haveli, Daman and Diu, Lakshadweep, Pondicherry and the National Capital Territory of Delhi.

1. Inserted by the Consumer Protection (Amendment) Rules, 1997, *w.e.f.* 27-2-1997.
2. Substituted for "authorised under rule 12" by the Consumer Protection (Second Ainend-. ment) Rules, 2005, *w.e.f.* 10-2-2005.
3. Inserted by the Consumer Protection (Amdt.) Rules, 2004, *w.e.f.* 5-3-2004.
4. Inserted by the Consumer Protection (Amdt.) Rules, 2006, *w.e.f.* 5-5-2006.

Sales Promotion through False Information

Will Result in Penalty and Prosecution

Check labels for correctness - Best before Date/Nutritional Information

Enlightening people about misleading/ misbranding information

Interactive approach for better transparency and quality improvement

Graded Penalty & Punishment-Safe Guarding Consumers

Food Safety and Standards (FSS) Act, 2006 which came into effect throughout the country on 5th August, 2011 repeals other Acts vis. Prevention of Food Adulteration Act 1954, Fruit Products Order (FPO), 1955, (SODEF) Solvent Extracted Oil, De-oiled Meal and Edible Flour (control) Order, 1967, Meat Food Products Order (MFPO), 1973, Edible Oils Packaging, 1998, Vegetable Oil Product Order, 1998, Milk and Milk Product Regulations, 2009.

Section 24 of the FSS Act puts restriction on misleading or deceiving advertisement and unfair trade practices, promoting the sale, supply, use and consumption of articles of food or adopt any unfair or deceptive practice or information which

(a) Falsely represents standards, quality, quantity or grade-composition;

(b) Makes a false or misleading representation about usefulness;

(c) Gives guarantee of the efficacy without adequate scientific justification thereof.

All persons/manufactures/dealers/importers of food items are required to comply with the above provisions of the law while advertising or disseminating information through direct or indirect promotional activity.

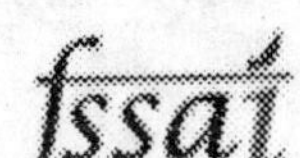

ISSUED IN PUBLIC INTEREST BY

Food Safety and Standards Authority of India

Kotla Road, FDA Bhawan, New Delhi-110002

Website : fssai.gov.in

Toll Free Helpline No. 1800 11 2100

RESERVE BANK OF INDIA
www.rbi.org.in

Banking Codes and Standards Board of India
www.bcsbi.org.in

CODE OF BANKS COMMITMENT TO MICRO AND SMALL ENTERPRISES

This is a voluntary Code, reflecting the bank's positive commitment to its Micro and small Enterprise (MSE) customers to provide easy, speedy and transparent access to banking services in their day-to-day operations and in times of finance difficulty.

The code does not replace or supercede regulatory or supervisory instructions issued by the Reserve bank of India (RBI). The provisions of the Code may, however, set higher standards than what is indicated in the regulatory one supervisory instructions and such higher standards will prevail.

Your bank is committed to make available to you free of cost:

1. A copy of the Code of Bank's commitment to MSEs which is your Charter of Rights.
2. A check list of our requirements along with a simple standardized, easy to understand application form for loan.

Your bank is committed to make available to your information about:

1. The interest rates applicable, and the fees/charges, if any, and any other matter which affects your interest, so that a meaningful comparison with those of other banks can be made informed decision can be taken by you.
2. The specific time frames for dealing with your loan application, disbursement, services etc.
3. The availability of collateral-free loan.
4. The parameters of credit assessment and post disbursement services.
5. Your obligations when you are in financial difficulty and how your bank can help you.
6. Nursing sick MSEs and debt restructuring.
7. The services which it has committed to give you.
8. The internal procedures for dealing with complaints.
9. The bank's policy for collection of dues, cheque collection, compensation, grievance redressal, etc.

The code of Bank's Commitment to micro & Small Enterprises tells you all this and much more. The Code will be available in English, Hindi, Assamese, Bengali, Gujarati, Kannada, Malayalam, Marathi, Oriya, Punjabi, Sindhi, Tamil, Telugu and Urdu.

You can access bcsbi.org.in for the full text of this Code in any of the above languages. The BCSBI monitors the Code. If you have any enquiries about the Code please contact:

The Banking Codes and Standards Board of India,
Reserve Bank of India Building
C-7, Bandra-Kurla Complex, Mumbai-400 051
Telephone: 022-26573715, Fax: 022-26573719
Email:ceo.bcsbi.org.in, Wbsite:www.bcsbi.org.in

OR

Indian Bank's Association
Centre 1, 6th floor, world trade Centre,
Cuffe Parade, Mumbai 400 005
Telepphone: 022-22174040, Fax: 022-2218222
Website:www.iba.org.in

Self-help groups create significant social impact. It is a social mobilization process of the poor for economic uplift and not merely a bank loan-enabler. Its success depends on unified action on the part of various stakeholders. This endeavour should result in comprehensive financing of target group for more effective performance.

Chapter 1 B

Consumer Protection Regulations, 2005

[GSR 342 (E), Dated 31-5-2005]

In exercise of the powers conferred by section 30A of the Consumer Protection Act, 1986 (68 of 1986), the National Consumer Disputes Redressal Commission with the previous approval of the Central Government, hereby makes the following regulations, namely:—

SHORT TITLE AND COMMENCEMENT

1. (1) These regulations may be called the Consumer Protection Regulations, 2005.

(2) They shall come into force on the date of their publication in the Official Gazette.

Definitions

2. In these regulations unless the context otherwise requires,—

(a) "Act" means the Consumer Protection Act, 1986 (68 of 1986);

(b) "Consumer Forum" means a District Forum, a Consumer Disputes Redressal Commission established in a State under clause *(b)* of section 9 (hereafter called the State Commission) or the National Consumer Disputes Redressal Commission;

(c) "Registrar" means the head of the ministerial establishment of the Consumer Forum and exercising such powers and functions as are conferred upon him by the President of the Consumer Forum;

(d) "rules" means the rules made under the Act;

(e) "section" means a section of the Act;

(f) words and expressions used in these regulations and not defined herein but defined either in the Act or in the rules shall have the same meaning respectively assigned to them either in the Act or in the rules, as the case may be.

Arrangements in Consumer Forum

3. (1) A Consumer Forum, being not a regular court, shall have the arrangements as to depict it distinct from a court,

(2) In the hall in which the Consumer Forum shall hear the parties, the dais may not be kept more than 30 çm. in height than the place earmarked for the parties so occupy.

(3) At the dais of the hall, the President and the members of the Consumer Forum shall use the same type of chairs at the same level and these chair's need not have high backs.

Dress code.

4. (1) The President and members of every Consumer Forum while presiding over the Benches,—

(a) shall wear simple and sober dress;

(b) shall not wear—

(i) flashy dress or dress display any affluence;

(ii) jeans or T-shirts; (m) as if they are holding Courts as Judges of a High Court or a District Court.

(2) The advocates shall be allowed to appear in the usual dress as prescribed by the High Court but without the gown. Hearing hours.

5. Subject to the provisions of the rules, the normal working hours of the Consumer Forum for hearing matters shall be from 10.30 a.m. to 1.00 p.m. and 2.00 p.m. to 4.00 p.m. on all working days of the Central Government in the case of the National Commission and on all working days of the State Government in the case of the State Commission and the District Forum.

Cause List.

6. (1) Cause list of the Consumer Forum for the following entire week shall be made ready before the close of the working hours of the preceding week and displayed on the notice board. The cause list in respect of a Consumer Forum having a website shall also be hosted on the website.

(2) Cause list shall be split into three different parts, namely:—

(i) Admission and after notice matters;

(ii) Matters where evidence is to be recorded; (m) Final disposal matters.

(3) Every cause list shall contain the following particulars, namely:—

Sr. No.	*No. of the matter*	*Names of the parties*	*Name of the party of counsel or agent appearing*
(1)	*(2)*	*(3)*	*(4)*

(4) If a date of hearing is given in the presence of parties or their agents it shall not be a ground for non-appearance for the reason that the cause list for concerned date does not show the matter or contains incorrect entry o is 6mission of the particulars of the matter.

Institution of complaints, appeals and revision petitions.

7. (1) Where a complaint is filed in District Forum or State Commission it shall be filed in three sets and where it is filed in the National Commission il shall be filed in four sets with additional sets equal to the number of opposite party (ies)/ respondent (s).

(2) Every complaint shall clearly contain particulars of dispute and the relief claimed and shall also be accompanied by copies of such documents as are necessary to prove the claim made in the complaint. Nomenclature to be given to the complaints, appeals and revision petitions.

8. (1) A complaint shall hereinafter be referred to as Consumer Complaint (C.C.) instead of O.P., e.g., C.C. No. 2 of 2005.

(2) An appeal shall be referred to as F.A., Revision Petition as R.P., Execution Application as E.A., Transfer Application T.A, and Review as RA containing the number and the year of filing.

Scrutiny of complaint, appeal, petition and revision petition.

9. (1) Every complaints appeal or revision petition after it is filed shall be numbered by the Registrar.

(2) If there is any defect in the filing of the complaints, appeal or revision petition, the particulars of such defects shall be recorded and the party or his agents shall be informed of the defects asking them for removing the defects within 15 days.

(3) In case the party disputes in the correctness of the defects pointed out the matter shall be placed before the Consumer Forum for appropriate orders.

(4) After the expiry of the time given, the matter shall, irrespective of the fact as to whether the defects have been removed or not, be placed before the Consumer Forum for appropriate orders.

(5) If the objections raised by the Registrar are substantial and are not removed within the time allowed for the purpose, those days shall not be" excluded for counting the period of limitation.

(6) As required by the second proviso to sub-section (3) of section 12, the admissibility of the complaint shall ordinarily be decided within twenty-one days from the date on which the complaint was received.

(7) In case any defect is pointed out by the Registrar, twenty-one days from the date on which such defect was removed shall be reckoned for the purpose of Pub-regulation (5).

(8) All pending complaints, appeals and revision petitions which have not come up for admission till the date of commencement of these regulations and are Pending for admission for more than 21 days shall be listed immediately by the Consumer Forum for admission and not later than 21 days from the date of 'commencement of these regulations. Issue of notice.

10. (1) Whenever the **Consumer Forum directs the issuance of a notice in** respect of **a complaint,** appeal or **revision** petition, **as** the **case** may be, **to** the opposite party (ies)/respondent (s), ordinarily such notice shall be issued for a period of 30 days and depending upon the circumstances of each case even for less than 30 days.

(2) When there is a question of raising presumption of service, 30 days notice shall be required.

(3) Whenever notices are sought to be effected by a courier service, it shall be ascertained that the courier is of repute.

(4) While appointing the courier for the purpose of effecting service, security deposit may also be taken.

(5) Along with the notice, copies of the complaint, memorandum of grounds of appeal, petitions as the case may be and other documents filed shall be served upon the opposite party (ies)/respondent (s).

(6) After the opposite party or respondent has put in appearance, no application or document shall be received by the Registrar unless it bears an endorsement I that a copy thereof has been served upon the other side.

Adjournment

11. (1) Every proceeding before a Consumer Forum shall be conducted as expeditiously as possible and as per the requirements of the Act.

(2) The Consumer Forum shall record the reasons for any adjournment made by it.

(3) The cost of adjournment, if asked by the opposite party or parties, shall not be less than five hundred rupees per adjournment and could be more depending upon the value and nature of the complaint as may be decided by the Consumer Forum.

(4) The complainant, appellant or petitioner, as the case may be, may also be burdened with cost unless sufficient cause is shown for seeking adjournment: **Provided** that in the circumstances of a particular case, the amount of cost imposed may be less than five hundred rupees but in no case less than one hundred rupees.

(5) The cost imposed may be given to the other party or parties to defray his or their expenses or be deposited in the Consumer Legal Aid Account to be maintained by the respective Consumer Forum, as the Consumer Forum may order.

(6) If any adjournment is granted without awarding cost, the order sheet shall mention the reasons thereof.

(7) All orders adjourning the matter shall be signed by the President and members constituting the Bench and not by the Court Master or Bench Clerk.

(8) Non-availability of a lawyer who is representing the party shall not be a ground for seeking adjournment of the matter unless absence is beyond the control of the lawyer such as his sudden illness or bereavement in the family-Hearing by Benches.

12. Where a Bench, constituted by the President of the State Commission or the National Commission as **Provided** under section 16 or section 20, as the; case may be, does not have a member with judicial background and any complex question of law arises and there is no precedent to decide the law point, the Bench so constituted may refer the matter to the President of the State Commission or the National Commission as the case may be to constitute another Bench of which the President shall be a member. Arguments.

13. (1) Arguments should be as brief as possible and to the point at issue.

(2) Where a party is represented by a counsel, it shall be mandatory to file a brief of written arguments two days before the matter is fixed for arguments.

(3) In case of default to file briefs, the cost shall be imposed at the same rates far laid down for grant of adjournments.

Limitation

14. (1) Subject to the provisions of sections 15, 19 and 24A, the period of limitation in the following matters shall be as follows;—

(*i*) Revision Petition shall be filed within 90 days from the date of the order or the date of receipt of the order as the case may be;

(*ii*) Application for setting aside the *ex parte* order under section 22A or dismissal of the complaint in default shall be maintainable if filed within thirty days from the date of the order or date of receipt of the order, as the case may be;

(*iii*) An application for review under sub-section (2) of section 22 shall be filed to the National Commission within 30 days from the date of the order or receipt of the order, as the case may be;

(*iv*) The period of limitation for filing any application for which no period of limitation has been specified in the Act, the rules of these regulations shall be thirty days from the date of the cause of action or the date of knowledge.

(2) Subject to the provisions of the Act, the Consumer Forum may condone the delay in filing an application or a petition referred to in sub-regulation (1) if valid and sufficient reasons to its satisfaction are given. Review.

15. (1) It shall set out clearly the grounds for review.

(2) Unless otherwise ordered by the National Commission, an application for review shall be disposed of by circulation without oral arguments, as far as practicable between the same members who had delivered the order sought to be reviewed.

Appearance of Voluntary Consumer Organisations

16. (1) Recognised Consumer Organisations have a right of audience before the Consumer Forum.

(2) An authorisation of a Voluntary Consumer Organisation may be by way of special power of attorney executed on a non-judicial paper or even on plain paper duly attested by a Gazetted Officer or a Notary Public.

(3) The Power of Attorney holder shall be entitled to engage a counsel, if authorised to do so.

(4) A Voluntary Consumer Organisation can engage a counsel or an advocate of its choice or it can itself represent through one of its office bearers as per the rules governing it.

(5) In case of a complaint where the Voluntary Consumer Organisation is a complainant along with the consumer himself and the dispute affects the complainant individually, he can withdraw the complaint:

Provided that if the issue involves unfair trade practice or restrictive trade practice a Voluntary Consumer Organisation may continue to proceed with the complaint even if the complainant wishes to withdraw the same.

(6) A Consumer Forum has to guard itself from touts and busy-bodies in the garb of power of attorney holders or authorised agents in the proceedings before it,

(7) While a Consumer Forum may permit an authorised agent to appear before it, but authorised agent shall not be, one who has used this as a profession : **Provided** that this sub-regulation shall not apply in case of advocates.

(8) An authorised agent may be debarred from appearing before a Consumer Forum if he is found guilty of misconduct or any other malpractice at any time.

Ex parte interim order,

17. Any *ex parte* interim order issued by the Consumer Forum shall stand vacated after 45 days if in the meanwhile the objections to the interim order are not heard and disposed of. Final order,

18. (1) An order on the top right hand corner shall show as to when the complaint was filed and the date of the order.

(2) The cause title of the order shall contain the names of all the parties with their addresses.

(3) In the body of the order it is desirable that after mentioning the complainant or the opposite party, their names as shown in the title be mentioned and parties thereafter may not be mentioned as complainant or opposite party No. 1 or opposite party No. 2, etc.

(4) The cause title shall also clearly show if the appellant or respondent was the complainant or opposite party.

(5) The order of a Consumer Forum disposing of a matter shall be as short and precise as practicable and unnecessary long quotations from the judgments ol the higher courts or otherwise shall be avoided.

(6) When a copy of the order is sent to a party, the mode by which it is sent and the date on which it is sent shall be stamped on the last page of the order.

(7) The Consumer Forum shall pass final order invariably within fifteen days of the conclusion of the arguments.

Return on institution and disposal of cases,

19. (1) A Consumer Forum is expected to dispose of at least 75 to 100 matters every month.

(2) A periodic monthly return of institution and disposal of cases shall be sent [by the District Forums to the State Commission.

(3) The State Commission shall submit a periodic monthly return of institution and disposal of cases to the National Commission.

(4) Notwithstanding anything contained in this regulation, the President of the National Commission may, at any time, call for any return or information relating lo its functioning from a State Commission or District Forums. Preservation of records.

20. (1) In the case of complaint, the record containing main files with original order sheet shall be preserved for a period of five years.

(2) In the case of records of first appeal and revision petitions, it shall be preserved for three years from the date of disposal of the appeal or revision as the case may be.

(3) Immediately after the consumer complaint, first appeal or revision petition, as the case may be, is disposed of, extra sets shall be given to the parties who may use the same for filing of appeal or revision petition and in that case the necessity to summon the record from the forums below can be dispensed with.

(4) The Registrar shall inform the parties while forwarding the certified copy of the final order, where they do not appear in person at the time of finally disposing of the matter to arrange to collect the extra sets.

(5) A period of at least one month shall be given for the purpose of collection of records by the party and in case of default the extra sets shall be weeded out. Certified copy.

21. (1) A copy of the order is to be given to the parties free of cost as required under the Act and the rules made there under.

(2) In case a party requires an extra copy, it shall be issued to him duly certified by the Registry on a payment of ₹ 20 irrespective of number of pages.

(3) A certified copy of an order shall clearly specify the date when free copy was issued, date of application, date when the copy was made ready and the date when it was so delivered to him.

(4) A fee of ₹ 20 shall be paid for obtaining another certified copy.

(5) Any party desiring to get a certified copy of any document on the file of the Consumer Forum, may get the same on payment of certification fee of twenty rupees per copy:

Provided that if any such document of which certified copy is sought, is over and above 5 pages, an extra amount of one rupee per page shall be charged over and above the fee of twenty rupees.

(6) Certified copy of any miscellaneous order passed by the Consumer Forum shall be supplied on payment of ₹ 5 per copy.

Inspection of Records

22. Parties or their agents can inspect the records of any matter by filing an I application on payment of ten rupees as fee.

Filing of Criminal Complaint

23. Wherever a complaint is required to be filed by the Consumer Forum under sub-section (5) of section 13, the Consumer Forum may authorize its Registrar to file the complaint. Practice **Directions,**

24. The National Commission shall be entitled to issue practice directions from time to time as may be necessary for the proper conduct of the cases before Consumer Forum including prescribing forms for complaints, notice returns, certificate to be issued to the collector and the like. Parcsha Yad-dast.

25. Where a party appears in person and is illiterate, the Court Master or Bench Clerk shall give to that party the next date of hearing in writing.

Miscellaneous

26. (1) In all proceedings before the Consumer Forum, endeavour shall be made by the parties and their counsel to avoid the use of provisions of Code of Civil Procedure, 1908 (5 of 1908): **Provided** that the provisions of the Code of Civil Procedure, 1908 may be applied which have been referred to in the Act or in the rules made there under.

(2) Every State Commission and every District Forum shall take steps for its computerisation and networking.

(3) The Consumer Forum shall give proper respect and courtesy to the parties who appear in person and shall provide separate accommodation in the hall for the convenience of the parties.

(4) The Consumer Forum shall not insist upon the parties to engage advocates,

(5) The fees collected for inspection of the documents and supply of certitieu copies shall be deposited in the account maintained for the purpose of depositing fee for filing a complaint as prescribed by the Central Government by rules.

(6) The cases filed by or against the senior citizens, physically challenged, widows and persons suffering from serious ailments shall be listed and disposed of on a priority basis.

ANALYSIS OF AMENDMENTS TO CONSUMER PROTECTION ACT BY CONSUMER PROTECTION (AMENDMENT) ACT, 2002

Consumer Protection Act, 1986 *was last amended in* 1993. *Subsequently, in* view *of experience gained in operation of the Act, major changes are now being made by the Consumer Protection (Amendment) Act, 2002. The amendments came into force from 15-3-2003.*

MAJOR CHANGES

- District Forum now can entertain complaints where value of goods or services and compensation claimed is upto ₹ 20 lakhs (against existing limit of ₹ 5 lakhs [amended section **11** (1)]. State Commission will now hear complaints where value of goods or services and compensation claimed is over ₹ 20 lakhs but less than ₹ 100 lakhs [against present limit of ₹ 5 lakhs to ₹ 20 lakhs] [section 17(1)]. National Commission will hear original complaint only if the value is ₹ 100 lakhs or more [section *21(a)(i)*].
- Prescribed fees will be payable along with every complaint filed [section 12(2)]. [Usually, such fee is termed as 'court fee'. This term is indeed not correct as consumer redressal forum is not a 'Court']. So far, no fee was payable. It was observed that highly inflated and even bogus claims were filed just because no fee was payable. This tendency may now reduce. - As per sections 18 and 22, these provisions will apply to State and National Commission also.
- Provision has been made for 'admission' of complaint. On receipt of complaint, the District Forum may, by order, allow the complaint to be proceeded with or rejected. Before rejecting a complaint, an opportunity of being heard has been given to the complainant. Once a complaint has been admitted by the District Forum, it shall not be transferred to any other court or tribunal or any authority set up by or under any other law for the time being in force [section 12(3)]. No guidance has been provided for 'admission' or 'rejection' of complaint, i.e., reasons for which a complaint can be rejected. - After admission of complaint, copy to be sent to opposite party within 21 days [section 13(1)]. —As per sections 18 and 22, these provisions will apply to State and National Commission also. Thus, it appears that appeal will have to be admitted first before proceeding further.
- Complaint should be decided within 3 months if no testing or analysis is required and within five months if testing/ analysis is required [section 13(3A)]. If complaint is not disposed of within the time, reason should be recorded in writing, while disposing of the complaint [third *proviso* to section 13(3A)]. In case of State Commission and National Commission, time limit of 90 days has been specified *vide* third *proviso* to section 19A. If matter is not decided, reasons should be recorded at the time of disposing of the appeal.
- Specific provision made for passing *ex parte* order by District Forum [section *13(2)(b)(ii)*]. As per sections 18 and 22, these provisions will apply to State and National Commission also.
- Cost of adjournment to be imposed [*proviso* to section 13(3A) in respect of district forum and section 19A in respect of State Commission and National Commission].
- District Forum can pass interim orders [section 13(3B)]. As per sections 18 and 22, these provisions will apply to State and National Commission also.
- Consumer Dispute Redressal Agency (CDRA) can now grant punitive damages [section *14(1)(d)*].
- CDRA can ask erring party selling hazardous goods or offering hazardous services to pay general damages when consumer number is large who are not identifiable conveniently. It can also issue cease and desist order [section *14(1)(hb)*].
- If a member who is hearing the case is unable to conduct proceedings till further and if bench is changed, it becomes necessary to re-hear the whole matter right from beginning. This was causing delays. Hence, proviso to section 14(2) provides that where a member is unable to conduct a proceeding till it is completed, the President and the other member shall continue the proceeding from the stage at which it was last heard by the previous member. As per sections 18 and 22, these provisions will apply to State and National Commission also.
- Appeal against order of District Forum can be entertained only if 50% amount or ₹ 25,000 whichever is less is deposited [second *proviso* to section 15]. In case of appeal against order of State Commission and National Commission, the deposit is ₹ 35,000 and ₹ 50,000 respectively.
- President of District Forum must be a member of the bench. [However, in absence of President, senior-most member can discharge function of President]. President of State Commission need not be member of each bench [section *16(1B)(ii)*]. Similarly, President of National Commission need not be member of each bench [section *20(1A)(ii)*].
- It is provided that in case of vacancy in office of President of District Forum, State Commission or National Commission, senior-most member shall perform the function of President [section 22D]. This is to ensure that if President is absent or his office is vacant, the work does not come to standstill.
- It is observed that opposite party usually tries to avoid serving of notice. Hence, it is provided that notice can be served by registered post or authorised courier or Fax or any other means. If opposite party refuses to accept the notice, it is deemed to have been served. Similarly, once notice is properly addressed and posted, it is deemed to have been served even if acknowledgement is not received within 30 days [section 28A].

OTHER CHANGES

- *Legal heir can continue as complainant* — Section 2(1)(b) which defines 'complainant' has been amended to provide that in case of death of a consumer, his legal heir or representative can continue as a complainant [section *2(1)(b)(v)]*. In the event of death of a complainant who is a consumer or of the opposite party against whom the complaint has been filed, the provisions of Order XXII of the First Schedule to the Code of Civil Procedure shall apply subject to the modification that every reference therein to the plaintiff and the defendant shall be construed as reference to a complainant or the opposite party, as the case may be [section 13(7)]. However, since section 12(1) has not been amended, it can be argued that a legal heir or representative of deceased consumer cannot file a complaint.
- *Complaint of UTP and RTP*— Definition of 'complaint' has been amended to provide that complaint of unfair trade practice (UTP) or restrictive trade practice (RTP) can be made against service provider also [section *2(1)(c)(i)* and *(iv)*].
- *Charging of higher prices* — Section *2(1)(c)(iv)* provided that 'complaint' includes an allegation that a trader has charged for the goods a price in excess of the price fixed by or under any law for the time being in force or displayed on the goods or any package containing such goods. To this following have been added - *(a)* Charging price higher than that displayed on the price list exhibited by him by or under any law for the time being in force *(b)* Charging price higher that the price agreed between the parties. Further, this provision, which was applicable only to trader and goods has been extended to services and service provider also.
- *Hazardous goods and services* — Provisions in respect of sale/supply of hazardous goods have been made more stringent. Now these provi-sions apply even in cases where trader was not required to display information regarding contents, manner and effect of such hazardous goods. Moreover, the provisions will apply even in cases where the trader could have known with due diligence that the goods so offered are unsafe to the public. The provisions have been extended to hazardous services also by inserting section 2(1)(*c*)(*vz).*
- *Services for commercial purposes excluded* — So far, 'consumer' included a person who availed services for commercial purposes, though person buying goods for commercial purposes was excluded from definition of 'consumer'. This anomaly has been removed and now section *2(1)(d)(ii)* as amended makes it clear that person availing services for commercial purposes will not be a 'consumer'. Corre-sponding amendment has been made to *Explanation* to this clause also.
- *Manufacturer includes brand name owner* — Definition of 'manufacturer' as contained in section 2(1)(j) has been amended to provide as follows - *(a)* A person who puts or causes to be put his own mark on any goods made or manufactured by any other manufacturer will also be 'manufacturer'. *(b)* An 'assembler' will be 'manufacturer' whether or not he claims that the end-product is manufactured by him. *(c)* A branch office will also be 'manufacturer' if the parts sent by parent are only assembled at branch office.
- *Regulations by NCDRC*— Section *2(1)(nn)* as inserted provides for "regulation" made by the National Commission. Section 30A authorises National Commission to make regulations for purposes of Act and in particular, in respect of cost of adjournment.
- *RTP definition brought near MRTP definition* — So far, definition of 'restrictive trade practice only covered trade practice in respect of 'full line forcing', *i.e.,* compelling a consumer to buy goods or avail services as a condition of buying, availing of hiring other goods or services. Now, the new definition states that "restrictive trade practice" means a trade practice which tends to bring about manipulation of price or its conditions of delivery or to affect flow of supplies in the market relating to goods or services in such a manner as to impose on the consumers unjustified costs or restrictions and shall include- *(a)* delay beyond the period agreed to by a trader in supply of such goods or in providing the services which has led or is likely to lead to rise in the price *(b)* any trade practice which requires a consumer to buy, hire or avail of any goods or, as the case may be, services as condition precedent to buying, hiring or availing of other goods or services. [section *2(1)(nnn)*]. Though this definition is different from 'Restrictive Trade Practice' under section 2(1)(0) of MRTP Act, the new definition is nearer the MRTP definition. Moreover, it is an 'inclusive definition', *i.e.,* any trade practice which manipulates such that it imposes unjustified cost of consumer will be RTP under Consumer Protection Act.
- *Any type of service will be covered* — Definition of 'service' as contained in section 2(1)(0) has been modified and it has been clarified that any type of service whether or not it has been included in the illustrations given in definition of 'service'. This is done by replacing the words "and includes the provision of", with the words "and includes, *but not limited to,* the provision of". [This was even otherwise clear, but has been made further clear by addition the words 'but not limited to', to remove any ambiguity that might have been in someone's mind or an artificial ambiguity that might be created by some ingenious lawyer].

- *Spurious goods and services* — As per definition in section 2(1)(00) (newly inserted), "spurious goods and services" mean such goods and services which are claimed to be genuine but they are actually not so. This insertion of definition has been made as revised definition of 'UTP' specifically provides that manufacture of spurious goods or offering spurious goods for sale or adopting deceptive practices in the provision of services will be an 'Unfair Trade Practice' [section 2(1)(*r)(6)* inserted].
- *Information about scheme of gifts and prizes* — If a seller, trader or service provider announces some scheme of gifts and prizes to allure consumers, he is now required to disclose final results of the scheme. If he does not do so, it will be an 'unfair trade practice'. This has been provided by inserting sub-clause *(3A)* to section 2(1)(*r*) in the definition of UTP, which provides that withholding from the participants of any scheme offering gifts, prizes or other items free of charge, on its closure the information about final results of the scheme will be an Unfair Trade Practice. [UTP]. As per *Explanation* to this sub-clause, the participants of a scheme shall be deemed to have been informed of the final results of the scheme where such results are within a reasonable time published, prominently in the same newspapers in which the scheme was originally advertised [section *2(1)(r)/(3A)]*. 'Thus, results of any scheme of gifts and prizes will be required to be announced in the same newspapers where the scheme was advertised.
- *Consumer Protection Councils* — Constitution of Central Consumer Protection Council (section 4) and State Consumer Protection Councils (section 7) have been made mandatory. Central Government is now empowered to nominate upto 10 official or non-official members to State Consumer Protection Council. [section *7(2)(c)]*. Provision of District Consumer Protection Council has been made by inserting sections 8A and 8B. It will be under chairmanship of Collector of the district.
- *Qualification at members of Consumer Disputes Redressal Agency* — Section *10(1)(b)* as amended provides that members of district forum shall be at least graduates and over 35 years of age, but below 65 years of age. [So far, qualification and minimum age was not prescribed]. It is also provided that a member shall be disqualified if he *(a)* has been convicted and sentenced to imprisonment for an offence which, in the opinion of the State Government, involves moral turpitude; or *(b)* is an undischarged insolvent; or *(c)* is of unsound mind and stands so declared by a competent court; or *(d)* has been removed or dismissed from the service of the Government or a body corporate owned or controlled by the Government; or *(e)* has, in the opinion of the State Government, such financial or other interest as is likely to affect prejudicially the discharge by him of his functions as a member; or *(f)* has such other disqualifications as may be prescribed by the State Government. Section 10(2) now provides that a member can be re-appointed, if he is otherwise qualified and is selected by the selection committee as provided in section 10(1A). Similar provisions for qualification and disqualification and selection by selection committee are provided in respect of State Commission [section *16(1)(b)* and section 16(3)] and National Commission. [section *20(1)(b)* and section 20(3)]. The difference is that in case of State Commission, age limit of member is 67 years. In case of National Commission, age limit is 70 years. In case of State Commission and National Commission, it is specifically provided that not more than 50% of members should have a judicial background.
- *Transitory provisions* — As a transitory provision, it has been specified that a person appointed as the President or as a member, before the commencement of the Consumer Protection (Amendment) Act, 2002, shall continue to hold such office as president or member, as the case may be, till the completion of his term [second *proviso* to section 10(2)]. Similar provision is made in respect of State Commission also [section 16(4)].
- *Appointment of whole-time member* — Proviso added to section 10(3) now makes provision for appointment of full time member to the District Forum. Similar provision is made in respect of State Commission also *[proviso* to section 16(2)].
- *Monetary limit enhanced* — District Forum now can entertain complaints where value of goods or services and compensation claimed is upto ₹ 20 lakhs (against existing limit of ₹ 5 lakhs) [amendment to section 11(1)]. State Commission will now hear complaints where value of goods or services and compensation claimed is over ₹ 20 lakhs but less than ₹ 100 lakhs [against present limit of ₹ 5 lakhs to ₹ 20 lakhs] [section 17(1)]. National Commission will hear original complaint only if the value is ₹ 100 lakhs or more [section *21(a)(l)*].
- *Manner in which complaint shall be made* — Section 12(1), as amended, provides that *(a)* recognised consumer association can file complaint even if the consumer is a member of such association or not *(b)* the Central Government or the State Government can file complaint either in its individual capacity or as a representative of interests of consumers in general.
- *Fees payable* — Section 12(2) provides that prescribed fees will be payable along with every complaint filed. So far, no fee was payable. It was observed that highly inflated and even bogus claims were filed just because no fee was payable. This tendency may now reduce. In case of appeal, it has been provided that some minimum amount is

deposited. Otherwise, appeal will not be entertained. As per sections 18 and 22, these provisions will apply to State and National Commission also.

- *Provision for admission of complaint and its non-transfer* — As per section 12(3), on receipt of complaint, the District Forum may, by order, allow the complaint to be proceeded with or rejected. Before rejecting a complaint, an opportunity of being heard has been given to the complainant. Admissibility of the complaint shall ordinarily be decided within twenty-one days from the date on which the complaint was received. Once a complaint has been admitted by the District Forum, it shall not be transferred to any other court or tribunal or any authority set up by or under any other law for the time being in force. No guidance has been provided for 'admission' or 'rejection' of complaint, *i.e.,* reasons for which a complaint can be rejected. It appears that District Forum may be able to refuse admission of complaint on any of the following grounds - *(a)* Lack of jurisdiction. *(b)* Non-payment of fees. *(c)* Frivolous and vexatious complaint. *(d)* Complainant is not consumer and/or controversy is not a 'consumer dispute'. *(e)* Limitation. *(f)* Matter already lying with other judicial forum (like Civil Court or MRTP Commission).

  As per sections 18 and 22, these provisions will apply to State and National Commission also. Thus, it appears that once appeal is filed, it will have to be admitted by State/National Commission, before proceeding further. The appeal may be rejected at admission stage itself on suitable grounds.

- *Copy of complaint to be sent within* 21 *days* — Section 13 has been amended to provide that copy of complaint shall be sent to opposite party only after complaint has been admitted. It is provided that copy should be sent to opposite party within 21 days. [Interestingly, the specified time limit of 21 days is only in respect of complaint relating to goods and not if it relates to services. This seems to be a drafting mistake].

- *Ex parte order can be passed* — Section 13(2)*(b)(ii)* as amended, now makes it abundantly clear that if opposite party does not reply or does not represent his case within prescribed time. It is also provided that where the complainant fails to appear on the date of hearing before the District Forum, the District Forum may either dismiss the complaint for default or decide it on merits [section 13(2)*(b)(iii)]* As per sections 18 and 22, these provisions will apply to State and National Commission also.

- *Tight schedule to decide on complaint* — Complaint should be decided within 3 months if no testing or analysis is required and within five months if testing/analysis is required [section 13(3A)]. If complaint is not disposed of within the time, reason should be recorded in writing, while disposing off the complaint [third *proviso* to section 13(3A)]. In case of State Commission and National Commission, time limit of 90 days has been specified *vide* third *proviso* to section 19A. If matter is not decided, reasons should be recorded at the time of disposing of the appeal.

- *Cost of adjournment* — Adjournment shall be granted only if sufficient cause is shown and recording reason in writing. Cost of adjournment shall be recovered *[provisos'* to section 13(3A) in respect of District Forum. Similar provision in first and second *provisos* to section 19A in respect of State and National Commission].

- *Interim orders can be passed* — Where during the pendency of any proceeding before the District Forum, it may pass such interim order as is just and proper in the facts and circumstances of the case [section 13(3B)]. As per sections 18 and 22, these provisions will apply to State and National Commission also.

- *Punitive damages and general damages* — Consumer Dispute Redressal Agency can now grant punitive damages [section *14(1)(d)].* It can also ask erring party selling hazardous goods or offering hazardous services to pay general damages when consumer number is large who are not identifiable conveniently. The minimum amount of sum so payable shall not be less than five per cent of the value of such defective goods sold or service provided, as the case may be, to such consumers [section *14(1)(hb)*]. As per sections 18 and 22, these provisions will apply to State and National Commission also.

- *Order correction of misleading advertisement* — Redressal Agency can order to issue corrective advertisement to neutralize the effect of misleading advertisement at the cost of the opposite party responsible for issuing such misleading advertisement [section *14(1)(hc)].*

- *Proceeding to continue even if a member changes* — If a member who is hearing the case is unable to conduct proceedings till further and if bench is changed, it becomes necessary to re-hear the whole matter right from beginning. This was causing delays. Hence, proviso to section 14(2) [as amended] provides that where a member, for any reason, is unable to conduct a proceeding till it is completed, the President and the other member shall continue the proceeding from the stage at which it was last heard by the previous member. As per sections 18 and 22, these provisions will apply to State and National Commission also.

- *Transfer of cases from one District Forum to another* — On the application of the complainant or of its own motion, the State Commission may, at any stage of the proceeding, transfer any complaint pending before the District Forum to another District Forum within the State in the interest of justice so requires [section 17 A]. In case of transfer from District Forum in one State to District Forum in another State, the order can be made only by National Commission [section 22B].

- *Pre-deposit for entertaining appeal* — No appeal by a person, who is required to pay any amount in terms of an order of the District Forum, shall be entertained by the State Commission unless the appellant has deposited in the prescribed manner fifty per cent of that amount or twenty-five thousand rupees, whichever is less [second *proviso* to section 15]. Similarly, in case of appeal against order of State Commission, appeal shall not be entertained unless appellant deposits ₹ 35,000 or 50% of the amount, whichever is less [*proviso* to section 19]. There is absolutely no provision to waive this pre-deposit of amount. Since the word used is 'entertained', it is not necessary to pay the amount before filing of appeal.
- *Benches of State Commission and National Commission* — The jurisdiction, powers and authority of the State Commission may be exercised by Benches thereof. A Bench may be constituted by the President with one or more members as the President may deem fit [section 16(IB)]. Thus, President of State Commission need not be member of each bench. Decision will be by majority. In case of equal division, matter will be referred to president who will either decide himself or refer to another member [section *16(1B)(iil)]* Similar provisions in respect of National Commission have been made *vide* section 20(IA)].
- *Jurisdiction of State Commission* - State Commission will have juris-diction as follows — *(a)* The opposite party or each of the opposite parties, where there are more than one, at the time of the institution of the complaint, actually and voluntarily resides or carries on business or has a branch office or personally works for gain; or *(b)* Any of the opposite parties, where there are more than one, at the time of the institution of the complaint, actually and voluntarily resides, or carries on business or has a branch office or personally works for gain, provided that in such case either the permission of the State Commission is given or the opposite parties who do not reside or carry on business or have a branch office or personally work for gain, as the case may be, acquiesce in such institution; or *(c)* the cause of action, wholly or in part, arises [section 17(2)]. Since the word 'or' is used in clauses *(a)* and *(b),* it is clear that State jurisdiction will have jurisdiction if anyone of the conditions namely *(a), (b)* or *(c)* is satisfied. Broadly, State Commission will have jurisdiction when at least part of cause of action arises or even when one of opposite parties has a branch office in the State.
- *Circuit Benches* — The State Commission shall ordinarily function in the State Capital but may perform its functions at such other place as the State Government may, in consultation with the State Commission, notify in the Official Gazette, from time to time [section 17B newly inserted]. Similar provision is made in respect of National Commission [section 22C].
- *Transfer of cases from one State Commission to another* — On the application of the complainant or of its own motion, the National Commission may, at any stage of the proceeding, in the interest of justice, transfer any complaint pending before the District Forum of one State to a District Forum of another State or before one State Commission to another State Commission [section 22B].
- *National Commission can review its orders if error apparent from records* — The National Commission shall have the power to review any order made by it, when there is an error apparent on the face of record [section 22(2)]. Thus, District Forum and State Commission have no power of review. Even, power of National Commission review its orders is limited only to error apparent from records and not all errors.
- *Power to set aside* ex parte *orders* — Where an order is passed by the National Commission *ex parte* against the opposite party or a complainant, as the case may be, the aggrieved party may apply to the Commission to set aside the said order in the interest of justice [section 22A]. District Forum and State Commission do not have such powers. The only remedy is to file appeal against the order.
- *Vacancy in the office of the President* — When the office of President of a District Forum, State Commission, or of the National Commission, as the case may be, is vacant or a person occupying such office is, by reason of absence or otherwise, unable to perform the duties of his office, these shall be performed by the senior-most member of the District Forum, the State Commission or of the National Commission, as the case may be. However, where a retired Judge of a High Court is a member of the National Commission, such member or where the number of such members is more than one, the senior-most person among such members, shall preside over the National Commission in the absence of President of that Commission [section 22D]. This is an excellent provision. It will ensure that work of District Forum or State/National Commission will not come to standstill when Presi-dent is absent or his office is vacant.

- *Enforcement of orders of the District Forum, the State Commission* or *the National Commission* — Where an interim order made under this Act is not complied with, the District Forum or the State/National Commission may order the property of the person, not complying with such order to be attached [section 25(1)]. The attachment shall remain in force for maximum three months, and if the non-compliance continues, the property attached may be sold. Out of the proceeds thereof, the District Forum or the State/National Commission may award such damages as it thinks fit to the complainant and shall pay the balance, if any, to the party entitled thereto [section 25(2)]. The drafting is faulty, as the provision applies only to interim order. Really, it should have been interim and/or final order. Thus, before passing final order, complaint should request the redressal forum to pass interim- order, as provisions of attachment are not available for execution of final order!

- *Recover amount as arrears of land revenue* — Where any amount is due from any person under an order made by a District Forum or State/National Commission, the District Forum or State/National Commission may issue a certificate for the said amount to the [illegible] to the Collector of the district for recovery of the amount as arrears of land revenue.

- *Penalty of imprisonment and fine* — Section 27 provided for penalty of imprisonment upto three years and fine upto ₹ 10,000; for disobey-ing order of District Forum and State/National Commission. However, it was not clear who will impose the penalty and how the penalty will be imposed. Now, section 27(2) provides that notwithstanding anything contained in the Code of Criminal Procedure, 1973 (2 of 1974), the District Forum or the State/National Commission shall have the power of a Judicial Magistrate of the first class for the trial of offences under this Act. They shall be deemed to be a Judicial Magistrate of the first class for the purpose of the Code of Criminal Procedure, 1973. As per section 27(3), all offences under this Act may be tried summarily by the District Forum or the State Commission or the National Commission, as the case may be.

- *Appeal against order of penalty* — An appeal under section 27, both on facts and on law, shall lie as follows *[The drafting is faulty. It should be appeal against order under section* 27, *as is correctly stated in the title of the section].* - *(a)* from order made by the District Forum to the State Commission; *(b)* from the order made by the State Commission to the National Commission; and *(c)* from the order made by the National Commission to the Supreme Court [section 27A(I)]. Except as aforesaid, no appeal shall lie to any court from any order of a District Forum or a State Commission or the National Commission [section 27 A(2)]. Appeal under this section shall be preferred within a period of thirty days from the date of an order [section 27(3)]. Appeal can be admitted even after 30 days, if the appellate authority (State Commis-sion or the National Commission or the Supreme Court, as the case may be) is satisfied that the appellant had sufficient cause for not preferring the appeal within the period of thirty days [*proviso* to section 27(3)]. Note that appeal u/s 27 A can be filed only when order is issued under section 27. Thus, if State Commission passes order on appeal against order of District Forum, further appeal cannot be filed as the order of State Commission is not under section 27. Similar is the situation when original order is passed under section 27 by State Commission or National Commission. In other words, in all cases, there will be only one appeal.

- *Service of notice* — It is general experience that opposite party avoids receipt of notice by all possible means. Hence, it is provided that notice can be issued by registered post or through recognised courier service or by other means of transmission, including FAX message. [Thus, serving notice by e-mail will be permissible] [section 28A(2)]. When an acknowledgement or any other receipt purporting to be signed by the opposite party or his agent or by the complainant is received by the District Forum or State/National Commission, it shall be declared that the notice has been received by opposite party [section 28A(3)].

- *Refusal to accept notice means notice has been duly served* — If postal employee or employee of authorised courier service makes endorse-ment to the effect that the opposite party or his agent or complainant had refused to take delivery of the postal article containing the notice or had refused to accept the notice by any other means when tendered or transmitted to him, the District Forum or the State Commission or the National Commission, as the case may be, shall declare that the notice had been duly served on the opposite party or to the complainant [section 28A(3)].

- *Notice served even if acknowledgement receipt misplaced* — Where the notice was properly addressed, pre-paid and duly sent by registered post acknowledgement due, notice will be deemed to have been served even if the acknowledgement has been lost or mislaid, or not received by the District Forum or State/National Commission within thirty days from the date of issue of notice *[proviso* to section 28A(3)].

- *Notice deemed to be served if properly addressed* — All notices required to be served on an opposite party or to complainant shall be deemed to be sufficiently served, if addressed in the case of the opposite party to the place where business or profession is carried and in case of complainant, the place where such person actually and voluntarily resides [section 28A(4)].

- *Removal of difficulties* — If any difficulty arises in giving effect to the provisions of the Consumer Protection (Amendment) Act, 2002, the Central Government may, by order, do anything not inconsistent with such provisions for the purpose of removing the difficulty, within two years from the Amendments [section 29(3)]. Every order made under sub-section (3) shall be laid before each House of Parliament [section 29(4)].
- *Power to make rules and regulations* — Section 30 authorises Central and State Government to make rules for carrying out provisions of the Act. Section 30A authorises National Commission to make regula-tions, with previous approval of Central Government. The rules and regulations are required to be placed before Parliament/State Legislature for 30 days [section 31].

Capturing Rural India "Consumerism"—

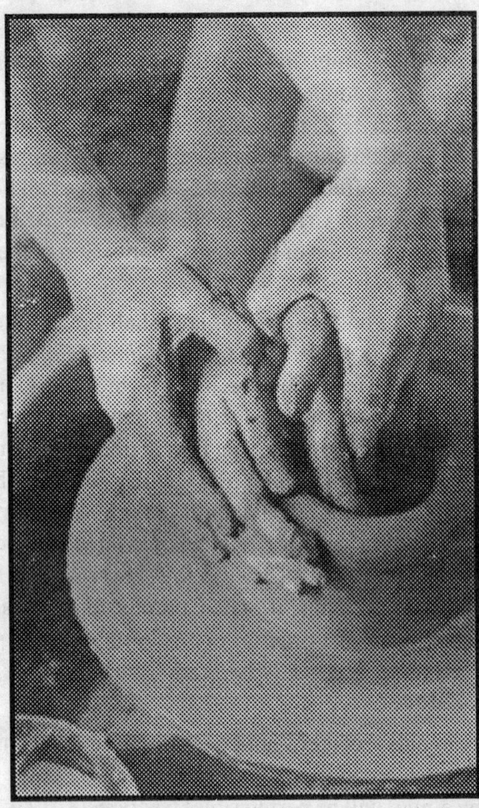

—✦—✦—✦—

Chapter 2

Consumer Welfare Fund

[GSR 895 (E), Dated 25-11-1992]

In exercise of the powers conferred by sub-section (2) of section 37, read with section 12D of the Central Excises and Salt Act, 1944 (1 of 1944), the Central Government hereby makes the following rules, namely :—

SHORT TITLE AND COMMENCEMENT

1.

(1) These rules may be called the Consumer Welfare Fund Rules, 1992.

(2) They shall come into force on the date of their publication in the Official Gazette.

Definitions

2. In these rules, unless the context otherwise requires,—

(a) "Act" means the Central Excises and Salt Act, 1944 (1 of 1944), or, as the case may be, the Customs Act, 1962 (52 of 1962);

(b) "Applicant" means any agency/organisation engaged in consumer welfare activities for a period of three years registered under the Companies Act, 1956 (1 of 1956) or under any other law for the time being in force, including village/mandal/Samiti level co-operatives of consumers especially Women, Scheduled Castes and Scheduled Tribes, or any industry as defined in the Industrial Disputes Act, 1947 (14 of 1947), recommended by the Bureau to be engaged for a period of five years in viable and useful research activity which has made, or is likely to make, significant contribution in formulation of standard mark of the products of mass consumption, *[the Central Government or the State Government]*, and includes a consumer for the purpose of reimbursing legal expenses as referred to in clause *(d)* of rule 8 of these rules;

(c) "Application" means an application in Form A-I, appended to these rules;

(d) "Bureau" means the Bureau of Indian Standards constituted under the Bureau of Indian Standards Act, 1986 (63 of 1986);

(e) "Central Consumer Protection Council" means the Central Consumer Protection Council established under sub-section (1) of section 4 of the Consumer Protection Act, 1986 (68 of 1986), for promotion and protection of rights of consumers;

(f) "Committee" means the Committee constituted under rule 5;

(g) "Consumer" has the same meaning as assigned to it in clause *(d)* of sub-section (1) of section 2 of the Consumer Protection Act, 1986 (68 of 1986), and includes consumer of goods on which duty has been paid;

(h) "Consumer Welfare Fund" means the fund established by the Central Government under sub-section (1) of section 12C of the Central Excises j and Salt Act, 1944 (1 of 1944);

(i) "Duty" means the duty paid under the Act;

[(J) "Proper Officer" means the officer having the power under the Act to make an order that the whole or any part of the duty is refundable;] (;) "Standard mark" shall have the same meaning as assigned to it in clause (0 of section 2 of the Bureau of Indian Standards Act, 1986 (63 of 1986);

(k) "Welfare of the Consumers" includes promotion and protection of rights of consumers;

(l) Words and expressions used in the rules and not defined but defined in the Consumer Protection Act, 1986 (68 of 1986) shall have the meanings respectively assigned to them in that Act. Establishment of Consumer Welfare Fund.

3. There shall be established a Consumer Welfare Fund with the Central Government into which credits of amounts of duty and income from investment along with other monies specified in sub-section (2) of section 12C of the Central Excises and Salt Act, 1944 (1 of 1944) shall be accredited; **Provided** that any amount having been credited to the Fund is ordered or directed as payable to any claimant by orders of proper officer, appellate authority or court, shall be paid from the Fund. Maintenance of Accounts and Records of Consumer Welfare Fund.

4. Proper and separate accounts in relation to the Consumer Welfare Fund shall be maintained by the Central Government and shall be subject to audit by the Comptroller and Auditor General of India. Constitution of the Committee.

5. (1) The Committee constituted by the Central Government under sub-rule (2), shall make recommendations for proper utilisation of the money credited to the Consumer Welfare Fund for the welfare of the consumers, to carry out the purposes of these rules.

(2) The Committee shall consist of the following Members, namely:—

(a) The Secretary, Department of Consumer Affairs, who shall be the chair-man of the committee];

(b) Secretary, Department of Expenditure in the Ministry of Finance or the Financial Adviser, Department of Consumer Affairs in the Ministry of Food, Civil Supplies and Public Distribution, who shall be the Vice-Chairman of the Committee;

(c) Chairman, Central Board of Excise and Customs or an officer not below the rank of a Joint Secretary in the Department of Revenue of Ministry of Finance;

(d) Member (Central Excise) of the Central Board of Excise and Customs or an officer not below the rank of a Joint Secretary in the Department of Revenue of Ministry of Finance;

(e) Secretary/Joint Secretary/Economic Advisor (Monitoring) Department of Rural Development;

[1b](f) Director General, Bureau of Indian Standards;

(g) the Additional Secretary or Joint Secretary incharge of Consumer Welfare Fund, in the Department of Consumer Affairs, who shall also be the Member Secretary of the Committee;

[**Provided** that the Chairman or Vice-Chairman, as the case may be, may invite representatives of the State Governments concerned and a nominee of the Consumer Co-ordination Council to the meetings as and when necessary.]

(3) The Committee shall be a Standing Committee. [Procedure for conduct of business.]

6. (1) The Committee shall meet as and when necessary, but not more than three months shall intervene between any two meetings.

(2) The Committee shall meet at such time and place as the Chairman, or in his absence the Vice-Chairman of the Committee may deem fit.

(3) The meeting of the Committee shall be presided over by the Chairman, and in the absence of the Chairman, the Vice-Chairman shall preside over the meetings of the Committee.

(4) Each meeting of the Committee shall be called, by giving notice in writing to every member of not less than ten days from the date of issue of such notice.

(5) Every notice of the meeting of the Committee shall specify the place and the day and hour of the meeting and shall contain a statement of business to be transacted thereat.

(6) No proceeding of the Committee shall be valid, unless it is presided over by the Chairman or Vice-Chairman and a minimum of [three] other members are present.

Powers and Functions of the Committee.

7. (1) The Committee shall have power—

(a) to require any applicant to produce before it, or before a duly authorised Officer of the Central Government, or as the case may be, the State Government, such books, accounts, documents, instruments, or commodities in custody and control of the applicant, as may be necessary for proper evaluation of the application;

(b) to require any applicant to allow entry and inspection of any premises, from which activities claimed to be for the welfare of consumers, are stated to be carried on, to a duly authorised officer of Central Government or, as the case may be, State Government;

(c) to get the accounts of the applicants audited, for ensuring proper utilization of the grant;

(d) to require any applicant, in case of any default, or suppression of material information on his part, to refund in lump sum, the sanctioned grant to the Committee, and to be subject to prosecution under the Act;

(e) to recover any sum due from any applicant in accordance with the provisions of the Act;

(f) to require any applicant, or class of applicants to submit a periodical report, indicating proper utilization of the grant;

(g) to reject an application placed before it on the basis of involvement of factual inconsistency, or inaccuracy in the material particulars;

(h) to recommend minimum financial assistance, by way of grant to an applicant, having regard to his financial status, and importance and utility of nature of activity under pursuit, after ensuring that the financial assistance **Provided** shall not be misutilised;

(i) to require Central Consumer Protection Council or the Bureau, to formulate broad guidelines for considering the projects/proposals for the purpose of incurring expenditure from the Consumer Welfare Fund;

(j) to identify beneficial and safe sectors, where investments out of Consumer Welfare Fund may be made and make recommendations, accordingly;

(k) to relax the conditions required for the period of engagement in consumer welfare activities of an applicant as specified in clause (b) of rule 2; (1) to make guidelines for the management and administration of the Consumer Welfare Fund.

(2) The Committee shall not consider an application, unless it has been inquired into, in material details and recommended for consideration accordingly, by the Member-Secretary.

Specification of Purposes for Utilization of Credits available in Consumer Welfare Fund

8. The Committee shall make recommendations :—

(a) for making available grants to any applicant;

(b) for making available grants recommended by the Bureau for activities relating to standard marks, which may be considered essential by the Central Government, for the welfare of the consumers;

(c) for investment of the money available in the Consumer Welfare Fund;

(d) for making available grants [on a selective basis], for reimbursing legal expenses, incurred by a complainant, or class of complainants in a consumer dispute, after its final adjudication;

(e) for making available grants for any other purpose recommended by the Central Consumer Protection Council'[as may be considered appropriate by the Committee.]

FORM – A I

[See rule 10(c) of the Consumer Welfare Fund Rules, 1992]

Important: Please fill up this form, furnishing correct details sought for, based on verifiable B-ue state of af f airs without causing suppression of any material information which, if resorted [o, shall entail prosecution under the Act.

Note: All applications must be submitted along with their enclosures in duplicate duly attested by any ga/etlcd officer of the Central or State Government.

1. Name and full postal address of the applicant	:	
2. Status of the applicant under clause (b) of rule 2	:	
3. Date of establishment	:	
4. Whether registered under the Societies Registration Act, 1860 (21 of 1860), or any other relevant Act	:	
5. If yes, number and year of registration (Attested copy of registration certificate to be enclosed)	:	
6. Whether the organisation is of national or state level	:	
7. Number of managing committee members together with list of names, addresses and occupation of the office bearers	:	

8. Brief details of the organisation, objectives and activities during the last three years :	
9. Purpose for which the amount is required (pleasestate the details of the project and its proposedimplementation) :	
10. Amount of grant required-itemwise detail sunder non-recurring, recurring to be enclosed :	
11. Time schedule of the activities arranged :	
12. The total amount incurred or invested by the applicant, or likely to be incurred by the applicant :	
13. Sources of funding of balance amount whether the organisation is getting financial assistance from any other official or non-official source, if yes, give details :	
14. Details of prosecution, if any, in a court of law launched against the applicant, during the last :	
15. Copies of the following documents (duly attested by a gazetted officer of the Central or State Government) to be attached : *(i)* Constitution of the organisation and articles of association; *(ii)* Annual reports of the organisation for last three years (please furnish separate annual reports for each year); *(iii)* Annual audited statement of accounts for each of last three years duly signed by Chartered Accountant. These statements must bear the registration number and official seal or stamp of the Chartered Accountant.	

DECLARATION

(To be signed by the applicant or its authorised agent)

The particulars heretofore given are true and correct. No material has been suppressed. It is certified that I/we have read the guidelines, terms and conditions governing the scheme and undertake to abide by them on behalf of our organisation/ institution. The financial assistance, if **Provided**, shall be put to the declared use, for promotion and protection of rights of consumers or for standard marks (strike out whichever is inapplicable).

Date : .... Applicant

Station : ....

To,
Member Secretary,
Committee (Consumer Welfare Fund),
Krishi Bhawan,
New Delhi.

Recommendation of Member-Secretary

Factual details furnished in the application have been verified in consultation with the Ministry/Department of agency who is/are administratively concerned in the matter and found to be correct/incorrect. The claims of the applicant are recommended for consideration by the committee (please give reasons in support of your recommendation).

Member-Secretary

Committee (Consumer Welfare Fund)

Recommendation of the Committee

Recommended for grant of ₹...............Rupees ....(in words) from the Consumer Welfare Fund as discussed in the meeting held on...............(date)

Chairman

Chapter 3

Investor Education and Protection Fund (Awareness and Protection of Investors) Rules, 2001

[GSR 750 (E) Dated 1-16-2001]

In exercise of the powers conferred by clauses (a) and (b) of sub-section (1) of section 642 of the Companies Act, 1956 (1 of 1956), read with sub-section (3) of section 205C of that Act, the Central Government hereby makes the following rules, namely:—

SHORT TITLE AND COMMENCEMENT

1. (1) These rules may be called the Investor Education and Protection Fund (Awareness and Protection of Investors) Rules, 2001.

(2) They shall come into force on the date of their publication in the Official Gazette.

Definitions

2. In these rules, unless the context otherwise requires:—

(a) "Act" means the Companies Act, 1956;

(b) "Fund" means the Investor Education and Protection Fund (IEPF) established under sub-section (1) of section 205C of the Companies Act, 1956 (1 of 1956);

(c) "Ministry" or "Department" means Ministry or Department of the Central Government dealing the Company Affairs;

(d) "Committee" Sub-Committee" means the Committee specified by the Central Government under sub-section (4) of section 205C of the Act to administer the Fund;

(e) "Form" means forms prescribed by these rules;

(f) Words and expressions used in these rules and not defined herein but defined in the Act shall have the meaning respectively assigned to them in the Act.**'credits to the Fund.**

(i) Any amount required to be credited by the companies to the Fund, as **Provided** in the Act shall be remitted into the concerned specified branches Punjab National Bank, within a becoming due to be credited to the Fund and the amount so credited shall by accounted for as **Provided** in rule 4 below.

(n) *(a)* The amount shall be tendered by the companies on behalf of the Centra] Government in such branches of Punjab National Bank along with Challan (in triplicate) and the Bank will return two copies duly stamped to the Company as token of having received the amount.

(b) Every Company shall file with the concerned Registrar of Companies one copy of the Challan referred to in *(a)* evidencing deposit of the amount to the Fund. The Company shall fill in the full description and the nature of the amount tendered and its Head of Account.

(c) (t) Every company shall, when effecting a credit to the account of the Fund, will separately furnish to the concerned Registrar of Companies a statement in Form 1 duly certified by a Chartered Accountant or a

Company Secretary or a Cost Accountant practising in India or by the statutory auditors of the company. **Provided** that each Company shall keep a record relating to folio number. Certificate Number, etc., in respect of persons to whom the amount of unpaid or unclaimed dividend, application money, matured deposit or debentures, interest accrued or payable, for a period of three years and the Committee or Sub-Committee shall have powers to inspect such records of that period.

(d) The Forms prescribed in these rules may be filed through electronic media or through any other computer readable media as referred under section 610A of the Companies Act, 1956 (1 of 1956).

(e) The electronic form shall be authenticated by the authorized signatories using digital signatures, as defined under the Information Technology Act, 2001 (21 of 2000).

(f) The Forms prescribed in these rules, when filed in physical form, may mauthenticated by authorized signatory by affixing his signature manually.

(if) On receipt of this statement, the concerned Registrar of Companies shall enter the details of such receipt in a register and reconcile the amount so remitted and collected, with the concerned Pay and Accounts Officer, on monthly basis.

(m) Each Registrar of Companies shall furnish an abstract of such receipt received during the month to Department of Company Affairs within seven days after the close of the month.

(iv) Department of Company Affairs shall maintain a consolidated abstract of receipts and shall reconcile them on a quarterly basis with Principal Pay and Accounts Office of the Department of Company Affairs.

Manner of Accounting

3. (i) (A) All amounts received shall be accounted for under the following

Heads of account, which shall thereafter be transferred to the Fund. Major Head 0075—Miscellaneous General Services.

Minor Head 104—Unclaimed and unpaid dividends, deposits and debentures etc. of Investors in Companies:

(a) Unpaid dividend.

(b) Unpaid application money received by Companies for allotment of securities and due for refund.

(c) Unpaid Matured Deposit.

(d) Unpaid Matured Debentures.

(e) Interest accrued on (a) to (d).

(f) Interest on unpaid dividend.

(g) Interest on unpaid application money received by Companies for allotment of securities and due for refund.

(h) Interest on unpaid matured deposits.

(i) Interest on unpaid matured debentures.

Note: (a) to (d) shall be sub-heads *(i)* to *(iv)* shall be detailed heads: (z) (B) Grants and donations given to the Fund by State Governments, Companies or any other Institutions will be credited under a separate Sub-Head under the Minor Head '800 - Other Receipts' below the Major Head '0075—Miscellaneous General Services'. (n) All expenditure for the purposes of carrying out the objects for which the Fund has been established shall be incurred under the functional Head expenditure head of Department of Company Affairs and equivalent amount will be shown as deduct entry by transfer of amount from the fund. (in) Surplus amount, if any, from the fund accounts shall not, for the present, be utilised for investment purpose.

Expenses of the Committee

4. (a) The official member of the committee or sub-committee shall be entitled to Travelling Allowance according to the rules regulating their official position.

(b) For Journeys performed by a non-official member of the Committee or sub-committee or a special invitee in connection with the work of the committee or a sub-committee shall be entitled for TA/DA as per supplementary Rules of Central Government.

(c) Committee shall have powers to recommend appointment/remuneration to any experts in such areas as may be considered necessary.

(d) Committee shall have powers to recommend appointment of Auditors and tor scrutinizing the accounts of the voluntarily agencies registered with it. Audit of Accounts.

5. The accounts of the Fund shall be audited by internal audit party of the Department of Company Affairs every year and will also be subject to audit by the office of Comptroller and Auditor General of India.

Constitution and Functions of the Committee

6. (a) The Committee shall consists of ten members, excluding the Chair-person who is. Secretary, to the Department of Company Affairs. The members shall be nominated by Reserve Bank of India, the Securities and Exchange Board of India and/or from any other Ministry or Department of Central Government dealing with investor protection activities and experts from the field of investors' education and protection. The non-official Members shall hold office for a period of two years. The Official members shall hold office for a period of two years or until they occupy their position whichever is earlier. The constitution of the Committee shall be notified in the Official Gazette.

(b) Functions of the Committee

(1) The Committee shall recommend the following activities relating to investors' education, awareness and protection:

(a) Education Programmes through Media;

(b) Organizing Seminars and Symposia;

(c) Proposals for registration of Voluntary Associations or Institution or other Organizations engaged in Investor Education and Protection activities;

(d) Proposals for projects for Investors' Education and Protection including research activities and proposals for financing such projects;

(e) Coordinating with institutions engaged in Investor Education, awareness, and protection activities; The Committee may also be entrusted with such other functions for carrying out the objects for which the Fund has been established;

(f) Proposals for selling up of institutional arrangements or infrastructure for taking up programmes; projects and action plans keeping in view the objectives and expenditure relating thereto, including research and training activities;

[(&)] CO The Committee may appoint one or more sub-committees whenever it considers necessary to facilitate efficient and speedy discharge of its functions.

Sub-committee shall be constituted from amongst the members.

The Chairperson of the Committee may nominate any one of the members of the sub-committee as its convenor and where no such nomination has been made, the members of the sub-committee elect a convenor amongst themselves.

The Committee may have Sub-Committee to examine the end use ot grants and assistance and recommend release of funds.

1. Inserted by the Investor Education and Protection Fund (Awareness and Protection of Investors) Amendment Rules, 2007, *w.e.f.* 20-2-2007.

2. Clause *(f)* re-lettered as clause *(g)*, *ibid.*

Power to Call upon a Company

7. *(i)* The Committee shall have *suo moto* powers to call upon any company to pay the amount due to the Fund.

(ii) Committee shall call upon any company to give estimates of the amounts to be credited to the Fund in Form 2.

Report by the Committee

8. The Committee shall furnish its activity report for every six months' period to the Central Government.

MEETINGS

9. (i) One third of the total members subject to five members in the case of meeting of committee and three members in case of sub-committee meeting shall constitute a quorum.

(ii) The Chairperson of the Committee and the convenor of a sub-committee, respectively, shall preside over the meetings of the Committee or the sub-committee as the case may be. In the event of the Chairperson or, as the case may be, the convenor being unable to attend the meeting for any reason, the members present may elect one amongst themselves to preside over the meeting.

(iii) The Chairperson of the Committee or the convenor of a sub-committee may, call meeting of the Committee or a sub-committee:

Provided that the Chairperson or the Convenor, as the case may be, shall also call a meeting if a requisition for that purpose is presented to him by at least five members in the case of the Committee and three members in the case of a sub-committee.

(iv) At least fourteen clear days' notice indicating the time and place of the meeting shall be sent to the members of the Committee or the sub-committee as the case may be:

Provided that in case of urgency, a special meeting of the Committee or sub-committee may be called at any time by the Chairperson or the convenor, who shall inform the members at least three clear days in advance of the subject matter for consideration at the meeting and the reasons for which he considers the meeting urgent:

Provided further that no other business shall be transacted at such a meeting. (v) The Chairman or the convenor, as the case may be, may invite any person to attend any meeting of the Committee or Sub-Committee as a special invitee but such person shall not be entitled to vote. **Agenda.**

10. (i) At least seven clear days before any meeting of the Committee or a Sub-Committee, except meetings referred to in proviso to sub-rule *(iv)* to rule 3 0, a list of business proposed to be transacted at the meeting shall be sent to the members of the Committee or of a sub-committee, as the case may be, *(if)* No business, not included in the list of business, shall be transacted at a meeting without the permission of the Chairperson presiding over the meeting.

VOTING

11. (z) Every question brought before any meeting of the Committee or Sub-Committee, as the.case may be, shall be decided by a majority vote of members present and voting at the meeting. No member shall vote by proxy.

(it) In the event of equality of votes, at a meeting, the Chairperson or the convenor, as the case may be or in his absence, the person presiding, shall have a second or casting vote.

MINUTES

12. The minutes of the meeting of the Committee or Sub-Committee shall be caused to be recorded and circulated among the members.

Conditions for Utilization of Funds by the Committee

13. (i) The Committee may register from time to time various Associations or institutions or organisations, engaged in activities relating to investor awareness, education and protection and proposing for investors programmes; organising seminar, symposia and undertake projects for Investor Protection including research activities.

(ii) Application for registration by such organisations referred to in sub-rule (i) be made in Form 3.

(iii) Application for release of funds for the activities listed in rule 7(1) from the organizations or institutes registered with the Department of Company Affairs shall be made in Form 4.

(iv) A copy of the summary or recommendations of the seminar or programme conducted and copy of Accounts for such activity by such organisation, e.g., registered associations or chambers of commerce or institutes shall be **Provided** to the Committee within ten days of the conclusion of the seminar or programme.

(v) The organisation or Associations registered shall be considered for grant of funds as a grant-in-aid cither as one time measure or in stages or by way of reimbursement depending upon the nature of the activity proposed.

(vi) The Committee shall be entitled to examine the end use of grants and assistance before recommending-release of funds.

(vii) The Committee shall cause to draw at the end of each financial year, a statement of Total Receipts from various sources indicated in section 205C or the Companies Act, 1956, and the grants disbursed or the expenditure incurred in connection with the activities organised by the Committee or Sub-Committee and other expenditure incurred for holding the meetings.

(viii) The Committee shall maintain the necessary records showing the amoun disbursed, date of disbursal, the name of Organisation or Voluntary agency, activities of the agency for which such disbursal was made.

FORM NO. 1

Statement of amounts credited to Investor Education and Protection Fund

[Pursuant to rule 3 of the Investor Education and Protection Fund (Awareness and Protection of Investors) Rules, 2001]

Note - All fields marked in *are to be mandatorily filled

1.

(a) 'Corporate Identity Number (CIN) of company

(b) Global Location Number (GLN) of company

2.

(a) Name of the company

(b) Address of the registered office of the company

Pre-fill

3. 'Date of payment of amount to the fund

4. 'Mode of payment

(DD/MM/YYYY)

(in ₹) (in ₹)

5. Details of the amount credited to the fund

(a) Amount in the unpaid dividend accounts of companies (in ₹)

(b) The application money received by companies for allotment of any securities and due for refund (in ₹)

(c) Matured deposits with companies

(d) Matured debentures with companies

(e) Interest accrued on the amounts referred to in clauses (a) to (d) above

(i) Unpaid dividend

(ii) Application money due for refund

(iiii) Matured deposit with companies

(iv) Matured debentures with companies

(f) Grants and donation

6. Financial year (s) to which the amount (s) relates

Details of filing Form 1 under section 205A(6) and 205A(7) of the Companies Act, 1956

Attachments

7. Details of amount credited to Investor Education & Protection Fund during the year

8. Details of amounts – State the details of amounts remaining unclaimed for six years since becoming due for payment for the following

(a) Unpaid dividend

(b) Unclaimed share application money

(c) Unclaimed matured deposits

(d) Unclaimed matured debentures

(e) Interest in respect of *(d)* to *(d)*

9. Relevant financial year in which amount is due for payment or redemption.

Signature of Person presenting the return:

Date & Place

Certificate from auditors Verified and found correct.

Place *Chartered Accountant/Cost Accountant/Company Secretary/Statutory Auditor* Date

FORM NO. 3
(See Rule 14)

Application for registration Note:

(1) Submission of the registration form does not necessarily guarantee automatic registration or funding.

(2) Committee reserves the right to reject any application in its own discretion without assigning any reason thereof.

(3) Committee may call for additional details as and when required for the purpose of granting registration.

(4) Any false information furnished or false representation made shall make the application/registration liable for rejection/ cancellation.

1. Name of Association:
2. Address:
   Tel No./Fax No./E-mail
3. Year of Establishment: Registration No. and Date:
4. Principal office bearer: Address:
   (a) How elected or appointed or nominated and what is the frequency
   of election to the. Hoard
   of election to the Board
   (b) Total number of employees
   (For the last three years)
5. Membership (For last three years)
   (a) Total Number i.e. Number of Members who are the Investors
   (b) Connected with Investment activities *i.e.,* Professionals
6. Financial Information
   (a) Source of Funds (Information for last three years)
   (i) Membership fees *(ii)* Annual subscription fees *(iii)* Any other fees *(iv)* Any other source of income
   (b) Uses of funds
   (i) Administrative expenses *(ii)* Salary and wages
   - Stationery and postage
   - Miscellaneous
   (iii) Expenses for holding seminars, meetings and other activities of the Fund
   (iv) Any other expenses excess of income over expenditure
7. Activities of the Association
   (a) Objectives of the Association
   (b) How has the Association met the objectives in the past/objectives of the present application
   (c) How does the Association communicates to the investors
   (d) Whether the Association holds meeting regularly (If yes, details of the number of meetings held during the last three years and the participation to be given)
   (e) Number of shareholders/conferences/seminars held during the last three years
   (f) Whether representatives of the Association are sent to attend shareholder' meeting of companies
   (g) Whether the association handles investors grievances? (if yes, then number of grievances received and settled during the last 12 months to be given)
   (h) Grievances redress system of the Association House Journal/publication of the Association
   (i) Whether any representation has been made by the Association in the past to the Stock exchanges/ Government/Companies in the interests of the investors in general and the members in particular.
   (k) Any other activity

(*l*) Whether any suits/proceedings are pending against the association or any of its office bearers/members in any court of law, if so details may be given.

(*m*) Whether the association agrees to abide by the rules/regulations/guidelines framed by Committee/Central Government from time to time for its effective functioning and better discipline.

(*n*) Whether any office bearer of the Association is a board member of any corporate entity.

Enclosures

(*i*) Copies of Memorandum and Articles of Association, rules/regulations/bye laws.

(*ii*) Latest membership and their addresses.

(*iii*) Copies of the audited statement of accounts for last three years

(*iv*) Copies of last 3 issues of the House magazine/journal, if any

(*v*) A copy of the statement authenticating registration of the Association

(*vi*) A statement elaborating details of activities of the Association.

Signature (with name)

President Vice-President Secretary Treasurer

FORM NO. 4

(*See* Rule 14J Application for Funds for Services/Programmes)

1. Name of Applicant:

2. Address: Registered Office Corporate Office Address:

3. Constitution. (Whether Association/Chamber of Commerce/Institute/Individual)

4. Date of Incorporation/registration

5. Details (Number/Date) of recognition granted by Committee under rule 14

Existing activities (0) Management:

Board of Directors: (n) Details relating to proposed serninar/programme/activity. Date when to be conducted: Venue:

Brief Literature on subject-matter:

6. Amount required for the proposed seminar/programme/activity and full justification for the same including following detail—

(*i*) The Nature of activity

(*ii*) List of proposed Guests/VIPs who would chair the dais

(*iii*) Description of expenses proposed to be incurred for the activity

(*iv*) Venue expenses

(*v*) Travelling, Boarding and lodging expenses of Guests for the activity,

(*vi*) Other expenses

(*vii*) Expected number of people who would attend the activity *(viif)* Any other information for the justification of the amount nature with name)

President: Vice-President Secretary Treasurer

Chapter 4

Monopolies and Restrictive Trade Practices (Recognition of Consumers' Association) Rules, 1987

[GSR 534 (E), Dated 1-6-1987]

In exercise of the powers conferred by section 67 read with clause (n) of section 2 of the Monopolies and Restrictive Trade Practices Act, 1969 (54 of 1969), the Central Government hereby makes the following rules, namely:—

SHORT TITLE AND COMMENCEMENT

1. (1) These rules may be called the Monopolies and Restrictive Trade Practices (Recognition of Consumers' Association) Rules, 1987.

(2) They shall come into force on the date of their publication in the Official Gazette.

Definitions

2. In these rules, unless the context otherwise requires,—

(a) "Act" means the Monopolies and Restrictive Trade Practices Act, 1969 (54 of 1969);

(b) "form" means a Form specified in the Schedule to these rules;

(c) "principal officer" in relation to a consumer association means any individual who is specifically authorised in writing or by means of a resolution adopted by such consumers' association in that behalf.

Application for recognition of Consumers' Association

3. (1) Every consumers' association which is desirous of being recognised as a registered consumers' association,—

(a) shall have not less than ten consumers as its members; and (for) shall make an application for such recognition in triplicate to the Central Government in the Department of Company Affairs in Form I.

(2) Every application made under sub-rule (1) shall be accompanied by J challan or a bank draft evidencing the payment of a fee of rupees five hundred-

(3) On receipt of an application made under sub-rule (1), the Department of Company Affairs shall note thereon the date of its receipt and shall **forthwith** communicate such date to the applicant.

(4) The Department of Company Affairs may, before issuing a certificate of recognition, require the applicant to furnish such additional information as it may consider necessary within a period of thirty days of the date of receipt of the latter seeking such additional information.

(4A) Every application made under sub-rule (1) shall be disposed of by the Department of Company Affairs within ninety days from the date of receipt of the application or, as the case may be, of the receipt of the additional information furnished under sub-rule (4).

(5) The certificate of recognition to be issued under sub-rule (4) shall be in Form II.

(6) Where a certificate of recognition issued under these rules is lost, destroyed or mutilated, a duplicate may be issued on an application made in this regard and on payment of a fee of rupees fifty.

Payment of Fees

4. Fees payable under these rules shall be paid in accordance with the procedure laid down in rule 10 of the Monopolies and Restrictive Trade Practices Rules, 1970.

Refusal to grant of Certificate of Recognition to Consumers' Association

5. Where a certificate of recognition of consumers' association has been refused, the applicant shall be informed of the reasons for such refusal.

Copies of Certificate of Recognition to be sent to certain Authorities

6. Every consumers' association which has been recognised as a "registered consumers' association" shall furnish a copy of the certificate of recognition issued to it to the concerned Consumer Disputes Redressal Commission established under clause *(b)* of section 9 of the Consumer Protection Act, 1986 (68 of 1986).

Verification of Application

Every application made under these rules shall be duly verified by the principal officer.

SCHEDULE FORM I

[See sub-rule (1) of rule 3]

Form of Application to be given to the Central Government in the Department of Company Affairs for recognition of Consumers' Association as "Registered Consumers' Association"

(To be submitted in triplicate)

(1) Name of the consumers' association:

(a) Registered Office:

(b) For correspondence:

(c) Branches:

(3) If registered under section 25 of the Companies Act, 1956, the date of registration:

(4) If registered under any other law, the Act under which registered and date of registration: (Certified copy of the certificate of registration to be enclosed)

(5) Total number of members of the association: (as on the date of application)

(6) Objects of the association (Certified copy of memorandum of association to be enclosed along with copy of the rules and regulations of the association).

(7) Names, addresses and occupations of persons on the board of directors/governing body/council/committee (by whatever name called), to whom the management of the affairs of the association is entrusted;

(8) Number of employees:

(a) Whole-time

(b) Part-time

(9) Year-wise details of the work done by the association during the last three years in the field of protection of consumers' interest:

(10) Copies of published annual reports and accounts of the association for the latest three years.

(11) Details of laboratory/organisation, if any, owned, run or operated by the association for purposes of protection of consumers' interest.

I,..................do hereby solemnly state that what is stated in item 1 to 11 above is true to the best of my knowledge and belief.

Place :

Date : Signature and designation of

Principal Officer

FORM II

[Set; sub-rule (5) of rule 3]
Certificate of Recognition
Government of India Department of Company Affairs

Certified that the Consumers' Association whose particulars are given below has, this day, been recognised as "registered consumers' association" in terms of clause *(n)* of section 2 of the Monopolies and Restrictive Trade Practices Act, 1969 (54 of 1969).

Particulars

(1) Name of the Consumers' Association:

(2) Address:

(3) Name of persons on the governing board/body/council to whom man-agement of the association is entrusted:

(4) Number of Members:

(5) Registration number:

Date : Signature

BUREAU OF INDIAN STANDARDS

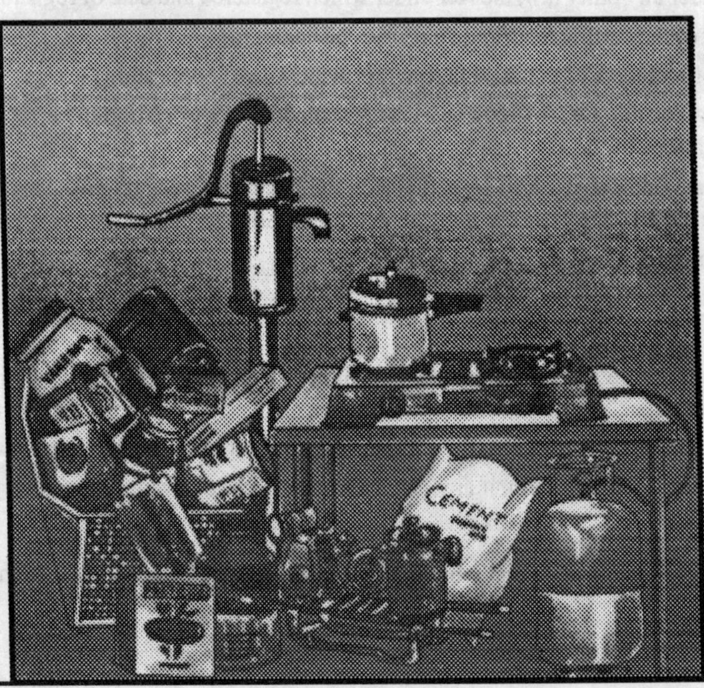

— ✦ — ✦ — ✦ —

Chapter 5

Consumer Protection Rules – Statewise Andaman and Nicobar Islands Consumer Protection Rules, 1987

In exercise of the powers conferred by sub-section (2) of section 30 of the Consumer Protection Act, 1986 (68 of 1986), read with Government of India, Ministry of Food and Civil Supplies, Department of Civil Supplies, Notification S.O. No. 469(E), dated 15th May, 1987, the Lieutenant Governor, (Administrator), Andaman and Nicobar Islands hereby makes the following Rules, namely —

SHORT TITLE AND COMMENCEMENT

1. (1) These rules may be called Andaman and Nicobar Islands Consumer Protection Rules, 1987.

(2) They shall come into force on such date as the Government may, by notification in the Official Gazette, appoint.

Definitions

2. In these rules, unless the context otherwise requires —

(a) "Act" means the Consumer Protection Act, 1986 (68 of 1986);

(b) "agent" means a person duly authorised by a party to present any complaint or appeal or reply on its behalf before the State Commission or the District Forum;

(c) "appellant" means a party which makes an appeal against the order of the District Forum;

(d) "Government" means the Andaman and Nicobar Administration;

(e) "Memorandum" means memorandum of appeal filed by the appellant;

(f) "Opposite party" means a person who answers complaint or claim;

(g) "President" means the President of the State Commission or District Forum as the case may be;

(h) "respondent" means the person who answers any memorandum or appeal.

Salaries and other allowances and terms and conditions of the president and members of the District Forum [Section 10(3)]

3. (1) The President of the District Forum shall receive the salary of the Judge of a District Court if appointed on whole-time basis or an honorarium of [₹ 250] per day if appointed on part-time basis. Other members if sitting on whole time basis, shall receive a consolidated honorarium of ₹ 2,000 per month and if sitting on part time basis, a consolidated of [₹ 150] per day for the sitting.

(2) The president and the members of the District Forum shall be entitled for such travelling allowance and daily allowance on official tour as are admissible to Grade-I Officer of the Government.

(3) The salary, honorarium and other allowances shall be defrayed out of the Consolidated Fund of India.

(4) Before appointment, the president and members of the District Forum shall have to take an undertaking that he does not and will not have any such financial or other interest as is likely to affect prejudicially his functions as a member.

(5) In addition to the provisions of section 10(2) of the Act, the Government may remove from the office, the President and member of a District Forum who:—

(*a*) has been adjudged an insolvent, or

(*b*) has been convicted of an offence which in the opinion of the Government, involves moral turpitude, or

(*c*) has become physically or mentally incapable of acting as such member, or

(*d*) has acquired such financial or other interest as is likely to affect prejudicially his functions as a member, or

(*e*) has so abused his position as to render his continuance in office prejudicial to the public interest:

Provided that the President or member shall not be removed from his office on the ground specified in clauses (*d*) and (*e*) of sub-rule (5) except on an inquiry held by the Government in accordance with such procedure as it may specify in this behalf and finds the member to be guilty of such ground.

(6) The terms and conditions of the service of the President and the members of the District Forum shall not be varied to their disadvantage during their tenure of Office.

(7) Where any vacancy occurs in the office of the President of the District Forum, the senior most (in order of appointment) member of District Forum, holding office for the time being, shall discharge the functions of the President until a person appointed to fill such vacancy assumes the office of the President of the District Forum.

(8) When the President of the District Forum is unable to discharge the functions owing to absence, illness or any other cause, the senior most (in order of appointment) member of the District Forum shall discharge the functions of the President until the day on which the President resumes the charge of his functions.

(9) The President or any member ceasing to hold office as such shall not hold any appointment in or be connected with the management or administration of an organisation which have been the subject of any proceeding under the Act during his tenure for a period of five years from the date on which he ceases to hold, such office.

Place of sitting and other matters relating to District Forum [Section 14(3)]

4. (1) The Office of the District Forum shall be located at Port Blair. Where the Government decides to establish a single District Forum having jurisdiction over more than and district, it shall notify the place and jurisdiction of the District, Forum so established.

(2) The working days and the office hours of the District Forum shall be the same as that of the Government.

(3) The official seal and emblem of the District Forum shall be such as the Government may specify,

(4) Sitting of the District Forum, as and when necessary, shall be convened by the President.

(5) No act or proceedings of the District Forum shall be invalid by reason only of the existence of any vacancy among its members only or any defect in its constitution.

(6) The Government shall appoint such staff, as may be necessary to assist the District Forum in its day to day work and perform such other functions as are **Provided** under these rules, or assigned to it by the President. The salary payable to such staff shall be defrayed out of the Consolidated Fund of India.

(7) Where the opposite party admits the allegation made by the complainant, the District Forum shall decide the complaint on the basis of the merit of the case and documents present before it.

(8) If during the proceedings conducted under section 13, District Forum fixes a date for hearing of the parties, it shall be obligatory on the complainant and opposite party or its authorised agent to appear before the District Forum on such date of hearing or any other date to which hearing could be adjourned. Where the complainant or his authorised agent fails to appear before the District Forum on such day, the District Forum may in its discretion either dismiss the complaint for default or decide it on merit. Where the opposite party or its authorised agent fails to appear on the day of hearing District Forum may decide the complaint *ex parte.*

(9) While proceeding under sub-rule (8), the District Forum may, on such terms as it may think fit and at any stage, adjourn the hearing of the complaint but not more than one adjournment shall ordinarily be given and the complaint should be decided within ninety days from the date of notice received by the opposite party where complaint does not require analysis or testing of the goods and within one hundred and fifty days if it requires analysis or testing of the goods.

(10) Order of the District Forum shall be signed and dated by the members or the District Forum constituting the Bench and shall be communicated to the parties free of charge.

Procedure to be adopted by the District Forum for analysis and testing of the goods [Section 13(l)(c)]

5. (1) Under section *13(\)(d),* if considered necessary, the District Forum may direct the complainant to provide more than one sample of the goods in clean containers with stopper properly fixed on them.

(2) On receiving the samples of such goods, the District Forum shall seal it and fix labels on the containers carrying following information—

(i) Name and address of the appropriate laboratory to whom sample will be sent for analysis and test;

(ii) Name and address of the District Forum;

(iii) Case Number;

(iv) Seal of the District Forum.

(3) The sample will be sent to the appropriate laboratory by the District Forum for sending report within fourty-five days or within such extended time as may be granted by the District Forum after specifying the nature of the defect alleged and date of submission of the report.

Salary and other allowances and terms and conditions of the president and members of the State Commission [Section 16(2)]

6. (1) The President of the State Commission shall receive the salary of the Judge of the High Court if appointed on whole-time basis or consolidated honorarium of [₹ 500] per day for the sitting if appointed on part-time basis. Other members, sitting on whole time basis, shall receive a consolidated honorarium of ₹ 3,000 per month and if sitting on part time basis, a consolidated honorarium of [₹ 300] per day for the sitting.

(2) The president and the members of the State Commission shall be eligible for such travelling allowance and daily allowance on official tour as are admissible to Grade-I Officer of the Government.

(3) The salary, honorarium and other allowances shall be defrayed out of the Consolidated Fund of India.

(4) The President and the member of the State Commission shall hold office for a term of five years or upto the age of sixty-five years whichever is earlier and shall not be eligible for re-nomination :

Provided that the President and member may—

(a) by writing under his hand and addressed to the Government resign his office any time;

(b) be removed from his office in accordance with provisions of sub-rule (5),

(5) The Government may remove from office, president or a member of the State Commission who—

(a) has been adjudged an insolvent, or

(b) has been convicted of an offence which in the opinion of the Government, involves moral turpitude, or

(c) has become physically or mentally incapable of acting as such member, or

(d) has acquired such financial or other interest as is likely to affect prejudicially his functions as a member, or

(e) has so abused his position as to render his continuance in office prejudicial to public interest:

Provided that the President or a member shall not be removed from his Office on the ground specified in clauses *(d)* and *(e)* of sub-rule (5) except on an inquiry held by the Government, in accordance with such procedure as it may specify in this behalf and finds the member to be guilty of such ground.

(6) Before appointment, President and a member of the State Commission shall have to take an undertaking that he does not and will not have'any such financial or other interests as is likely to affect prejudicially his functions as such member.

(7) The terms and conditions of the service of the President and the members of the State Commission shall not be varied to their disadvantage during their tenure of office.

(8) Every vacancy caused hy resignation and removal of the President or any other member of the State Commission under sub-rule (4) or otherwise shall be filled by fresh appointment.

(9) Where any such vacancy occurs in the Office of the President of the State Commission, the seniormost (in order of appointment) member, holding office for the time being shall discharge the functions of the President until a person appointed to fill such vacancy assumes the office of the President of the State Commission.

(10) When the President of the State Commission is unable to discharge the functions owing to absence, illness or any other cause, the seniormost (in order of appointment) member of the State Commission shall discharge the func-tions of the President until the day on which the President resumes the charge of his functions.

(11) The President or any member ceasing to hold office as such shall not hold any appointment in or be connected with the management or administration of an organisation which have been the subject of any proceeding under the Act during his tenure for a period of five years from the date on which he ceases to hold such office.

Place of sitting and other matters relating to State Commission [Section 14(3) read with section 18]

7. (1) Office of the State Commission shall be located at Port Blair.

(2) The working days and the Office hours of the State Commission shall be the same as that of the Government.

(3) The official seal and emblem of the State Commission shall be such as the Government may specify.

(4) Sitting of the State Commission, as and when necessary, shall be convened by the President.

(5) No act or proceedings of the State Commission shall be invalid by reasons I only of the existence of any vacancy among its members or any defect in its I constitution thereof.

(6) The Government shall appoint such staff, as may be necessary to assist the State Commission in its work and perform such other functions as are **Provided** under these rules or assigned to it by the president. The salary payable to such staff shall be defrayed out of the Consolidated Fund of the Government.

(7) Where the opposite party admits the allegation made by the complainant, the State Commission shall decide the complaint on the basis of the merit of the case and documents present before it.

(8) If during the proceedings conducted under section 13, State Commission. fixes a date for hearing of the parties, it shall be obligatory on the complainant and opposite party or his authorised agent to appear before the State Commission on such date of hearing or any other date to which hearing could be adjourned. Where the complainant or his authorised agent fails to appear before the State Commission on such day, the State Commission may in its discretion either dismiss the complaint for default or decide it on merits. Where the opposite party or its authorised agent fails to appear on the day of hearing, the State Commission may decide the complaint *ex parte*.

(9) While proceeding under sub-rule (8) the State Commission may, on such terms as it may think fit and at any stage, adjourn the hearing of the complaint but not more than one adjournment shall ordinarily be given and the complaint should be decided within ninety days from the date of notice received by the opposite party where complaint does not require analysis or testing of the goods and within one hundred and fifty if it requires analysis or testing of the goods.

(10) Orders of the Stale Commission shall be signed and dated by the members of the State Commission constituting the Bench and shall be communicated to the parties free of charge.

Procedure for hearing appeal [Section 15]

8. (1) Memorandum shall be presented by the appellant or his authorised agent to the State Commission in person or sent by registered post addressed to the Commission.

(2) Every memorandum filed under sub-rule (1) shall be in legible handwriting preferably typed and shall set forth concisely under distinct heads, the grounds of appeal without any argument or narrative and such ground shall be numbered consecutively.

(3) Each memorandum shall be accompanied by the certified copy of the order, of the District Forum appealed against and such of the documents as may be required to support grounds of objection mentioned in the memorandum.

(4) When the appeal is presented after the expiry of period of limitation as specified in the Act, Memorandum shall be accompanied by an application supported by an affidavit setting forth the fact on which appellant relies to satisfy the State Commission that he has sufficient cause for not preferring the appeal within the period of limitation.

(5) The appellant shall submit four copies of the memorandum to the State Commission for official purposes.

(6) On the date of hearing or any other day to which hearing may be adjourned, it shall be obligatory for the parties or their authorised agents to appear before the State Commission. If appellant or his authorised agent fails to appear on such date, the State Commission may, in its discretion, either dismiss the appeal or decide it on the merit of the case. If respondent or his authorised agent fails to appear on such date, the State Commission shall proceed *ex parte* and shall decide the appeal *ex parte* on merits of the case.

(7) The appellant shall not, except by leave of the State Commission, urge or be heard in support of any ground of objections not set forth in the memorandum but the State Commission, in deciding the appeal, shall not confine to the grounds of objection set forth in the memorandum of taken by leave of the State Commission under this rule :

Provided that the Commission shall not rest its decision on any other grounds unless the party who may be affect thereby, has been given, at least one opportunity of being heard by the State Commission.

(8) State Commission may, on such terms as it may think fit and at any stage, adjourn the hearing of appeal, but not more than one adjournment shall ordinarily be given and the appeal should be decided within ninety days from the first date of hearing.

(9) The Order of the State Commission on appeal shall be signed and dated by the members of the State Commission constituting the Bench and shall be communicated to the parties free of charge.

Chapter 6

Andhra Pradesh Consumer Protection Rules, 1987

[Notification No. G.O. MS. No. 473, Food and Agriculture (CS-III), dated 2-9-1987]

In exercise of the powers conferred by sub-section (2) of section 30 of the Consumer Protection Act, 1986 (68 of 1986), the State Government hereby makes the following Rules, namely —

SHORT TITLE AND COMMENCEMENT

1. (1) These rules may be called the Andhra Pradesh State Consumer Protection **Rules,** 1987.

(2) They shall come into force on such date as the State Government may by notification in the Official Gazette.

Definitions

2. In these rules, unless the context otherwise requires,—

(a) "Act" means the Consumer Protection Act, 1986 (68 of 1986);

(b) "Agent" means a person duly authorised by a party to present any complaint or appeal or reply on its behalf before the State Commission or the District Forum;

(c) "Appellant" means a party which makes an appeal against the order of the District Forum;

(d) "Memorandum" means memorandum of appeal filed by the appellant;

(e) "Opposite party" means a person who answers complaint or claim;

(f) "President" means the President of the State Commission or District Forum as the case may be;

(g) "Respondent" means the person who answers any memorandum of appeal;

(h) "State" includes Union Territories.

Constitution of the State Consumer Protection Council and the working groups

2A. (1) The State Government shall, by notification in the Official Gazette constitute the State Consumer Protection Council (hereinafter referred to as the State Council) which shall consist of not more than 100 members nominated by the State Government from among the following categories of persons namely —

(a) the Minister-in-charge of Department of Civil Supplies who shall be the Chairman of the State Council.

(b) the Ex-Officio Secretary to Government, Food and Agriculture (Civil Supplies) shall be the Vice-Chairman of the State Council;

(c) one Legislator from each political party;

(d) representatives of the State Government Departments concerned with consumer interest;

(e) representatives of the consumer organisations or consumers;

(f) representatives of women;

(g) representatives of farmers, trade and industries;

(*h*) persons capable of representing consumer interests not specified above; and

(i) the Ex-Officio Joint Secretary, Food and Agriculture (Civil Supplies) Department shall be the Member-Secretary of the State Council.

(2) The term of the Council shall be three years from the date of its constitution,

(3) Any member may, by writing under his hand to the Chairman of the State Council resign from the Council. The vacancies as so caused or caused otherwise shall be filled from the same category by the State Government; and such person shall hold office so long as the member whose place he fills would have been entitled to hold office if the vacancy has not occurred.

Procedure of the State Council

2B. The State Council shall observe the following procedure in regard to the transaction of its business —

(1) The State Council shall meet at least once in every three months.

(2) The meeting, of the State Council shall be presided over by the Chairman. In the absence of the Chairman, the Vice-Chairman shall preside over the meeting of the State Council. In the absence of the Chairman and the Vice-Chairman the State Council shall elect a member to preside over the meeting of the Council.

(3) Each meeting of the State Council shall be called by giving not less than ten days' time from the date of issue of notice in writing to every member.

(4) Every notice of a meeting of the State Council shall specify the place and the day and hour of the meeting and shall contain statement of business to be transacted thereat.

(5) No proceedings of the State Council shall be invalid merely by reasons of existence of any vacancy in or any defect in the constitution of the Council.

(6) For the purpose of performing its functions under the Act, State Council may deem necessary and every working group so constituted shall perform such functions as are assigned to it by the State Council for its consideration.

(7) The non-official members shall be entitled to draw travelling allowance and dearness allowance as per orders issued in G.O. Ms. No. 196, Finance and Planning (Fin. Wing-T.A.). Department, dated 19-7-1988, read with G.O. Ms. No. 115, Finance and Planning (Fin. Wing-T.A.) Department, dated 16th April, 1979 and G.O. Ms. Nos. 125 and 132, Finance and Planning (Fin. Wing-T.A.) Department, dated 13-4-1982 and 16-4-1982, respectively.

(8) The resolutions passed by the State Council shall be recommendatory in nature.

(9) If any non-official member absented himself from the consecutive meetings off the Andhra Pradesh State Consumer Protection Council, without reasonable cause, he shall ceases to be the member as such and his name shall be removed by the Chairman of the council from the Membership of Andhra Pradesh State Consumer Protection Council.

[z]Salaries and other allowances and terms and conditions of the President and members of District Forum

3. (1) The President of the District Forum shall receive a consolidated amount of honorarium of ₹ 10,000 (rupees Ten thousand only) per month and if a retired district judge is appointed on whole time basis, shall receive an honorarium of last salary drawn minus pension or ₹ 10,000 (Rupees Ten thousand per month) whichever is beneficial to him.

(2) The President and members of the District Forum shall be entitled for such travelling allowance and daily allowance on official tour as are admissible to Grade-1 Officer of the State Government.

(3) The salary, honorarium and other allowances shall be defrayed out of the ansolidated Fund of the State Government.

(4) Before appointment, the President and members of the District Forum shall have to take an undertaking that he does not and will not have any such financial or other interests as is likely to affect prejudicially his functions as a member. In addition to provisions to sub-section (2) of section 10, the State Government may remove from the office of the President and member of a District Forum who —

(*a*) has been adjudged an insolvent, or

(*b*) has been convicted of an offence which in the opinion of the State Government, involves moral turpitude, or

(*c*) has become physically or mentally incapable of acting as such member, or

(*d*) has acquired such financial or other interest as is likely to affect prejudicially his functions as a member, or

(*e*) has so abused his position as to render, his continuance in office prejudicial to the public interest, or

(*f*) has absented himself from three consecutive sittings of the District Forum without reasonable cause]:

Provided that the President or member shall not be removed from his office on the ground specified in clauses *(d)* and *(e)* of sub-rule

(5) except on an enquiry held by State Government in accordance with the procedure as it may specify in this behalf and finds the member to be guilty of such ground.

(6) The terms and conditions of the service of the President and the members of the District Forum shall not be varied to their disadvantage during their tenure of office.

(7) Where any vacancy occurs in the office of the President of the District Forum, the Additional District Judge in District and Additional Chief Judge, City Civil Court in Hyderabad shall discharge the functions of the President until new incumbent assumes the office of the President of the District Forum.

(8) When the President of the District Forum is unable to discharge the functions owing to absence, vacation, illness or anyother cause the Additional District Judge in District and Additional Chief Judge in the City Civil Court in Hyderabad shall discharge the functions of the President until the new incumbent assumes the office of the President of the District Forum.

(9) The President or members ceasing to hold office as such shall not hold any appointment in or be connected with the management or administration or an organisation which have been the subject of any proceeding under the Act during his tenure for a period of 5 years from the date on which he ceases to hold such office.

Place of sitting and other matters relating to District Forum

4. (1) The Office of the District Forum shall be located at the head-quarters of the District, [or at such place as may be notified by the State Government]. Where the State Government decides to establish a Single District Forum having jurisdiction over more than one district, it shall notify the place and jurisdiction of the District Forum so established.

(2) The working days and the office hours of the District Forum shall be the same as that of the State Government.

(3) The official seal and emblem of the District Forum shall be such as the State Government may specify.

(4) Sitting of the District Forum, as and when necessary, shall be convened by the President.

(5) No act or proceedings of the District Forum shall be invalid by reason only of the existence of any vacancy among its members or of any defect in it constitution.

(6) State Government shall appoint such staff, as may be necessary to assist the District Forum in its day to day work and perform such other functions as are **Provided** under these rules, or assigned to it by the President. The salary payable to such staff shall be defrayed out of the Consolidated Fund of the State Government.

(7) Where the opposite party admits allegations made by the complainant the District forum shall decide the complaint on the basis of the merits of the case and documents present before it.

(8) If during the proceedings conducted under section 13, the District Forum fixes a date for hearing of the parties it shall be obligatory on the complainant and opposite party or its authorised agent to appear before the District Forum of such date of hearing or any other date to which hearing could be adjourned. Where the complainant or his authorised agent fails to appear before the District Forum on such day, the District Forum may in its discretion either dismiss the complaint for default or decide it on merit. Where the opposite party or its authorised agent fails to appear on the day of hearing, the District Forum may decide the complaint *ex parte.*

(9) While proceeding under sub-rule (8), the District Forum may, on such terms as it may think fit and at any stage, adjourn the hearing of the complaint but not more than one adjournment shall ordinarily be given and the complaint should be decided within 90 days from the date of notice received by the opposite party where complaint docs not require analysis or testing of the goods and within 150 days if it requires analysis or testing of the goods.

(10) Orders of the District Forum shall be signed and dated by the members of the District Forum constituting the Bench and shall be communicated to the parties free of charge.

Procedure to be adopted by the District Forum for analysis and testing of the goods

5. (1) Under section 13(l)(c), if considered necessary, the District Forum may direct the complainant to provide more than one sample of the goods in clean containers with stopper properly fixed on them,

(2) On receiving the samples of such goods, the District Forum shall seal it and fix labels on the containers carrying following information—

(i) name and address of the appropriate laboratory to whom sample will be sent for analysis and test;

(ii) name and address of the District Forum;

(iii) case number;

(iv) seal of the District Forum.

(3) The sample will be sent to the appropriate laboratory by the District Forum for sending report within 45 days or within such extended time as may be granted by the District Forum after specifying the nature of the defect alleged and date of submission of the report.

Salary and other allowances and terms and conditions of the President and members of the State Commission

6. (1) President of the State Commission shall receive the salary of the Judge of the High Court if appointed on whole-time basis or a consolidated honorarium of ₹ 200 per day for the sitting if appointed on part-time basis. Other members, if sitting on whole-time basis, shall receive a consolidated honorarium of [₹ 5,000] per month.

(2) The President and the members of the State Commission shall be eligible for such travelling allowance and daily allowance on official tour as are admissible to Grade-I Officer of the State Government.

(3) The salary, honorarium, other allowances shall be defrayed out of the Consolidated Fund of the State Government.

(4) President and the member of the State Commission shall hold office for a term of five years, or upto the age of [68] years whichever is earlier and shall not be eligible for renomination:

Provided that President and members may,—

(a) by writing under his hand and addressed to the State Government resign his office any time;

(b) be removed from his office in accordance with provisions of sub-rule (5).

(5) The State Government may remove from office. President or a member of the State Commission who—

(a) has been adjudged an insolvent, or

(b) has been convicted of an offence which in the opinion of the State Government, involves moral turpitude, or

(c) has become physically or mentally incapable of acting as such member, or

(d) has acquired such financial or other interest as is likely to affect prejudicially his functions as a member, or

(e) has so abused his position as to render his continuance in office prejudicial to the public interest:

Provided that the President or a member shall not be removed from his office on the ground specified in clauses *(d)* and *(e)* of sub-rule (5) except on a enquiry held by the State Government, in accordance with such procedure as it may specify in this behalf and find the member to be guilty of such ground.

(6) Before appointment, President and a member of the State Commission have to take an undertaking that he does not and will not have any financial or other interests as is likely to affect prejudicially his functions such member.

(7) The terms and conditions of the service of the President and the members of the State Commission shall not be varied to their disadvantage during their tenure of office.

(8) Every vacancy caused by resignation and removal of the President or any other member of the State Commission under sub-rule (4) or otherwise shall be filled by fresh appointment.

(9) Where any such vacancy occurs in the office of the President of the State Commission, the seniormost (in order of appointment) member, holding office for the time being, shall discharge the functions of the President until a person appointed to fill such vacancy assumes the office of the President of the State Commission.

(10) When the President of the State Commission is unable to discharge the functions owing to absence, illness or any other cause, the senior most (in order of the appointment) member of the State Commission shall discharge the functions of the President until the day on which the President resumes the charge of his functions.

(11) The President or any member ceasing to hold office as such shall not hold any appointment in or be connected with the management or administration of an organisation which have been the subject of any proceeding under the Act during his tenure for a period of 5 years from the date on which he ceases to hold such office.

Place of sitting and other matters relating to State Commission

7. (1) Office of the State Commission shall be located at the capital of the State,

(2) The working days and the office hours of the State Commission shall be the same as that of the State Government.

(3) The official seal and emblem of the State Commission shall be such as the [State Government may specify].

(4) Sitting of the State Commission, as and when necessary, shall be convened by the President.

(5) No act or proceedings of the State Commission shall be invalid by reason only of the existence of any vacancy among its members or any defect in its constitution thereof.

(6) State Government shall appoint such staff; as may be necessary to assist the State Commission in its day to day work and perform such other functions as are **Provided** under these rules or assigned to it by the President. The salary payable to such staff shall be defrayed out of the consolidated fund of the State Government.

(7) Where the opposite party admits the allegation made by the complainant the State Commission shall decide the complaint on the basis of the merit of the case and documents present before it.

(8) If during the proceedings conducted under section 13, the State Commission fixes a date for hearing of the parties, it shall be obligatory on the complainant and opposite party or his authorised agent to appear before the State Commission on such date of hearing or any other date to which hearing could be adjourned. Where the complainant or his authorised agent fails to appear before the State Commission on such day, the State Commission may in its discretion either dismiss the complaint for default or decide it on merits. Where the opposite party or its authorised agent fails to appear on the day of hearing, the State Commission may decide the complaint *ex parte.*

(9) While proceeding under sub-rule (8) the State Commission may on such I terms as it may think fit and at any stage, adjourn the hearing of the complaint but not more than one adjournment shall ordinarily be given and the complaint should be decided within 90 days from the date of notice received by the opposite party where complaint does not require analysis or testing of the goods and within 150 days if it requires analysis or testing of the goods.

(10) Orders of the State Commission shall be signed and dated by the members of the State Commission constituting the Bench and shall be communicated to the parties free of charge.

Procedure for hearing appeal

8. (1) Memorandum shall be presented by the appellant or his authorised agent to the State Commission in person or sent by registered post addressed to the Commission.

(2) Every memorandum filed under sub-rule (1) shall be in legible handwriting preferably typed and shall set forth concisely under distinct heads, the grounds of appeal without any argument or narrative and such ground shall be numbered consecutively.

(3) Each memorandum shall be accompanied by the certified copy of the order of the District Forum appealed against and such of the documents as may be required to support grounds of objection mentioned in the memorandum.

(4) When the appeal is presented after the expiry of period of limitation as specified in the Act, memorandum shall be accompanied by an application supported by an affidavit setting forth the fact on which appellant relies to satisfy the State Commission that he has sufficient cause for not preferring the appeal within the period of limitation.

(5) The appellant shall submit four copies of the memorandum to the State Commission for official purposes.

(6) On the date of hearing or any other day to which hearing may be adjourned, it shall be obligatory for the parties or their authorised agents to appear before the State Commission. If appellant or his authorised agent fails to appear on such date, the State Commission may, in its discretion, either dismiss the aPPJ3 or decide it on the merits of the case. If respondent or his authorised agents is to appear on such date, the State Commission shall proceed *ex parte* and shall decide the appeal *ex parte* on merits of the case.

(7) The appellant shall not, except by leave of the State Commission, urge or I heard in support of any ground of objections not set forth in the memorandum but the State Commission, in deciding the appeal, shall not confine to t grounds of objection set forth in the memorandum or taken by leave of the State Commission under this rule: **Provided** that the Commission shall not rest its decision on any other grounds unless the party who may be affected thereby, has been given, at least one opportunity of being heard by the State Commission.

(8) State Commission may, on such terms as it may think fit and at any stage, adjourn the hearing of appeal, but not more than one adjournment shall ordinarily be given and the appeal should be decided within 90 days from the first date of hearing.

(9) Order of the State Commission on appeal shall be signed and dated by the embers of the State Commission constituting the Bench and shall be communicated to the parties free of charge.

Chapter 7

Arunachal Pradesh Consumer Protection Rules, 1987

In exercise of the powers conferred by sub-section (2) of section 30 of the Consumer Protection Act, 1986 (68 of 1986), the Government of Arunachal Pradesh hereby makes the following Rules, namely:—

SHORT TITLE AND COMMENCEMENT

1. (1) These rules may be called the Arunachal Pradesh Consumer Protection Rules, 1987.

(2) They shall come into force at once.

Definition

2. In these rules, unless the context otherwise requires—

(a) "Act" means the Consumer Protection Act, 1986 (68 of 1986);

(b) "agent" means a person duly authorised by a party to present any, complaint or appeal or reply on its behalf before the State Commission or the District Forum;

(c) 'appellant' means a party which makes an appeal against the order of the District Forum; [1](Chairman" means a Chairman of the State Consumer Protection council established under sub-section (1) of section 7 of the Consumer Protection Act, 1986 (No. 68 of 1986);

(d) "memorandum" means memorandum of appeal filed by the appellant;

(e) "opposite party" means a person who answers complaint or claim;

(f) "president" means the President of the State Commission or District Forum as the case may be;

(g) "respondent" means the person who answers any memorandum of appeal;

(h) "State" means the State of Arunachal Pradesh; ("State Government" means the Government of Arunachal Pradesh).

2A.

(1) While establishing and appointing the District Forum and its members the State Government should strictly follow the provisions of section 9 and section 10 of the Act.

(2) That State Government may prescribe the pay scale for the regular staff of District Forum as are admissible to other State Government employees of the same category. For the part-time appointees of the Forum, remuneration of @ 20% of their basic pay (on the basic of Nos. of cases received and disposed) shall be payable to him. These staff will also be entitled to TA/DA on official tour as admissible to their respective category of employees.

(B) The salary payable to such staff shall be defrayed out of the consolidated fund of the state]. Salaries and other allowances and terms and conditions of the President and members of the District Forum [Section 10(3)].

3. (1) The President of the District Forum shall receive an honorarium of ₹ 150 per day of sitting. Other members of the District Forum shall however, receive a consolidated honorarium of ₹ '100 per day of sitting'.

(2) The President and the members of the District Forum shall be entitled to travelling allowance and daily allowance on official tour as are admissible to Grade-1 officer of the State Government.

(3) The honorarium and other allowances shall be defrayed out of the Consolidated Fund of the State Government.

(4) Before appointment, the President and the members of the District Forum shall have to take a undertaking that he does not and will not have any such financial or other interests as is likely to affect prejudicially, his functions as a member.

(5) In addition to the provisions of section 10(2), the State Government may remove from the office, the President and the member of a District Forum who:—

(*a*) has been adjudged an insolvent, or

(*b*) has been convicted of an offence which in the opinion of the State Government, involves moral turpitude, or

(*c*) has become physically or mentally incapable of acting as such member, or

(*d*) has acquired such financial or other interest as it may affect prejudicially his functions as a member, or

(*e*) has so abused his position as to render his continuance in office prejudi-cial to the public interest:

Provided that the President or the member shall not be removed from his office on the ground specified in clauses (*d*) and (e) of sub-rule (5) exception an Inquiry held by the State Government in accordance with such procedure as it may specify in this behalf and finds the member to be guilty of such ground. [(5A) The President and the members of the District Forum shall hold office or a term of five years or upto the age of 65 years, whichever is earlier and shall not be eligible for re-appointment:

Provided that the President and members may, by writing under his hand and addressed to the State Government, resign his office any time.

(6) The terms and conditions of the service of the President and the members of the District Forum shall not be varied to their disadvantage during their tenure of office.

(7) Where any vacancy occurs in the office of the President of the District Forum, the seniormost (in order of appointment) member of District Forum holding office for the time being, shall discharge the functions of the President until a person appointed to fill such vacancy assumes the office of the President of the District Forum.

(8) When the President of the District Forum is unable to discharge the functions owing to absence, illness or any other cause, the seniormost (in order of appointment) member of the District Forum shall discharge the functions of the President until the day on which the President resumes the charge of his functions,

(9) The President or any member ceasing to hold office as such shall not hold any appointment in or be connected with the management or administration of an organisation which have been the subject of any proceeding under the Act during his tenure for a period of five years from the date on which he ceases to hold such office.

Place of sitting and other matters relating to District Forum [Section 14(3)]

4. (1) The office of the District Forum shall be located at the headquarter of the District.

(2) The working days and the office hours of the District Forum shall be the same as that of the State Government.

(3) The official seal and emblem of the District Forum shall be such as the State Government may specify.

(4) Sitting of the District Forum, as and when necessary, shall be convened by the President.

(5) No act or proceedings of the District Forum shall be invalid by reason only of the existence of any vacancy among its members or any defect in its constitution.

(6) State Government shall appoint such staff, as may be necessary, to assist the District Forum in its day to day work and perform such other functions as are **Provided** under these rules, or assigned to it by the President. The salary payable to such staff shall be defrayed out of the Consolidated Fund of the State Government.

(7) Where the opposite party admits the allegation made by the complainant, the District Forum shall decide the complaint on the basis of the merit of the case and documents present before it.

(8) If during the proceedings conducted under section 13, District Forum fixes a date for hearing of the parties, it shall be obligatory on the complainant and opposite party or its authorised agent to appear before the District Forum on such date of hearing or any other date to which hearing could be adjourned. Where the complainant or his authorised agent fails of appear before the district Forum on such day, the District Forum may in its discretion either dismiss the complaint for default or decide it on merit. Where the opposite party or its authorised agent fails to appear on the day of hearing, the District forum may decide the complaint *ex parte*.

(9) While proceeding under sub-section (8), the District Forum may, on such terms as it may think fit and at any stage, adjourn the hearing of the complaint but not more than one adjournment shall ordinarily be given and the complaint should be decided within 90 days from the date of notice received by the opposite party where complaint does not require analysis or testing of the goods and within 150 days if it requires analysis or testing of the goods.

(10) Orders of the District Forum shall be signed and dated by the members of the District Forurn constituting the bench and shall be communicated to the parties free of charge.

(11) Subject to the other provisions of the Act, the District Forum may entertain, complaints as mentioned under section 11 of the Act.

(12) The District Forum shall, in disposal of any complaint before it as far as possible, follow the procedure laid down in sub-sections (1) and (2) of section 13.

(13) While admitting/entertaining a complaint, the District Forum shall, as far; as possible follow the procedures laid down under section 24A of the Act.

(14) Order of the District Forum should be signed by the President and at least pne member of the District Forum,

(15) The District Forum shall also have the power to direct that any order passed by it, where no appeal has been preferred under section 15 of the Act be published in the Official Gazette or through other media and no legal proceeding shall lie against the District Forum or any other media for such publication.]

Procedure to be adopted by the District Forum for analysis and testing of the goods [Section 13(l)(c)]

5. (1) Under section 13(l)(c), if considered necessary, the District Forum may direct the complainant to provide more than one sample of the goods in clean containers with stopper properly fixed on them.

(2) On receiving the samples of such goods, the District Forum shall seal it and fix labels on the containers carrying following information:

(i) name and address of the appropriate laboratory to whom sample will be sent for analysis and test;

(ii) name and address of the District Forum;

(iii) case number;

(iv) seal of District Forum,

(3) The sample will be sent to the appropriate laboratory by the District Forum lor sending report within 45 days or, within such extended, time as may be granted by the District Forum after specifying the nature of the defect alleged and date of submission of the report.

5A. (1) While establishing and appointing the State Commission and its members, the State Government shall strictly follow the provisions of section 16 of the Act.

(2) The State Government may also prescribe the pay scale for the regular staff of State Commission as are admissible to other State Government employees of the same category. For the part time, appointees, of the Commission remuneration of @ 20% of their basic pay (on the basis of number of cases received and disposed) shall be payable to them. These staff will also be entitled to TA/DA on official tour as admissible to their respective category.

(3) The salary payable to such staff shall be defrayed out of the Consolidated Fund of the State.

Allowances and terms and conditions of the President and members of the State Commission [Section 16(2)]

6. (1) The President of the State Commission shall receive a consolidated honorarium of ₹ 200 per day of sitting. Other members, shall receive consolidated honorarium of ₹ 150 per day of sitting.

(2) The President and the members of the State Commission shall be eligible for such TA/DA as admissible to the Judges of the High Court and shall be entitled to travel by air.

(3) The honorarium, other allowances shall be defrayed out of the Consolidated Fund of the State Government.

(4) The President and the member of the State Commission shall hold office for a term of five years or upto the age of 65 years whichever is earlier and shall not be eligible for renomination:

Provided that President and member may:—

(*a*) by writing under his hand and addressed to the State Government resign his office any time;

(*b*) be removed from his office in accordance with provisions of sub-rule (5).

(5) The State Government may remove, from office. President or a member of the State Commission who:—

(*a*) has been adjudged an insolvent, or

(*b*) has been convicted of an offence which in the opinion of the State Government, involves moral turpitude, or

(*c*) has become physically or mentally incapable of acting as such member, or

(*d*) has acquired such financial or other interest as is likely to affect prejudicially his functions as a member, or

(*e*) has so abused his position as to render his continuance in office prejudicial to the public interest:

Provided that the president or a member shall not be removed from his office on the ground specified in clauses (*d*) and (*e*) of sub-rule (5) except on any inquiry held by State Government in accordance with such procedure as it may specify in this behalf and finds the member to be guilty of such ground.

(6) Before appointment, President and member of the State Commission shall have to take an undertaking that he does not and will not have any such financial or other interests as is likely to affect prejudicially his functions as such member.

(7) The terms and conditions of the service of the President and the members of the State Commission shall not be varied to their disadvantage during their tenure of office.

(8) Every vacancy caused by resignation and removal of the President or any Bier member of the State Commission under sub-section (4) or otherwise shall be filled by fresh appointment.

(9) Where any such vacancy occurs in the office of the President of the State Commission, the seniormost (in order of appointment) member, holding office in the time being shall discharge the functions of the President until a person jointed to fill such vacancy assumes the office of the President of the State Commission.

(10) When the President of the State Commission is unable to discharge the functions owing to absence, illness or any other cause, the seniormost (in order of appointment) member of the State Commission shall discharge the functions of the President until the day on which the President resumes the charge if his functions.

(1l) The President or any member ceasing to hold office as such shall not hold ly appointment in or be connected with the management of administrations an organisation which have been to subject of any proceeding under the Act during the tenure for a period of 5 years from the date on which he ceased to hold such office.

Place of sitting and other matters relating to State Commission [Section 14(3) read with section 18]

7. (1) Office of the State Commission shall be located at the capital of the State.

(2) The working days and the office hours of the State Commission shall be the same as that of the State Government,

(3) The official seal and emblem, of the State Commission shall be such as the State Government may specify.

(4) Sitting of the State Commission, as and when necessary, shall be convened by the President.

(5) No act or proceedings of the State Commission shall be invalid by reasons only of the existence of any vacancy among its members or any defect in its constitution thereof.

(6) State Government shall appoint such staff, as may be necessary, to assist the State Commission in its work and perform such other functions as are **Provided** under these rules or assigned to it by the President. The salary payable to such staff shall be defrayed out of the Consolidated Fund of the State Government.

(7) Where the opposite party admits the allegation made by the complainant the State Commission shall decide the complaint on the basis of the merit of the case and documents present before it.

(8) If during the proceedings conducted under section 13, State Commission fixes a date for hearing of the parties, it shall be obligatory on the complainant and opposite party or his authorised agent to appear before the State Commis-sion on such date of hearing or any other date to which hearing could be adjourned. Where the Complainant or his authorised agent fails to appear before the State Commission on such day, the State Commission may in its discretion either dismiss the complaint for default or decide it on merits. Where the opposite party or its authorised agent fails to appear on the day of hearing, the State Commission may decide the complaint *ex. parte*.

(9) While proceedings under sub-rule (8) the State Commission may, on such terms as it may think fit and at any stage, adjourn the hearing of the complaint but not more than one adjournment, shall ordinarily be given and the complaints should be decided within 90 days from the date of notice received by the opposite party where complaint does not require analysis or testing of the goods and within 150 days if it requires analysis or testing of the goods.

(10) Orders of the State Commission shall be signed and dated by the members of the State Commission constituting the Bench and shall be communicated to the parties free of charge.

(11) Subject to the other provisions of the Act, the State Commission may entertain complaint as mentioned under section 17 of the Act.

(12) A complaint containing the following particulars shall be presented by the complainant in person or his agent to the State Commission or be sent by registered post addressed to the State Commission:—

(a) the name, description and the address of the complainant;

(b) the name, description and address of the opposite party or parties as the case may be, so far as they can be ascertained;

(c) the fact relating to complaint and when and where it arouse;

(d) document in support of the allegations contained in complaint;

(e) the relief which the complainant claims.

(13) The State Commission shall, in disposal of any complaint before it as far as possible, follow the procedures laid down in section 18 of the Act.

(14) Orders of the State Commission shall be issued at least with the signature of two members including the President and a member.

(15) While admitting/entertaining a complaint, the State Commission shall as far as possible, follow the procedures laid down under section 24A of the Act.

(16) The State Commission shall also have the power to direct that any order assed by it, where no appeal has been preferred under section 14, be published the Official Gazette or through other media and no legal proceedings shall be against the State Commission or any other media for such publication.

Procedure for hearing appeal [Section 15]

8. (1) Memorandum shall be presented by the appellant or his authorised agent to the State Commission in person or sent by registered post addressed to the Commission.

(2) Every memorandum filed under sub-rule (1) shall be in legible handwriting referable typed and shall set forth concisely under distinct heads, the grounds f appeal without any argument or narrative and such ground shall be umbered consecutively.

(3) Each memorandum shall be accompanied by the certified copy of the order of the District Forum appealed against and such of the documents as may be required to support grounds of objection mentioned in the memorandum.

(4) When the appeal is presented after the expiry of period of limitation as specified in the Act, memorandum shall be accompanied by an application supported by an affidavit setting forth the fact of which appellant relies to satisfy the State Commission that he has sufficient cause for not preferring the appeal within the period of limitation.

(5) The appellant shall submit four copies of the memorandum of the State Commission for official purpose.

(6) On the date of hearing or any other day to which hearing may be adjourned, it shall be obligatory for the parties or their authorised agents to appear before foe State Commission. If appellant or his authorised agent fails to appear on such date, the State Commission may, in its discretion, either dismiss the appeal or decide it on the merit of the case. If respondent or his authorised agents fails to appear on such date the State Commission shall proceed *ex. parte* and shall decide the apeal *ex. parte* on merits of the case.

(7) The appellant shall not, except by leave of the State Commission, urge or be heard in support of any ground of objections not set forth in the memorandum but the State Commission, in deciding the appeal, shall not confine to the grounds, of objection set forth in the memorandum or taken by leave of the State Commission under this rule:

Provided that the Commission shall not rest its decision on any other grounds Unless the party who may be of seated thereby, has been given, at least one opportunity of being heard by the State Commission.

(8) State Commission, on such terms as it may think fit and at any stage adjourn i.e., learning of appeal, but not more than one adjournment shall ordinarily be given and the appeal should be decided within 90 days from the first date of earing.

(9) Order of the State Commission on apeall shall be signed and dated by the members of the State Commission constituting the Bench and shall be communicated to the parties free of charge.

The constitution of the State Consumer Protection Council and the Working Group

9. (1) The State Government shall, by notification in the Official Gazette, constitute the State Consumer Protection Council (hereinafter referred to as the State Council) which shall consist of the following members, namely–

(*a*) The Minister-in-charge of Consumer Affairs who shall be the Chairman of the State Council;

(*b*) 3 (three) members of the Legislative Assembly;

(*c*) Nine official representative of the State Government departments and autonomous organisation concerned with consumer interests;

(*d*) Representatives of the Consumer organisation or Consumers;

(*e*) Representatives of Women (at least two);

(*f*) Representatives of farmers, trade and industries;

(*g*) Representatives of education/analytical/medical Science.

(2) The term of council shall be of 3 (three) years.

(3) Any member may by writing under his hand to the Chairman of the State Council, resign from the Council. The vacancies, so caused or otherwise shall be filled from the same category by the State Government and such person shall hold office so long as the member in whose place he fills would have been entitled to hold office if the vacancy had not occurred.

Procedure of the State Council

10. Under sub-section (4) of section 7 of the Act, the State Council shall observe the following procedure in regard to the transaction of its business—

(*i*) The meeting of the State Council shall be presided over by the Chairman. In the absence of Chairman, the State Council shall elect a member of the Council to preside over that meeting of the Council. At least 2 (two) meetings should be held in a year.

(*ii*) Each meeting of the State Council shall be convened by giving notice in writing which shall not be less than ten days from the date of issue, to every member.

(*iii*) Every notice of a meeting of the State Council shall specify the place and the day and hour of the meeting and shall contain statement of business to be transacted thereat.

(*iv*) For the purpose of performing its functions under the Act, the State Council may constitute from amongst its members, such working groups as it may deem necessary and every working group so constituted shall perform such functions as are assigned to it by the State Council. The findings of such working group shall be placed before the State Council for its consideration.

(*v*) The non-official members shall be entitled to actual expenditure on each journey or ₹ 250 (Rupees two hundred fifty) only whichever is less (for-each journey) and a daily allowance of ₹ 80 (Rupees eighty) only per day for attending the meeting of the State Council or any working group.

(*vi*) The rate of honorarium will be ₹ 150 (Rupees one hundred fifty) only each per day of sitting for both the official and non-official members. However, the honorarium, to be paid to the Chairman will be ₹ 200 (Rupees two hundred) only.

(*vii*) The resolutions passed by the State Council shall be recommendatory in nature.

Chapter 8

Assam Consumer Protection Rules, 1989

[No. SDA/35/87/64, Dated 16-12-1989

In exercise of the powers conferred by sub-section (2) of section 30 of the Consumer Protection Act, 1986 (68 of 1986), the State Government in the Department of Food and Civil Supplies, Assam makes hereby the following Rules, namely—

SHORT TITLE AND COMMENCEMENT

1. (1) These rules may be called "The Assam State Consumer Protection Rules, 1989",

(2) They shall come into force from the date of their Notification in the Official Gazette.

Definition

2. *(a)* "Act" means the Consumer Protection Act, 1986 (68 of 1986);

(b) "Agent" means a person duly authorised by a party to present any complaint or appeal or reply on its behalf before the State Commission or the District Forum;

(c) "Appellant" means a party which makes an appeal against the order of the District Forum;

(d) "Memorandum" means memorandum of appeal filed by the appellant;

(e) "Opposite Party" means a person who answers complaint or claim;

(f) "President" means the President of the State Commission or District Forum as the case may be;

(g) "Respondent" means the person who answers any memorandum or appeal;

(h) "State" means the State of Assam; (z) "State Government" means the Government of Assam.

Salaries and other allowances and terms and conditions of the President affiliated Members of the District Forum [Section 10(3) of the Act]

3. (1) The President of the District Forum shall receive the salary of the Judgement of a District Court if appointed on whole-time basis or an honorarium ₹ 150/- per day of sitting if appointed on part-time basis. Other members sitting on whole-time basis shall receive a consolidated honorarium of ₹ 2,000/- per month and if sitting on part-time basis, a consolidated honorarium of ₹ 100 per day for the sitting.

(2) The President and the Members of the District Forum shall be entitled to such travelling allowance and daily allowance on official tour as are admissible Grade-I Officer of the State Government.

(3) The salary, honorarium and other allowances shall be defrayed out of the consolidated Fund of the State Government.

(4) Before appointment, the President and Members of the District Forum shall live to give an undertaking that he does not and will not have any such financial or other interests as is likely to affect prejudicially his functions as the resident and a Member.

(5) In addition to the provisions of section 10(2), State Government may remove the office, the President and Member of a District Forum who—

(*a*) has been adjudged an insolvent, or

(*b*) has been convicted of an offence which in the opinion of the State Government involved moral turpitude, or

(*c*) has become physically or mentally incapable of acting as such member, or

(*d*) has acquired such financial or other interests as is likely to affect prejudicially his functions as a member, or

(*e*) has so abused his position as to render his continuance in office prejudicial to the public interest:

Provided that the President or Member shall not be removed from his office on; ground specified in clauses *(d)* and *(e)* of sub-rule (5) except on an inquiry led by State Government in accordance with such procedure as it may specify 'this behalf and finds the Member to be guilty of such ground.

(6) The terms and conditions of the service of the President and the Members the District Forum shall not be varied to their disadvantage during their lure of office.

(7) Where any vacancy occurs in the office of the President of the District Forum, the senior most (in order of appointment) Member of District Forum, leading office for the time being shall discharge the functions of the President until a person appointed to fill such vacancy assumes the office of the President District Forum.

(8) When the President of the District Forum is unable to discharge the functions owing to absence, illness or any other cause the senior most (in order 'the appointment) Member of the District Forum shall discharge the functions of the President till the President resumes the charge of his functions. [1]The President or any Member ceasing to hold office as such shall not hold by appointment in or be connected with the management or administration 'an organisation which has been the subject of any proceeding under the Act during his tenure for a period of 5 years from the date on which he ceases to hold such office'.

Place of sitting and other matters relating to District Forum [Section 14(3) of the Act]

4. (1) The Office of the District Forum shall be located at the Head Quarter of the District.

(a) Persons who are appointed President/Members of any District Forum can also be appointed as President/Members of another District Forum but hearing of cases arising out of the territorial limits of any District Forum can be conducted only in that District and not while sitting in another District.

(2) The working days and the office hours of the District Forum shall be the same as that of the State Government.

(3) The official seal and emblem of the District Forum shall be such as the State Government may specify.

(4) Sitting of the District Forum, as and when necessary shall be convened by the President.

(5) No Act or proceeding of the District Forum shall be invalid by reason only of the existence of any vacancy among its Members or any defect in its constitution.

(6) State Government shall appoint such staff, as may be necessary to assist the District Forum in its day to day work and perform such other functions, as are **Provided** under these Rules, or assigned to it by the President. The salary payable to such staff shall be defrayed out of the Consolidated Fund of the State Government.

(7) Where the opposite party admits the allegation made by the complainant, the District Forum shall decide the complaint on the basis of the merit of the case and documents present before it.

(8) If during the proceedings conducted under section 13, District Forum fixes a date for hearing of the parties, it shall be obligatory on the complainant and opposite party or its authorised agent to appear before the District Forum on such date of hearing or any other date to which hearing could be adjourned. Where the complainant or his authorised agent fails to appear before the District Forum on such day, the District Forum may in its discretion either dismiss the complaint for default or decide it on merit. Where the opposite party or its authorised agent fails to appear on the day of hearing, the District Forum may decide the complaint *ex parte.*

(9) While proceeding under sub-rule (8), the District Forum may, on such terms as it may think fit and at any stage, adjourn the hearing of the complaint but not more than one adjournment shall ordinarily be given and the complaint should be decided within 90 days from the date of notice received by opposite party where complaint does not require analysis or testing of I goods and within 150 days if it requires analysis or testing of the goods.

(10) Orders of the District Forum shall be signed and dated by the Members of the District Forum constituting the Bench and shall be communicated to the parties free of charge.

Procedure to be Adopted by the District Forum for Analysis and Testing of the Goods [Section 13(l)(c) of the Act]

5. (1) If considered necessary, the District Forum may direct the complainant to provide more than one sample of the goods in clean containers with stopper properly fixed on them.

(2) On receiving the samples of such goods, the District Forum shall seal it and fix labels on the containers carrying following information—

(i) Name and address of the appropriate laboratory to which sample will be sent for analysis and test;.

(ii) Name and address of the District Forum;

(iii) Case number;

(iv) Seal of the District Forum.

(3) The sample will be sent to the laboratory, name(s) of which will be notified by the State Government from time to time, by the District Forum for sending report within 45 days or within such extended time as may be granted by the District Forum after specifying the nature of the defect alleged and date of submission of the report.

Salary and other Allowances and Terms and Conditions of the President and Members of the State Commission [Section 16(2)]

6. (1) President of State Commission shall receive the salary of the Judge of the High Court if appointed on whole-time basis or a consolidated honorarium of ₹ 200 per day for the sitting if appointed on part-time basis. Other Members, if sitting on whole-time basis shall receive a consolidated hono-rarium ₹ 3,000 per month and if sitting on part-time basis, a consolidated honorarium of ₹ 150 per day for the sitting.

(2) The President and the Members of the State Commission shall be eligible for such travelling and daily allowances on official tour as are admissible to that of the High Court or Senior Grade Officer of the State Government.

(3) The salary, honorarium, other allowance shall be defrayed out of the Consolidated Fund of the State Government.

(4) President and the Member of the State Commission, shall hold office for a term of five years or up to the age of 65 years, whichever is earlier and shall not be eligible for renomination:

Provided that the President and Member may,—

(a) by writing under his hand and addressed to the State Government resign his office any time;

(b) be removed from his office in accordance with the provision of sub-rule (5).

(5) (I) The State Government may remove from office,- the President or a Member of the State Commission who—

(a) has been adjudged an insolvent, or

(b) has been convicted of an offence which in the opinion of the State Government, involves moral turpitude, or

(c) has become physically or mentally incapable of acting as such Member, or

(d) has acquired such financial or other interest as is likely to affect prejudicially his function as a Member, or

(e) has so abused his position as to render his continuance in office prejudicial to the public interest.

(II) The President or any Member ceasing to hold office as such shall not hold any appointment in or be connected with the management or administrations of an organisation which have been the subject of any proceeding under the Act during his tenure for a period of 5 years from the date on which he ceases to hold such office.

Provided that the President or a Member shall not be removed from his office on the ground specified in clauses *(d)* and *(e)* of sub-rule (5) except on an inquiry held by the State Government in accordance with such procedure as it may specify in this behalf and finds the Member to be guilty of such ground.

(6) Before appointment the President and a Member of the State Commission shall have to give an undertaking that he does not and will not have any such financial or other interests as is likely to affect prejudicially his functions as such President or Member.

(7) The terms and conditions of the service of the President and the Members of the State Commission shall not be varied to their disadvantage during their tenure of office.

(8) Every vacancy caused by resignation and removal of the President or any other Member of the State Commission under sub-rule (4) or otherwise shall be filled by fresh appointment.

(9) Where any such vacancy occurs in the office of the President of the State Commission, the seniormost (in order of appointment) Member, holding office for the time being, shall discharge the functions of the President until a person appointed to fill such vacancy assumes the office of the President of the State Commission.

(10) When the President of the State Commission is unable to discharge the functions owing to absence, illness, or any other cause, the seniormost (in order of the appointment) Member of the State Commission shall discharge the functions of the President until the day on which the President resumes the charge of this functions.

Place of Sitting and other Matters Relating to State Commission [Section 14(3) Read with Section 18 of the Act]

7. (1) The office of the State Commission shall be located at the State Capital.

(2) The working days and the office hours of the State Commission shall be the same as that of the State Government.

(3) The official seal and emblem of the State Commission shall be such as the State Government may specify.

(4) Sitting of the State Commission, as and when necessary, shall be convened by the President.

(5) No Act or proceedings of the State Commission shall be invalid by reason only of the existence of any vacancy among its Member or any defect in its Constitution thereof.

(6) The State Government shall appoint such staff, as may be necessary to assist the State Commission in its work and perform such other functions as are **Provided** under these rules or assigned to it by the President. The salary payable to such staff shall be defrayed out of the Consolidated Fund of the State Government.

(7) Where the opposite party admits the allegations made by the complainant, the State Commission shall decide the complaint on the basis of the merit of the case and documents present before it.

(8) If during the proceedings conducted under section 13, State Commission fixes a date for hearing of the parties, it shall be obligatory on the complainant and opposite party or his authorised agent to appear before the State Commission on such date of hearing or any other date to which hearing could be adjourned. Where the complainant or his authorised agent fails to appear before the State Commission on such date the State Commission may in its discretion either dismiss the complaint for default or decide it on merits. Where the opposite party or its authorised agent fails to appear on the day of hearing, the State Commission may decide the complaint *ex parte.*

(9) While proceeding under sub-rule (8), the State Commission may, on such terms as it may think fit and at any stage, adjourn the hearing of the complaint but not more than one adjournment shall ordinarily be given and the complaint should be decided within 90 days from the date of notice received by the opposite party where complaint does not require analysis or testing of the goods and within 150 days if it requires analysis or testing of the goods.

(10) Orders of the State Commission shall be signed and dated by the Members of the State Commission constituting the Bench and shall be communicated to the parties free of charge.

Procedure for hearing appeal [Section 15]

8. (1) Memorandum shall be presented by the appellant or his authorized agent to the State Commission in person or sent by registered post addressed to the Commission.

(2) very memorandum filed under sub-rule (1) shall be in legible handwriting typed and shall set forth concisely under distinct heads, the grounds of appeal without any argument or narrative and such ground shall be numbered consecutively.

(3) Each memorandum shall be accompanied by the certified copy of the order of the District Forum appealed against and such of the documents as may be required to support grounds of objection mentioned in the memorandum.

(4) When the appeal is presented after the expiry of period of limitation as specified in the Act, memorandum shall be accompanied by an application supported by an affidavit setting forth the fact of which appellant relies to satisfy the State Commission that he has sufficient cause for not preferring the appeal within the period of limitation.

(5) The appellant shall submit four copies of the memorandum of the State Submission for official purpose.

(6) On the date of hearing or any other day to which hearing may be adjourned, shall be bligatory for the parties or their authorised agents to appear before State Commission. If appellant or his authorised agent fails to appear on each date, the State Commission may, in its discretion, either dismiss the appeal decide it on the merit of the case. If respondent or his authorised agents fails appear on such date the State Commission shall proceed *ex parte* and shall decide the appeal *ex parte* on merits of the case.

How to file complaint with the Forum or Commission?

- File within 2 years from the date of cause of action in the district where the seller has his business or lives.
- Submit complaint on plain paper with supporting documents (receipt, bill etc.)
- Engagement of lawyer is not mandatory.
- MINIMAL FEE IS PAYABLE.

Chapter 9

Bihar Consumer Protection Rules, 1987

[Notification No. G.S.R. 32/1, Dated 28-9-1987]

In exercise of the powers conferred by sub-section (2) of section 30 of the Consumer Protection Act, 1986 (68 of 1986), the Governor of Bihar is pleased to make the following rules, namely —

SHORT TITLE AND COMMENCEMENT

1. (1) These rules may be called the Bihar Consumer Protection Rules, 1987.

(2) It shall come into force on such date as the State Government may, by notification in the Official Gazette, appoint.

Definitions

2. In these rules unless the context otherwise requires:—

(*a*) "Act" means the Consumer Protection Act, 1986 (68 of 1986);

(*b*) "Agent" means a person duly authorised by a party to present any complaint or appeal or reply on its behalf before the State Commission or the District Forum;

(*c*) "Appellant" means a party which makes an appeal against the order of the District Forum;

(*d*) "Memorandum" means memorandum of appeal filed by the appellant;

(*e*) "Opposite party" means a person who answers complaint or claim;

(*f*) "President" means the President of the State Commission or District Forum as the case may be;

(*g*) "Respondent" means the person who answers any memorandum of appeal;

(*h*) "State" means the State of Bihar.

Salaries and other allowances and terms and conditions of the President and Members of the District Forum

3. (1) The President of the District Forum shall receive the salary of the District Judge, if appointed on whole-time basis or an honorarium of ₹ 150 per day for the sitting, if appointed on part-time basis. Other members if sitting on whole-time basis shall receive a consolidated honorarium of ₹ 2,000 per month and if sitting on part-time basis, a consolidated honorarium of ₹ 100 per day for the sitting.

(2) The President and the members of the District Forum shall be entitled for such travelling allowance and daily allowance on official tour as are admissible to Class I officers of the State Government.

(3) The salary, honorarium and other allowances shall be defrayed out of the Consolidated Fund of the State Government.

(4) Before appointment, the President and the members of the District Forum shall have to give an undertaking that he does not and will not have any such financial or other interests as is likely to affect prejudicially his functions as a member.

(5) In addition to provisions of section 10(2), State Government may remove from the office, the President and member of a District Forum who—

(a) has been adjudged an insolvent, or

(b) has been convicted of an offence which in the opinion of the State Government, involves moral turpitude, or

(c) has become physically or mentally incapable of acting as such member, or

(d) has acquired such financial or other interest as is likely to affect prejudicially his functions as a member, or

(e) has so abused his position as to render his continuance in office prejudicial to the public interest:

Provided that the President or member shall not be removed from his office on the ground specified in clauses *(d)* and *(e)* of sub-rule (5) except on an enquiry held by the State Government in accordance with such procedure as it may specify in this behalf and finds the member guilty of such ground.

(6) The terms and conditions of the service of the President and the members of the District Forum shall not be varied to their disadvantage during their tenure of office.

(7) Where any vacancy occurs in the office of the President of the District Forum, the senior most (in order of appointment) member of District Forum, holding office for the time being, shall discharge the functions of the President until a person appointed to fill such a vacancy assumes the office of President of the District Forum.

(8) When the President of the District Forum is unable to discharge his functions owing to absence, illness or any other cause, the seniormost (in on of appointment) member of the District Forum shall discharge the function of the President until the day on which the President resumes the charge or functions.

(9) The President or any member ceasing to hold office as such shall not by any appointment in or be connected with the management or administration of an organization which has been the Subject of any proceeding under the Act during his tenure for a period of 5 years from the date on which he ceases to hold such office.

Place of sitting and other matters relating to District Forum

4. (1) The office of the District Forum shall be located at the old divisional headquarters, namely, Patna, Ranchi, Bhagalpur and Muzaffarpur. Where State Government decides to establish a single District Forum having jurisdiction over more than one district, it shall notify the place and jurisdiction of the District Forum so established.

(2) The working, days of the District Forum shall be notified by the State Government from time to time.

(3) The Official seal and emblem of the District Forum shall be such as the State Government may specify.

(4) Sitting of the District Forum, as and when necessary, shall be convened by the President as **Provided** in sub-rule (2).

(5) No act or proceedings of the District Forum shall be invalid by reason only of the existence of any vacancy among its members or any defect in its constitution.

(6) State Government shall appoint such staff, as may be necessary to assist the District Forurn in its day to day work and perform such other functions as are **Provided** under these rules, or assigned to it by the President. The salary payable to such staff shall be defrayed out of the Consolidated Fund of the State. Government.

(7) Where admission of facts have been made either in the pleading or otherwise, whether orally or in writing, the District Forum may at any stage of the case, either on the application of any party or of its own motion and without Waiting for the determination of any other question between the parties, make such order or decide the complaint as it may think fit, having regard to such admissions.

(8) If during the proceedings conducted under section 13, District Forum fixes date for hearing of the parties, it shall be obligatory on the complainant and opposite party or its authorised agent to appear before the District Forum on such date of hearing or any other date to which hearing is adjourned. Where the complainant or his authorised agent fails to appear before the District Forum on such day. District Forum may in its discretion either dismiss the complaint for default or decide it on merits. Where the opposite party or its authorised agent fails to appear on the day of hearing, the District Forum may decide the complaint *ex parte.*

(9) While proceeding under sub-rule (8), the District Forum may, on such terms it may think fit and at any stage, adjourn the hearing of the complaint but not more than one adjournment shall ordinarily be given and the complaint should be decided within 90 days from the date of notice received by the opposite party where complaint does not require analysis or testing of the goods and within 150 days if it requires analysis or testing of the goods.

(10) Orders of the District Forum shall be signed and dated by the members of the District Forum constituting the Bench and shall be communicated to the parties free of charge.

Procedure to be adopted by the District Forum for analysis and testing of the goods

5. (1) Under section 13(l)(c), if considered necessary, the District Forum may direct the complainant to provide more than one sample of the goods in clean containers with stopper properly fixed on them.

(2) On receiving the samples of such goods, the District Forum shall seal it and fix labels on the containers carrying following information —

(i) Name and address of the appropriate laboratory to whom sample will be sent for analysis and test;

(ii) Name and address of the District Forum;

(iii) Case Number;

(iv) Seal of the District Forum.

(3) The sample will be sent to appropriate laboratory by the District Forum for sending report within 45 days or within such extended time as may be granted by the District Forum after specifying the nature of the defect alleged and date of submission of the report.

Salary and other allowances and terms and conditions of the President and members of the State Commission

6. (1) The President of the State Commission shall receive the salary of the Judge of the High Court if appointed on whole-time basis or a consolidated honorarium of ₹ 200 per day for the sitting if appointed on part-time basis. Other members, if sitting on whole-time basis, shall receive a consolidated honorarium of ₹ 3,000 per month and "if sitting on part-time basis, a consolidated honorarium of ₹ 150 per day for the sitting.

(2) The President and the members of the State Commission shall be eligible for such travelling allowance and daily allowance on official tour as are admissible to Class I officers of the State Government.

(3) The salary, honorarium and other allowances shall be defrayed out of the Consolidated Fund of the State Government.

(4) The President and the members of the State Commission shall hold office for a term of five years or upto the age of 65 years whichever is earlier and shall not be eligible for re-nomination:

Provided that President and member may—

(a) by writing under his hand and address to the State Government resign his office any time;

(b) be removed from his office in accordance with provision of sub-rule (5)

(5) The State Government may remove from office, President or a member of the State Commission who—

(a) has been adjudged an insolvent, or

(b) has been convicted of an offence which in the opinion of the State Government, involves moral turpitude, or

(c) has became physically or mentally incapable of acting as such member, or

(d) has acquired such financial or other interest as is likely to affect prejudicially his functions as a member, or

(e) has so abused his position as to render his continuance in office prejudicial to the public interest:

Provided that the President or a member shall not be removed from his office on the ground specified in clauses (d) and (e) except on an enquiry held by State [Government. In accordance with such procedure as it may specify in this behalf land finds the member guilty of such ground].

(6) Before appointment, President and a member of the State Commission shall have to Lake an undertaking that he does not and will not have any such financial or other interests as is likely to affect prejudicially his functions as such member.

(7) The terms and conditions of the service of the President and the members of the Stale Commission shall not be varied to their disadvantage during tenure of office.

(8) Every vacancy caused by resignation and removal of the President or any other member of the State Commission under sub-rule (4) or otherwise shall be filled by fresh appointment.

(9) Where any such vacancy occurs in the office of the President of the State Commission, the senior most (in order of appointment) member, holding office for the time being, shall discharge the functions of the President until a person appointed to fill such vacancy assumes the office of the President of the State Commission.

(10) When the President of the State Commission is unable to discharge the functions owing to absence, illness or any other cause, the seniormost (in order of appointment) member of the State Commission shall discharge the functions of the President until the day on which the President resumes the charge of his functions.

(11) The President or any member ceasing to hold office as such shall not hold any appointment in or be connected with the management or administration of an organisation which has been the subject of any proceeding under the Act during his tenure for a period of 5 years from the date on which he ceases to hold such office.

Place of sitting and other matters relating to State Commission

7. (1) Office of the State Commission shall be located at Patna.

(2) The working days and the office hours of the State Commission shall be as notified by the State Government from time to time.

(3) The official seal and emblem of the State Commission shall be such as the State Government may specify.

(4) Sitting of the State Commission as and when necessary, shall be convened by the President as **Provided** in sub-rule (2).

(5) No act or proceedings of the State Commission shall be invalid by reasons only of the existence of any vacancy among its members or any defect in its constitution thereof.

(6) State Government shall appoint such staff, as may be necessary to assist the State Commission in its day to day work and perform such other functions as are **Provided** under these rules or assigned to it by the President. The salary payable to such staff shall be defrayed out of the Consolidated Fund of the State Government.

(7) Where admission of facts have been made either in the pleading or otherwise, whether orally or in writing, the State Commission may at any stage of the case, either on the application of any party or of its own motion and without waiting for the determination of any other question between the parties, make such order or decide the complaint as it may think fit, having regard to such admissions.

(8) If during the proceedings conducted under section 13, State Commission fixes a date for hearing of the parties, it shall be obligatory on the complainant and opposite party or his authorised agent to appear before the State Commission on such date of hearing or any other date to which hearing is adjourned. Where the complainant or his authorised agent fails to appear before the State Commission on such day, the State Commission may in its discretion either dismiss the complaint for default or decide it on merits. Where the opposite party or its authorised agent fails to appear on the day of hearing, the State Commission may decide the complaint *ex parte*.

(9) While proceedings under sub-rule (8) the State Commission may, on such terms as it may think fit and at any stage, adjourn the hearing of the complaint but not more than one adjournment shall ordinarily be given and the complaint should be decided within 90 days from the date of notice received by the opposite party where complaint does not require analysis or testing of the goods and within 150 days if it requires analysis or testing of the goods.

(10) Orders of the State Commission shall be signed and dated by the members of the State Commission constituting the Bench and shall be communicated to the parties free of charge.

Procedure for hearing appeal

8. (1) Memorandum shall be presented by the appellant or his authorised agent to the State Commission in person or be sent by registered post addressed to the Commission.

(2) Every memorandum filed under sub-rule (1) shall be in legible handwriting preferably typed and shall set forth concisely under distinct heads, the grounds of appeal without any argument or narrative and such ground shall be numbered consecutively.

(3) Each memorandum shall be accompanied by the certified copy of the order of the District Forum appealed against and such of the documents as may be required to support grounds of objection mentioned in the memorandum.

(4) When the appeal is presented after the expiry of period of limitation as specified in the Act, memorandum shall be accompanied by an application supported by an affidavit setting forth the fact on which appellant relies to satisfy the State Commission that he has sufficient cause for not preferring the appeal within the period of limitation.

(5) The appellant shall submit four copies of the memorandum to the State Commission for official purposes.

(6) On the date of hearing or any other day to which hearing may be adjourned it shall be obligatory for the parties or their authorised agents to appear before the State Commission. If appellant or his authorised agent fails to appear on such date, the State Commission may, in its discretion, either dismiss the appeal or decide it on the merit of the case. If respondent or his authorised agents fails to appear on such date, the State Commission shall proceed *ex parte and* shall decide the appeal *ex parte* on merit of the case.

(7) The appellant shall not except by leave of the State Commission, urge or be heard in support of any ground of objection not set forth in the memorandum but the State Commission, in deciding the appeal, shall not confine to the grounds of objection set forth in the memorandum or taken by leave of the State Government under this rule;

Provided that the Commission shall not rest its decision on any other grounds unless the party who may be affected thereby, has been given, at least one opportunity of being heard by the State Commission.

(8) State Commission may, on such terms as it may think fit and at any stage, adjourn the hearing of appeal, but not more than one adjournment shall ordinarily be given and the appeal should be decided within 90 days from the first date of hearing.

(9) Order of the State Commission on appeal shall be signed and dated by the members of the State Commission constituting the Bench and shall be communicated to the parties free of charge.

Chapter 10

Chandigarh Consumer Protection Rules, 1987

[DFSO-CCPC-87/7312, Dated 21-10-1987]

In exercise of the powers conferred by sub-section (2) of section 30 of the Consumer Protection Act, 1986 (68 of 1986), read with Government of India, Ministry of Food and Civil Supplies, Department of Civil Supplies, Notification bearing SO No. 469(E), dated the 15th May, 1987, the Administrator, Union Territory, Chandigarh, is pleased to make the following rules, namely —

SHORT TITLE AND COMMENCEMENT

1. (1) These rules may be called the Chandigarh Consumer Protection Rules, 1987.

(2) They shall come into force on such date as the Administrator, may, by notification in the Chandigarh Administration Gazette.

Definitions

2. In these rules, unless the context otherwise requires —

(*a*) "Act" means the Consumer Protection Act, 1986 (68 of 1986);

(*b*) "Agent" means a person duly authorised by a party to present any complaint or appeal or reply on its behalf before the State Commission or the District Forum;

(*c*) "Appellant" means a party which makes an appeal against the order of the District Forum;

(*d*) "Memorandum" means memorandum of appeal filed by the appellant;

(*e*) "Opposite party" means a person who answers complaint or claim;

(*f*) "President" means the President of the State Commission or District Forum as the case may be;

(g) "Respondent" means the person who answers any memorandum or appeal; and

(*h*) "State" means Union Territory of Chandigarh.

Salaries and allowances and terms and conditions of the President and members of the District Forum under section 10(3)

3. (1) The President of the District Forum shall receive the salary of the Judge of the District Court if appointed on whole-time basis or an honorarium of ₹ 200 (Rupees two hundred only) per day for sitting, if appointed on part-time basis. Other members if sitting on whole-time basis, shall receive a consolidated honorarium of '[₹ 9,000 (Rupees nine thousand only)] per month and if sitting on part-time basis an honorarium of ₹ 150 (Rupees one hundred and fifty) per day for the sitting.]

(2) The President and the members of the District Forum shall be entitled for such travelling allowance and daily allowance on official tour as are admissible to Grade I Officer of the Administration of Union Territory of Chandigarh.

(3) Before appointment, the President and members of the District Forurn shall have to take an undertaking that he does not and will not have any such financial or other interests as is likely to affect prejudicially his functions as a member.

(4) In addition of provisions of section 10(2), the Administrator, may remove from the office, the President and members of a District Forum who,—

(*a*) has been adjudged an insolvent; or

(*b*) has been convicted of an offence which in the opinion of the Administrator, Union Territory of Chandigarh, involves moral turpitude; or

(*c*) has become physically or mentally incapable of acting as such member; or

(*d*) has acquired such financial or other interest as is likely to effect prejudicially his functions as a member; or

(*e*) has so abused his position as to render his continuance in office, prejudicial to the public interest:

Provided that the President or member shall not be removed from his office on the ground specified in clauses (*d*) and (*e*) except on an inquiry held by Government in accordance with such procedure as it may specify in this behalf and finds President or the member to be guilty of such ground.

(5) The terms and conditions of the service of the President and the members of the District Forum shall not be varied to their disadvantage during their tenure of Office.

(6) Where any vacancy occurs in the office of the President of the District Forum, the seniormost (in order of appointment) member of District Forum, holding office for the time being, shall discharge the functions of the President until a person appointed to fill such vacancy assumes the office of the President of the District Forum.

(7) When the President of the District Forum is unable to discharge the functions owing to absence, illness or any other cause, the seniormost (in order to the appointment) member of the District Forum shall discharge the functions of the President until the day on which the President resumes the charge of his functions.

(8) The President or any member ceasing to hold office as such shall not hold any appointment in or be connected with the management or administration of an organisation which have been the subject of any proceeding under the Act during his tenure for a period of 5 years from the date on which he ceases to hold such office.

Place of sitting and other matters relating to District Forum [Section 14(3)]

4. (1) The office of the District Forum shall be located at Chandigarh.

(2) The working days and the office hours of the District Forum shall be the same as that of Union Territory Administration of Chandigarh.

(3) The official seal and emblem of the District Forum shall be such as the Administrator of Union Territory, may specify.

(4) Sitting of the District Forum, as and when necessary, shall be convened by the President.

(5) No act or proceedings of the District Forum shall be invalid by reason only of the existence of any vacancy among its members or any defect in its constitution.

(6) The Chandigarh Administration shall appoint such staff, as may be necessary to assist the District Forum in its day to day work and perform such other functions as are **Provided** under these rules, or assigned to it by the President.

(7) Where the opposite party admits the allegation made by the complainant, the District Forum shall decide the complaint on the basis of the merits of the case and documents present before it.

(8) If during the proceedings conducted under section 13, the District Forum fixes a date for hearing of the parties, it shall be obligatory on the complainant and opposite party or his authorised agent to appear before the District Forum on such date of hearing or any other date to which hearing could be adjourned. Where the complainant or his authorised agent fails to appear before the District Forum on such day, the District Forum may in its discretion either dismiss the complaint for default or decide it on merits. Where the opposite party or its authorised agent fails to appear on the day of hearing, the District Forum may decide the complaint *ex parte*.

(9) While proceeding under sub-rule (8), the District Forum may, on such terms as it may think fit and at any stage, adjourn the hearing of the complaint but not more than one adjournment shall ordinarily be given and the complaint should be decided within 90 days from the date of notice received by the opposite party where complaint does not require analysis or testing of the goods and within 150 days if it requires analysis or testing of the goods.

(10) Orders of the District Forum shall be signed and dated by the members of the District Forum constituting the Bench and shall be communicated to the parties free of charge.

Procedure to be adopted by the District Forum for analysis and testing of the goods [Section 13(l)(c)]

5. (1) Under section 13(l)(c) if considered necessary, the District Forum may direct the complainant to provide more than one sample of the goods ir clean containers with stopper properly fixed on them.

(2) On receiving the samples of such goods, the District Forum shall seal it and fix labels on the containers carrying following information—

(i) name and address of the appropriate laboratory to whom sample will be sent for analysis and test;

(ii) name and address of the District Forum;

(iii) case number;

(iv) seal of the District Forum.

(3) The sample will be sent to the appropriate laboratory by the District Forum for sending report within 45 days or within such extended time as may be granted by the District Forum after specifying the nature of the defect alleged and date of submission of the report.

Salary and other allowances and terms and conditions of the President and members of the State Commission [Section 16(2)]

6. (1) The President of the State Commission shall receive the salary of the Judge of High Court if appointed on whole-time basis or a consolidated honorarium of ₹ 350 (Rupees three hundred and fifty) per day for the sitting if appointed on part-time basis. Other members, if sitting on whole-time basis shall receive a consolidated honorarium of [₹ 10,000] (Rupees ten thousand only) per month and if sitting on part-time basis a consolidated honorarium of ₹ 250 (Rupees two hundred and fifty only) per day for the sitting.]

(2) The President and the members of the State Commission shall be eligible for such travelling allowance and daily allowance on official tour as are admissible to Grade I Officer of the Union Territory Administration of Chandigarh.

(3) The salary, honorarium and other allowances shall be defrayed out of the Consolidated Fund of the State Government.

(4) President and the member of the State Commission shall hold office for, a term of 5 years or upto the age of 70 years, whichever is earlier and shall not be eligible for renomination on his completion of a term of 5 years or on his attaining the age of 70 years

Provided that President and member may —

(a) by writing under his hand and addressed to the Administrator, Union Territory of Chandigarh, resign his office any time;

(b) be removed from his office in accordance with provision of sub-rule (5)] (5) The Administrator of Union Territory of Chandigarh may remove from Office, President or a member of the State Commission who, —

(a) has been adjudged an insolvent; or

(b) has been convicted of an offence which in the opinion of the Administrator of Union Territory, Chandigarh, involves moral turpitude; or

(c) has become physically or mentally incapable of acting as such member; or

(d) has acquired such financial or other interest as is likely to effect prejudicially his functions as a member; or

(e) has so abused his position as to render his continuance in office, prejudicial to the public interest:

Provided that the President or a member shall not be removed from his office on the ground specified in clauses *(d)* and *(e)* of sub-rule

(5) Except on an inquiry held by the Government in accordance with such procedure as it may specify in this behalf and finds the President or the member to be guilty of such ground.

(6) Before appointment, the President and members of the State Commission shall have to take an undertaking that he does not and will not have any such financial or other interests as is likely to affect prejudicially his functions as such member.

(7) The terms and conditions of the service of the President and the members of the State Commission shall not be varied to their disadvantage during their tenure of office.

(8) Every vacancy caused by resignation and removal of the President or any other member of the State Commission under sub-rule (4) or otherwise shall be filled by fresh appointment.

(9) Where any vacancy occurs in the office of President of the State Commission, the senior most (in order of appointment) member holding office for the time being, shall discharge the functions of the President until a person appointed to fill such vacancy assumes the office of the President of the State Commission.

(10) When the President of the State Commission is unable to discharge the functions owing to absence, illness or any other cause, the senior most (in order to the appointment) member of the State Commission shall discharge the functions of the President until the day on which the President resumes the charge of his functions.

(11) When the President or any member ceasing to hold office as such shall not hold any appointment in or be connected with the management or administration of an organisation which have been the subject of any proceeding under the Act during his tenure for a period of 5 years from the date on which he ceases to hold such office.

Place of sitting and other matters relating to State Commission [Section 14(3) read with section 18]

7. (1) Office of the State Commission shall be located at Chandigarh.

(2) The working days and the office hours of the State Commission shall be the same as that of the Union Territory Administration of Chandigarh.

(3) The official seal and emblem of the State Commission shall be such as the Administration of Union Territory, may specify.

(4) Sitting of the State Commission, as and when necessary, shall be convened by the President.

(5) No act or proceedings of the State Commission shall be invalid by reason only of the existence of any vacancy among its members or any defect in its constitution thereof.

(6) The Administration of Union Territory, shall appoint such staff, as may be necessary to assist the State Commission in its day to day work and perform **Provided** under these rules or assigned to it by the

(7) Where the opposite party admits the allegation made by the complainant, the Slate Commission shall decide the complaint on the basis of the merit of the Base and documents present before it.

(8) If during the proceedings conducted under section 13, State Commission Bees a date for hearing of the parties, it shall be obligatory on the complainant and opposite party or his authorised agent to appear before the State Commission on such date of hearing or any other date to which hearing could be adjourned. Where the complainant or his authorised agent fails to appear before the State Commission on such day, the State Commission may in its discretion either dismiss the complaint for default or decide it on merits. Where the opposite party or its authorised agent fails to appear on the day of hearing, the State Commission may decide the complaint *ex parte.*

(9) While proceeding under sub-rule (8), the State Commission may, on such terms as it may think fit and at any stage, adjourn the hearing of the complaint but not more than one adjournment shall ordinarily be given and the complaint should be decided within 90 days from the date of notice received by the opposite party where complaint does not require analysis or testing of the goods and within 150 days if it requires analysis or testing of the goods. (30) Orders of the State Commission shall be signed and dated by the members of the State Commission constituting the Bench and shall be communicated to the parties free of charge.

Procedure for hearing appeal [Section 15]

8. (1) Memorandum shall be presented by the appellant or his authorised agent to the State Commission in person or sent by registered post addressed to the Commission.

(2) Every memorandum filed under sub-rule (1) shall be in legible handwriting preferably typed and shall set forth concisely under distinct heads, the grounds of appeal without any argument or narrative and such grounds shall be numbered consecutively.

(3) Each memorandum shall be accompanied by the certified copy of the order of the District Forum appealed against and such of the documents as may be required to support grounds of objection mentioned in the memorandum.

(4) When the appeal is presented after the expiry of the period of limitation as specified in the Act, the memorandum shall be accompanied by an application supported by an affidavit setting forth the fact on which the appellant relies to satisfy the State Commission that he has sufficient cause for not preferring the appeal within the period of limitation.

(5) The appellant shall submit four copies of the memorandum to the State commission for official purposes.

(6) On the date of hearing or on any other day to which hearing may be adjourned, it shall be obligatory for the parties or their authorised agents to appear before the State Commission, If appellant or his authorised agent fails to appear on such date, the State Commission may, in its discretion, either dismiss the appeal or decide it on the merit of the case. If respondent or his authorised agent fails to appear on such date, the State Commission shall proceed *ex parte* and shall decide the appeal *ex parte* on the merits of the case

(7) The appellant shall not, except by leave of the State Commission, urge or be I heard in support of any ground of objection not set forth in the memorandum but the State Commission, in deciding the appeal, shall not confine to the grounds of objection set forth in the memorandum or taken by leave of the State Commission under this rule:
Provided that the Commission shall not rest its decision on any other grounds unless the party who may be affected thereby, has been given, at least one opportunity of being heard by the State Commission.

(8) State Commission may, on such terms as it may think fit and at any stage, adjourn the hearing of the appeal, but not more than one adjournment shall ordinarily be given and the appeal should be decided within 90 days from the first date of hearing.

(9) Order of the State Commission on appeal shall be signed and dated by the members of the State Commission constituting the Bench and shall be communicated to the parties free of charge.

Chapter 11

Delhi Consumer Protection Rules, 1987

[F.50(131)/86. F & S/CA, Dated 29-9-1987]

In exercise of the powers conferred by sub-section (2) of section 30 of the Consumer Protection Act, 1986 (68 of 1986), read with the Government of India, Ministry of Food and Civil Supplies, New Delhi's Notification No. SO 469(E), dated the 15th May, 1987, the Administrator of the Union Territory of Delhi, hereby makes the following rules, namely—

SHORT TITLE AND COMMENCEMENT

1. (1) These rules may be called the Delhi Consumer Protection Rules, 1987.

(2) They shall come into force on the date of their publication in the Official Gazette.

Definitions

2. In these rules, unless the context otherwise requires,—

(*a*) "Act" means the Consumer Protection Act, 1986 (68 of 1986);

(*b*) "Administration" means the administration of the Union Territory of Delhi;

(*c*) "Administrator" means the Administrator of the Union Territory of Delhi, appointed by the President under Article 239 of the Constitution;

(*d*) "Agent" means a person duly authorised by a party to present any complaint or appeal or reply on its behalf before the State Commission or the District Forum;

(*e*) "Appellant" means a party which makes an appeal against the order of the District Forum;

(*f*) "Memorandum" means memorandum of appeal filed by the appellant;

(*g*) "Opposite party" means a person who answers complaint or claim;

(*h*) "President" means the President of the State Commission or District Forum, as the case may be;

(*i*) "Respondent" means the person who answers any memorandum of appeal;

(*j*) "State" means the Union Territory of Delhi;

(*k*) "State Commission" means the Delhi State Commission constituted under clause *(b)* of section 9;

(*l*) Words and expressions used in the Rules and not defined but defined in Act shall have the meanings respectively assigned to them in the Act.

Salaries and other allowances and terms and conditions of the President and Members of the District Forum

3. (1) *(a)* The President of the District Forum shall receive the salary, allowances and other perquisites as are admissible to a sitting judge of the District Court, if appointed on whole-time basis, or an honorarium of two hundred rupees per day, if appointed on part-time basis.

Note: When a retired District Judge is appointed as President of the District Forum, his salary, allowances and other perquisites, shall be subject to the rules governing the payment of pension to such retired District Judge.

(*b*) A member of District Forum, when appointed on whole-time basis, shall receive a consolidated honorarium of four thousand rupees per month, and if appointed on part-time basis, a consolidated honorarium of one hundred and fifty rupees per day of sitting.

(2)

(*i*) The President and the Members of the District Forum shall be entitled to such travelling allowance and daily allowances on official tour as are admissible to Grade A officers of the Administration.

(*ii*) For the purpose of attending the sitting of the District Forum, a Member shall be entitled to actual conveyance charges subject to a ceiling of one hundred rupees per day of sitting.

(3) The salary, honorarium and other allowances shall be defrayed out of the Consolidated Fund of India.

(4) Before appointment, the President and Member of the District Forum shall have to take an undertaking that he does not and will not have any such financial or other interests as is likely to affect prejudicially his functions as the President or a Member, as the case may be.

(5) In addition to provisions of section 10(2), the Administrator, may remove from the office, the President and Member of a District Forum who—

(*a*) has been adjudged an insolvent, or

(*b*) has been convicted of an offence which, in the opinion of the Administrator, involves moral turpitude, or

(*c*) has become physically or mentally incapable of acting as such President or Member, as the case may be, or

(*d*) has acquired such financial or other interests as is likely to affect prejudicially his functions as the President or a Member, as the case may be, or

(*e*) has so abused his position as to render his continuance in office prejudicial to public interest :

Provided that the President or Member shall not be removed from his office o the grounds specified in clauses (*d*) and (*e*) of sub-rule (5) except on an inquiry; held by the Administrator in accordance with such procedure as he may specify in this behalf and if the President or Member is found guilty of such grounds in the inquiry.

(6) The terms and conditions of the service of the President and the Members of the District Forum shall not be varied to their disadvantage during their tenure of office.

(7) Where any vacancy occurs in the office of the President of the District Forum, the seniormost (in order of appointment) Member of the District Forum, holding office for the time being, shall discharge the functions of the president until a person appointed to fill such vacancy assumes the office of the president of the District Forum.

(8) When the President of the District Forum is unable to discharge the functions owing to absence, illness or any other cause, the seniormost (in order of appointment) Member of the District Forum shall discharge the functions of the President until the day on which the President resumes the charge of his functions.

(9) The President or any Member ceasing to hold office as such shall not hold any appointment in or be connected with the management or administration of an organisation which has been the subject of any proceeding under the Act during his tenure for a period of five years from the date on which he ceases to hold such office.

Place of sitting and other matters relating to District Forum

4. (1) The office of the District Forum shall be located at such place in the Union Territory of Delhi as may be specified by the Administration in this behalf. Where two or more District Forums are constituted for Delhi, the Administrator may, by general or special order, regulate the distribution of business among them.

(2) The working days and the office hours of the District Forum shall be the same as those of the District Courts of Delhi.

(3) The official seal and emblem of the District Forum shall be such as the Administrator may specify.

(4) Sitting of the District Forum, as and when necessary, shall be convened by the President.

Explanation—When the President and/or a member attends office work on a day other than sitting of the Forum for official work in connection with the Working of District Forum, the President/member shall be deemed to have had sitting for that day for the purpose of drawing honorarium **Provided** the President of the District Forum certifies that such attendance of the member(s) or himself was in public interest.

(5) No act or proceedings of the District Forum shall be invalid by reason only or the existence of any vacancy among its members or any defect in its constitution.

(6) The Administrator shall appoint such staff, as may be necessary to assist the District Forum in its day to day work and perform such other functions as are **Provided** under these rules, or assigned to it by the President. The salary payable to such staff shall be defrayed out of the Consolidated Fund of India.

(7) Where the opposite party admits the allegation made by the complainant, the District Forum shall decide the complaint on the basis of the merit of the case and documents present before it.

(8) If during the proceeding conducted under section 13, the District Forum fixes a date for hearing of the parties, it shall be obligatory on the complainant and opposite party or its authorised agents to appear before the District Forum on such date of hearing or any other date to which hearing could be adjourned. Where the complainant or his authorised agent fails to appear before the District Forum on such day, the District Forum may, in its discretion, either dismiss the complaint for default or decide it on merit. Where the opposite party or its authorised agent fails to appear on the day of hearing, the District Forum may decide the complaint *ex parte.*

(9) While proceeding under sub-rule (8), the District Forum may, on such terms as it may think fit and at any stage adjourn the hearing of the complaint but not more than one adjournment shall ordinarily be given and the complaint should be decided, as far as possible, within 90 days from the day of notice received by the opposite party, where complaint does not require analysis or testing of the goods, and within 150 days, where it requires analysis or testing of goods.

(10) Orders of the District Forum shall be signed and dated by the Members of the District Forum constituting the Bench and shall be communicated to parties free of charge.

Procedure to be adopted by the District Forum for analysis and testing of the goods

5. (1) Under section 13(1)(c), if considered necessary, the District Forum may direct the complainant to provide more than one sample of the goods in clean containers with stopper properly fixed on them.

(2) On receiving the samples of such goods, the District Forum shall seal it and fix labels on the containers carrying following information—

(i) Name and address of the appropriate laboratory to which sample will be sent for analysis and test;

(ii) Name and address of the District Forum;

(iii) Case Number;

(iv) Name and description of the goods/articles;

(v) Sea! of the District Forum.

(3) The sample will be sent to the appropriate laboratory by the District Forum for sending the report within 45 days or within such extended time, as may be granted by the District Forum, after specifying the nature of the defect alleged and date of submission of the report.

Salary and other allowances and terms and conditions of the President and Members of the State Commission

6. (l) *(a)* The President of the State Commission shall receive the salary, allowances and other perquisites as are admissible to a sitting Judge of the High Court, if appointed on whole-time basis, or an honorarium of three hundred and fifty rupees per day, if appointed on part-time basis.

Note: When a retired Judge of a High Court is appointed as President of the State Commission, his salary, allowances and other perquisites, shall be subject to the rules governing the payment of pension to such retired Judge.

(b) A member of the State Commission, when appointed on whole-time basis, shall receive a consolidated honorarium of five thousand rupees per month, and, if appointed on part-time basis, a consolidated honorarium of two hundred and fifty rupees per day of sitting.

(2) *(a)* The President and the Members of the State Commission shall be entitled to such travelling allowance and daily allowances, on official tour as are admissible to Group A Officers of the Administration.

(b) For the purpose of attending the sitting of the State Commission, a Member shall be entitled to actual conveyance charges subject to a ceiling of one hundred rupees per day of sitting.

(3) The salary, honorarium and other allowances shall be defrayed out of the Consolidated Fund of India.

(4) The President and the Members of the State Commission shall hold office for a term of five years or upto the age of 65 years, whichever is earlier and shall not be eligible for re-appointment:

Provided that the President or a Member may,

(a) by writing under his hand and addressed to the Administrator resign his office any time;

(b) be removed from his office in accordance with the provision of sub-rule

(5) The Administrator may remove from Office, the President or a Member of the State Commission who,

(a) has been adjudged an insolvent; or

(b) has been convicted of an offence which, in the opinion of the Administrator, involves moral turpitude; or

(c) has become physically or mentally incapable of acting as such President or Member, as the case may be; or

(d) has acquired such financial or other interests as is likely to affect prejudicially his functions as President or a Member, as the case may be; or

(e) has so abused his position as to render his continuance in office prejudicial to public interest:

Provided that the President or a Member shall not be removed from his office on the grounds specified in clauses *(d)* and (e) of sub-rule (5), except on an inquiry held by the Administrator in accordance with such procedure as he may specify in this behalf and if the President or the Member is found guilty of such grounds in the inquiry.

(6) Before appointment, the President and a Member of the State Commission shall have to take an undertaking that he does not and will not have any such financial or other interests as are likely to affect prejudicially his functions as such President or Member.

(7) The terms arid conditions of the service of the President and the Members of the State Commission shall not be varied to their disadvantage during their tenure of office.

(8) Every vacancy caused by resignation and removal of the President or any other Member of the State Commission under sub-rule (4) or otherwise shall be filled by fresh appointment.

(9) Where any such vacancy occurs in the office of the President of the State Commission, the senior most (in order of appointment) Member, holding office for the time being, shall discharge the functions of the President until a person appointed to fill such vacancy assumes the office of the President of the State Commission.

(10) When the President of the State Commission is unable to discharge the functions owing to absence, illness or any other cause, the senior most (in order of appointment) Member of the State Commission shall discharge the functions of the President until the day on which the President resumes the charge of his functions.

(11) The President or any Member ceasing to hold office as such shall not hold any appointment in or be connected with the management or administration of an organisation which has been the subject of proceeding under the Act during his tenure for a period of five years from the date on which he ceases to hold such office.

Place of sitting and other matters relating to State Commission

7. (1) The office of the State Commission shall be located at such place in the Union Territory of Delhi as may be specified by the Administrator in this behalf.

(2) The working days and the office hours of the State Commission shall be the same as those of the Delhi High Court.

(3) The official seal and emblem of the State Commission shall be as the Administrator may specify.

(4) Sitting of the State Commission, as and when necessary, shall be convened by the President.

Explanation—When the President and/or a member attends office work on day other than sitting of the Commission for official work in connection with the working of State Commission, the President/Member shall be deemed to have had sitting for that day for the purpose of drawing honorarium **Provided** the President of the State Commission certifies that such attendance of the member(s) or himself was in public interest.

(5) No act or proceedings of the State Commission shall be invalid by reason only of the existence of any vacancy among its members or any defect in its constitution.

(6) The Administrator shall appoint such staff, as may be necessary, to assist the State Commission in its day to day work and perform such other functions as are **Provided** under these rules, or assigned to it by the President. The salary payable to such staff shall be defrayed out of the Consolidated Fund of India.

(7) Where the opposite party admits the allegation made by the complainant, the State Commission shall decide the complaint on the basis of the merit of the case and documents present before it.

(8) If during the proceeding conducted under section 13, the State Commission fixes a date for hearing of the parties, it shall be obligatory on the complainant and opposite party or its authorised agent to appear before the State Commission

on such date of hearing or any other date to which hearing could be adjourned. Where the complaint or his authorised agent fails to appear before the State Commission on such day, the State Commission may, in its discretion, either dismiss the complaint for default or decide it on merits. Where the opposite party or its authorised agent fails to appear on the day of hearing, the State Commission may decide the complaint *ex parte*.

(9) While proceeding under sub-rule (8), the State Commission may, on such terms as it may think fit and at any stage, adjourn the hearing of the complaint, but not more than one adjournment shall ordinarily be given and the complaint shall be decided, as far as possible, within 90 days from the day of notice received by the opposite party, where the complaint does not require analysis or testing of the goods, and within 150 days, where it requires analysis or testing of goods.

(10) Orders of the State Commission shall be signed and dated by the Members the State Commission constituting the Bench and shall be communicated to the parties free of charge.

Procedure for hearing appeal

8. (1) The Memorandum shall be presented by the appellant or his authorised agent to the State Commission in person or sent by registered post addressed to the Commission.

(2) Every memorandum filed under sub-rule (1) shall be in legible handwriting, preferably typed, and shall set forth concisely under district-heads, the grounds of appeal without any argument or narrative and such ground shall be numbered consecutively.

(3) Each memorandum shall be accompanied by the certified copy of the order of the District Forum appealed against and such of the documents, as may be required to support grounds of objection mentioned in the memorandum.

(4) When the appeal is presented after the expiry of period of limitation as specified in the Act, memorandum shall be accompanied by an application supported by an affidavit setting forth the fact on which appellant relies to satisfy the State Commission that he has sufficient cause for not preferring the appeal within the period of limitation.

(5) The appellant shall submit four copies of the memorandum to the State Commission for official purposes.

(6) On the date of hearing or any other day to which hearing may be adjourned, it shall be obligatory for the parties or their authorised agents to appear before the State Commission. If appellant or his authorised agent fails to appear on such date, the State Commission may, in its discretion, either dismiss the appeal or decide it on the merit of the case. If respondent or his authorised agent fails to appear on such date, the State Commission shall proceed *ex parte* and shall decide the appeal *ex parte* on merits of the case.

(7) The appellant shall not except by leave of the State Commission, urge or be heard in support of any ground of objections not set forth in the memorandum, but the State Commission, in deciding the appeal, need not confine to the grounds of objection set forth in the memorandum or taken by leave of the State Commission under this rule:

Provided that the Commission shall not rest its decision or any other grounds unless the party who may be affected thereby, has been given, at least one; opportunity of being heard by the State Commission.

(8) State Commission may, on such terms as it may think fit and at any stage, adjourn the hearing of the appeal, but not more than one adjournment shall ordinarily be given and the appeal should be decided as far as possible within 90 days from the first day of hearing.

(9) The order of the State Commission on appeal shall be signed and dated by the members of the State Commission constituting the Bench and shall be communicated to the parties free of charge.

Chapter 12

Dadra and Nagar Haveli Consumer Protection Rules, 1987

In exercise of the powers conferred by sub-section (2) of section 30 of the Consumer Protection Act, 1986 (68 of 1986) the Administration, Dadra and Nagar Haveli, hereby makes the following Rules, namely —

SHORT TITLE AND COMMENCEMENT

1. (1) These rules may be called the Dadra and Nagar Haveli Consumer Protection Rules, 1987.

(2) They shall come into force on such date as the Administrator, may by notification in the Official Gazette.

Definitions

2. In these rules unless the context otherwise requires —

(a) "Act" means the Consumer Protection Act, 1986 (68 of 1986);

(b) "Agent" means a person duly authorised by a party to present any complaint or appeal or reply on its behalf before the State Commission or the District Forum;

(c) "Appellant" means a party which makes an appeal against the order of the District Forum;

(d) "Memorandum" means memorandum of appeal filed by the appellant;

(e) "Opposite party" means a person who answers complaint or claim;

(f) "President" means the President of State Commission or District Forum as the case may be;

(g) "Respondent" means the person who answers any memorandum of appeal;

(h) "State-Commission" means the Consumer Disputes Redressal Commission established under section 9(6) for the Dadra and Nagar Haveli, Salaries and other allowances and terms and conditions of the President and Pnembers of the District Forum [Section 10(3)].

3. (1) The President of the District Forum shall received the salary of the Judge of a District Court if appointed on whole-time basis or an honorarium of ₹ 150 per day if appointed on part time basis. Other member if sitting on whole time basis, shall receive a consolidated honorarium of ₹ 2,000 per month and if sitting on part time basis, a consolidated honorarium of ₹ 100 per day for the sitting.

(2) The president and the members of the District Forum shall be entitled such travelling allowance and daily allowance on official tour as are admissible to Grade-I Officer of the Central Government.

(3) The salary, honorarium and other allowances shali be defrayed out of the Consolidated Fund of India.

(4) Before appointment, the President and members of the District Forum shall have to take an undertaking that he does not and will not have any such financial or other interest as is likely to effect prejudicially his functions as a member.

(5) In addition of provision of section 10(2) Administrator may remove from the office the President and member of a District Forum who —

(a) has been adjudged an insolvent, or

"BEAWARE OF DISCOUNTS AND SALE"

(*b*) has been convicted of an offence which in the opinion of the Administrator, involves moral turpitude, or

(*c*) has become physically or mentally incapable of acting as such member, or

(*d*) has acquired such financial or other interest, is likely to effect prejudicially his functions as a member, or

(*e*) has so abused his position as to render his continuance in office prejudicial to the public interest:

Provided that the President or member shall not be removed from his office on the ground specified in clauses (*d*) and (*e*) of sub-rule (5) except on an inquiry held by Administrator in accordance with such procedure as he may specify in this behalf and finds the member to be guilty of such ground.

(6) The terms and conditions of the service of the President and the members of the District Forum shall not be varied to their disadvantage during their tenure of office.

(7) Where any vacancy occurs in the office of the President of the District Forum, the senior most (in order of appointment) member of District Forum, holding office for the time being, shall discharge the functions of the President until person appointed to fill such vacancy assumes the office of the President of the District Forum.

(8) When the President of the District Forum is unable to discharge the functions owing to absence, illness or any other cause, the senior most (in order of appointment) member of the District Forum shall discharge the functions or the President until the day on which the President resumes the charge of his functions.

(9) The President or any member ceasing to hold office as such shall not hold any appointment in or be connected with the management or administration of an organisation which have been the subject of any proceeding under the Act during his tenure for a period of 5 years from the date on which he ceases to hold such office.

Place of sitting and other matters relating to District Forum [Section 14(3)]

4. (1) The office of the District Forum shall be located at Silvassa, the headquarter of the Union Territory of Dadra and Nagar Haveli.

(2) The working days and the office hours of the District Forum shall be same as that of Administration of Dadra and Nagar Haveli.

(3) The official seal and emblem of the District Forum shall be such as the Administrator may specify.

(4) Sitting of the District Forum, as and when necessary, shall be convened by President.

(5) No act or proceedings of the District Forum shall be invalid by reason only of the existence of any vacancy among its members or any defect in its constitution.

(6) Administrator shall appoint such staff as may be necessary to assist the District Forum in its day to day work and perform such other functions as arc **Provided** under these rules, or assigned to it by the president. The salary payable to such staff shall be defrayed out of the Consolidated Fund of India.

(7) Where the opposite party admits the allegation made by the complaint the District Forum shall decide the complaint on the basis of the merit of the case and documents present before it,

(8) If during the proceedings conducted under section 13, District Forum fixes a date for hearing of the parties, it shall be obligatory on the complainant arid opposite party or its authorised agent to appear before the District Forum on such date of hearing or any other date to which hearing could be adjourned. Where the complainant or his authorised agent fails to appear before the District Forum on such day, the District Forum may in its discretion either dismiss the complaint for default or decide it on merit. Where the opposite party or its authorised agent fails to appear on the day of hearing the District Forum may decide the complaint *ex parte*.

(9) While proceeding under sub-rule (8), the District Forum may, on such terms as it may think fit and at any stage, adjourn the hearing of the complaint but not more than one adjournment shall ordinarily be given and the complaint should be decided within 90 days from the date of notice received by the opposite party where complaint does not require analysis or testing of the goods and within 150 days if it requires analysis or testing of goods.

(10) Orders of the District Forum shall be signed and dated by the members of the District Forum constituting the Bench and shall be communicated to the Parties free of charge.

Procedure to be adopted by the District Forum for analysis and testing of the goods [Section 13(l)(c)]

(1) Under section 13(l)(c), if considered necessary, the District Forum may direct the complainant to provide more than one sample of the goods in clean containers with stopper properly fixed on them.

(2) On receiving the samples of such goods, the District Forum shall seal it and fix lables on the containers carrying following information.

(i) name and address of the appropriate laboratory to whom samples will sent for analysis and test;
(ii) name and address of the District Forum;
(iii) case number;
(iv) seal of the District Forum.

(3) The sample will be sent to the appropriate laboratory by the District Forum for sending report within 45 days or within such extended time as may be granted by the District Forum after specifying the nature of the defect alleged and date of submission of the report.

Salary and other allowances and terms and conditions of the President and members of the State Commission [Section 16(2)]

6. (1) President of the State Commission shall receive the salary of the Judge of the High Court if appointed on whole time basis or a consolidated honorarium of ₹ 200 per day for the sitting if appointed on part time basis. Other members, if sitting on whole time basis, shall receive a consolidated honorarium of ₹ 3,000 per month and if sitting on part time basis, a consolidated honorarium of ₹ 150 per day for the sitting.

(2) The President and the members of the State Commission shall be eligible for such travelling allowances on official tour as are admissible to Grade-1 officers of the Central Government.

(3) The salary, honorarium, other allowances shall be defrayed out of the Consolidated Fund of India.

(4) President and the members of the State Commission shall hold office for a term of five years or upto the age of 65 years whichever is earlier and shall not be eligible for renomination:

Provided that President and member may—

(a) by writing under his hand and addressed to the Administrator resign his office any time;
(b) be removed from his office in accordance with provisions of sub-rule (5).

(5) The Administrator may remove from office, President or a member of the State Commission who,

(a) has been adjudged an insolvent, or
(b) has been convicted of an offence which in the opinion of the Administrator involves moral turpitude, or
(c) has become physically or mentally incapable of acting as such or
(d) has acquired such financial or other interest as is likely to affect prejudicially his functions as a member, or
(e) has abused his position so as to render his continuance in office prejudicial to the public interest:

Provided that the President or a member shall not be removed from his on the ground specified in clauses *(d)* and *(e)* of sub-rule (5) except on an inquiry held by Administrator, in accordance with such procedure as it may specify in behalf and finds the member to be guilty of such ground.

(6) Before appointment, President and a member of the State Commission shall to take an undertaking that he does not and will not have any such financial or other interests as is likely to affect prejudicially his functions as member.

(7) The terms and conditions of the service of the President and the members State Commission shall not be varied to their disadvantage during their ire of office.

(8) Every vacancy caused by resignation and removal of the President or any other member of the State Commission under sub-rule (4) or otherwise shall be filled by fresh appointment.

(9) Where any such vacancy occurs in the office of the President of the State Commission, the senior most (in order of appointment) member holding office the time being, shall discharge the functions of the President until a person minted to fill such vacancy assumes the office of the President of the State Commission.

(10) When the President of the State Commission is unable to discharges the functions owing to absence, illness or any other cause, the seniormost (in order the appointment) member of the State Commission shall discharge the functions of the President until the day on which, the President resumes the charge of his functions.

(11) The President or any member ceasing to hold office as such shall not hold any appointment in or be connected with the management or administration organisation which have been the subject of any proceeding under the during his tenure for a period of 5 years from the date on which he ceases to hold such office.

Place of sitting and other matters relating to State Commission [Section 14(3) with section 18]

7. (1) Office of the State Commission shall be located at the capital place of Union Territory of Dadra and Nagar Haveli or at such other place as the Administrator may by order specify.

(2) The working days and the office hours of the State Commission shall be the as that of the Administration of Union Territory.

(3) The official seal and emblem of the State Commission shall be such as the Administrator may specify.

(4) Sitting of the State Commission, as and when necessary, shall be convened the President.

(5) No act or proceedings of the State Commission, shall be invalid by reason only of the existence of any vacancy among its members or any defect in its institution thereof.

(6) Administrator shall appoint such staff, as may be necessary to assist the State Commission in its work and perform such other functions as are **Provided** under these rules or assigned to it by the President. The salary payable to such staff shall be defrayed out of the Consolidated Fund of India.

(7) Where the opposite party admits the allegation made by the complainant the State Commission shall decide the complaint on the basis of the merit of the case arid documents present before it.

(8) If during the proceedings conducted under section 13, State Commission fixes a date for hearing of the parties, it shall be obligatory on the complainant and opposite party or his authorised agent to appear before the State Commission on such date of hearing or any other date to which hearing could be adjourned. Where the complainant or his authorised agent fails to appear on the day of hearing the State Commission may in its discretion either dismiss the complaint for default or decide it on merits where the opposite or its authorised agent, fails to appear on the day of hearing, the State Commission decide the complaint *ex parte.*

(9) While proceeding under sub-rule (8), of the State Commission may on such terms as it may think fit and at any stage, adjourn the hearing of the complaint but not more one adjournment shall ordinarily be given and the complaint should be decided within 90 days from the date of notice received by the opposite party where complaint does not require analysis or testing of the goods and within 150 days if it requires analysis or testing of the goods.

(10) Orders of the State Commission shall be signed and dated by the members of the State Commission constituting the Bench and shall be communicated to the parties free of charge.

Procedure for hearing appeal [Section 15]

8. (1) Memorandum shall be presented by the appellant or his authorised agent by the State Commission in person or sent by registered post addressed to the Commission.

(2) Every memorandum filed under sub-rule (1) shall be in legible handwriting preferably typed and shall set forth concisely under distinct heads, the grounds of appeal without any argument of narrative and such ground shall be numbered consecutively.

(3) Each memorandum shall be accompanied by the certified copy of the order of District Forum appealed against and such documents as may be required to support grounds of objection mentioned in the memorandum.

(4) When the appeal is presented after the expiry of period of limitation as specified in the Act, memorandum shall be accompanied, by an application supported by an affidavit setting forth the fact on which appellant relies to satisfy the State Commission that he has sufficient cause for not preferring the appeal within the period.

(5) The appellant shall submit four copies of the memorandum to the State Commission for official purposes.

(6) One the date of hearing or any other day to which hearing may be adjourned it shall be obligatory for the parties or their authorised agent, to appear before the State Commission. If the appellant or his authorised agent fails to appear on such date the State Commission may in its discretion, either dismiss the appeal or decide it on the merit of the case. If respondent or his authorised agent fails to appear on such date, the State Commission shall proceed *ex parte,* and shall decide the appeal *ex parte* on merits of the case.

(7) The appellant shall not except by leave of the State Commission, urge or be heard in support of any ground of objection not set forth in the memorandum but the State Commission, in deciding the appeal, shall not confine to the grounds of objection set forth in the memorandum of appeal taken by leave of the State Commission under this rule:

Provided that the Commission shall not rest its decision on any other ground unless the party who may be affected thereby, has been given, at least one opportunity of being heard by the State Commission.

(8) State Commission may, on such terms as it may think fit and at any stage, adjourn the hearing of appeal, but not more than one adjournment shall ordinarily be given and the appeal should be decided within 90 days from the first day of hearing.

(9) Order of the State Commission on appeal shall be signed and dated by the members of the State Commission constituting the Bench and shall be communicated to the parties free of charge.

Chapter 13

Goa Consumer Protection Rules, 1987

[Notification No. 11/14-2/87-PS & WD, Dated 22-6-1987]

In exercise of the powers conferred by sub-section (2) of section 30 of the Consumer Protection Act, 1986 (68 of 1986), the Government of Goa, hereby makes the following rules, namely —

SHORT TITLE AND COMMENCEMENT

1. (1) These rules may be called Goa Consumer Protection Rules, 1987.

(2) They shall come into force on such date as the Government may, by notification in the Official Gazette.

Definitions

2. In these rules, unless the context otherwise requires—

(a) "Act" metans the Consumer Protection Act, 1986 (68 of 1986);

(b) "Agent" means a person duly authorised by a party to present any complaint or appeal or reply on its behalf before the State Commission or the District Forum;

(c) "Appellant" means a party which makes an appeal against the order of the District Forum;

(d) "Government" means the Government of Goa;

(e) "Memorandum" means memorandum of appeal filed by the appellant;

(f) "Opposite party" means a person who answers complaint or claim;

(g) "President" means the President of the State Commission or District Forum as the case may be;

(h) "Respondent" means the person who answers any memorandum or appeal;

(i) "State" includes Union territory.

Salaries and other allowances and terms and conditions of the President and members of the District Forum.

3. (1) The President of the District Forum shall receive the salary of the judge of District Court if appointed on whole time basis or an honorarium of [₹ 300] per day if appointed on part-time basis. Other members if sitting on whole time basis, shall receive a consolidated honorarium of [₹ 4,000] per month and if sitting on part-time basis, a consolidated honorarium of [₹ 200] per day for the sitting.

(2) (2A) The President and the members of the District Forum shall be entitled for such travelling allowances and daily allowances on official tour as admissible to Grade 1 Officer of the Government.

(2B) The President and the members of the District Forum shall be entitled for conveyance charges of ₹ 75 (Rupees seventy-five only) per day of sitting subject to a maximum of ₹ 2,000 (Rupees two thousand only) per month, and further subject to the condition that they are not **Provided** with [Government conveyance] and are not paid any T.A./D.A. for attending the sitting of the Forum.]

(3) The salary, honorarium and other allowances shall be defrayed out of the Consolidated Fund of the Government.

(4) Before appointment, the President and members of the District Forum shall have to take an undertaking that he does not and will not have any such financial or other interests as is likely to affect prejudicially his functions as a member.

(5) Notwithstanding anything contained in sub-section (2) of section 10 of the Act, the Government may remove from the office, the President and members of a District Forum who—

(a) has been adjudged as an insolvent, or

(b) has been convicted of an offence which in the opinion of the Government, involves moral turpitude, or

(c) has become physically or mentally incapable of acting as such member, or

(d) has acquired such financial or other interest as is likely to affect prejudicially his functions as a member, or

(e) has so abused his position as to render his continuance in office prejudicial to the public interest:

Provided that the President or member shall not be removed from his office on the ground specified in clauses *(d)* and *(e)* of sub-rule (5) except on an inquiry held by the Government in accordance with such procedure as it may specify in this behalf and finds the members to be guilty of such ground.

(6) The terms and conditions of the service of the President and the members of the District Forum shall not be varied to their disadvantage during their tenure of office.

(7) Where any vacancy occurs in the office of the President of the District Forum, the senior most (in order of appointment) member of District Forum, holding office for the time being, shall discharge the functions of the President until a person appointed to fill such vacancy assumes the office of the President of the District Forum.

(8) When the President of the District Forum is unable to discharge the functions owing to absence, illness or any other cause, the senior most (in order of the appointment) member of the District Forum shall discharge the func-tions of the President until the day on which the President resumes the charge of his functions.

(9) The President or any member ceasing to hold office as such shall not hold any appointment in or be connected with the management or administration of an organisation which have been the subject of any proceeding under the Act during his tenure for a period of 5 years from the date on which he ceases to hold such office.

Place of sitting and other matters relating to District Forum

4. (1) The office of the District Forum shall be located at the headquarters of the District. Where the Government decides to establish a single District Forum having jurisdiction over more than one District, it shall notify the place and jurisdiction of the District Forum so established.

(2) The working days and the office hours of the District Forum shall be the same as that of the Government.

(3) The official seal and emblem of the District Forum shall be such as the Government may specify.

(4) Sitting of the District Forum, as and when necessary, shall be convened by the President.

(5) No act or proceedings of the District Forum shall be invalid by reason only of the existence of any vacancy among its members or any detect in its constitution.

(6) The Government shall appoint such staff, as may be necessary to assist the District Forum in its day to day work and perform such other functions as are **Provided** under these rules, or assigned to it by the President. The salary payable to such staff shall be defrayed out of the Consolidated Fund of the Government.

(7) Where the opposite party admits the allegations made be the complainant, the District Forum shall decide the complaint on the basis of the merit of the case and documents present before it.

(8) If during the proceedings conducted under section 13 of the Act, District Forum fixes a date for hearing of the parties, it shall be obligatory on the complainant and opposite party or its authorised agent to appear before the District Forum on such date of hearing or any other date to which hearing could be adjourned. Where the complaint or his authorised agent fails to appear before the District Forum on such day, the District Forum may in its discretion either dismiss the complaint for default or decide it on merit. Where the opposite party or its authorised agent fails to appear on the day of hearing, the District Forum may decide the complaint *ex parte*.

(9) While proceeding under sub-rule (8), the District Forum may, on such terms as it may think fit and at any stage, adjourn the hearing of the complaint but not more than one adjournment shall ordinarily be given and the complaint shall be decided within 90 days from the date of notice received by the opposite party where complaint does not require analysis or testing of the goods and within 150 days if it requires analysis or testing of the goods.

(10) Orders of the District Forum shall be signed and dated by the members of the District Forum constituting the Bench and shall be communicated to the parties free of charge.

Procedure to be adopted by the District Forum for analysis and testing of the goods

5. (1) The District Forum may, if considered necessary under clause (c) of sub-section (1) of section 13 of the Act, direct the complainant to provide more than one sample of the goods in clean containers with stopper properly fixed on them.

(2) On receiving the samples of such goods, the District Forum shall seal it and fix labels on the containers carrying following information —

(i) Name and address of the appropriate laboratory to whom sample will be sent for analysis and test;

(ii) Name and address of the District Forum;

(iii) Case number;

(iv) Seal of the District Forum.

(3) The sample shall be sent to the appropriate laboratory by the District Forum for sending report within 45 days or within such extended time as may be granted by the District Forum after specifying the nature of the defect alleged and date of submission of the report.

Salary and other allowances and terms and conditions of the President and members of the State Commission

6. (1) President of the State Commission shall receive the salary of the judge of the High Court if appointed on whole-time basis or a consolidated honorarium of [₹ 400] per day for the sitting if appointed on part-time basis. Other members, if sitting on whole-time basis, shall receive a consolidated honorarium of [₹ 5,000] per month and if sitting on part-time basis, a consolidated honorarium of [₹ 300] per day for the sitting.

(2) (2A) The President of the State Commission shall be eligible for a daily allowance of ₹ 90 per day for the actual number of days spent on the commission work, and the members of the State Commission shall be eligible for such travelling allowances and daily allowances on official tour as are admissible to Grade I officer of the Government.

(2B) The President and members of State Commission shall be entitled for conveyance charges of ₹ 75 (Rupees seventy-five only) per day of sitting subject to a maximum of ₹ 2,000 (Rupees two thousand only) per month, and further subject to the condition that they are not **Provided** with [Government conveyance] and are not paid any T.A./D.A. for attending the sitting of the Commission.

(3) The salary, honorarium and other allowances shall be defrayed out of the Consolidated Fund of the Government.

(4) President and the members of the State Commission shall hold office for a term of five years or upto the age of 65 years whichever is earlier and shall not be eligible for renomination:

Provided that President and member may,—

(a) by writing under his hand and addressed to the Government resign his office any time;

(b) be removed from his office in accordance with provisions of sub-rule (5).

(5) The Government may remove from office, President or a member of the State Commission who:—

(a) has been adjudged as an insolvent, or

(b) has been convicted of an offence which, in the opinion of the Government, involves moral turpitude; or

(c) has become physically or mentally incapable of acting as such President or member, as the case may be; or

(d) has acquired such financial other interest as is likely to affect prejudicially his functions as a member; or

(e) has so abused his position as to render his continuance in office prejudicial to the public interest:

Provided that the President or a member shall not be removed from his office on the grounds specified in clauses *(d)* and *(e)* of sub-rule (5) except on an enquiry held by the Government in accordance with such procedure as it may specify in this behalf and finds the member to be guilty of such ground.

(6) Before appointment, President and a member of the State Commission shall have to take an undertaking that he does not and will not have such financial other interests as is likely to affect prejudicially his functions as such member.

(7) The terms and conditions of the service of the President and the members the State Commission shall not be varied to their disadvantage during their more of office.

(8) Every vacancy caused by resignation and removal of the President or any pier member of the State Commission under sub-rule (4) or otherwise shall filled by fresh appointment. Where any such vacancy occurs in the office of the President of the State commission, the senior most (in order of appointment) member, holding office the time being, shall discharge the functions of the President until a person pointed to fill such vacancy assumes the office of the President of the State Commission.

(9) When the President of the State Commission is unable to discharge the functions owing to absence, illness or any other cause, the senior most (in order 'the appointment') member of the State Commission shall discharge the functions of the President until the day on which the President resumes the large of his functions.

(11) The President or any member ceasing to hold office as such shall not hold any appointment or be connected with the management or administration of an organisation which have been the subject of any proceeding under the Act during his tenure for a period of 5 years from the date on which he ceases to hold such office.

Place of sitting and other matters relating to State Commission

7. (1) Office of the State Commission shall be located at the capital of the State.

(2) The working days and the office hours of the State Commission shall be the same as that of the Government.

(3) The official seal and emblem of the State Commission shall be such as the Government may specify.

(4) Sitting of the State Commission, as and when necessary, shall be convened by the President.

(5) No act or proceedings of the State Commission shall be invalid by reasons of the existence of any vacancy among its members or any defect in its institution thereof.

(6) The Government shall appoint such staff, as may be necessary to assist the State Commission in its day to day work and perform such other functions as **Provided** under these rules or assigned to it by the President. The salary payable to such staff shall be defrayed out of the Consolidated Fund of the Government.

(7) Where the opposite partly admits the allegations made by the complainant, the State Commission shall decide the complaint on the basis of the merit of the case and documents present before it.

(8) If during the proceedings conducted under section 13, State Commission fixes a date for hearing of the parties, it shall be obligatory on the complainant and opposite party or his authorised agent to appear before the State Commission on such date of hearing or any other date to which hearing could be adjourned. Where the complainant or his authorised agent fails to appear before the State Commission on such day, the State Commission may in its discretion either dismiss the complaint for default or decide it on merits. Where the opposite party or its authorised agent fails to appear on the day of hearing, the State Commission may decide the complaint *ex partes.*

(9) While proceedings under sub-rule (8), the State Commission may, on such terms as it may think fit and at any stage, adjourn the hearing of the complaint but not more than one adjournment shall ordinarily be given and the complaint shall be decided within 90 days from the date of notice received by the opposite party where complaint does not require analysis or testing of the goods, and within 150 days if it requires analysis or testing of the goods.

(10) Orders of the State Commission shall be signed and dated by the members of the State Commission constituting the Bench and shall be communicated to the parties free of charge.

Procedure for hearing appeal

8. (1) Memorandum shall be presented by the appellant or his authorised agent to the State Commission in person or sent by registered post addressed to the Commission.

(2) Every memorandum filed under sub-rule (1) shall be in legible handwriting preferably typed and shall set forth concisely under distinct heads, the grounds of appeal without any argument or narrative and such grounds shall be numbered consecutively.

(3) Each memorandum shall be accompanied by the certified copy of the order of the District Forum appealed against and such of the documents as may be, required to support grounds of objection mentioned in the memorandum.

(4) When the appeal is presented after the expiry of period of limitation as specified in the Act, memorandum shall be accompanied by an application supported by an affidavit setting forth the fact on which appellant relies to satisfy the State Commission that the has sufficient cause for not preferring the appeal within the period of limitation.

(5) The appellant shall submit four copies of the memorandum to the State Commission for official purposes.

(6) On the date of hearing or any other day to which hearing may be adjourned it shall be obligatory for the parties or their authorised agents to appear before the State Commission. If appellant or his authorised agent fails to appear such

date, the State Commission may, in its discretion, either dismiss the appeal decide it on the merit of the case. If respondent or his authorised agent fails to appear on such date, the State Commission shall proceed *ex parte* and shall decide the appeal *ex parte* on merits of the case.

(7) The appellant shall not, except by leave of the State Commission urge or be heard in support of any ground of objections not set forth in the memorandum but the State Commission, in deciding the appeal, may not confine to the grounds of objection set forth in the memorandum or taken by leave of the State Commission under this rule:

Provided that the State Commission shall not rest its decision on any other grounds unless the party who may be affected thereby, has been given at least one opportunity of being heard by the State Commission.

(8) State Commission may, in such terms as it may think fit and at any stage adjourn the hearing of appeal, but not more than one adjournment Shall ordinarily be given and the appeal should be decided within 90 days from the first date of hearing.

(9) Orders of the State Commission on appeal shall be signed and dated by the members of the State Commission constituting the Bench and shall be communicated to the parties free of charge.

Chapter 14

Gujarat Consumer Protection Rules, 1988

[GSR/GHTH/88/91/CPA/1287/1408/D, Dated18-2-1988]

In exercise of the powers conferred by sub-section (2) of section 30 of the Consumer Protection Act, 1986 (68 of 1986), the Government of Gujarat hereby makes the following rules, namely —

SHORT TITLE AND COMMENCEMENT

1. (1) These rules may be called the Gujarat Consumer Protection Rules, 1988.

(2) They shall come into force on the date[1] of their publication in the Official Gazette.

Definitions

2. In these rules, unless the context otherwise requires,—

(*a*) "Act" means the Consumer Protection Act, 1986 (68 of 1986);

(*b*) "agent" means a person duly authorised by a party to present any complaint, appeal or reply on its behalf before the State Commission or the District Forum;

(*c*) "appellant" means a party which makes an appeal against the order of the District Forum;

(*d*) "memorandum" means any memorandum of appeal filed by the appellant;

(*e*) "opposite party" means a person who answers complaint or claim;

(*f*) "President" means the President of the District Forum or the State Commission, as the case may be;

(*g*) "respondent" means the person who answers any memorandum of appeal;

(*h*) "section" means the section of the Act;

(*i*) "State" means the State of Gujarat;

(*j*) words and other expressions used in these rules but not defined therein shall have the same meaning respectively assigned to them in the Act.

Salaries or honorarium and other allowances and other terms and conditions of service of the President and members of the District Forum under sub-section (3) of section 10.

3. (1) The President of the District Forum shall receive the salary of a District Judge if appointed on full time basis or an honorarium of ₹ 150 per day if appointed on part-time basis. Other members, if sitting on whole time basis shall receive, a consolidated honorarium of ₹ 2,000 per month and if sitting on part-time basis, a consolidated honorarium of ₹ 100 per day for the sitting.

(2) The President and the members of the District Forum shall be entitled to such travelling allowance arid daily allowance, on official tours, as are admissible to Class-I Officers of the State Government.

(3) The salary or honorarium as the case may be, and other allowances shall be defrayed out of the Consolidated Fund of the Slate.

(4) Before appointment, the President and each Member of the District Forum shall have to take an undertaking that he does not, and will not have, any such financial or other interest as is likely to affect prejudicially his functions as the President or Member.

(5) The State Government may remove from office, the President or any Member of a District Forum who,—

(a) has been adjudged an insolvent, or

(b) has been convicted of an offence which, in the opinion of the State Government, involves moral turpitude, or

(c) has become physically or mentally incapable of acting as the President or a Member, or

(d) has acquired such financial or other interest as is likely to affect prejudicially his functions as the President or a Member, or

(e) has so abused his position as to render his continuance in office prejudicial to the public interest, or

(f) has absented himself from three consecutive sittings of the District Forum without reasonable cause:

Provided that the President or any Member shall not be removed from his office on the ground specified in clauses *(d)* and *(e)* of sub-rule (5) except on an inquiry held by the State Government in accordance with such procedure as it may specify in this behalf and finds the President or a Member to be guilty on such ground.

(6) Where any vacancy occurs in the office of the President of the District Forum, the seniormost (in order of appointment) member of District Forum, holding office for the time being, shall discharge the functions of the President until a person appointed to fill such vacancy assumes the office of the President of the District Forum.

(7) When the President of the District Forum is unable to discharge the functions owing to absence, illness or any other cause, the seniormost (in order of appointment) member of the District Forum shall discharge the functions of the President until the day on which the President resumes the charge of his functions.

(8) The President or any member ceasing to hold office as such shall not hold any appointment in, or be connected with, the management or administration of an organisation which has been the subject of any proceeding under the Act during his tenure for a period of five years from the date on which he ceases to hold such office.

(9) The terms and conditions of the service of the President and the Members of the District Forum shall not be varied to their disadvantage during their tenure of office.

Procedure to be adopted by the District Forum for analysis and testing of the goods

4. (1) For the purpose of analysis or test, the District Forum shall obtain from the complainant a sample of the goods in clean, dry container with tight stopper, cover or lid properly fixed on them. If necessary the District Forum may direct the complainant to provide more than one sample of the goods. (2) After obtaining the sample of the goods under sub-rule (1), the District Forum shall carefully seal the stopper, cover or lid of the container by means of sealing wax and affix label on the container which shall bear,— (z) the name and address of the appropriate laboratory to which the sample is to be sent for analysis or test; *(ii)* the name and address of the District Forum; *(iii)* the nature of the goods kept in the sealed container; *(iv)* the case number and date; and (*v*) the seal of the District Forum,

(3) The container shall then be completely wrapped in fairly strong pack paper and the ends of the paper shall be neatly folded and affixed by means of gum or other adhesive. A slip of the size that goes round from the bottom to the top of the container bearing the signature of such persons as may be authorised by the District Forum in this behalf for the purpose of authentication of the sample and the case number shall be pasted on the wrapper.

(4) The wrapper shall be further secured by means of strong twine or thread or both above and across the container and the knots of the twine or thread shall then be fastened on the wrapper by means of a sealing wax on which there shall be at least four distinct and clear impressions of the seal of the District Forum.

Place of sitting, conduct of meeting and other matters relating to District Forum

5. (1) The office of the District Forum shall be located at the head quarter of the District. Where State Government decides to establish a single District Forum having jurisdiction over more than one district, it shall by notification in the Official Gazette, specify the place and the jurisdiction to the District Forum so established.

(2) The working days and the office hours of the District Forum shall be the same as that of the State Government,

(3) The official seal and emblem of the District Forum shall be such as the State Government may specify.

(4) Sitting of the District Forum, as and when necessary, shall be convened by the President.

(5) No act or proceedings of the District Forum shall be invalid by reason only of the existence of any vacancy among its members or any defect in its constitution.

(6) The State Government shall appoint such staff, as may be necessary to assist the District Forum in its day to day work and perform such other functions as are **Provided** under these rules, or assigned to it by the President, The salary payable, to such staff shall be defrayed out of the Consolidated Fund of the State.

(7) Where the opposite party admits the allegation made by the complainant the District Forum shall decide the complaint on the basis of the merit of the case and document present before it.

(8) If during the proceedings conducted under section 13, the District Forum fixes a date for hearing of the parties, it shall be obligatory on the complainant and the opposite party or their respective authorised agents to appear before the District Forum on the date of hearing or any other date to which hearing could be adjourned. Where the complainant or his authorised agent fails to appear before the District Forum on such day, the District Forum may, in its discretion, either dismiss the complaint for default or decide it on merit. Where the opposite party or its authorised agent fails to appear on the day of hearing, the District Forum may decide the complaint *ex parte*.

(9) While proceeding under sub-rule (8), the District Forum may, on such terms las it may think fit and at any stage adjourn the hearing of the complaint but not more than one adjournment shall ordinarily be given and the complaint shall be decided within 90 days from the date of notice received by the opposite party where the complaint does not require analysis or testing of the goods and within 150 days, if it requires analysis or testing of the goods.

(10) Orders of the District Forum shall be signed and dated by the members of the District Forum constituting the Bench and shall be communicated to the arties free of charge.

Procedure for hearing appeal

6. (1) Memorandum shall be presented by the appellant or his authorised agent to the State Commission in person or sent by registered post addressed to the Commission in the form appended to these rules.

(2) Every memorandum filed under sub-rule (1) shall be in legible handwriting preferably typed and shall set forth concisely under distinct heads, the grounds of appeal without any argument or narrative and such ground shall be numbered consecutively.

(3) Each memorandum shall be accompanied by the certified copy of the order of the District Forum appealed against and such of the documents as may be required to support grounds of objection mentioned in the memorandum.

(4) When the appeal is presented after the expiry of period of limitation as specified in the Act, memorandum shall be accompanied by an application supported by an affidavit setting forth the fact on which appellant relies to satisfy the State Commission that he has sufficient cause for not preferring the I appeal within the period of limitation.

(5) The appellant shall submit four copies of the memorandum to the State Commission for the official purpose.

(6) On the dale of hearing or on any other day to which hearing may be adjourned, it shall be obligatory for the parties or their authorised agent to appear before the State Commission. If appellant or his authorised agents fails to appear on such date, the State Commission may, in its discretion, either dismiss the appeal or decide it on merit of the case. If respondent or his authorised agent fails to appear on such date, the State Commission shall proceed *ex parte* and shall decide the appeal *ex parte* on merits of the case. Salary or honorarium and other allowances and terms and conditions of the President and members of the State Commission.

7. (1) The President of the State Commission shall receive the salary of the Judge of the High Court if appointed on whole-time basis or consolidated honorarium of ₹ 200 per day for the sitting if appointed on part-time basis. Other members, if sitting on whole-time basis, shall receive a consolidated honorarium of ₹ 3,000 per month and if sitting on part-time basis, a consolidated honorarium of ₹ 150 per day for the sitting.

(2) The President and the members of the State Commission shall be eligible for such travelling allowance and daily allowance on official tours as are admissible to class I Officers of the State Government.

(3) The salary or honorarium as the case may be and other allowances shall be defrayed out of the Consolidated Fund of the State.

(4) The President and the members of the State Commission shall hold office for a term of five years or upto the age of '[70] years whichever is earlier and shall not be eligible for renomination:

Provided that the President and the Member may— (a) by writing under his hand and addressed to the State Government resign his office any time; (b) be removed from his office in accordance with provisions of sub-rule (5)

(5) The State Government may remove from office, the President or a Member of the State Commission who—

(*a*) has been adjudged an insolvent, or

(*b*) has been convicted of an offence which in the opinion of the Government, involves moral turpitude, or

(*c*) has become physically or mentally incapable of acting as such member, or

(*d*) has acquired such financial or other interest as is likely to effect prejudicially his functions as the President or a Member, or

(*e*) has so abused his position as to render his continuance in office prejudicial to the public interest:

Provided that the President or a member shall not be removed from his office on the ground specified in clauses (*d*) and (*e*) of sub-rule (5) except on an inquiry heid by State Government in accordance with such procedure as it may specify in this behalf and finds the members to be guilty of such ground.

(6) Before appointment the President and a Member of the State Commission shall have to take an undertaking that he does not, and will not, have any such financial or other interests as is likely to affect prejudicially his functions as such member.

(7) The terms and conditions of the service of the President and the members of the State Commission shall not be varied to their disadvantage during their tenure of office.

(8) Every vacancy caused by resignation and removal of the President or any other member of the State Commission under sub-rule (4) or otherwise shall be filled by fresh appointment.

(9) Where any such vacancy occurs in the office of the President of the State Commission, the seniormost (in order of appointment) Member, holding office for the time being shall discharge the functions of the President until a person appointed to fill such vacancy assumes the office of the President of the State Commission.

(10) When the President of the State Commission is unable to discharge the functions owing to absence, illness or any other cause, the seniormost (in order of appointment) Member of the Slate Commission shall discharge the func-tions of the President until the day on which the President resumes the charge of his functions.

(11) The President or any Member ceasing to hold office as such shall not hold any appointment in or be connected with the management or administration of an organisation which has been the subject of any proceeding under the Act during his tenure for a period of 5 years from the date on which he ceases to hold such office.

Place of sitting, conduct of meeting and other matters relating to State Commission

8. (1) Office of the State Commission shall be located at [Ahmedabad].

(2) The working days and the office hours of the State Commission shall be the same as that of the State Government.

(3) The official seal and emblem of the State Commission shall be such as the State Government may specify.

(4) Sitting of the State Commission, as and when necessary, shall be convened by the President.

(5) No act or proceeding of the State Commission shall be invalid by reason only of the existence of any vacancy among its members or any defect in its constitution.

(6) The State Government shall appoint such staff, as may be necessary to assist the State Commission in its work and perform such other functions as are **Provided** under these rules or assigned to it by the President. The salary payable to such staff shall be defrayed out of the Consolidated Fund of the State,

(7} Where the opposite party admits the allegation made by the complainant the State Commission shall decide the complaint on the basis of the merit of the case and documents present before it,

(8) If during the proceedings conducted under section 13, the State Commission fixes a date for hearing of the parties, it shall be obligatory on the complainant and opposite party or his authorised agent to appear before the State Commission on such date of hearing or any other date to which hearing could be adjourned. Where the complainant or his authorised agent fails to appear before the State Commission on such day, the State Commission may, in its discretion, either dismiss the complaint for default or decide it on merits. Where the opposite party or its authorised agent fails to appear on the day of hearing the State Commission may decide the complaint *ex parte.*

(9) While proceeding under sub-rule (8) the State Commission may on such terms as it may think fit and at any stage adjourn the hearing of the complaint but not more than one adjournment shall ordinarily be given and the complaint should be decided within 90 days from the date of notice received by the opposite party where complaint does not require analysis or testing of the goods and within 150 days if it requires analysis or testing of the goods.

(10) Orders of the State Government shall be signed and dated by the members of the State Commission constituting the Bench and shall be communicated to the parties free of charge.

FORM

[*See* Rule 6] Appeal under section 15 of the Consumer Protection Act, 1986

To,

The President

Consumer Disputes Redressal Commission

[Ahmedabad]

Name of Appellant ....

Full address of the appellant ....

Number and date of the order against which the appeal is made ....

Date of receipt of such order by the appellant ....

Whether appeal is made in time?

If not the reason therefore may be stated

(1) A certified copy of the order appealed against is attached hereto.

(2) Statement of facts of the case (If necessary attach a separate sheet of paper).

(3) The appellant has not preferred any appeal against the aforesaid order, before any authority, at any time.

(4) Enter here the ground relied for the purpose of this appeal. (If necessary attach a separate sheet of paper)

(5) The appellant, therefore, prays..

The appellant......................................named above, does hereby declare that what is stated herein is true to the best of his knowledge and belief.

Signature

(To be signed by the appellant or by agent duly authorised in writing in this behalf by the appellant)

Dated the.......day of.........20......

"Always Check the Label and Packaging for Quality Products"

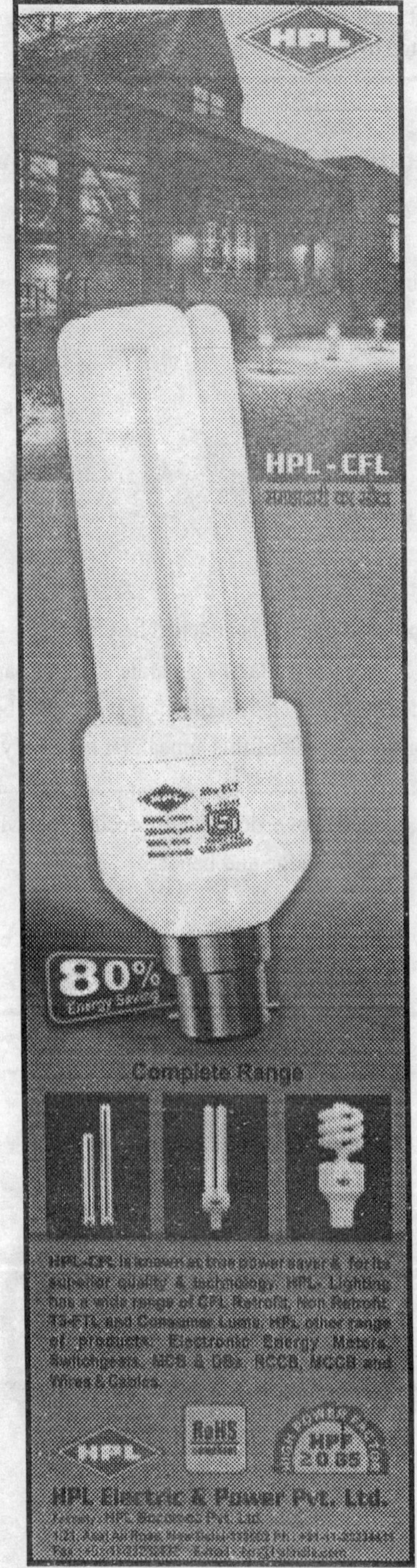

"Buyers Be Aware"

Chancellor
Horvard Luxury

—✦—✦—✦—

Chapter 15

Haryana Consumer Protection Rules, 1988

[GSR 37/C.A. 68/86/S. 30-88, Dated 25-4-1988]

In exercise of the powers conferred by sub-section (2) of section 30 of thei Consumer Protection Act, 1986 (68 of 1986), the Governor of Haryana hereby makes the following rules, namely —

SHORT TITLE AND COMMENCEMENT

1. These rules may be called the Haryana Consumer Protection Rules, 1988.

Definitions

2. In these rules, unless the context otherwise requires —

(*a*) "Act" means the Consumer Protection Act, 1986 (68 of 1986);

(*b*) "agent" means a person duly authorised by a party to present any complaint, appeal or reply on its behalf before the State Commission or the District Forum;

(*c*) "appellant" means a party which makes an appeal against the order of the District Forum;

(*d*) "memorandum" means any memorandum of appeal filed by the appellant;

(*e*) "opposite party" means a person who answers complaint or claim;

(*f*) "President" means the President of the State Commission or District Forum as the case may be;

(*g*) "respondent" means the person who answers any memorandum appeal;

(*h*) "State" means the Haryana State;

(*i*) "Government" means the Haryana Government in the Administrate Department.

Salaries and allowances and terms and conditions of the President and members of the District Forum [Section 10(3)]

3. (1) The President of the District Forum shall receive the salary of the Judge of the District Court if appointed on whole time basis or an honorarium ₹ [200] per day if appointed on part-time basis. Other members if sitting whole-time basis, shall receive a consolidated honorarium of ₹ 2,000 per month and if sitting on part time basis, a consolidated honorarium of ₹ [150] per day for the sitting, and if a sitting District Judge is appointed on part time basis, shall receive a consolidated honorarium of ₹ 150 per day for the sitting.

(2) The President and the members of the District Forum shall be entitled to such travelling allowance and daily allowance on official tour as are admissible to Class I Officers of the State Government.

(3) The salary, honorarium and other allowances shall be defrayed out of the head "2408 - Food Storage and Warehousing (Directorate Staff)".

(4) Before appointment, the President and members of the District Forum shall have to take an undertaking that he does not and will not have any such financial or other interests as is likely to affect prejudicially his functions as a member.

(5) In addition to the provisions of section 10(2) of the Consumer Protection Act, [986 the State Government may remove from the office, the President and member of a District Forum who,—

(a) has been adjudged as insolvent; or

(b) has been convicted of an offence which in the opinion of the State Government involves moral turpitude; or

(c) has become physically or mentally incapable of acting as such member; or

(d) has acquired such financial or other interest as is likely to effect prejudicially his functions as a member; or

(e) has so abused his position as to render his continuance in office prejudicial to the public interest:

Provided that the President or member shall not be removed from his office on the ground specified in clauses *(d)* and *(e)* of sub-rule

(6) except on an inquiry held by State Government in accordance with such procedure as it may specify in this behalf and finds the member to be guilty of such ground.

(7) The terms and conditions of the service of the President and the members of the District Forum shall not be varied to their disadvantage during their tenure of office.

(8) Where any vacancy occurs in the office of the President, of the District Forum, the seniormost (in order of appointment) member of the District Forum with judicial background, shall discharge the functions of the President until a person appointed to fill such vacancy assumes the office of the President of the District Forum.

(9) When the President of the District Forum is unable to discharge the frictions owing to absence, illness or any other cause, the senior most member of the District Forum with judicial background, if authorised so to do by the President in writing, shall discharge the functions of the President until the day on which the President resumes the charge of his functions.

(10) The President or any member ceasing to hold office as such shall not hold any appointment in or be connected with the management or administration of an organisation which have been the subject of any proceeding under the Act. during his tenure for a period of 5 years from the date on which he ceases to hold such office.

Place of sitting and other matters relating to District Forum [Section 14(3)]

4. (1) The office of the District Forum shall be located at the headquarters of the District. The State Government may enlarge the jurisdiction of District Forum by way of setting up of such forums at divisional levels or a forum for 3 to 4 districts or may set up a District Forum for every district.

(2) The working days and the office hours of the District Forum shall be the same as that of the State Government.

(3) The official seal and emblem of the District Forum shall be as follows— The President, Consumer Dispute Redressal Forum...............

(4) Sitting of the District Forum, as and when necessary, shall be convened by; the President.

(5) No act or proceedings of the District Forum shall be invalid by reason only of the existence of any vacancy among its members or any defect in its constitution.

(6) The President and the other members of the District Forums shall be entitled to such subordinate staff to assist the District Forum in its day to day work and perform such other function as are **Provided** under these rule, or assigned to it by the President which is admissible to a District Judge and other judicial member of the District. The salary payable to such staff shall be defrayed out of the head "2048—Food Storage and Warehousing (Field Staff)".

(7) Where the opposite party admits the allegation made by the complainant, the District Forum shall decide the complaint on the basis of the merit of the case and documents present before it.

(8) If during, the proceedings conducted under section 13, District Forum fixes a date for hearing of the parties, it shall be obligatory on the complainant and opposite party or its authorised agent to appeal before the District Forum of such date of hearing or any other date to which hearing could be adjourned Where the complainant or his authorised agent fails to appear before the District Forum on such day, the District Forum may in its discretion either dismiss the complaint for default or decide it on merit. Where the opposite party or its authorised agent fails to appear on the day of hearing, the District Forum may decide the complaint *ex parte.*

(9) While proceeding under sub-rule (8), the District Forum may on such terms as it may think fit and at any stage, adjourn the hearing of the complaint but no more than one adjournment shall ordinarily be given and the complaint should be decided within 90 days from the date of notice received by the opposite party where complaint does not require analysis or testing of the goods and within 150 days if it requires analysis or testing of the goods.

(10) Orders of the District Forum shall be signed and dated by the members of the District Forum constituting the Bench and shall be communicated to the parties free of charge.

Procedure to be adopted by the District Forum for analysis and testing of goods [Section 13(l)(c)]

5. (1) Under section 13(l)(c), if considered necessary, the District Forum may direct the complainant to provide more than one sample of the goods in clean containers with stopper properly fixed on them.

(2) On receiving the samples of such goods, the District Forum shall seal it and fix labels on the containers carrying following information:—

(i) name and address of the appropriate laboratory to whom sample will be sent for analysis and test;

(ii) name and address of the District Forum;

(iii) case number;

(iv) seal of the District Forum.

(3) The sample will be sent to the appropriate laboratory by the District Forum for sending report within 45 days or within such extended time as may be granted by the District Forum after specifying the nature of the defect alleged and date of submission of the report.

Salary and other allowances and terms and conditions of the President and members of the State Commission [Section 16(2)]

6. (1) President of the State Commission shall receive the salary of the Judge of the High Court if appointed on whole time basis or a consolidated honorarium of ₹ 200 per day for the sitting if appointed on part time basis. Other members, if sitting on whole time basis, shall receive a consolidated honorarium of ₹ 3,000 per month and if sitting on part time basis, a consolidated honorarium of [₹ 250] per day for the sitting.

(2) The President and the members of the State Commission shall be eligible for such travelling allowance and daily allowance on official tour as arc admissible to Class I Officers of the State Government.

(3) The Salary, honorarium and other allowances shall be defrayed out of the head "2408.—Food Storage and Warehousing (Directorate Staff)".

(4) President and the members of the State Commission shall hold office for a term of five years or upto the age of [70] years whichever is earlier and shall not be eligible for renomination.

Provided that President and members may

(a) by writing under his hand and addressed to the State Government resign his office any time; and

(b) be removed from his office in accordance with provisions of sub-rule (5).

(5) The State Government may remove from office, President or a member of 1 the State Commission who,—

(a) has been adjudged as insolvent; or

(b) has been convicted of an offence which in the opinion of the State Government, involves moral turpitude; or

(c) has become physically or mentally incapable of acting as such member; or

(d) has acquired such financial or other interest as is likely to effect prejudicially his functions as a member; or

(e) has so abused his position as to render his continuance in office prejudicial to the public interest:

Provided that the President or member shall not be removed from his office on the ground specified in clauses *(d)* and *(e)* of sub-rule (5) except on an inquiry held by State Government in accordance with such procedure as it may specify in this behalf and finds the member to be guilty of such ground.

(6) Before appointment, the President and members of the State Commission shall have to take an undertaking that he does not and will not have any such financial or other interests as is likely to affect prejudicially his functions as such member.

(7) The terms and conditions of the service of the President and the members of the State Commission shall not be varied to their disadvantage during their tenure of office.

(8) Every vacancy caused by resignation and removal of the President or any other member of the State Commission under sub-rule (4) or otherwise shall be filled by fresh appointment.

(9) Where any vacancy occurs in the office of the President of the State Commission, the senior most member of the State Commission with judicial background, shall discharge the functions of the President until a person appointed to fill such vacancy assumes the office of the President of the State Commission.

(10) When the President of the State Commission is unable to discharge the functions owing to absence, illness or any other cause, the seniormost member of the State Commission with judicial background, if authorised so to do by the President in writing, shall discharge the functions of the President until the day on which the President resumes the charge of his functions.

(11) The President or any member ceasing to hold office as such shall not hold any appointment in or be connected with the management or administration of any organisation which have been the subject of any proceeding under the Act during his tenure for a period of 5 years from the date on which he ceases to hold such office.

Place of sitting and other matters relating to State Commission [Section 14(3) read with section 18]

7. (1) Office of the State Commission shall be located at Chandigarh.

(2) The working days and the office hours of the State Commission shall be the same as that of the State Government.

(3) The official seal and emblem of the State Commission shall be as follows— The President, Consumer Dispute Redressal Commission, Haryana, Chandigarh.

(4) Sitting of the State Commission, as and when necessary, shall be convened by the President.

(5) No act or proceedings of the State Commission shall be invalid by reason only of the existence of any vacancy among its members or any defect in its constitution thereof.

(6) The President and other members of the Commission shall be entitled for such subordinate staff to assist the State Commission in its work and perform such other functions as are **Provided** under these rules or assigned to it by the President which is admissible to Judge of a High Court. The salary payable to such staff shall be defrayed out of the head "2408 - Food Storage and Warehousing (Directorate Staff)."

(7) Where the opposite party admits the allegation made by the complainant, the State Commission shall decide the complaint on the basis of the merit of the case and documents present before it.

(8) If during the proceedings conducted under section 13, State Commission I fixes a date for hearing of the parties, it shall be obligatory on the complainant and opposite party or his authorised agent to appear before the State Commission on such date of hearing or any other date to which hearing could be adjourned. Where the complainant or his authorised agent fails to appear before the State Commission on such day, the State Commission may in its discretion either dismiss the complaint for default or decide it on merit. Where the opposite party or its authorised agent fails to appear on the day of hearing, the State Commission may decide the complaint *ex parte*.

(9) While proceeding under sub-rule (8), the State Commission may on such terms as it may think fit and at any stage, adjourn the hearing of the complaint, but not more than one adjournment shall ordinarily be given and the complaint should be decided within 90 days from the date of notice received by the opposite party where complaint does not require analysis or testing of the goods and within 150 days if it requires analysis or testing of the goods.

(10) Orders of the State Commission shall be signed and dated by the members of the State Commission constituting the Bench and shall be communicated to the parties free of charge.

Procedure for hearing the appeal [Section 15]

8. (1) Memorandum shall be presented by the appellant or his authorised agent to the State Commission in person or be sent by registered post addressed to the Commission.

(2) Every memorandum filed under sub-rule (1) shall be in legible handwriting preferably typed and shall set forth concisely under distinct heads, the grounds of appeal without any argument or narrative and such grounds shall be numbered consecutively.

(3) Each memorandum shall be accompanied by the certified copy of the order of the District Forum appealed against and such of the documents as may be required to support grounds of objection mentioned in the memorandum.

(4) When the appeal is presented after the expiry of the period of limitation as specified in the Act, the memorandum shall be accompanied by an application supported by an affidavit setting forth the fact on which the appellant relies to satisfy the State Commission that he has sufficient cause for not preferring the appeal within the period of limitation.

(5) The appellant shall submit four copies of the memorandum to the State Commission for official purpose.

(6) On the date of hearing or on any other day to which hearing may be adjourned, it shall be obligatory for the parties or their authorised agents to appear before the State Commission. If appellant or his authorised agent fails to appear on such date, the State Commission may, in its discretion, either dismiss the appeal or decide it on the merit of the case. If respondent or his authorised agent fails to appear on such date, the State Commission shall proceed *ex parte* and shall decide the appeal *ex parte* on the merits of the case.

(7) The appellant shall not, except by leave of the State Commission, urge or be heard in support of any ground of objection not set forth in the memorandum but the State Commission, in deciding the appeal, shall not confine to the grounds of objection set forth in the memorandum or taken by leave of the State Commission under this rule:

Provided that the Commission shall not rest its decision on any other grounds unless the party who may be affected thereby, has been given, at least one opportunity of being heard by the State Commission.

(8) State Commission may, on such terms as it may think fit and at any stage, adjourn the hearing of the appeal, but not more than one adjournment shall Irdinarily be given and the appeal should be decided within 90 days from the first date of hearing.

(9) Order of the State Commission on appeal shall be signed and dated by the Members of the State Commission constituting the Bench and shall be communicated to the parties free of charge.

—✦—✦—✦—

Chapter 16

Himachal Pradesh Consumer Protection Rules, 1988

[Notification No. FDS A (3)-4/82--IH, Dated 25-4-1988]

In exercise of the powers conferred by sub-section (2) of section 30 of the Consumer Protection Act, 1986 (68 of 1986), the Government of Himachal Pradesh hereby makes the following rules, namely:—

PRELIMINARY

SHORT TITLE AND COMMENCEMENT

1. (1) These rules may be called the Himachal Pradesh Consumer Protection Rules, 1988.

(2) They shall come into force with effect from 1-5-1988.

Definitions

2. In these rules, unless the context otherwise requires,—

(a) "Act" means the Consumer Protection Act, 1986 (68 of 1986);

(b) "agent" means a person duly authorised by a party to present an; complaint, or appeal or reply on its behalf before the District Forum or the State Commission, as the case may be;

(c) "appellant" means a party which makes an appeal against the order of the District Forum;

(d) "memorandum" means any memorandum of appeal filed by the appellant;

(e) "opposite party" means a person who answers complaints or claims;

(f) "President" means the President of the District Forum or State Commission as the case may be;

(g) "respondent" means the person who answers any memorandum appeal;

(h) "State Government" means the Government of Himachal Pradesh.

(i) The words and expressions used in these rules and not defined therein defined in the Act shall have the same meanings respectively assigned to in the Act.

DISTRICT FORUM

Place of Sitting of the District Forum

3. The office of the District Forum shall be located at the headquarters of the District and where the State Government decides to establish a single District Forum having jurisdiction over more Districts than one, it shall notify the place and jurisdiction of the District Forum so established.

Working Days and Office Hours of the District Forum

4. The working days and office hours of the District Forum shall be the same as those of the offices of the State Government.

Seal and Emblem

5. The official seal and emblem of the District Forum shall be such as the State Government may specify.

Sitting of the District Forum

6. The sitting of the District Forum, as and when necessary, shall be convened by the President and it may, in the interest of speedy disposal of the complaint, hold its sittings at any place within its jurisdiction.

Staff of the District Forum

7. The State Government shall appoint such staff as may be necessary to assist the District Forum in its day-to-day work and to perform such functions as are assigned to it by the President. The salary payable to such staff shall be defrayed out of the Consolidated Fund of the State Government.

The terms and conditions of the staff so appointed for this purpose shall be such as may be laid down by the State Government from time to time.

Salaries, Honorarium and other Allowances of the President and the Members of the District Forum

8. (1) Where the President of the District Forum is a sitting Judge of the District Court he shall enjoy all benefits which he should have enjoyed as a sitting Judge of the District Court. Where the President is not a sitting Judge of the District Court, he shall be entitled to the salary payable as District Judge but the pay plus pension of a retired person shall not exceed the last pay drawn by him, if appointed on whole-time basis or an honorarium of ₹ 150 per day if appointed on part-time basis. Other members, if appointed on whole-time basis, shall receive a consolidated honorarium of ₹ 1,250 per month or if appointed on part-time basis a consolidated honorarium of ₹ 100 per day for each sitting.

(2) The President and the members of the District Forum shall be entitled to Ravelling and daily allowance on official tours at the same rates as are admissible to the highest Grade I Officer of the State Government.

(3) The honorarium or the salary, as the case may be, and other allowances shall be defrayed out of the Consolidated Fund of the State Government.

Terms and Conditions of Services of the President and Members of the District Forum

9. (1) Before appointment, the President and members of the District Forum shall have to give an undertaking that he does not and will not have any such financial or other interest as is likely to affect prejudicially his functions as such President or a member, as the case may be.

(2) The terms and conditions of the service of the President and the members shall not be varied to their disadvantage during their tenure of office.

(3) A casual vacancy caused by resignation or removal of the President or any other member of the District Forum shall be filled by fresh appointment.

(4) No act or proceeding of District Forum shall be invalid by reason only of the existence of any vacancy among its President or members or any defect in the constitution thereof.

(5) In case of difference of opinion among the members of the District Forum, the majority opinion shall prevail and the opinion or orders of the District Forum shall be expressed in terms of the views of the majority.

(6) The President or any member ceasing to hold office, as such, shall not hold any appointment in or be connected with the management or administration of an organisation which has been the subject of any proceeding under the Act during his tenure for a period of 5 years from the date on which he ceases to hold such office.

Removal of President or Members of the District Forum from Office in Certain Circumstances

10. The State Government may remove any person from the office of the President or the member, as the case may be, who,—

(a) had been adjudged as an insolvent; or

(b) has been convicted of an offence which, in the opinion of the State Government, involves moral turpitude; or

(c) has become physically or mentally incapable of acting as such President or member; or

(d) has acquired such financial or other interest as is likely to affect prejudicially his functions as such President or member; or

(*e*) has so abused his position as to render his continuance in office prejudicial to the public interest:

Provided that the President or any member shall not be removed from his office on the grounds specified in clauses (*d*) and (*e*) of this rule except on any enquiry held by the State Government in accordance with such procedure a it may specify in this behalf and find the President or the member, as the case may be, guilty on such grounds.

Procedure on Receipt of Complaint

11. (1) Where the opposite party admits the allegations made by the complainant, the District Forum shall decide the complaint on merits or case and the documents presented to it.

(2) If during the proceedings conducted under section 13, the District Forum fixes a date for hearing of the parties, it shall be obligatory on the complainant Lid the opposite party or their authorised agents to appear before the District Forum on such date of hearing or any other date to which hearing is adjourned. here the complainant or his authorised agent fails to appear before the strict Forum on such day, District Forum may in its discretion either dismiss the complaint for default or decide it on merit. Where the opposite party or its authorised agent fails to appear on the day of hearing, the District Forum may decide the complaint *ex parte.*

(3) While proceeding under sub-rule (2), the District Forum may, on such terms Bit may think fit, at any stage of the proceedings, adjourn the hearing of the complaint but the complaint shall be decided as far as possible within a period & three months from the date of notice received by the opposite party where Complaint does not require analysis or testing and within five months if it requires analysis or testing of the goods.

(4) Orders of the District Forum shall be duly signed, sealed and dated by the members of the District Forum constituting the Bench and shall be communicated to the parties free of cost.

Procedure to be Adopted for Analysis and Testing of Goods

12. (1) Under clause (c) of sub-section (1) of section 13 of the Act, if considered necessary, the District Forum may direct the complainant to provide more than one sample of the goods in clean containers with stopper properly Eked on them.

(2) On receiving the sample of such goods, the District Forum, shall seal it and fix labels on the containers carrying following information—

(i) name and address of the appropriate laboratory to whom sample will be sent for analysis and test;

(ii) name and address of the District Forum; case number; and Seal of the District Forum.

(4) The sample will be sent to the appropriate laboratory by the District Forum sending report within 45 days or within such extended time as may be Wanted by the District Forum after specifying the nature of the defect alleged date of submission of the report.

STATE COMMISSION

Salary, Honorarium and Other Allowances of the President and Members of the State Commission

13. (1) Where the President of the State Commission is a sitting Judge of the High Court, he shall enjoy all the benefits which he should have enjoyed as sitting Judge of the High Court. Where the President is not a sitting Judge of the High Court, he shall receive a consolidated honorarium of ₹ 7,000 per month, if appointed on whole-time basis or last pay drawn by him minus, Pension granted to him or an honorarium of ₹ 300 per day if appointed on part-time basis. Other members, if appointed on whole-time basis shall receive a consolidated honorarium of ₹ 1,500 per month or if appointed on part-time basis a consolidated honorarium of ₹ 250 per day for the sitting : **Provided** that a member shall be eligible to any pension granted to him by the Government or any authority but honorarium plus pension shall not exceed the last pay drawn.

(2) The President and the members shall also be entitled to semi-furnished accommodation.

(3) The President and the members shall be entitled to travelling and daily allowance on official tours at the same rates as are admissible to the highest Grade I Officer of the State Government.

(4) The honorarium or the salary, as the case may be, and other allowances shall be defrayed out of the Consolidated Fund of the State Government.

Terms and Conditions of Service of the President and Members of the State Commission

14. (1) Before appointment, the President and a member of the State Commission shall have to give an undertaking that he does not and will not have any such financial or other interest as is likely to affect prejudicially his functions as such President or member, as the case may be.

(2) The President and the members shall hold the office for a term of two years and shall not be eligible for re-appointment:

Provided that no President or a member shall hold office as such for a term exceeding 5 years or after he has attained the age of 65 years, whichever is earlier.

(3) Notwithstanding anything contained in sub-rule (2), the President or a member may—

(*a*) by writing under his hand and addressed to the Secretary (Food and Supplies) to the Government of Himachal Pradesh, resign his office at any time; and]

(*b*) be removed from his office in accordance with the provision of rule 15 of these rules.

(4) The terms and conditions of service of the President and the members shall not be varied to their disadvantage during their tenure of office.

(5) A casual vacancy caused by resignation or removal of the President or any other member of the State Commission under sub-rule (3) or otherwise shall be filled by fresh appointment.

(6) No act or proceedings of the State Commission shall be invalid by reason only of the existence of any vacancy among its President or members or an) defect in the constitution thereof.

(7) In case of difference of opinion among the members of the State commission, the opinion of the majority shall prevail and the opinion or orders or the Commission shall be expressed in terms of the views of the majority.

(8) The President or any member ceasing to hold office as such shall not hold any appointment in or be connected with the management or administration of an organisation which have been the subject of any proceeding under the Act during his tenure for a period of 5 years from the date on which he ceases to hold such office.

Removal of President or Members from Office in Certain Circumstances

15. (1) The State Government may remove from office, the President or any member who,—

(*a*) has been adjudged as insolvent; or

(*b*) has been convicted of an offence which, in the opinion of the State Government, involves moral turpitude; or

(*c*) has become physically or mentally incapable of acting as such President or member; or

(*d*) has acquired such financial or other interest as is likely to affect prejudicially his functions as the President or a member; or

(*e*) has so abused his position as to render his continuance in office prejudicial to the public interest.

(2) Notwithstanding anything contained in sub-rule (1), the President or any member shall not be removed from his office on the grounds specified in clauses *(d)* and *(e)* of that sub-rule except on an inquiry held by the State Government in accordance with such procedure as it may specify in this behalf and find the President or any member guilty on such grounds.

Place of Sitting of the State Commission

16. The office of the State Commission shall be located in the capital of the State.

Working Days and Office Hours of the State Commission

17. The working days and office hours of the State Commission shall be the same as that of the offices of the State Government.

Seal and Emblem of the State Commission

18. The official seal and emblem of the State Commission shall be such as the state Government shall specify.

State Government may specify sitting of the State Commission

19. The sitting of the State Commission, as and when necessary, shall be convened by the President and it may, in the interest of speedy disposal tt the complaint or appeal, hold its sittings at any place within its jurisdiction.

State Staff of the Commission

20. The State Government shall appoint such staff as may be necessary to assist the State Commission in its day to day work and to perform such Fictions as are assigned to it by the President. The salary payable to such staff shall be defrayed out of the Consolidated Fund of the State Government.

Procedure to be followed by the State Commission

21. (1) A complaint containing the following particulars shall be presented by the complainant in person or by his agent to the State Commission or be sent by registered post addressed to the State Commission—

(*a*) the name, description and the address of the complainant;

(*b*) the name, description and address of the opposite party or parties, as the case may be, so far as they can be ascertained;

(*c*) the facts relating to complaint and when and where it arose;

(*d*) documents in support of the allegations contained in the complaint;

(*e*) the relief which the complainant claims.

(2) The Slate Commission shall, in disposal of any complaint before it, as far as possible, follow the procedure laid down in sub-sections (1) and (2) of section 13 of the Act in relation to the complaint received by the District Forum.

(3) On the date of hearing or any other date to which the hearing could be adjourned, it shall be obligatory on the parties or their agents to appear before the State Commission. Where the complainant or his agent fails to appear before the State Commission on such date, the State Commission may in its discretion either dismiss the complaint for default or decide it on merits. Where the opposite party or its agent fails to appear on the date of hearing, the State Commission may decide the complaint *ex parte.*

(4) The State Commission may, on such terms as it deems fit and at any stage of the proceedings, adjourn the hearing of the complaint, but the complaint shall be decided, as far as possible within a period of three months from the date of notice received by the opposite party where the complaint does not require analysis or testing of commodities and within five months if it requires such analysis or testing.

(5) If the proceedings conducted under sub-rule (3), the State Commission is satisfied with the allegations contained in the complaint, it shall issue orders to the opposite party or parties, as the Case may be, directing him or them to take one or more of the things mentioned in sub-section (1) of section 14 of the Act.

Procedure of Hearing the Appeal

22. (1) Memorandum shall be presented by the appellant or his agent to the State Commission in person or be sent by registered post addressed to the Commission.

(2) Every memorandum filed under sub-rule (1) shall be in legible handwriting preferably typed, and shall set forth concisely under distinct heads, the ground of appeal without any argument or narrative and such grounds shall numbered consecutively.

(3) Each memorandum shall be accompanied by a certified copy of the order of the District Forum appealed against and such of the documents as may required to support grounds of objection mentioned in the memorandum.

(4) When the appeal is presented after the expiry of the period of limitation specified in the Act, the memorandum shall be accompanied by an application supported by an affidavit setting forth the facts on which the appellant relies to satisfy the State Commission that he has sufficient cause for not preferring the appeal within the period of limitation.

(5) The appellant shall submit four copies of the memorandum to the Commission for official purpose.

(6) On the date of hearing or on any other day to which the hearing may be adjourned, it shall be obligatory for the parties or their agents to appear before the State Commission. If the appellant or his agent fails to appear on such date, the State Commission may in its discretion, either dismiss the appeal or decide it *ex parte* on merits. If the respondent or his agent fails to appear on such date, the State Commission shall proceed *ex parte* and shall decide the appeal on merits of the case.

(7) The appellant shall not, except by leave of the State Commission, urge or be heard in support of any ground or objection not set forth in the memorandum but the State Commission, in deciding the appeal, may not confine to the grounds of objection set forth in the memorandum:

Provided that the State Commission shall not rest its decision on any grounds other than those specified in the memorandum unless the party who may be affected thereby, has been given an opportunity of being heard by the State Commission.

(8) The State Commission, on such terms as it may think fit, and at any stage, adjourn the hearing of the appeal, but not more than one adjournment shall ordinarily be given and the appeal should be decided as far as possible within 90 days from the first date of hearing.

(9) The order of the State Commission, on appeal, shall be signed and dated by the members of the State Commission and communicated to the parties free of charge.

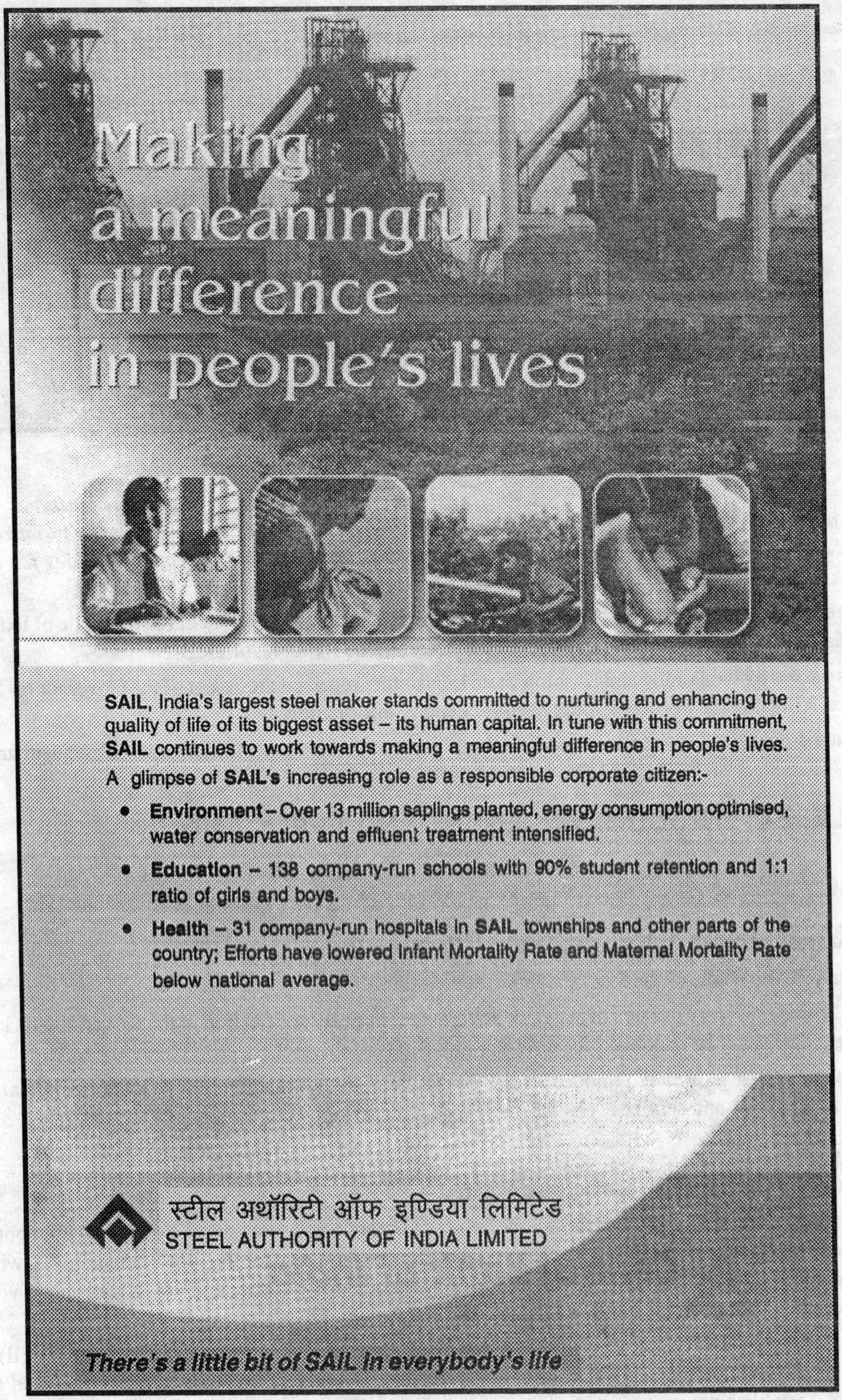
Making
a meaningful
difference
in people's lives
SAIL, India's largest steel maker stands committed to nurturing and enhancing the quality of life of its biggest asset – its human capital. In tune with this commitment, SAIL continues to work towards making a meaningful difference in people's lives.
A glimpse of SAIL's increasing role as a responsible corporate citizen:-
• Environment – Over 13 million saplings planted, energy consumption optimised, water conservation and effluent treatment intensified.
• Education – 138 company-run schools with 90% student retention and 1:1 ratio of girls and boys.
• Health – 31 company-run hospitals in SAIL townships and other parts of the country; Efforts have lowered Infant Mortality Rate and Maternal Mortality Rate below national average.
स्टील अथॉरिटी ऑफ इण्डिया लिमिटेड
STEEL AUTHORITY OF INDIA LIMITED
There's a little bit of SAIL in everybody's life

Chapter 17

Jammu and Kashmir Consumer Protection Act, 1987

[Act No. XVI of 1987]

An Act to provide for better protection of the interest of consumers and for that purpose to make provision or the establishment of consumer councils, and other authorities for the settlement of consumers disputes for matters connected therewith.

Be it enacted by the Jammu and Kashmir State Legislature in the thirty eighth year of the Republic of India and amended by the Jammu and Kashmir State Legislature in the forty eighth year of the Republic of India.

The Acts as passed by the Jammu and Kashmir State Legislature received the assent of the Governor on 19th Aug., 1987 and its amendments on 30th May, 1997 is hereby published for general information.

(The Acts stand published in the Jammu and Kashmir Gazette on 22nd Aug. 1987 and its subsequent amendments on 2nd June 1997).

SHORT TITLE, EXTENT, COMMENCEMENT AND APPLICATION

PRELIMINARY

1. *(i)* This Act may be called the Jammu and Kashmir Consumer Protection Act, 1997.

(ii) It extends to the whole of the State of Jammu and Kashmir.

(iii) It shall come into force on such date as the Government may, by notification in the Government Gazette, appoint and different dates may be appointed for different provisions of this Act.

(iv) Save as otherwise expressly provided by the Government by notification in the Government Gazette, this Act shall apply to all goods and services.

Definitions

2. In this Act, unless the context, otherwise requires;—

(a) "appropriate laboratory" means a laboratory or organisation recognised by the Government and includes any such laboratory or organisation established by or under any law for the time being in force, which is maintained, financed or aided by the Government for carrying out analysis or test of any goods with a view to determining whether such goods suffer from any defect.

(aa) "Branch Office" means (I) any establishment described as branch by opposition party or (II) any establishment carrying on the same or substantially the same activity as that carried on by the head office of the same establishment;

(b) "Complainant" means—

(i) a consumer; or

(ii) any voluntary consumer association registers under the Companies Act, 1956 or under any other law for the time being in force; or

(iii) the Government who makes a complaint;

(iv) one or more consumers where there are numerous consumers having the same interest;

(c) "complaint" means any allegation in writing made by a complainant that

(i) as a result of any unfair trade practice or restrictive trade practice has been adopted by any trader, the complainant has suffered loss or damage;

(ii) the goods bought by him or agreed to be bought by him in the complaint suffer from one or more defects;

(iii) the services hired or availed or agreed to be hired or availed of by him in the complaint suffer from deficiencies in any respect;

(iv) a trader has charged for the goods mentioned in the complaint a price in excess of the price fixed by or under any law for the time being in force or displayed on the goods or any package containing such goods;

(v) goods which be hazardous to life and safety when used or being offered for sale to the public in contravention of the provision of any law for the time being in force requiring traders to display information in regard to the contents, manner and effect of use of such goods. With a view to obtaining any relief provided by or under this Act;

(d) "consumer" means any person who;

(i) buys any goods for a consideration which has been paid or promised or partly paid and partly promised or under any system of deferred payment and includes any user of such goods other than the person who buys such goods for consideration paid or promised partly paid or partly promised or under any system of deferred payment when such use is made with the approval of such person, but does not include a person who obtains such goods for resale or for any commercial purpose; or

(ii) hires or avails of any service for a consideration which has been paid or promised or partly paid and partly promised, or under any system of deferred payment and includes any beneficiary of such services other than the person who hires the services for consideration paid or promised or partly paid and partly promised or under system of deferred payment, when such services are availed with the approval of the first mentioned person.

Explanation—For the purpose of sub-clause (z) "Commercial purpose" does not include use by a consumer of goods bought and used by him exclusively for the purposes of earning his livelihood, by means of self-employment;

(e) "Consumer dispute" means a dispute where the person against whom a complaint has been made, denies or disputes the allegations contained in the complaint;

(f) "Defect" means any fault, imperfection or shortcoming in the quality, quantity, potency, purity or standards which is required to be maintained by or under any law for the time being in force under any contract expressed or implied or ordered as is claimed by the trader in any manner whatsoever in relation to any goods;

(g) "Deficiency" means any fault, imperfection shortcoming or inadequacy in the quality, quantity, nature and manner of performance which is required to be maintained by or under any law for the time being in force or has been undertaken to be performed by a person in pursuance of a contract or otherwise in relation to any service;

(h) "Divisional Forum" means a Consumer Disputes Redressal Forum estab-lished under clause *(a)* of section 7;

(i) "Goods" means goods as defined in the Jammu and Kashmir Sale of Goods Act, Samvat 1996;

(j) "Government" means the Government of Jammu and Kashmir;

(k) "Manufacturer" means a person who—

(i) makes or manufactures any goods or parts thereof, or

(ii) does not make or manufacture any goods but assembles parts thereof made or manufactured by others and claims the end-products to be goods manufactured by himself, or

(iii) puts or causes to be put his own mark on an)' goods made or manufactured by any other manufacturer and claims such goods to be goods made or manufactured by himself;

(kk) "Member" includes the President and a Member of the State Commission or Divisional Forum as the case may be.

Explanation—Where a manufacturer dispatches any goods or part thereof to any branch office maintained by him, such branch office shall not be deemed to be the manufacturer even though the parts so despatched to it are assembled at such branch office and are sold or distributed from such branch office;

(1) "notification" means a notification published in the Government Gazette;

(l) "person" includes—

(i) a firm whether registered or not

(ii) a Hindu undivided family

(iii) a co-operative society

(iv) every other association of persons whether registered under the Jammu and Kashmir Societies Registration Act, Sam vat 1998 or not;

(m) "prescribed" means prescribed by rules made by the Government under this Act;

(n) "restrictive trade practice" means any trade practice which requires a consumer to buy, hire or availing of any goods, or as the case may be, services as a condition precedent for buying, hiring, or availing of other goods or services;

(o) "service" means service of any description which is made available to potential users and includes the provision of facilities in connection with banking, financing, insurance, transport, processing, supply of electrical or other energy, board or lodging or both housing construction entertainment, amusement or the purveying a news or other information, under a contract of personal services;

(p) "State Commission" means a Consumer Disputes Redressal Commission established in the State under clause *(b)* of section 7;

(q) "trader in relation to any goods" means a person who sell or distributes any goods for sale and includes the manufacturer thereof, and where such goods are sold or distributed in package from includes the packer thereof;

(r) "unfair trade practice" means a trade practice which for the purpose of promoting the sale, use or supply of any goods or for the provision of any services, adopts one or more of the following practices and thereby causes loss, injury or to the consumers of such goods or services whether by eliminating or restricting competition or otherwise "adopts any unfair methods or unfair or deceptive practice including any of the following practices" namely the practices of making any statement, whether orally or in writing or by visible representation which :—

(i) falsely represents that the goods are of a particular standard, quality, grade composition, style or model;

(ii) falsely represents that the services are of a particular standard, quality or grade;

(iii) falsely represents any rebuilt second hand renovate reconditioned or old goods as new goods;

(iv) represents that the people or goods or services have sponsorship, approval, performance, characteristics, accessories, users or benefits which such goods or services do not have;

(v) represents that the seller or the supplier has a sponsorship or approval or affiliation which such seller or supplier does not have;

(vi) makes a false or misleading representation concerning the need for, or the usefulness of any goods or services;

(vii) gives to the public any warranty or guarantee, of the performance, efficiency or length of life of a product or of any goods that is not based on an adequate or proper test there:

Provided that where a defence is raised to the effect that such warranty or guarantee is based on adequate or proper test, the burden of proof of such defence shall lie on the person raising such defence; makes to the public a representation in a form that purports to be—

(viii) a warranty or guarantee of a product of any goods or services; or

(ix) a promise to replace, maintain or repair an article or any part thereof or to repeal or continue a service until it has achieved a specified result. If such purported warranty or guarantee or promise is materially misleading or if there is no reasonable prospect that such warranty, guarantee or promise will be carried out;

(x) materially misleads the public concerning the price at which a product or like products or goods or services, have been or are ordinarily sold or provided, and for this purpose, a representation as to price shall be deemed to refer to the price at which the product or goods or services has or have been sold by sellers or unless it is clearly specified to be the price at which the product has been sold or services have been provided by the person by whom or on whose behalf the representation is made;

(xi) gives false or misleading facts disparaging the goods, services or trade of another person.

Explanation—For the purpose of clause (1), a statement that is—

(a) expressed on an article offered or displayed for sale, or on its wrapper or container; or

(b) expressed on anything attached to, inserted in, or accompanying, an article offered or displayed for sale, or on anything on which the article is mounted for display or sale; or

(c) contained in or on anything that is sold, sent, delivered, transmitted[1] or in any other manner whatsoever made available to a member of the public, shall be deemed to be a statement made to the public by, and only by, the person who had caused the statement to be so expressed made or contained.

(2) Permits the publication of any advertisement whether in any newspaper or otherwise, for the sale or supply at a bargain price, of goods or services that are not intended to be. offered for sale or supply at the bargain price, or for a period that is, and in quantities that are, reasonable, having regard to the nature of the market in, which the business is carried on, the nature and size of business and the nature of the advertisement.

Explanation—For the purpose of clause (2), "bargain price" means—

(a) a price that is stated in any advertisement to be a bargain price, by reference to an ordinary price or otherwise; or

(b) a price that a person who reads, hears or sees the advertisement, would reasonably understand to be a bargain price having regard to the practices at which the product advertised or like products arc ordinarily sold;

(3) Permits—

(a) the offering of gifts, prizes or other items with the intention of not providing them as offered or creating the impression that something is being given or offered free of charge when it is fully or partly covered by the amount charged in the transaction as a whole;

(b) the conduct of any contest, lottery, game of chance of skill, for the purpose of promoting, directly or indirectly, the sale, use or supply of any product or any business interest,

(4) Permits the sale or supply of goods intended to be used or are of a kind likely to be used, by consumers, knowing or having reason to believe that the goods do not comply with the standards prescribed by competent authority relating to performance, composition, contents design, constructions, finishing or packaging as are necessary to prevent or reduce the risk of injury to the person using the goods.

(5) permits the hoarding or destruction of goods, or refuses to sell the goods or to make them available for sale, or to provide any service, if such hoarding or destruction or refusal raised or tends to raise or is intended to raise the cost of those or other similar goods or services, Act not in derogation of any other law.

3. The provisions of this Act shall be in addition to and not in derogation of the provision of any other law for the time being in force.

CONSUMER PROTECTION COUNCILS

The State Consumer Protection Council

4. (i) The Government may by notification in the Government Gazette establish with effect from such date as it may specify in such, notification a Council to be known as the State Consumer Protection Council (hereinafter referred to as the State Council).

(ii) The State Council shall consist of the following members, namely —

(a) The Minister in charge of the Department of Food and Civil Supplies in the Government, who shall be its Chairman, and

(b) Such member of other official or non-official members representing such interests as may be prescribed.

Procedure for Meetings of the State Council

5. (i) The State Council shall meet as and when necessary, but not less than three meetings of the Council shall be held every year.

(ii) The State Council shall meet at such time and place as the Chairman may think fit and shall observe such procedure in regard to the transaction of its business as may be prescribed.

Objects of the State Council

6. The objects of the State Council shall be to promote and protect the rights of the consumers such as—

(a) the right to be protected against the marketing of goods which arc hazardous to life and prosperity;

(b) the right to be informed about the quality, quantity potency, purity, standard and price of goods so as to protect the consumer against unfair trade practices;

(c) the right to be assured wherever possible access to a variety of goods and services at competitive prices;

(d) the right to be heard and to be assured that consumers interests will receive due consideration at appropriate;

(e) the right to seek redressal against unfair trade practices, restrictive trade practice or unscrupulous exploitation of consumers;

(f) right to consumer education.

Constitution of District Consumer Protection Council

6A. *(i)* The Government may by notification in the Government Gazette establish with effect from such date as it may specify in such notification, a Council to be known as the District Consumer Protection Council, which hereinafter shall be referred to as District Council.

(ii) The District Council shall consist of the following members, namely—

(a) Deputy Commissioner of the District, who shall be its Chairman; and

(b) Such number of other officials or non-official members representing such interests as may be prescribed.

(iii) The District Council shall meet as and when necessary, but not. less than four meetings of the Council shall be held every year,

(iv) The objects of the District Council shall be the same as that of State Council.

CONSUMER DISPUTES REDRESSAL AGENCIES

Establishment of Consumer Disputes Redressal Agencies

7. There shall be established for the purposes of this Act, the following agencies namely;

(a) A Consumer Disputes Redressal Forum to be known as the "Divisional Forum" established by the Government in each division of the State;

(b) A Consumer Disputes Redressal Commission to be known as the "State Commission" established by the Government.

Composition of the Divisional Forum

8. *(i)* Each Divisional Forum shall consist of:

(a) a person who is or has been, or is qualified to be a District Judge to be nominated by the Government to be its President;

(b) the two member who are persons of ability, integrity and standing and have adequate knowledge or experience of dealing with problems relating lo economic, law, commerce, accountancy, industrial public affairs or administration, one or whom to be preferably a lady."; (1-A) Every appointment under sub-section (1) shall be made by the Government on the recommendations of a Selection Committee consisting of the following namely—

(i) The President of the State Commission ... Chairman

(ii) The Secretary to Government Law Department ... Member

(iii) The Secretary to Government Food, Supplies and Transport Department (In charge Consumer Affairs) ... Member

(ii) Every member of the Divisional Forum shall hold office for a term of five years or up to the age of 62 years whichever is earlier, and shall not be eligible for reappointment:

Provided that a member may resign his office in writing under his hand addressed to the Government on such resignation being accepted, his office shall become vacant and may be filled by the appointment of a person possessing any of the qualification mentioned in sub-section (1) in relation to the category of the member who has resigned,

(iii) The salary or honorarium and other allowances in the other terms and payable to and including tenure of office of the members of the Divisional Forum shall be such as may be prescribed by the Government.

Jurisdiction of the Divisional Forum

9. (i) Subject to the other provisions of this Act, the Divisional Forum shall have jurisdiction to entertain complaints where the value of the goods or services and the compensation if any claimed does not exceed ₹ 5.00 lacs.

(ii) A complaint shall be instituted in a Divisional Forum within its local limits of whose jurisdiction;

(a) the opposite party or each of the opposite parties where there are more than one, at the time of the institution of the complaint, actually and voluntarily resides or carries on business, directly or through a branch office; or personally work for gains,

(b) any of the opposite parties, where there are more than one, at the time of the institution of the complaint, actually and voluntarily resides or carry on business directly or through a branch office or personally works for gain, provided that in such case either the permission of the Divisional Forum is given or the opposite parties who do not reside or carry on business directly or through branch office or personally work for gain, as the case may be, acquiesce in such institution, or.

(c) the cause of action wholly or in part, arises.

Manner in which complaint shall be made

10. Complaint in relation to any goods sold or delivered or agreed to be sold or delivered or any service provided or agreed to be provided may be filled with a Divisional Forum by,—

(a) the consumer lo whom such goods are sold or delivered or agreed to be sold or delivered or such service provided or agreed to be provided;

(b) any recognised consumer association whether the consumer to whom the goods sold or delivered or agreed lo be sold or delivered or services provided or agreed to be provided is a member of such association or not;

(c) one or more consumers where there arc numerous consumers having the same interest, with the permission of the Divisional Forum on behalf of or for the benefit of all consumers so interested;

(d) the government.

Explanation—For the purpose of the section "recognised consumer association" means any voluntary association registered under the Companies Act, 1956, or any other law for the time being in force."

Procedure on receipt of complaint

11. (1) The Divisional Forum shall on receipt of a complaint, if it relates to any goods:

(a) Refer a copy of the complaint to the opposite party mentioned in the complaint directing him to give his version of the case within a period of thirty days or such extended period not exceeding than fifteen days as may be granted by the Divisional Forum;

(b) where the opposite party on receipt of a complaint referred to him under clause *(a)* denies or disputes the allegations contained in the complaint, or omits or fails to take any action to represent his case within the time given by the Divisional Forum, the Divisional Forum shall proceed to settle the consumers dispute in the manner specified in clauses (c) to *(g):*

(c) where the complaint alleges a defect in the goods which cannot be determined without proper analysis or test of the goods, the Divisional Form shall obtain a sample of the goods from the complainant, seal it and authenticate in the manner prescribed and refer the sample so sealed to the appropriate laboratory along with a direction that such laboratory make an analysis, or test, whichever may be necessary, with a view to finding out whether such goods from any defect alleged in the complaint or suffer from any other defect and to report its findings thereon to the Divisional Forum within a period of forty-five days of the receipt of the reference or within such extended period as may be granted by the Divisional Forum;

(d) before any sample of the goods is referred to any appropriate laboratory under clause *(b),* the Divisional Forum may require the complaint to deposit to the credit of the Forum such fees as may be specified, for payment to the appropriate laboratory, for carrying out the necessary analysis or test in relation to the goods in question;

(e) the Divisional Forum shall remit the amount deposited to its credit under clause *(d)* lo the appropriate laboratory to enable it to carry out the analysis or rest mentioned in clause *(c)* and on receipt of the report from the appropriate laboratory, the Divisional Forum shall forward a copy of the report along with such remarks as the Divisional Forum may feel appropriate to the opposite party;

(f) if any of the parties disputed the correctness of the findings of the appropriate' laboratory or disputes the correctness of the methods of analysis or test adopted by the appropriate laboratory, the Divisional Forum shall require the opposite party or the complainant to submit in writing his objection in regard to the report made by the appropriate laboratory;

(g) the Divisional Forum shall thereafter give a reasonable opportunity to the complainant as well as the opposite party of being heard as to the correctness or otherwise of the report made by the appropriate laboratory and also as to the objection made in the relation thereto under clause (*f*) and issue an appropriate order under section.

(2) The Divisional Forum shall, if the complaint received by it under specified section 10 relates to goods in respect of which the procedure specified in sub-section (1) cannot be followed, or if the complaint relates to any services—

(a) refer a copy of such complaint to the opposite party directing him to give his version of the case within a period of thirty days or such extended period not exceeding fifteen days as may be granted by the Divisional Forum;

(b) where the opposite party on receipt of a copy of the complaint, referred to him under clause (a) denies or disputes the allegations contained in the complaint or omits or fails to take any action to represent his case within the time given by the Divisional Forum, the Divisional Forum shall proceed to settle the consumer disputes,—

(i) On the basis of evidence brought to its notice by the complainant and the opposite party, where the opposite party denies or disputes the allegation contained in the complaint, or

(ii) On the basis of evidence brought to its notice by the complainant where the opposite party omits or fails to take any action to represent his case within the time given by the Forum.

(3) No proceedings complying with the procedure laid down in sub-sections (1) and (2) shall be called in question any court on the ground that the principles of natural justice have not been complied with.

(4) For the purpose of this section, the Divisional Forum shall have the same powers as are vested in a civil court under the Code of Civil Procedure, Samvat 1977 while trying a suit in respect of the following matters, namely —

(i) the summoning and enforcing the attendance of any defendant....? examining the witness on oath;

(ii) the discovery and production of any document or other material object producible as evidence;

(iii) the reception of evidence on affidavits;

(iv) the requisitioning of the report of the concerned analysis or test from the appropriate laboratory or from any other relevant source;

(v) issuing of any commission for the examination of any witness and, *(vi)* any other matter which may be prescribed.

(5) Every proceeding before the Divisional Forum shall be deemed to be a judicial proceeding within the meaning of sections 193 and 228 of the Ranbir Penal Code, and the Divisional Forum shall be deemed to be a civil court for the purposes of section 195 and Chapter XVII of the Code of Criminal Procedure, Samvat 1989.

(6) Where the complainant is consumer referred in sub-clause *(iv)* of clause *(b)* of section 2 the provisions of rule 8 of order 1 of the First Schedule to the Code of Civil Procedures, Samvat 1977 shall apply subject to the modification that every reference therein to a suit or a decree shall be construed as a reference to a complaint or the order of the Divisional Forum thereon."

Finding of the Divisional Forum

12. (1) if, after the proceeding conducted under section II, the Divisional Forum is satisfied that the goods complained against suffer from any of the defect specified in the complaint or that any of the allegations contained in the complaint about the services arc removed, it shall issue an order, to the opposite party directing him to do one or more of the following things namely —

(a) to remove the defect pointed out by the appropriate laboratory from the goods in question;

(b) to replace the goods with new goods of similar description which shall be free from any defect;

(c) to return to the complainant the price, or as the case may be the charges', paid by the complainant;

(d) to pay such amount as may be awarded by it as compensation to the' consumer for loss to the expenditure or injury suffered by the consumer due to the negligence of the opposite party;

(e) to remove the defects or deficiencies in the services in question;

(f) to discontinue the unfair trade practice or the restrictive trade practice or not to repent them;

(g) not to offer the hazardous goods from being offered for sale;

(h) to withdraw the hazardous goods from being offered for sale; *(i)* to provide for adequate costs to parties;

(2) Every order made by the Divisional Forum under sub-section (1) shall be signed by the majority of members constituting it and it shall be deemed to be the order of the Divisional Consumer Forum

Provided that where the proceeding is conducted by the President and one member and they differ on any point they shall state the point or points on which they differ and refer the same to other member for hearing on such point or points and the opinion of the majority shall be the order of the Divisional Forum.

(3) Subject to the foregoing provisions the procedure relating to the conduct of the meetings of the Divisional Forum, its sitting and other matters shall be such as may be prescribed by the Government.

Appeal

13. Any person aggrieved by an order made by the Divisional Forum may prefer an appeal against such order to the State Commission within a period of thirty days from the date of the order in such form and manner as may be prescribed:

Provided that the State Commission may entertain an appeal after the expiry of the said period of 30 days if it is satisfied that there was sufficient cause for not filing it within that period:

Provided further that no appeal shall lie unless the memorandum of appeal is accompanied by a certificate issued by the President Divisional Forum to the effect that appellant has deposited with him 25% of the amounts payable under the order.

Composition of the State Commission

14. (1) Each State Commission shall consist of—

(a) a person who is or has been a Judge of a High Court, appointed by the Government, who shall be its President.

(b) two or more members who shall be persons of ability, integrity and having profound knowledge of law and experience in law and consumer affairs:

Provided that every appointment made under this section shall be made by the Government on the recommendation of the Selection Committee consisting of the following namely;—

(i)	Chief Secretary	...	Chairman
(ii)	Secretary to Government, Law Department	...	Member
(iii)	Secretary to Government, Food and Supplies Department (In-charge Consumer Affairs)	...	Member

(2) The salary or honorarium and other allowances payable to, and the other terms and conditions of service (including tenure of office) of the members of the State Commission shall be as such as may be prescribed by the Government.

Jurisdiction of the State Commission

15. Subject to the other provisions of this Act, the State Commission shall have jurisdiction —

(a) to entertain—

(i) complaints where the value of the goods or service and compensations, if any, claimed exceeds Rupees 5.00 lacs but does not exceed Rupees 30.00 lacs; and

(ii) appeals against the orders of Divisional Forum within the State; and

(b) to call for the records and pass appropriate orders in any consumer dispute which is pending before or has been decided by any Divisional Forum within the State, where it appears to the State Commission that such Divisional Forum has exercised a jurisdiction not vested in it by law or has failed to exercise, jurisdiction so vested or has acted in exercise of its jurisdiction illegally or with material irregularity.

Procedure applicable to the State Commission

16. The procedure specialised in sections, 10, 11 and 12 and under the rules made thereunder for the disposal of complaints by the Divisional Forum shall, with such modifications as may be necessary be applicable for the disposal of disputes by the State Commission.

Validity of orders

16A. Notwithstanding anything contained in section 16. No order passed by the State Commission and Divisional Forum shall be called in question simply on the ground that it has not been signed by all the members of the Divisional Forum or State Commission on the case may be and all such orders shall have and shall always be deemed to have been valid if signed by Majority of the members.

Appeals

17. Any person aggrieved by any order by the State Commission in exercise of its powers conferred by sub-clause (1) of clause (a) of section 15 may prefer an appeal against such order to the High Court within a period of thirty days from the date of the order in such form and manner as may be prescribed:

Provided that such appeal shall be heard by not less than two judges of the High Court:

Provided further that the High Court may entertain an appeal after the expiry of the said period of thirty days if it is satisfied that there was sufficient cause for not filing it within that period:

Provided also that no appeal shall lie unless the memorandum of appeal is accompanied by a certificate issued by the Chairman State Commission to the effect that the appellant has deposited 25 % of the amount payable under the order.

Finality or orders

18. Every order of a Divisional Forum, or the State Commission shall if no appeal had been preferred against such order under the provisions of this Act, be final.

Limitation period

18A. (1) The Divisional Forum or the State Commission may not admit a complaint unless it is filed within two years from the date on which the cause of action arises.

(2) Notwithstanding anything contained in sub-section (1), a complaint may be entertained after the period specified in sub-section (1) if the complainant satisfies the Divisional Forum or the State Commission, as the case may be, that he had sufficient cause for not filing the complaint within such period:

Provided that no such complaint shall be entertained unless the Divisional Forum or the State Commission, as the case may be, records its reason for condoning such delay.

Enforcement of order by the Forum or the State Commission

19. Every order made by the Divisional Forum, or the State Commission may be enforced by the Divisional Forum or the State Commission as the case may be in the same manner as if it were a decree or order made by a court in a suit pending therein and it shall by lawful for the Divisional Forum or the State Commission to send in the event of its inability to execute it, such order to the court within the local limits of jurisdiction—

(a) in the case of an order against a company, the registered office of the company is situated, or

(b) in the case of an order against any other person, the place where the person concerned voluntarily resides or carries on business or personally works for gain, is situated, and thereupon the court to which the order is so sent, shall execute the orders as if it were a decree or order sent to it for execution.

Dismissal of frivolous or vexatious complaints

20. Where a complaint instituted the Divisional Forum or the State Commission as the case may be is found to be frivolous or vexatious, it shall, for reasons to be recorded in writing, dismiss the complaint and make an order that the complainant shall pay to the opposite party such cost not exceeding ten thousand rupees, as may be specified in the order.

Penalties

21. Where a Trader or a person against whom the complaint is made or fails or omits to comply with any order made by the Divisional Forum or the State Commission, as the case may be, such trader or person shall be punishable with imprisonment for a term which shall not be less than one month but which may be extend to three years, or with fine which shall not be less than two thousand rupees but which may extend to ten thousand rupees, or with both:

Provided that the Divisional Forum, or the State Commission, as the case may be, may, if it is satisfied that the circumstances of any case so require, impose a sentence of imprisonment or fine, or both, for a term lesser than the minimum term and amount lesser than the minimum amount, specified in this section.

MISCELLANEOUS

Protection of action taken is in good faith

22. No suit, prosecution or other legal proceedings shall lie against the members of the Divisional Forum or the State Commission or any Officer or reason acting under the direction of the Divisional Forum or the State Commission for executing any order made by it or in respect of anything which is in good faith done or intended to be done by such member, officer or person under this Act, or under any rule or order made thereunder.

Power to remove difficulties

23. (i) If any difficulty arises in giving effect to the provisions of this Act, the Government may by order in the Government Gazette make such provisions nor inconsistent with the provisions of this Act as appear to it to be necessary or expedient for removing the difficulty:

Provided that no such order shall be, made after the expiry of a period of two years from the commencement of this Act.

(ii) Every order made under this section shall, as soon as may be after it is made, be laid before each House of the State Legislature.

Vacancies of defects in appointment not to invalidate orders

23A. No act or proceeding of the Divisional Forum or the State Commission, as the case may be, shall be invalid by reason only of the existence of any vacancy amongst its member or any defect in the constitution thereof,

Power to make rules

24. The Government may, by notification make rules for carrying out the provisions contained in clause *(b)* of sub-section (2) of section 4, sub-section (2) of section 5, sub-section (3) of section 8, clause *(c)* of sub-section (3) and clause (h)of sub-section (4) of section 11, sub-section (3) of section 12, section 13, sub-section (2) of section 11 of this Act.

Laying of rules

25. Every rule made by the Government under this Act shall be laid, as soon as, may be after it is made, before each House of State Legislature, while it is in session, for a total period of thirty days which may be comprised in one session or in two or more successive sessions, and if, before the expiry of the session immediately following the session or the successive session aforesaid, both Houses agree in making any modification in the rule or both houses agree that the rule should not be made, the rule shall thereafter have effect only in such modified form or be of no effect, as the case may be, so, however, that any such modification or annulment shall be without prejudice to the validity of anything previously done under that rule.

SRO 86, dated 10-3-1988 *-In exercise, of the powers conferred by section 24 of the Jammu and Kashmir Consumer Protection Act, 1987 (Act No. XV! of 1987), the Government hereby make the following rules, namely:—* **Short title and commencement.**

1. (1) These rules may be called the Jammu and Kashmir Consumer Protection Rules, 1987.

(2) They shall come into force from the date of their publication in the Government Gazette.

Definitions

2. In these rules, unless the context otherwise require —

(a) "Act" means the Jammu and Kashmir Consumer Protection Act, 1987;

(b) "Agent" means a person duly authorised by a party to present any complaint, appeal or reply on its behalf before the State Commission;

(c) "Appellant" means a party which makes an appeal against the order of the Divisional Forum;

(d) "Chairman" means the Chairman of the State Consumer Protection Council established under section 4 of the Act;

(e) "Memorandum" means any memorandum of appeal filed by the appellant;

(f) "Opposite party" means a person who answers complaint or claim;

(g) "Respondent" means a person who answers any memorandum of appeal;

(h) "Section" means section of the Act;

(i) "Words and expressions" used in the rules but not defined herein shall have the same meanings as assigned to them in the Act.

The Constitution of the State Consumer Protection Council

3. (1) The Government may by notification in the Government Gazette establish the State Consumer Protection Council which in addition to the Chairman shall consist of the following members, namely—

(a)	The Minister of State for Food and Supplies Department	....	Vice-Chairman.
(b)	One Member from Legislative Assembly and Two from Legislative Council	....	Members
(c)	Three Representatives of Autonomous Organisations concerned with Consumer interests	....	Members
(d)	Three Representatives of the Consumer Organisation or Consumers	....	Members
(e)	Two Representatives of Women	....	Members
(f)	Three Representatives of Farmers, Traders and Industrialists, one from each category	....	Members
(g)	Three persons capable to represent Consumer interests not specified above		Members
(h)	The Secretary to Government, Food and Supplies Department.	....	Member-Secretary.

Procedure of the State Council

4. (i) The Stale Council shall observe the following procedure in regard to the transaction of its business—

(a) The meeting of the State Council shall be presided over by the Chairman, in his absence by the Vice-Chairman, in the absence of the Chairman and the Vice-Chairman the Council shall elect a member to preside over the meeting.

(b) Each meeting of the State Council shall be called by giving not less than ten days notice in writing to every member.

(c) The notice shall specify the place, the day, hour and statement of business to be transacted thereat.

(d) No proceedings of the State Council shall be held invalid merely by reasons of any vacancy or defect in the constitution of the Council.

(e) For the purpose of performing its functions under the Act, the State Council may constitute from amongst its members, such working groups as it may deem necessary and every working group so constituted shall perform such functions as are assigned to it by the State Council. The findings of such working groups shall be placed before the State Council for its consideration.

(f) The non-official members shall be entitled to A-class to and for Bus fare and an allowance of one hundred rupees per day for attending the meetings of the State Council or any working group. Members of Legis-lature shall be entitled to travelling and daily allowances at such rates as are admissible to such members under the Salaries and Allowances of Members of Jammu and Kashmir State Legislature Act, 1966.

(g) The resolution passed by the State Council shall be recommendatory in nature.

Term of Office of the State Council

5. *(i)* The term of office of the members shall be three years.

(ii) Any member may, in writing under his hand addressed to the Chairman of the State Council, resign from the Council. The vacancies, so caused or otherwise, shall be filled up from the same category by the Government and such member shall hold office so long as the member in whose place he is appointed would have been entitled to hold office had the vacancy not occurred.

The Salary or Honorarium and other allowance payable to the members of the Divisional Forum

6. *(i)* Under sub-section (3) sitting of section 8 where the President of the Divisional Forum is a sitting Judge of the Session Court, he shall enjoy all the benefits which he should have enjoyed as sitting Judge of the Session Court. Where the

President is not a sitting Judge of the Session Court, he shall receive a honorarium equivalent to the amount of salary as he was drawing at the time of his retirement *minus* the pension per month. Other members, if sitting on whole time basis, shall receive a consolidated honorarium of ₹ 1,500 per month or if sitting on part time basis, a consolidated honorarium of ₹ 50 per day per sitting.

(*ii*) The President and the members shall be entitled to travelling and daily allowances on official tours at the same rates as are admissible to Class II Officers of the Government,

Terms and conditions of service of the President and Members of the Divisional Forum

7. (*i*) Prior to appointment, the President and the Members of the Divisional Forum shall have to give an undertaking to the effect that he does not and will nol have any such financial or other interest as is likely to affect prejudicially his functions as such.

(*ii*) The President and the Members shall hold office for a period not exceeding 5 years or up to the age of 62 years whichever is earlier, but shall not eligible for reappointment.

(*iii*) Notwithstanding anything contained in sub-rule (*if*) the President or a Member may—

(*a*) by writing under his hand address to the Government resign his office at any time.

(*b*) be removed from his office in accordance with the provisions of rule 13.

(*iv*) The terms and conditions of service of the President and the Members shall not be varied to their disadvantage during their tenure of office.

(*v*) A casual vacancy caused by resignation or removal of the President or any member of the Divisional Forum shall be filled by fresh appointment.

(*vi*) Where any such casual vacancy occurs in the office of the President of the Divisional Forum, the senior-most Member (in order of appointment) holding office for the time being, shall discharge the functions of the President until a person appointed to fill such vacancy assumes the office of the President of the Divisional Forum.

(*vii*) When the President of the Divisional Forum is unable to discharge the functions owing to absence, illness or any other case, the senior-most Member (in order of appointment) shall discharge the functions of the President until the day on which the President assumes the charge of his functions.

(*viii*) No act or proceeding of the Divisional Forum shall be held invalid by reason of any vacancy of its President or Member or any defect in the constitution thereof.

(*ix*) In case of a difference of opinion among the Members of the Divisional Forum, the opinion of the majority shall prevail.

(*x*) The President or any Member ceasing to hold office as such shall not hold any appointment in or be connected with the management or administration of an organisation which has been the subject of any proceedings under the Act during his tenure for a period of 5 years from the date on which he ceases to hold such office.

Manager prescribed under clause (c) of sub-section (1) of section 11

8. (1) Samples of goods for test or analysis shall be sent by the Divisional Forum by registered post in a sealed packet, enclosed, together with a memorandum in Form 1, in a outer cover addressed to the.....

(2) The packet as well as the outer cover, shall be marked with a distinguishing number.

(3) A copy of the memorandum in Form 1 and a specimen impression of the seal used to seal the packet shall be sent separately by registered post to the ....

(4) On receipt of the packet is shall be opened by an officer authorised in writing in that behalf by the... who shall record the condition of the seal on the packet.

(5) After test or analysis, the result of the test or analysis together with full protocols of the tests applied shall be supplied forthwith to the Divisional Forum in Form 2.

Procedure of the Divisional Forum

9. (*i*) Under sub-section (3) of section 12 of the Act, the office of the Divisional Forum shall be located in two divisions i.e., Jammu/Kashmir. Working days and office hours of the Divisional Forum shall be the same as that of the State Government.

(*ii*) The Divisional Forum shall observe the following procedure in regard to the transaction of its business.

(*iii*) The meeting of the Divisional Forum shall be presided over by the President. In his absence the senior-most member (in order of appointment) shall preside over the meeting.

(iv) Each meeting of the Divisional Forum shall be called by giving not less than 10 days notice in writing to every member.

(v) The notice shall specify the place, the day, hour and statement of business to be transacted thereat.

Procedure for hearing the appeal

10. *(i)* Under section 13 of the Act memorandum shall be presented by the appellant or his agent to the State Commission in person or be sent by registered post addressed to the Commission.

(ii) Every memorandum filed under sub-rule (1) shall be in legible handwriting preferably typed and shall set forth concisely under distinct heads, the grounds of appeal without any argument or narrative and such grounds shall be numbered consecutively.

(iii) Each memorandum shall be accompanied by a certified copy of the order of the Divisional Forum appealed against and such of the documents as may be required to support grounds of the memorandum.

(iv) When the appeal is presented after the expiry of the period of limitation as specified in the Act, the memorandum of appeal shall be accompanied by an application supported by an affidavit setting forth the facts on which the appellant relies to satisfy the State Commission that he has sufficient cause for not preferring the appeal with the period of limitation.

(v) The appellant shall submit six copies of the memorandum of appeal to the Commission for official purpose.

(vi) On the date of hearing or on any other day to which hearing may be adjourned, it shall be obligatory for the parties or their agents to appear before the State Commission. If appellant, or his agent fails to appear on such date, the State Commission may, on its discretion, either dismiss the appeal or decide *ex parte* on merits. If the respondent or his agent fails to appear on such date, the Slate Commission shall proceed *ex parte* and shall decide the appeal on merits of the case.

(vii) The appellant shall not, except by leave of the State Commission, argue or be heard in support of any objection not set forth in the memorandum but the State Commission. While deciding an appeal, may not confine to the grounds of objection set forth in the memorandum:

Provided that the Commission shall not rest its decision on any other ground other than those specified in the memorandum unless the party who may be affected thereby, has been given, an opportunity of being heard by the State Commission.

(viii) The State Commission, on such terms as it may think fit and at any stage, adjourn the hearing of the appeal, but not more than one adjustment shall ordinarily be given and the appeal should be decided as far as possible, within 90 days from the first date of hearing,

(ix) The order of the State Commission on appeal shall be signed and dated by the Members of the State Commission and shall be communicated to the parties free of charge.

Salaries, honorarium and other allowances of the President and Members of the State Commission

11. *(i)* Where the President of the State Commission is a sitting Judge of the Hon'ble High Court, he shall enjoy all the benefits which he should have enjoyed as sitting Judge of the Hon'ble High Court where the President is not a sitting Judge of High Court he shall receive a honorarium equivalent to the amount of salary as he was drawing at the time of his retirement *minus* the pension per month. Other Members, if sitting on whole-time basis, shall receive a consolidated honorarium of ₹ 3,000 per month or if sitting on part-time basis, a consolidated honorarium of ₹ 100 per day per sitting.

(ii) The President and the members shall be entitled to travelling and daily allowances on official tours at the same rates as are admissible to Class I Officer of the Government,

(iii) The honorarium or the salary, as the case may be, and other allowances shall be defrayed out of the contingency fund of the Government.

Terms and conditions of service of the President and Members of the State Commission

12. *(i)* Prior to their appointment, the President and the Members of the State Commission shall have to give an undertaking to the effect that he does not and will not have any financial or other interest as is likely to affect prejudicially his functions as such.

(ii) The President and the members shall hold office for a period of not exceeding 5 years or such period as may be specified by the Government in the notification, but shall be eligible for reappointment:

Provided that the President or a Member shall not hold office as such for a total period exceeding 10 years or after he attains the age of 65 years whichever is earlier.

(iii) Notwithstanding anything contained in sub-rule *(ii)* the President or a Member may —

(a) by writing under his hand addressed to the Government resign his office at any time;

(b) be removed from his office in accordance with the provisions of rule 13.

(iv) The terms and conditions of service of the President and the Members shall not be varied to their disadvantage during their tenure of office.

(v) Any causal vacancy caused by resignation or removal of the President or any other member of the State Commission under sub-rule (3) or otherwise shall be filled of by fresh appointment.

(vi) Where any such casual vacancy occurs in the office of the President of the State Commission, the senior-most Member (in order of appointment) holding office for the time being, shall discharge the functions of the President until a person appointed to fill such vacancy assumes the office of the President of the State Commission.

(vii) When the President of the State Commission is unable to discharge the functions owing to absence, illness or any other cause, the senior-most Member (in order of appointment) shall discharge the functions of the President until the day on which the President resumes the charge of his functions.

(viii) No act or proceedings of the State Commission shall be held invalid by reason of any vacancy of its President or Members or any defect in the constitution thereof.

(ix) In case of any difference of opinion among the members of the State Commission opinion of the majority shall prevail.

(x) The President or any Member ceasing to hold office as such shall not hold any appointment in or be connected with the management on administration of an organisation which has been the subject of any proceedings under the Act during his tenure for a period of 5 years from the dale on which he ceases to hold such office.

Removal of President or Members from office in certain circumstances

13. *(i)* The Government may remove from office, the President or any Member who—

(a) has been adjudged an insolvent; or

(b) has been convicted of an offence which in the opinion of the Government involves moral turpitude; or

(c) has become physically or mentally incapable of acting as the President or the Member; or

(d) has acquired such financial or other interests as is likely to affect prejudicially his functions as the President or a Member; or

(e) has so abused his position as to render his continuance in office prejudicial to the public interest.

(ii) Notwithstanding anything contained in sub-rule (1) the President or any Member shall not be removed from his office on the grounds specified in clauses *(d)* and *(e)* of sub-rule except on an inquiry held by the Government in accordance with such procedure as it may specify in this behalf.

By order of the Government of Jammu and Kashmir.

(Sd.)...........
Secretary to Government, Food, Supplies and
Transport Department

....

FORM 1

[*See* rule 8]

Memorandum to the Laboratory

Serial Number : ....

To the .... Laboratory...

From........................

I send herewith, under the provisions of clause (c) of sub-section (1) of section 11 of the Jammu and Kashmir Consumers Protection Act, 1987 sample(s) of good(s) purporting to be for test or analysis and request that a. report of the result of the test or analysis may be supplied to............................

2. The distinguishing number on the packet is..............
3. Particulars of offence alleged............................
4. Matter on which opinion is required...................
5. A fee of ₹...................has been deposited in..........................

Dated :................. Senders Name

FORM 2

[*See* rule 8]

Certificate of test or analysis by the .... Laboratory. Certified that the good(s) bearing number.. purporting to be a sample of.. received on .... with Memorandum No............ .... dated .... from.............................. has been tested/ analysed and that the result of such test/analysis is as stated below;

2. The condition of the seals on the packet on receipt was as follows :—

3. In the opinion of the undersigned, the sample of the good(s) is ....for the reasons given below :—

Dated :.............. ....Laboratory

Details of results of test or analysis with protocols of the test applied,

..................................Laboratory

Chapter 18

Karnataka Consumer Protection Rules, 1988

[GSR 256, Dated 4-11-1988]

In exercise of the powers conferred by sub-section (2) of section 30 of the Consumer Protection Act, 1986 (68 of 1986), the Government of Karnataka hereby makes the following rules, namely— **Short title and commencement.**

1. (1) These rules may be called the Karnataka Consumer Protection Rules, 1988.

(2) They shall come into force[1] on the date of their publication in the Official Gazette.

Definitions

2. In these rules, unless the context otherwise requires,—

(*a*) "Act" means the Consumer Protection Act, 1986 (68 of 1986).

(*b*) "Section" means section of the Act.

Salaries and other allowances and terms and conditions of the service of the President and Members of the District Forum

3. (1) The President of the District Forum shall receive the salary of a District Judge if appointed on whole time basis or honorarium of rupees two hundred per day, if appointed on part time basis. Other members, if appointed on whole time basis, shall receive a consolidated honorarium of rupees three thousand per month and if appointed on part time basis, shall receive a consolidated honorarium of rupees one hundred and fifty per day of sitting.

(2) The President and the members of the District Forum shall be entitled for such travelling allowance and daily allowance on official tour as are admissible to the officer of Category I of the State Government.

(3) The salary, honorarium and other allowances shall be defrayed out of the consolidated fund of the State.

(4) Before appointment, the President and the members of the District Forum shall give an undertaking in writing that they do not and will not have any financial dealings or other interest which is likely to affect prejudicially their functions as such President or member, as the case may be.

(5) The State Government may remove from office the President or member of a District Forum, if he—

(*a*) has been adjudged an insolvent; or

(*b*) has been convicted of an offence which in the opinion of the State Government, involves moral turpitude; or

(*c*) has become physically or mentally incapable of acting as such President or member; or

(*d*) has acquired such financial or other interest as it likely to affect prejudicially his functions as such President or member; or

(*e*) has so abused his position as to render his continuance in office prejudicial to the public interest; or

(*f*) absents for three consecutive sittings without obtaining permission of the President, in the case of member and the State Government in the case of President:

Provided that no order of removal from office of the President or member on the ground specified in clauses *(d)* and *(e)* shall be made unless the President or the member, as the case may be, has been given an opportunity of being heard.

(5A) The President, in the case of member and the State Government in the case of the President, may sanction leave:

Provided that a District Judge appointed as President on deputation shall be covered by the leave rules applicable to him:

Provided further that a retired District Judge appointed as President shall avail leave in accordance with the provisions of Karnataka Civil Services Rules:

Provided also that a member shall be entitled for leave not exceeding fifteen days in a calendar year with honorarium but such leave with or without honorarium shall not exceed five days at a time excluding general holidays.

(6) The terms and conditions of service of the President and members of the District Forum shall not be varied to their disadvantage during their tenure of office.

(7) and (8) [on offer *vide Notification No. PCS 151 SLF 97, dated 11-4-1998*].

(9) The President or any member after ceasing to hold office, shall not hold any appointment in or be connected with the management or administration of an organisation which had been subjected to any proceeding under the Act during his tenure, for a period of five years from the date on which he ceases to hold such office.

Place of sitting and procedure as to conduct meeting, etc., of District Forum

4. (1) The Office of the District Forum shall be located at the headquarters of the District. Where State Government decides to establish a single District Forum having jurisdiction over more than one District, it shall notify the place and jurisdiction of the District Forum so established.

(2) The working days and office hours of the District Forum shall be the same as that of the offices of the State Government.

(3) The official seal and emblem of the District Forum shall be such as the State Government may specify.

(4) Sitting of the District Forum as and when necessary, shall be fixed by the President.

(5) No act or proceedings of the District Forurn shall be invalid by reason only of the existence of any vacancy in the office of members or any defect in its constitution.

(6) The State Government shall appoint such staff as may be necessary to assist the District Forum in its day to day work and to perform such other functions as are **Provided** under the Act or the rules framed thereunder, or assigned to them by the President. The salary payable to the staff shall be defrayed out of the Consolidated Fund of the State.

(7) In case where the opposite party admits the allegations made by the complainant, the District Forum shall decide such complaint on merits and on the basis of documents produced.

(8) If during the proceedings conducted under section 13, the District Forum fixes a date for hearing of the parties, it shall be obligatory on the part of the complainant and the opposite party or their authorised agent to appear before the District Forum on such date of hearing or any other date to which hearing would be adjourned. Where the complainant or his authorised agent fails to appear before the date specified above, the District Forum may in its discretion either dismiss the complaint for default or decide it on merit. Where the opposite party or its authorised agent fails to appear on the date of hearing, the District Forum may decide the complaint *ex parte.*

(9) While proceeding under sub-rule (8), the District Forum may, at any time and on such terms as it may think fit, adjourn the hearing of the complaint but not more than one adjournment shall ordinarily be granted. The complaint shall be decided as for as possible within ninety days from the date of notice received by the opposite party where complaint does not require analysis or testing of the goods and within one hundred and fifty days if it requires analysis or testing of the goods.

(10) Order of the District Forum shall be signed and dated by the President and members of the District Forum and shall be communicated to the parties.

Manner of authentication of samples

5. (1) The samples of the goods received under clause *(c)* of sub-section (1) of section 13, shall be affixed with lables containing—

(i) the name and address of the appropriate laboratory to whom the sample will be sent for analysis and test;

(ii) the name and address of the District Forum; and mil the case number.

(2) The sample shall be authenticated by putting on the label the seal of the District Forum with signature of an officer authorised by the District Forum in this behalf.

Salary and other allowances, and terms and conditions of service of the President and members of the State Commission

6. (1) The President of the State Commission shall receive the salary of a judge of the High Court, if appointed on whole time basis, or a consolidated honorarium of rupees two hundred per day of the sitting if appointed on part lime basis. Other members appointed on the whole time basis, shall receive a consolidated honorarium of rupees three thousand per month and if appointed im part time basis a consolidated honorarium of rupees one hundred and fifty per day of sitting.

(2) The President and the members of the State Commission shall be eligible for such travelling allowance and daily allowance on official tour as are admissible on the Category of Officers of the State Government.

(3) The salary, honorarium and other allowances shall be defrayed out of the consolidated fund of the State.

(4) [*Omitted vide Notification No. PCS 76 SLF 93, dated 8-6-1994*\].

(5) The President or member of the State Commission may—

(a) by writing under his hand and addressed to the State Government resign his office at any time; or

(b) be removed from office in accordance with the provisions of sub-rule (6).

(6) The State Government may remove from office the President or a member of the State Commission who—

(a) has been adjudged an insolvent, or

(b) has been convicted of an offence which in the opinion of the State Government, involves moral turpitude, or

(c) has become physically or mentally incapable of acting as such President or Member, or

(d) has acquired such financial or other interest as is likely to affect prejudicially his functions as such President or member, or

(e) has so abused his position as to render his continuance in office prejudicial to the public, interest:

Provided that no order of removal from office of the President or a member on the ground specified in clauses *(d)* and *(e)* of sub-rule (6) shall be made unless the President or member as the case may be has been given an opportunity of being heard.

(7) Before appointment, President and the members of the State Commission shall have to give an undertaking that they do not and will not have any such financial or other interests as is likely to affect prejudicially their functions as such president or member as the case may be.

(8) The terms and conditions of service of the President and the members of the State Commission shall not be varied to their disadvantage during their tenure of office.

(9) Every Vacancy caused by resignation, removal or otherwise of the President or any other member of the State Commission shall be filled by fresh appointment.

(10) and (11) [*Omitted vide Notification No. PCS 151 SLF 99, dated 11-4-1998*].

(12) The President or any member ceasing to hold office shall not hold any appointment in, or be connected with the management or administrations of, any organisation which has been subjected to any proceeding under the Act during his tenure, for a period of five years from the date on which he ceases to hold such office.

Appeal

7. (1) Every appeal preferred under section 15 shall be in the form of a memorandum and be presented by the appellant or his authorised agent to the State Commission in person or be sent by registered post addressed to theCommission.

(2) Every memorandum filed under sub-rule (1) shall set forth concisely under distinct heads, the grounds of appeal and shall be numbered consecutively-

(3) Each memorandum shall be accompanied by a certified copy of the order of the District Forum appealed against and such of the documents as may be required to support the grounds urged in the memorandum.

(4) When the appeal is presented after the expiry of the period of limitation as specified in the Act, the memorandum shall be accompanied by an application supported by an affidavit setting forth the facts on which the appellant relies to satisfy the State Commission that he has sufficient cause for not prefer the appeal within the period of limitation,

(5) The appellant shall submit four copies of the memorandum to the State Commission for official purposes.

Chapter 19

Kerala Consumer Protection Rules, 1998

[S.R.O. No. 566/98, Dated 5-6-1998]

In exercise of the powers conferred by sub-section (2) of section 30 of the Consumer Protection Act, 1986 (68 of 1986) and in supersession of the Consumer Protection (Kerala) Rules, 1987, published under Notification No. 377/C1/87/F&CSD dated the 16th October, 1987as S.R.O. No. 1373/87 in the Kerala Gazette Extraordinary No. 822 dated the 16th October, 1987, as subse-quently amended, the Government of Kerala hereby make the following Rules, namely :—

SHORT TITLE AND COMMENCEMENT

1. (1) These rules may be called the Kerala Consumer Protection Rules, 1998.

(2) They shall come into force at once.

Definitions

2. In these rules, unless the context otherwise requires,—

(*a*) "Act" means the Consumer Protection Act, 1986;

(*b*) "agent" means a person duly authorised by a party to present any complaint, appeal or revision or other petition or reply on his/her behalf before the State Commission or the District Forum;

(*c*) "appellant" means a party who makes an appeal against the order of the District Forum;

(*d*) "Government" means the Government of Kerala;

(*e*) "memorandum" means memorandum of appeal filed by the appellant;

(*f*) "opposite party" means a person who has to answer a complaint or a claim;

(*g*) "President" means the President of the State Commission or the District Forum, as the case may be;

(*h*) "respondent" means a person who has to answer any memorandum ot appeal;

(*i*) "section" means a section of the Act; (*f*) "State" means the State of Kerala; (&) words and expressions used but not defined in these rules, but denned the Act, shall have the meanings, respectively assigned to them in the Act

Composition of the State Consumer Protection Council

3. (1) The Consumer Protection Council for the State of Kerala established under section 7 of the Act, (hereinafter referred to as the State Council) shall consist of the following members, namely:—

(*a*) the Minister in charge of Consumer Affairs in the State of Kerala who shall be the Chairman;

(*b*) ten members of the Kerala Legislative Assembly, nominated by the Government;

(*c*) five representatives of the Government Departments and Undertakings concerned with consumer interests, nominated by the Government;

(*d*) seven representatives of the Consumer Organisations is the State, seven nominated by the Government, of whom three shall be women;

(e) five representatives of farmers, manufacturers, traders and industrialists, five nominated by the Government;

(f) five representatives of the recognised trade unions of the State nominated by the Government;

(g) three persons capable of representing consumer interests in the State other than those specified above, three nominated by the Government;

(h) the Commissioner of Civil Supplies—*ex-officio;*

(f) the Secretary to Government of Kerala, Food and Civil Supplies Department—*ex-officio;*

(f) the Director off Civil Supplies, Kerala—*ex-officio;*

(k) the Secretary, Consumer Disputes Redressal Commission—*ex-officio;*

(l) the additional Secretary to Government, Food and Civil Supplies Department, who shall be the Member Secretary of the State Council.

(2) The term of office, of the nominated members, shall be three years from the date of their nomination of such member,

(3) Any nominated member may, by writing under his hand addressed to the Chairman of the State Council, resign his office. Any casual vacancy that may arise due to resignation or otherwise of such a member shall be filled from among the same category and such person shall hold office only for the remainder of the term of office of the person in whose place he was nominated.

Procedure for the Meetings of the State Council

4. The State Council shall observe the following procedure with regard to the transaction of its business—

(1) Every meeting of the State Council shall be convened by the Member Secretary, in accordance with the directions of the Chairman.

(2) The meetings of the State Council shall be presided over by the Chairman. In the absence of the Chairman, the members present shall elect a person from among themselves to preside over that meeting.

(3) The quorum for a meeting of the State council shall be ten.

(4) Every meeting of the State Council shall be called only after giving not less than seven days notice in writing of the date of meeting, to each member:

Provided that a meeting of the State Council may be convened with less than seven days notice if the circumstances so warrant. However each member shall be informed of the date, time and place of meeting sufficiently early so that he could attend the same.

(5) Every notice of the meeting of the State Council shall specify the place, date and hour of the meeting and shall contain a statement of the business to be transacted thereof.

(6) No proceedings of the State Council shall be invalid merely by reason of the existence of any vacancy in, or any defect in the constitution of the Council.

(7) For the purpose of performing its functions under the Act, the State Council may constitute, from amongst its members, such working groups as it may deem necessary and each such working group so constituted shall perform such functions as are assigned to it by the State Council, for its consideration.

(8) The resolutions passed by the State Council shall be recommendatory in nature.

(9) The non-official members other than the members of the Legislative Assembly shall be eligible for travelling allowance and daily allowance for attending the meetings of the State Council as are admissible to Class I Officers of the State Government. Members of the State Legislative Assembly shall be entitled to travelling and daily allowances at such rates as are admissible to them under the Payment of Salaries and Allowances Act (14 of 1951). On receipt of a claim, payment of travelling allowance to non-official members shall be made by the Secretary of the State Commission from the Travelling Allowance Head of Account of the Consumer Disputes Redressal Commission.

Location of Office and Other Matters Relating to State Commission

5. (1) The Office of the State Commission shall beat Thiruvananthapuram.

(2) The working days and office hours of the Office of the State Commission shall be the same as that of the Offices of the State Government.

(3) The Official seal and emblem of the State Commission shall be such as the Government may specify.

(4) The President of the State Commission shall be the Head of Office and shall have administrative control over the staff of the State Commission and Fora and shall have disciplinary control over the staff subject to the provisions contained in rule 19 of the Kerala Civil Services (Classification, Control and Appeal) Rules, 1960.

(5) Sittings of the State Commission shall be convened by the President. The sittings shall ordinarily be at the Office of the State Commission;

Provided however that sittings may also be convened at other centres also according to necessity.

(6) The State Government shall appoint such staff, as may be necessary, to assist the State Commission in its day-today work and perform such other functions as are

Provided under the Act of these rules or assigned to them by President.

(7) Where the opposite party admits the allegations made by the complainant in a complaint filed before it, the State Commission shall decide the complaint on the basis of the merit of the case, based on the documents presented before it.

(8) If during the proceedings conducted under section 13 of the Act, the State Commission fixes a date for hearing of the parties, it shall be obligatory on the part of the complainant and the opposite party or their authorised agent to appear before the State Commission on such date or on any other, date to which the hearing stands adjourned. When the complainant or his authorised agent fails to appear before the State Commission on such date, the State Commission may, in its discretion, either dismiss the complaint for default or decide it on merits. Where the opposite party or his authorised agent fails to appear on the day of hearing, the State Commission may decide the complaint *ex parte.*

(9) While proceeding, under sub-rule (8), the State Commission may, on such terms, as it may think fit, and at any stage adjourn the hearing of the complaint, but not more than three adjournments shall ordinarily be given, and the complaint shall be decided within 90 days from the date of receipt of notice by the opposite party, where the complaint does not require analysis or testing of the goods and within 150 days, if analysis or testing of goods is required.

Salary honorarium and other allowances and the terms and conditions of appointment of the President and members of the State Commission

6. (1) The President of the State Commission shall be entitled to salary, allowances and other perquisites as are admissible to a sitting Judge of the High Court, if appointed on whole-time basis or to an honorarium of ₹ 500 per day for each sitting if appointed on part-time basis. The other members, if appointed on whole time basis, shall receive a consolidated honorarium of ₹ 10,000 per month or if appointed on part-time basis, an honorarium of ₹ 400 per day for each sitting.

(2) The President shall be entitled to travelling and daily allowance for the official tour conducted by him at the same rates as are admissible to sitting Judge of the High Court.

(3) The other members of the State Commission shall be entitled to travelling and daily allowances for the official tour conducted by them at the same rates as are admissible to a Class 1 Officer of the State Government. The members who are required to travel within a short distance, which do not render them eligible for daily allowances, shall receive a monthly conveyance allowance of ₹ 1,500. The members who are separately entitled to any other kind of Travelling Allowance or Dearness Allowance or **Provided** with departmental vehicle shall not be eligible for conveyance allowance. Conveyance allowance shall not be drawn during leave or holidays prefixed or suffixed to leave Conveyance allowance shall not be drawn for the days for which regular Travelling Allowance or Dearness Allowance is drawn.

(4) The President, who is not a sitting Judge of the High Court, and a member may,—

(*a*) by writing under his hand and addressed to the State Government resign his office at any time;

(*b*) be removed from his office in accordance with the provisions of rule 7.

(5) Before appointment, the President and each member of the State Commis-sion shall have to make a declaration to the effect that he does not have any financial or other interests as is likely to affect prejudicially his functions as the President or as such member.

(6) The terms and conditions of the services of the President and the members of the State Commission shall not be varied to their disadvantage during their tenure of office.

(7) A casual vacancy, caused by the resignation or removal or otherwise, of the President or any member of the State Commission shall be filled by fresh appointment.

Removal of President or Members from office in certain circumstances

7. The Government may remove from office, the President, who is not a sitting Judge of the High Court, or any member of the State Commission who,—

(a) has been adjudged as an insolvent; or

(B) has been convicted of an offence, which in the opinion of the Government, involves moral turpitude; or

(c) has become physically or mentally incapable of acting as the President or as such member; or

(d) has acquired such financial or other interest as is likely to affect prejudicially his functions as the President or as such member; or

(e) has so abused his position as to render his continuance in office prejudicial to public interest:

Provided that the President or a member shall not be removed from his office on the grounds specified in clauses *(d)* and *(e)* unless such grounds have proved on an inquiry held by the Government, in accordance with such procedure, as it may specify in this behalf.

The Location of Office and Other Matters Relating to District Forum

8. (1) The office of the District Forum shall be at the headquarters of the respective District or at such other places as may be notified by the Government. Where the Government decide to establish more than one District Forum in a District, it shall notify the headquarters and jurisdiction or each such District Forum, so established.

(2) The working days and the office hours of the Office of a District Forum shall be the same as that of the Offices of the State Government.

(3) The Official seal and emblem of the District Forum shall be such as the Government may specify.

(4) The President shall be the head of office of the District Forum and shall have administrative control subject to the provisions contained in rule 19 of 1 Kerala Civil Services (Classification, Control and Appeal) Rules, 1960, shall have disciplinary control over the staff.

(5) The sittings of a District Forum shall be convened by the President. The sittings shall ordinarily be at the office of the District Forum **Provided** however that sittings may also be convened at such other places also if necessary warrants.

(6) The State Government shall appoint such staff, as may be necessary, to assist the District Forum in its day to day work and to perform such other function as are **Provided** under the Act or these Rules or assigned to them by the President.

(7) While entertaining a complaint under section 13, if the opposite party admits the allegation made by the complainant, the District Forum shall decide the complaint on the basis of the merits of the case based on the documents presented before it.

(8) If a District Forum, either *suo moto* or on the application of a party finds that it is not proper to try any complaint filed before it, the President of the Forum shall report the matter, giving reasons for the same, to the President of the State Commission for transfer of the case to some other District Forum in the State and the President of the State Commission shall pass appropriate orders on such requisition.

(9) If during the proceedings conducted under section 13, the District Forum fixes a date for hearing of the parties, it shall be obligatory on the complainant and the opposite party or their authorised agent to appear before the District Forum on such date or any other date to which the hearing stands adjourned. Where the complainant or his authorised agent fails to appear before the District Forum on such date, the District Forum may, in its discretion, either dismiss the complaint for default or decide it on merits. Where the opposite party or its authorised agent fails to appear on the day of hearing, the District Forum may decide the complaint *ex parte*.

(10) While proceeding under sub-rule (9) the District Forum may, on such terms as it may think fit and at any stage, adjourn the hearing of the complaint, but not more than three adjournments shall, ordinarily, be given, and the complaint should be decided within 90 days from the date of receipt of notice, by the opposite party where, the complaint does not require analysis or testing of the goods and within 150 days, if it requires analysis or testing of the goods.

Salary, Honorarium and Other Allowances and Terms and Conditions of the President and Members of the District Forum

9. (1) The President of a District Forum shall be entitled to salary and allowances at the following rates, namely: —

(a) if he is a sitting District Judge

(b) if he is a person qualified to be appointed as District Judge and is appointed —

(*i*) on full time basis Same salary and allowances to which he is entitled to as District Judge. Minimum of the pay in the scale of pay admissible to the District Judge plus allowances attached thereto.

(*ii*) on part-time basis

(c) if he is a retired District Judge, appointed on full time basis An honorarium of ₹ 400 per day for each sitting. Minimum of the pay and allowances in the scale of pay of the District Judge, less the amount of pension including dearness relief to which he is entitled to or the salary and allowances prescribed under rule 100 of Part 1C of the Kerala Service Rules or an honorarium of ₹ 7,500 per month, whichever is higher.

(2) The other members of the District forum, if appointed as full time members shall be entitled to a consolidated honorarium of ₹ 6,500 per month. If appointed as part-time members, they shall be entitled to an honorarium of ₹ 300 per day for each sitting.

(3) The President of a District Forum, if appointed on full time basis, shall be entitled to the leave admissible to the District Judge as per the Kerala Service Rules.

(4) The President, who is not a sitting Judge of the District Court, may:—

(*a*) by writing under his hand and addressed to the State Government resign his office at any time;

(*b*) be removed from his office in accordance with the provisions of rule 10.

(5) Before appointment, the President and members of a District Forum shall make a declaration to the effect that he does not have any financial or other interests as is likely to affect prejudicially his functions as the President or as such member.

(6) The terms and conditions of services of the President and the members shall not be varied to their disadvantage during their tenure of office.

(7) A casual vacancy in the District Forum caused by the resignation or removal or otherwise of the President or any members shall be filled by fresh appointment.

(8) The President or any member ceasing to hold office as such shall not hold any appointment in or connected with the management or administration or any organisation which have been the subject of any proceeding under the Act during his tenure for a period of 5 years from the date on which he ceases to hold such office.

Removal of the President or members from office in certain circumstances.

(9) The Government may remove from office, the President, who is not sitting judge of a District Court or a member of a District Forum who-

(*a*) has been adjudged as an insolvent; or

(*b*) has been convicted of an offence which, in the opinion of the Government involves moral turpitude; or

(*c*) has become physically or mentally incapable of acting as the President as such member; or

(*d*) has acquired such financial or other interest as is likely to affect prejudicially his functions as the President or as such member;

(*e*) has so abused his position as to render his continuance in office prejudicial to public interest:

Provided that the President or a member shall not be removed from his office on the grounds specified in clauses (*d*) and (*e*) unless such grounds have been proved on an inquiry held by Government in accordance with such procedure as it may specify in this behalf.

Procedure to be followed by the District Forum and the State Commission for Authentication of the Goods Obtained for Analysis

10. (1) The District Forum or, as the case may be, the State Commission, if consider necessary, direct the complainant to provide more than one sample of the goods in clean containers with stopper properly fixed on them.

(2) On receipt of the samples of such goods, the District Forum or, as the case may be, the State Commission shall seal it and fix labels on the containers carrying the following information—

(*i*) name and address of the appropriate laboratory to which sample shall be sent for analysis and test;

(*ii*) name and address of the District Forum or, as the case may be,

(*iii*) case number; and

(*iv*) Seal of the District Forum or as the case may be, the State Commission.

(3) After specifying the nature of the defect alleged, the sample shall be sent to the appropriate laboratory by the District Forum or as the case may be, the State Commission with a request to send the report within 45 days from the date of receipt of the same or within such extended time, as may be granted by the District Forum or, as the case may be, the State Commission.

Forum and Manner of Appeal Memorandum

11. (1) The memorandum of appeal shall be presented by the appellant or his authorised agent to the State Commission in person or shall be sent by registered post addressed to the President of the State Commission.

(2) Every memorandum of appeal filed under sub-rule (1) shall be legible, preferably typed and shall set forth concisely under distinct heads the grounds of appeal, without any argument or narration; and the grounds shall be numbered consecutively.

(3) Each memorandum of appeal shall be accompanied by a certified copy of the order of the District Forum appealed against and such other documents as pay be required in support of the grounds or objections mentioned in the Memorandum.

(4) When the appeal is presented after the expiry of the period of limitation as specified in the Act, the memorandum shall be accompanied by an application to condone the delay, supported by an affidavit setting forth the facts on which the appellant relies to satisfy the State Commission than he has sufficient cause for not preferring the appeal within the period of limitation.

(5) The appellant shall submit four copies of the memorandum of appeal to the State Commission for official purposes with additional copies of memorandum equivalent to the number of respondents. The appellant shall also submit additional copies of documents if so required by the Commission.

(6) On the date of hearing or on any other day to which hearing stands adjourned, it shall be obligatory for the parties or their authorised agents to appear before the State Commission. If appellant or his authorised agent fails to appear on such date, the State Commission may in its discretion, either dismiss the appeal or decide it on the merits of the case. If the respondent or his authorised agent fails to appear on such date, the State Commission shall decide the appeal *ex parte* on the merits of the case.

(7) The appellant shall not, except by leave of the State Commission, urge or be heard in support of any ground of objection not set forth in the memorandum of appeal but the State Commission in deciding the appeal, may not confine to the grounds of objection set forth in the memorandum of appeal or taken by leave of the State Commission under this rule:

Provided that the State Commission shall not rest any decision on any other grounds unless the party who may be affected thereby, has been given, at least an opportunity of being heard by the State Commission.

(8) The State Commission may, on such terms as it may think fit and at any stage, adjourn the hearing of the appeal, but not more than three adjournments shall, ordinarily, be given and the appeal shall be decided within 90 days from the first date of hearing.

(9) The orders of the State Commission, on complaint appeal revision or other petitions, shall be signed and dated by the President and the members of the State Commission constituting the Bench and shall be communicated to the parties free of charges.

Chapter 20

Lakshadweep Consumer Protection Rules, 1989

[F. No. 15/7/88-WM]

In exercise of the powers conferred by sub-section (2) of section 30 of the Consumer Protection Act, 1986 (68 of 1986), the Administrator, Union Territory of lakshadweep hereby makes the following rules namely —

SHORT TITLE AND COMMENCEMENT

1. (1) These rules may be called Lakshadweep Consumer Protection Rules, 1989.

(2) They shall come into force on such date as the Administrator may, by notification in the Official Gazette, prescribe.

Definitions

2. In these rules, unless the context otherwise requires —

(*a*) "Act" means the Consumer Protection Act, 1986 (68 of 1986);

(*b*) "agent" means a person duly authorised by a party to present any complaint or appeal or reply on its behalf before the State Commission or the District Forum;

(*c*) "appellant" means a party which makes an appeal against the order of the District Forum;

(*d*) "Memorandum" means memorandum of appeal filed by the appellant;

(*e*) "opposite party" means a person who answers complaint or claim;

(*f*) "President" means the president of the State Commission or District Forum as the case may be; Respondent" means the person who answers any memorandum or appeal;

(*g*) "Administrator" means Administrator of the Union Territory of Lakshadweep.

Salaries and other allowances and terms and conditions of the President and members of the District Forum

3. (1) President, District Forum may receive honorarium of ₹ 300 (three hundred) only per sitting subject to a minimum of ₹ 1,000 (one thousand) per month. Substituted by the Lakshadweep Consumer Protection (Amendment) Rules 1994 *w.e.f.* 30-3-1994. Other members of the Forum may receive honorarium of ₹ 100 (Rupees one hundred) only per day for each sitting of the Forum.

(2) The President and members of the District Forum shall be entitled for TA/DA on official tour as are admissible to Grade I Officers of the Central Government.

(3) The salary, honorarium and other allowances shall be defrayed out of the consolidated Fund of the Union Territory Government.

(4) Before appointment, the President and each member of the District Forum shall have to take an undertaking that he does not and will not have any such financial or other interests as is likely to affect prejudicially his functions as a member.

(5) In addition of provisions of section 10(2) of the Act, Administrator may remove from the Office the President and member of the District Forum who —

(a) has been adjudged as insolvent, or

(b) has been convicted of an offence which in the opinion of the Administrator involves moral turpitude, or

(c) has become physically or mentally incapable of acting as such member, or

(d) has acquired such financial or other interest as is likely to affect prejudicially his functions as a member, or

(e) has so abused his position as to render his continuance in Office prejudicial to the public interest **Provided** that the President or member shall not be removed Irom his Office on the ground specified in clauses *(d)* and *(e)* of sub-rule (5) except on an inquiry held by the Admínistrator in accordance with such procedure as he may specify on his behalf and finds the member to be guilty of such ground.

(6) The terms and conditions of the service of the President and the members of the District Forum shall not be varied to their disadvantage during their tenure of Office.

(7) Where any vacancy occurs in the Office of the President of the District Forum, the senior most (in order of appointment) member of District Forum holding Office for the time being, shall discharge the functions of the President until a person appointed to fill such vacancy assumes the Office or the President of the District Forum,

(8) When the President, of the District Forum is unable to discharge the functions owing to absence, illness or any other cause, the seniormost (in 01 of appointment) member of the District Forum shall discharge the functions of the President until the day on which the President resumes the charge or functions.

(9) The President or any member ceasing to hold Office as such shall not hold By appointment in or be connected with the management or Administration an organisation which have been the subject of any proceedings under the during his tenure for a period of 5 years from the date on which he ceases to hold such Office.

Place of sitting and other matter relating to District Forum

4. (1) The Office of the District Forum shall be located at Kavaratti.

(2) The working days and the office hours of the District Forum shall be same as that of the Administration.

(3) The Official seal and emblem of the District Forum shall be such as the Administration may specify.

(4) Sitting of the District Forum, as and when necessary shall be convened by the President.

(5) No act or proceedings of the District Forum shall be invalid by reason only the existence of any vacancy among its members or any defect in its constitution.

(6) Administrator may appoint such staff, as may be necessary to assist the District Forum in its day to day work and perform such other functions as are **Provided** under these rules, or assigned to it by the President. The salary payable to such staff shall be defrayed out of the consolidated fund of the Union Territory Government.

(7) Where the opposite party admit the allegation made by the complainant, the District Forum shall decide the complaint on the basis of the merit of the case and documents present before it.

(8) If during the proceedings conducted under section 13, District Forum fixes a date for hearing of the parties, it shall be obligatory on the complainant and opposite party or its authorised agent to appear before the District Forum on such date of hearing or any other date to which hearing could be adjourned. Where the complainant or his authorised agent fails to appear before the state commission on such day, the state commission may in its District Forum on such day, the District Forum may in its discretion either dismiss the complaint for default or decide it on merit. Where the opposite Party or its authorised agent fails to appear on the day of hearing, the District forum may decide the complaint *ex parte,*

(9) While proceeding under sub-rule (8). The District Forum may, on such as it may think fit and at any stage, adjourn the hearing of the complaint more than one adjournment shall ordinarily be given and the complaint be decided within 90 days from the date of notice received by the opposite party where complaint does not require analysis or testing of the goods and within 150 days of it require analysis or testing of the goods.

(10) Orders of the District Forum shall be signed and dated by the members of the District Forum constituting the Bench and shall be communicated to the parties free of charge.

Procedure to be adopted by the District Forum for analysis and testing of the goods [Section I3(l)(c)]

5. (l) Under section 13(l)(c), if considered necessary, the District Forum may direct the complainant to provide more than one sample of the goods in clean containers with stopper properly fixed on them.

(2) On receiving the samples of such goods, the District Forum shall seal it and fix labels on the containers carrying following information—

(*i*) Name and address of the appropriate laboratory to whom sample will be sent for analysis and test;

(*ii*) Name and address of the District Forum;

(*iii*) Case number;

(*iv*) Seal of the District Forum.

(3) The sample will be sent to the appropriate laboratory by the District Forum for sending report, within 45 days or within such extended time as may be granted by the District Forum, after specifying the nature of the defect alleged and date of submission of the report.

Salary and other allowances and terms and conditions of the President and members of the State Commission [Section 16(2)]

6. (1) President of State Commission may receive honorarium of ₹ 2,000 per month or ₹ 500 per day of sitting whichever is more. For each sitting of the Commission, other members of the Commission may receiving honorarium of ₹ 150/- per day.

(2) The President of State Commission shall be entitled to such TA/DA on official tour as are admissible to the judges of High Court. The members of State Commission shall be entitled for such TA/DA on official tour as are admissible to Grade I officers of Central Government. The President and members are entitled for air travel between islands and mainland and inter island journey in connection with business of the Commission. The President of State Commission is also entitled for a residential telephone.

(3) The salary honorarium and other allowances shall be defrayed out or consolidated fund of the Administration.

(4) President and members of State Commission shall hold Office for a team five years or up to the age of 70 years whichever is earlier and shall not eligible for renomination:

Provided that the President and members may—

(*a*) by writing under his hand and addressed to the Administration resign his Office any time.

(*b*) be removed from his Office in accordance with provisions of sub-rule (5)

(5) The Administrator may remove from Office President or a member State Commission who

(*a*) has been adjudged an insolvent, or

(*b*) has been convicted of an offence which in the opinion of the Administrator, involves moral turpitude, or

(*c*) has become physically or mentally incapable of acting as such member, or

(*d*) has acquired such financial or other interest as is likely to effect prejudicially his functions as a member, or

(*e*) has so abused his position as to render his continuance on Office prejudicial to the public interest;

Provided that the President or a member shall not be removed from his Office the ground specified in clauses (*d*) and (*e*) of sub-rule (5) except on an inquiry held by the Administration, in accordance with such procedure as it may specify in this behalf and finds the member to be guilty of such ground. (6) Before appointment, President and members of the State Commission shall live to take an undertaking that he does not and will not have any such financial or other interest as is likely to affect prejudicially his functions as such member.

(7) The terms and conditions of the service of the President and the members if the State Commission shall not be varied to their disadvantage during their tenure of Office.

(8) Every vacancy caused by resignation and removal of the President or any her member of the State Commission under sub-rule (4) or otherwise shall be filled by fresh appointment.

(9) Where any such vacancy occurs in the Office of the President of the State Commission, the seniormost (in order of appointment) member holding Office for the time being, shall discharge the functions of the President until a person appointed to fill such vacancy assumes the Office of the President of the State Commission.

(10) When the President of the State Commission is unable to discharge the functions owing to absence, illness or any other cause, the seniormost (in order to the appointment) member of the State Commission shall discharge the functions of the President until the day on which the President resumes the charge of his functions.

(11) The President or any member ceasing to hold Office as such shall not hold any appointment in or be connected with the management or Administrations of an organisation which have been the subject of any proceeding under the Act during his tenure for a period of five years from the date on which he ceases to hold such Office.

Place of sitting and other matters relating to State Commission [Section 14(3) read with section 18]

7. (1) Office of the State Commission shall be located at the capital of the Union Territory.

(2) The working day and the Office hours of the State Commission shall be the as that of the Administration.

(3) The Official seal and emblem of the State Commission shall be such as the Administration may specify.

(4) Sitting of the State Commission, as and when necessary, shall be convened' by the President.

(5) No act or proceedings of the State Commission shall be invalid by reason only of the existence of any vacancy among its member or any defect in its constitution thereof.

(6) The Administrator shall appoint such staff as may be necessary to assist the State Commission in its work and perform such other functions as are **Provided** under these rules or assigned to it by the President. The salary payable to such staff shall be defrayed out of the consolidated Fund of the Administration.

(7) Where the opposite party admits the allegation made by the complainant, the State Commission shall decide the complaint on the basis of the merit of the case and documents present before it.

(8) If during the proceedings conducted under section 13, State Commission fixes as date for hearing of the parties, it shall be obligatory on the complainant and opposite party or his authorised agent to appear before the State Commission on such date of hearing or any other date to which hearing could be adjourned. Where the complainant or his authorised agent fails to appear before the State Commission on such day, the State Commission may in its discretion either dismiss the complaint for default or decide it on merits. Where the opposite party or its authorised agent fails to appear on the day of hearing, the State Commission may decide the complaint *ex parte.*

(9) While proceeding under sub-rule (8), the State Commission may, on such-terms as it may think fit and at any State, adjourn the hearing of the complaint, but not more than one adjournment shall ordinarily be given and the complaint should be decided within 90 days from the date of notice received by the opposite party where complaint does not require analysis or testing of goods and within 150 days if it require analysis or testing of the goods.

(10) Order of the State Commission shall be signed and dated by the members of the State Commission constituting the Bench and shall be communicated to the parties free of charge.

Procedure for hearing appeal [Section 15]

8. (1) Memorandum shall be presented by the appellant or his authority agent to the State Commission in person or sent by registered post addressed to the Commission.

(2) Every memorandum filed under sub-rule (1) shall be in legible handwriting preferably typed and shall set forth concisely under distinct heads, the ground of appeal without an argument or narrative and such ground shall be numbered consecutively.

(3) Each memorandum shall be accompanied by the certified copy of the or of the District Forum appealed against and such of the documents as may required to support grounds of objection mentioned in the memoranda.

(4) When the appeal is presented after the expiry of period of limitation as specified in the Act, Memorandum shall be accompanied by an application supported by an affidavit setting forth the fact on which appellant relies to satisfy the State Commission that he has sufficient cause for not preferring the appeal within the period of limitation.

(5) The appellant shall submit four copies of the memorandum to the State Commission for Official purposes.

(6) On the date of hearing or any other day to which hearing may be adjourned, it shall be obligatory for the parties or their authorised agents to appear before the State Commission. If appellant or his authorised agent fails to appear on such date, the State Commission may, in its discretion either dismiss the appeal or decide it on the merit of the case. If respondent or his authorised agent fails to appear on such date, the State Commission shall proceed *ex parte* and shall decide the appeal *ex parte* on merits of the case.

(7) The appellant shall not except by leave of the State Commission, urge or be heard in support of any ground of objections not set forth in the memorandum but the State Commission in deciding the appeal, shall not confine to the grounds of objection set forth in the memorandum or taken by leave of the State Commission under this rule;

Provided that the Commission shall not rest its decision on any other grounds unless the party who may be affected thereby, has been given at least one opportunity of being heard by the State Commission.

(8) State Commission may, on such terms as it may think fit and at any stage, adjourn the hearing of appeal, but not more than one adjournment shall ordinarily be given and the appeal should be decided within 90 days from the first date of hearing.

(9) Order of the State Commission on appeal shall be signed, dated by the members of the State Commission constituting the Bench and shall be communicated to the parties free of charge.

Chapter 21

Madhya Pradesh Consumer Protection Rules, 1989

[Notification No. F. 4-2-87-XXIX-2, Dated 29-9-1987

In exercise of the powers conferred by sub-section (2) of section 30 of the Consumer Protection Act, 1986 (68 of 1986), the State Government hereby makes the following rules, namely— **Short title and commencement.**

1. (1) These rules may be called the Madhya Pradesh Consumer Protection Rules, 1987.

(2) They shall come into force on such date as the State Government may, by notification in the Official Gazette.

Definitions

2. In these rules, unless the context otherwise requires —

(*a*) "Act" means the Consumer Protection Act, 1986 (68 of 1986);

(*b*) "agent" means a person duly authorised by a party to present any complaint or appeal or reply on its behalf before the State Commission or the District Forum;

(*c*) "appellant" means a party which makes an appeal against the order of the District Forum;

(*d*) "memorandum" means memorandum of appeal filed by the appellant;

(*e*) "opposite party" means a person who answers complaint or claim;

(*f*) "President" means the President of the State Commission or District Forum as the case may be;

(*g*) "respondent" means the person who answers any memorandum appeal;

(*h*) "State" includes Union Territories.

Salaries and Other Allowances and Terms and Conditions of the President and Members of the District Forum

3. (1) The President of the District Forum shall receive the salary of the Judge of the District Court if appointed on whole-time basis or an honorarium ₹ 150/- per day if appointed on part-time basis. Other members if sitting basis, shall receive a consolidated honorarium of ₹ 2,000/- per and if sitting on part-time basis, a consolidated honorarium of ₹ 100/- day for the sitting.

(2) The President and the Members of the District Forum shall be entitled to each travelling allowance and daily allowance on official tour as are admissible Grade I Officer of the State Government.

(3) The salary, honorarium and other allowances shall be defrayed out of the Consolidated Fund of the State Government.

(4) Before appointment, the President and Members of the District Forum shall have to take an undertaking that he does not and will not have any such financial or other interests as is likely to affect prejudicially his functions as a member.

(5) In addition to the provisions of section 10(2) of the Act, the State Government may remove from the office, the President and any Member of a District Forum who,—

(*a*) has been adjudged as insolvent; or

(*b*) has been convicted of an offence which in the opinion of the State Government involves moral turpitude; or

(*c*) has become physically or mentally incapable of acting as such member; or

(*d*) has acquired such financial or other interest as is likely to affect prejudicially his functions as a member; or

(*e*) has so abused his position as to render his continuance in office prejudicial to the public interest;

(*f*) is absent himself from three consecutive sittings of the Forum, except for a reasonable cause:

Provided that the President or Member shall not be removed from his office on the ground specified in clauses (*d*) and (*e*) of sub-rule (5) except on an inquiry held by State Government in accordance with such procedure as it may specify this behalf and finds the member to be guilty of such ground.

(6) The terms and conditions of the service of the President and the Members of the District Forum shall not be varied to their disadvantage during their tenure of office.

(7) Where any vacancy occurs in the office of the President of the District forum, the senior-most (in order of appointment) Member of the District forum, holding office for the time being, shall discharge the functions of the president until a person appointed to fill such vacancy assumes the office of the Resident of the District Forum.

(8) When the President of the District Forum is unable to discharge the functions owing to absence, illness, or any other cause, the seniormost (in order of appointment) Member of the District Forum shall discharge the functions of the President until the day on which the President resumes the charge of his functions.

(9) The President or any Member ceasing to hold office as such shall not hold any appointment in or be connected with the management or administration of an organisation which has been the subject of any proceeding under the Act during his tenure for a period of 5 years from the date on which he ceases to hold such office.

Place of Sitting and Other Matters Relating to District Forum

4. (1) The Office of the District Forum shall be located at the headquarter of the District. Where State Government decides to establish a single District Forum having jurisdiction over more than one District, it shall notify the place and jurisdiction of District Forum so established.

(2) The working days and the office hours of the District Forum shall be the same as that of the State Government.

(3) The official seal and emblem of the District Forum shall be such as the State Government may specify.

(4) Sitting of the District Forum, as and when necessary, shall be convened by the President.

(5) No act or proceeding of the District Forum shall be invalid by reason only of the existence of any vacancy among its members or any defect in its constitution.

(6) The State Government shall appoint such staff, as may be necessary to assist the District Forum in its day to day work and perform such other functions as are **Provided** under these rules, or assigned to it by the President. The salary payable to such staff shall be defrayed out of the Consolidated Fund of the State Government.

(7) Where the opposite party admits the allegation made by the complainant, the District Forum shall decide the complaint on the basis of the merits of the case and documents present before it.

(8) If during the proceedings conducted under section 13, District Forum fixes a date for hearing of the parties, it shall be obligatory on the complainant and opposite party or its authorised agent to appear before the District Forum on such date of hearing or any other date to which hearing could be adjourned. Where the complainant or his authorised agent fails to appear before the District Forum on such day, the District Forum may in at its discretion either dismiss the complaint for default or decide it on merit. Where the opposite party or its authorised agent fails to appear on the day of hearing, the District Forum may decide the complaint *ex parte*.

(9) While proceeding under sub-rule (8), the District Forum may, on such term as it may think fit and at any stage, adjourn the hearing of the complaint but not more than one adjournment shall ordinarily be given and the complaint should be decided within 90 days from the date of notice received by the opposite party where complaint does not require analysis or testing goods and within 150 days if it requires analysis or testing of the goods.

(10) Orders of the District Forum shall be signed and dated by the Members of the District Forum constituting the Bench and shall be communicated to the parties free of charge.

Procedure to be Adopted by the District Forum, Forum for Analysis and Testing of the Goods

5. (1) Under section 13(l)(c), if considered necessary, the District Forum may direct the complainant to provide more than one sample of the goods in clean containers with stopper properly fixed on them.

(2) On receiving the sample of such goods, the District Forum shall seal it and 'fix labels on the containers carrying following information;—

(*i*) name and address of the appropriate laboratory to whom sample will be sent for analysis and test;

(*ii*) name and address of the District Forum;

(*iii*) case number;

(*iv*) seal of the District Forum.

(3) The sample will be sent to the appropriate laboratory by the District Forum for sending report within 45 days or within such extended time as may be granted by the District Forum after specifying the nature of the defect alleged and date of submission of the report.

Salary and other allowances and terms and conditions of the President and Members of the State Commission

6. (1) The President of the State Commission shall receive the salary of the Judge of the High Court if appointed on whole-time basis or a consolidated honorarium of ₹ 200 per day for the sitting if appointed on part-time basis. Other members, if sitting on whole time basis, shall receive a consolidated Honorarium of ₹ 3,000 per month and if sitting on part-time basis, a consolidated honorarium of ₹ 150/- per day for the sitting.

(2) The President and the Members of the State Commission shall be eligible for such travelling allowance and daily allowance on official tour as are admissible to Grade I Officer of the State Government.

(3) The salary, honorarium and other allowances shall be defrayed out of the Consolidated Fund of the State Government.

(4) The President and the Members of the State Commission shall hold office for a term of five years or upto the age of 65 years whichever is earlier and shall I not be eligible for renomination;

Provided that President and/or Members may —

(*a*) by writing under his hand and addressed to the State Government resign his office any time; and

(*b*) be removed from his office in accordance with the provisions of sub-rule (5).

(5) The State Government may remove from Office, President or any Member of the State Commission who,—

(a) has been adjudged as insolvent; or

(*b*) has been convicted of an offence which in the opinion of the State Government, involves moral turpitude; or

(*c*) has become physically or mentally incapable of acting as such member

(*d*) has acquired such financial or other interest as is likely to affect prejudicially his functions as a member; or

(*e*) has so abused his position as to render his continuance in office, prejudicial to the public interest;

(f) is absent himself from five consecutive sittings of the Commission, except for a reasonable cause:

Provided that the President or Member shall not be removed from his office on the ground specified in clauses (*d*) and (*e*) of sub-rule (5) except on an inquiry held by the State Government, in accordance with such procedure as it may specify in this behalf and finds the member to be guilty of such ground.

(6) Before appointment, the President and Member of the State Commission shall have to take an undertaking that he does not and will not have any such financial or other interests as is likely to affect prejudicially his functions as such member.

(7) The terms and conditions of the service of the President and the Members of the State Commission shall not be varied to their disadvantage during their tenure of office.

(8) Every vacancy caused by resignation and removal of the President or any other Member of the State Commission under sub-rule (4) or otherwise shall be filled by fresh appointment.

(9) Where any such vacancy occurs in the office of the President of the State Commission, the senior most (in order of appointment) member, holding office for the time being, shall discharge the functions of the President until a person appointed to fill such vacancy assumes the office of the President of the State Commission.

(10) When the President of the State Commission is unable to discharge the functions owing to absence, illness or any other cause, the senior-most (in order of the appointment) Member of the State Commission shall discharge to functions of the President until the day on which the President resumes the charge of his functions.

(11) The President or any Member ceasing to hold office as such shall not hole any appointment in or be connected with the management or administration of an organisation which have been the subject of any proceeding under the Act. during his tenure for a period of 5 years from the date on which he ceases hold such office.

Inserted by the Madhya Pradesh Consumer Protection (Amendment) Rules, 1999, *w.e.f.* 27-10-1999, place of sitting and other matters relating to State Commission

7. (1) The office of the State Commission shall be located at the Capital of the State.

(2) The working days and the office hours of the State Commission shall be same as that of the State Government.

(3) The official seal and emblem of the State Commission shall be such as the State Government may specify.

(4) Sitting of the State Commission, as and when necessary, shall be convened by the President.

(5) No act or proceedings of the State Commission shall be invalid by reasons only of the existence of any vacancy among its members or any defect in its constitution thereof.

(6) The State Government shall appoint such staff, as may be necessary to assist the State Commission in its work and perform such other functions as are **Provided** under these rules or assigned to it by the President. The salary payable to such staff shall be defrayed out of the Consolidated Fund of the State Government.

(7) Where the opposite party admits the allegation made by the complainant, the State Commission shall decide the complaint on the basis of the merit of the case and documents present before it.

(8) If during the proceedings conducted under section 13, the State Commission fixes a date for hearing of the parties, it shall be obligatory on the complainant and opposite party or his authorised agent to appear before the State Commission on such date of hearing or any other date to which hearing could be adjourned. Where the complainant or his authorised agent fails to appear before the State Commission on such day, the State Commission may its discretion either dismiss the complaint for default or decide it on merits. Where the opposite party or its authorised agent fails to appear on the day of hearing, the State Commission may decide the complaint *ex parte*.

(9) While proceeding under sub-rule (8), the State Commission may on such terms as it may think fit and at any stage, adjourn the hearing of the complaint but not more than one adjournment shall ordinarily be given and the complaint should be decided within 90 days from the date of notice received by the opposite party where complaint does not require analysis or testing of the goods and within 150 days if it requires analysis or testing of the goods.

(10) Orders of the State Commission shall be signed and dated by the members of the State Commission constituting the Bench and shall be communicated to the parties free of charge.

Procedure for Hearing Appeal

(1) Memorandum shall be presented by the appellant or his authorised agent to the State Commission in person or be sent by registered postal addressed to the Commission.

(2) Very memorandum filed under sub-rule (1) shall be in legible handwriting preferably typed and shall set forth concisely under distinct heads, the grounds of appeal without any argument or narrative and such grounds be numbered! consecutively.

(3) Each memorandum shall be accompanied by the certified copy of the order of the District Forum appealed against and such of the documents as may be required to support grounds of objection mentioned in the memorandum.

(4) When the appeal is presented after the expiry of the period of limitation as I specified in the Act, the memorandum shall be accompanied by an application supported by an affidavit setting forth the fact on which the appellant relies to satisfy the State Commission that he has sufficient cause for not preferring the appeal within the period of limitation.

(5) The appellant shall submit four copies of the memorandum to the State Commission for official purposes.

(6) On the date of hearing or any other day to which hearing may be adjourned, it shall be obligatory for the parties or their authorised agents to appear before the State Commission. If appellant or his authorised agent fails to appear only such date, the State Commission may, in its discretion, either dismiss the appeal or decide it on the merit of the case. If respondent or his authorised agent fails to appear on such date, the State Commission shall proceed *ex parte* and shall decide the appeal *ex parte* on the merits of the case.

(7) The appellant shall not, except by leave of the State Commission, urge or be heard in support of any ground of objections not set forth in the memorandum but the State Commission, in deciding the appeal, shall not confine to the grounds of objection set forth in the memorandum or taken by leave of the State Commission under this rule:

Provided that the State Commission shall not rest its decision on any other grounds unless the party who may be affected thereby, has been given at least one opportunity of being heard by the State Commission.

(8) The State Commission may, on such terms as it may think fit and at any stage, adjourn the hearing of the appeal, but not more than one adjournment shall ordinarily be given and the appeal should be decided within 90 days from the first date of hearing.

(9) Order of the State Commission on appeal shall be signed and dated by the Members of the State Commission constituting the Bench and shall be communicated to the parties free of charge.

Chapter 22

Maharashtra Consumer Protection Rules, 2000

[No. CPC. 5598/CR/1668/CP-3, Dated 16-2-2000]

In exercise of the powers conferred by sub-section (4) of section 7, sub-section (3) of section 10, clause (c) of sub-section (1) of section 13, sub-section (3) of section 14, section 15 and sub-section (2) of section 16 of the Consumer Protection Act, 1986 (68 of 1986) and of all the other powers enabling it in that behalf, and in supersession of all previous rules, notifications orders, in this behalf, the Government of Maharashtra hereby makes the following rules, namely—**Short title and commencement.**

1. (1) These rules may be called the Maharashtra Consumer Protection Rules, 2000.

(2) It shall come into force on the 16th February, 2000.

Definition

2. In these rules, unless the context otherwise requires,—

(a) "Act" means the Consumer Protection Act, 1986 (68 of 1986);

(b) "Agent" means a person duly authorised by a party to present any complaint, appeal or reply on its behalf before the State Commission or District Forum;

(c) "Appellant" means a party preferring an appeal against the order of the District Forum;

(d) "Defendant" means a person responding to the complaint or the claim;

(e) "Memorandum" means the memorandum of appeal filed by the appellant;

(f) "President" means the President of the State Commission or as the case may be the District Forum;

(g) "Respondent" means the person who answers to the memorandum;

(h) "Section" means the section of the Act; (i) words and expressions used but not defined in the Act shall have the meanings respectively assigned to them in the Act.

Salaries and Other Allowances and Terms and Conditions of the President and their Members of the District Forum

3. (1) The President of the District Forum shall receive the salary at the minimum stage, of the District Judge appointed in the State Judicial Service, if appointed on whole-time basis. However, if on a part-time basis, or on a sitting basis the President shall be paid ₹ 200 per day as honorarium. Such of the President who is appointed after selection from the retired District Judges, shall get his pay fixed as per rule 157(2) of the Maharashtra Civil Services (Pension) Rules, 1982. Deputation allowance in addition to pay the allowances shall be payable to such of the President who is appointed from the cadre of sitting District Judges. The members of the District Forum, if appointed on whole-time basis, shall be paid a consolidated honorarium offers ₹ 4,000 per mensem. For attending sittings of the Forum on per sitting basis a sitting fee of ₹ 200 or such amount as the Government may decide, from time to time, shall be paid.

Explanation—(1) Whenever the President attends the work of the Forum, it I shall be treated as a sitting.

(2) When a member is present and attends the work of the Forum like giving dates, admitting cases, etc., it shall be treated as a sitting.

(2A) The President and the members of the District Forum shall be entitled for such conveyance allowance and daily allowance, on official tour at such rate, as may be specified by the State Government, from time to time:

Provided that, the members of the District Forum, except the members of the Mumbai District Forum, shall be entitled to conveyance allowance at the rate that Government decides from time to time.

(3) Before appointment, the President and Members of the District Forum shall have to make an undertaking that he does not and will not have any such financial or other interests, as is likely to affect prejudicially, his functions as a President or a Member, and he shall not have any association with any political party.

(4) In addition of provisions of sub-section (2) of section 10, State Government may remove from the office, the President and Member of a District Forum who,—

(a) has been adjudged an insolvent; or

(b) has been convicted of an offence which in. the opinion of the State Government, involves moral turpitude; or

(c) has become physically or mentally incapable of acting as such member,

(d) has acquired such financial or other interest as is likely to affect prejudicially his functions as a member, or

(e) has so abused; his position as to render his continuance in office prejudicial to the public interest; or

(f) has remained absent for not less than three consecutive sittings of the District Forum, without permission, of the President of the State Commission, in case he is President of the District Forum and of the Preside i the concerned District Forum, in case he is a member. Under special circumstances such permission may be obtained *post facto,* however strictly within thirty days from the first day of such absence, failing which he shall be treated as absent:

Provided that the President or Member shall not be removed from his office on the ground specified in clauses *(d)* and *(e)* of this sub-rule except on an inquiry held by the State Government in accordance with such procedure as it may specify in this behalf and finds the Member to be guilty of such ground.

(5) The terms and conditions of the service of the President and the Members of the District Forum shall not be varied to their disadvantage during their tenure of office.

(6) Where any vacancy occurs in the office of the President of the District Forum, by resignation, removal or he is unable to discharge the functions owing to absence, illness or any other cause, the seniormost (in order of appointment) member of the District Forum, who is qualified to be appointed as President of the Forum under clause (a) of sub-section (1) of section 10, holding office for the time being, shall discharge the functions of the President until the person appointed to fill such vacancy assume the office of the President of the District Forum. In absence of both the members of the District Forum, or if none of the member is qualified to hole the office of the President, the President or any seniormost (in order of appointment) member of the District Forum of adjacent district, qualified to be appointed as a President shall discharge the functions of the president of the District Forum;

Provided that if the member of the District Forum of and adjacent District is qualified to be appointed as President, preference shall be given to such member over the President of such adjacent district:

Provided further that the Government shall, by order specify the District which shall be treated as adjacent District for such purposes:

Provided also that where there are more than one Forum in the District, the President of any other Forum, in the District or any member of any other Forum in the District, who is qualified to be appointed as a President shall discharge the functions of the President:

Provided also that, where the President or member of the adjoining District Forum attends the work of the District Forum such President or the member shall be paid travelling allowance and daily allowance in accordance with these Rules.

Explanation—If the members, are not eligible under clause *(d)* of sub-section of section 10 of the Act, such members shall attend the work of the Forum like giving of dates for hearing of complaints, accepting applications, complaints, etc., and bring the same to the notice of the President. Every such work shall be deemed to be a sitting. However, they shall not hear and dispose of the complaints, shall be the duty of the Registrar and the other members of the staff to assist the members in discharging such function.

(7) The President or any member ceasing to hold office as such shall not hold any appointment in or be connected with the management or administration of an organisation which have been the subject of any proceeding under the Act during his tenure for a period of 5 years from the date on which he ceases to hold such office.

(8) The President of the District Forum shall discharge the judicial functions while the Registrar of the District Forum shall discharge the administrative functions.

Place of Sitting and other Matters Relating to District Forum

4. (1) The office of the District Forum shall be located at the headquarter of the District, where the State Government decides to establish a single District Forum having jurisdiction over more than one district, it shall notify the place and jurisdiction of the District Forum so established.

(2) The working days and the office hours of the District Forum shall be the same as that of the State Government:

Provided that, if any of the members of the Forum is a part timer, the President shall fix the timings in consultation with such member. However, while fixing such timings the President shall ensure that two of the members shall be present at one time at least for two hours in a day.

(3) The official seal and emblem of the District Forum shall be such as the Stale Government may specify.

(4) Sitting of the District Forum, as and when necessary, shall be convened by the President.

(5) State Government shall appoint such staff, as may be necessary to assist the District Forum in its day to day work and perform such other functions as are **Provided** under these rules, or assigned to it by the President.

(6) Where the opposite party (Defendant) admits the allegation made by the, complainant, the District Forum shall decide the complaint on the basis of the merit of the case and documents present before it.

(7) If during the proceedings conducted under section 13, District Forum fixes a date for hearing of the parties, it shall be obligatory on the complainant and opposite party (Defendant) or its authorised agent to appear before the District Forum on such date of hearing or any other date to which hearing could be adjourned. Where the complainant or his authorised agent fails to appear before the District Forum on such day, the District Forum may in its discretion either dismiss the complaint for default or decide it on merit. Where the opposite party (Defendant) or its authorised agent fails to appear on the day of hearing, the District Forum may decide the complaint *ex parte.*

(8) While proceeding under sub-rule (7), the District Forum may, on the, reasonable grounds at any stage, adjourn the hearing of the complaint but not more than one adjournment shall ordinarily be given and the complaint should be decided as far as possible within 90 days from the date of notice received by the opposite party (Defendant) where complaint does not require analysis or testing of the goods and as far as possible within 150 days if it requires analysis or testing of the goods.

(9) Orders of the District Forum shall be signed and dated by the members o the District Forum constituting the Bench and shall be communicated to the parties free of charge.

(10) When the hearing takes place at the time when all members of the District Forum are present, the opinion of the majority shall be the order of the Forum.

Procedure to be Adopted by District Forum for Analysis and Testing of Goods

5. (1) Under clause (c) of sub-section (1) of section 13, if considered necessary, the District Forum may direct the complainant to provide more than one sample of the goods in clean containers with stopper properly fixed on them.

(2) On receiving the samples of such goods, the District Forum shall seal it and fix labels on the containers carrying following information—

(*i*) name and address of the appropriate laboratory to whom sample will be sent for analysis and test;

(*ii*) name and address of the District Forum;

(*iii*) case number;

(*iv*) seal of the District Forum.

(3) The sample will be sent to the appropriate laboratory by the District Forum for report within 45 days or within such extended time as may be granted by the District Forum after specifying the nature of the defect alleged and date of submission of the report.

Procedure of District Forum

6. (1) The language of the District Forum shall be Marathi. *Explanation.—For* the purposes of this sub-rule language includes language of hearings, and orders.

(2) The complaint before the District Forum shall be made in writing and may filed in the District Forum or sent by post. The complaint and the documents shall be in triplicate and shall be accompanied by as many copies of the complaint and

documents as the number of defendants. The Registrar shall on receipt of the complaint scrutinize the same and file the same in the Register maintained for this purpose.

(3) The District Forum is the authority to decide any complaint, including the preliminary hearing, necessary, if any.

(4) The defendant shall give his reply and documents in quadruplicate.

(5) The President and member of the District Forum shall endeavour the speedy trial for disposal of the matters.

(6) The President of the District Forum shall, after receipt of the execution application of the judgment forward the same to the Civil Court for necessary execution.

(7) The Registrar shall provide the members of the Forum information with regard to official work and correspondence of the Forum with the Government. It shall be the duty of the Registrar to place with the members the files with respect to the matters with the Forum so that the members can devote their time for the working of the Forum.

Salary and Allowances and the terms and Conditions of the President and Members of the State Commission

7. (1) President of the State Commission shall receive the salary at par of the salary of the Judge of the High Court, if appointed on whole time basis or a consolidated honorarium of ₹ 400/- per day for the sitting, if appointed on part-time basis. Other members, if sitting as whole time basis shall receive a consolidated honorarium of ₹ 4,000 per mensem and if sitting on a part-time basis a consolidated honorarium of ₹ 400 or such sum as may be decided by the Government, from time to time.

(2) The President and the members of the State Commission shall be entitled for such conveyance allowance and daily allowance on official tour, at such rate, as specified by the State Government, from time to time.

(3) President and the member of the State Commission shall hold office for a term of five years or upto the age of 67 years whichever is earlier and shall not be eligible for re-appointment:

Provided that President and member may—

(a) by writing under his hand and addressed to the State Government resign his office any time;

(b) be removed from his office in accordance with provisions of sub-rule (4).

(4) The State Government may remove from office, President or a member of the State Commission who,—

(a) has been adjudged an insolvent; or

(b) has been convicted of an offence which in the opinion of the State Government, involves moral turpitude; or

(c) has become physically or mentally incapable of acting as such member; or

(d) has acquired such financial or other interest as is likely to affect prejudicially his functions as a member; or

(e) has so abused his position as to render his continuance in office prejudicial to the public interest; or

(f) has remained absent from three consecutive sittings of the State Commission, without permission of the State Government, in case he is President of the Commission and of the President of the State Commission, in case he is a member under special circumstances such permission may be obtained *post facto,* however, strictly within 30 days from the first day or such absence, failing which, he shall be treated as absent : **Provided** that the President or a member shall not be removed from his office on the ground specified in clauses *(d)* and *(e)* of this sub-rule except on an inquiry held by State Government in accordance with such procedure as it may specify in this behalf and finds the member to be guilty of such ground.

(5) Before appointment, the President and members of the State Commission shall have to make an undertaking that he does not have and will not have any such financial or other interests, as is likely to affect prejudicially his functions as a President or a member and he shall not have any association with any political party.

(6) The terms and conditions of the service of the President and the member; of the State Commission shall not be varied to their disadvantage during their tenure of office.

(7) Every vacancy caused by resignation and removal of the president or any of the member of the State Commission under sub-rule (3) or otherwise shall he filled by fresh appointment.

(8) Where any vacancy occurs in the office of the president of the State Commission, by resignation, removal or he is unable to discharge the functions owing to absence, illness or any other cause, the seniormost (in order of appointment) member of the State Commission, holding office for the time being; shall be the acting President until a person appointed to fill such vacancy assumes the office of the President of the State Commission. However, such acting President and the other member shall not hear and decide contested matters. They can dispose of *ex parte* matters and

can give further dates of hearing. However, in the *ex parte* matters, the opinion of such acting President and Member should be unanimous.

(9) The President or any member ceasing to hold office as such shall not hold any appointment in or be connected with the management or administration of an organisation which have been the subject of any proceeding under the Act during his tenure for a period of 5 years from the date on which he ceases to hold such office.

Place of Sitting and Other Matters Relating to State Commission

8. (1) Office of the State Commission shall be located at Mumbai.

(2) The working days and the office hours of the State Commission shall be the same as that of the State Government.

(3) The official seal and emblem of the State Commission shall be such as the State Government may specify.

(4) Sitting of the State Commission, as and when necessary, shall be convened by the President.

(5) State Government shall appoint such staff, as may be necessary to assist the State Commission in its work and perform such other functions as are **Provided** under these rules or assigned to it by the President.

(6) Where the opposite party (defendant) admits the allegation made by the complainant, the State Commission shall decide the complaint on the basis of the merit of the case and documents present before it.

(7) If during the proceedings conducted under section 13, State Commission fixes a date for hearing of the parties, it shall be obligatory on the complainant and opposite party (Defendant) or his authorised agent to appear before the State Commission on such date of hearing or any other date to which hearing could be adjourned. Where the complainant or his authorised agent fails to appear before the State Commission on such day, the State Commission may in its discretion either dismiss the complaint for default or decide it on merits. Where the opposite party (Defendant) or its authorised agent fails to appear on the day of hearing, the State Commission may decide the complaint *ex parte.*

(8) While proceeding under sub-rule (8), the State Commission may, on such terms as it may think fit at any stage, adjourn the hearing of the complaint but not more than one adjournment shall ordinarily be given and the complaint should be decided within 90 days from the date of notice received by the opposite party (Defendant) where complaint does not require analysis or testing of the goods and within 150 days if it requires analysis or testing of the goods.

(9) Orders of the State Commissions shall be signed and dated by the members of the State Commission constituting the Bench and shall be communicated to the parties free of charge.

Procedure for Hearing Appeal

9. (1) Memorandum shall be presented by the appellant or his authorised agent to the State Commission in person or sent by the registered post addressed to the Commission.

(2) Every memorandum filed under sub-rule (1) shall be in legible handwriting preferably typed and shall set forth concisely under distinct heads, the grounds of appeal without any argument or narrative and such grounds shall be numbered consecutively.

(3) Each memorandum shall be accompanied by the certified copy of the order of the District Forum appealed against and such of the documents as may be required to support grounds of objection mentioned in the memorandum.

(4) "When the appeal is presented after the expiry of period of limitations as specified in the Act, memorandum shall be accompanied by an application supported by an affidavit setting forth the fact on which appellant relies to satisfy the State Commission that he has sufficient cause for not preferring the appeal within the period of limitation.

(5) The appellant shall submit four copies of the memorandum to the State Commission for official purposes.

(6) On the date of hearing or any other day to which hearing may be adjourned, it shall be obligatory for the parties or their authorised agents to appear before the State Commission. If appellant or his authorised agent fails to appear on such date, the State Commission may, in its discretion, either dismiss the appeal or decide it on the merit of the case. If respondent or his authorised agents fails to appear on such date, the State Commission shall proceed *ex parte* and shall decide the appeal *ex parte* on merits of the case.

(7) The appellant shall not except by leave of the State Commission, urge or be heard in support of any ground of objections not set forth in the memorandum, but the State Commission, in deciding the appeal, shall not confine to the grounds of objection set forth in the memorandum or taken by leave of the State Commission under this rule:

Provided that the Commission shall not rest its decision on any other grounds unless the party who may be affected thereby, has been given at least one opportunity of being heard by the State Commission.

(8) State Commission may, on such terms as it may think fit and at any stage adjourn the hearing of appeal if there are reasonable grounds, but not more than one adjournment shall ordinarily be given and the appeal should decided as far as possible within 90 days from the first date of hearing.

(9) Order of the State Commission on appeal shall be signed and dated by the members of the State Commission constituting the Bench and shall be communicated to the parties free of charge.

Repeal and Savings

10. On the commencement of these rules the Maharashtra Consumer Protection Rules, 1987, in so far as they relate to matters **Provided** by these rules, are hereby repealed:

Provided that,—*(a)* such repeal shall not affect previous operation of any notifications or orders made; or anything done or any action taken under the rules so repealed; of any proceedings under the rules so repealed which were pending at the commencement of these rules shall be continued and disposed off as far as may be, in accordance with the provisions of these rules, as if, such proceedings were proceedings under these rules.

Consumerism gaining momentum

Chapter 23

Meghalaya Consumer Protection Rules, 1989

[F. 91/87/55, dated 6-1-1989]

In exercise of the powers conferred by sub-section (2) of section 30 of the Consumer Protection Act, 1986 (68 of 1986), the Government of Meghalaya hereby makes the following rules, namely —

SHORT TITLE, EXTENT AND COMMENCEMENT

1. These rules may be called Meghalaya Consumer Protection Rules, 1989. It extends to the whole State of Meghalaya. They shall come into force on such date as the State Government may by notification in the Official Gazette.

Definitions

2. In these rules unless there is anything repugnant to subject or context —

(a) "Act" means the Consumer Protection Act, 1986 (68 of 1986);

(b) "District Forum" means the District Forum constituted under section 9 of the Act;

(c) "President" means the President of District Forum or, as the case may be, of the State Commission;

(d) "State Commission" means the State Commission constituted under section 9(6) of the Act;

(e) "State Government" means the Government of the State of Meghalaya;

(f) all words and expressions used and not defined shall have the meaning respectively assigned to them in the Act.

Location of District Forum and the State Commission

3. (1) The District Forum shall be located at the Headquarter of the District where the jurisdiction of the District Forum extends to more than one District, the Headquarter of the Forum shall be at such place as the State Government may from time to time decide.

(2) The State Commission shall be located at the capital of the State.

Conditions for appointment as President and members of the State Commissioner of the District Forum

4. (1) No person shall be appointed as or continue to be a President or of the State Commission or as the case may be, of a District Forum one who —

(a) has been adjudged and insolvent;

(b) has been convicted of an offence for which in the opinion of the State Government, involves moral turpitude;

(c) has become physically or mentally incapable of acting as such President or Member;

(d) has acquired such financial or other interest as is likely to affect prejudicially his functions in the State Commission or, as the case may be, in the District Forum; or

(*e*) has so abused his position so as to render his continuance in office prejudicial to the public interest;

Provided that the President or Member shall not be removed from his office on the ground specified in clauses (*d*) and (*e*) except after an inquiry is held by State Government in accordance with such procedure as it may specify in this behalf and finds the member to be guilty of such conduct.

(2) The President and a member of the District Forum before appointment shall furnish an undertaking that he does not and will not have any such financial or other interest which is likely to affect prejudicially his function as a President or a Member.

(3) Where the President of the State Commission or as the case may be, of the District Forum is unable to discharge his function owing to absence or illness or adequacy otherwise occurs in his office, the seniormost (in order of appointment) member holding office for the time being shall discharge the function of the President until the President resumes the office or a person is appointed to fill up the vacancy.

(4) The President or a member of the State Commission or of a District Forum shall not, for a period of 5 years from the date he ceases to hold office as such, hold any appointment in or be connected with the management or administration or any organisation which has been the subject of any proceeding under the Act either before the State Commission or the District Forum, as the case may be, during his tenure as such President or Member.

(5) The President and any member of the State Commission and of a District Forum shall hold office for a term of five years from the date of appointment or until they attain, in the case of those of the State Commission, sixty-seven years of age and, in the case of those of the District Forum, sixty-five years, whichever respectively occurs earlier and such President or member shall not be eligible for reappointment.

(6) Notwithstanding any thing contained in sub-rule (5) the President or any member of the State Commission or a District Forum may—

(*a*) by writing under his hand addressed to the State Government resign his office from the date his resignation is so accepted by the State Government; or

(*b*) be removed from his office under the provisions of sub-rule (1)].

Honorarium and other allowances of the President and Members of the State Commission and also of the District Forum

5. (a) For the State Commission:

(*i*) The President of the State Commission, if not a sitting judge of the High Court, shall, if appointed on whole time basis be paid on honorarium or rupees five thousand per month and, if on part time basis, rupees two hundred for each day of attending work of the commission;

(*ii*) The President of the State Commission, if he is a serving Judge of a High Court shall draw pay and allowances as admissible to him as Judge of the High Court;

(*iii*) A sitting fee of Rupees One hundred seventy-five only per day shall be paid to a non-official member for attending meeting of the State Commission;

(*iv*) The President and Member while travelling on duty connected with the State Commission shall be entitled to travelling allowances at rates admissible to grade I officers of the State Government;

Provided that in case of a serving Judge that rates shall as admissible to him as Judge of that High Court.

(b) The District Forum:

(*i*) The President of a District Forum, other than one drawn from any service under the Government or Court, shall, if appointed on whole time basis, be paid an honorarium of rupees two thousand per month and, if on part time basis, rupees one hundred fifty for each day of attending work of the forum:

(*it*) The President of the District Forum drawn from any service under the Government or Court shall draw pay and allowance as admissible to him in his parent office:

Provided that no pay or allowances shall be admissible in case the appointment of such officer is on part time basis;

(*iii*) A sitting fee of rupees seventy-five only per day shall be paid to a non-official member for attending meeting of the District Forum; A sitting fee of rupees three hundred shall be paid to the President of the District Forum for East Khasi Hills District when such President is a District Judge;

(*iv*) The President and member while travelling on duty connected with the District Forum shall be entitled to travelling allowances at rates admissible to Grade I Officers of the State Government.

Appointment of officers and staffs of the District Forum and State Commission

6. The State Government shall appoint such officers and staffs as may be necessary to assist the District Forum or as the case may be, the State Commission, in the day to day work and their salary be defrayed out of the Consolidated Fund of the State.

Procedure to be adopted by the District Forum for analysis and testing of the goods

7. (1) The District Forum may, if considered necessary, direct the complaint to provide more than one sample of the goods in clean container with stopper properly fixed on them.

(2) On receiving the samples of such goods by the District Forum the same shall be sealed and a label affixed on the container indicating the following particulars—

(*a*) name and address of the laboratory to which samples will be sent for analysis and test; name and address of the District Forum; case number; and (*d*) seal of the District Forum.

(3) The District Forum shall send the samples to the laboratory for making its report within 45 days from the date of its receipt or within such further time as may be granted by the District Forum, specifying the nature of the defect dated in the samples.

Proceedings before the District Forum

8. (1) In any proceeding before the District Forum only the parties thereto may appear either by themselves or through their authorised agents.

(2) Where the opposite party admits the allegation made by the complainant, the District Forum shall decide the matter before it on the basis of the merits of the case.

(3) If any proceeding it shall be obligatory on the complainant and the opposite party to appear before the District Forum on the date fixed by it. In case of any both of them fail to so appear, the District Forum may in its discretion dismiss the complaint or hear the matter *ex parte* and decide it on its merits.

(4) The District Forum may, on such terms as it may think fit and at any stage, adjourn the hearing but not more than one adjournment shall ordinarily be given. The complaint shall be decided within ninety days or within one hundred and fifty days where the complaint requires analysis or testing of goods, from the date of receipt of notice by the opposite party. The order of the District Forum shall be signed and dated by the President and the members hearing the complaint and shall be communicated to the party free of cost.

Other matters relating to District as well as the State Commission

9. (1) The official seal and emblem of the District Forum and of the State Commission shall be such as the State Government may specify.

(2) Sitting of the District Forum or the State Commission as and when necessary, shall be convened by the President.

(3) No act of proceeding of the District or of the State Commission shall be invalid by reason only of the existence of any vacant in its membership or defect in its constitution.

Procedure for preferring appeal to the State Commission

10. (1) Memorandum for appeal under section 15 of the Act may be presented to the State Commission by the appellant in person or by his authorised agent or it may be sent to it under Registered post.

(2) Every memorandum filed under sub-section (1) shall be typed or in legible handwriting. It shall set forth concisely in distinct paragraphs the grounds of appeal without arguments or narratives.

(3) Certified copy of the order of the District Forum appealed against and also such other documents as may be required to support the grounds of appeal should accompany the memorandum.

(4) The memorandum of appeal should normally be submitted within the period of limitation specified in the Act:

Provided that for sufficient cause the appeal could not prepared in time, an application for condoning the period of limitation should simultaneously be made to the State Commission:

(5) The memorandum of appeal submitted to the State Commission should be accompanied with four extra copies.

(6) The appellant or his authorised agent should appear on the date fixed for hearing, failing which the State Commission may, in discretion, either dismiss the appeal or decide it *ex parte* on its merit.

(7) No argument shall be made by the appellant in support of any ground or objection not set forth in the memorandum of appeal except with leave of the State Commission:

Provided that the State Commission may not confine its decision only to the grounds or objection set forth in the memorandum or grounds tendered by leave of the State Commission under this rule:

Provided further that the State Commission may not base its decision on an; ground tendered by the appellant with leave of the State Commission unless the affected party has been given an opportunity of being heard before given its final decision.

(8) The State Commission may, on such term as it may think fit or at any stage adjourn the hearing of appeal, but not more than one adjournment shall ordinarily be given. The appeal should be decided within ninety days from the first date of hearing.

(9) The order of the State Commission shall be signed and dated by the President and members of the State Commission hearing the appeal and the order shall be communicated to the parties concerned free of cost.

Mark	Carat	
958	Corresponds to 23 Carat	A millesimal fineness number indicative of gold content on a scale of 1000
916	Corresponds to 22 carat	
875	Corresponds to 21 Carat	
750	Corresponds to 18 Carat	
585	Corresponds to 14 Carat	
375	Corresponds to 9 Carat	

ASSAYING AND HALLMARKING CENTRE'S MARK

A & HMCS Mark	The Identification Mark of BIS recognized Assaying and Hallmarking Centre where the jewellery has been assayed and hallmarked

YEAR OF MARKING

Code Letter	Code letter represents the year of hallmarking of gold jewellery e.g. 'N' for 2011

JEWELLER'S MARK

Jeweller's Mark	Identification Mark of BIS Certified Jeweller/Jewellery Manufacturer

— ✦ — ✦ — ✦ —

Chapter 24

Mizoram Consumer Protection Rules, 2000

[No. A. 52012/1/96-L&J (SCDF)/121$_T$ Dated 1-12-2000]

In exercise of the powers conferred by sub-section (2) of section 30 of the Consumer Protection Act, 1986 (68 of 1986), as amended from time to time, the Governor of Mizoram is pleased to make the following rules, namely—

SHORT TITLE AND COMMENCEMENT

1. (1) These rules may be called the Mizoram Consumer Protection Rules, 2000.

(2) They shall come into force on the date of their Publication in the Mizoram Gazette.

Definitions

2. In these Rules, unless the context otherwise requires—

(a) "Act" means the Consumer Protection Act, 1986 (68 of 1986), as amended from time to time;

(b) "agent" means a person duly authorised by a party to present any complaint or appeal or reply on its behalf before any District Forum or the State Commission as the case may be;

(c) "appellant" means a party which makes an appeal from an order of District Forum;

(d) "Government" means the State Govt. of Mizoram;

(e) "memorandum" means memorandum of appeal filed by an appellant,

(f) "opposite party" means a person who answer a complaint or claim;

(g) "President" means the President of the State Commission or the District Forum, as the case may be;

(h) "respondent" means the person who answers any memorandum appeal;

(i) "section" means section of the Act;

(j) "State" means the State of Mizoram;

(k) words and expressions used in these Rules and not defined, but defined in the Act shall have the meaning respectively assigned to them in the Act.

Constitution of the State Consumer Protection Council - under section 7(2) of the Act

3. (1) The State Government shall, by notification in the Official Gazette, constitute the State Consumer Protection Council (hereinafter referred to as the State Council) which shall consist of the following members, namely—

(a) the Minister-in-charge of Food and Civil Supplies in the State Government who shall be Chairman of the State Council;

(b) five members of Mizoram Legislative Assembly - at least one each from the recognised/registered political parties;

(c) representatives from consumer organisations or consumers - not less than five;

(d) representatives of the women organisations or women - not less than two;

Information to be furnished with the complaint

- Name and full address of complainant.
- Name and full address of opposite party.
- Description of goods and/or services.
- Date of cause of action.
- Nature of deception.
- Date & proof of purchase of hiring.
- Type of redressal prayed for.

REMEDIES AVAILABLE

- Removal of the defects or deficiencies.
- Refund of money.
- Replacement of the goods.
- Compensation for loss or injury suffered by the consumer.
- Prohibition of marketing of goods/services hazardous to health or environment.

Time limit for disposal of complaint by the Forum

- Normality three months from the date of receipt of notice by the opposite party.
- Five months for the cases where laboratory tests are required.

(*e*) representatives of Banks and other Central Government organisations or bodies concerned with consumer interests like telecommunications, Post and Telegraphs, FCI etc. - not exceeding five;

(*f*) representatives of State Govt. Departments, organisations or bodies concerned with consumer interests like Food and Civil Supplies, Power and Electricity, Public Health Engineering, Transport, Health and Family Welfare Departments and the like - not exceeding ten;

(*g*) representatives of farmers, trade, transport and industries - not exceeding five;

(*h*) persons capable of representing consumer interests not specified above - not exceeding five;

(*i*) Secretary, Law and Judicial Department, Govt. of Mizoram;

(*j*) Secretary, Food and Civil Supplies Department, Government of Mizoram shall be the Member-Secretary of the State Council.

(2) The term of the Council shall be three years in the first instance and subject to extension from time to time.

(3) Any member may by writing under his hand to the Chairman of the State Council, resign from the Council. The vacancies, so caused or otherwise, shall be filled from the same category by the State Government and such person shall hold office so long as the member whose place he fills would have been entitled to hold office, if the vacancy had not occurred.

Procedure of the State Council under section 7(4) of the Act under sub-section (3) of section 4- the State Council shall observe the following procedure in regard to the transaction of its business

4. (1) The meeting of the State Council shall be presided over by the Chairman. In the absence of the Chairman, the State Council shall elect a member to preside over the meeting of the Council.

(2) Each meeting of the State Council shall be called by giving not less than ten days from the date of issue, a notice in writing to every member.

(3) Every notice of a meeting of the State Council shall specify the place and the day and hour of the meeting and shall contain statement of business to be transacted thereat.

(4) No proceedings of the State Council shall be invalid merely by reasons of existence of any vacancy in or any defect in the Constitution of the Council.

(5) The non-official members shall be entitled to Railway fare in first class air-condition by all trains including Rajdhani Express or to actual expenses by actual mode of travel, whichever is availed of and whichever is less, when such member is required to attend the meeting from any place outside Mizoram, or to actual bus fare to and from when such member is required to attend the meeting from any place inside the State of Mizoram. Out station non-official members shall be entitled to a daily allowance of one hundred and fifty rupees per day for attending the meetings of the State Council. Local non-official members shall be paid actual conveyance hire charges subject to a ceiling of one hundred rupees per day. Members of the Mizoram Legislative Assembly shall be entitled to travelling and daily allowances at such rates as are admissible to such members.

(6) The resolutions passed by the State Council shall be recommendatory in nature.

DISTRICT FORUM

Salaries, honorarium and other allowances of the President and members of District Forum under section 10(3) of the Act

5. (1) The President of the District Forum shall be appointed from amongst the persons who were or are qualified to be a District Judge and shall receive the salary of a member of the Mizoram Judicial Service in Grade-I (Junior) if appointed on whole time and regular basis, or an honorarium of ₹ 300 (Rupees three hundred) only per sitting a day, if appointed otherwise. Other members, if sitting on whole time and regular basis, shall receive a consolidated honorarium of ₹ 7,000 (Rupees seven thousand) only per month, or if appointed otherwise, and honorarium of ₹ 250 (Rupees two hundred fifty) only per sitting a day.

(2) The President and the members of the District Forum shall be entitled to travelling and daily allowances on official tour at the same rates as are admissible to the officers in Grade-I (Junior) in the Mizoram Judicial service and to the officers to the Government in the rank of Joint-Secretary respectively.

(3) The President and members of the District Forum if so appointed on whole time and regular basis shall also receive the transfer traveling allowance if they join such District Forum from outside the District Headquarters as is admissible to them at the rates mentioned in sub-rule (2).

The salary or the honorarium as the case may be, and other allowances shall be defrayed out of the consolidated fund of the State.

Other terms and conditions of services of the President and Members of the District Forum under section 10(3) of the Act

6. (1) Before appointment, the President and Members of the District Forum shall be required each to give an undertaking that he or she does not and will not have any such financial or other interests as is likely to effect prejudicially his or her functions as such President or Member, as the case may be, that he is not in any other salaries employment or engagement whether political or otherwise, and that he shall not take up any such other assignment during his tenure as the President or Member as the case may be.

(2) The terms and conditions of service of the President and the members shall not be varied to their disadvantage during their tenure of office.

(3) The President or any other Member ceasing to hold office as such shall not hold any appointment in or be connected with the management or administration of an organisation which has been the subject of any proceeding under the Act during his tenure for a period of five years from the date on which he ceases to hold such office.

Removal of President or Members of the District Forum from office in certain circumstances under section 10(3) of the Act

7. (1) Notwithstanding anything contained in section 10(2) of the Act, the Government may remove from the office the President and a Member of a District Forum who —

(a) has been adjudged an insolvent, or

(b) has been convicted of an office which in the opinion of the State Government involves moral turpitude, or

(c) has become physically or mentally incapable of acting as such President or Member; or

(d) has acquired such financial or other interest as in likely effect prejudicially his functions as such President or Member; or

(e) has no abused his position as to render his continuance in office prejudicial to the public interest; or

(f) has remained absent in three consecutive sittings of the District Forum except for reasons beyond his control; or

(g) has failed to resign from office after attaining the age of 65 years, or completion of his tenure of 5 years as the case may be.

(h) Notwithstanding anything contained in sub-rule (1), the President or any Member shall not be removed from his office on the grounds specified in causes *(d), (e)* and *(g)* except on an inquiry held by the State Government in accordance with such procedure as it may specify in this behalf and finds the resident or a Member to be guilty of such ground.

Place of sitting and other matters relating to District Forum under section 14(3) of the Act

8. (1) The office of the District Forum shall be located at the headquarters of the District and where the State Government decides to establish a single District Forum having jurisdiction over more than one District, it shall notify the place and jurisdiction of the District Forum so established.

(2) The working days, office hours and holdings of the District Forum shall be the same as that of the State Government.

(3) The office seal and emblem of the District Forum shall be as the State Government may specify.

(4) Sitting of the District Forum shall be convened to be held on every working day by the President, and he may, in the interest of speedy disposal of the complaint, hold its sittings at any place within its jurisdiction with prior approval of the Government.

Staff of the District Forum

9. (1) The State Government shall appoint such staff as may be specified by notification(s) from time to time and as may be necessary, to assist the District Forum in its day to day works and to perform such functions as are assigned by the President.

(2) The salaries payable to such staff shall be defrayed out of the Consolidated Fund of the State Government.

(3) The terms and conditions of the staff so appointed for this purpose shall be the same as those of the other employees of the State Government in equivalent rank or grade or as may be specified by the State Government from time to time.

Procedure to be followed for making complaints before the District Forum and the State Commission

10. Subject to the provisions contained in sections 12, 13, hand ISA of the Act, a complaint containing the following particulars shall be presented by the complaint in person or by his authorised agent to the District Forum or the State Commission, as the case may be, or be sent by registered post with A/D, addressed to the District Forum or the State Commission, as the case may be—

(1) Name, description and address of the complainant.

(2) Name, description and address of the opposite party or parties, as the case may be, so far as they can be ascertained;

(3) Material facts and circumstances relating to complaint and when and where the cause of action for the same arose;

(4) Documents in support of the allegation contained in the complaint;

(5) Reliefs claimed.

Procedure of receipt of complaint, subject to the provisions contained in sections 12, 13, 14 and ISA of the Act

11. (1) Where the opposite party admits the allegations made by complainant, the District Forum shall decide the complaint on the basis of the merits of the case and the documents presented before it.

(2) If during the proceedings conducted under section 13, the District For fixed a date for hearing of the parties, it shall be obligatory on the complainant and the opposite party of their authorised agents to appear before the District Forum on such date of hearing or any other date to which the hearing could be adjourned.

(3) Where the complainant or his authorised agent fails to appear before the District Forum on such day, the District Forum may in its discretion, either dismiss the complaint for default or decide it on merit.

(4) Where the opposite party or its authorized agent fails to appear on the day of hearing, the District Forum may decide the complaint *ex parte.*

(5) While proceeding under sub-rule (2), the District Forum may, on such terms *as* it may think fit and at any stage of the proceeding, adjourn the hearing of the complaint but not more than one adjournment shall ordinarily be given and the complaint shall be decided within 90 days from the complaint does not require analysis to testing of the goods involve, and within 150 days if it requires analysis or testing of the goods involved.

(6) The order of the District Forum shall be communicated to the parties concerned free of cost.

Procedure to be adopted by the District Forum or the State Commission for analysis and testing of the goods under section 13(l)(c) of the Act

12. (1) Under section 13(l)(c) of the Act, if considered necessary, the District Forum or State Commission, as the case may be, direct the complainant to provide two or more separate samples of the goods in clean containers with stopper properly fixed on them with a slip of paper wrapped and posted on each of the containers, in which the signature or thumb-impression of the person, trader or manufacturer from whom the goods were purchased shall be affixed:

Provided that if the person or trader or manufacturer from whom the goods were purchased, refuses to affix his signature or thumb-impression, the signature or thumb-impression of a witness shall be taken in the same manner,

(2) On receiving the samples of such goods, the District Forum or the State Commission, as the case may be shall fix labels on the containers carrying the following information—

(*a*) Name and address of the appropriate Laboratory to whom the sample will be sent for analysis and test;

(*b*) Name and address of the District Forum;

(*c*) Case number;

(*d*) Particulars of the goods sent for analysis and test;

(*e*) Date of despatch;

(*f*) Seal of the District Forum.

(3) The quantity of sample, in case of food samples, for analysis shall be such as specified under rule 22 of the Prevention of Food Adulteration Rules, 1955,

(4) The amount of fees for carrying out the analysis of samples shall be decided in consultation with the concerned appropriate laboratory.

STATE COMMISSION

Salary, and other allowances of the President and Members of the State Commission

13. (1) The President of the State Commission shall receive the salary of the judge of the Gauhati High Court, if appointed on whole time basis or a consolidated honorarium of ₹ 350 (Rupees three hundred fifty) per day for the sitting if appointed on part-time basis other members, if appointed on whole time and regular basis shall receive salary of a member of in the Grade [(Senior) of Mizoram Judicial Service if appointed from amongst the members of such Service or a consolidated honorarium of ₹ 7500 (Rupees seven thousand five hundred) only per month, as the case may be, or if appointed on part-time basis, a consolidated honorarium of ₹ 300 (Rupees three hundred) only per day for the sitting.

(2) The President and the Members of the State Commission shall be entitled to such travelling and daily allowances on official tour as are admissible to a Judge of the Gauhati High Court and to the Grade-I Officer in the rank of the Additional Secretary of the Government respectively.

(3) The President and other Members of the State Commission shall also receive the transfer travelling allowance, as is admissible to a Judge of the Gauhati High Court and to the Class-I Officer in the rank of Secretary of the Government respectively, if so appointed on whole time and regular basis.

(4) The Salary, honorarium and other allowances shall be defrayed out of the Consolidated Fund of the State.

Other terms and conditions of service of the President the Members of the State Commission

14. (1) Before appointment, the President if he is a retired High Court Judge and a Member of the State Commission shall have to give an undertaking in writing that he does not and will not have any such financial or other interests as is likely to effect prejudicially his functions as such President or Members as the case may be, and that he is not affiliated to any political party or any consumer association.

(2) The President or any Member ceasing to hold office as such shall not hold any appointment in or be connected with the management or administration of an organisation which has been the subject of any proceeding under the Act. during his tenure for a period of 5 years from the date on which he ceases hold such office.

Removal of President or Members from office in certain circumstances

15. (1) The State Government may remove from office, any Member who-

(a) has been adjudged as an insolvent; or

(b) has been convicted of an offence which, in the opinion of the Government, involves moral turpitude; or

(c) has become physically or mentally incapable of acting as the Preside Member; or

(d) has acquired such financial or other interest as is likely to effects prejudicially his functions as the President or a Member; or

(e) has so abused his position as to render his continuance in office prejudicially to the public interest; or

(f) has remained absent in three consecutive sittings except for reasoned beyond his control; or

(g) has failed to resign from office after attaining the age of sixty-seven years or completion of five years, as the case may be:

Provided that no removal of the President from the State Commission shall be made except with the express approval of the Chief Justice of the High Court option.

(2) Notwithstanding anything contained in sub-rule (1) no Member shall be removed from his office on the grounds specified in clauses *(d)*, *(e)* and *(f)* of sub-rule (1) except on an inquiry held by the State Government in accordance with such procedure as it may specify in this behalf and find any Member guilty of such ground.

Place of sitting and other matters relating to the State Commission, under section 18 read with section 14(3) of the Act

16. (1) The office of the State Commission shall be located at Aizawl.

(2) The working days, office hours and holidays of the State Commission shall be as that of the State Government.

(3) The official seal and emblem of the State Commission shall be such as the State Government may specify.

(4) Sitting of the State Commission shall be convened by the President, and he may, in the interest of speedy disposal of the complaint or appeal, hold its sitting at other suitable place within the State with prior approval of the State Government.

Staff of the State Commission

17. (1) The State Government shall appoint such staff as may be specified in Schedule I to the Rules, subject to additions or alterations by notification(s) from time to time, and as may be necessary to assist the State Commission in its day-to-day work and to perform such functions as are assigned to it by the President.

(2) The salary payable to such staff shall be defrayed out of the Consolidated Fund of the State Government.

(3) The terms and conditions of the staff so appointed for this purpose shall be same as those of the other employees of the State Government in equivalent rank or grade or as may be specified by the State Government from time to time.

Procedure on receipt of complaint, subject to the provisions contained in sections 12, 13, 14, 18 and ISA of the Act

18. (1) Where the opposite party admits the allegation made by the complainant, the State Commission shall decide the complaint on the basis of the merit of the case and documents presented before it.

(2) If during the proceedings conducted under section 13 read with the State Commission fixes a date forbearing of the parties it shall be obligatory on the complaint and the opposite party or his authorise agent to appear before the State Commission on such date of hearing or any other date of which the hearing could be adjourned.

(3) Where the complaint or his authorised agent fails to appear before the State Commission on such day, the State Commission may, in its discretion, either dismiss the complaint for default or decide it on merit.

(4) Where the opposite party or its authorised agent fails to appear on the day of hearing, the State Commission may decide the complaint *ex parte.*

(5) While the proceeding under sub-rule (2), the State Commission may, on such terms as it may think fit and at any stage of the proceedings, adjourn the hearing of the complaint but not more than one adjournment shall ordinarily be given and the complaint shall be decided within 90 days from the date of notice received by the opposite party where the complaint does not require analysis or testing of the goods and within 150 days it requires analysis or testing of the goods involved.

(6) The order of the State Commission shall be communicated to the parties concerned free of cost.

Procedure for hearing appeal

19. (1) Memorandum shall be presented by the appellant or his agent to the State Commission in person or be sent by registered post addressed to the State Commission.

(2) Every memorandum filed under sub-rule (1) shall be in legible handwriting, preferably typed, and shall set forth concisely under distinct heads, the grounds of appeal without any argument or narrative and such grounds shall be numbered consecutively.

(3) Each memorandum shall be accompanied by a certified copy of the order of the District Forum appealed against and such of the documents as may be required to support grounds of objection mentioned in the memorandum.

(4) When the appeal is presented after the expiry of the period of limitation as specified in the Act, such memorandum shall be accompanied by an application supported by an affidavit setting forth the facts on which appellant relies to satisfy the State Commission that he has sufficient cause for not preferring the appeal within the period of limitation.

(5) The appellant shall submit four copies of the memorandum to the State Commission for official purpose.

(6) On the date of hearing or any other day to which hearing may be adjourned, it shall be obligatory for the parties or their authorised agents to appear before the State Commission on such date, if appellant or his authorized agent tails appear on such date, the State Commission may in its discretion either dismiss the appeal or decide *ex parte* on the merit. If respondent or his authorised agent fails to appear on such date, the State Commission shall proceed *ex parte* and shall decide the appeal on merits of the case.

(7) The appellant shall not, except by leave of the State Commission, urge or be heard in support of any ground of objection not set forth in the memorandum but the State Commission, in deciding the appeal, may not confine to the grounds of objection set forth in the memorandum:

Provided that the State Commission shall not rest its decision on any other ground other than these specified in the memorandum, unless the party who may be effected thereby has been given an opportunity of being heard by the State Commission.

(8) State Commission may, on such terms as it may think fit and at any stage adjourn the hearing of appeal, but not more than one adjournment shall ordinarily be given and the appeal should be decided as far as possible, within 90 days from the first date of hearing.

(9) Order of the State Commission on appeal shall be communicated two the parties concerned free of cost.

Repeal and Saving

20. The Mizoram Consumer Protection Rules, 1987 with all amendments and notifications relating thereto shall stand repealed with effect from the date of commencement of these Rules :

Provided that any order made or anything done under the Rules so repealed shall be deemed to have been made or done under the corresponding provisions of these Rules.

—✦—✦—✦—

Chapter 25

Nagaland Consumer Protection Rules, 1987

[SPLY-4/2/87, Dated 28-1-1988]

In exercise of the powers conferred by sub-section (2) of section 30 of the Consumer Protection Act, 1986 (68 of 1986), the State Government hereby makes the following rules, namely:—

SHORT TITLE AND COMMENCEMENT

1. (1) These rules may be called the Nagaland Consumer Protection Rules, 1987.

(2) They shall come into force on such date as the State Government may, by notification in the Official Gazette.

Definitions

2. In these rules, unless the context otherwise requires,—

(a) "Act" means the Consumer Protection Act, 1986 (68 of 1986);

(b) "agent" means a person duly authorised by a party to present any complaint or appeal or reply on its behalf before the State Commission or the District Forum;

(c) "appellant" means a party which makes an apeal against the order of the District Forum;

(d) "memorandum" means memorandum of appeal filed by the appellant;

(e) "opposite party" means a person who answers complaint or claim;

(f) "President" means the President of the State Commission or District Forum as the case may be;

(g) "respondent" means the person who answers any memorandum ot appeal;

(h) "State" includes Union Territories.

Salaries and other allowances and terms and conditions of the President and Members of the District Forum

3. (1) The President of the District Forum shall receive the salary of the Judge of the District Court if appointed on whole-time basis or an honorarium or ₹ 150/- per day if appointed on part-time basis. Other members if sitting o whole-time basis, shall receive a consolidated honorarium of ₹ 2,000/- month and if sitting on part-time basis, a consolidated honorarium of ₹ 100/- per day for the sitting.

(2) The President and the Members of the District Forum shall be entitled to such travelling allowance and daily allowance on official tour as are admissible to Grade-I Officer of the State Government.

(3) The salary, honorarium and other allowances shall be defrayed out of the Consolidated Fund of the State.

(4) Before appointment, the President and Members of the District Forum shall have to take an undertaking that he does not and will not have any such financial or other interests as is likely to affect prejudicially his functions as a member.

(5) In addition to the provisions of section 10(2) of the Act, the State Government may remove from the office, the

President and any Member of a District Forum who,—

(*a*) has been adjudged as insolvent; or

(*b*) has been convicted of an offence which in the opinion of the State Government involves moral turpitude; or

(*c*) has become physically or mentally incapable of acting as such member; or

(*d*) has acquired such financial or other interest as is likely to affect prejudicially his functions as a member; or

(*e*) has so abused his position as to render his continuance in office prejudicial to the public interest:

Provided that the President or Member shall not be removed from his office on the ground specified in clauses (*d*) and (*e*) of sub-rule (5) except on an inquiry held by the State Government in accordance with such procedure as it may specify in this behalf and finds the member to be guilty of such ground.

(6) The terms and conditions of the service of the President and the Members of the District Forum shall not be varied to their disadvantage during their tenure of office.

(7) Where any vacancy occurs in the office of the President of the District Forum, the senior-most (in order of appointment) Member of District Forum, holding office for the time being, shall discharge the functions of the President until a person appointed to fill such vacancy assumes the office of the President of the District Forum.

(8) When the President of the District Forum is unable Lo discharge the functions owing to absence, illness, or any other cause, the senior-most (in order of appointment) Member of the District Forum shall discharge the functions of the President until the day on which the President resumes the harge of his functions.

(9) The President or any Member ceasing to hold office as such shall not hold appointment in or be connected with the management or administration an organisation which have been the subject of any proceeding under the during his tenure for a period of 5 years from the date on which he ceases hold such office.

Place of Sitting and Other Matters Relating to District Forum

4. (1) The office of the District Forum shall be located at the headquarter the District. Where State Government decides to establish a single District Forum having jurisdiction over more than one District, it shall notify the place and jurisdiction of the District Forum so established.

(2) The working days and the office hours of the District Forum shall be the same as that of the State Government.

(3) The official seal and emblem of the District Forum shall be such as the State Government may specify.

(4) Sitting of the District Forum, as and when necessary, shall be convened by the President.

(5) No act or proceedings of the District Forum shall be invalid by reasons only of the existence of any vacancy among its members or any defects in its Constitution.

(6) The State Government shall appoint such staff, as may be necessary to assist I the District Forum in its day to day work and perform such other functions as are **Provided** under these rules, or assigned to it by the President. The salary payable to such staff shall be defrayed out of the Consolidated Fund of the State.

(7) Where the opposite party admits the allegation made by the complainant, the District Forum shall decide the complaint on the basis of the merit of the case and documents present before it.

(8) If during the proceedings conducted under section 13, District Forum fixes I a date for hearing of the parties, it shall be obligatory on the complainant and] opposite party or its authorised agent to appear before the District Forum on I such date of hearing or any other date to which hearing could be adjourned Where the complainant or his authorised agent fails to appear before the District Forum on such day, the District Forum may in its discretion either dismiss the complaint for default or decide it on merit. Where the opposite party or its authorised agent fails to appear on the day of hearing, the District Forum may decide the complaint *ex parte.*

(9) While proceeding under sub-rule (8), the District Forum may, on such terms as it may think fit and at any stage, adjourn the hearing of the complaint but not more than one adjournment shall ordinarily be given and the complaint should be decided within 90 days from the date of notice received by the opposite party where complaint does not require analysis or testing of the goods and within 150 days if it requires analysis or testing of the goods.

(10) Orders of the District Forum shall be signed and dated by the Members of the District Forum constituting the Bench and shall be communicated to the parties free of charge.

Procedure to be Adopted by the District Forum for Analysis and Testing Goods

5. (1) Under section 13(l)(c), if considered necessary, the District Forum direct the complainant to provide more than one sample of the goods clean containers with stopper properly fixed on them.

(2) On receiving the samples of such goods, the District Forum shall seal it and fix labels on the containers carrying following information:—

(i) name and address of the appropriate laboratory to whom sample will be sent for analysis and test;

(ii) name and address of the District Forum;

(iii) case number;

(iv) seal of the District Forum.

(3) The sample will be sent to the appropriate laboratory by the District Forum for sending report within 45 days or within such extended time as may be granted by the District Forum after specifying the nature of the defect alleged and date of submission of the report.

Salary and Other Allowances and Terms and Conditions of the President and Members of the State Commission

6. (1) The President of the State Commission shall receive the salary of the Judge of the High Court if appointed on whole-time basis or a consolidated honorarium of ₹ 200/- per day for the sitting if appointed on part-time basis. Other members, if sitting on whole-time basis, shall receive a consolidated honorarium of ₹ 3,000 per month and if sitting on part-time basis, a consolidated honorarium of ₹ 150 per day for the sitting.

(2) The President and the Members of the State Commission shall be eligible for such travelling allowance and daily allowance on official tour as are admissible to Grade-I Officer of the State Government.

(3) The salary, honorarium, other allowances shall be defrayed out of the Consolidated fund of the State Government.

(4) The President and the Member of the State Commission shall hold office for a term of five years or upto the age of 65 years whichever is earlier and shall not be eligible for renomination:

Provided that President and Member may:—

(a) by writing under his hand and addressed to the State Government resign his office any time; and

(b) be removed from his office in accordance with the provision of sub-rule (5).

(5) The State Government may remove from office, President or a Member of the State Commission who,—

(a) has been adjudged as insolvent; or

(b) has been convicted of an offence which in the opinion of the State Government, involves moral turpitude; or

(c) has become physically or mentally incapable of acting as such member;

(d) has acquired such financial or other interest as is likely to affect prejudi-cially his functions as a member; or See section 16(3) of the Consumer Protection Act, 1986.

(e) has so abused his position as to render his continuance in office prejudicial to the public interest:

Provided that the President or Member shall not be removed from his office of the ground specified in clauses *(d)* and *(e) of* sub-rule (5) except on an inquiry, held by State Government, in accordance With such procedure as it may specify in this behalf and finds the member to be guilty of such ground.

(6) Before appointment, the President and Members of the State Commission shall have to take an undertaking that he does not and will not have any such financial or other interests as is likely to affect prejudicially his functions as such member.

(7) The terms and conditions of the service of the President and the Members of the State Commission shall not be varied to their disadvantage during their tenure of office.

(8) Every vacancy caused by resignation and removal of the President or any other Member of the State Commission under sub-rule (4) or otherwise shall be filled by fresh appointment.

(9) Where any such vacancy occurs in the office of the President of the State Commission, the senior most (in order of appointment) member, holding office for the time being, shall discharge the functions of the President until a person appointed to fill such vacancy assumes the office of the President of the State Commission.

(10) When the President of the State Commission is unable to discharge the functions owing to absence, illness or any other cause, the seniormost (in order of appointment) Member of the State Commission shall discharge the functions of the President until the day on which the President resumes the charge of his functions.

(11) The President or any Member ceasing to hold office as such shall not hold any appointment in or be connected with the management or administration of an organisation which have been the subject of any proceedings, under the Act during his tenure for a period of 5 years from the date on which he ceases to hold such office.

Place of Sitting and Other Matters Relating to State Commission

7. (1) Office of the State Commission shall be located at the capital of the State.

(2) The working days and the office hours of the State Commission, shall be same as that of the State Government.

(3) The official seal and emblem of the State Commission shall be such as the State Government may specify.

(4) Sitting of the State Commission, as and when necessary, shall be convened by the President.

(5) No act or proceedings of the State Commission shall be invalid by reason only of the existence of any vacancy among its members or any defect in the constitution thereof.

(6) Slate Government shall appoint such staff, as may be necessary to assist the State Commission in its work and perform such other functions as are **Provided** under these rules or assigned to it by the President. The salary payable to such staff shall be defrayed out of the Consolidated Fund of the State Government.

(7) Where the opposite party admits the allegation made by the complainant, the State Commission shall decide the complaint on the basis of the merit of the case and documents present before it.

(8) If during the proceedings conducted under section 13, State Commission fixes a date for hearing of the parties, it shall be obligatory on the complainant and opposite party or his authorised agent to appear before the State Commission on such date of hearing or any other date to which hearing could be adjourned. Where the complainant or his authorized agent fails to appear before the State Commission on such day, the State Commission may in its discretion cither dismiss the complaint for default or decide it on merit. Where the opposite party or its authorised agent fails to appear on the day of hearing, the State Commission may decide the complaint *ex parte.*

(9) While proceeding under sub-rule (8), the State Commission may on such terms as it may think fit and at any stage, adjourn the hearing of the complaint but not more than one adjournment shall ordinarily be given and the complaint should be decided within 90 days from the date of notice received by the opposite party where complaint does not require analysis or testing of the goods and within 150 days if it requires analysis or testing of the goods.

(10) Orders of the State Commission shall be signed and dated by the members of the State Commission constituting the Bench and shall be communicated to the parties free of charge.

Procedure for Hearing Appeal [Section 15]

8. (1) Memorandum shall be presented by the appellant or his authorised agent to the State Commission in person or be sent by registered post addressed to the Commission.

(2) Every memorandum filed under sub-rule (1) shall be in legible handwriting, preferably typed and shall set forth concisely under distinct heads, the grounds of appeal without any argument or narrative and such grounds shall be numbered consecutively.

(3) Each memorandum shall be accompanied by the certified copy of the order of the District Forum appealed against and such of the documents as may be required to support grounds of objection mentioned in the memorandum.

(4) When the appeal is presented after the expiry of the period of limitation as specified in the Act, the memorandum shall be accompanied by an application supported by an affidavit setting forth the fact on which the appellant relies to satisfy the State Commission that he has sufficient cause for not preferring the Peal within the period of limitation.

(5) The appellant shall submit four copies of the memorandum to the State Commission for official purposes.

(6) On the date of hearing or on any other day to which hearing may be so journed, it shall be obligatory for the parties or their authorized agent to appear before the State Commission. If appellant or his authorised agent fag to appear on such date, the State Commission, may, in its discretion either dismiss the appeal or decide it on the merit of the case. If respondent or his authorized agent fails to appear on such date, the State Commission shall proceed *ex parte and* shall decide the appeal *ex parte on* the merits of the case

(7) The appellant shall not, except by leave of the State Commission, urge or be heard in support of any ground of objection not set forth in the memorandum but the State Commission, in deciding the appeal, shall not confine to the grounds of objection set forth in the memorandum or taken by leave of the State Commission under this rule: **Provided** that the State Commission shall not rest its decision on any other grounds unless the party who may be affected thereby, has been given, at least one opportunity of being heard by the State Commission.

(8) State Commission may, on such terms as it may think fit and at any stage, adjourn the hearing of the appeal, but not more than one adjournment shall ordinarily be given and the appeal should be decided within 90 days from the first date of hearing.

(9) Order of the State Commission on appeal shall be signed and dated by the Members of the State Commission constituting the Bench and shall be communicated to the parties free of charge.

Chapter 26

Orissa Consumer Protection Rules, 1987

[No. PL 1C 9/87/944, Dated 15-3-1988]

In exercise of the powers conferred by sub-section (2) of section 30 of the Consumer Protection Act, 1986 (68 of 1986) the Government of Orissa hereby makes the following rules, namely —

SHORT TITLE AND COMMENCEMENT

1. (1) These Rules may be called the Orissa Consumer Protection Rules, 1987.

(2) They shall come into force on the date of their publication in the Orissa Gazette.

Definitions

2. In these rules unless the context otherwise requires —

(a) "Act" means the Consumer Protection Act, 1986 (68 of 1986);

(b) "agent" means a person duly authorised by a party to present any complaint or appeal or reply on its behalf before the District Forum or the State Commission;

(c) "appellant" means a party which makes an appeal against the order of the District Forum;

(d) "memorandum" means memorandum of appeal filed by the appellant;

(e) "opposite party" means a person who answers complaint or claim;

(f) "President" means the President of the State Commission or District Forum as the case may be;

(g) "respondent" means the person who answers any memorandum of appeal;

(h) "State Government" means the Government of Orissa.

Salary or Honorarium and Other Allowances and Terms and Conditions of the "President and Members of the District Forum [Section 10(3)]

3. (1) The President of the District Forum shall receive the salary or an honorarium at the following rates—

(a) If a person who is a serving District. The salary of a District Judge is appointed on whole time basis.

(b) If a person who is a serving District Judge is appointed on part-time basis.

(c) If a retired person who had been a District Judge is appointed on whole-time basis.

(d) If a person is qualified to be a District Judge is appointed on whole-time basis.

Honorarium at the rate of rupees one hundred and fifty per day of sitting.

A consolidated salary of rupees five thousand per month, over and above the pension.

A consolidated salary of rupees five thousand per month.

(2) The other members of the District Forum shall receive a consolidated salary of rupees three thousand per month if appointed on whole time basis.

(3) The salary honorarium and other allowances shall be defrayed out of the Consolidated Fund of the State Government.

(4) Before appointment, the President and members of the District Forum shall have to give an undertaking that he does not and will not have any such financial or other interests as is likely to affect prejudicially his functions as a member.

(5) The State Government may remove from the office, the President and member of a District Forum who,—

(a) has been adjudged as insolvent; or

(b) has been convicted of an offence which in the opinion of the State Government, involves moral turpitude; or

(c) has become physically or mentally incapable of acting as such member;

(d) has acquired such financial or other interest as is likely to affect prejudicially his functions as a member; or

(e) has so abused his position as to render his continuance in office prejudicial to the public interest:

Provided that the President or member shall not be removed from his office on the ground specified in clauses *(d)* and *(e)* except on an inquiry held by the State Government in accordance with such procedure as it may deem proper and finds the member to be guilty of such ground.

(6) The terms and conditions of the service of the President and the members of the District Forum shall not be varied to their disadvantage during their tenure of office.

(7) Where any vacancy occurs in the office of the President of the District Forum, the seniormost (in order of appointment) member of District Forum holding office for the time being, shall discharge the functions of the Preside] until a person appointed to fill such vacancy and assumes the office of President of the District Forum,

(8) When the President of the District Forum is unable to discharge the functions owing to absence, illness or any other cause, the senior-most (in order of appointment) member of the District Forum shall discharge the functions of the President until the day on which the President resumes the charge of his functions.

(9) The President or any member ceasing to hold office as such shall not hold any appointment in or be connected with the management or administration of an organisation which have been the subject of any proceeding under the Act during his tenure for a period of 5 years from the date on which he ceases to hold such office.

Place of sitting and other matters relating to District Forum [Section 14(3)]

4. (1) The Office of the District Forum shall be located at the headquarter of the District. The office of the District Forum Puri [Koraput and Ganjam District shall however, be located at Bhubaneshwar, Jaipur and Berhampur respectively].

(2) The working days and the office hours of the District Forum shall be the same as that of the State Government.

(3) The official seal and emblem of the District Forum shall be such as the State Government may specify.

(4) Sitting of the District Forum, as and when necessary, shall be convened by the President.

(5) No act or proceedings of the District Forum shall be invalid by reason only or the existence of any vacancy among its members or any defect in its constitution.

(6) State Government shall appoint such staff, as may be necessary to assist the District Forum in its day to day work and perform such other functions as may be assigned to them by the President under these rules. The salary payable to such staff shall be defrayed out of the Consolidated Fund of the State Government.

(7) Where the opposite party admits the allegation made by the complainant, the District Forum shall decide the complaint on the basis of the merit of the case and documents present before it.

(8) If during the proceedings conducted under section 13, District Forum fixes a date for hearing of the parties, it shall be obligatory on the complainant and opposite party or its authorised agent to appear before the District Forum on such date of hearing or any other date to which hearing could be adjourned. Where the complainant or his authorised agent fails to appear before the District Forum on such day, the District Forum may in its discretion either dismiss the complaint for default or decide it on merit. Where the opposite party or its authorised agent fails to appear on the day of hearing, the District Forum may decide the complaint *ex parte.*

(9) While proceeding under sub-rule (8), the District Forum may, on such terms as it may think fit and any stage, adjourn the hearing of the complaint but not more than one adjournment shall ordinarily be given and the complaint should be decided within 90 days from the date of notice received by the opposite party where complaint does not require analysis or testing of the goods and Within 150 days if it requires analysis or testing of goods.

(10) Order of the District Forum shall be signed and dated by the members of the District Forum hearing the complaint and shall be communicated to the parties free of charge.

(11) Substituted by Orissa Exty, Gazette No. 558, dated 24-6-1990, *vide* Notification No. 11166 PL-1C 7/89, dated 20-4-1990 (*w.e.f.* 24-4-1990).

Procedure to be Adopted by the District Forum for Analysis and Testing of the Goods [Section 13(4)(c)]

5. (1) The District Forum if it considers necessary, may direct the complainant to provide more than one sample of the goods in clean containers with stopper properly fixed on them.

(2) On receiving the samples of such goods, the District Forum shall seal them and fix labels on the containers carrying following information, namely—

(i) name and address of the appropriate laboratory to whom samples will be sent for analysis and test;

(ii) name and address of the District Forum;

(iii) case number;

(iv) seal of the District Forum.

(3) The District Forum shall send the samples to the appropriate laboratory for sending a report within 45 days or within such extended Urne as may be granted by the District Forum after specifying the nature of the defect alleged and date of submission of the report.

Salary or Honorarium and Other Allowances and Terms and Conditions of the President and Members of the State Commission [Section 16(2)]

6. (1) *(a)* The President of the State Commission shall receive the salary of the Judge of a High Court if appointed on whole time basis or an honorarium of rupees two hundred only per day of sitting if appointed on part-time basis.

(b) Other members of State Commission if appointed on whole time basis, shall receive a consolidated salary of rupees five thousand per month.

(2) The President and the members of the State Commission shall be eligible for such travelling allowance and daily allowance on official tour as are admissible to Class-I officer of the State Government under the Orissa Travelling Allowances Rules.

(3) The salary, honorarium and other allowances shall be defrayed out of the Consolidated Fund of the State Government.

(4) President and the members of the State Commission shall hold office for a term of five years or upto the age to 65 years whichever is earlier and shall not be eligible for re-appointment:

Provided that the President and member may by writing under his hand and addressed to the State Government resign his office at any time.

(5) The State Government may remove from office President or a member of the State Commission who,—

(a) has been adjudged as insolvent; or

(b) has been convicted of an offence which in the opinion of the State Government involves moral turpitude; or

(c) has become physically or mentally incapable of acting as such member; or

(d) has required such financial or other interest as is likely to affect prejudicially his functions as a member; or

(e) has so abused with position as to render his continuance in office prejudicial to the public interest:

Provided that the President or a member shall not be removed from his office on the ground specified in clauses *(d)* and *(e)* except on an inquiry held by State Government in accordance with such procedure as il may deem proper and finds the member to be guilty of such grounds.

(6) Before appointment. President/member of the Stale Commission shall have to give an undertaking that he does not and shall not have any such financial or other interests as is likely to affect prejudicially his functions as such member.

(7) The terms and conditions of the service of the President and the members of the State Commission shall not be varied to their disadvantage during their tenure of office.

(8) Every vacancy caused by resignation and removal of the President or any other member of the State Commission under sub-rules (4) and (5) or otherwise shall be filled by fresh appointment.

(9) Where any such vacancy occur in the office of the President of the State Commission, the scniormost (in order of appointment) member, holding office for the time being shall discharge the functions of the President until a person appointed lo fill such vacancy assumes the office of the President of the State Commission.

(10) When the President of the State Commission is unable to discharge the functions owing to absence, illness or any other cause, the seniormost (in order to the appointment) member of the State Commission shall discharge the functions of the President until the day on which the President resumes his functions.

(11) The President or any member ceasing to hold office as such shall not hold any appointment in or be connected with the management or administration of an organisation which have been the subject of any proceeding under the Act during his tenure for a period of 5 years from the date on which he ceases to hold such office:

Provided that where the President is the sitting Judge of the High Court of the State, no undertaking shall be necessary.

Place of Sitting and Other Matters Relating to State Commission [Section 14(3)]

7. (1) Office of the State Commission shall be located at [Cuttack].

(2) The working days and the office hours of the State Commission shall be the same as that of the State Government.

(3) The official seal and emblem of the State Commission shall be such as the State Government may specify.

(4) Sitting of the State Commission, as and when necessary, shall be convened by the President.

(5) No act or proceedings of the State Commission shall be invalid by reasons only of the existence of any vacancy among its members or any defect in its constitution thereof.

(6) State Government shall appoint such staff, as may be necessary to assist the State Commission in its work and perform such other functions as are **Provided** under these rules or assigned to it by the President. The salary payable to such staff shall be defrayed out of the Consolidated Fund of the State Government.

(7) The provision contained in sub-rules (7) to (10) of rule 4 shall *mutatis mutandis* apply to the appeal preferred before the State Commission subject to the modifications specified in rule 8.

Procedure for Hearing Appeal [Section 15]

8. (1) Memorandum shall be presented by the appellant or his authorised agent to the State Commission in person or be sent by registered post addressed to the Commission.

(2) Every memorandum filed under sub-rule (1) shall be in legible handwriting preferably typed and shall set forth concisely under distinct heads, the grounds of such appeal without any argument or narrative and such ground shall be numbered consecutively.

(3) Each memorandum shall be accompanied by the certified copy of the order of the District Forum appealed against and such of the documents as may be required to support grounds of objection mentioned in the memorandum.

(4) When the memorandum is presented after the expiry of period of limitation as specified in the Act, such memorandum shall be accompanied by an application supported by an affidavit setting forth the fact on which appellant relies to satisfy the State Commission that he has sufficient cause for not preferring the appeal within the period of limitation.

(5) The appellant shall submit four copies of the memorandum to the State Commission for official purposes,

(6) On the date of hearing or any other date to which hearing has been adjourned, it shall be obligatory for the parties or their authorised agent to appear before the State Commission on such date. If appellant or his authorised agent fails to appear on such date, the State Commission may, in its discretion, either dismiss the appeal or decide it on the merit of the case. If respondent or his authorised agent fails to appear on such date, the State Commission shall proceed *ex parte* and shall decide the appeal *ex parte* on merits of the case.

(7) The appellant shall not, except by leave of the State Commission, urge or be heard in support of any ground of objection not set forth in the memorandum but the State Commission, in deciding the appeal, shall not confine to the grounds of objection set forth in the memorandum or taken by leave of the State Commission under this rule :

Provided that the State Commission shall not rest its decision on any other grounds unless the party who may be affected thereby, has been given, at least one opportunity of being heard by the State Commission.

(8) State Commission may, on such terms as it may think fit and at any stage, adjourn the hearing of appeal, but not more than one adjournment shall ordinarily be given and the appeal should be decided within 90 days from the first date of hearing.

(9) Order of the State Commission on appeal shall be signed and dated by the members of the State Commission hearing the appeal and shall be communicated to the parties free of charge.

Chapter 27

Pondicherry Consumer Protection Rules, 1987

[G.O.Ms. No. 16, Dated 22-8-1987]

In exercise of the powers conferred by sub-section (2) of section 30 of the Consumer Protection Act, 1986 (68 of 1986), read with Government of India Notification SO No. 469(E), dated 15th May, 1987, the Lieutenant-Governor, Pondicherry is hereby pleased to make the following rules, namely —

SHORT TITLE AND COMMENCEMENT

1. (1) These rules may be called the Puducherry Consumer Protection Rules, 1987.

(2) They shall come into force on such date as the Government may, by notification in the Official Gazette.

Definitions

2. In these rules, unless the context otherwise requires,—

(a) "Act" means the Consumer Protection Act, 1986 (68 of 1986);

(b) "agent" means a person duly authorised by a party to present any complaint or appeal or reply on its behalf before the State Commission or the District Forum;

(c) "appellant" means a party which makes an appeal against the order of the District Forum;

(d) "Government" means the Government of Puducherry;

(e) "memorandum" means memorandum of appeal filed by the appellant;

(f) "opposite party" means a person who answers complaint or claim;

(g) "President" means the President of the State Commission, or District Forum as the case may be;

(h) "Respondent" means the person who answers any memorandum of appeal.

Salaries and other allowances and other terms and conditions of the President and members of the District Forum [Section 10(3)]

3. (1) The President of the District Forum shall receive the salary of a Judge of a District Court if appointed on whole time basis or consolidated honorarium of ₹ 1,500 *plus* ₹ 250 per day for sitting if appointed on part-time basis. Other members, if sitting on whole time basis, shall receive a consolidated honorarium of ₹ 3,500 per month and if sitting on part-time basis, a consolidated honorarium of Rs. 750 *plus* ₹ 100 per day for the sitting.

(2) The President and the members of the District Forum shall be entitled for such travelling allowance and daily allowance on official tour as are admissible to Grade-I Officer of the Government.

(3) The salary, honorarium and other allowances shall be defrayed out of the Consolidated Fund of the Government.

(4) Before appointment, the President and Members of the District Forum shall have to take an undertaking that he does not, and will not have any such financial or other interest as is likely to affect prejudicially his functions as a Member.

(5) In addition to the provisions of section 10(2) of the Act, the Government may remove from the office, the President and member of a District Forum

(*a*) has been adjudged as insolvent, or

(*b*) has been convicted of an offence which in the opinion of the Government, involves moral turpitude, or

(*c*) has become physically or mentally incapable of acting as such Member, or

(*d*) has acquired such financial or other interest as is likely to affect prejudicially his functions as a Member, or

(*e*) has so abused his position as to render his continuance in office prejudicial to the public interest:

Provided that the President or Member shall not be removed from his office on the ground specified in clauses (d) and (e) of sub-rule (5) except on an inquiry held by the Government in accordance with such procedure as it may specify in this behalf and finds the Member to be guilty of such grounds.

(6) The terms and conditions of the service of the President and the members of the District Forum shall not be varied to their disadvantage during their tenure of office.

(7) Where any vacancy occurs in the office of the President of the District Forum, the seniormost (in order of appointment) member of District Forum, holding office for the time being, shall discharge the functions of the Preside 11 until a person appointed to fill such vacancy assumes the Office of the President of the District Forum.

(8) When the President of the District Forum is unable to discharge the functions owing to absence, illness or any other cause, the seniormost (in order of the appointment) Member of the District Forum shall discharge the functions of the President until the day on which the President resumes the charge of his functions.

(9) The President or any member ceasing to hold office as such shall not any appointment in or be connected with the management or administration of an organisation which have been the subject of any proceeding under Act. during his tenure for a period of five years from the date on which he ceases to hold such office.

Place of Sitting and Other Matters Relating to District Forum [Section 14(3)]

4. (1) The office of the District Forum shall be located at Pondicherry. Where the Government decides to establish a single District Forum having jurisdiction over more than one district, the place and jurisdiction of the District Forum so established shall be notified by the Government.

(2) The working days and the office hours of the District Forum shall be same as that of the Government.

(3) The official seal and emblem of the District Forum shall be such as the Government may specify.

(4) Silting of the District Forum, as and when necessary, shall be convened by the President.

(5) No act or proceeding of the District Forum shall be invalid by reason only of the existence of any vacancy among its members or any defect in its constitution.

(6) The Government shall appoint such staff, as may be necessary to assist the District Forum in its day to day work and perform such other functions as are **Provided** under these rules, or assigned to it by the President. The salary payable to such staff shall be defrayed out of the Consolidated Fund of the Government.

(7) Where the opposite party admits the allegation made by the complainant, the District Forum shall decide the complaint on the basis of the merit of the case and documents present before it.

(8) If during the proceedings conducted under section 13, District Forum fixes a date for hearing of the parties, it shall be obligatory on the complainant and opposite party or its authorised agent to appear before the District Forum on such date of hearing or any other date to which hearing could be adjourned. Where the complainant or his authorised agent fails to appear before the District Forum on such day, the District Forum may in its discretion either dismiss the complaint for default or decide it on merit. Where the opposite party or its authorised agent fails to appear on the date of hearing, the District Forum may decide the complaint *ex parte*.

(9) While proceeding under sub-rule (8), the District Forum may, on such terms it may think fit and at any stage, adjourn the hearing of the complaint but not more than one adjournment shall ordinarily be given and the complaint should be decided within 90 days from the date of notice received by the opposite party, where complaint does not require analysis or testing of the goods and within 150 days if it requires analysis or testing of the goods.

(10) Orders of the District Forum shall be signed and dated by the members of District Forum constituting the Bench and shall be communicated to the Parties free of charge.

Procedure to be Adopted by the District Forum for Analysis and Testing of the Goods [Section 13(l)(c)]

5. (1) Under section 13(1)(c), if considered necessary, the District Forum may direct the complainant to provide more than one sample of the goods in clean container with stopper properly fixed on them.

(2) On receiving the samples of such goods, the District Forum shall seal it and fix lables on the containers carrying following information :—

(i) Name and address of the appropriate laboratory to whom sample will be sent for analysis and test;

(ii) Name and address of the District Forum;

(iii) Case number;

(iv) Seal of the District Forum.

(3) The sample will be sent to the appropriate laboratory by the District Forum for sending report within 45 days or within such extended time as may be granted by the District Forum after specifying the nature of the defect alleged and date of submission of the report.

Salary and Other Allowances and Terms and Conditions of the President and Members of the State Commission [Section 16(2)]

6. (1) President of the State Commission shall receive the salary of the Judge of the High Court if appointed on wholetime basis or a consolidated honorarium of ₹ 2,000 plus ₹ 500 per day for the sitting, if appointed on part-time basis. Other members, if sitting on whole time basis shall receive a consolidated honorarium of ₹ 3,500 per month and if sitting on part-time basis a consolidated honorarium of Rs. 1,500 plus ₹ 200 per day for the sitting.

(2) The President and the Members of the State Commission shall be eligible for such travelling allowance and daily allowance on official tour as are admissible to a Judge of a High Court and to a Grade-I Officer of the Government, respectively.

(3) The salary, honorarium, other allowances shall be defrayed out of the Consolidated Fund of the Government.

(4) 'President and the Member of the State Commission shall hold office for a term of five years or up to the age of 67 years whichever is earlier and shall not be eligible for renomination;

Provided that President and member may—

(a) by writing under his hand and addressed to the Government resign his/her office any time; and

(b) be removed from his office in accordance with provisions of sub-rule (5) **Provided further** that notwithstanding anything contained in this sub-rule, a person appointed as a President or as a member before the commencement of the Consumer Protection (Amendment) Act, 1993, shall continue to hold such office as President or member, as the case may be, till the completion of his/ her term.

(5) The Government may remove from office, President or a Member of the State Commission who,—

(a) has been adjudged as insolvent, or

(b) has been convicted of an offence which in the opinion of the Government, involves moral turpitude, or

(c) has become physically or mentally incapable of acting as such member, or

(d) has acquired such financial or other interest as is likely to affect prejudicially his functions as a member, or

(e) has so abused his position as to render his continuance in office prejudicial to the public interest:

Provided that the President or a member shall not be removed from his office on the ground specified in clauses *(d)* and *(e)* of sub-rule (5) except on an inquiry held by the Government, in accordance with such procedure as it may specify in this behalf and finds the member to be guilty of such grounds,

(6) Before appointment, President and a member of the State Commission shall have to take an undertaking that he does not and will not have any such financial or other interests as is likely to affect prejudicially his functions as such member.

(7) The terms and conditions of the service of the President and the members of the State Commission shall not be varied to their disadvantage during their tenure of office.

(8) Every vacancy caused by resignation and removal of the President or any other member of the State Commission under sub-rule (4) or otherwise shall be filled by fresh appointment.

(9) Where any such vacancy occurs in the office of the President of the State Commission, the seniormost (in order of appointment) member, holding office for the time being, shall discharge the functions of the President until a person appointed to fill such vacancy assumes the office of the President of the State Commission.

(10) When the President of the State Commission is unable to discharge the functions owing to absence, illness or any other cause, the seniormost (in order of the appointment) member of the State Commission shall discharge the functions of the President until the day on which the President resumes the charge of his functions.

(11) The President or any member ceasing to hold office as such shall not hold any appointment in or be connected with the management or administration of an organisation which have been the subject of any proceeding under the Act during this tenure for a period of five years from the date on which he ceases to hold such office.

Place of Sitting and Other Matters Relating to State Commission [Section 14(3) read with section 18]

7. (1) Office of the State Commission shall be located at Pondicherry.

(2) The working days and the office hours of the State Commission shall be the same as that of the Government or as fixed by the President of the State Commission.

(3) The official seal and emblem of the State Commission shall be such as the Government may specify.

(4) Sitting of the State Commission, as and when necessary, shall be convened by the President.

(5) No act or proceedings of the State Commission shall be invalid by reasons only of the existence of any vacancy among its members or any defect in its constitution thereof.

(6) The Government shall appoint such staff, as may be necessary to assist the State Commission in its work and perform such other functions as are **Provided** under these rules or assigned to it by the President. The salary payable to such staff shall be defrayed out of the Consolidated Fund of the Government,

(7) Where the opposite party admits the allegation made by the complainant, the State Commission shall decide the complaint on the basis of the merit of the case and documents present before it.

(8) If during the proceedings conducted under section 13, the State Commission fixes a date for hearing of the parties, it shall be obligatory on the complainant and opposite party or his authorised agent to appear before the State Commission on such date of hearing or any other date to which hearing could be adjourned. Where the complainant or his authorised agent fails to appear before the State Commission on such day, the State Commission may in its discretion either dismiss the complaint for default or decide it on merits. Where the opposite party or its authorised agent fails to appear on the day of hearing, the State Commission may decide the complaint *ex parte*.

(9) While proceedings under sub-rule (8) the State Commission may, on such terms as it may think fit and at any stage, adjourn the hearing of the complaint but not more than one adjournment shall ordinarily be given and the complaint should be decided within 90 days from the date of notice received by the opposite party where complaint does not require analysis or testing of the goods and within 150 days if it requires analysis or testing of the goods.

(10) Orders of the State Commission shall be signed and dated by the members of the State Commission constituting the Bench and shall be communicated to the parties free of charge.

Procedure for Hearing Appeal [Section 15]

8. (1) Memorandum shall be presented by the appellant or his authorised agent to the State Commission in person or be sent by registered post addressed to the Commission.

(2) Every memorandum filed under sub-rule (1) shall be in legible handwriting preferably typed and shall set forth concisely under distinct heads, the grounds of appeal without any argument or narrative and such grounds shall numbered consecutively.

(3) Each memorandum shall be accompanied by the certified copy of the order of the District Forum appealed against and such of the documents as may be required to support grounds of objection mentioned in the memorandum.

(4) When the appeal is presented after the expiry of period of limitation as specified in the Act, memorandum shall be accompanied by an application supported by an affidavit setting forth the fact on which appellant relies to satisfy the State Commission that he has sufficient cause for not preferring the appeal within the period of limitation.

(5) The appellant shall submit four copies of the memorandum to the State Commission for official purposes.

(6) On the date of hearing or any other day to which hearing may be adjourned, it shall be obligatory for the parties or their authorised agents to appear before the State Commission. If applicant or his authorised agent fails to appear on such date, the State Commission may, in its discretion, either dismiss the appeal or decide it on the merit of the case. If respondent or his authorised agents fails to appear on such date, the State Commission shall proceed *ex parte* and shall decide the appeal *ex, parte* on merits of the case.

(7) The appellant shall not except by leave of the State Commission, urge or be heard in support of any ground of objections not set forth in the memorandum but the State Commission, in deciding the appeal, may not confine to the grounds of objection set forth in the memorandum or taken by leave of the State Commission under this rule:

Provided that the Commission shall not rest its decision on any other grounds unless the party who may be affected thereby, has been given, at least one opportunity of being heard by the State Commission.

(8) State Commission may, on such terms as it may think fit and at any stage, adjourn the hearing of appeal, but not more than one adjournment shall ordinarily be given and the appeal should be decided within 90 days from the first date of hearing.

(9) Order of the State Commission on appeal shall be signed and dated by the members of the State Commission constituting the Bench and shall be communicated to the parties free of charge.

Chapter 28

Consumer Protection (Punjab) Rules, 1987

[No. G.S.R. 85/C.A./68/86/5.3.87, Dated 17-11-1987]

In exercise of the powers conferred by sub-section (2) of section 30 of the Consumer Protection Act, 1986 (68 of 1986), the President of India is pleased to make the folio-wing rules, namely—

SHORT TITLE AND EXTENT

1. (1) These rules may be called the Consumer Protection (Punjab) Rules, 1987.

(2) They extend to whole of the State of Punjab.

Definitions

2. In these rules, unless the context otherwise requires,—

(a) "Act" means the Consumer Protection Act, 1986 (68 of 1986);

(b) "agent" means a person duly authorised by a party to present any complaint or appeal or reply on its behalf before the State Commission or the District Forum;

(c) "appellant" means a party which makes an appeal against the order of the District Forum;

(d) "memorandum" means memorandum of appeal filed by the appellant;

(e) "opposite party" means a person who answers complaint or claim;

(f) "respondent" means the person who answers any memorandum of appeal;

(g) "State" means the State of Punjab; and

(h) "section" means a section of the Act.

Salaries and Other Allowances and Terms and Conditions of the President and Members of the District Forum Under Section 10(3)

3. (1) The President of a District Forum,—

(a) if appointed on whole-time basis, shall draw his pay in the grade of pay admissible to a Judge of a District Court; and

(b) if appointed on part-time basis, shall be paid an honorarium of two hundred rupees per day for the sitting of the District Forum,

(1A) The Members of the District Forum other than the President,—

(c) if appointed on whole-time basis, shall be paid a consolidated honorarium of four thousand rupees per mensem; and

(d) if appointed on part-time basis, shall be paid an honorarium of one hundred and fifty rupees per day for the sitting of the District Forum.

(2) The President and the members of the District Forum shall be entitled for such travelling allowance and daily allowance on official tour as are admissible to Class I Officers of the State Government.

(3) The salary, honorarium and other allowances shall be defrayed out of the Consolidated Fund of the State Government.

(4) Before appointment, the President and members of the District Forum shall have to give an undertaking that he does not and will not have any such financial or other interests as is likely to affect prejudicially his functions as such.

(5) In addition to the provisions of sub-section (2) of section 10, State Government may remove from the office the President and members of a District Forum who,—

(a) has failed to attend five sittings of the District Forum in a calendar month; or

(b) has been adjudged as insolvent; or

(c) has been convicted of an offence which in the opinion of the State Government, involves moral turpitude; or

(d) has become physically or mentally incapable of acting as such member; or

(e) has acquired such financial or other interest as is likely to effect prejudicially his functions as a member; or

(f) has so abused his position as to render his continuance in office, prejudicial to the public interest:

Provided that the President or member shall not be removed from his office on the ground specified in clauses *(d)* and *(e)* except on an inquiry held by State Government in accordance with such procedure as it may specify in this behalf and finds the President or the member to be guilty of such ground.

(6) The terms and conditions of the service of the President and the members; of the District Forum shall not be varied to their disadvantage during their tenure of office.

(7) Where any vacancy occurs in the office of the President of the District Forum, the seniormost (in order of appointment) member of District Forum, holding office for the time being, shall discharge the functions of the President until a person appointed to fill such vacancy assumes the office of the President of the District Forum.

(8) When the President of the District Forum is unable to discharge the functions owing to absence, illness or any other cause, the seniormost (in order of appointment) member of the District Forum shall discharge the functions of the President until the day on which the President resumes the charge of his functions.

(9) The President or any member ceasing to hold office as such shall not hold an appointment in or be connected with the management or administration of an organisation which have been the subject of any proceeding under the Act during his tenure for a period of 5 years from the date on which he ceases to hold such office.

Place of Sitting and Other Matters Relating to District Forum [Section 14(3)]

4. (1) The office of the District Forum shall be located at the headquarter of the district. Where State Government decided to establish a single District Forum having jurisdiction over more than one district, it shall notify the place and jurisdiction of the District Forum so established.

(2) The working days and the office hours of the District Forum shall be the same as that of the State Government.

(3) The official seal and emblem of the District Forum shall be such as the State Government may specify.

(4) Sitting of the District Forum, as and when necessary, shall be convened by the President.

(5) No act or proceedings of the District Forum shall be invalid by reasons only of the existence of any vacancy among its members or any defect in its constitution.

(6) The State Government shall appoint such staff, as may be necessary to assist the District Forum in its day to day work and perform such other functions as are **Provided** under these rules, or assigned to it by the President. The salary payable to such staff shall be defrayed out of the Consolidated Funds of the State Government.

(7) Where the opposite party admits the allegation made by the complainant, the District Forum shall decide the complaint on the basis of the merit of the case and documents present before it.

(8) If during the proceedings conducted under section 13, the District Forum fixes a date for hearing of the parties, it shall be obligatory on the complainant and opposite party or his authorised agent to appear before the District Forum on such date of hearing or any other date to which hearing could be adjourned. Where the complainant or his authorised agent fails to appear before the District Forum on such day, the District Forum may in its discretion either dismiss the complaint for default or decide it on merits. Where the opposite party or his authorised agent fails to appear on the day of hearing, the District Forum may decide the complaint *ex parte*.

(9) While proceeding under sub-rule (8), the District Forum may, on such terms as it may think fit and at any stage, adjourn the hearing of the complaint but not more than one adjournment shall ordinarily be given and the complaint I shall be

decided within 90 days from the date of notice received by the opposite party where complaint does not require analysis or testing of the goods and within 150 days if it requires analysis or testing of the goods.

(10) Orders of the District Forum shall be signed and dated by the members of I the District Forum constituting the Bench and shall be communicated to the parties free of charge.

Procedure to be Adopted by the District Forum for Analysis and Testing of the Goods [Section 13(I)(c)]

5. (1) Under, clause *(c)* of sub-section (1) of section 13, if considered necessary, the District Forum may direct the complainant to provide more than one sample of the goods in clean containers with stopper properly fixed on them.

(2) On receiving the samples of such goods, the District Forum shall seal it and fix lables on the containers carrying following information—

(i) name and address of the appropriate laboratory to whom sample will be sent for analysis and test;

(ii) name and address of the District Forum;

(iii) case number;

(iv) seal of the District Forum.

(3) The sample will be sent to the appropriate laboratory by the District Forum for sending report within 45 days or within such extended time as may be granted by the District Forum after specifying the nature of the defect alleged and date of submission of the report.

Salary and Other Allowances and Terms and Conditions of the President and Members of the State Commission [Section 16(2)]

6. (1) The President of the State Commission,—

(a) if appointed on whole-time basis, shall draw his pay in the grade of any admissible to a Judge of the High Court; and

(b) if appointed on part-time basis, shall be paid an honorarium of three hundred and fifty rupees per day for the sitting of the State Commission.

(1A) The Members of the State Commission other than the President,—

(a) if appointed on whole-time basis, shall be paid a consolidated honorarium of five thousand rupees per day mensem; and

(b) if appointed on part-time basis, shall be paid an honorarium of two hundred and fifty rupees per day for the sitting of the State Commission.

(2) The President and the members of the State Commission shall be eligible for such travelling allowance and daily allowance on official tour as are admissible to Class I Officer of the State Government.

(3) The salary, honorarium and other allowances shall be defrayed out of the Consolidated Fund of the State Government.

(4) President and the member of the State Commission shall hold office for a term of five years or upto the age of [sixty seven years] whichever is earlier and shall not be eligible for renomination;

Provided that President and members may—

(a) by writing under his hand and addressed to the State Government resign his office any time;

(b) be removed from his office in accordance with provisions of sub-rule (5),

(5) The State Government may remove from Office, President or a member of the State Commission who,—

(a) has failed to attend five sittings of the State Commission in a calendar month; or

(b) has been adjudged as insolvent; or

(c) has been convicted of an offence which in the opinion of the State Government, involves normal turpitude; or

(d) has become physically or mentally incapable of acting as such member; or

(e) has acquired such financial or other interest as is likely to effect prejudicially his functions as a member; or

(f) has so abused his position as to render his continuance in office, prejudicial to the public interest:

Provided that the President or a member shall not be removed from his office on the ground specified in clauses *(d)* and *(e)* except on an inquiry held by the State Government in accordance with such procedure as it may specify in this behalf and finds President or the member to be guilty of such ground.

(6) Before appointment, President and a member of the State Commission shall have to give an undertaking that he does not and will not have any such financial or other interests as is likely to affect prejudicially his functions as such member.

(7) The terms and conditions of the service of the President and the members of the State Commission shall not be varied to their disadvantage during their tenure of Office.

(8) Every vacancy caused by resignation and removal of the President or any other member of the State Commission under sub-rule (4) or otherwise shall be filled by fresh appointment.

(9) Where any vacancy occurs in the office of the President of the State Commission, the seniormost (in order of appointment) member, holding office for the time being, shall discharge the functions of the President until a person appointed to fill such vacancy assumes the office of the President of the State Commission.

(10) When the President of the State Commission is unable to discharge the functions owing to absence, illness or any other cause, the seniormost (in order of the appointment) member of the State Commission shall discharge the functions of the President until the day on which the President resumes the charge of his functions.

(11) The President or any member ceasing to hold office as such shall not hold any appointment in or be connected with the management or administration of an organisation which have been the subject of any proceeding under the Act during his tenure for a period of 5 years from the date on which he ceases to hold such office.

Place of Sitting and Other Matters Relating to State Commission [Section 14(3) Read with Section 18(1)]

7. (1) Office of the State Commission shall be located at the Capital of State.

(2) The working days and the office hours of the State Commission shall be the same as that of the State Government.

(3) The official seal and emblem of the State Commission shall be such as the State Government may specify.

(4) Sitting of the State Commission, as and when necessary, shall be convened by the President.

(5) No act or proceedings of the State Commission shall be invalid by reason only of the existence of any vacancy among its members or any defect in its constitution thereof.

(6) The State Government shall appoint such staff, as may be necessary to assist the State Commission in its work and perform such other functions as are **Provided** under these rules or assigned to it by the President. The salary payable to such staff shall be defrayed out of the Consolidated Fund of the State Government.

(7) Where the opposite party admits the allegation made by the complainant, the State Commission shall decide the complaint on the basis of the merit of the case and documents present before it.

(8) If during the proceedings conducted under section 13, the State Commission fixes a date for hearing of the parties, it shall be obligatory on the complainant and opposite party or his authorised agent to appear before the State Commission on such date of hearing or any other date to which hearing could be adjourned. Where the complainant or his authorised agent fails to appear before the State Commission on such day, the State Commission may in its discretion either dismiss the complainant for default or decide it on merits. Where the opposite party or its authorised agent fails to appear on the day of hearing, the State Commission may decide the complaint *ex parte*.

(9) While proceeding under sub-rule (8), the State Commission may, on such terms as it may think fit and at any stage, adjourn the hearing of the complaint should not more than one adjournment shall ordinarily be given and the complaint should be decided within 90 days from the date of notice received by the goods and within 150 days if it requires analysis or testing of the good.

(10) Orders of the State Commission shall be signed and dated by the members, of the State Commission constituting the Bench and shall be communicated to the parties free of charge.

Procedure for Hearing the Appeal [Section 15]

8. (1) The Memorandum of appeal shall be presented by the appellant or his authorised agent to the State Commission in person or sent by registered post addressed to the State Commission.

(2) Every memorandum filed under sub-rule (1), shall be in legible handwriting preferably typed and shall set forth concisely under distinct heads, the grounds of appeal without any argument or narrative and such grounds shall be numbered consecutively.

(3) Each memorandum of appeal shall be accompanied by the certified copy of the order of the District Forum appealed against and such of the documents as may be required to support grounds of objection mentioned in the memorandum.

(4) When the appeal is presented after the expiry of the period of limitation as specified in the Act, the memorandum shall

be accompanied by an application supported by an affidavit setting forth the fact on which the appellant relies to satisfy the State Commission that he has sufficient cause for not preferring the appeal within the period of limitation.

(5) The appellant shall submit four copies of the memorandum to the State Commission for official purpose.

(6) On the date of hearing or any other day to which hearing may be adjourned, it shall be obligatory for the parties or their authorised agents to appear before the State Commission. If appellant or his authorised agent fails to appear on such date, the State Commission may, in its discretion, either dismiss the appeal or decide it on the merit of the case. If respondent or his authorised agents fails to appear on such date, the State Commission shall proceed *ex parte* and shall decide the appeal *ex parte* on the merits of the case.

(7) The appellant shall not, except by leave of the State Commission urge, or be heard in support of any ground of objection not set forth in the memorandum but the State Commission, in deciding the appeal, shall not confine to the grounds of objection set forth in the memorandum or taken by leave of the State Commission under this rule **Provided** that the State Commission shall not rest its decision on any other grounds unless the party who may be affected thereby, has been given, at least one opportunity of being heard by the State Commission.

(8) State Commission may, on such terms as it may think fit and at any staff adjourn the hearing of appeal, but not more than one adjournment shall ordinarily be given and the appeal should be decided within 90 days from the first date of hearing.

(9) Order of the State Commission on appeal shall be signed and dated by the members of the State Commission constituting the Bench, and shall be communicated to the parties free of charge.

Consumer Problems

Chapter 29

Consumer Protection (Rajasthan) Rules, 1987

[Notification No. F. 20(40) FS/Meeting/87, Dated 21-07-1987]

In exercise of the powers conferred by sub-section (2) of section 30 of the Consumer Protection Act, 1986 (68 of 1986), the State Government hereby makes the following rules, namely—

SHORT TITLE AND COMMENCEMENT

1. (1) These rules may be called the Consumer Protection (Rajasthan) Rules, 1987.

(2) They shall come into force on such date of its publication in the Official Gazette.

Definitions

2. In these rules, unless the context otherwise requires, —

(a) "Act" means the Consumer Protection Act, 1986 (68 of 1986);

(b) "agent" means a person duly authorised by a party to present any complaint or appeal or reply on its behalf before the State Commission or the District Forum;

(c) "appellant" means a party which makes an appeal against the order of the District Forum;

(d) "memorandum" means memorandum of appeal filed by the appellant;

(e) "opposite party" means a person who answers complaint or claim;

(f) "President" means the President of the State Commission or District Forum as the case may be;

(g) "respondent" means the person who answers any memorandum appeal;

(h) "State" means the State of Rajasthan.

Salaries and Other Allowances and Terms and Conditions of the President and Members of the District Forum [Section 10(3)]

3. (1) The President of the District Forum shall receive the salary of the Judge of a District Court if appointed on whole-time basis or an honorarium of ₹ 150 per day if appointed on part-time basis. Other members if sitting on whole-time basis, shall receive a consolidated honorarium of ₹ 2,000 per month and if sitting on part-time basis, a consolidated honorarium of ₹ 100 per day for the sitting.

(2) The President and the members of the District Forum shall be entitled for such travelling allowance and daily allowance on official tour as are admissible to Grade 1 Officer of the State Government.

(3) The salary, honorarium and other allowances shall be defrayed out of the Consolidated Fund of the State Government.

(4) Before appointment, the President and Members of the District Forum shall have to take an undertaking that he and his relatives as defined in the Companies Act, 1956 (1 of 1956) does not and will not have any such financial or other interests as is likely to affect prejudicially his functions as a member.

(5) In addition to the provisions of section 10(2) of the Act, the State Government may remove from the office, the President and member of a District Forum who,—

(*a*) has been adjudged as insolvent; or

(*b*) has been convicted of an offence which, in the opinion of the State Government, involves moral turpitude; or

(c) has become physically or mentally incapable of acting as such member; or

(*d*) has acquired such financial or other interest as is likely to effect prejudicially his functions as a member; or

(*e*) has so abused his position as to render his continuance in office prejudicial to the public interest:

Provided that the President or Member shall not be removed from his office on the ground specified in clauses (*d*) and (*e*) of '[sub-rule (5)] except on an inquiry held by the State Government in accordance with such procedure as it may specify in this behalf and finds the member to be guilty on such ground.

(6) The terms and conditions of the service of the President and the members of the District Forum shall not be varied to their disadvantage during their tenure of office,

(7) Where any vacancy occurs in the office of the President of the District Forum, the seniormost (in order of appointment) member of District Forum, holding office for the time being, shall discharge the functions of the President until a person appointed to fill such vacancy assumes the office of the President of the District Forum.

(8) When the President of the District Forum is unable to discharge the functions owing to absence, illness, or any other cause, the seniormost (in order of appointment) member of the District Forum shall discharge the functions of the President until the day on which the President resumes charge of his functions.

(9) The President or any member ceasing to hold office as such shall not hold any appointment in or be connected with the management or administration of an organisation which have been the subject of any proceeding under the Act during his tenure for a period of 5 years from the date on which he ceases to hold such office.

Place of Sitting and Other Matters Relating to District Forum [Section 14(3)]

4. (1) The office of the District Forum shall be located at the headquarters of the District. Where the State Government decides to establish a single District Forum having jurisdiction over more than one district, it shall notify the place and jurisdiction of the District Forum so established.

(2) The working days and the office hours of the District Forum shall be the same as that of the State Government.

(3) The official seal and emblem of the District Forum shall be such as the State Government may specify.

(4) Sitting of the District Forum, as and when necessary, shall be convened by the President.

(5) No act or proceedings of the District Forum shall be invalid by reason only of the existence of any vacancy among its Members or any defect in its constitution.

(6) The State Government shall appoint such staff, as may be necessary to assist the District Forum in its day-to-day work and perform such other functions as are **Provided** under these Rules, or assigned to it by the President. The salary payable to such staff shall be defrayed out of the Consolidated Fund of the State Government.

(7) Where the opposite party admits the allegation made by the complainant, the District Forum shall decide the complaint on the basis of the merit of the case and documents present before it.

(8) If during the proceedings conducted under section 13 of the Act. The District Forum fixes a date for hearing of the parties, it shall be obligatory on the complainant and opposite party or its authorised agent to appear before the District Forum on such date of hearing or any other date to which hearing could be adjourned.

(9) Where the complainant or his authorised agent fails to appear before the District Forum on such day, the District Forum may in its discretion either dismiss the complaint in default or if a substantial portion of the evidence o the complainant has already been recorded decide it on merit. Where opposite party or its authorised agent fails to appear on the day of hearing the District Forum may decide the complaint *ex parte*.

(10) Where any part to a complaint to whom time has been granted fails produce his evidence or to cause the attendance of his witness, or to perform any other act necessary to the further progress of the complaint, for which time has been allowed, the District Forum may notwithstanding such default:—

(*a*) if the parties are present, proceed to decide the complaint forthwith; or

(*b*) if the parties are, or any of them is absent, proceed under sub-rule (9).

(11) The District Forum may, on such terms as it may think fit at any stage, adjourn the hearing of the complaint but not more than one adjournment shall ordinarily be given and the complaint should be decided within 90 days from the date of

notice received by the opposite party where complaint does not require analysis or testing of the goods and within 150 days if it requires analysis or testing of the goods.

(12) Orders of the District Forum shall be pronounced and shall be signed and dated by the members of the District Forum consisting the Bench.

Procedure to be Adopted by the District Forum for Analysis and Testing of the Goods [Section 13(l)(c)]

5. (1) Under section 13(l)(c) of the Act, if considered necessary, the District Forum may, direct the complainant to provide more than one sample of the goods in clean containers with stopper properly fixed on them.

(2) On receiving the samples of such goods, the District Forum shall seal it and fix labels on the containers carrying following information—

(i) name and address of the appropriate laboratory to whom sample shall be sent for analysis and test;

(ii) name and address of the District Forum;

(iii) case number;

(iv) seal of the District Forum.

(3) The sample will be sent to the appropriate laboratory by the District Forum for sending a report within 45 days or within such extended time as may be granted by the District Forum after specifying the nature of the defect alleged and date of submission of the report.

Salary and Other Allowances and Terms and Conditions of [service of] the President and Members of the State Commission [Section 16(2)]

6. (1) The President of the State Commission shall receive the salary of the Judge of the High Court if appointed on whole-time basis or a consolidated honorarium of ₹ 200 per day for the sitting if appointed on part time basis. Other members if sitting on whole-time basis, shall receive a consolidated honorarium of ₹ 3,000 per month and if sitting on part time basis, a consolidated honorarium of ₹ 150 per day for the sitting.

(2) The President and the members of the State Commission shall be paid travelling allowance and daily allowance as per Travelling Allowance Rules applicable to the Judges of the Rajasthan High Court. Other members of the State Commission shall be eligible for such travelling allowance and daily allowance as are admissible to Grade-1 Officer of the State Government and shall also be entitled to travel by Air.

(3) The salary, honorarium, and other allowances shall be defrayed out of the Consolidated Fund of the State Government.

(4) The President and the members of the State Commission shall hold office for a term of five years or upto the age of [65] years whichever is earlier and shall not be eligible for renomination:

Provided that President and members may—

(a) by writing under his hand and addressed to the State Government resign his office any time;

(b) be removed from his office in accordance with provisions of sub-rule (5)-

(5) The State Government may remove from Office, President or a Member of the State Commission who,—

(a) has been adjudged as insolvent; or

(b) has been convicted of an offence which in the opinion of the State Government, involves moral turpitude; or

(c) has become physically or mentally incapable of acting as such member; or

(d) has acquired such financial or other interest as is likely to affect prejudicially his functions as a member or President; or

(e) has so abused his position as to render his continuance in office prejudicial to the public interest:

Provided that the President or Member shall not be removed from his office on the ground specified in clauses (d) and (e) except on an inquiry held by the Government, in accordance with such procedure as it may specify in this behalf and finds the member to be guilty of such ground.

(6) Before appointment, President and a member of the State Commission shall have to take an undertaking that he does not and will not have any such financial or other interests as is likely to affect prejudicially his functions as such member.

(7) The terms and conditions of the service of the President and the members of the State Commission shall not be varied to their disadvantage during their tenure of office.

(8) Every vacancy caused by resignation and removal of the President or any other member of the State Commission under [sub-rule (4)] or otherwise shall be filled by fresh appointment.

(9) Where any such vacancy occurs in the office of the President of the State Commission, the seniormost (in order of appointment) member, holding office for the time being, shall discharge the functions of the President until a person appointed to fill such vacancy assumes the office of the President of the State Commission.

(10) When the President of the State Commission is unable to discharge the functions owing to absence, illness or any other cause, the seniormost (in order of appointment) member of the State Commission shall discharge the functions of President until the day on which the President resumes the charge of his functions.

(11) The President or any Member ceasing to hold office as such shall not hold any appointment in or be connected with the management or administration of an organisation which have been the subject of any proceeding under the Act during his tenure for a period of 5 years from the date on which he ceases to hold such office.

Place of Sitting and Other Matters Relating to State Commission [Section 14(3) Read with Section 18]

7. (1) Office of the State Commission shall be located at the capital of the State.

(2) The working days and the office hours of the State Commission shall be same as that of the State Government.

(3) The official seal and emblem of the State Commission shall be such as the State Government may specify.

(4) Sitting of the State Commission, as and when necessary, shall be convened by the President.

(5) No act or proceedings of the State Commission shall be invalid by reasons only of the existence of any vacancy among its members or any defect in its constitution.

(6) The State Government shall appoint such staff, as may be necessary to assist the State Commission in its work and perform such other functions as are **Provided** under these rules or assigned to it by the President. The salary Payable to such staff shall be defrayed out of the Consolidated Fund of the State Government.

(7) Where the opposite party admits the allegation made by the complainant, the State Commission shall decide the complaint on the basis of the merit of the cases and documents present before it.

(8) If during the proceedings conducted under section 13 of the Act, the State Commission fixes a date for hearing of the parties, it shall be obligatory on the complainant and opposite party or his authorised agent to appear before the State Commission on such date of hearing or any other date to which hearing could be adjourned.

(9) Where the complainant or his authorised agent fails to appear before the State Commission on such day, the State Commission may in its discretion either dismiss the complaint in default or if a substantial portion of the evidence of the complainant has already been recorded decide it on merits Where the opposite party or his authorised agent fails to appear on the day of hearing, the State Commission may decide the complaint *ex parte.*

(10) Where any party to a complaint to whom time has been granted fails to produce his evidence or to cause the attendance of his witness, or to perform any other act necessary to the further progress of the complaint, for which time has been allowed, the State Commission may, notwithstanding such default,—

(*a*) if the parties are present, proceed to decide the complaint forthwith; or

(*b*) if the parties are, or any of them is absent, proceed under sub-rule (9).

(11) The State Commission may, on such terms as it may think fit at any stage, adjourn the hearing of the complaint but not more than one adjournment shall ordinarily be given and the complaint should be decided within 90 days from the date of notice received by the opposite party where complaint does not require analysis or testing of the goods and within 150 days, if it requires analysis or testing of the goods.

(12) Orders of the State Commission shall be pronounced and shall be signed and dated by the members of the State Commission constituting the Bench and shall be communicated to the parties free of charge.

Procedure for Hearing Appeal [Section 15]

8. (1) The Memorandum shall be presented by the appellant or his authorised agent to the State Commission in person or be sent by registered post addressed to the Commission.

(2) Every memorandum filed under sub-rule (1), shall be in legible handwriting preferably typed and shall set forth concisely under distinct heads, the grounds of appeal without any argument or narrative and such grounds shall be numbered consecutively.

(3) Each memorandum shall be accompanied by the certified copy of the order of the District Forum appealed against and such of the documents as may be required to support grounds of objection mentioned in the memorandum.

(4) When the appeal is presented after the expiry of period of limitation as specified in the Act, memorandum shall be accompanied by an application supported by an affidavit setting forth the fact on which appellant relies satisfy the State Commission that he has sufficient cause for not preferring the appeal within the period of limitation.

(5) The appellant shall submit four copies of the memorandum to the State Commission for official purposes.

(6) On the date of hearing or any other day to which hearing may be adjourned, it shall be obligatory for the parties or their authorised agents to appear before the State Commission. If appellant or his authorised agent fails to appear on such date, the State Commission may, decide the appeal on the merit of the case. If respondent or his authorised agent fails to appear on such date, the State Commission shall proceed *ex parte* and shall decide the appeal *ex parte* on the merits of the case.

(7) The appellant shall not except by leave of the State Commission urge or be heard in support of any ground of objection not set forth in the memorandum or taken by leave of the State Commission under this rule:

Provided that the Commission shall not rest its decision on any other grounds unless the party who may be affected thereby, has been given, at least one opportunity of being heard by the State Commission.

(8) State Commission may, on such terms as it may think fit and at any stage, adjourn the hearing of appeal, but not more than one adjournment shall ordinarily be given and the appeal should be decided within 90 days from the first date of hearing.

(9) Order of the State Commission on appeal shall be pronounced and shall be signed and dated by the members of the State Commission constituting the Bench and shall be communicated to the parties free of charge.

Coke, Pepsi alter recipes to avoid cancer warning

New York: Coca-Cola and PepsiCo are changing the way they make the caramel coloring used in their sodas as a result of a California law that mandates drinks containing a certain level of carcinogens bear a cancer warning label.

The firms said the changes will be expanded nationally to streamline their manufacturing processes. The changes have already been made for drinks sold in California.

The American Beverage Association, which represents the broader industry, said its member companies will continue to use caramel coloring in certain products but that adjustments were made to meet California's new standard.

HEALTH SCARE?

A representative for Coca Cola, Diana Garza-Ciarlante, said the company directed its caramel suppliers to modify their manufacturing processes to reduce the levels of the chemical 4-methylimidazole, which can be formed during the cooking process and as a result may be found in trace amounts in many foods.

"While we believe that there is no public health risk that justifies any such change we did ask our caramel suppliers to take this step so that our products would not be subject to the requirement of a scientifically unfounded warning." Garza-Giarlante said.

The Center for Science in the Public Interest, a consumer advocacy group, in February had filed a petition with the US Food and Drug Administration to ban the use of ammonia-sulfite caramel coloring. A spokesman for FDA said the plea is being reviewed. But he noted that a consumer would have to drink more than 1,000 cans of soda a day to reach the doses administered that have shown links to cancer in rodents.

The American Beverage Association said California added the coloring to its list of carcinogens with no studies showing that it causes cancer in humans. It noted that the listing was based on a single study in lab mice and rats.

Source : TOI

Chapter 30

Sikkim Consumer Protection Rules, 1990

[No. 19/FCS, Dated 30-1-1990]

In exercise of the powers conferred by sub-section (2) of section 30 of the Consumer Protection Act, 1986 (68 of 1986), State Government hereby makes the following Rules, namely—

SHORT TITLE AND COMMENCEMENT

1. (1) These rules may be called the Sikkim Consumer Protection Rules, 1990.

(2) They shall come into force on such date as the State Government may, by notification in the Official Gazette, appoint.

Definitions

2. In these rules, unless the context otherwise requires—

(a) "Act" means the Consumer Protection Act, 1986 (68 of 1986);

(b) "agent" means a person duly authorised by a party to present any complaint or appeal or reply on its behalf before the State Commission of the District Forum;

(c) "appellant" means a party which makes an appeal against the order of the District Forum;

(d) "memorandum" means memorandum of appeal filed by the appellant;

(e) "opposite party" means a person who answers complaint or claim;

(f) "President" means the President of the State Commission or District Forum as the case may be;

(g) "respondent" means the person who answers any memorandum or appeal.

Salaries and Other Allowances and Terms and Conditions of the President and Members of the District Forum

3. (1) The President of the District Forum shall receive the salary of the judge of a District Court if appointed on whole-time basis or an honorarium of one hundred fifty rupees per day for the sitting if appointed on part-time basis. Other members shall receive two thousand rupees a consolidated honorarium of one hundred rupees per day for the sitting.

(2) The President and the members of the District Forum shall be entitled for such travelling allowance and daily allowance on official tour as are admissible to Grade I Officers of the State Government.

(3) The salary, honorarium and other allowances shall be defrayed out of the Consolidated Fund of the State Government.

(4) Before appointment, the president and members of the District Forum shall have to take an undertaking that he does not and will not have any such financial or other interests as is likely to affect prejudicially his functions as a member.

(5) In addition to the provisions of sub-section (2) of section 10 of the Act, the State Government may remove from the office the President and member of a District Forum—

(a) has been adjudged as insolvent; or

(*b*) has been convicted of an offence which the opinion of the State Government involves moral turpitude; or

(*c*) has become physically or mentally incapable of acting as such member; or

(*d*) has acquired such financial or other than as it is likely to affect prejudicially his functions as a member; or

(*e*) has so abused his position as to his continuance in office prejudicial to the public interest; or

(*f*) has absented himself from three consecutive sitting of the District Forum without reasonable cause:

Provided that the president or member, not be removed from his office or the ground specially in clauses (*d*) and (*e*) of sub-rule (5) exceptional inquiry held by the Slate Government in accordance with such procedure as it may specify in this behalf and finds the members to be guilty of such ground.

(6) The terms and conditions of the service of the President and the members of the District Forum shall not be varied to their disadvantage during their tenure of office.

(7) Where any vacancy occurs in the office of the President of the District forum, the seniormost (in order of appointment) member of District Forum, holding office for the time being, shall discharge the functions of the presidential person, appointed to fill such vacancy assumes the office of the President of the District Forum.

(8) When the President of the District Forum is unable to discharge the functions owing to absence, illness or any other cause, the seniormost (in order of the appointment) member of the District Forum shall discharge the functions of the president until the day on which the president resumes the charge of his functions.

(9) The President or any member ceasing to hold office as such shall not hold appointment in or be connected with the management or administration of an organisation which have been the subject of any proceeding under the Act during his tenure for a period of five years from the date on which he ceases to hold such office.

Place of Sitting and Other Matters Relating to District Forum

4. (1) The office of the District Forum shall be located at the headquarter of the District. Where the State Government decides to establish a single District Forum having jurisdiction over more than one district, it shall notify the place and jurisdiction of the District Forum established.

(2) The working days and the office hours of the District Forum shall be the same as that of the State Government.

(3) The official seal and emblem of the District Forum shall be such as the State Government may specify.

(4) Sitting of the District Forum, as and when necessary, shall be convened by the President.

(5) No act or proceedings of the District Forum shall be invalid by reason only of the existence of any vacancy among its members or any defect in its constitution.

(6) The State Government shall appoint such staff, as may be necessary to assist the District Forum in its day to day work and perform such other functions as are **Provided** under these rules, or assigned to it by the President. The salary payable to such staff shall be defrayed out of the Consolidated Fund of the State Government.

(7) Where opposite party admits the allegation made by the complainant, the District Forum shall decide the complaint on the basis of the merit of the case and documents present before it.

(8) If during the proceeding conducted under section 13 of the Act, District Forum fixed a date for hearing of the parties, it shall be obligatory on the complainant and opposite party or its authorised agent to appear before the District Forum on such date of hearing or any other date to which hearing could be adjourned. Where the complainant or his authorised agent fails to appear before the District Forum on such day, the District Forum may in its discretion either dismiss the complaint for default or decide it on merit. Where the opposite party or its authorised agent fails to appear on the day of hearing the District Forum may decide the complaint *ex parte.*

Provided that where a complaint is dismissed or default of the complainant or his authorised agent or a complaint is decided *ex, parte* for default of the opposite party or his authorised agent, the District Forum shall have the power to set aside the order of dismissal or *ex, parte* decision on such terms as to costs or otherwise as it thinks fit on being satisfied that failure to appear before the forum was for sufficient cause.

(9) While proceeding under sub-rule (8), the District Forum may, on such terms as it may think fit and at any stage, adjourn the hearing of the complaint not more than one adjournment shall ordinarily be given and the complaint should be decided within ninety days from the date of notice received by the opposite party where complaint does not require analysis or testing of the goods and within one hundred fifty days if it requires analysis or testing of the goods.

(10) Orders of the District Forum shall be signed and dated by the members of the District Forum constituting the Bench and shall be communicated to the parties free of charge.

Procedure to be Adopted by the District Forum for Analysis and Testing of the Goods

5. (1) If the District Forum thinks it necessary so to do, it may direct the complainant to provide more than one sample of the goods in clean containers with stopper properly fixed on them.

(2) On receiving the samples of such goods, the District Forum shall seal it and fix labels on the containers carrying following information:—

(i) name and address of the appropriate laboratory to whom sample will be sent for analysis and test;

(ii) name and address of the District Forum;

(iii) case number;

(iv) seal of the District Forum.

(3) The sample will be sent to the appropriate laboratory by the District Forum for sending report within forty-five days or within such extended time as may be granted by the District Forum after specifying the nature of the defect alleged and date of submission of the report.

Salary and Other Allowances and Terms and Conditions of the President and Members of the State Commission

6. (1) President of the State Commission shall receive the salary of the judge of the High Court if appointed on whole time basis or a consolidated honorarium of two hundred rupees per day for the sitting if appointed on part-time basis. Other members shall receive a consolidated honorarium of one hundred and fifty rupees per day for the sitting.

(2) The President and the members of the State Commission shall be eligible for such travelling allowance and daily allowance on official tour as are admissible to Grade-I Officer of the State Government:

Provided that if the President is a sitting Judge of the High Court, he shall be eligible for such travelling allowance and daily allowance as are admissible to him by virtue of his office as Judge of the High Court.

(3) The salary, honorarium, other allowances shall be defrayed out of the Consolidated Fund of the State Government.

(4) President and the members of the State Commission shall hold office for a terms of five years or upto the age of sixty-five years whichever is earlier and shall not be eligible for renomination:

Provided that the President and a member may—

(a) by writing under his hand and addressed to the State Government resign his office any time;

(b) be removed from his office in accordance with provisions of sub-rule (5).

(5) The State Government may remove from office, President or a member of the State Commission who—

(a) has been adjudged as an insolvent, or

(b) has been convicted of an offence which in the opinion of the State Government, involves moral turpitude, or

(c) has become physically or mentally incapable of acting as such member, or

(d) has acquired such financial or other interest as is likely to affect prejudiially his functions as a member, or

(e) has so abused his position as to render his continuance in office prejudicial to the public interest:

Provided that the president or a member shall not be removed from his office on the ground specified in clauses *(d)* and *(e)* of this sub-rule except on an inquiry held by State Government in accordance with such procedure assist may specify in this behalf and finds the member to be guilty of such ground:

Provided further that clauses *(c), (d)* and *(e)* shall not be applicable to the President if he is a sitting Judge of the High Court.

(6) Before appointment. President and a member of the State Commission shall have to take an undertaking that he does not and will not have any such financial or other interests as is likely to affect prejudicially his functions as such members.

(7) The terms and conditions of the service of the President and the members of the State Commission shall not be varied to their disadvantage during their tenure of office.

(8) Every vacancy caused by resignation and removal of the President or any other member of the State Commission under sub-rule (4) or otherwise shall be filled by fresh appointment.

(9) Where any such vacancy occurs in the office of the President of the State Commission, the seniormost (in order of appointment) members, holding office for the time being, shall discharge the functions of the President until a person appointed to fill such vacancy assumes the office of the President or the State Commission.

(10) When the President of the State Commission is unable to discharge the functions owing to absence, illness or any other cause, the seniormost (in order to the appointment) member of the State Commission shall discharge the functions of the president until the day on which the president resumes charge of his functions.

(11) The President or any member ceasing to hold office as such shall not hold any appointment in or be connected with the management or administrations of an organisation which have been the subject of any proceeding under the Act during his tenure for a period of 5 years from the date on which he ceases to hold such office.

Place of Sitting and Other Matters Relating to State Commission

7. (1) Office of the State Commission shall be located at the capital of the State.

(2) The working days and the office hours of the State Commission shall be the same as that of the State Government;

Provided that if the President of the State Commission is a sitting Judge of the High Court, the working days and the office hours of the Commission shall be the same as that of the High Court.

(3) The official seal and emblem of the State Commission shall be such as the State Government may specify.

(4) Sitting of the State Commission as and when necessary, shall be convened by the President.

(5) No act of proceedings of the State Commission shall be invalid by reasons only of the existence of any vacancy among its members or any defect in its constitution thereof.

(6) The State Government shall appoint such staff, as may be necessary to assist the State Commission in its work and perform such other functions as are **Provided** under these rules, or assigned to it by the President. The salary payable to such staff shall be defrayed out of the Consolidated Fund of the State Government.

(7) Where the opposite party admits the allegation made by the complainant, the State Commission shall decide the complaint on the basis of the merit of the case and documents present before it.

(8) If during the proceedings conducted under section 13, the State Commission fixes a date for hearing of the parties, it shall be obligatory on the complainant and opposite party or his authorised agent to appear before the State Commission on such date of hearing or any other date to which hearing could be adjourned. Where the complainant or his authorised agent fails to appear before the State Commission on such day, the State Commission may in its discretion either dismiss the complaint for default or decide it on merit. Where the opposite party or its authorised agent fails to appear on the day of hearing, the State Commission may decide the complaint *ex parte:*

Provided where a complaint is dismissed for default of the complainant or his authorised agent or a complaint is decided *ex parte* for default of the opposite party or his authorised agent, the State Commission shall have the power to set aside the order of dismissal or *ex parte* decision on such terms as to costs or otherwise as it thinks fit on being satisfied that the failure to appear before the Commission was for sufficient cause.

(9) While proceeding under sub-rule (8), the State Commission may, on such terms as it may think fit and at any stage, adjourn the hearing of the complaint but not more than one adjournment shall ordinarily be given and the complaint should be decided within ninety days from the date of notice received by the opposite party where complaint does not require analysis or testing of the goods and within one hundred fifty days if it requires analysis or testing of the goods.

(10) Orders of the State Commission shall be signed and dated by the members of the State Commission constituting the Bench and shall be communicated to the parties free of charge.

Procedure for Hearing Appeal

8. (1) Memorandum of appeal shall be presented by the appellant or his authorised agent to the State Commission in person or sent by registered post addressed to the Commission.

(2) Every memorandum filed under sub-rule (1) shall be in legible handwriting preferable types and shall set forth concisely under distinct heads, the grounds of appeal without any argument or narrative and such ground shall be numbered consecutively.

(3) Each memorandum shall be accompanied by the certified copy of the order of the District Forum appealed against and such of the documents as may be required to support grounds of objection mentioned in the memorandum.

(4) When the appeal is presented after the expiry of period of limitation as specified in the Act, memorandum shall be accompanied by an application supported by an affidavit setting forth the fact on which appellant relies to satisfy the State Commission that he has sufficient cause for not preferring the appeal with the period of limitation.

(5) The appellant shall submit four copies of the memorandum to the State Commission for official purposes.

(6) On the date of hearing or any other day to which hearing may be adjourned, it shall be obligatory for the parties of their authorised agents to appear before the State Commission, if appellant or his authorised agent fails to appear on such date, the State Commission may, in its discretion, either dismiss the appeal or decide it on the merit of the case. If respondent or his authorised agents fails to appear on such date, the State Commission shall proceed *ex parte* and shall decide the appeal *ex parte* on merits of the case:

Provided where an appeal is dismissed for default of the appellant or his authorised agent or is decided *ex parte* for default of the respondent or his authorised agent, the State Commission shall have the power to set aside the order of dismissal or *ex parte* decision on such terms as to costs or otherwise as it thinks fit on being satisfied that the failure to appear before the Commission was for sufficient cause.

(7) The appellant shall not, except by leave of the State Commission, urge or be heard in support of any ground of objections not set forth in the memorandum but the State Commission, in deciding the appeal, shall not confine to the grounds of objection set forth in the memorandum or taken by leave of the State Commission under this rule:

Provided that the Commission shall not rest its decision on any other grounds unless the party who may be affected thereby, has been given, at least one opportunity of being heard by the State Commission.

(8) State Commission may, on such terms as it may think fit and at any stage, adjourn the hearing of appeal, but not more than one adjournment shall ordinarily be given and the appeal should be decided within 90 days from the first date of hearing.

(9) Order of the State Commission on appeal shall be signed and dated by the members of the State Commission constituting the Bench and shall be communicated to the parties free of charge.

Coke, Pepsi alter recipes to avoid cancer warning

New York: Coca-Cola and PepsiCo are changing the way they make the caramel coloring used in their sodas as a result of a California law that mandates drinks containing a certain level of carcinogens bear a cancer warning label.

The firms said the changes will be expanded nationally to streamline their manufacturing processes. The changes have already been made for drinks sold in California.

The American Beverage Association, which represents the broader industry, said its member companies will continue to use caramel coloring in certain products but that adjustments were made to meet California's new standard.

A representative for Coca-Cola, Diana Garza-Ciarlante, said the company directed its caramel suppliers to modify their manufacturing processes to reduce the levels of the chemical 4-methylimidazole, which can be formed during the cooking process and as a result may be found in trace amounts in many foods.

"While we believe that there is no public health risk that justifies any such change, we did ask our caramel suppliers to take this step so that our products would not be subject to the requirement of a scientifically unfounded warning," Garza-Giarlante said.

The Centre for Science in the Public Interest, a consumer advocacy group, in February had filed a petition with the US Food and Drug Administration to ban the use of ammonia-sulfite caramel coloring. A spokesman for FDA said the plea is being reviewed. But he noted that a consumer would have to drink more than 1,000 cans of soda a day to reach the doses administered that have shown links to cancer in rodents.

The American Beverage Association said California added the coloring to its list of carcinogens with no studies showing that it causes cancer in humans. It noted that the listing was based on a single study in lab mice and rats.

Source: GOP

"Right to Information"

Chapter 31

Tamil Nadu Consumer Protection Rules, 1988

[No. S.R.O.A-158/88, Dated 30-6-1988]

In exercise of the powers conferred by sub-section (2) of section 30 of the Consumer Protection Act, 1986 (68 of 1986), read with S.O. No. 390(E), published in Part II Section 3, sub-section (A) of the Gazette of India, Extraordinary, dated 15th April, 1987and S.O. No. 568(E), published in Part-II - Section 3, sub-section (a.) of the Gazette of India Extraordinary, dated the 10th June, 1987, the Governor of Tamil Nadu hereby makes the following rules :—

SHORT TITLE AND COMMENCEMENT

1. (1) These rules may be called the Tamil Nadu Consumer Protection Rules, 1988.

(2) They shall come into force at once.

Definitions

2. In these rules, unless, the context otherwise requires,—

(*a*) "Act" means the Consumer Protection Act, 1986 (68 of 1986);

(*b*) "agent" means a person duly authorised by a party to present any complaint or appeal or reply on its behalf, before the State Commission or the District Forum;

(*c*) "appellant" means a party which makes an appeal against the order of the District Forum;

(*d*) "memorandum" means memorandum of appeal filed by the appellant;

(*e*) "Opposite party" means a person who answers complaint or claim;

(*f*) "President" means the President of the State Commission or District Forum as the case may be;

(*g*) "respondent" means the person who answers any memorandum of appeal;

(*h*) "section" means section of the Act;

(*i*) "State" means the State of Tamil Nadu;

(*j*) words and expression used in the rules and not defined, but defined in the Act shall have the same meaning respectively assigned to them in the Act.

Salaries and Other Allowances and Terms and Conditions of the President and Members of the District Forum

3. (1) The President of the District Forum shall receive the salary of the Judge of a District Court, if appointed on whole time basis or an hono-rarium of ₹ 150 (Rupees one hundred and fifty) per day subject to a maximum of ₹ 2,100 (Rupees two thousand one hundred only) per month, if appointed on part-time basis. [The President of a District Forum shall receive the transfer travelling allowance if he joins such District Forum from outside the District]. Other members if sitting on whole time basis, shall receive a consolidated honorarium of ₹ 2,000 (Rupees two thousand) per month and if sitting on part-time basis, a consolidated honorarium of ₹ 750 (Rupees seven hundred and fifty) per month in addition to ₹ 100 (Rupees one hundred) per day for the sitting. The members residing away from the headquarters shall also receive the conveyance allowance of ₹ 150 (Rupees one hundred and fifty only) per month.

(2) The President and the members of the District Forum shall be entitled for such travelling allowance and daily allowance on official tour as are admissible to Grade I Officer of the Government of Tamil Nadu.

(3) The salary or honorarium, as the case may be, and other allowances shall be defrayed out of the Consolidated Fund of the Government of Tamil Nadu.

(4) Before appointment, the President and members of the District Forum shall have to take an undertaking that he does not and will not have any financial or such other interests as is likely to affect prejudicially his functions as a member.

(5) In addition to provisions of sub-section (2) of section 10, Government of Tamil Nadu may remove from office, the President and members of a District Forum who—

(a) has been adjudged as an insolvent, or

(b) has been convicted of an offence which in the opinion of the Government of Tamil Nadu involves moral turpitude, or

(c) has become physically or mentally incapable of acting as the President or member, or

(d) has acquired financial or other interests likely to affect prejudicially his functions as the President or a member, or

(e) has so abused his position as to render his continuance in office prejudi-cial to the public interest:

Provided that the President or member shall not be removed from his office on the ground specified in clauses *(d)* and *(e)* of sub-rule (5) except on an inquiry held by Government of Tamil Nadu in accordance with such procedure as it may specify in this behalf and finds the President or a member to be guilty of such ground.

(5A) The Government of Tamil Nadu may, after giving a reasonable oppor-tunity of being heard, remove from office, a member of a District Forum who has not attended two consecutive sittings of the District Forum without sufficient causes.

(6) The terms and conditions of the service of the President and the members of the District Forum shall not be varied to their disadvantage during their tenure of office.

(7) Where any vacancy occurs in the office of the President of the District Forum, the seniormost (in order of appointment) member of District Forum, holding office for the time being, shall discharge the functions of the President until a person appointed to fill such vacancy assumes the office of the President of the District Forum.

(8) When the President of the District Forum is unable to discharge the functions owing to absence, illness or any other cause, the seniormost (in order of the appointment) member of the District Forum shall discharge the functions of the President until the day on which the President resumes the charge of his functions.

(9) The President or any member ceasing to hold office as such shall not hold any appointment in or be connected with the management or administration of an organisation which has been the subject of any proceeding under the Act during his tenure for a period of 5 years from the date on which he ceases to hold such office.

(10) In case of difference of opinion among the members of the District Forum, the opinion of the majority shall prevail and the opinions or orders of the forum shall be expressed in terms of the views of the majority.

(11) (1) The President and the members shall hold office for a term of five years or upto the age of 65 years whichever is earlier, and shall not be eligible for reappointment.

(2) Notwithstanding anything contained in sub-rule *(i)* the president or the member may—

(a) by writing under his hand and addressed to the Government of Tamil Nadu resign his office at any time and on such resignation being accepted, his office shall become vacant;

(b) be removed from his office in accordance with sub-rule (5) of rule 3.

Place of Sitting and Other Matters Relating to District Forum

4. (1) The office of District Forum shall be located at the headquarters of the District where the state Government decides to establish a single District Forum having jurisdiction over more than one district, it shall notify the place and jurisdiction of the District Forum so established.

(2) The working days and the office hours of the District Forum shall be the same as that of the Government of Tamil Nadu.

(3) The official seal of the District Forum shall be as follows :—

Seal.—The seal shall have two concentric arcs bearing the inscriptions, namely "DISTRICT CONSUMER DISPUTES REDRESSAL FORUM" and name of the District at the Centre.

(4) Sitting of the District Forum, as and when necessary, shall be convened by the President.

(5) No act or proceedings of the District Forum shall be invalid by reason only 'of the existence of any vacancy among its President or members or any defect in its constitution.

(6) State Government shall appoint such staff, as may be necessary to assist the District Forum in its day-to-day work and to perform such other functions as are **Provided** under the Act and these rules are assigned to it by the President. The salary payable to such staff shall be defrayed out of the Consolidated Fund of the State Government.

(7) Where the opposite party admits the allegation made by the complainant, the District Forum shall decide the complaint on the basis of the merit of the case and documents present before it.

(8) If during the proceedings conducted under section 13, the District Forum fixes a date for hearing of the parties, it shall be obligatory on the complainant and opposite party or its authorised agent to appear before the District Forum on such date of hearing or any other date to which hearing could be adjourned. Where the complainant or his authorised agent fails to appear before the District Forum on such day, the District Forum may in its discretion either dismiss the complaint for default or decide it on merit. Where the opposite party or its authorised agent fails to appear on the day of hearing, the District Forum may decide the complaint *ex parte.*

(9) While proceeding under sub-rule (8) the District Forum may, on such terms as it may think fit and at any stage, adjourn the hearing of the complaint but not more than one adjournment shall ordinarily be given and the complaint should be decided within 90 days from the date of notice received by the opposite party where complaint does not require analysis or testing of the goods and within 150 days if it requires analysis or testing of the goods.

(10) Orders of the District Forum shall be signed and dated by the members of the District Forum constituting the Bench and shall be communicated to the Parties free of charge.

Procedure to be Followed for Making Complaints before the District Forum/ State Commission

5. A complaint containing the following particulars, shall be presented by the complainant in person or by his authorised agent to the District Forum/ State Commission, or be sent by registered post addressed to the District Forum/ State Commission —

(a) the name, description and address of the complainant;

(b) the name, description and address of the opposite party or parties as the case may be, so far as they can be ascertained;

(c) the facts relating to complaint and when and where it arose;

(d) document in support of the allegations contained in the complaint;

(e) the relief which complainant claims.

Procedure to be Adopted by the District Forum for Analysis and Testing of the Goods

6. (1) Under clause (c) of sub-section (1) of section 13 if considered necessary, the District Forum may direct the complainant to provide two separate samples of the goods packed in clean dry bottles or jars or other suitable containers which shall be sufficiently tight to prevent leakage, evaporation, or in the case of dry substance entrance of moisture, with a paper slip wrapped and pasted on the container in which the signature or thumb-impression of the person, trader or manufacturer, from whom the goods are purchased shall be affixed:

Provided that in case the person or trader or manufacturer from whom the goods are purchased, refuses to affix his signature or thumb impression, the signature or thumb impression of a witness shall be taken in the same manner.

(2) On receiving the samples of such goods, the District Forum shall fix labels on the containers carrying the following information —

(i) Name and address of the appropriate laboratory to whom the sample will be sent for analysis and test;

(ii) Name and address of the District Forum;

(iii) Case Number;

(iv) Nature of articles sent for analysis and test;

(v) Seal of the District Forum.

(3) The container of sample shall be completely wrapped in fairly strong thick paper, the ends of the paper shall be neatly folded in and affixed by means of gum or adhesive. The paper cover shall be further secured by means of strong twine or thread both above and across the container and the twine or thread shall then be fastened on the paper cover by means of scaling wax on which there shall be at least four distinct and clear impressions of the seal of which one shall be at the top of the packet, one at the bottom of the packet and the other two on the body of the packet. The knots of the twine or thread shall be covered by means of sealing wax bearing the impressions of the seal of the District Forum.

(4) One of the sealed containers will be retained by the District Forum for future reference and another will be sent to the appropriate laboratory by the District Forum for sending report within 45 days or within such extended time as ma be granted by the District Forum, after specifying the nature of the defect alleged and date of submission of the report.

(5) The quantity of sample, in case of food samples, for analysis shall be as specified under rule 22 of the Prevention of Food Adulteration Rules, 1954

(6) A specimen impression of the seal used to seal the container of the sample packet will be sent to the appropriate laboratory separately by the District Forum.

(7) The amount of fees for carrying out the analysis of samples shall be decided in consultation with the concerned appropriate laboratory.

Salary and Other Allowances and Terms and Conditions of the President and Members of the State Commission

7. (1) [The President of the State Commission shall receive the salary, allowances and other perquisites as are applicable to a judge of the High Court, if appointed on whole-time basis] or a consolidated honorarium of ₹ 200 (Rupees two hundred only) per day for the sitting if appointed on part time basis. Other members if sitting on whole-time basis, shall receive a consolidated honorarium of ₹ 3,000 (Rupees three thousand only) per month and if sitting on part-time basis, a consolidated honorarium of ₹ 150 (Rupees one hundred and fifty only) per day for the sitting. The members shall also receive the conveyance allowance of ₹ 1,000 (Rupees one thousand only) per month.

(2) The President and the members of the State Commission shall be eligible for such travelling allowance and daily allowance on official tour as are admissible to Grade I Officer of the Tamil Nadu Government.

(3) The salary, honorarium, other allowances shall be defrayed out of the Consolidated Fund of the Government of Tamil Nadu.

(4) The President and the members of the State Commission shall hold office for a term of five years or upto the age of [75 years] whichever is earlier and shall not be eligible for renomination :

Provided that President and members may —

(a) by writing under his hand and addressed to the State Government resign his office any time;

(b) be removed from his office in accordance with provisions of sub-rule (5).

(5) The Government of Tamil Nadu may remove from office President or member of the State Commission who,—

(a) has been adjudged as insolvent, or

(b) has been convicted of an offence which in the opinion of the Government of Tamil Nadu involves moral turpitude, or

(c) has become physically or mentally incapable of acting as President or a member, or

(d) has acquired such financial or other interest as is likely to affect prejudicially his functions as President or a member, or

(e) has so abused his position as to render his continuance in office prejudicial to public interest:

Provided that the President or a member shall not be removed from his office on the ground specified in clauses *(d)* and *(e)* and sub-rule (5) except on an inquiry held by the Government of Tamil Nadu in accordance with such procedure as it may specify in this behalf and finds the President or a member to be guilty on such ground.

(5A) The Government of Tamil Nadu may, after giving reasonable opportu-nity of being heard, remove from office a member of the State Commission who has not attended two consecutive sittings of the State Commission without sufficient causes.

(6) Before appointment, President and members of the State Commission shall have to take an undertaking that he does not and will not have any such financial or other interests as is likely to affect prejudicially his functions as President or a member.

(7) The terms and conditions of the service of the President and the members of the State Commission shall not be varied to their disadvantage during their tenure of office.

(8) Every vacancy caused by resignation and removal of the President or any other member of the State Commission under sub-rule (4) or otherwise shall be filled by fresh appointment.

(9) Where any such vacancy occurs in the office of the President of the State Commission, the senior most member (in order of appointment) holding office for the time being, shall discharge the functions of the President until a person appointed to fill such vacancy assumes the office of the President of the State Commission.

(10) When the President of the State Commission is unable to discharge the functions owing to absence, illness or any other cause, the seniormost (in order of appointment) member of the State Commission shall discharge the functions of the President until the day on which the President resumes the charge of his functions.

(11) The President, or any member ceasing to hold office, as such shall not hold any appointment in or be connected with the management or administration of an organisation which have been the subject of any proceeding under the Act, during his tenure for a period of five years from the date on which he ceases to hold such office.

(12) In case of difference of opinion among the members of the State Commission, the opinion of the majority shall prevail and the opinion or orders of the commission shall be expressed in terms of the views of the majority,

Places of Sitting and Other Matters Relating to State Commission

8. (1) The office of the State Commission shall be located at Madras.

(2) The working days and the office hours of the State Commission shall be the same as that of the Government of Tamil Nadu.

(3) The emblem and official seal of the State Government shall be as follows—

Emblem—The State Commission as Head of the Department shall use the State Emblem in their official letter heads, namely "single colour black Emblem in full with designation within two concentric arcs of two-thirds of a circle."

Seal—The seal shall have two concentric arcs of two-thirds of a circle with the inscriptions, namely, "STATE CONSUMER DISPUTES REDRESSAL COMMISSION" and with the State Emblem at the Centre.

(4) Sitting of the State Commission, as and when necessary, shall be convened by the President.

(5) No act or proceedings of the State Commission shall be invalid by reasons only of the existence of any vacancy among its President or members or any defect in its constitution thereof.

(6) Government of Tamil Nadu shall appoint such staff, as may be necessary to assist the State Commission in its work and to perform such other functions as are Provided under the Act and these rules or assigned to it by the President. The salary payable to such staff shall be defrayed out of the Consolidated Fund of the Government of Tamil Nadu.

(7) Where the opposite party admits the allegation made by the complainant, the State Commission shall decide the complaint on the basis of the merit of the case and documents presented before it.

(8) If during the proceedings conducted under section 13, State Commission fixes a date for hearing of the parties, it shall be obligatory on the complainant and opposite party or his authorised agent to appear before the State Commis-sion on such date of hearing or any other date to which hearing could be adjourned. Where the complainant or his authorised agent fails to appear before the State Commission on such day, the State Commission may in its discretion either dismiss the complaint for default or decide it on merits. Where the opposite party or. its authorised agent fails to appear on the day of hearing, the State Commission may decide the complaint *ex parte*.

(9) While proceeding under sub-rule (8) the State Commission may, on such terms as it may think fit and at any stage, of the proceedings adjourn the hearing of the complaint but not more than one adjournment shall ordinarily be given and the complaint shall be decided within 90 days from the date of notice received by the opposite party where the complaint does not require analysis or testing of the goods and within 150 days if it requires analysis or testing of the goods.

(10) Orders of the State Commission shall be signed and dated by the members of the State Commission constituting the Bench and shall be communicated to the parties free of charge.

Procedure for Hearing Appeal

9. (1) Memorandum shall be presented by the appellant or his authorised agent to the State Commission in person or be sent by registered post addressed to the Commission.

(2) Every memorandum filed under sub-rule (1) shall be in legible handwriting preferably typed and shall set-forth concisely under distinct heads, the grounds of appeal without any argument or narrative and such ground shall be numbered consecutively.

(3) Each memorandum shall be accompanied by the certified copy of the order of the District Forum appealed against and such of the documents as may be required to support grounds of objection mentioned in the memorandum.

(4) When the appeal is presented after the expiry of period of limitation as specified in the Act, Memorandum shall be accompanied by an application supported by an affidavit setting forth the fact on which appellant relies to satisfy the State Commission that he has sufficient cause for not preferring the appeal within the period of limitation.

(5) The appellant shall submit four copies of the memorandum to the State Commission for official purposes.

(6) On the date of hearing or any other day to which hearing may be adjourned, it shall be obligatory for the parties or their authorised agents to appear before the State Commission. If appellant or his authorised agent fails to appear on such date, the State Commission may, in its discretion, either dismiss the appeal or decide in on the merit of the case. If respondent or his authorised agent fails to appear on such date, the State Commission shall proceed *ex pane* and shall decide the appeal *ex parte* on merits of the case.

(7) The appellant shall not, except by leave of the State Commission, urge or be heard in support of any ground of objections not set forth in the memorandum but the State Commission, in deciding the appeal, shall not confine to the grounds of objection set forth in the memorandum or taken by leave of the State Commission under this rule:

Provided that the State Commission shall not rest its decision on any other grounds other than those specified unless the party who may be affected thereby, has been given at least one opportunity of being heard by the State Commission.

(8) State Commission may, on such terms as it may think fit and at any stage, adjourn the hearing of appeal, but not more than one adjournment shall ordinarily be given and the appeal should be decided within 90 days from the first date of hearing,

(9) Order of the State Commission on appeal shall be signed and dated by the members of the State Commission constituting the Bench and shall be communicated to the parties free of charge.

"Consumers Be Aware Before Buying A Product, Look For Quality"

Chapter 32

Tripura Consumer Protection Rules, 1987

[No. CP-72/XXIX-10-CP(8)-87, Dated 31-8-1987]

In exercise of the powers conferred by sub-section (2) of section 30 of the Consumer Protection Act, 1986 (68 of 1986), State Government hereby makes the following rules, namely —

SHORT TITLE AND COMMENCEMENT

1. (1) These rules may be called the Tripura Consumer Protection Rules, 1987.

(2) They shall come into force on the Second day of October, 1987.

Definitions

2. In these rules, unless the context otherwise requires —

(a) "Act" means the Consumer Protection Act, 1986 (68 of 1986);

(b) "agent" means a person duly authorised by a party to present any complaint or appeal or reply on its behalf before the State Commission or the District Forum;

(c) "appellant" means a party which makes an appeal against the order of the District Forum;

(d) "memorandum" means memorandum of appeal filed by the appellant;

(e) "Opposite party" means a person who answers complaint or claim;

(f) "President" means the President of the State Commission or District Forum as the case may be;

(g) "Respondent" means person who answers any memorandum of appeal;

(h) "State" includes union territories.

Salaries and Other Allowances and Terms and Conditions of the President and Members of the District Forum [Section 10(3)]

3. (1) The President of the District Forum shall receive the salary of the Judge of a District Court if appointed on whole time basis or an honorarium of ₹ 150 per day if appointed on part-time basis. Other members if sitting on whole time basis, shall receive a consolidated honorarium of ₹ 2,000 per month and if sitting on part-time basis, a consolidated honorarium of ₹ 100 per day for the sitting.

(2) The President and the members of the District Forum shall be entitled for such travelling allowance and daily allowance on official tour as are admissible to Grade-I Officer of the State Government.

(3) The salary, honorarium and other allowances shall be defrayed out of the Consolidated Fund of the State Government.

(4) Before appointment, the President and Members of the District Forum shall have to take an undertaking that he does not and will not have any such financial or other interests as is likely to affect prejudicially his functions as a Member.

(5) In addition of provisions of section 10(2), State Government may remove from the office, the President and member of a District Forum who—

(*a*) has been adjudged as insolvent, or

(*b*) has been convicted of an offence which in the opinion of the State Government, involves moral turpitude, or

(*c*) has become physically or mentally incapable of acting as such Member, or

(*d*) has acquired such financial or other interest as is likely to affect prejudicially his functions as his Member, or

(*e*) has so abused his position as to render his continuance in office prejudicial to the public interest:

Provided that the President or Member shall not be removed from his office on the ground specified in clauses (*d*) and (*e*) of sub-rule (5) except on an inquiry held by the State Government in accordance with such procedure as it may specify in this behalf and finds the Member to be guilty of such ground.

(6) The terms and conditions of the service of the President and the members of the District Forum shall not be varied to their disadvantage during their tenure of office.

(7) Where any vacancy occurs in the office of the President of the District Forum, the seniormost (in order of appointment) Member of District Forum, holding office for the time being, shall discharge the functions of the President until a person appointed to fill such vacancy assumes the Office of the President of the District Forum.

(8) When the President of the District Forum is unable to discharge the functions owing to absence, illness or any other cause, the seniormost (in order of appointment) Member of the District Forum shall discharge the functions of the President until the day on which the President resumes the charge of his functions.

(9) The President or any member ceasing to hold office as such shall not hold any appointment in or be connected with the management or administration of an organisation which have been the subject of any proceeding under the Act during his tenure for a period of 5 years from the date on which he ceases to hold such office.

Place of sitting and other matters relating to District Forum [Section 14(3)]

4. (1) The office of the District Forum shall be located at the headquarter of the District. Where State Government decides to establish a single District Forum having jurisdiction over more than one district, it shall notify the place and jurisdiction of the District Forum so established.

(2) The working days and the office hours of the District Forum shall be the same as that of the State Government.

(3) The official seal and emblem of the District Forum shall be such as the State Government may specify.

(4) Sitting of the District Forum, as and when necessary, shall be convened by the President.

(5) No act or proceedings of the District Forum shall be invalid by reason only of the existence of any vacancy among its members or any defect in its constitution.

(6) State Government shall appoint such staff, as may be necessary to assist the District Forum in its day to day work and perform such other functions as are **Provided** under these rules, or assigned to it by the President. The salary payable to such staff shall be defrayed out of the Consolidated Fund of the State Government.

(7) Where the opposite party admits the allegation made by the complainant, the District Forum shall decide the complaint on the basis of the merit of the case and documents present before it.

(8) If during the proceedings conducted under section 13, District Forum fixes a date for hearing of the parties, it shall be obligatory on the complainant and opposite party or its authorised agent to appear before the District Forum on such date of hearing or any other date to which hearing could be adjourned. Where the complainant or his authorised agent fails to appear before the District Forum on such day, the District Forum may in its discretion either dismiss the complaint for default or decide it on merit. Where the opposite party or its authorised agent fails to appear on the day of hearing, the District Forum may decide the complaint *ex parte*.

(9) While proceeding under sub-rule (8), the District Forum may on such terms as it may think fit and at any stage, adjourn the hearing of the complaint but not more than one adjournment shall ordinarily be given and the complaint should be decided within 90 days from the date of notice received by the opposite party where complaint does not require analysis or testing of the goods and within 150 days if it requires analysis or testing of the goods.

(10) Orders of the District Forum shall be signed and dated by the members of the District Forum constituting the Bench and shall be communicated to the parties free of charge.

Procedure to be adopted by the District Forum for analysis and testing of the goods [Section 13(l)(c)]

5. (1) Under section 13(l)(c), if considered necessary, the District Forum may direct the complainant to provide more than one sample of the goods in clean containers with stopper properly fixed on them:

(2) On receiving the samples of such goods, the District Forum shall seal it and fix labels on the containers carrying following information —

(i) Name and address of the appropriate laboratory to whom sample will be sent for analysis and test;

(ii) Name and address of the District Forum;

(iii) Case number;

(iv) Seal of the District Forum.

(3) The sample will be sent to the appropriate laboratory by the District Forum for sending report within 45 days or within such extended time as may be granted by the District Forum after specifying the nature of the defect alleged and date of submission of the report.

Salary and Other Allowances and Terms and Conditions of the President and Members of the State Commission [Section 16(2)]

6. (1) President of the State Commission shall receive the salary of the Judge of the High Court if appointed on whole-time basis or a consolidated honorarium or ₹ 200 per day for the sitting if appointed on part-time basis. Other members, if sitting on whole time basis, shall receive a consolidated honorarium of ₹ 3,000 per month and if sitting on part-time basis, a consolidated honorarium of ₹ 150 per day for the sitting.

(2) The President and the Members of the State Commission shall be eligible for such travelling allowance and daily allowance on official tour as are admissible to Grade-I Officer of the State Government.

(3) The salary, honorarium, other allowances shall be defrayed out of the Consolidated Fund of the State Government.

(4) President and the Member of the State Commission shall hold office for a term of five years or up to the age of 65 years whichever is earlier and shall not be eligible for renomination:

Provided that President and member may—

(a) by writing under his hand and addressed to the State Government resign his office any time;

(b) be removed from his office in accordance with provisions of sub-rule (5).

(5) The State Government may remove from office, President or a Member of the State Commission who—

(a) has been adjudged as insolvent, or

(b) has been convicted of an offence which in the opinion of the State Government, involves moral turpitude, or

(c) has become physically or mentally incapable of acting as such member, or

(d) has acquired such financial or other interest as is likely to affect prejudicially his functions as a member, or

(e) has so abused his position as to render his continuance in office prejudicial to the public interest. Provided that the President or a member shall not be removed from his office on the ground specified in clauses *(d)* and *(e)* of sub-rule (5) except on an inquiry held by State Government, in accordance with such procedure as it may specify in this behalf and finds the members to be guilty of such ground.

(6) Before appointment, President and a member of the State Commission shall have to take an undertaking that he does not and will not have any such financial or other interests as is likely to affect prejudicially his functions as such member.

(7) The terms and conditions of the service of the President and the members of the State Commission shall not be varied to their disadvantage during their tenure of office.

(8) Every vacancy caused by resignation and removal of the President or any other member of the State Commission under sub-rule (4) or otherwise shall filled by fresh appointment.

(9) Where any such vacancy occurs in the office of the President of the State Commission, the seniormost (in order of appointment) member, holding office for the time being, shall discharge the functions of the President until a person appointed to fill such vacancy assumes the office of the President of the State Commission.

(10) When the President of the State Commission is unable to discharge the functions owing to absence, illness or any other cause, the seniormost (in order to the appointment) member of the State Commission shall discharge the functions of the President until the day on which the President resumes the charge of his functions.

(11) The President or any member ceasing to hold office as such shall not hold any appointment in or be connected with the management or administrations of an organisation which have been the subject of any proceeding under the Act during this tenure for a period of 5 years from the date on which he ceases to hold such office.

Place of Sitting and Other Matters Relating to State Commission Section 14(3) Read with Section 18]

7. (1) Office of the State Commission shall be located at the capital of the State.

(2) The working days and the office hours of the State Commission shall be the same as that of the State Government.

(3) The official seal and emblem of the State Commission shall be such as the State Government may specify.

(4) Sitting of the State Commission, as and when necessary, shall be convened by the President.

(5) No Act or Proceedings of the State Commission shall be invalid by reasons only of the existence of any vacancy among its members or any defect in its constitution thereof.

(6) State Government shall appoint such staff, as may be necessary to assist the State Commission in its work and perform such other functions as are provided under these rules or assigned to it by the President. The salary payable to such staff shall be defrayed out of the Consolidated Fund of the State Government.

(7) Where the opposite party admits the allegation made by the complainant, the State Commission shall decide the complaint on the basis of the merit of the case and documents present before it.

(8) If during the proceedings conducted under section 13, State Commission fixes a date for hearing of the parties, it shall be obligatory on the complainant and opposite party or his authorised agent to appear before the State Commission such date of hearing or any other date to which hearing could be adjourned. Where the complainant or his authorised agent fails to appear before the Slate Commission on such day, the State Commission may in its discretion either dismiss the complaint for default or decide it on merits. Where the opposite party or its authorised agent fails to appear on the day of hearing the State Commission may decide the complaint *ex parte*.

(9) While proceedings under sub-rule (8) the State Commission may, on such terms as it may think fit and at any stage adjourn the hearing of the complaint but not more than one adjournment shall ordinarily be given and the complaint should be decided within 90 days from the date of notice received by the opposite party where complaint does not require analysis or testing of the goods and within 150 days if it requires analysis or testing of the goods.

(10) Orders of the State Commission shall be signed and dated by the members of the State Commission constituting the Bench and shall be communicated to the parties free of charge.

Procedure for Hearing Appeal [Section 15]

8. (1) Memorandum shall be presented by the appellant or his authorised agent to the State Commission in person or sent by registered post addressed to the Commission.

(2) Every memorandum filed under sub-rule (1) shall be in legible handwriting preferably typed and shall set forth concisely under distinct heads, the grounds of appeal without any argument or narrative and such ground shall be numbered consecutively.

(3) Each memorandum shall be accompanied by the certified copy of the order of the District Forum appealed against and such of the documents as may be required to support grounds of objection mentioned in the memorandum.

(4) When the appeal is presented after the expiry of period of limitation as specified in the Act, memorandum shall be accompanied by an application supported by an affidavit setting forth the fact on which appellant relies to satisfy the State Commission that he has sufficient cause for not preferring the appeal within the period of limitation.

(5) The appellant shall submit four copies of the memorandum to the State Commission for official purposes.

(6) On the date of hearing or any other day to which hearing, may be adjourned, it shall be obligatory for the parties or their authorised agents to appear before the State Commission. If appellant or his authorised agent fails to appear such date, the State Commission may, in its discretion, either dismiss the appeal or decide it on the merit of the case. If respondent or his authorised agents t to appear on such date, the State Commission shall proceed *ex parte* and shall decide the appeal *ex parte* on merits of the case.

(7) The appellant shall not, except by leave of the State Commission, urge or 'heard in support of any ground of objections not set forth in the memorandum but the State Commission, in deciding the appeal, shall not confine to the grounds of objection set forth in the memorandum or taken by leave of the State Commission under this rule:

Provided that the Commission shall not rest its decision on any other grounds unless the party who may be affected thereby, has been given, at least one opportunity of being heard by the State Commission.

(8) State Commission may, on such terms as it may think fit and at any stage, adjourn the hearing of appeal, but not more than one adjournment shall ordinarily be given and the appeal should be decided within 90 days from the first date of hearing.

(9) Order of the State Commission on appeal shall be signed and dated by the members of the State Commission constituting the Bench and shall be communicated to the parties free of charge.

Chapter 33

Uttar Pradesh Consumer Protection Rules, 1987

[No. CP-72/XIX-10-CP(8)-87, Dated 31-8-1987]

In exercise of the powers under sub-section (2) of section 30 of the Consumer Protection Act, 1986 (68 of 1986) the Governor is pleased to make the following rules, namely —

SHORT TITLE AND COMMENCEMENT

1. (1) These rules may be called the Uttar Pradesh Consumer Protection Rules, 1987.

(2) They shall come into force on the date of their publication in the Official Gazette.

Definitions

2. In these rules, unless the context otherwise requires,—

(a) "Act" means the Consumer Protection Act, 1986 (68 of 1986);

(b) "agent" means a person duly authorised by a party to present any complaint or appeal or reply on its behalf before the State Commission or the District Forum;

(c) "appellant" means a party which makes an appeal against the order of the District Forum;

(d) "memorandum" means memorandum of appeal filed by the appellant;

(e) "opposite party" means a person who answers complaint or claim;

(f) "President" means the President of the State Commission or District Forum as the case may be;

(g) "respondent" means the person who answers any memorandum or appeal;

(h) "State" includes Union Territories.

Constitution of the State Council [Section 7(2)]

2A. (1) The State Council established in Government Notification No. C.I 594/XX1X-8-97-C.P. 41-90, dated March 14, 1997, shall consist of the following members, namely —

(i) Official members —

(a) The Minister Incharge of Food and Civil Supplies Department, Uttar Pradesh — *Chairman*

(b) Principal Secretary or Secretary, as the case may be, to the State Government in Food and Civil Supplies Department — *Member*

(c) Principal Secretary or Secretary, as the case may be, to the State Government in Industries Department — *Member*

(d) Principal Secretary or Secretary, as the case may be, to the State Government in Medical and Health Department — *Member*

(e) Principal Secretary or Secretary, as the case may be, to the State Government in Agriculture Department — *Member*

(f) Commissioner, Food and Civil Supplies Department — *Member*

(g) Principal Secretary or Secretary, as the case may be, to the State Government in Transport Department — *Member*

(h) Principal Secretary, Judicial and Legal Remembrance to the State Government — *Member*

(i) General Manager, Telecommunication — *Member*

(j) Director General, Consumer Protection, Uttar Pradesh — *Member*

(k) Principal Secretary or Secretary, as the case may be, to the State Government in Avas Vibhag — *Member*

(l) Director of Information, Uttar Pradesh — *Member*

(m) Drug Controller, Uttar Pradesh — *Member*

(n) Managing Director, Uttar Pradesh Food and Essential Commodities Corporation, Uttar Pradesh — *Member*

(o) Managing Director, Provincial Cooperative Federation, Uttar Pradesh — *Member*

(p) Principal Secretary or Secretary, as the case may be, to the State Government in Institutional Finance Department — *Member*

(q) Managing Director, Rajya Mandi Parishad, Uttar Pradesh — *Member*

(r) Executive Director, Uttar Pradesh Employees Welfare Corporation — *Member*

(s) Regional Officer, Indian Standard Organisation, Uttar Pradesh — *Member*

(t) State Co-ordinator, Indian Oil Corporation, Uttar Pradesh — *Member*

(u) Principal Secretary or Secretary, as the case may be, to the State Government in Nagar Vikas Vibhag, Uttar Pradesh — *Member*

(v) Secretary, Uttar Pradesh State Electricity Board, Lucknow — *Member*

(w) Divisional Manager, Northern Railway, Lucknow — *Member*

(x) Anchalik Prabandhak Life Insurance Corporation — *Member*

(y) Secretary, Co-operative Department, Uttar Pradesh Shasan — *Member*

(ii) Non-Official Members:—

(a) Member, Legislative Assembly nominated by the State Government with the "approval of the Speaker — *Five members*

(b) Member, Legislative Council nominated by the State Government with the approval of the Chairman — *Three members*

(c) The representatives of voluntary organisations/agencies, representing the Consumer interests nominated by the State Government — *Eight members*

(d) Representatives of Farmers/Services undertakings/Manufacturers/Retailers and Major Trade Organisations such as Avadh Chamber of Commerces, Udyog Vyapar Mandal, Punjab-Haryana Chamber of Commerce, etc. — *Eight members*

(e) Noted persons working in the field of Consumer protection or in public interest in the important areas of Society nominated by State Government — *Sixteen members*

(2) (A) The members of the Legislative Council and Legislative Assembly shall hold office till they are members of the Legislative Council or the Legislative Assembly, as the case may be, and the rest of the non-official members shall hold office for a period of three years from the date of their nomination.

Procedure of the State Council [Section 7(4)]

2B. (a) State Council shall observe the following procedure in regard to the transaction of its business, namely—

(a) The meeting of the State Council shall be presided over by the chairman In the absence of the chairman the State Council shall select a member preside over the meeting of the Council.

(b) Each meeting of the State Council shall be called by giving, not less than ten days from the date of issue, notice in writing to every member.

(c) Every notice of a meeting of the State Council shall specify the place and the day and hour of the meeting and shall contain statement of business to be transacted in the meeting.

(d) No proceedings of the State Council shall be invalid merely by reasons of existence of any vacancy or any defect in the Constitution of the Council.

(e) For the purpose of performing its functions under the Act, the State Council may constitute from amongst its members, such working groups as it may deem necessary and every working group, so constituted shall perform such functions as are assigned to it by the State Council. The findings of such working groups shall be placed before the State Council for its consideration.

(f) The non-official member shall be entitled to first class railway fare for attending a meeting and for return journey and a daily allowance of one hundred rupees per day for attending a meeting of the State Council or any working group members of Legislative Assembly/Legislative Council shall be entitled to travelling and daily allowances at such rates as are admissible to such members.

(g) The resolutions passed by the State Council shall be recommendatory in nature.

Salaries and Other Allowances and Terms and Conditions of the President and Member of the District Forum [Section 10(3)]

3. (1) (a) The President of the District Forum shall receive the salary of the Judge of a District Court if appointed on whole time basis or an honorarium of ₹ 200 per day if appointed on part time basis, Other members if sitting on whole time basis, shall receive a consolidated honorarium of ₹ 4,000 per month and is sitting on part time basis, a consolidated honorarium of ₹ 150 per day for the sitting.

(b) The President of the District Forum shall receive House Rent Allowance of ₹ 800 per month if appointed on whole time basis and no Government Accommodation is Provided to him.

(c) A member of the District Forum shall get House Rent Allowance of ₹ 600 per month if no Government accommodation is Provided to him.

(2) The President and the Members of the District Forum shall be entitled to such travelling allowance and daily allowance on official tour as are admissible Bo Grade 1 Officer of the State Government.

(3) The salary, honorarium and other allowances shall be defrayed out of the Consolidated Fund of the State Government.

(4) Before appointment, the President and Members of the District Forum shall have to take an undertaking that he does not and will not have any such financial or other interests as is likely to affect prejudicially his functions as a member.

(5) In addition to provisions of section 10(2), State Government may remove from the office the president and member of a District Forum who,—

(a) has been adjudged as insolvent, or

(b) has been convicted of an offence which in the opinion of the State Government involves moral turpitude, or

(c) has become physically or mentally incapable of acting as such member, or

(d) has acquired such financial or other interest as it likely to affect prejudicially his functions as a member, or

(e) has so abused his position as to render his continuance in office prejudicial to the public interest, or

(f) does not pass judgment or order possible under Act, and in conformity with the earlier judgment and the act and does not display absolute, integrity good conduct and dutifulness, or

(g) is guilty of an explained absence upto 7 days without permissions:

Provided that the President or member shall not be removed from his office on the ground specified in clauses (b) and (c) of this sub-rule except on an inquiry held by State Government in accordance with such procedure as it may specify in this behalf and the member is found to be guilty of such ground.

(6) The terms and conditions of the service of the President and the Members of the District Forum shall not be varied to their disadvantage during their tenure of office,

(7) Where any vacancy occurs in the office of the President of the District Forum, the seniormost (in order of appointment) Member of District Forum, holding office for the time being, shall discharge the functions of the President until a person appointed to fill such vacancy assumes the office of the President of the District Forum.

(8) When the President of the District Forum is unable to discharge the functions owing to absence, illness, or any other cause, the seniormost (in order of appointment) Member of the District Forum shall discharge the functions of the President until the day on which the President resumes the charge of his functions.

(9) The President or any Member ceasing to hold office as such shall not hold any appointment in or be connected with the management or administration of an organisation which have been the subject of any proceeding under the Act during his tenure for a period of 5 years from the date on which he ceases to hold such office.

Place of Sitting and Other Matters relating to District Forum [Section 14(3)]

4. (1) The Office of the District Forum shall be located at the headquarter of the District. When State Government decides to establish a single District Forum having jurisdiction over more than one District, it shall notify the place and jurisdictions of the District Forum so established.

(2) The working days and the office hours of the District Forum shall be the same as that of the State Government.

(3) The official seal and emblem of the District Forum shall be as the State Government specify,

(4) Sitting of the District Forum, as and when necessary, shall be convened by the President.

(5) No act or proceeding of the District Forum shall be invalid by reasons only of the existence of any vacancy among its members or any defect in its constitution.

(6) The State Government shall appoint such staff, as may be necessary to assist the District Forum in its day to day work and perform such other functions as are Provided under these rules, or assigned to it by the President, The salary payable to such staff shall be defrayed out of the Consolidated Fund of the State Government,

(7) Where the opposite party admits the allegation made by the complainant the District Forum shall decide the complaint on the basis of the merit of the case and documents present before it.

(8) If during the proceedings conducted under section 13, District Forum fixes a date for hearing of the parties, it shall be obligatory on the complainant and opposite party or its authorised agent to appear before the District Forum on such date of hearing or any other date to which hearing could be adjourned. Where the complainant or his authorised agent fails to appear before the District Forum on such day, the District Forum may in its discretion either dismiss the complaint for default or decide it on merit. Where the opposite party or its authorised agent fails to appear on the day of hearing, the District Forum may decide the complaint *ex parte.*

(9) While proceeding under sub-rule (8), the District Forum may on such terms as it may think fit and at any stage, adjourn the hearing of the complaint but not more than one adjournment shall ordinarily be given and the complaint should be decided within 90 days from the date of notice received by the opposite party where complaint does not require analysis or testing of the goods and within 150 days if it requires analysis or testing of the goods.

(10) Orders of the District Forum shall be signed and dated by the Members of the District Forum constituting the Bench and shall be communicated to the parties free of charge.

Procedure to be Adopted by the District Forum for Analysis and Testing of Goods [Section 13(1)(c)]

5. (1) Under section 13(1)(c), if considered necessary, the District Forum may direct the complainant to provide more than one sample of the goods in clean containers with stopper properly fixed on them.

(2) On receiving the samples of such goods, the District Forum shall seal it and fix labels on the containers carrying following information—

(i) name and address of the appropriate laboratory to whom sample will be sent, for analysis and test;

(ii) name and address of the District Forum;

(iii) case number;

(iv) seal of the District Forum.

(3) The sample will be sent to the appropriate laboratory by the District Forum for sending report within 45 days or within such extended time as may be granted by the District Forum after specifying the nature of the defect alleged and date of submission of the report.

Salary and Other Allowances and Terms and Conditions of the President and Members of the State Commission [Section 16(2)]

6. (1) *(a)* The President of the State Commission shall receive the salary of the judge of the High Court appointed on whole time basis, or a consolidated honorarium of ₹ 250 per day for the sitting if appointed on part time basis. Other members if sitting on whole time basis shall receive a consolidated honorarium of ₹ 6,000 per month and if sitting on part time basis a consolidated honorarium of ₹ 200 per day for the sitting.

(b) The President and the Members of the State Commission shall be entitled to rent free Government accommodation. If no such accommodation is Provided to "the President or Member of the State Commission he shall get house rent allowance of ₹ 1,500 per month.

(2) The President and the Members of the State Commission shall be eligible for such travelling allowance and daily allowance on official tour as are admissible to Grade I Officer of the State Government.

(3) The salary, honorarium and other allowances shall be defrayed out of the Consolidated Fund of the State Government,

(4) *(a)* The President of the State Commission shall hold office for a term of five years or upto the age of 70 years whichever is earlier and shall not he eligible renomination;

(b) The Member of the State Commission shall hold office for a term of five years or upto the age of 65 years whichever is earlier and shall not be eligible for renomination:

Provided that President and Members may—

(a) by writing under his hand and addressed to the State Government resign his office any time; and

(b) be removed from his office in accordance with provisions of sub-rule (5).]

(5) The State Government may remove from Office, President or a Member of the State Commission who,—

(a) has been adjudged as insolvent; or

(b) has been convicted of an offence which in the opinion of the State Government, involves moral turpitude; or

(c) has become physically or menially incapable of acting as such member; or

(d) has acquired such financial or other interest as is likely to affect prejudicially his functions as a member; or

(e) has so abused his position as to render his continuance in office prejudicial to public interest:

Provided that the President or Member shall not be removed from his office on the ground specified in clauses *(d)* and *(e)* of sub-rule (5) except on an inquiry held by State Government in accordance with such procedure as it may specify in this behalf and finds the member to be guilty of such ground.

(6) Before appointment, the President and Members of the State Commission shall have to take an undertaking that he does not and will not have any such financial or other interests as is likely to affect prejudicially his functions as such member.

(7) The terms and conditions of the service of the President and the Members of the State Commission shall not be varied to their disadvantage during their tenure of office.

(8) Every vacancy caused by resignation and removal of the President or any other Member of the State Commission under sub-rule (4) or otherwise shall be filled by fresh appointment.

(9) Where any such vacancy occurs in the office of the President of the State Commission, the seniormost (in order of appointment) member holding office for the time being, shall discharge the functions of the President until a person appointed to fill such vacancy assumes the office of the President of the State Commission.

(10) When the President of the State Commission is unable to discharge the functions owing to absence, illness or any other cause, the seniormost (in order of appointment) member of the State Commission shall discharge the func-tions of President until the day on which the President resumes the charge of his functions.

(11) The President or any Member ceasing to hold office as such shall not hold any appointment in or be connected with the management or administration of an organisation which have been the subject of any proceeding under the Act during his tenure for a period of 5 years from the date on which he ceases to hold such office.

Place of sitting and other matters relating to State Commission [Section 14(3) read with section 18]

7. (1) Office of the State Commission shall be located at the capital of the State.

(2) The working days and the office hours of the State Commission shall be same as that of the State Government.

(3) The official seal and emblem of the State Commission shall be such as the State Government may specify.

(4) Sitting of the State Commission, as and when necessary, shall be convened by the President.

(5) No act or proceedings of the State Commission shall be invalid by reason only of the existence of any vacancy among its members or any defect in its constitution thereof.

(6) The State Government shall appoint such staff, as may be necessary to assist the State Commission in its work and perform such other functions as are provided under these rules or assigned to it by the President. The salary payable to such staff shall be defrayed out of the Consolidated Fund of the State Government.

(7) Where the opposite party admits the allegation made by the complainant, the State Commission shall decide the complaint on the basis of the merit of the case and documents present before it.

(8) If during the proceedings conducted under section 13, State Commission fixes a date for hearing of the parties. It shall be obligatory on the complainant and opposite party or his authorised agents to appear before the State Commission on such date of hearing or any other date to which hearing could be adjourned. Where the complainant or his authorised agent fails to appear before the State Commission on such day, the State Commission may in its discretion either dismiss the complaint for default or decide it on merits, where the opposite party or its authorised agent fails to appear on the day of hearing, the State Commission may decide the complaint *ex, parte.*

(9) While proceeding under sub-rule (8), the State Commission may on such terms as it may think fit and at any stage, adjourn the hearing of the complaint but not more than one adjournment shall ordinarily be given and the complaint should be decided within 90 days from the date of notice received by the opposite party where complaint does not require analysis or testing of the goods and within 150 days if it requires analysis or testing of the goods. (10) Orders of the State Commission shall be signed and dated by the members of the State Commission constituting the Bench and shall be communicated to the parties free of charge.

Procedure for hearing appeal [Section 15]

8. (1) Memorandum shall be presented by the appellant or his authorised agent to the State Commission in person or be sent by registered post addressed to the Commission,

(2) Every memorandum filed under sub-rule (1) shall be in legible handwriting preferably typed and shall set forth concisely under distinct heads, the grounds of appeal without any argument or narrative and such grounds shall be numbered consecutively.

(3) Each memorandum shall be accompanied by the certified copy of the order of the District Forum appealed against and such of the documents as may be required to support grounds of objection mentioned in the memorandum.

(4) When the appeal is presented after, the expiry of the period of limitation as specified in the Act, the memorandum shall be accompanied by an application supported by an affidavit setting forth the fact on which the appellant relies to satisfy the State Commission that he has sufficient cause for not preferring the appeal within the period of limitation.

(5) The appellant shall submit four copies of the memorandum to the State Commission for official purposes.

(6) On the date of hearing or any other day to which hearing may be adjourned, it shall be obligatory for the parties or their authorised agents to appear before the State Commission. If appellant or his authorised agent fails to appear on such date, the State Commission may, in its discretion either dismiss the appeal or decide it on the merit of the case. If respondent or his authorised agent fails to appear on such date, the State Commission shall proceed *ex parte* and shall decide the appeal *ex parte* on the merits of the case.

(7) The appellant shall not, except by leave of the State Commission, urge or be heard in support of any ground of objection not set forth in the memorandum but the State Commission, in deciding the appeal, need not confine to the grounds of objection set forth in the memorandum or taken by leave of the State Commission under this rule:

Provided that the Commission shall not rest its decision on any other grounds unless the party who may be affected thereby, has been given, at least one opportunity of being heard by the State Commission;

(8) The State Commission may, on such terms as it may think fit and at any stage, adjourn the hearing of the appeal, but not more that one adjournment shall ordinarily be given and the appeal should be decided within 90 days from the first date of hearing.

(9) Order of the State Commission on appeal shall be signed and dated by the Members of the State Commission constituting the Bench and shall be communicated to the parties free of charge.

9. (1) *(a)* On complaint received against the full time President, member of Districts Forum and the State Commission, an enquiry shall be held by Principal Secretary or Secretary as the case may be to Government of Uttar Pradesh Food and Civil Supplies Department or by an officer of Government nominated by him.

(b) On complaint received against such Part time President who are working District Judge or Additional District Judge inquiry shall be held by the High Court.

(c) The complaints received against the President of the State Commission shall be inquired into by any retired Chief Justice of any High Court nominated by the State Government.

(2) On being found guilty on the basis of the findings of the aforesaid inquiry the State Government may remove the President or member of the District Forum and the State Commission from their office on grounds specified in sub-rule (5) of rule 3 and sub-rule (5) of rule 6 as the case may be of the said Rules.

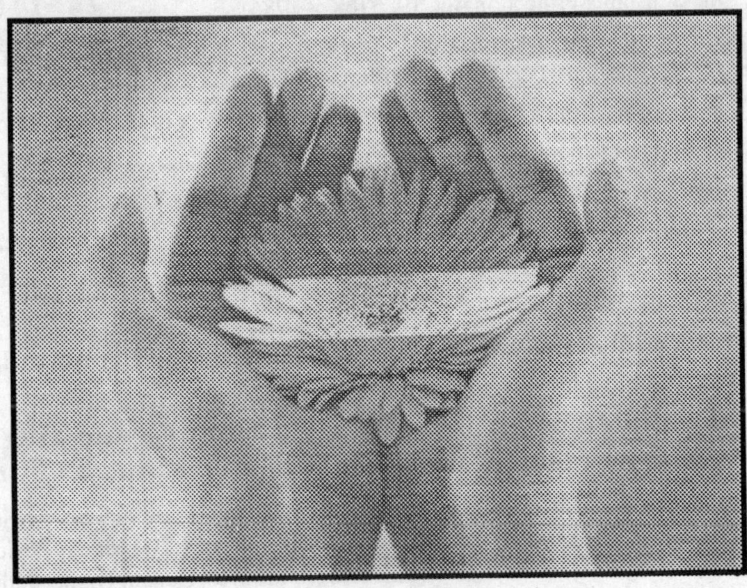

—✦—✦—✦—

Chapter 34

West Bengal Consumer Protection Rules, 1987

[Notification No. 7601-FS/4F-25/82 PT. II, Dated 20-7-1987]

In exercise of the powers conferred by sub-section (2) of section 30 of the Consumer Protection Act, 1986 (68 of 1986), the Governor is pleased hereby to make the following rules —

SHORT TITLE AND COMMENCEMENT

1. (1) These rules may be called the West Bengal Consumer Protection Rules, 1987.

(2) They shall come into force on such date as the State Government may, by notification in the Official Gazette.

Definitions

2. (1) In these rules, unless the context otherwise requires,—

(a) "Act" means the Consumer Protection Act, 1986 (68 of 1986);

(b) "agent" means a person duly authorised by a party to present any complaint or appeal or reply on its behalf before the State Commission or the District Forum;

(c) "appellant" means a party which makes an appeal against the order of the District Forum;

(d) "memorandum" means memorandum of appeal filed by the appellant;

(e) "opposite party" means a person who answers complaint or claim;

(f) "President" means the President of the State Commission or District Forum, as the case may be;

(g) "respondent" means the person who answers any memorandum of appeal;

(h) "section" means a section of the Act.

(2) Words and expressions used in these rules and not defined but defined in the Act shall have the same meanings respectively assigned to them in the Act.

Salaries, Honorarium and Other Allowances, Payable to and the Other Terms and Conditions of Service of the President and Members of the District Forum [Section 10(3)]

3. (1) *(i)* If a sitting District Judge or a serving member of the West Bengal Higher Judicial Service is appointed as President of the District Forum on whole time basis, he shall receive a special pay of ₹ 200 per day besides the pay and allowances admissible to him as a sitting Judge or as a serving member of the West Bengal Higher Judicial Service.

(ii) If a sitting District Judge or a serving member of the West Bengal Higher Judicial Service appointed as a President of the District Forum on whole-time basis stands superannuated (on attaining the age of superannuation) during his tenure as President of the District Forum, he shall continue to receive the pay and allowances last drawn by him less pension and the pension equivalent to gratuity if any.

EXAMPLE OF PACKAGE INFORMATION

(*iii*) If a retired District Judge or a retired member of the West Bengal Higher Judicial Service or a person who has resigned from the Higher Judicial Service is appointed as President of the District Forum on whole-time basis, he shall receive the pay and allowances last drawn by him less pension and the pension equivalent to gratuity, if any.

(*iv*) If the President of the District Forum is appointed on part-time basis, he shall receive art honorarium of ₹ 150 per day.

(*v*) Other members, if sitting on whole-time basis, shall receive a consolidated honorarium of ₹ 2,000 per month and if sitting on part-time basis shall receive a consolidated honorarium of ₹ 100 per day.

(2) The President and the members of the District Forum shall be entitled to such travelling allowance and daily allowance on official tour as are admissible to a [Group A] Officer of the State Government.

(3) The salary, honorarium and other allowances shall be defrayed out of the Consolidated Fund of the State Government.

(4) Before appointment, the President and any member of the District Forum shall have to give an undertaking that he does not and will not have any such financial or other interests as is likely to affect prejudicially his functions as a member,

(5) The State Government may remove from the office, the President and any member of a District Forum who,—

(a) has been adjudged as insolvent, or

(b) has been convicted of an offence which, in the opinion of the State Government, involves moral turpitude, or

(c) has become physically or mentally incapable of acting as such member, or

(d) has remained absent in three consecutive sittings of the District Forum without obtaining previous permission of the State Government, except for reasons beyond his control, or]

(d) has acquired such financial or other interest as is likely to affect prejudicially his function as member, or

(e) has so abused his position as to render his continuance in office prejudicial to the public interest:

Provided that the President or any other member shall not be removed from his office on the ground specified in clauses *(d)* and *(e)* except on an inquiry held by the State Government in accordance with the procedure laid down in sub-rule (10).

(5A) The State Government may transfer the President of a District Forum from one District Forum to any other District Forum in the interest of public service.

(5B) The terms and conditions of service of the President and the members of the District Forum, which have not been specified in these rules, shall be such as are applicable to Group 'A' Officers of the State Government under the West Bengal Service Rules, Part I and Part II.

(6) The terms and conditions of service of the President and the member of the District Forum shall not be varied to their disadvantage during their tenure of office.

(7) Where any vacancy occurs in the office of the President of the District Forum, the seniormost (in order of appointment) member of the District Forum, holding office for the time being, shall discharge the functions of the President until a person appointed to fill such vacancy assumes the office of the President of the District Forum.

(8) When the President of the District Forum is unable to discharge his functions owing to absence, illness or any other cause, the seniormost (in order of appointment) member of the District Forum shall discharge the functions of the President until the day on which the President resumes the charge of his functions.

(9) The President or any member ceasing to hold office as such shall not hold any appointment in or be connected with the management or administration of an organisation which have been the subject of any proceeding under the Act during his tenure for a period of five years from the date on which he ceases to hold such office.

(10) *(a)* For the purpose of the inquiry under the proviso to sub-rule (5), the State Government shall draw up, or cause to be drawn up,—

(i) the substance of imputations of misconduct or misbehaviour into defi-nite and distinct articles of charge;

(ii) a statement of misconduct or misbehaviour in support of each article of charge which shall contain—

(a) a statement of relevant facts including any admission or confession by the President or the member, as the case may be, of the District Forum;

(b) a list of documents by which, and a list of witnesses by whom, the articles of charge are proposed to be sustained.

(b) The State Government shall deliver, or cause to be delivered, to the President or the member as the case may be, of the District Forum a copy of the articles of charge and the statement of imputations of misconduct or misbehaviour prepared under clause *(a)*.

(c) The State Government shall, in all cases for the purpose of inquiry, appoint an inquiring authority and forward to it—

(i) a copy of the articles of charge and the statement of imputations of misconduct or misbehaviour;

(ii) a copy of statement of witnesses, if any;

(iii) evidence proving the delivery of the documents referred to in clause (a) to the President or the member, as the case may be, of the District Forum.

(*d*) The inquiring authority shall issue a notice to the President or the member, as the case may be, of the District Forum, to submit, within ten working days from the date of receipt of the notice, a written statement of his defence together with the following—

(*i*) a list of witnesses to be examined on his behalf;

(*ii*) a notice asking for the discovery or production of any documents which are in possession of the State Government but not mentioned in clause (a). The inquiring authority shall also inform the President or the member through the aforesaid notice that, for the purpose of preparing his defence, he may, within five working days from the date of receipt by him of the notice, inspect he documents specified in the list referred to in clause *(a),*

(*e*) The inquiring authority shall, on receipt of the notice. for discovery or production of documents, forward the same or copies thereof to the authority in whose custody or possession the documents are kept, with a requisition for |he production of the documents by such date as may be specified in such requisition:

Provided that the inquiring authority may, for reasons to be recorded by it in 'riling, refuse to requisition such of the documents as are, in its opinion, not relevant to the case.

(*f*) On receipt of the requisition referred to in clause (e), every authority having the custody or possession of the requisitioned documents shall produce the lame before the inquiring authority:

Provided that if the authority having the custody or possession of the requisitioned documents is satisfied for reasons to be recorded by it in writing that the production of all or any of such documents would be against the public interest or security of the State, it shall inform the inquiring authority accordingly and he inquiring authority shall, on being so informed, communicate the information to the President or the member and withdraw the requisition made by it or the production or discovery of such documents.

(*g*) The President or the member, as the case may be, of the District Forum shall appear in person before the inquiring authority on such day and at such time Within fourteen working days from the date of receipt of notice as referred to in clause *(d), as* the inquiring authority may specify in this behalf, to defend the charges brought against him.

(*h*) The inquiring authority shall issue a notice requiring the State Government or its representative to appear before it on such date and at such time as are specified in clause *(g),* to present its case.

(*i*) The President or the member, as the case may be, of the District Forum and the State Government or its representative shall appear before the inquiring authority on the date of hearing or any other date on which the hearing may be adjourned.

(*j*) If the President or the member, as the case may be, of the District Forum, without prior leave of the inquiring authority, fails to appear on the specified date and time, the inquiring authority may require the State, Government or his representative to present his case and conduct the inquiry *ex parte.*

(*k*) If prior leave of the inquiring authority has been taken, the case shall be adjourned to a later date. The inquiring authority shall not ordinarily allow more than one adjournment.

(*l*) If the President or the member, as the case may be, of the District Forum, who has not admitted any of the articles of charge in his written statement of defence, the authority shall ask him whether he is guilty or has any defence to make and if he pleads guilty to any of the articles of charge, the inquiring authority shall record the plea, sign the record and obtain the signature of the President or the member, as the case may be, of the District Forurn thereon. The inquiring authority shall return a finding of guilt in respect of those articles of charge to which the President or the member, as the case may be, of the District I Forum pleads guilty.

(*m*) If the President, or the member, as the case may be, of the District Forum I refuses or omits to plead guilty, or claims to be tried, the inquiring authority shall, after giving both the parties reasonable opportunities of being heard, conduct the inquiry.

(*n*) After completion of the inquiry, a report shall be prepared which shall be forwarded to the State Government. The report shall contain—

(*i*) the articles of charge and the statement of imputation of misconduct or misbehaviour;

(*ii*) the defence of the President or the member, as the case may be, of the District Forum in respect of each article of charge;

(*iii*) an assessment of the evidence in respect of each article of charge; and *(iv)* the finding on each article or charge and the reasons therefor.

Procedure to be Adopted by the District Forum for Analysis and Testing of the Goods [Section 13(l)(c)]

4. (1) Where a complaint alleges that a defect in the goods which cannot be determined without proper analysis or test of the goods, the District Forum may direct the complainant to provide more than one sample of the goods clean containers with stopper properly fixed on them.

(2) On receiving the samples of such goods, the District Forum shall seal it and fix labels on the containers carrying following information—

(i) name and address of the appropriate laboratory to whom sample will be sent for analysis and test;

(ii) name and address of District Forum;

(iii) case number; and

(iv) seal of the District Forurn.

(3) The sample shall be sent to the appropriate laboratory by the District Forum for sending report within 45 days or within such extended time as may be granted by the District Forum keeping in view the provision of sub-rule (9) of rule 4 after specifying the nature of the defect alleged and date of submission of the report.

Procedure Relating to the Conduct of the Meetings of the District Forum, its Sittings and Other Matters [Section 14(3)]

5. (1) The office of the District Forum shall be located at the headquarters of the District. Where the State Government decides to establish a single District Forum having jurisdiction over more than one District, it shall notify the place and jurisdiction of the District Forum so established.

(2) The working days and the office hours of the District Forum shall be the same as that of the State Government.

(3) The official seal and emblem of the District Forum shall be such as the State Government may specify.

(4) The sitting of the District Forurn, as and when necessary, shall be convened by the President.

(5) No act or proceedings of the District Forum shall be invalid by reason only of the existence of any vacancy amongst its members or any defect in its constitution.

(6) The State Government shall appoint such staff, as may be necessary to assist the District Forum in its day to day work and to perform such other functions as are provided under these rules or assigned to it by the President.

(7) Where the opposite party admits the allegation made by the complainant, the District Forum shall decide the complaint on the basis of the merit of the case and documents placed before it.

(8) If during the proceedings conducted under section 13, the District Forum fixes a date for hearing of the parties, it shall be obligatory on the complainant and the opposite party or their authorised agents to appear before the District Forum on such date of hearing or any other date to which hearing could be adjourned. Where the complainant or his authorised agent fails to appear before the District Forum on such day, the District Forum may in its discretion either dismiss the complaint for default or decide it on merit. Where the opposite party or their authorised agents fails to appear on the day of hearing, the District Forum may decide the complaint *ex. parte.*

(9) While proceeding under sub-rule (8), the District Forum may, on such terms as it may think fit and at any stage, adjourn the hearing of the complaint but not more than one adjournment shall ordinarily be given and the complaint should be decided within ninety days from the date of notice received by the opposite party where complaint does not require analysis or testing of the goods and within one hundred and fifty days if it requires analysis or testing of the goods.

(10) Orders of the District Forum shall be signed and dated by the members of the District Forum and shall be communicated to the parties free of charge.

Salary, Honorarium and Other Allowances Payable to, and the Other Terms and Conditions of Service of the President and Members of the State Commission [Section 16(2)]

6. (1) The President of the State Commission shall receive the salary admis-sible to Judge of the High Court if appointed on whole time basis or a consolidated honorarium of ₹ 200 per day for the sitting if appointed on part-time basis. Other members, if sitting on whole time basis, shall receive a consolidated honorarium of ₹ 3,000 per month and if sitting on part-time basis, a consolidated honorarium of ₹ 150 per day for the sitting.

(2) The President and the members of the State Commission shall be entitled to such travelling allowance and daily allowance on official tour as are admissible to a '[Grade A] Officer of the State Government.

(3) The salary, honorarium and other allowances shall be defrayed out of the Consolidated Fund of the State Government.

(4) The President and the members of the State Commission shall hold office for a term of five years or up to the age of 2[67] years whichever is earlier and. shall not be eligible for reappointment 23:

Provided that the President and any member may—

(a) by writing under his hand and addressed to the State Government resign" his office any time; and

(b) be removed from his office in accordance with provisions of sub-rule (5).

(5) The State Government may remove from office of the President or a member of the State Commission who,—

(a) has been adjudged as insolvent, or

(b) has been convicted of an offence which, in the opinion of the State Government, involves moral turpitude, or

(c) has become physically or mentally incapable of acting as such member, or

(ca) has remained absent in three consecutive sittings of the State Commission without obtaining previous permission of the State Government, except for reasons beyond his control, or]

(d) has acquired such financial or other interest as is likely to affect prejudicially his functions as a member, or

(e) has so abused his position as to render his continuance in office prejudicially to the public interest:

(5) Provided that the President or any other member shall not be removed from his office on the ground specified in clauses (d) and (e) except on an inquiry held by the State Government in accordance with the procedure laid down in sub-rule (12).

(5A) The terms and conditions of service of the President and the members of the State Commission, which have not been specified in these rules, shall be such as are applicable to Group 'A' officers of the State Government under the West Bengal Service Rules, Part I and Part II.

(6) Before appointment, the President and members of the State Commission shall have to give an undertaking that he does not and will not have any such financial or other interests as is likely to affect prejudicially his functions as a member of the State Commission.

(7) The terms and conditions of service of the President and the members of the State Commission shall not be varied to their disadvantages during their tenure of office.

(8) Every vacancy caused by resignation or removal of the President or any other member of the State Commission under sub-rule (4) or otherwise shall be filled by fresh appointment.

(9) Where any such vacancy occurs in the office of the President of the State Commission the seniormost (in order of appointment) member, holding office for the time being, shall discharge the functions of the President until a person appointed to fill such vacancy assumes the office of the President of the State Commission.

(10) When the President of the State Commission is unable to discharge his functions owing to absence, illness or any other cause, the senior most (in order of appointment) member of the State Commission shall discharge the functions of the President until the day on which the President resumes the charge of his functions.

(11) The President or any member ceasing to hold office as such shall not hold any appointment in or be connected with the management or administration of an organisation which have been the subject of any proceeding under the Act during his tenure for a period of five years from the date on which he ceases to hold office.

(12) (a) For the purpose of the inquiry under the proviso to sub-rule (5), the State Government shall draw up or cause to be drawn up—

(i) the substance of imputation of misconduct or misbehaviour into definite and distinct articles of charge;

(ii) a statement of misconduct or misbehaviour in support of each article of charge containing—

(A) a statement of relevant facts including any admission or confession by the President or the member, as the case may be, of the State Forum,

(B) a list of documents by which and a list of witnesses by whom, the articles of charge are proposed to be sustained.

(b) The State Government shall deliver, or cause to be delivered, to the President or to the member as the case may be, of the State Forum a copy of the articles of charge and the statement of imputations of misconduct or misbehaviour prepared under clause (a).

(c) The State Government shall in all cases for the purpose of inquiry appoint an inquiring authority and forward to it—

(i) a copy of the articles of charge and the statement of imputations of misconduct or misbehaviour;

(ii) a copy of statement of witnesses if any;

(iii) evidence proving the delivery of the documents referred to in clause (a) to the President or the member, as the case may be, of the State Forum.

(d) The inquiring authority shall issue a notice to the President or the member, as the case may be, of the State Forum, to submit, within ten working days from the date of receipt of the notice, a written statement of his defence together with the following:

(i) a list of witnesses to be examined on his behalf;

(ii) a notice asking for the discovery or production of any documents which are in possession of the State Government but not mentioned in clause (a). The inquiring authority shall also inform the President or the member through the aforesaid notice that, for the purpose of preparing his defence, he may, within five working days from the date or receipt by him of the notice, inspect the documents specified in the list referred to in clause (a).

(e) The inquiring authority shall, on receipt of the notice for discovery or production of documents forward the same or copies thereof to the authority in whose custody or possession the documents are kept, with a requisition for the production of the documents by such date as may be specified in such requisition:

Provided that the inquiring authority may, for reasons to be recorded by it in writing, refuse to requisition such of the documents as are, in its opinion, not relevant to the case.

(f) On receipt of the requisition referred to in clause (e) every authority having the custody or possession of the requisitioned documents shall produce the same before the inquiring authority:

Provided that if the authority having the custody or possession of the requisitioned documents is satisfied for reasons to be recorded by it in writing that the production of all or any of such documents would be against the public interest or security of the State, it shall inform the inquiring authority accordingly and the inquiring authority shall, on being so informed, communicate the information to the President or the member and withdraw the requisition made by it for the production or discovery of such documents.

(g) The President or the member as the case may be, of the State Forum snail appear in person before the inquiring authority on such day and at such time within fourteen working days from the date of receipt of notice as referred to in clause (d), as the inquiring authority may specify in this behalf, to defend the charges brought against him.

(h) The inquiring authority shall issue notice requiring the State Government or his representative to appear before it on such date and at such time as specified in clause (g), to present their case.

(i) The President or the member, as the case may be, of the State Forum and the State Government or its representative shall appear before the inquiring authority on such date of hearing or any other date to which the hearing may be adjourned.

(j) If the President or the member, as the case may be, of the State Forum, without prior leave of the inquiring authority, fails to appear on the specified date and time, the inquiring authority shall require the State Government or his representative to present his case and conduct the inquiry exparte.

(k) If prior leave of the inquiring authority has been taken, the case shall be adjourned to a later date. The inquiring authority shall, however, not ordinarily allow more than one adjournment.

(l) If the President or the member, as the case may be, of the State Forum, who has not admitted any of the articles of charge in his written statement of defence, the authority shall ask him whether he is guilty or has any defence to make and if he pleads guilty to any of the articles of charge, the inquiring authority shall record the plea, sign the record and obtain the signature of the President or the member, as the case may be, of the State Forum thereon. The inquiring authority shall return a finding of guilt in respect of those articles of charge to which the President or the member, as the case may be, of the State Forum pleads guilty.

(m) If the President or the member, as the case may be, of the State Forum refuses or omits to plead guilty, or claims to be tried, the inquiring authority shall, after giving both the parties reasonable opportunities of being heard, conduct the inquiry.

(n) After completion of the inquiry, a report shall be prepared which shall be forwarded to the State Government. The report shall contain—

(i) the articles of charge and the statement of imputation of misconduct or misbehaviour;

(ii) the defence of the President or the member, as the case may be, of the State Forum in respect of each article of charge;

(iii) an assessment of the evidence in respect of each article of charge; and

(iv) the finding on each article of charge and the reasons therefore.

Place of Sitting and Other Matters Relating to State Commission [Section 14(3) Read with Section 18]

7. (1) Office of the State Commission shall be located at the Capital of the State;

(2) The working days and the office hours of the State Commission shall be the same as that of the State Government.

(3) The official seal and emblem of the State Commission shall be such as the State Government may specify.

(4) Sitting of the Slate Commission, as and when necessary, shall be convened by the President.

(5) No act or proceedings of the State Commission shall be invalid by reasons only of the existence of any vacancy among its members or any defect in its constitution thereof.

(6) The State Government shall appoint such staff, as may be necessary to assist the State Commission in its works and perform such other functions as are provided under these rules or assigned to it by the President.

(7) Where the opposite party admits the allegation made by the complainant, the State Commission shall decide the complaint on the basis of the merit of the case and documents placed before it.

(8) If during the proceedings conducted under section 13, the State Commis-sion fixes a date for hearing of the parties, it shall be obligatory on the complainant and opposite party or their authorised agents to appear before the State Commission on such date of hearing or any other date to which hearing could be adjourned. Where the complainant or his authorised agent fails to appear before the State Commission on such day, the State Commission may in its discretion either dismiss the complaint for default or decide it on merits. Where the opposite party or its authorised agent fails to appear on the day of hearing, the State Commission may decide the complaint *ex parte.*

(9) While proceeding under sub-rule (8), the State Commission may, on such terms as it may think fit and at any state, adjourn the hearing of the complaint but not more than one adjournment shall ordinarily be given and the complaint should be decided within ninety days from the date of notice received by the opposite party where complaint does not require analysis or testing of the goods and within one hundred and fifty days if it requires analysis or testing of the goods.

(10) Orders of the State Commission shall be signed and dated by the members, of the State Commission and shall be communicated to the parties free of charge.

Form and Manner of Appeal Under Section 15

8. (1) Every appeal under section 15 shall be filed in the form of a memorandum in legible handwriting, preferably typed, setting forth concisely under distinct heads, the grounds of appeal without any argument or narrative numbering such grounds consecutively.

(2) The memorandum of appeal shall be presented by the applicant or his authorised agent to the State Commission in person or be sent by registered post addressed to the State Commission.

(3) Each memorandum shall be accompanied by the certified copy of the order of the District Forum appealed against and such of the documents as may be required to support grounds of objection mentioned in the memorandum.

(4) When the appeal is presented after the expiry of period of limitation as specified in the Act, the memorandum shall be accompanied by an application supported by an affidavit setting forth the fact on which appellant relies to satisfy the State Commission that he has sufficient cause for not preferring the appeal within the period of limitation.

(5) The appellant shall submit four copies of the memorandum to the State Commission for official purposes.

(6) On the date of the hearing or any other day to which hearing may be adjourned, it shall be obligatory for the parties or their authorised agents to appear before the State Commission. If the appellant or his authorised agent fails to appear on such date, the State Commission may, in its discretion, either dismiss the appeal or decide it on the merit of the case. If respondent or his authorised agent fails to appear on such date, the State Commission shall decide the appeal *exparte* on merits of the case.

(7) The appellant shall not, except by leave of the State Commission, urge or be heard in support of any ground or objections not set forth in the memorandum but the State Commission, in deciding the appeal, shall not confine to the grounds of objection set forth in the memorandum or taken by leave of the State Commission under this rule:

Provided that the Commission shall not rest its decision on any other grounds unless the party, who may be affected thereby, has been given at least one opportunity of being heard by the State Commission.

(8) The State Commission may, on such terms as it may think fit and at any stage, adjourn the hearing of appeal, but not more than one adjournment shall ordinarily be given and the appeal should be decided within ninety days from the first date of hearing.

(9) Order of the State Commission on appeal shall be signed and dated by the Members of the State Commission (constituting the Bench) and shall be communicated to the parties free of charge.

✦ — ✦ — ✦

Chapter 35

Extract of Monopolies and Restrictive Trade Practices Act, 1969

[54 of 1969]

An Act to provide that the operation of the economic system does not result in the concentration of economic power to the common detriment, for the control of monopolies, for the prohibition of monopolistic and restrictive trade practices and for matters connected therewith or incidental thereto. Be it enacted by Parliament in the Twentieth Year of the Republic of India as follows —

SHORT TITLE, EXTENT AND COMMENCEMENT

PRELIMINARY

1. (1) This Act may be called the Monopolies and Restrictive Trade Practices Act, 1969.

(2) It extends to the whole of India except the State of Jarnmu and Kashmir.

(3) It shall come into force on such date as the Central Government may, '[by notification], appoint.

Definitions

2. In this Act, unless the context otherwise requires,—

(a) "agreement" includes any arrangement or understanding, whether or not it is intended that such agreement shall be enforceable (apart from any provision of this Act) by legal proceedings;

(b) "goods" means goods as defined in the Sale of Goods Act, 1930 (3 of 1930). and includes,—

(*i*) products manufactured, processed or mined in India;

(*ii*) shares and stocks including issue of shares before allotment;

(*iii*) in relation to goods supplied, distributed or controlled in India, goods imported into India;]

(c) "monopolistic trade practice" means a trade practice which has, or is likely to have, the effect of,—

(i) [maintaining the prices of goods or charges for the services] at an unreasonable level by limiting, reducing or otherwise, controlling the production, supply or distribution of goods or the supply of any services or in any other manner;

(*ii*) unreasonably preventing or lessening competition in the production, supply or distribution of any goods or in the supply of any services;

(*iii*) limiting technical development or capital investment to the common detriment or allowing the quality of any goods produced, supplied or distributed, or any service rendered, in India to deteriorate;

(*iv*) increasing unreasonably,—

(*a*) the cost of production of any goods; or

(*b*) charges for the provision, or maintenance, of any services;

(*v*) increasing unreasonably,—

(*a*) the prices at which goods are, or may be, sold or resold, or the charges at which the services are, or may be, **Provided**; or

(*b*) the profits which are, or may be, derived by the production, supply or distribution (including the sale or purchase) of any goods or by the provision of any services;

(*vi*) preventing or lessening competition in the production, supply or distribution of any goods or in the provision or maintenance of any services by the adoption of unfair methods or unfair or deceptive practices;

(d) "price", in relation to the sale of any goods or to the performance of any services, includes every valuable consideration, whether direct or indirect, and includes any consideration which in effect relates to the sale of any goods or to the performance of any services although ostensibly relating to any other matter or thing;

(e) "registered consumers' association" means a voluntary association of persons registered under the Companies Act, 1956 (1 of 1956), or any other law for the time being in force which is formed for the purpose of protecting the interest of consumers generally and is recognised by the Central Government as such association on an application made in this behalf in such form and such manner as may be prescribed;

(f) "restrictive trade practice" means a trade practice which has, or may have, the effect of preventing, distorting or restricting competition in any manner and in particular, which tends to obstruct the flow of capital or resources into the 'stream of production, or which tends to bring about manipulation of prices, or conditions of delivery or to affect the flow of supplies in the market relating to goods or services in such manner as to impose on the consumers unjustified costs or restrictions;

(g) "retailer", in relation to the sale of any goods, includes every person, other than a wholesaler, who sells the goods to any other person; and in respect of the sale of goods by a wholesaler, to any person for any purpose other than re-sale, includes that wholesaler;

(h) "service" means service '[***] which is made available to potential users and includes the provision of facilities in connection with [2][banking, financing, insurance, [3][chit fund, real estate,] transport, processing], supply of electrical or other energy, boarding or lodging or both, enter tainment, amusement or the purveying of news or other information, but does not include the rendering of any service free of charge or under a contract of personal service.

Explanation — For the removal of doubts, it is hereby declared that any dealings in real estate shall be included and shall be deemed always to have been included within the definition of "service";]

(i) "trade" means any trade, business, industry, profession or occupation relating to the production, supply, distribution or control of goods and includes the provision of any services;

(j) "trade practice" means any practice relating to the carrying on of any trade, and includes —

(k) anything done by any person which controls or affects the price charged by, or the method of trading of, any trader or any class of traders,

(l) a single or isolated action of any person in relation to any trade;

(m) "wholesaler", in relation to the sale of any goods, means a person who [4][sells the goods, either in bulk or in large quantities, to any person for the purposes of re-sale, whether in bulk or in the same or smaller quantities;]

Powers of the Commission

3. (1) The Commission shall, for the purposes of any inquiry under this Act, have the same powers as are vested in a civil court under the Code of Civil Procedure, 1908 (5 of 1908), while trying a suit, in respect of the following pattrns, namely—

(*a*) the summoning and enforcing the attendance of any witness and: examining him on oath;

(*b*) the discovery and production of any document or other material object producible as evidence;

(*c*) the reception of evidence on affidavits;

(*d*) the requisitioning of any public record from any court or office;

(*e*) the issuing of any commission for the examination of witnesses;

(*f*) the appearance of parties and consequence of non-appearance.

(2) Any proceeding before the Commission shall be deemed to be a judicial proceeding within the meaning of sections 193 and 228 of the Indian Penal Code (45 of 1860), and the Commission shall be deemed to be a civil court for the purposes of section 195 [and Chapter XXVI of the Code of Criminal Procedure, 1973 (2 of 1974)].

(3) The Commission shall have power to require any person—

(*a*) to produce before, and allow to be examined and kept by, an officer of the Commission specified in this behalf, such books, accounts or other documents in the custody or under the control of the person so required as may be specified or described in the requisition, being documents relating to any trade practice, the examination of which may be required for the purposes of this Act; and

(*b*) to furnish to an officer so specified such information as respect the trade practice as may be required for the purposes of this Act or such other information as may be in his possession in relation to the trade carried on by any other person.

(4) For the purpose of enforcing the attendance of witnesses the local limits of the Commission's jurisdiction shall be the limits of the territory of India.

(5) Where, during any inquiry under this Act, the Commission has any grounds to believe that any books or papers of, or relating to any undertaking in relation to which such inquiry is being made or which the owner of such undertaking may be required to produce in such inquiry, are being, or may be, destroyed, mutilated, altered, falsified or secreted, it may, by a written order, authorise any officer of the Commission to exercise the same powers of entry, search and seizure in relation to the undertaking, or the books or papers, aforesaid as may be exercised by the Director General while holding a preliminary investigation under section 11.

Power of the Commission to Grant Temporary Injunctions

3A. (1) Where, during an inquiry before the Commission, it is proved, whether by the complainant, Director General, any trader or class of traders or any other person, by affidavit or otherwise, that any undertaking or any person is carrying on, or is about to carry on, any monopolistic or any restrictive, or unfair, trade practice and such monopolistic or restrictive, or unfair, trade practice is likely to affect prejudicially the public interest or the interest of any trader, class of traders or traders generally or of any consumer or consumers generally, the Commission may, for the purposes of staying or preventing the undertaking or, as the case may be, such person from causing such prejudicial effect, by order grant a temporary injunction restraining such undertaking or person from carrying on any monopolistic or restrictive, or unfair, trade practice until the conclusion of such inquiry or until further orders.

(2) The provisions of rules 2A to 5 (both inclusive) XXXIX of the First Schedule to the Code of Civil Procedure, 1908 (5 of K 3), shall, as far as may be, apply to a temporary injunction issued by the Commission under this section, as they apply to a temporary injunction issued by a civil court, and any reference in any such rule to a suit shall be construed as a reference to an inquiry before the Commission.

Explanation — For the purposes of this section, an inquiry shall be deemed to have commenced upon the receipt by the Commission of any complaint, reference or, as the case may be, application or upon its own knowledge or information reduced to writing by the Commission.

Explanation II — For the removal of doubts it is hereby declared that the power of the Commission with respect to temporary injunction includes power to grant a temporary injunction without giving notice to the opposite party.

Power of the Commission to Award Compensation

3B. (1) Where, as a result of the monopolistic or restrictive, or unfair, trade practice, carried on by a undertaking or any person, any loss or damage is caused to the Central Government, or any State Government or any trader or class of traders or any consumer, such Government or, as the case may be, trader or class of traders or consumer may, without prejudice to the right of such Government, trader or class of traders or consumer to institute a suit for the recovery of any compensation for the loss or damage so caused, make an application to the Commission for an order for the recovery from that undertaking or owner thereof or, as the case may be, from such person, of such amount as the Commission may determine, as compensation for the loss or damage so caused.

(2) Where any loss or damage referred to in sub-section (1) is caused to numerous persons having the same interest, one or more of such persons may, with the permission of the Commission, make an application, under that sub-section, for and on behalf of, or for the benefit of, the persons so interested, and thereupon the provisions of rule 8 of Order I of the First Schedule to the Code of Civil Procedure, 1908 (5 of 1908), shall apply subject to the modification that every reference therein to a suit or decree shall be construed as a reference to the application before the Commission and the order of the Commission thereon.

(3) The Commission may, after an inquiry made into the allegation, made in the application filed under sub-section (1), make an order directing the owner of the undertaking or other person to make payment, to the applicant, of the amount determined by it as realisable from the undertaking or the owner thereof, or, as the case may be, from the other person, as compensation for the loss or damage caused to the applicant by reason of any monopolistic or restrictive, or unfair, trade practice carried on by such undertaking or other person.

(4) Where a decree for the recovery of any amount as compensation for any loss or damage referred to in sub-section (1) has been passed by any court in favour of any person or persons referred to in sub-section (1) or, as the case may be, sub-section (2), the amount, if any, paid or recovered in pursuance of the order made by the Commission under sub-section (3) shall be set off against the amount payable under such decree and the decree shall, notwithstanding anything contained in the Code of Civil Procedure, 1908 (5 of 1908), or any other law for the time being in force, be executable for the balance, if any, left after such set off.

Enforcement of the Order Made by the Commission Under Section 3A or 3B

3C. Every order made by the Commission under section 12A granting a temporary injunction or under section 12B directing the owner of an undertaking or other person to make payment of any amount, may be enforced by the Commission in the same manner as if it were a decree or order made by a court in a suit pending therein and it shall be lawful for the Commission to send, in the event of its inability to execute it, such order to the court within the local limits of whose jurisdiction,—

(a) in the case of an order against a company, the registered office of the company is situated, or

(b) in the case of an order against any other person, the place where the person concerned voluntarily resides or carries on business or personally works for gain, is situated, and thereupon the court to which the order is so sent shall execute the order as if it were a decree or order sent to it for execution.

Orders of Commission may be Subject to Conditions, etc.

4. (1) In making any order under this Act, the Commission may make such provisions not inconsistent with this Act, as it may think necessary or Desirable for the proper execution of the order and any person who commits breach of or fails to comply with any obligation imposed on him by any such Provision shall be deemed to be guilty of an offence under this Act. Any order made by the Commission may be amended or revoked at any me in the manner in which it was made.

(2) An order made by the Commission may be general in its application or may limited to any particular class of traders or a particular class of trade Practice or a particular trade practice or a particular locality.

Power of the Commission to Cause Investigation to Find Out Whether or not Orders made by it have been Complied with

4A. (1) The Commission may, if it has any reasonable cause to believe that any person has omitted or failed to comply with any order made by it under this Act or any obligation imposed on him by or under any order made by the Commission under this Act, authorise the Director General or any officer of the Commission to make an investigation into the matter and the Director General, or the officer so authorised, may, for the purpose of making such investigation, exercise all or any of the powers conferred on the Director General by section 11.

(2) On the conclusion of the investigation, the Director General or, as the case may be, the officer so authorised, shall submit to the Commission a report of the investigation to enable the Commission to take such action in the matter as it may think fit.

Power to Punish for Contempt

4 B. The Commission shall have, and exercise, the same jurisdiction, powers and authority in respect of contempt of itself as a High Court has and may exercise and, for this purpose, the provisions of the Contempt of Courts Act, 1971 (70 of 1971) shall have effect subject to the modifications that—

(a) the reference therein to a High Court shall be construed as including a reference to the Commission;

(b) the references to the Advocate-General in section 15 of the said Act shall be construed as a reference to such Law Officer as the Central Government may, by notification[3] in the Official Gazette, specify in this behalf.

RESTRICTIVE TRADE PRACTICES AND UNFAIR TRADE PRACTICES

Registration of Agreements Relating to Restrictive Trade Practices

Registrable Agreements Relating to Restrictive Trade Practices

5. (1) Every agreement falling within one or more of the following categories shall be deemed, for the purposes of this Act, to be an agreement relating to restrictive trade practices and shall be subject to registration in accordance with the provisions of this Chapter, namely —

(*a*) any agreement which restricts, or is likely to restrict, by any method the persons or classes of persons to whom goods are sold or from whom goods are bought;

(*b*) any agreement requiring a purchaser of goods, as a condition of such purchase, to purchase some other goods;

(*c*) any agreement restricting in any manner the purchaser in the course of his trade from acquiring or otherwise dealing in any goods other than those of the seller or any other person;

(*d*) any agreement to purchase or sell goods or to tender for the sale or purchase of goods only at prices or on terms or conditions agreed upon between the sellers or purchasers;

(*e*) any agreement to grant or allow concessions or benefits, including alloavances, discounts, rebates or credit in connection with, or by reason of, dealings;

(*f*) any agreement to sell goods on condition that the prices to be charged on re-sale by the purchaser shall be the prices stipulated by the seller unless it is clearly stated that prices lower than those prices may be charged;

(*g*) any agreement to limit, restrict or withhold the output or supply of any goods or allocate any area or market for the disposal of the goods;

(*h*) any agreement not to employ or restrict the employment of any method, machinery or process in the manufacture of goods;

(*i*) any agreement for the exclusion from any trade association of any person carrying on or intending to carry on, in good faith the trade in relation to which the trade association is formed;

(*j*) any agreement to sell goods at such prices as would have the effect of eliminating competition or a competitor;

(*k*) any agreement restricting in any manner, the class or number of whole-salers, producers or suppliers from whom any goods may be bought;

(*l*) any agreement as to the bids which any of the parties thereto may offer at an auction for the sale of goods or any agreement whereby any party thereto agrees to abstain from bidding at any auction for the sale of goods;

(*m*) any agreement not hereinbefore referred to in this section which the Central Government may, [2][by notification] specify for the time being as being one relating to a restrictive trade practice within the meaning of this sub-section pursuant to any recommendation made by the Commission in this behalf;

(*n*) any agreement to enforce the carrying out of any such agreement as is referred to in this sub-section.

(2) The provisions of this section shall apply, so far as may be, in relation to agreements making provision for services as they apply in relation to agreements connected with the '[production, storage, supply,] distribution or control of goods.

(3) No agreement falling within this section shall be subject to registration in accordance with the provisions of this Chapter if it is expressly authorised by or under any law for the time being in force or has the approval of the Central Government or if the Government is a party to such agreement.

Registration of Agreements

6. (1) The Central Government shall, [2][by notification], specify a day, here-inafter referred to as the appointed day] on and from which every agreement falling within section 33 shall become registrable under this Act;

Provided that different days may be appointed for different categories of agreements.

(2) Within sixty days from the appointed day, in the case of an agreement existing on that day, and in the case of an agreement made after the appointed day, within sixty days from the making thereof, there shall be furnished to the [Director General] in respect of every agreement falling within section 33, the following particulars, namely—

(*a*) the names of the persons who are parties to the agreement; and

(*b*) the whole of the terms of the agreement.

(3) If at any time after the agreement has been registered under this section, the agreement is varied (whether in respect of the parties or in respect of the terms thereof) or determined otherwise than by efflux of time, particulars of the variation or determination shall be furnished to the [Director General] within one month after the date of the variation or determination.

(4) The particulars to be furnished under this section in respect of an agreement shall be furnished—

(*a*) in so far as the agreement or any variation or determination of the agreement is made by an instrument in writing, by the production of the original or a true copy of that agreement; and (*b*) in so far as the agreement or any variation or determination of the agreement is not so made, by the production of a memorandum in writing signed by the person by whom the particulars are furnished.

(5) The particulars to be furnished under this section shall be furnished by or on behalf of any person who is a party to the agreement or, as the case may be, was a party thereto immediately before its determination, and where the particulars are duly furnished by or on behalf of any such person, the provisions of this section shall be deemed to be complied with on the part of all such persons.

Explanation I — Where any agreement subject to registration under this section relates to the '[production, storage, supply,] distribution or control of goods or the performance of any services in India and any party to the agreement carries on business in India, the agreement shall be deemed to be an agreement within the meaning of this section, notwithstanding that any other party to the agreement does not carry on business in India.

Explanation II — Where an agreement is made by a trade association, the agreement for the purposes of this section shall be deemed to be made by all persons who are members of the association or represented thereon as if each such person were a party to the agreement.

Explanation III — Where specific recommendations, whether expressed or implied, are made by or on behalf of a trade association to its members, or to any class of its members, as to the action to betaken or not to be taken by them in relation to any matter affecting the trade conditions of those members, this section shall apply in relation to the agreement for the constitution of the association notwithstanding any provision to the contrary therein as if it contained a term by which each such member and any person represented on the association by any such member agreed with the association to comply with those recommendations and any subsequent recommendations affecting those recommendations.

Unfair Trade Practices

Definition of Unfair Trade Practice

7A. In this Part, unless the context otherwise requires, "unfair trade practice" means a trade practice which, for the purpose of promoting the sale, use or supply of any goods or for the provision of any services, [adopts any unfair method or unfair or deceptive practice including any of the following practices,] namely —

(1) the practice of making any statement, whether orally or in writing or by visible representation which,—

(*i*) falsely represents that the goods are of a particular standard, quality, [quantity,] grade, composition style or model;

(*ii*) falsely represents that the services are of a particular standard, quality or grade;

(*iii*) falsely represents any re-built, second-hand, renovated, reconditioned or old goods as new goods;

(*iv*) represents that the goods or services have sponsorship, approval performance, characteristics, accessories, uses or benefits which such goods, or services do not have;

(*v*) represents that the seller or the supplier has a sponsorship or approval or affiliation which such seller or supplier does not have'

(*vi*) makes a false or misleading representation concerning the need for or the usefulness of, any goods or services;

(*vii*) gives to the public any warranty or guarantee of the performance efficacy or length of life of a product or of any goods that is not based on an adequate or proper test thereof:

Provided that where a defence is raised to the effect that such warranty or guarantee is based on adequate or proper test, the burden of proof of such defence shall lie on the person raising such defence;

(*viii*) makes to the public a representation in a form that purports to be a warranty or guarantee of a product or of any goods or services; or

(*ix*) a promise to replace, maintain or repair an article or any part thereof or to repeat or continue a service until it has achieve a specified result, it such purported warranty or guarantee or promise is materially mislead-ing or if there is no reasonable prospect that such warranty, guarantee or promise will be carried out;

(*x*) materially misleads the public concerning the price at which a product or like products or goods or services, have been, or are, ordinarily sold or **Provided**, and, for this purpose, a representation as to price shall be deemed to refer to the price at which the product or goods or services has or have been sold by sellers or **Provided** by suppliers generally in the relevant market unless it is clearly specified to be the price at which the product has been sold or services have been **Provided** by the person by whom or on whose behalf the representation is made;

(*xi*) gives false or misleading facts disparaging the goods, services or trade or another person. *Explanation :* For the purposes of clause, a statement that is—

(*a*) expressed on an article offered or displayed for sale, or on it wrapper or container; or

(*b*) expressed on anything attached to, inserted in, or accompanying, an article offered or displayed for sale, or on anything on which article is mounted for display or sale; or

(*c*) contained in or on anything that is sold, sent, delivered, transmitte or in any other manner whatsoever made available to a member of the public, shall be deemed to be a statement made to the public by, and only by, the person who had caused the statement to be so expressed, made or contained;

(2) permits the publication of any advertisement whether in any newspaper or otherwise, for the sale or supply at a bargain price, of goods or services that are not intended to be offered for sale or supply at the bargain price, or for a period that is, and in quantities that are, reasonable, having regard to the nature of the market in which the business is carried on, the nature and size of business, and the nature of the advertisement.

Explanation — For the purpose of clause (2), "bargain price" means—

(*a*) a price that is stated in any advertisement to be a bargain price, by reference to an ordinary price or otherwise, or

(*b*) a price that a person who reads, hears, or sees the advertisement, would reasonably understand to be a bargain price having regard to the prices at which the product advertised or like products are ordinarily sold;

(3) permits—

(*a*) the offering of gifts, prizes or other items with the intention of not providing them as offered or creating the impression that something is being given or offered free of charge when it is fully or partly covered by the amount charged in the transaction as a whole,

(*b*) the conduct of any contest, lottery, game of chance or skill, for the purpose of promoting, directly or indirectly, the sale, use of supply of any product or any business interest;

(4) permits the sale or supply of goods intended to be used, or are of a kind likely to be used, by consumers, knowing or having reason to believe that the goods do not comply with the standards prescribed by competent authority relating to performance, composition, contents, design, constructions, finishing or packaging as are necessary to prevent or reduce the risk of injury to the person using the goods;

(5) permits the hoarding or destruction of goods, or refuses to sell the goods or to make them available for sale, or to provide any service, if such hoarding or destruction or refusal raises or tends to raise or is intended to raise, the cost of those or other similar goods or services.

Inquiry into Unfair Trade Practices by Commission

7 B. The Commission may inquire into any unfair trade practice,—

(*a*) upon receiving a complaint of facts which constitutes such practice '[from any trade association or from any consumer or a registered consumers' association, whether such consumer is a member of that consumers' association or not]; or

(*b*) upon a reference made to it by the Central Government or a State Government; or

(*c*) upon an application made to it by the Director General; or

(*d*) upon its own knowledge or information.

Investigation by Director General Before an Issue of Process in Certain Cases

7C. The Commission may, before issuing any process requiring the attendance of the person against whom an inquiry (other than an inquiry upon an application by the Director General) may be made under section 36B, by an order, require the Director General to make, or cause to be made, a preliminary investigation in such manner as it may direct and submit a report to the Commission, for the purpose of satisfying itself that the matter requires to be inquired into.

Powers which may be Exercised by the Commission Inquiring into an Unfair Trade Practice

7D. (1) The Commission may inquire into any unfair trade practice which may come before it for inquiry and, if, after such inquiry, it is of opinion that the practice is prejudicial to the public interest, or to the interest of any consumer or consumers generally, it may, by order direct that—

(*a*) the practice shall be discontinued or shall not be repeated;

(*b*) any agreement relating to such unfair trade practice shall be void or shall stand modified in respect thereof in such manner as may be specified in the order;

(*c*) any information, statement or advertisement relating to such unfair trade practice shall be disclosed, issued or published, as the case may be, in such manner as may be specified in the order.

(2) The Commission may, instead of making any order under this section, permit any party to carry on any trade practice, if it so applies and takes such steps within the time specified by the Commission as may be necessary to ensure that the trade practice is no longer prejudicial to the public interest or to the interest of any consumer or consumers generally, and, in any such case, if the Commission is satisfied that necessary steps have been taken within the time so specified, it may decide not to make any order under this section in respect of that trade practice.

(3) No order shall be made under sub-section (1) in respect of any trade practice which is expressly authorised by any law for the time being in force.

Power Relating to Restrictive Trade Practices may be Exercised or Performed in Relation to Unfair Trade Practices

7E. Without prejudice to the provisions of section 12A, section 12B and section 36D, the Commission, Director General or any other person authorised in this behalf by the Commission or Director General, may exercise, or perform, in relation to any unfair trade practice, the same power or duty which it or he is empowered, or required, by or under this Act to exercise, or perform, in relation to a restricted trade practice.

CONTROL OF CERTAIN RESTRICTIVE TRADE PRACTICES

Investigation into Restrictive Trade Practices by Commission

8. (1) The Commission may inquire into any restrictive trade practice, whether the agreement, if any, relating thereto has been registered under section 35 or not, which may come before it for inquiry and, if, after such inquiry it is of opinion that the practice is prejudicial to the public interest the Commission may, by order, direct that—

(*a*) the practice shall be discontinued or shall not be repeated;

(*b*) the agreement relating thereto shall be void in respect of such restrictive trade practice or shall stand modified in respect thereof in such manner as may be specified in the order.

(2) The Commission may, instead of making any order under this section, permit the party to any restrictive trade practice, if he so applies, to take such steps within the time specified in this behalf by the Commission as may be necessary to ensure that the trade practice is no longer prejudicial to the public interest, and, in any such case, if the Commission is satisfied that the necessary steps have been taken within the time specified, it may decide not to make any order under this section in respect of that trade practice.

(3) No order shall be made under sub-section (1) in respect of—

(*a*) any agreement between buyers relating to goods which are bought by the buyers for consumption and not for ultimate resale whether in the same or different form, type or specie or as constituent of some other goods;

(*b*) a trade practice which is expressly authorised by any law for the time being in force.

(4) Notwithstanding anything contained in this Act, if the Commission, during the course of an inquiry under sub-section (1), finds that '[the owner of any undertaking is indulging in monopolistic trade practices], it may, after passing such orders under sub-section (1) or sub-section (2) with respect to the restrictive trade practices as it may consider necessary, submit the case along With its findings thereon to the Central Government["*] for such action as that government may take under section 31.

Presumption as to the Public Interest

9. (1) For the purposes of any proceedings before the Commission under section 37, a restrictive trade practice shall be deemed to be prejudicial to the public interest unless the Commission is satisfied of any one or more of the following circumstances, that is to say –

(*a*) that the restriction is reasonably necessary, having regard to the character of the goods to which it applies, to protect the public against injury (whether to persons or to premises) in connection with the consumption, installation or use of those goods;

(*b*) that the removal of the restriction would deny to the public as purchasers, consumers or users of any goods, other specific and substantial benefits or advantages enjoyed or likely to be enjoyed by them as such, whether by virtue of the restriction itself or of any arrangements or operations resulting therefrom;

(c) that the restriction is reasonably necessary to counteract measures taken by any one person not party to the agreement with a view to preventing or restricting competition in or in relation to the trade or business in which the persons party thereto are engaged;

(d) that the restriction is reasonably necessary to enable the persons party to the agreement to negotiate fair terms for the supply of goods to, or the acquisition of goods from, any one person not party thereto who controls a preponderant part of the trade or business of acquiring or supplying such goods, or for the supply of goods to any person not party to the agreement and not carrying on such a trade or business who, either alone or in combination with any other such persons, controls a preponderant part of the market for such goods;

(e) that, having regard to the conditions actually obtaining or reasonably foreseen at the time of the application, the removal of the restriction would be likely to have a serious and persistent adverse effect on the general level of unemployment in an area, or in areas taken together, in which a substantial proportion of the trade, or industry to which the agreement relates is situated;

(f) that, having regard to the conditions actually obtaining or reasonably foreseen at the time of the application, the removal of the restriction would be likely to cause a reduction in the volume or earnings of the export business which is substantial either in relation to the whole export business of India or in relation to the whole business (including export business) of the said trade or industry;

(g) that the restriction is reasonably required for purposes in connection with the maintenance of any other restriction accepted by the parties, whether under the same agreement or under any other agreement between them, being a restriction which is found by the Commission not to be contrary to the public interest upon grounds other than those specified in this paragraph or has been so found in previous proceedings before the Commission;

(h) that the restriction does not directly or indirectly restrict or discourage competition to any material degree in any relevant trade or industry and is not likely to do so;

(i) that such restriction has been expressly authorised and approved by the Central Government;

(j) that such restriction is necessary to meet the requirements of the defence of India or any part thereof, or for the security of the State; or

(k) that the restriction is necessary to ensure the maintenance of supply of goods and services essential to the community,] and is further satisfied (in any such case) that the restriction is not unreasonable having regard to the balance between those circumstances and any detriment to the public or to persons not parties to the agreement (being purchasers, consumers or users of goods produced or sold by such parties, or persons engaged or seeking to become engaged in the trade or business of selling such goods or of producing or selling similar goods) resulting or likely to result from the operation of the restriction.

(2) In this section, "purchasers", "consumers" and "users" include persons purchasing, consuming or using for the purpose or in the course of trade or business or for public purposes; and references in this section to any one person include references to any two or more persons being inter-connected undertakings or individuals carrying on business in partnership with each other.

Special Conditions for Avoidance of Conditions for Maintaining Resale Prices

10. (1) Without prejudice to the provisions of this Act with respect to registration and to any of the powers of the Commission or of the Central Government under this Act, any term or condition of a contract for the sale of goods by a person to a wholesaler or retailer or any agreement between a person and a wholesaler or retailer relating to such sale shall be void insofar as it purports to establish or provide for the establishment of minimum prices to be charged on the resale of goods in India.

(2) After the commencement of this Act, no supplier of goods whether directly or through any person or association of persons acting on his behalf shall notify to dealers or otherwise publish on or in relation to any goods, a price stated or calculated to be understood as the minimum price which may be charged on the resale of the goods in India.

(3) This section shall apply to patented articles (including articles made by a patented process and articles made under any trade mark) as it applies to other goods and notice of any term or condition which is void by virtue of this section or which would be so void if included in a contract of sale or agreement relating to the sale of such article shall be of no effect for the purpose of limiting the right of a dealer to dispose of that article without infringement of the patent or trade mark, as the case may be;

Provided that nothing in this section shall affect the validity as between the Parties and their successors, of any term or condition of a licence granted by the proprietor of a patent or [trade mark or by a licensee of patent or trade mark] or of any assignment of a patent or trade mark, so far as it regulates the price at which articles produced or processed by the licensee or the assignee may be sold by him.

Explanation—In this section and in section 40, the term "supplier", in relation to supply of any goods, means a person who supplies goods to any person for the ultimate purpose of resale and includes a wholesaler, and the term "dealer" includes a supplier and a retailer.

Prohibition of Other Measures for Maintaining Resale Prices

11. (1) Without prejudice to the provisions of this Act with respect to registration and to any of the powers of the Commission or of the Central Government under this Act, no supplier shall withhold supplies of any goods from any wholesaler or retailer seeking to obtain them for resale in India on the ground that the wholesaler or retailer—

(*a*) has sold in India at a price below resale price, goods obtained, cither directly or indirectly, from that supplier, or has supplied such goods, either directly or indirectly, to a third party who had done so; or

(*b*) is likely if the goods are supplied to him to sell them in India at a price below that price or supply them, either directly or indirectly, to a third party who would be likely to do so.

(2) Nothing contained in sub-section (1) shall render it unlawful for a supplier to withhold supplies of goods from any wholesaler or retailer or to cause or procure another supplier to do so if he has reasonable cause to believe that the wholesaler or the retailer, as the case may be, has been using as loss leaders any goods of the same or a similar description whether obtained from that supplier or not.

(3) A supplier of goods shall be deemed to be withholding supplies of goods from a dealer if he—

(*a*) refuses or fails to supply those goods to the order of the dealer;

(*b*) refuses to supply those goods to the dealer except at prices, or on terms or conditions as to credit, discount or other matters which are less favourable than those at or on which he normally supplies those goods to other dealers carrying on business in similar circumstances; or

(*c*) treats a dealer, in spite of a contract with such dealer for the supply or goods, in a manner less favourable than that in which he normally treats other dealers in respect of time or methods of delivery or other matters arising in the performance of the contract.

(4) A supplier shall not be deemed to be withholding supplies of goods on an) of the grounds mentioned in sub-section (1), if, in addition to that ground, has any other ground which alone would entitle him to withhold such supplies

Explanation I— "Resale price", in relation to sale of goods of any description, means any price notified to the dealer or otherwise published by or on behalf of the supplier of the goods in question (whether lawfully or not) as the price or minimum price which is to be charged on, or is recommended as appropriate for, a sale of that description or any price prescribed or purporting to be prescribed for that purpose by any contract or agreement between the wholesaler or retailer and any such supplier.

Explanation II—A wholesaler or retailer is said to use goods as loss leaders when he re-sells them otherwise than in a genuine seasonal or clearance saje not for the purpose of making a profit on the resale but for the purpose of attracting to the establishment at which the goods are sold, customers likely to purchase other goods or otherwise for the purpose of advertising his business.

Power of Commission to Exempt Particular Classes of Goods from Sections 39 and 40

12. (1) The Commission may, on a reference made to it by the [1][Director General] or any other person interested, by order, direct that goods of any class specified in the order shall be exempt from the operation of sections 39 and 40 if the Commission is satisfied that in default of a system of maintained minimum resale prices applicable to those goods—

(*a*) the quality of goods available for sale or the varieties of goods so available would be substantially reduced to the detriment of the public as consumers or users of those goods, or

(*b*) the prices at which the goods are sold by retail would, in general and in the long run, be increased to the detriment of the public as such consumers or users, or

(*c*) any necessary services actually **Provided** in connection with or after the sale of the goods by retail would cease to be so **Provided** or would be substantially reduced to the detriment of the public as such consumers or users.

(2) On a reference under this section in respect of goods of any class which have been the subject of proceedings before the Commission under section 31, the Commission may treat as conclusive any evidence of fact made in those proceedings.

1. Substituted for "Registrar" by the MRTP (Amdt.) Act, 1984, *W.e.f.* 1-8-1984.

Risk Management Principles for Electronic Banking Prescribed by Basel Committee's Electronic banking Group

A. Board and Management oversight

- Effective management oversight of e-banking activities.
- Establishment of a comprehensive security control process.
- Comprehensive due diligence and management oversight process for outsourcing relationships and other third-party dependencies.

B. Security controls

- Authentication of e-banking customers
- Non-repudiation and accountability for e-banking transactions.
- Appropriate measures to ensure segregation of duties.
- Proper authorization controls within e-banking systems, databases and applications.
- Data integrity of e-banking transaxtions, records, and information.
- Establishment of clear audit trails for e-banking transactions.
- Confidentiality of key bank information.

C. Legal and Reputational Risk Management

- Appropriate disclosures for e-banking services.
- Privacy of customer information.
- Capacity, business continuity and contingency planning to ensure availability of e-banking systems and services.
- Incident response planning.

Source: www.bis.org

—✦—✦—✦—

PART II

Chapter 1

Introduction — Research

This study is an attempt to examine the state-of-art of consumerism and consumer protection in India through opinion survey of consumers, companies and voluntary organizations.

Consumers are the life-blood of economic phenomenon. The objective of all production is sale by increasing number of consumers. Thus, consumers occupy a very important place in the success and failure of a business, without consumers no business would survive. Consumers' satisfaction is the ultimate aim of all business activities. Mass production of goods for ever-expanding markets and in anticipation or expectation of demand involves considerable risk or loss. It leads to over-production of goods and very keen competition between manufacturers and merchants to capture the market or demand. Industrial revolution gave us mass production which in turn demanded mass distribution techniques. Instead of sellers' market, we come across buyers' market. It is said in buyers' market, consumers enjoy supremacy and the consumer becomes the 'king' in the market. But in real practice, we see a different picture in India. He is mostly neglected and exploited by unscrupulous businessmen. Adulteration of goods, poor quality, false measures and weights, lack of service and courtesy and false advertisement are instances, where consumers is generally victimized by clever and dishonest businessmen.

Consumerism provides business with a challenge to take the offensive and to re-examine its marketing philosophy, practices and programmes which affect short and long term customer satisfaction, in a manner, it is consistent with public welfare. So enduring is today's consumer protection movement that it can be counted on to operate as a major force of influence in the years ahead.

Corporate managers no longer ask whether consumerism is here to stay, rather they are worried about how to respond correctly to the problems and dissatisfactions of consumer. To an increasing numbers of executives, consumerism is viewed as an opportunity in the market arena rather than as a threat. Correspondingly new programmers designed to meet the challenges of consumerism need to be analyzed, planned, and implanted.

Indian business played a notable part in the freedom movement. Since Independence, it has been mainly responsible for upgrading the country to tenth position in the world. What is equally significant is that the Industrial corporations, by producing a variety of commodities of daily use on an unprecedented mass scale have improved the lifestyle or standard of millions of consumer's. For this, the consumer, in general, owes a debt to Indian entrepreneurship.

However, there is a general feeling among consumers of all sections' of society that their rights are not adequately recognized and interests not properly safeguard. The main cause of this thinking is the high prices of almost all consumer goods. It is natural that when a person pays more, his expectations from the product purchases also become greater. Considering these things, the rhetoric of consumer protection is based on the reality of dissatisfactions.

The marketplace, a few decades ago, was a happy meeting ground where buyers and sellers had confidence in one e another. It even promoted trust among fellowmen. Today, it has become so complex and depersonalized that a customer finds himself at sea. He spends his money but hardly anybody cares for him. The good old marketplace of friendly exchanges between the familiar shoppers and a welcoming grocer is now a place of distrust and suspicion.

Industry is urged to take the consumer more seriously not only with regard to his personal requirements but in terms of his larger environment also. Some manufacturers look upon him as a "sales prospect" rather than as an individual to be cared for and helped in making satisfying purchase choices.

The consumer has a feeling that a section of industry considers only one 'aspect' while producing goods – will the product sell and how big will be the margin of profit?

Presently in India, high prices have made the consumer more conscious about the quality and standard of a product. Even a little gap between marketing claim and actual performance upsets him. This might have been ignored when prices were not high. Of course, there are many manufacturers who have maintained high standards of quality and excellence in performance.

Customers are not taken seriously in the marketplace. They feel hurt when they are treated as if they have low mental capabilities and lack an understanding of the worth of merchandise, while the petty retailer poses as a superior person. Is this what consumer sovereignty means in the present technological age of unparalleled mass production? The consumer even suffers incivility on many occasions. The surly salesman at the counter shows him practically no consideration, and this adds to his frustration.

Today in India, consumer consciousness is increasing.

There is growing awareness of rights among consumers. They want to express their views and to be heard by the marketer. Collectively, they seek to raise their voice for the protection of their legitimate interests. Today's consumer is not only price conscious but also quality conscious. His stress on wholesomeness shows concern for social health. He is sophisticated. He is giving a higher call for quality of life. His concern for environment hygiene is a result of the new age of consumer sensibility.

Drucker (1969) cited the growing consumer movement as evidence that the marketing concept is not really practiced:

"I have come to the conclusion that ..... The only way one can really define (consumerism) within the total marketing concept is as the shame of the total marketing concept. It is essentially a mark of failure of the concept. Consumerism means that the consumer looks upon the manufacturer as somebody who is interested, but who really does not know what the consumer's realities are. He regards the manufacturer as somebody who has not made the effort to find out, who does not understand the world in which the consumer lives, and who expects the consumer to be able to make distinctions which the consumer is neither is able nor willing to make."

THE CONSUMER : A SOCIAL PHENOMENON

"The customer is the king": the saying, like the idea behind, it is an age-old one. It is supposed to express the pre-eminence of the person who wishes to purchase….. Over the one whose trade is to supply. But the application of this concept is necessarily limited. It covers only a fleeting relationship between the "client king" and the supplier, a relationship during which the independent will of the purchaser is opposed to the sellers persuasion to buy, often ceasing as soon as the transaction is completed. From this moment onwards, the client ceases to be king , sometimes to become a "consumer victim".

Awareness of consumer's relative weakness in relation to the supplier of goods or services, before se well as after the act of purchase, is not new. The concept of consumer protection was not invented in this century. The Magna Carta, drawn up in England in the year 1215, bears witness to this. But we can find examples even further back in history, such as the Hammourabi code which protected consumers in Babylon in the 18th century before Christ (EEC Document, 1986, p.l)

With the passage of time development of modern economic systems, consumer protection in all its forms has required even more complex regulations and controls on marketing activities.

In today's growing and changing market-place there is an important role of the following in protecting the interest of the consumers.

- The manufactures/trading institutions
- The Government
- The voluntary organizations
- The consumer themselves

With the tremendous growth of our industrial society during the twentieth century, a need arose for government to act as a protector of consumers against exploitation by manufacturers. Initially the primary concern was the health and safety of consumers. But as industrialization developed and merchandising and marketing practices grew more complex, the consumer needed to become more and better informed and protected.

PRESENT STATE OF CONSUMER AFFAIRS IN INDIA

In the olden days, the mothers milked the cows; the daughters set it out in pans to separate the cream, one of the sons sold it in the market. Today the agricultural department is mobilized, the milk is homogenized, the supplies are motorized, and the dairies are organized. The result is that the Indian consumer is victimized (Hidayatullah, 1984).

It is estimated that due to unhealthy trade practices restored to by the businessman, the consumers in India are cheated to the extent of ₹ 1,600 crores every year (Rayudu, 1983, P.23).

In an environment of limited choice, inadequate supplies, incomplete information, gullible customers, and unlimited demand, it is inevitable that the Indian consumer gets cheated. Some glaring examples of how he is affected are given below in the following categories: Black Marketing, Inflation, Public distribution system, Adulteration, Weights and Measures, Environmental Pollution and Advertisement.

1. Blackmarketing, Hoarding and Profiteering

In a black market economy the ruling price is not necessarily the consequence of the market stabilizer as is the case with conditions of competition. Generally, the black market is operated by some group of people and not by a single individual. Therefore, we generally find a fluctuating price level with an upward slant. In order to attain maximum profits, artificial manipulation of either demand or supply or both is common in a Black market. The Black market operators do not care for productivity, growth and equal distribution but aim at maximization of profits only.

Presently in India, wholesalers and particularly retailers are in the habit of hoarding, profiteering and black marketing. Almost all goods are subject to price control are invariably available in black market in all big cities. Today, it is the seller's market for consumer goods and not the buyer's market. Many items of consumer goods like edible oil, sugar, kerosene and cooking gas are in short supply through quiet often artificial and manipulated. When goods are not available and the customer has to stand in queues to get what he wants there is little scope for complaint by him of quality and measure and has to pay excess amount to get the goods and services.

2. Inflation

It is noted that a moderate rise in the prices of goods is in the interests of the economy as it serves as an incentive for producers to produce more.

However, most developing countries, including India are facing undue rise in the price of goods, particularly essential goods. Though inflation not only reduces the real income of the poor but creates problems to the government and the economy as a whole.

A developing country like India is compelled to incur heavy expenditures on various items under a programme of planned development. However, there are serious limitations to raising the output of essential goods. We are facing shortages in respect of crucial inputs like capital. Our villages do not even have the minimum infrastructural facilities. Naturally, there is always a mismatch between supply of money and the availability of goods. While money supply is increasing by about 10 per cent per anum, real national income is increasing at around 2 per cent per anum. To this extent, inflation is a mandatory phenomenon.

However, inflation in the Indian context is not really a monetary phenomenon. It is multi-dimensional as price rise is due to social, cultural, political and psychological factors. India is having a mixed economy

With both public and private sector functioning side by side. The private sector is still predominant; its activities are governed by profit motive. Our economy suffers from inequalities in income and wealth. No wonder, our production pattern turns to be preposterous in the market, there are enough comfort and luxuries, but shortages of essential goods! It is difficult to control inflation so long as this situation continues.

Scarcity of resources and goods on one hand and inflationary trends partly inherent in increased state expenditure on the other, make situation in the developing countries unfavorable for the common people (Yogender, 1980, p.17). Basically, inflation rises because there is more income to spend, and less goods to spend it on. Measures like price control, taxation and rationing only relive the symptoms. A lasting solution lies in increasing production on a broader basis and to utilize the market where possible, within the framework of social goals (Narayanan, 1979).

3. Functioning of Public Distribution System — Fair Price Shops

The existing infrastructure of the Public Distribution System not only in Delhi but in other parts of the country has undoubtedly helped in the proper distribution of foodgrains including pulses, kerosene, soft coke, soap, cycle tyres and tubes, sugar, vegetable oil. Most of these items are at present, being sold through retail outlets, co-operative societies or the super bazaars.

During the sixth plan period, the public distribution system admittedly helped in checking the social menace of rising prices particularly of essential commodities. The system also helped in containing the inflation. The seventh plan strategy has also recognized the public distribution system as a permanent feature for controlling the price rise and also for reducing the fluctuations in the distribution of essential goods. Even the 20- point programme as envisaged by our Late Prime Minister Mrs. Indira Gandhi has given due recognition to this system for ensuring adequate and equitable distribution of essential commodities to the poor and needy sections of the society.

According to Government records, the public distribution system had been functioning in the country for many decades and since then a large number of commodities besides food grains, had been coming under its ambit. The public commodities system operates on a national level with the sole objective of making available all essential goods to the consumers, especially those belonging to the weaker sections of our society at fair prices (Wig, 1986).

The very purpose of public distribution system through a chain of fair price shops is defeated if ration commodities are either not available to those in need or are of so poor a quality that it leaves consumers disgusted. For example, a report on public distribution system in West Bengal By CAF (1987) revealed that –

(a) Quality of rice was bad, broken and full of dust and no par boiled rice was allocated. There was an instance of superior quality Basmati rice getting spoiled as it was left in the warehouse for 3 years, the officers being unable to decide its price. In comparison to rice, quality of wheat was found to be generally better.

(b) People were obliged to buy rice from open market, Because the rice supplies through ration shops was largely unfit for human consumption. Oil not being supplied regularly, the consumers could not comment on the quality of oil. Sugar was often given on due slips but there was no provision for due slips for oil or rice. Edible cooking oil was found to be very much in short supply.

(c) Consumers believe that the good quality goods are lifted against fictitious ration cards, by unscrupulous persons with the connivance of the shopkeepers and sold in the open market.

(d) There is no system of checking weights' at ration shops.

(e) There is no co-ordination between ration shops and rationing officers.

The PDS thus needs to be strengthened, recognized and revitalized properly for the attainment of objectives for which it was started in every part of the country (Trivedi, 1979). The sixth plan declared: An efficient public distribution system requires annexus between production, procurement, transportation, storage and distribution of the selected commodities (Planning Commission, 1981).

The PDS cannot be effective unless it is backed up by scientific mode of classification to identify the consumers. The down-trodden class consumers are generally found indulging in black-marketing of sugar. They take their respective quota from the shop and sell at higher rates elsewhere and then purchase wheat and rice. This flaw in distribution system can be eliminated if only the actual requirement of a consumer is classified and identified to supply the required quantities of commodities (Roy and Srivastava, 1982, p.30).

At present, the system suffers from regular supplies and innumerable bogus ration cards (Shankaraiah, Ojha and Sadanndam, 1982, p.17).

The voluntary consumer organizations should ensure effective functioning of the PDS and provide more effective consumer protection. It rightly declared that "there is need for strengthening the intelligence, early warning and demand-supply management information system". (Planning Commission, 1981, p.81). Thus, the sixth plan laid stress not only on increasing the output of essential goods but efficient management of the supply of those goods in order to safeguard the interest of the customers, particularly the vulnerable section. Our present Prime Minister Mr. P.V. Narashima Rao has also time and again reiterated to reach out the Fair Price Shops (FPS) facility to the remotest villages which needs their attention

4. Adulteration

Adulteration of food articles is rampant in the country and has become a grave menace to the health and well-being of the community. It makes a heavy dent in the already low nutritional standards and the benefits of many are spent are insidiously undermined. A major offensive against this evil is overdue (Govt. of India Gazette, 1976).

A survey conducted by the Consumer Council on India reveals that as much as 774 and 1063 deaths took place in the year 1972 and 1973 respectively due to adulteration of food articles. Sixty-five percent of deaths were attributed to liquor poisoning (Consumer Bulletin, 1974, p.18-19).

Adulteration is not confined to food articles alone. 'Surma' an eye cosmetic, when recently tested, has indicated the presence of one to five per cent of lead in the samples which can damage the eyes. In view of the high price of petrol, it is being adulterated. It is difficult to detect adulteration of petrol as long as the kerosene content does not exceed 10 per cent.

5. Weights and Measures - Deceving of Consumers by Traders

Usage of wrong weights and measures is illegal, but the practice is widely prevalent. But most consumers are blissfully ignorant. The enormous loss incurred by consumers by this method would surprise most consumers.

The traders are benefited in more than one way; they charge exorbitant prices, keep the quality below the prescribed standard and use wrong weights and measures. The weights and measures (Law revision) committee, popularly known as the Maitra committee, came to sad conclusion, "even one percent error in commercial transactions carried out in the country by inaccurate weights and measures cause the consumers a loss of over ₹ 170 crores in cities; the farmers stand to lose about ₹ 150 crores by a mal-practice". Normally, the error and short weight is about 5 per cent and there the loss to the urban consumers and farmers will be about five times as much. A report later released in January 1977, has disclosed that under-weighing alone cheated the consumers to the tune of ₹ 3,000 crores annually (Sundaram, 1985, pp.55-56).

Almost the entire consumer trade revolves round weights and measures. While buying or selling one blindly depends on the genuineness of the weights and measures being used. The implications of these weights and measures themselves being fake can be mind-boggling.

What is of serious concern to the consumer is not only that a number of weights and measures are truly tampered with, but with one cannot depend even on packaged and tinned commodities where the net weight given is in some cases less than the actual weight.

The Standard Weights and measures Enforcement Act 1985, puts certain obligations on the manufacturer and seller of packaged commodities. All packed items must have the name and address of the manufacturer, name of the item packed, quantity of item, month and year of manufacture, maximum retail price. The manufacturer, distributor and retailer are liable to be prosecuted if any of the items are missing.

6. Environmental Pollution

With the tremendous technological advances, our environment is being polluted constantly by various sources endangering the lives of human and other living beings.

The pollution in the air is due to smoke and gasses emitted by automobiles, factories, power plants, etc. The water is contaminated by the effluents released by the factories in the rivers, lakes and ponds. The pesticides used by the farmers have caused widespread contamination in agricultural products like vegetables, fruits, cereals and pulses. In fact, a sample survey has revealed that 50 per cent of vegetables consumed by us are contaminated with pesticides (Financial Express, 1985). Besides this, animal foods like meat, milk, eggs and fish have invariably been found to contain levels of pesticides higher than the safe limits. To control the environmental pollution, Government has from time to time enacted various Acts. The Water (Prevention and Control of Pollution) Act, 1974. The Air (Prevention and control of pollution) Act, 1981 and The Environment protection act, 1986. Since protection of our environment is a must for our survival, every one of us should work for its success. This can be achieved by creating awareness among the masses about the seriousness of the problem along with the stricter enforcement of various Acts.

7. Advertisement

The advertising policy in India is based mostly on the commercial expediency rather than ethical principle. Spurious toiletries and cosmetics products, medicines and food items are a common feature in the market. Most of these spurious goods are sold under false advertisement, promising wild reliefs while in fact creating the opposite. In the cloth trade, for example, tall promises of fast color and durability are common, while often they do not stand few washes. Similarly, advertisement of some tooth pastes, cosmetics and figure-improving and body building apparatus make claims for the products without explaining how the claimed qualities produce the benefits suggested. Most of the mail order companies indulge in false and deceptive advertisement (Verma, 1978, p.5).

It may be pointed out that in India alone, Mail order frauds run into several hundred crores of rupees (Garg, 1981, p.5).

In addition, many such advertisements are not only false in their content and promises but also a disgrace to public decency and morality.

PRESENT STATE OF CONSUMERS AFFAIRS IN INDIA

In India, a number of measures to safeguard the consumer interest through legislative protection have been taken. For example , Essential Commodities Act, governs the production, procurement and distribution of all essential commodities. This Act has been amended in 1974 give more protection to consumers by ensuring quicker and more effective actions against the in social activities of the profiteers and blackmarketeers and hoarders.

Dishonest, deceptive and otherwise unprincipled business practices victimize Indian consumers in many ways. Consumers are hurt in the pocket by overcharging, by the purchase of inferior merchandise and by exortionate credit policies. Their health is endangered by impure foods and drugs or by the valueless medical devices. They or their children are often injured by poorly made appliances, unsafe articles and other defective items.

There are various Acts introduced in India from time to time which protects the interests of the consumers. Chief of them are:

1. Agricultural Produce Act, 1937
2. Fruits Products Order, 1955
3. Essential Commodities Act, 1955
4. Maharashtra Scheduled Articles Order, 1969
5. Weights and Measures Act, 1976
6. Prevention of Food Adulteration Act,1954
7. Prevention of Food Rules,1955
8. The Drug and Cosmetics Act,1940
9. Drug and Magic Remedies, 1954
10. The Dangerous Drug Act
11. Poisons Act
12. Bureau of Standards Act
13. Standards and Weights Measures (Packaged Commodities Rules, 1977)
14. Household Electrical Appliances Act, 1976
15. Indian Sales of Goods Act, 1930
16. M.R.T.P Act, 1969
17. Consumer Protection Act, 1986

Legislation is not a total answer to consumer complaints about business. What is needed is vigilant and united consumer organizations in various parts of the country.

Several consumer associations are doing useful work in this field. To name a few following societies deserve mention:

1. Karnataka Consumer Services Society, Bangalore
2. Consumer Guidance Centre, Cochin
3. Southern Consumers Union,Madras
4. Citizen Action Group
5. Consumer Education and Research Centre, Ahmedabad
6. Consumer Guidance Bureau, Bhilai
7. Consumer Guidance Society of India, Bombay
8. Consumer Action Forum, Calcutta
9. Consumer's Association, Bhimavaram (West Godavari Dist.), Andhra Pradesh
10. Consumer Protection Association, Agartala (Tripura)

These voluntary organisations in India are creating consumer awareness by imparting consumer education. Some are conducting research work while others are imparting training to the consumers.

President John F Kennedy, in his 1962 declaration of rights for the consumers (Engel, Kollet and Blackwell, 1973, p.614) stated that consumers have:

1. The right to safety
2. The right to be informed
3. The right to choose
4. The right to be heard

Lately in India, the Consumer Protection Act,1986 was enacted to include the following two additional rights.

1. Right to seek redressal
2. Right to Consumer Education

NEED OF THE STUDY

This research proposal, fit within the priority expressed by the Indian Government in a developing country such as ours. Late Mr. L.K. Jha, the then Advisor to the Prime Minister stated that the whole apparatus of economic policies should be given the right orientation to provide a better deal to the consumer (Assocham Bulletin,1936, p.130)

In developed countries, almost every month the consumers notice the announcement of a new victory in the form of a new trading agreement, a new institution. Programmes about consumers affairs, publication in newspapers, TV, Radio and Government media are making the consumer movement official (Basu, 1986).

The consumers are certainly entitled to have certain basic rights such as the right to safety; the right to be informed, the right to choose and the right to be heard. But these rights have limited coverage as large number of consumers are not aware of these rights. At the same time, consumers in India are highly disorganized. Because of these factors, the business community resort to all kinds of unhealthy trade practices such as hoarding, blackmarketing, charging exorbitant prices, adultearation, supplying sub-standards products, using deceptive and misleading advertisements and so on.

Consumerism and consumer protection has been a neglected aspect in our country. Not much has been conducted on these issues. Verma (1980) made an attempt in studying the regulation of restrictive trade practices, but consumerism and other Acts and Regulations related to consumer protection were not covered.

Though consumer regulation is a complex subject, yet it is quite fascinating. Moreover, it contains the diverse disciplines of commerce, economics, law and business administration. It is, therefore, inexplicable as to why it has not so far received adequate attention from research scholars in India. Hardly anu in-depth study on the subjects has so far been undertaken. The issues taken in this study will provide support to the SOCIAL WELFARE aspect in the fields of trade, commerce and socio-economic planning. The findings can be of use to various institutions, universities and organizations connected with Consumer Movement in India and abroad.

Specific Objectives of the Study

1. To trace and document the historical development in consumerism and consumer protection movement in India and abroad.
2. To analyse the consumer's opinion, regarding consumerism and consumer protection legislation in India.
3. To study the activities of Indian Companies in the changed circumstances and observe the reaction of the marketing executives with respect to consumerism.
4. To analyze the working of the various types of consumer associations in India.
5. To identify the parameters needed to implement consumerism and consumer protection in India.

Organisation of the Study

The present study has been divided into eight chapters.

Chapter-I, that is the present chapter is introductory in nature, which explains/elaborates consumerism and consumer protection. It also discusses the present situation about the problems of the Indian consumers; also how the marketing executives are facing present social challenges. It also gives the need of the study and specifies the objectives of the study.

Chapter-II, deals with the evolution of consumerism and consumer protection in India and abroad. We have discussed the historical background of Consumer Protection, Cosumer Movement. We have explained how the consumer movement started in India and its impact on the society, the various legislations implemented by the Governments for the welfare of the Indian consumers and the various Acts introduced for protection of customers.

In Chapter-III, we have discussed the various studies made by different writers/authors related to consumerism and consumer protection in India and overseas. This chapter reviews the available literature on social marketing, consumer welfare and discusses various research findings related to the above mentioned topics.

Chapter-IV, deals with research methodology used for the present study. It describes the universe of the study, sample design, method of data collection and data analysis and some limitations of the study.

Chapter-V, is devoted to the empirical study done on Indian consumer on various consumer issues. It deals with the opinions and attitudes of the Indian buyers/users towards consumerism and consumer movement and the findings have been discussed in detail in this chapter.

Chapter-VI, deals with opinions expressed by the company executives of the Indian industries/manufacturers concerning consumerism and consumer protection and how they are coping with one another with the present marketing challenges and social changes.

In Chapter-VII, we have examined the opinions expressed by the voluntary organizations and their modus operandi in rendering various services to the Indian consumers while bringing in consumer awareness, imparting consumers education.

The major findings and conclusions that have emerged from this study, are in **Chapter-VIII.** It gives the summary of the findings and conclusions and ends up with suggestions and recommendations for the marketing organizations, voluntary organizations, Government departments and the consumer themselves.

Chapter 2

Evolution of Consumerism and Consumer Protection

HISTORICAL BACKGROUND

Throughout the history of human affairs critics have charged that middleman add mark-ups to the cost of a product substantially in excess of the value added by their services. The Greek philosopher Plato had a strong prejudice against traders. He held that they practiced the acquisitive arts as against the productive arts bringing nothing new into being. His favourite pupil Aristotle also condemned retailers as making their wealth in an unnatural way and gaining profits at the expense of the buyer. These prejudices persisted in the middle ages in the writings of various philosophers and commentators who saw the middlemen as an unproductive profiteer.

Consumer protection is not the outcome of the twentieth century legislations. Even during the period of ancient Rome, protection was available to the consumer. In the Middle Ages, established consumer standards also played their part, and a merchant of shoddy goods was dragged round the town on a hurdle with his wares tied round his neck (Willbeforce, Campbel and Elles, 1966). In Scythia, in the 5th century B.C., the philosopher Anacharis asserted that 'the market is the place where men may deceive each other.' And the medieval proverb '*caveat emptor*' (let the buyer beware) seems to be still a good advice today.

The problems relating to restrictive trade practices and the legislative measures to curb them are not exclusively a modern phenomenon. They have their foundation in human greed and are traceable from the earliest times in trade and commerce. As to the practices, the advantages of cornering the market were known to the ancient Egyptians;papyri are in existence which show the existence of private monopolies in woold and cloth, and a schedule of merchandise which dates from about 300 B.C., is known, which shows an attempt to fix prices as against those prevailing in free market.

The Romans took more drastic measures to curb restrictive trade practices. According to Bible, the earliest Roman legislation is the *Lex Julia de Annona* enacted in about 50 B.C. This law was stipulated to protect the corn trade against unnatural rises in prices, and to impose heavy fines against anyone who by any means affected a rise in the price of corn. Further, the law was intended to check not only individual cases of profiteering, but also combinations to raise the price of corn. At a later period, there was an edict of Diocletian in 301 A.D., which was intended to bring down the price of goods in day-to-day use. It also provided remedies for some of special cases of buying up merchandise; the concealment of foodstuffs and the artificial creation of scarcity. However, another important development in the Roman law was the promulgation of the Constitution of Zeno in 483 A.D. This Constitution was intended to protect the consumers against the artificial increase in the prices of foodstuffs and other commodities of daily use. It also prevented the combinations of artisans, labourers and traders and provided for very heavy penalties for breaches, including confiscation of property and lifelong punishment. However, it was not every effective, as Justinian was later compelled to base the economy of the state on official monopolies managed by paid officials.

INDIAN HISTORICAL ANTECEDENTS

It is revealing to note that in ancient India during the reign of Mauryas as long ago as 300 B.C., the act of adulteration was considered 'adharma' and viewed with disgrace, and distribution of adulterated articles of good and drugs was prohibited. The law provided protection to the consumers from the evil effects of adulteration and provided severe punishment for adulteration of grains, food articles and medicines.

In Kautilya's Arthashastra (India) which dates back to a period placed various between 300 B.C. and 300 A.D., there are provisions for heavy penalties where artisans combine for production of goods to reduce the quality thereof or to charge profits in excess of labour involved or to depress prices to harm suppliers. There is also a precept to the ruler to be vigilant so that the traders do not buy and sell in concert on a large scale (Sinha, 1976, pp. 69 -71).

The ancient writings tend to show that monopolistic and restrictive trade practices were also operative in ancient India. In order to prevent such practices, some centuries before Christ, there had been regulations prohibiting under penalty of very heavy fines, the making of collective agreements to influence natural market prices of goods by withholding them from trade. Restrictive trade practices are as old as trade itself. Those practices represent attempts of businessmen to enrich themselves at the cost of the consumer. In order to protect the consumer, the State has sought to regulate the anti-competitive activities of traders and manufacturers since ancient times (Willbeforce *et. al.*, 1966).

CONSUMER MOVEMENT – HISTORICAL PERSPECTIVE AWARENESS FOR PROTECTION OF CONSUMERS

Consumer Movement first took root in the USA, the land of the world renowned consumer activist, Ralph Nader. In that country, 100% of consumer products, and 90% of consumer services (the only exception being the postal serice) are produced, manned and maintained by the private sector. Very stringent laws were made for ensuring safety and reliability of all consumer products and services used by the US citizen. The market force generated by intense competition ensured that the quality of those products and services remained always at concert pitch (Gaedeke, 1969).

The movement for consumer protection began to crystallize as early as the late nineteenth century. This was reflected in the formation of various local and regional consumer groups, in exposing scandals and by concerted federal legislations (Faedeke, 1970, pp. 31-40). There in 1872, the first consumer protection law was passed, making it a federal crime to defraud through the use of mails.

The current wave of consumerism is not unprecedented in the history of business. Historically, consumerism started in U.S.A. and it has three periods of consumer unrest. Common feature of the three periods provide a new perspective on the current consumer movement. It may help in identifying causes of consumer unrest, the forms it will take and probable course.

First Era

By 1870s, some of the abuses and excesses of rapid industrialization led some states of U.S.A. and the Federal Government to enact laws to regulate them. By then the Supreme Court had begun to interpret the Constitution to invalidate the regulation of business. '*Caveat emptor*' (let the buyer beware) was the law of product sales, and this interpretation was retained and extended as the courts took a strict, hands-off policy towards private countracts, no matter how unfair or oppressive the terms.

The posture of the law began to change in the last two decades of the 19th century. The Sherman Antitrust Act (1890) was a forerunner of a new wave of consumer-oriented laws. When the Clayton Act was added to Antitrust legislation in 1914, the Government's role as protector of the public domain was confirmed. Joining the procession of early consumer legislations were the Food and Drop Act (1906), the Federal Trade Commission Act (1914), and the Federal Power Commission Act (1920).

These pieces of legislation came about because consumer advocates, trade unions, journalists, and the executives clamoured for them before a reluctant Congress. The first Consumers' Leage of middle and upper-class advocates, formed in 1891, led to establishing the National Consumer League in 1898. The leagues joined with other groups including the National Child Labour Association, the League of Women Voters, and the labour unions, and got laws passed and enforced affecting safety and working conditions, maximum hours, child labour, and minimum wages.

Perhaps the most important result of the first era of consumerism was recognition by American Society that the consumer had valid interest which was not always served by the existing market mechanisms.

Consumerism ebbed during World War, but not before courts had begun to be consumer conscious. The rule of '*caveat emptor*' began evolving towards '*caveat vendior*' (let the seller beware) – a rule applied against powerful industries, such as utilities and insurance.

Second Era

The depression of the 1930s ushered in the second phase of consumerism. During the 1920s, educators had developed guidelines for consumer education. Consumers Research, Inc., was formed in 1929 to meet the enquiries about products, which flooded in on the heels of the best seller. By 1933, people were eager to critically examine the issues of brand proliferation, unwise spending, and misleading advertising (Kallet and Schlink, 1933). The National Recovery Act (1933) gave the first formal recognition to the consumer interest in Federal law by providing labour and consumer advisory boards in the code making process.

It was in 1937 that the tragic death of ninety three consumers from taking Elixir Sulfanilimide, a sulfa-based drug, provided the final jmpetus behind the passage of the Food, Drug and Cosmetic Act 1938. The new Act amended the Food and Drugs Act of 1906, expanding the jurisdiction of the Food and Drug Administration (FDA) to include cosmetics and therapeutic devices. It provided for the seizure of these items, as well as foods and drugs that were deemed to be adulterated or misbranded (Lamb, 1936).

In addition, it established standards to identify, quality, and fill for food products; allowed the introduction of new drugs only after prior FDA approval; and established general criteria of adulteration for food, drugs, and cosmetics.

The other major piece of consumer protection legislation to emerge from the 1930s was the Wheeler Lea Amendment to the Federal Trade Commission Act. The passage of this legislation in 1938 expanded the mandate of the FTC to include "unfair and deceptive acts or practices in commerce", which gave the FTC jurisdiction over a wide range of practices considered to be harmful to the consumer, including deceptive advertising. In 1935, consumer groups formed consumers' Union, which fought for recognition of consumer interests throughout the years of World War II. A period thus emerged which saw the rise of an articulate consumer consciousness, generally labeled as the "Consumer Movement" (Dameron, 1939, pp. 276-277).

Third Era

Consumerism in America began to move into its third phase at the end of the 1950's. Actually, the beginning of the third era of the consumer movement often is dated from late Mr. John F. Kennedy's Consumer Message to the Congress in the Spring of 1962. On March 15, 1962, Late President John F. Kennedy sent to the Congress a special message on protecting the consumer interest. His central theme was that "consumers are the only important group in the economy who are not effectively organized, whose views are often not heard." In the preamble to his Consumer Message to the Congress in March, 1962, President Kennedy enunciated the now favoured Consumer Bill of Rights:

1. The right to safety
2. The right to be informed
3. The right to choose; and
4. The right to be heard.

The Kefauver-Harris Amendment (1962) to the Federal Food, Drug and Cosmetic Act (1938) was established in 1962. This amendment laid down new procedures for testing the safety and effectiveness of all new drugs prior to marketing, and it applied retrospectively to all drugs which had been marketed since 1938. Subsequently, the amendment was to play a major role in consumer protection measures relating to drug products.

In 1965, a landmark year in consumer protection, Senator Abraham Ribicoff, convened a Senate Committee to hold hearings on automobile safety. In the process, he uncovered what was appeared to be an amazing lack of concern on the part of auto industry/manufacturers about safety-related design defects. To some extent this lack of concern may have been a reflection of lack of information on the part of industrialists. For example, questioning of General Motors executives in which they admitted to having insufficient information on highway safety. Another example of industry ignorance was the confession by Chrysler Vice-President that he didn't know whether dealers who had been informed about a serious defect in the steering gear of some of their cars had taken the trouble to inform the buyers about the problem (U.S. Congress, 1965, p. 784).

An important spokesman for the consumer at these hearings was an obscure lawyer named Ralph Nader who, in the public interest, had taken upon himself the task of holding automobile manufacturers accountable for defects in their products. Within the next few years, Ralph Nader was to figure prominently in many congressional hearings on a wide variety of subjects relating to consumer protection. He was the central figure in publicizing U.S. Department of Agriculture data on the unwholesome conditions prevailing in some meat processing plants. The effect of his disclosures was the passage of the Wholesome Meat Act of 1967. Since then, Ralph Nader has become an institution in the struggle to safeguard the public interest, including consumer protection, with his sponsorship of the Centre for Study of Responsive Law in 1968, and later the Public Interest Research Group.

In his Consumer Message of October 30, 1969 President Nixon offered a "Buyers Bill of Rights".

I believe that the buyer in America today has the right to make an intelligent choice among products and services. The buyer has the right to accurate information on which to make his free choice.

The buyer has the right to expect that his health and safety is taken into account by those who seek his patronage.

The buyers has the right to register his dissatisfaction and have his complaint heard and weighed, when his interests are badly served.

Now we shall study the "Consumer Movement" in other parts of the world.

THE INTERNATIONAL CONSUMER MOVEMENT

The Modern Consumer Movement has its Roots in The United States whose Consumers' Union is the largest consumer organization in the world with more than two million members. European organizations and those in Australia and New Zealand emerged after World War II. In the developing countries too the spirit of consumerism has awakened. There are now thousands of groups in more than 70 countries.

The pattern of consumer protection in Europe bears a remarkable similarity to the U.S. experience. Industrialized nations on both continents generated extensive brand name advertising and were faced with many of the same problems of packaging and of ensuring the purity of food and drugs. The idea of supplying the consumer with the results of product testing by brand name crossed the Atlantic following World War II. Starting in Great Britain, the Netherlands, and Belgium, it spread to the Scandinavian countries, Austria, West Germany, and France and was soon exported to Australia, Japan and Israel (Gaedeka and Etcheson, 1972).

In Great Britain, the consumer movement began to gather momentum during the years following the second world war through voluntary action mostly by women's organizations. For the first time one of the leading political parties came into the picture in a significant manner when in 1955 the Labour Party put out a pamphlet entitled "Battle for the Consumer". Another significant development of the late fifties was the establishment of a Retail Trading Standards Association with the primary objectives of helping to resolve disputes between retailers and their consumers. In fact, a consumer revolution was gradually taking place in Britain. It was this development that compelled the Government to appoint the Molony Committee to report on what changes in the law were desirable "for further protection of the consuming public" and to make recommendations, inter alia for more and better standard of safety, quality and performance.

On the basis of the report of the Molony Committee which has rightly been regarded as a great landmark in the history of consumer legislation and consumer movement, the Government appointed a Consumers' Council in 1963. The Council was envisaged to be authoritative and considered voice of the consumer and it soon came to exercise a healthy influence on the Government as well as the trade. In the following years, several legislative enactments were passed for the benefit of the consumer. Today, there is a Ministry for Consumer Protection in Great Britain which looks after the consumer interest in a systematic manner.

Except for Belgium and the Netherlands, European consumer testing organizations have followed the pattern set by the Scandinavian countries rather than by British and the U.S. In Norway, substantial Government grants are given to a consumer organization, Forbrukerradet, operated by representatives of seven leading national organizations. In Denmark, consumer activities are divided between a Government operated Household Advice Centre, which undertakes extensive programmes in the field of nutrition and household equipment, and a consumer testing organization supported by its individual members as well as some 21 member organizations and the Government. Perhaps the most notable of the European efforts is Austria's Verein fur Konsumenten-Information. This organization not only issues a monthly testing publication but also operates a demonstration centre in central Vienna where the consumer may view available brands and receive impartial guidance. Among the Asian countries, Japan has demonstrated as to how a consumer revolution can take place along with rapid economic development and the emergence of a mass consumption society. After a series of administrative and legislative measures during the fifties for the protection of the consumer, in 1968, the basic law for the protection of the consumer was clarified and a commission for the protection of the consumer was established as an organ directly responsible to the Prime Minister. In Japan, consumer protection is not confined to the national government alone. It is also the responsibility of all the municipalities and other local governments. For example, in 1961, the Tokyo Municipality set up a Consumption Economy Section and this example was emulated by other local bodies. Side by side with the legislative measures, a large number of voluntary consumer organizations have also sprung up devoting increasing attention to the other aspects, namely, information, education, guidance and stronger organization of consumers. But it has to be emphasized that the movement in Japan took its roots through the various forms or measures or protection of the consumer taken by the government.

A number of embryonic movements had been formed in Korea, the Philippines, Malaysia and India. Perhaps the strongest organizations in the pacific area, however, were those in Australia and New zealand. The Consumers Institutes of New Zealand receives a heavy government subsidy. The Australian consumer movement was independent in character and received no government money. Local consumer movements existed in leading Australian cities, and New South Wales and Victoria had consumer councils. In the Latin American countries we find consumerism has made immense progress in countries like Argentina, Brazil, Colombia, Costa Rica, Jamaica, Mexico, Nicaragua, etc. In these countries, there are various consumer associations, consumer councils and other groups working for the consumer welfare in their respective countries.

In African countries, consumer movement has taken place in Nigeria, Kenya, South Africa, Zimbabwe and also in other parts of the continent and the remaining countries are following suit with their gradual development. Now the consumer movement has become a global phenomenon.

In conclusion, we note that the world consumer movement has grown most rapidly in more advanced nations that have the discipline of quality control, welltrained government inspection services, and discerning consumers.

THE INDIAN SCENARIO

Role of Indian Voluntary Organizations in Consumerism and Consumer Protection

Indian consumer is a gentleman. He may be grinded under the yoke of high costs of commodities, may be fleeced by the profiteer, blackmarketeer or hoarder, but still he does not complain or protest.

Through the years of experience, he has learnt to suffer in silence rather than make a noise which does not help him rather he is ridiculed not only by the Trade but even at places by the bureaucracy handling the affairs. He feels that unless the society as a whole changes socially, no fruitful result will come out of his cry. Besides, he feels the law of the country so cumbersome that if one puts a complaint he get nothing out of it rather is put to harassment through protracted procedure in getting the culprit to book.

Consumer feels that he has to work very hard to build public opinion awakening the consumer of his rights and responsibilities to himself and to the society. It is with this background that the consumer has got up to build public opinion.

Of late, the public opinion is building up in an organized manner in different parts of our country and consumer welfare movement has started taking deep roots especially in States of Delhi, Gujarat, Karnataka, Tamil Nadu, West Bengal, Jammu and Kashmir, etc.

Indian consumer wants that he gets articles of necessity, essential commodities and service in terms of quality and quantity in proportion to what he pays for acquiring the same; but he does not get whether it be food stuffs, milk, spices, or other services.

Over and above whatever commodity we purchase is found adulterated, even the life saving medicines are not spared by the anti-social elements who manufacture spurious drugs that have proved injurious and even fatal to human health. The consumer is consuming these items knowing that he is being deceived, and harmed with the poor stuff both in terms of quality and quantity. There is no effective weights and measures control. Prices are also not properly displayed and controlled. In a nutshell, it can be said that the consumer of today though hard-hit but are not fully aware and united and unless they come to face this unhealthy situation unitedly, there is no alternative to remaining a poor spectator of helplessness and exploitation by the greedy who do not hesitate even to play with the lives of human beings.

Hence these non-political, non-secretarial, social associations, charitable organization, should stand committed to project and protect the interests of the consumers by adopting peaceful, democratic, dignified and constitutional ways and means. The organization must create awareness among the consumers, regarding their rights and responsibilities, act as a watch-dog to resist the exploiters of the consumers. One of the objectives is to educate the consumers about the application of various government acts/laws/standards meant for their welfare, so that working of the concerned government departments can be made more useful and effective through mutual cooperation and public participation, in an organized and rational manner.

India with more than 400 consumer action groups as against one lac in USA has long way to go but the process of consumerism has been stimulated and it is expected to be a reckoning force in the very near future.

A major obstacle to consumer movement in India is that there are different classes of consumers, and that very often sectional interest of these classes clash with each other. When we look at different classes of consumers in rural and urban areas, we find wide difference as regards (i) purchasing power; (ii) living styles and consumption patterns and (iii) educational, cultural and social background. The big consumer organizations are not in a position to work for the poor, illiterate rural consumers, nor are they able to safeguard the interests of the unorganized urban poor (Economic Times, 1982).

In India, consumer movement is gaining strength though it is not very powerful. There is the Consumer Guidance Society of India with Headquarters in Mumbai and branches in Delhi, Hyderabad, Thane and Dandeli. There is the Consumers Council of India in New Delhi. It is an all India organization which wants to strengthen and popularize consumer protection measures, apart from studying consumer problems to evolve remedies. There is also Consumer Education and Research Centre at Ahmedabad. Other such organizations are Citizen Service Group, Mumbai, Surat Grahak Mandal, Surat, Karnataka Consumers' Service Society, Bengaluru etc. However, measures have yet to be taken to effectively promote consumerism in a big way. There is need for organized efforts on the part of the consumers to make their voice heard and grievances redressed. Consumer organizations can check acts like adulteration, cheating in weights and measures, failure to honour guarantees.

There are often success stories, The Calcutta Consumers Action Forum's success some years ago in persuading makers of baby foods to utilize ideal capacity also in ensuring that wholesome fish is supplied to hospitals – clearly reveals what a pressure group can achieve if the public conscience is aroused and opinion mobilized.

The Consumer Education and Research Centre (CERC) which came into being in 1978 has been bringing relief to hundreds of aggrieved consumers. The CERC, under the leadership of Prof. Manubhai Shah, had taken a variety of individual complaints – rise in the price of milk, a rise in the fare on public transport, rejection of a claim by the LIC, etc. The Centre operates with a high degree of professionalism, skill expertise, patience and even more hard work. During the last five years, the CERC has fought legal battle against giants like the Gujarat Electricity Board, Indian Airlines, Ahmedabad Telephones and Gujarat Government.

Role of Manufacturers

The marketing system in India is subject to a variety of governmental influences. Public policy towards marketing consists of the totality of all governmental influences, ranging from indicative guidelines to direct intervention. Public policy shapes the structure of the marketing system in the long run and guides its functioning in the short run. A systematic view of public policy is also necessary for the policy makers because, after all, they manage the entire marketing system at the macro level.

The present marketing concept calls for a customer orientation backed by integrated marketing aimed at generating consumer satisfaction as the key to attaining long run profitable volume (Patel, 1975). It may be noted that the new social marketing concept does not imply losses to the firms but offers a new opportunity of marketing.

In recent years, the consumrs are attaching importance to the quality and beneficial effects of products they purchase. The manufacturers must recognize the changing psychological orientation of consumers. They should keep the consumers' interest foremost and try to improve upon the manufacturing process by adopting modern technology, introduce new products and strive for zero defects in them, promptly replace defective products, provide satisfactory after-sales service, etc. In fact consumerism not only requires management commitment but also employee-education, social actions and company's investments. The true leaders of Indian Industry are no doubt trying constantly to satisfy the consumer and enhance his total well being for what is good in the long run for consumers is good for business (Dholakia, Bhandari and Khurana, 1976).

Role of the Government In India

When India became Republic, the Constitution of India in particular and other policies in general gave many direction to achieve the socialist pattern of society in India. In other words, along with the policy of giving topmost priority to the Public Sector and to achieve welfare state (through Directive Principles of State Policy), Government of India wanted to achieve higher growth along with social justie. On the other hand, Government did realize that during the development process, the consumer does not suffer and hence did come out with many legislations and laws to protect the public from exploitation.

The Indian Law

In India, we have an array of controls and regulations to protect the consumers from the unscrupulous trade practices. The legislative enactments which provide protection to the consumers in one form or the other and their implementation in the Indian context is elaborated under the heading 'Legal Aspects of Marketing'.

The purpose of this section is to review some of the recent legislations which reflects the growing importance of consumer protection and the considerable latter-day influence of consumerism.

Government regulation thus serves two groups: the consumers and the business competitors. The consumer is served by the efforts of the law to prevent monopoly and, consequently, the higher prices and lower quality that may accompany monopoly. Business firms are served in two ways; market conduct by powerful business rivals which might deprive firms of free access to the market – place is subject to regulatory control, and business competitors are protected from rivals who choose to resort to practices which may deceive consumers. Without regulation against deceptive selling tactics, those competitors who wished to avoid their use might not survive the competition on the basis of their efficiency: to survive, they might be forced to adopt similar tactics. In short, government regulation serves to maintain a healthy competition free of exclusion and deception. Much of the legal control over competition has been sought by business itself.

Development of Consumerism in India – A Comparative Study

In the West, consumerism has emerged after the countries concerned reached a level of affluence which is characteristic of what may be called the post-industrial society. There was adequate production and distribution of essential as well as luxury products. Under these circumstances, the objectives of consumerism were to seek more information about the merits of competing products and services and to represent the collective views of consumers in order to influence the producers.

As a result, the consumer movement in the West has resulted in greather concerns for the claims being made by producers about their sophisticated products and in evaluation of alternative products and services available to the consumer.

In India, the basic reasons for the origin of consumerism have been quite different as compared to the West.

It was the shortage of essential consumer products and the inflation of early 1973-74 that gave a fillip to the consumer movement. It was not because the consumer was confronted with an abundance of products rather than encountered shortage, adulteration and black market prices.

Indian industry by and large has not achieved the level of affluence in technology or advertising to provide the range of alternative products and claims. It has largely been a market of shortages or high prices, although there are exceptions.

The Indian housewife has tended to be a more discriminating customer than her Western counterpart because she has less money for discretionary spending and has more time to compare and decide on her purchases. Therefore, she is not easily taken in by appeals to impulses and desires.

As a result, the thrust of the Consumer Movement in India has been on availability, purity and pricing of essential articles. Since the vast majority of consumers in India have to keep a precarious balance between income and expenditure, the need to protect the interests of the consumer in these directions will assume greater significance.Therefore, consumerism has to be accepted as an enduring phenomenon in our country.

Like other social phenomena, consumerism also will pass through a process of evolution. The first phase in the West was one of protests and investigations. In India too, there has been an element of protest and militancy although not on the same scale as in the West because the origin of consumerism in India has been related to shortages and inflation, and also the Government has been very responsive to consumer needs and have taken legislative action (Thomas, 1977).

Consumer can be called soverign as it is his dollar choice in the market which decides the success or failure of manufacturers. The plight of consumer in a developing country like ours is not that of a sovereign. This may be due to lot of socialistic ideologies, belief, social controls and public sector monopolies. The consumer is just a hapless non-entity ignored by the business class and neglected by the state. The consumer is a pawn in the hands of manufacturers. His dollar vote does not come across in any rational manner to decide who should be producing what. Consequently, the consumer cannot exercise his will and free choice (Poduval, 1981, pp.41-48).

Practices of Developed Countries vs. Less Developed Country such as India

Consumerism in developed countries has received much attention in recent business literature. In these countries, consumers' basic rights such as freedom of choice, to be informed, to be heard, to be safe and to be represented seem to be accepted both by business firms and public policy makers alike. However, very little attention so far, has been paid to consumerism especially among less developed countries like India where consumerism is in an early stage of development.

An interesting comparison between the different characteristics of the macro consumer environment of developed and less developed country, like India has been shown as below:

Consumer-related Factors

India	*Developed Country*
1. Low standards of living	1. High standards of living.
2. Low level of aspiration	2. High level of aspiration.
3. Sellers' market conditions prevail	3. Buyers' market conditions prevail.
4. Low information outreach	4. Actively seek information.
5. Consumers are dominated by decisions of sellers.	5. Consumers make most of the decisions.
6. Lower level of expectations from products.	6. Higher level of expectations from products.

There are also differences in the market system of different countries. Such differences in market characteristics should have significant effect upon the marketing practices of companies. In addition to this, there is also unwillingness on the part of business firms in the way of protecting consumer rights in less developed countries. The single most important characteristic of the typical less developed countries' consumer is that of low purchasing powers.

There is a predominance of fatalism among consumers of less developed countries. In our country, the culture, attitudes, value system and other social characteristics have been slower to change. Social, psychological and cultural changes take longer, than economic changes and require consumers to perceive that their attempts at change will be ultimately successful. The consumer movement is less likely to flourish without generalized consumer beliefs. Consumerism needs sustained public support which is critically lacking in India. In addition to sustained public support, consumerism in less developed countries requires some underlying cultural set and sufficient development in terms of social-economic and cultural variables that make it acceptable to the persons as well as society to become involved in consumer issues. Less developed nations like India by and large tend to be dominated by physiological and safety/security needs, whereas the more advanced countries tend to be dominated by love/ affection and self/esteem needs. This difference in dominance of needs does generate cross-cultural differences in product/ service value. As a result of this, more non-functional values in a product/service will be manifested in those cultures which are dominated by higher order needs, whereas more functional values will be dominant in less developed countries like India (Sheth, 1980, p.11).

The consumer protection measures which have made much progress in developed countries seem less relevant for the present conditions of most of the less-developed countries. In these countries, India being no exception, it seems to be mainly the middle class that get the protection rather than those who are poor, uneducated and live in the villages or in remote areas where there is lack of communication.

Consumers of poor nations like India who mostly attain their psychological and safety needs are dominated by the decisions of the sellers. In the present situation because of lack of education, poor availability of media and scarcity of most consumer goods, Indian consumers do not search out for information. Even if the information is available, due to the low level of education and lack of awareness they would not be able to utilise if profitably to make the comparisons among alternative products and services offered to them.

Summary of Problems Faced by Consumers in India

Comparing India with the developed countries, we find that the problems faced by consumers are entirely different and this is due to the fact that the economy, the consumer profile, their buying behavior, the market structure, in short, almost everything is diametrically opposite. Some of the comparisons are as follows

Developed Countries	*India*
1. Product profile very different. Too many brands available. So, there is a wide range of choice.	1. Product choice is very limited, as brands available are few. The cost pattern is drastically different.
2. Advertising and media are very superior	2. Inferior advertising, not upto the mark.
3. Consumers are very affluent	3. Consumers are not affluent. Inflationary tendencies also affect.
4. Less time to spend on buying	4. Lots of time available to spend on buying.
5. All commodities are plentiful	5. Commodities are scarce, even essential ones.
6. Not much of Government interference or control except for standardization. Government not involved extensively in marketing.	6. Too much of Government control. No proper standardization. Govt. itself a large market.
7. Consumer movement very advanced.	7. Consumer movement restricted to urban areas only.
8. Consumer requirement are very special	8. Only basic needs to be fulfilled. Other requirements are not very special.

On the basis of the foregoing discussion, it can be concluded the current consumer movement in India has grown in importance for various reasons which are as follows:

1. The increased complex and various demands of the consumer.
2. The continuation of unfair, unsafe, and misleading business practices.
3. Poor business practices by the manufacturers/traders
4. Heightened government intervention/regulations.
5. Insensitivity of some business people to consumer need.
6. High inflation rates.
7. Shortages of essential goods and services.
8. Unsatisfactory processing of complaints.
9. Excessive exploitation of consumers by business community.
10. The emergence of consumer groups/voluntary organizations.
11. The desire of many companies to please consumers by understanding and reacting to their wants and behaviour.
12. Demands of citizens for better and quality products and prompt services.

LEGAL ASPECTS OF MARKETING

Indian Legislation

The consumer in India is like a minor – he need special protection. This is not because of a paucity of laws to protect his interests. It is either because he is too shy or because he is unware of them.

Today, a consumer can take shelter under the Law of Torts; the Indian Contract, 1872; the sale of Goods Act, 1930; The Monopolies and Restictive Trade Practices Act,1969; The Bereau of Indian Standards Act, 1986; and The Consumer Protection Act 1986.

Besides the six consumer laws as cited above there are about thirty consumer laws pertaining to every aspects of a consumer's life which can protect him from getting a raw deal.

We shall discuss about these laws in the chronological order in brief while giving special emphasis on Consumer Protection Act 1986.

1. The Law of Torts

As per this law, it is the duty of the manufacturer to take 'reasonable care' that the product sold to a consumer ultimately reaches him in the same form and is free from any defect. It should also not result in an injury to the life and property of the consumer.

The law makes the manufacturer liable for damages especially if the retail dealer did not have an opportunity of inspection and could not have by a simple test ascertained the unsuitability of the good for sale to consumers.

2. The Indian Contract Act, 1972

This Act came into force in 1972. It sowed the seed of consumer protection.

Under this law, if a consumer enters into a contract with the manufacturer or trader, and the contract is breached, the consumer is entitled to be duly compensated for the loss or damage suffered by him in the usual or normal course of things.

But, these contracts should be in writing otherwise it is difficult to prove the exact terms and conditions thereof , subsequently.

3. The Sale of Goods Act, 1930

The Sale of Goods Act, 1930 provides consumer with the rights as a buyer, Section 12 to 18 (both inclusive) are relevant

(i) The Section 12 of the Act, it is mentioned that 'a stipulation in a contract of sale with reference to goods which are the subject thereof may be a condition or a warranty.

(ii) Section 13 explains when a condition is to be treated as a warranty.

(iii) By Section 14 of the Act the consumer is entitled to a good title.

(iv) Section 15 deals with the 'Sale by description'.

(v) According to section 16 of the act, the goods should be of the quality and fitness specified.

(vi) By setion 17 of the Act, the goods should be in accordance with the samples displayed.

(vii) Section 18 of the Act states, 'Where there is a contract for the sale of unascertained gods, no property in the goods is transferred to the buyer unless and until the goods are ascertained'.

Thus, as a result of the above provision in the Sale of Goods Act, 1930, the consumer is entitled to goods in a fit, proper and consumable condition. The Act also provides legal remedy in the case of contract or warranty between the buyer and the seller by way of claiming damages against the defaulting party.

4. Agricutural Product (Grading and Marketing) Act, 1937

This act covers unprocessed and semi processed agricultural products. The certification mark under the Act is popularly known as AGMARK. It is affixed on various agricultural commodities, such as spices, ghee, edible oils, butter, food grains and tobacco. The various commodities are graded on the basis of size, amount of foreign matter, insect infestation and other such parameters as have a bearing on the final quality of the product.

5. Drugs and Cosmetics Act, 1940

Drugs and Cosmetics Act 1940 and rules made thereunder regulates the import, manufacture, sale and distribution of drugs and cosmetics. It has been laid down that no person/firm can stock, sell or distribute drugs without having a proper license by the State Government for the purpose. It is mandatory under the law that every dealer must issue a cash memo for the drug sold to a consumer. Section 26 of the Drugs & Cosmetics Act 1940 has been amended and a recognised consumer association has also been authorized to pick up a sample of drug/cosmetics for the purpose of test and analysis. Any dealer/manufacturer found stocking/manufacturering sub-standard drug will be punished under law.

6. Fruits Product Order, 1946

It provides for compulsory licensing of manufacturers of fruits and vegetables products to ensure minimum standards in respects of quality , packing, labeling, and for sanitey conditions. Production and sale of fruit and vegetable products like jams, jellies, squashes, pickles, processed vegetable and synthetic beverages are covered ender this order. A manufacturing license is a must. The manufacturer has to comply with conditions laid down for labeling, packing, and marking as well as also comply with the hygienic conditions as quality requirements.

7. Prevention of Food Adulteration Act, 1954

This act protects the consumers against adulterated and contaminated food stuff. It makes it a criminal offence to sell any food product which is adulterated or misbranded. Under this Act any article of food is considered adulterated if it turns out different from that which it is declared to be or retains any substance which makes it injurious or is prepared or kept in unhygienic conditions or contains impurities. The Act was amended in 1986 to confer powers to the consumer and registered consumer associations to draw sample of foodstuff for analysis and to send it to public analyst for testing. The Act provides for stringent penalties.

8. The Drugs and Magic Remedies (Objectionable Advertisement) Act, 1954

The Act prohibits misleading advertisements relating to drugs, advertisements of drug alleged to posses magic qualities and remedies for treatment of certain scheduled diseases and disorders. Section 7 of this Act provides that whoever contravenes any of the provision of this Act or rules made thereunder shall on conviction be punishable with imprisonment which may extend to six months or with fine or with both. In case of subsequent offence, with imprisonment of one year or fine or both,

9. The Essential Commodities Act, 1955

Under the provisions of this Act the Central/State Government have been empowered to regulate the production, supply, distribution and pricing of essential commodities through promulgation of various control orders issued under Section 3 of this Act. It provides for stringent punishment including imprisonment and fine of any person who contravenes or abets contravention of any provision of any control order issued under the E.C Act, this Act was amended in 1986 to give a consumer or a recognized consumer association the right to lodge such a complaint in the court directly.

10. The Trade and Merchandise Mark Act, 1958

The Trade and Merchandise Marks Act,1958 provides for the registration of trademarks and prevents the use of frauldulent marks on merchandise. The act provides penalty for applying false trademarks and trade descriptions. Such punishment includes imprisonment for a term which may extend to two years or fine or with both.

11. The Monopolies and Restrictive Trade Practices Act, 1969

The MRTP Commission has been set up under this Act to prevent any company to indulge in any monopolistic, restrictive or unfair trade practices. By an amendment in 1986 the Commission has been empowered to enquire into any restrictive or unfair trade practice upon receiving a complaint from any trade association, or from any consumer, or a registered consumer association. Based on the recommendations of the Sachart Committee, the MRTP (Amendment) Act 1984 was passed in My 1984 and its new provisions provide for the regulation of the unfair trade practice.

When the Monopolies and Restrictive Trade Practices Act, 1969 was amended in 1984, on the recommendations of the sachar Committee, provisions in favour of consumer interest and relating to 'unfair trade practices' were incorporated in it.

12. The Water (Prevention and Control of Pollution) Act, 1974

This Act prohibits or restricts the discharge of industrial wastes in rivers , streams, and wells, thus preventing and controlling water pollution there by maintaining the purity of wate. Both fine and imprisonment have been provided for under this Act.

13.

A. The Standards of Weights and Measures Act, 1976

The Standards of Weights & Measures Act,1976 was enacted to standardise the numerous kinds of weights and measures which are used in trade and commerce. It prohibits manufacture of non standard weights and measures, storage and use of non standard weights and measures and counterfeiting of seals. It provides for penalties which include imprisonment and fine for contravention of the provisions of this Act. For uniform enforcement of this Act, Standard of Weights and Measure (Enforcement) Act 1985, was passed by the Parliament.

It provides for more effective protection to consumers and covers all instruments used in commercial transaction, industrial production and instruments used for human health and safety. The Act contains deterrent provisions for the offenders particularly for those indulging in under weighment.

B. The Standards of Weights and Measures (Packaged Commodities) Rules, 1977

The Standards of Weights & Measures (packaged commodities) Rules, 1977 have been framed under this Act which make it mandatory that all packages intended for retail sale shall have the same name and address of the manufacturers/packer, the name of the commodity packed, the net weight or measure of the commodity, the month and year of packing written.

14. The Air (Prevention and Control of Pollution) Act 1981

The above act provides for the prevention and control and abatement of air pollution. In case of contravention of any of the provisions of the Act, punishment and fine is also provided.

15. Household Electrical Appliances Quality Control Order 1981 and 1988:

The Household Electric Appliances Quality Control Order 1981, promulgated under Section 3 of the Essential Commodities Act, 1955, prohibits the manufacturing, sale and storage for sale of 40 household electrical appliances (like rubber insulated cables, electric shaver, hot plates, toaster, kettles and jugs, thermostat for the use of water heaters etc.) not conforming to prescribed standards of such appliances prescribed by the Bureau of Indian Standards.

Forther, the Household Electrical Appliances Quality Control Act, 1988 provides for compulsory certification of seven of these household electrical appliances namely electric iron, water heater, radiator, stove, switches, three pin plug and sockets. This order safeguards the right to safety of the consumer covered in the Consumer Protection Act 1986.

16. The Bureau of Indian Standards Act, 1986

The Bureau of Indian Standards Act, 1986 was passed by the Parliament to replace the Indian Standards Institutions Certification Marks Act, 1957. a Bureau of Indian Standards has been established under this act for standardization, marking and quality certification of goods. The Bureau operates a Certification Marks Scheme under the provisions of this Act to certify the products conforming to the relevant standards set by the Bureau of Indian Standards. The Act prohibits the improper use of standard marks.

The Bureau of Indian Standards Certification Marks Scheme has been mandatory for a number of products involving hazards to health and safety of life. These include vanaspati, food additives, cement, LPG cylinders, oil pressure stoves and appliances used in mines and other hazardour areas.

17. The Environment Protection Act, 1986

The lacunaes and procedural difficulties involved in implementing the various Central and State Antipollution laws have led to the enactment by Central Government of the comprehensive environment Protection Act in 1986. This act has some outstanding features. Two of these are listed below:

1. If a public complaint is made to the Government about a particular problem, the Central Government or any authority or officer authorized on this behalf by that Government has to take immediate action in this matter. If no action is taken within 60 days, the complaint can go to court both against the pollutant and the concerned Government.
2. If any solid, liquid or gaseous substance is present in certain concentration which injures the environment, penalty is quite stringent. The first offence leads to an imprisonment of five years or a fine of one lakh rupees or both. If the contravention still continues one year after the date of conviction, additional fine of rupees five thousand for every day and a maximum imprisonment of upto seven years is laid down in the Act.

18. The Consumer Protection Act, 1986

A. Objectives of the Act

The Consumer Protection Act, 1986 (68 of 1986) is a milestone in the history of socio-economic legislation in the country. It is one of the most progressive and comprehensive pieces of legislation enacted for the protection of consumers. The law has been enacted after indepth study of consumer protection laws and arrangements in the U.K, U.S.A, Australia and New Zealand. Before its formulation, consultations with the representatives of consumers, trade and industry were held. Various ideas and suggestions were also considered in a number of ministerial meetings within the Government.

The main objective of this new law is to provide for the better protection of the consumers. The Act enshrines certain rights of the consumers and provides for the setting up of Consumers Protection Councils in the Centre and the States. The objectives of these consumer councils will be to promote the rights of the consumers.

B. Extent and Coverage of the Act

(i) The Act applies to all goods and services unless specifically exempted by the Central Government.

(ii) It covers all the sectors whether private, public or corporate.

(iii) The provisions of the Act are compensatory.

(iv) It enshrines the following rights of the consumers:

(a) The right to be protected against the marketing of goods which are hazardous to life and property.

(b) The right to be informed about the quality, quantity, potency, purity, standard and price of goods so as to protect the consumer against unfair trade practices.

(c) The right to be assured of access to a variety of goods at a competitive prices.

(d) The right to be heard and to be assured that consumers interest will receive due consideration at appropriate forums.

(e) The right to seek reddressal against unfair trade practices or unscrupulous exploitation of consumers.

(f) The right to consumer education.

(v) The Act envisages establishment of consumer protection council at the Central and State levels whose main object will be to promote and protect the rights of the consumers.

(vi) To provide simple, speedy, and inexpensive redressal of consumer grievances, the Act envisages a three tier quasi judicial machinery at the national, state and district levels. At the national level, there will be a National Consumer Dispute Redressal Commission (to be known as the 'National Commission'). At the State levels there will be Consumer Disputes Redressal Commission (to known as State Commission) and at the District Level there will be the District Forums.

(vii) The provisions of this Act are in addition to and not in derogation of the provisions of any other law for the time being in force.

19. The Railway Claims Tribunal Act, 1987

This Act provides for the establishment of Railway Claims Tribunal. The Tribunal has been setup for ' inquiring into and determining claims against a railway administration for loss, destruction, damage, deterioration or non delivery of animals or goods entrusted to it, to be carried by rail or for the refund of fares or freight or for compensation for death or injury to passengers occurring as a result of railway accidents and for matters connected therewith or incidental thereto'.

20. The Textiles (Consumer Protection) Regulation, 1988

According to a notification, effective form 15th June 1988, issued by the Textile Commissioner, Ministry of Textiles (Consumer Protection) Regulation, 1988, shall be therewith reference to standards perscribed by the Bureau of Indian Standards. The above regulations deals with the marking of tops, yarns and pieces of cloths to be compiled with by the manufacturer including the person who gets them manufactured.

Other Indian Laws & Legislations in the Consumer interests are namely:

1. The Indian Penal Code Act, 1860.
2. The Emblems and Names (Prevention of Improper Use) Act, 1950.
3. The Forward Contract Regulation Act, 1956.
4. The Motors Cars (Distribution and Sales) Control Order, 1959
5. The Essential Services Maintenance Act, 1968.
6. The Maharashtra Schedules Articles Order 1969.
7. The Kerosene (Fixation of Ceiling Prices) Order, 1970
8. The Defence and Internal Security Act, 1971.
9. The Higher Purchase Act, 1972.
10. The Consumer Prduct Safety Act, 1972.
11. The Vegetable Oil Products (Standard of Quality) Order, 1972.
12. The Display of Prices Order, 1973.

13. The Fertilizer (Movement Control) Order, 1973
14. The Vegetable Oil Product Producers (Regulation of Refined Oil Manufacturer) Order, 1973
15. The Supply of Goods (Implied Term) Act, 1973.
16. The Wheat (Price Control) Act, 1974.
17. The Cigarette (Regulation and Registration of Products) Supply and Distribution Act , 1975.
18. The Paper (Production and Regulation) Control Order, 1979.
19. The Prevention of Black Marketing and Maintenance of Supplies of Essential Commodities Act, 1980.

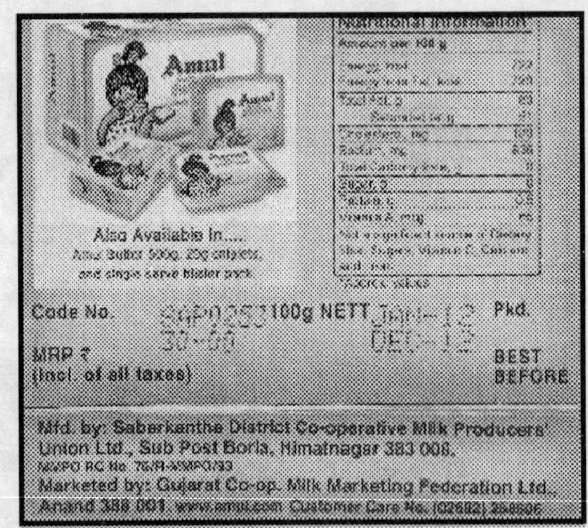

ALWAYS CHECK
MRP - DATE OF PACKAGING - WEIGHT. ETC.
THIS IS A SAMPLE ONLY

— ✦ — ✦ — ✦ —

Chapter 3

Review of Literature

In this chapter, we shall touch upon various studies connected with consumerism and consumer protection. We shall discuss the research reports and surveys that have been conducted in various countries including India. The development that took place in the marketing world for the welfare of the consumers are narrated in the chronological order.

In India, from research viewpoint, Consumerism is an area which is quite new and unexplored. There is hardly any empirical study available that deals exclusively with consumerism. So, in reviewing the literature, the interest is focused on studies conducted in India and abroad, dealing not only empirical investigations but also on such theoretical studies which offer relevant findings to generate some understanding of analogous nature.

Keith (1960, pp.35-38) opines that the centre of all business activity orientation should be the consumer or customer. If other companies experience the marketing revolution as did Pillsbury company of U.S.A they will move through perhaps for eras: (a) production (b) sales (c) marketing and (d) marketing control. In the last era of the revolution marketing will become the basic motivating force for the entire corporation until every activity is aimed at satisfying the needs and desires of the consumer.

E.A. Clasen, Vice President of the Pillsbury Company (USA) commented:

"I truly believe that the actions taken within the Pillsbury Company, as well as the leadership shown on the National Business Council for Consumer Affairs in USA, are consistent with the philosophies and thoughts expressed by Mr. Keith as early as 1960."

In effect he believed that (1) if a policy be clearly stated, (2) a procedure could be put into effect that would be understood and endorsed by operating units within a company, and (3) a monitoring system could be established that left no doubt, but that the top management was involved would develop the finest form of self-regulation. This system sould not only be in tune with the increasing level of consumer expectations, but would assure a highly competitive approach under the free enterprise system.

The most common understanding of 'Consumerism' is in reference in the activities designed to protect individuals from practices that infringe upon their rights as consumers.

Day and Akker (1970, pp.12-19) feel that the scope of consumerism will probably eventually subsume or be subsumed by two other areas of social concern. (A) Distortions and inequities in the economic environment have been a concern since the end of the 19th century. (B) The declining quality of the physical environment is a recent concern. They are of the opinion that there are a number of underlying reasons for upsurge in consumerism. Also a number of causes are associated with the discontented consumer.

1. Problems of the market place, such as proliferation of products, make it impossible for the consumer to have all the information he needs to make a useful price and quality comparison.

2. Changes in the social fabric, such as the new visibility of the low income consumer as a dissatisfaction with the impersonalisation of society, have been a catalyst for consumerism.
3. The consumer has found more effective ways to express feelings and press for change than ever before.
4. The Legal and Political structure has been much more willing to take action than ever before.

The writers are optimistic that consumerism activity is not likely to decline significantly in the future; therefore, effective programmes to protect the rights of the consumer should be developed using information gained from planned research.

Buskirk and Rothe (1970, pp.61-65) discussed certain implications of the consumer movement for corporate policy and made definite recommendations on what corporations should do in the current situation.

The guidelines for the Corporate Policy as suggested by them are:

1. Establish a separate corporate division for consumer affairs.
2. Change corporate practices that are perceived as deceptive.
3. Educate channel members to the need for a consumerism effort throughout the channel system.
4. Incorporate the increased costs of consumerism efforts into the corporate operating budget.

An analysis of the above guidelines by the authors suggests that an effective consumerism programme will be directed primarily at the communication problem between forms and consumers. The main purpose of the consumerism programme will be to enhance the quality of communications between the consumer and the firm and to incorporate valid complaints into corporate decisions.

Kotler (972, pp.48-57) argued that consumerism is inevitable, enduring, beneficial promarketing and profitable. This is quite contrary to the intuitive assessment of the businessman. After discussing his own assessment the author advances a new concept of social marketing to replace the time honored marketing concept.

The writer states that ***"Consumerism mobilizes the energies of consumers, businessman and government leaders to seek solution to several complex problems in a technologically advanced society. One of these is the difference between the serving consumer desires efficiently and serving their long run interests."***

To the marketers, the author says that products and marketing practices must be found which combine short run and long run values for the consumer. He says that a societal marketing concept is an advance over the original marketing concept and a basis for earning increased consumer goodwill and profits. The enlightened marketer attempts to satisfy the consumer and enhance his social well being on the theory that what is good in the long run for consumers is good for business.

An explanatory study conducted by Barksdale and Darden (1972, pp. 28-35) reports the reactions of a national sample of consumers to these issues.

The information supplied by the cross section of consumers in the study suggested several broad conclusions:-

1. Most consumers recognize and value highly particular aspects of the free enterprise system, such as price paid, efforts to fit products to consumer needs, variety of products offered and convenient availability of products.
2. Many consumers register a high level of apprehension about certain business policies and considerable discontent about specific marketing activities. The most obvious example is the lack of confidence in advertising.
3. Many respondents conceded that some of the imperfections in the operations of the marketing system result from the ineptness, carelessness and apathy of consumers.
4. In general, respondents thought that consumer problems are important and deserve more attention than they now receive. This attitude may help explain the impatience reflected in the opinions expressed about certain business practices.
5. Respondents' overwhelming support for additional government regulations as a means of solving consumer problems.

Business leaders may have definite reasons for opposing protective legislation for consumers, but apparently the buying public does not agree. Business appears to be facing the choice of voluntary or legislative control.

The authors are of the opinion that business must educate the public about the operation of the marketing system, the benefits of free enterprise, and the limitations of government. Business must also re-examine and modify its policies and practices to improve products and services offered to consumers. The consumer movement has emphasized the responsibility of consumers to complain when justified. This situation has created a responsibility for business to increase the attention given to consumers and to initiate programs that will improve customer relations. If businessman do not voluntarily respond to consumer problems and complaints, they may be faced with further government control through legislation.

Greenland (1974, pp.4-6) stated that the food marketer was currently under attack by individuals consumers, civic groups, government agencies, legislatures, politicians, labour unions and the mass media. He was surrounded by consumerist overkill and things were to get worse. In order to defend himself, he should rely on such tools as courageous management. Forthight media relations and honest advertising and sound marketing principles in the first place. Greenland pointed out wisely that the problems was not consumerism but policies of consumerism.

The writer states that ***"the first and foremost step in regaining credibility with the public is to back up product claims with facts about performance".***

Greyser and Diamond (1974) studied the attitudes and reactions of the executive community regarding consumerism. The respondents came from a variety of industries, company sizes, functional areas and levels of management. A survey of 3418 managers indicated that they saw consumerism as permanent, and were optimistic about its effect on the marketplace to boot.

The major findings of the study are as follows:-

1. Consumerism is here to stay is the overwhelming executive consensus. The combination of consumer concern over rising prices and over the problems of the products, performance and quality are viewed as the chief reasons for consumerism's growth.
2. The traditional buyer beware philosophy of the market place is seen as fast eroding. Executive think the balance between buyer beware and seller is still tilted toward the former, but pendulum is swinging swiftly towards seller beware.
3. Despite their problems, consumers are still seen as being able to make sensible buying decisions. Although many respondents think that marketers sometimes manipulate consumers into unwanted purchases, executives strongly contend that consumers still hold the ultimate weapon of not buying products.
4. Businessman support propositions to make advertising more factual and informative. They see consumerism as leading to major modifications in advertising content that will make it more truthful.
5. Business is considered primarily responsible for both causing consumer problems and resolving them. Business self regulation is still the most favoured route.
6. Improving product quality and performance is viewed as the most constructive consumer–oriented program that companies can undertake.
7. While much progress has been made in the past decade on key consumer related issues, even further progress is foreseen in decades ahead. Increased sensitivity to consumer problem has shown the most progress; quality of repair and maintenance services has furthest to go.
8. Consumerism can be positive competitive marketing tool and opportunity for business. Executives also generally think consumerism is both good for business and for the consumer.

How do consumers perceive consumerism… and what are the implications of these perceptions for marketing managers has been discussed by Kangun, Cox Higginbotham and Burton (1975, pp. 3-10).

Their study indicated that:-

1. consumerism, like marketing, is perceived to encompass a wide variety of issues and is broadening its domain;
2. consumers perceive the specific consumerism issues to be important ; and
3. consumerism is here to stay and grow in strength in future.

For many marketing managers, *caveat emptor* is an inappropriate philosophy today. Bcause the pressures to attend to consumer problems are likely to remain, the obligations of marketers particularly consumer goods marketers, will change drastically. Further it behoves marketing managers to be sensitive to the demands of consumers since marketing is an interface between the company and its external environment. Two frameworks for evaluating possible alternative courses of action for marketing are

1. company action, and
2. industry wide action.

The authors strongly feel that the question for business is not whether to undertake efforts to identify and correct consumer problem but how to make such efforts effective, particularly if firms are to survive the joint pressure exerted by consumerists and government. Consumer education, the establishment of product standards in terms of quality, and the development of programs for handling consumer complaints are all areas where industry wide efforts may be productive.

Again consumerism issues for which broad consensus does not exist and the costs would be high are not likely to addressed voluntarily by a business firm. The pollution issues appears to be an area where government action may necessary and desirable.

Barksdale and French (1975, pp.55-67) opined that Marketing Managers nad Consumer Advocates did not see any conflict between objectives of consumerism and goals of marketing management. Other studies indicated that the consumer movement was viewed as a positive force which had performed a valuable service for both business and public. The changes fostered by consumerism had touched all aspects of marketing except physical distribution. This did not mean that improvements had met expectations of consumer activities or eliminated the call for additional changes. The thrust of consumerism had gone beyond exposure of abusive practices to more or less organized efforts aimed at presenting the consumer's view to legislative bodies, regulatory agencies, and courts of law. More important, consumerists had been successful in convincing government to act upon their proposal.

Blood (1976, pp.6) has the feeling that UK marketers had learned that consumerism represents both a challenge and an opportunity for alert and intelligent entrepreneurs. Experience had shown that serious consumer organizations were quite willing to discuss their problems rationally and that they welcomed meeting business representatives who could offer sincere and constructive proposals. Consumers seems to be beginning to rease the importance of marketing in the business world of today.

Zahn (1977, pp.24) pointed out that European Economic Community (EEC) had begun a new role as an advocate of the European customs. A primary move in this direction was the adaptation of several directives regarding colorants in food stuffs. And a directive concerning the use of anti fungicides in citrus fruits. The organization's most recent concern had been with maximum levels of erucic acid in oils and greases in human foodstuffs. It was expected that the EEC eventually expand into all marketing areas. Action was now planned in the areas of consumer credit practices, door to doot sales, distribution practices, licensing and trade names. The purpose of these efforts was to create a truly common market for more European products.

A survey conducted by Andreasen and Best (1977, pp.99-104) disclosed much dissatisfaction among purchasers of goods and services and mediocre work by business in handling their complaints.

A telephone interview survey of some 2,400 metropolitan household regarding their attitude towards 26 products and 8 service categories, ranging from air conditioners to mail order merchandises to medical and dental cases, revealed that:

1. The reduction of consumers' complaints was sufficiently important to continued market success to warrant the formation of a top level complaint review committee, including senior marketing, production accounting, and service personnel made responsible (and given authority) for improving performance. This committee they believed, could significantly improve coordination while lodging responsibility with those word carried the most weight.
2. In as much as half the serious complaints were never mentioned to business, the obvious solution was to market the complaint handling system to customers. Business would encourage customers to speak out when things go wrong and make it more convenient for them to do so. Through advertising, point of sale promotion and product inserts business could tell customers that it wanted to know when things went wrong.
3. Another, avenue for improving complaint performance was in dealing with the complaints received. Careful, speedy process to handle letters, telephone calls and even visits could improve consumers' satisfaction. Many complaint managers believe that the faster a communication was handled the more satisfied the customer is, whatever the problem or the outcome is.
4. To gain full value from the voice of the customers, the company should want to hear from him and should believe that he was right until otherwise proved.
5. The positive attitude should first be adopted at the top because the staff would act only when it believed that the top management was fully committed. It was a commitment they believe management ahould adopt if it was to maximize its success in the increasingly " consumerist" business environment of the future.

Jacob (1977) pointed out that quality goods and services and a clean environment were a necessity for consumer health and safety. No doubt, the promotion of quality was the duty of not only the government and the producers but also of the consumers themselves. However, the Indian consumer today was more or less unware of this pivotal role he should play in the promotion of quality. Little did he realize that his voice, his intelligence and information on consumer goods and his choices count and that these could be a decisive factor in the planning, production, and distribution of goods and services.

A study conducted by Greyser (1977/78, pp.28-34) had shown that the consumerism phenomenon had become a permanent fixture in the American marketplace. Generally those surveyed felt that the consumer movement was moving ahead and the majority was optimistic about its accomplishment so far. They were still very displeased with the treatment of consumers and felt that product quality was getting worse. Improvements were seen in safety and labeling, and they did express optimism for future progress in all areas. The majority of respondents were in favour of a consumer protection agency and did not feel that business could effectively regulate themselves. In listing areas that concern consumers the most, high prices were cited most often. Attitudes on consumerism were varied among leadership groups with business managers on one side and consumer activists on the other. The general public's thinking was somewhere near the middle but did lean toward the consumer activist.

Jones (1978, pp.16-19) opined that consumer leaders needed to be able to negotiate with business on the services to be supplied to consumers. Business should deal with these leaders as equals in order to keep them from turning to government mandates and to courts for legal decisions. The tensions between the consumer interests and the goals of enterprise are health. They might force business to eliminate those practices that are not worth the consumer dissatisfaction they may endanger. The consumer movement should help business planners to evaluate past performance and to prevent costly mistakes in judgement as to what consumers are likely to accept, demand, tolerate or oppose.

Nicholas (1978, pp8-9), President and Chairman of the Beech Nut Food Corp., pointed out that if a consumer could be persuaded to use one of the products, other products should be developed to be used in subsequent period. He went on to warn never to underestimate the intimate knowledge that consumer groups had of the negative aspects, of the products or the lack of knowledge they had about the positive aspect of the product. Oher things to remember were:

1. Realise that if a product is changed so that it is inconsistent with the way the consumer believes it to be, it can put the company out of business.
2. Do not put ingredients about which consumer activists are complaining.
3. Be innovative in the product market.

Foxall (1978, pp.264-274) assessed that consumerism had been welcomed not only by consumers, journalists and educators but even by businessmen. Consumerism could generate additional costs through funds required of taxpayers, through firms being required to produce more reliable products, through firms being man hours of work to deal with inaccurate and wasteful complaints and through the retarding of manufacturing processes and marketing programs which reflected the notion that governments, managers, and consumers must be prepared to pay indiscriminately for what ever program and measures consumerists decide were necessary to protect buyer. The author pointed out that if consumer protection officials were not properly trained and they lack knowledge of the consumer, they could misappropriate public funds and increase business costs and buyers, prices.

Straver (1978, pp.316-325) believed that the consumer movement was here to stay. Increased government regulation would occur and marketing managers would have increased opportunity to respond to the consumerist phenomena. In a recent study of how consumers perceived consumerism, it was found that women felt more strongly about the inclusion of pricing under consumerism than did student who wished to include pollution under consumerism. Consumer representation in government did not get the level of support that consumer unions sometimes claim for their cause. Business had responded to the consumer movement in a variety of ways some companies had taken action on particular issue and others had tried to ignore the existence of the consumer problem. For the consumer movement to be effective, it should realize that unreasonable aggressiveness could harm the entire movement.

Barnhill, Barksdale and Perreault (1981, pp.59-80) conducted a survey to compare the attitudes of American and Canadian consumers' towards consumerism. A random sample of 365 consumers was drawn. Results indicate that American and Canadian consumers have a highly skeptical attitude towards business philosophy, marketing practices, consumerism and government. Both American and Canadian consumers believed they were being exploited. Consumers of both nations indicated that government should (1) set minimum product standards, (2) conduct publicly reports brand tests, and (3) increase regulation of advertising, sales, and marketing activities. Canadians appear to feel that government could provide the means to rectify exploitation.

Mc Daniel (1981, pp.14-18) attempted a study to determine (1) the seriousness of the problem of marketing malpractice, (2) the perceptions of consumers as to their protection from such malpractices, (3) the need perceived by the consumers for stronger protection measures and (4) the type of consumer most dissatisfied with marketing malpractices. The study was conducted in southwestern metropolitan area. Serious problems viewed by the consumers studied included:

1. deceptive advertising and pricing
2. deceptive practices by repair personnel
3. misleading warranties
4. poor or unsafe product performance
5. indifference to consumer complaints
6. lack of support for a product or its claims, and
7. deceptive credit practices by retailers.

The proposed solution, according to consumers, was stronger consumer protection effects. Another alternative was to create a 'marketing quality control department', in each firm at the corporate levels and at various sub levels in the marketing channel.

Resnik and Harmon (1983, pp.86-97) examined manager and consumer perceptions of appropriate responses to complaints letters. The responses were analyzed separately and then compared to determine how effectively the managers could deal with consumer requirements. Insights are provided into how to deal more expeditiously and judiciously with complaints.

Customers satisfaction was found to be the primary response objective for managers. Correspondingly they felt that consumers would be satisfied with the responses they were prepared to give. In order to achieve this satisfaction, managers appears willing to go beyond consumer expectation in resolving the complaint. Managers' personal contact rather than that the contact by letter that consumer expected.

In the opinion of the authors, the managers in the study were doing a good job identifying appropriate responses and tended to behave in a manner that accommodated consumer satisfaction as their primary objective.

Gupta (1986, pp.149-158) pointed out the implications of the rising consumer awareness for manager for the policy makers and for the consumers themselves.

She feels that imposing rules and regulations from above is likely to have little effect, if consumers themselves do not believe in the utility of these regulations. Thus, education and awareness must accompany and process of making regulations and legislations. In fact, consumer education and dissemination of information should form part of any policy to help the consumer.

The author is of the opinion that business, consumers and government live on each other, live off each other and because of each other. Producers and the government are merely a means to consumer satisfaction. Therefore, in any development process it is important that both consumers and producers must work together in the attainment of their goals.

In an opinion survey conducted in Australia by Trade Practices Commission (1987), it was found that, whilst there was a high degree of general satisfaction among consumers about the goods and services they buy, there was nevertheless a quite strong feeling among a broad cross section of the community that suppliers of goods and services (including government services) should work harder to give better value for money, more particularly by general improvement in the quality of goods with better 'in store' attention to customers and better after sale service. Almost all the consumers surveyed reported some awareness of consumer affairs agencies with over half indicating that they would approach their local agency for advice or assistance concerning a consumer problem.

Nicoulaud (1987, pp.7-16) made an attempt to study consumerism issues and marketing manager's responsibility toward the enhancement of consumer's rights. A random sample of 85 companies in the food and electrical appliances industry in France, Denmark and the UK was taken. Product quality enhancement and more and improved information were seen as two main consumer issues of the late 1980. The managers responses included that:

1. business should be given the responsibility for providing adequate information to aid consumers in making buying decisions.
2. government should be given the responsibility to protect consumers from their own buying mistakes and
3. consumers themselves should take the responsibility for protecting themselves from their own views about buying decisions.

Firms in Europe have implemented various consumer affairs programmes in response to consumerism and have perceived the most constructive to be:

1. Upgrading quality.
2. Conducting more consumer research.
3. Marking post sales calls on consumers and
4. Supporting industry self regulation.

Singh (1989, pp. 91-105) conducted a survey regarding Food Adulteration in the state of Jammu and Kashmir. The study had revealed that people were generally aware of the incidence of food adulteration, which was largely an extension of the present socio economic cum political atmosphere generated by the changing value system of the society, and knew that dealing in adulterated food articles constituted to be an offence under the law.

The consumers belonging to lower socio economic groups found it difficult to get genuine food articles despite their best efforts. The main reason for the poor rate of initiation of prosecutions was the ignorance of consumers if the remedies provided by the law, on the one hand and the pick and choose method adopted by the Food Inspector on the other.

Recently, Singh (1990 pp.8-11) in an explanatory study conducted on a sample of 105 respondents living in the metropolitan city of Delhi has examined that consumer attitudes towards various business marketing activities and their views on the role played by manufacturers and government in protecting the interest of consumers. From the response of consumers, he has observed that general dissatisfaction prevails among consumers regarding their rights and interests and there is great deal of resentment against manufacturers and government. Most of the consumers feel that the basic object of the manufacturers should be customer satisfaction, that the manufacturers should not give false and exaggerated information about any product in advertisements, that they should exercise greater responsibility to protect environment and consumer health and safety even if such measures increased prices of products. Similarly, majority are of the opinion that government should exercise more responsibility relating to various marketing activities of manufacturers such as advertising, product quality, sales, pricing, etc. In a later study which is also of exploratory nature Singh (1990, pp. 146-152) has examined the perception of consumers as to what issues should be considered as part of consumerism. The study was based on opinions of 100 consumers sampled conveniently from the city of Amritsar. The sample was composed of 40 servicemen, 30 businessmen and 30 housewives. The result of the analysis show that despite minor differences of opinion among various occupational groups in certain issues, consumerism is generally considered to include issues such as health and safety, pricing, product quality, repair and servicing, environmental pollution, truth in advertising and correct weights and measures. However, majority of consumers are ignorant about consumer movement. Thus it is the imperative need of the hour to create awareness about consumerism and according to opinion of consumers this can be achieved through mass media, efforts of voluntary organizations and government.

Recently Mehta (1992,pp.20) has observed that while the consumers in India has not become 'King' as a result of Consumer Protection Act,1986 (COPRA) which is a landmark in protecting Indian consumers' rights., he is certainly not without remedy. Although Indian consumers is yet not fully conscious of his rights and obligations, he is not totally oblivious of the same.

Mehta has also pointed out that despite small but significant gains achieved under COPRA, this Act has not been properly implemented due to lack of interest of the State Government, paucity of funds, non availability of right personnel to man the consumer bodies, lack of accommodation and dilatory procedure requiring State Government to obtain sanction from the Centre or from the high court. Further, he feels that COPRA needs improvement in many areas. The National Commission , State Commission and District Forums should have the powers for initiating *suo motu* proceedings in public interest. Such power could also be given to registered consumer organizations. Thus growing interest of Indian Consumers about their rights and proper implementation of modified COPRA should go a long way in boosting the consumer movement in India.

The above review of literature has shown that studies regarding Consumerism and Consumer Protection have mostly been carried out abroad. In India very few people have attempted to explore this field. No worth while empirical studies was thus felt. Accordingly, the present study was undertaken with a view to bring out the state of art in our consumer protection movement, suggest remedial measures and also set a trend for future research work in this direction.

Pallavi Purkayastha, who was murdered by a guard in her Mumbai apartment last Thursday

—✦—✦—✦—

Chapter 4

Research Methodology

The present study is an attempt to examine the consumerism and consumer protection in India. For this the following three categories of population have been considered:

1. Consumers
2. Companies
3. Voluntary Organisations

Separate opinion surveys have been conducted for each of these categories. Questionnaires have been developed and presented on few respondents. Pre testing has helped in making improvements in the questionnaires. The revised questionnaires have since been used in collecting the necessary information. The methodologies adopted for these surveys have been discussed below:

A. CONSUMERS OPINION SURVEY

Universe

The universe of the study consists of the consumers living in the metropolitan city of Delhi. The population essentially consists of government employees, other married people, commercial business communities, traders, industrialists, small scale entrepreneurs and other various income groups having different educational background. Being a cosmopolitan city, it consists of people from various religions having different background, different culture, speaking different languages and belonging to various states of India. Thus conclusion drawn from any such survey carried out on Delhi population will more or less reflect All India Phenomena.

Sample and Sampling Design

The domain of the survey has been restricted to Delhi Metropolitan city. Selection of individuals was made on the basis of information obtained from the office of Chief Electoral Officer, Delhi. For the purpose of General Election, 1989, Delhi, was divided in seven parliamentary constituencies. The required information relate to number of polling stations in each parliamentary constituency, the number and list of voters under eah polling station. For our study we have considered areas pertaining to only six constituencies. Viz., New Delhi, South Delhi, East Delhi, Karol Bagh, Chandni Chowk and Delhi Sadarand excluded areas falling under outer Delhi parliamentary constituency.

A satisfied two stage sampling design has been adopted to select 600 individuals for the purpose of the survey. The six parliamentary constituencies have been to for six strata. The polling station comprise the first state units where as individuals the second stage units. For carrying out the sampling in two stages, in all 50 polling stations have been selected at a random out of total 4664 in the first stage. The number of polling stations to be selected from each stratum has been fixed in proportion to the number available in each of these and varies between 5 (Karol Bagh, Chandni Chowk and New Delhi) to 18 (East Delhi).

In the second stage, within each of the fifty selected polling stations the number of respondents sampled are in proportion to the number of voter available in each of them, in fact for any polling station the number of voter to selected equals to

$$600 \times \frac{\text{Number of voters available in that polling station}}{\text{Total number of voters in all the fifty polling station}}$$

The selection of sample units for both the stages has been with equal probability with the help of random number tables. In this way, a fairly representative of 600 individuals was obtained. In this connection it may be further mentioned that use of satisfied random sampling was made only to ensure representation of different types of people and not with the intention of giving the results for each stratum

Data Collection

As stated earlier, data were collected by interviewing the selected respondents with the help of pre tested questionnaire. The questionnaires was of structured and not a non disguised type. To develop the list of information item for framing the questionnaire we reviewed the existing literature on marketing, consumerism and consumer protection, also consulted various personalities in the areas of marketing and consumer protection. The preliminary draft of the questionnaire was pre tested on 25 households/individuals. This helped in improving upon the questionnaire and also gave an indication as to the kind response that will be forthcoming. With a few deletions, additions and alterations the final questionnaire was developed which has been in Appendix –I.

Data Analysis

There may be a number of variables which can effect the consumerism and consumer protection. However, for the present study we have considered only one variable, *viz.*, education. Four educational categories have been considered here, they are:

1. Upto Matric E1
2. Graduates E2
3. Post Graduates E3, and
4. Professionally Qualified E4

The responses of the individuals have been given in all the tables in terms of both the numbers and percentages. Figures in tables within parenthesis represent percentages while those without parenthesis are simple frequencies.

The weighted average scores were calculated at appropriate places where the respondents were asked to rank, rate different statements, either according to degree of their importance or according to the extent they agree with the statements as to the extent they agree with the statements as the case may be. Five types of responses were envisaged to denote the degree of importance/degree of agreement, *viz.*,

(i) Most important/strongly agree.
(ii) Important/agree
(iii) Neither important nor unimportant/neither agree nor disagree
(iv) Unimportant/disagree and
(v) Most unimportant/strongly disagree.

These being quantitative in nature, a scoring system was adopted to quantity them. Scores of 2, 1, 0, –1, –2 were allotted to (i) to (iv) respectively.

The weighted average scores $\overline{W}$ is given by

$$\overline{W} = \frac{1}{\Sigma f_w} \qquad \Sigma_{W=-2}^{2} Wf_w$$

Where W is the weight/score given to the type of response and f_w is the number of respondents for the type of response for which the weight/score w is given. Such weighted average scores have been calculated separately for Σj (j=1,…,4) and total for different statements.

Statistical Techniques

Appropriate non parametric statistical tests based on Chi-square (Wright, 1976) and Kendall's Coefficient of Concordance (Siegal, 1956)) have been used to test the various null hypothesis regarding consumer's opinion on a number of statements relating to consumerism and consumer protection. These have helped in sharpening the conclusions drawn on the basis of simple description of facts in terms of frequencies, averages and percentages.

B. AN OPINION SURVEY OF COMPANIES IN INDIA

The universe of the survey consists of manufacturers of industrial as well as consumer products. Convenience and Judgement sampling of 100 industrial units (consisting of small medium and large units) was selected covering most of the states.

Data Collection

Data were collected with the help of a questionnaire which was pre tested and improved upon. The specimen of the final questionnaire is given in Appendix –II. Questionnaire were then mailed to the manufacturing organizations selected for the study. Some of the senior executives and also marketing executives were contacted personally to elicit information from them regarding their marketing objectives, to have their views on consumerism and consumer protection, as to how they react to consumer complaints and try to solve them. During the discussions we have tried to observe the manufacturers'/marketing organizations views for consumer protection laws, their policies towards consumer welfare, their method of satisfying their customers and the services rendered to their clients.

Data Analysis

The data collected from 100 organisation were first classified into three categories on the basis of their annual turnover. Organizations having annual turnover up to Rupees One Crore were classified as small scale organizations (S). Those with annual turnover between "₹ 1 crore to 10 crores" were categorized as medium scale organizations (M) and organizations with turnover "above 10 crores" were classified as large scale organizations (L).

The analysis was then carried out on the basis of above three categories. The response from the organizations have been tabulated in terms of both the numbers both the numbers and percentages. Figures in tables within parenthesis represent percentages while those without parenthesis are simple frequencies.

C. SURVEY OF VOLUNTARY ORGANIZATIONS

The universe of the survey consists of voluntary organizations who are working for the welfare of the consumers.

From the list of voluntary organizations available form the Ministry of Civil Supplies, Government of India, a random sample of 100 organizations was selected. However an effort has been made to include voluntary organizations from the most of the states of India to make the sample more representative. Due to no response, the final sample consisted of only 38 voluntary organizations.

Data Collection

The questionnaire prepared for the collecting the information as given in Appendix-III, was mailed to each of these organizations. Besides this some of the major voluntary organizations at Ahmedabad, Mumbai, Kolkata, etc., were contacted personally and their officials were interviewed to elicit information related to their field of work. We tried to find out their objectives in running the organizations, welfare of the consumers, their attitude towards consumer problems, Government Legislations, their method of working for bringing awareness amongst consumers, whether they have received complaints from the consumers and how they handled the grievances, whether they have any educational programmes for imparting knowledge to the consumers through seminars, mass media, etc.

Data Analysis

We have based our analysis on 38 organizations which have responded. Analysis has been done on the basis of two categories – organizations in existence for less the 10 years (category A) and others in existence for 10 years and above.

Limitations of the Study

Any survey conducted through pre designed questionnaire suffers from the basic limitations of the possibility of difference between what is recorded and what is the truth, no matter how carefully the questionnaire has been designed and field investigation has been conducted. However in order to minimize this error, respondents were interviewed personally, and through persuasions and helpful discussion it has been possible to a large extent to elicit reliable information from them. But there is no foolproof method of making it completely error free.

Besides this the consumer opinion has been restricted to respondents from Delhi city only. Though Delhi is cosmopolitan city and conclusion drawn on the basis of this survey has definitely some limitations for its applicability on the All India level of course, to a large extent these do give an overall picture of the country.

In case of survey on voluntary organization the interferences being based on the responses from only 38 such organizations have the obvious limitations for their wider applicability.

ENGAGEMENT OF LAWYER IS NOT MANDATORY IN CONSUMER FORUMS.

IT ONLY REQUIRE THREE SHEETS OF PAPERS

At Consumer Courts you are the lawyer of yours.

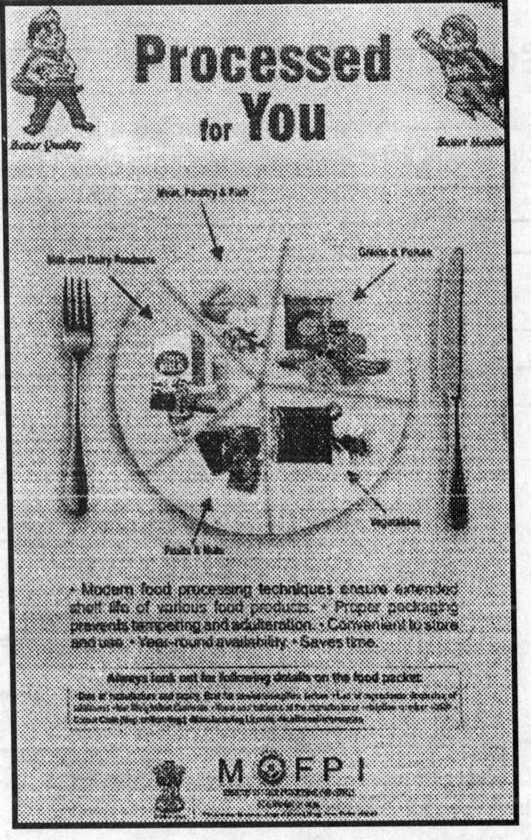

— ✦ — ✦ — ✦ —

Chapter 5

Consumerism and Consumer Movement Opinion and an Opinion Survey of Consumers

This Chapter presents the findings of the survey which has been conducted to know consumers' opinion about consumerism and consumer movement. The data have been collected with the help of a comprehensive questionnaire (Appendix I) prepared for this survey from a sample of 600 respondents. Section I of this chapter gives the sample description of the respondents surveyed. Detailed analysis of consumer opinions regarding consumerism is presented in Section II.

SECTION I

This section related to general information about sex, age, educational qualification, average monthly family income and occupation of the respondents. The distribution of the respondents by the above attributes have been given in Tables 5.1 to 5.5

Table 5.1 : Sex wise distribution of the respondents

Sex	*No. of respondents*
Male	442 (73.67)
Female	158 (26.33)
Total	**600 (100.00)**

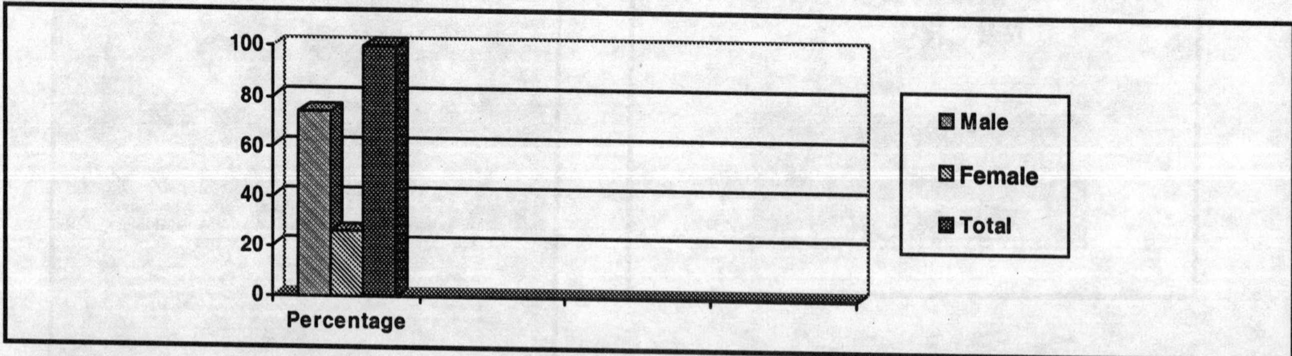

Note: Figures in the parenthesis show percentage while figures without parenthesis are show simple frequencies in this table and on all subsequent tables.

From the above figure we find that male and female are approximately in the ratio 3:1. the age wise distribution of respondents made on the basis of four age groups, *viz.*, 0 – 20 (A1), 21 – 40 years (A2), 41 – 60 years (A3) and above 60 years (A4) has been shown in Table 5.2.

Table 5.2 : Age wise distribution of respondents

Age Group	*No. of respondents*	
0 – 20 years (A1)	16	(2.67)
21 – 40 years (A2)	434	(72.33)
41 – 60 years (A3)	123	(20.50)
Above 60 years (A4)	16	(2.67)
Non response	11	(1.83)
Total	**600**	**(100.00)**

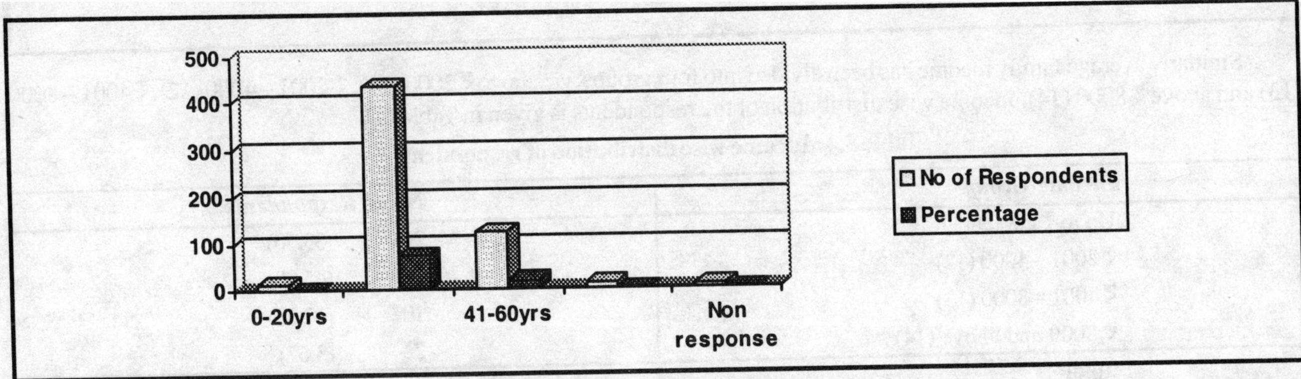

The above Table reveals that an overwhelming majority of 72.33 percent belongs to the age group A2, i.e., 21 – 4- years and another 20.50 per cent to A3 (41 – 60 years). Together they comprise 92.83 per cent of the consumers. The remaining 7.17 per cent only belong to age groups A1 and A4 including few non-responders.

The educational qualifications have been classified into four categories, *viz.*, up to Matric (E1), Graduates (E2), Post Graduate (E3) and Professionally Qualified (E4). Table 5.4 gives the education wise distribution of the respondents.

Table 5.3 : Education wise distribution of respondents

Educational Category	*No. of Respondents*	
Up to Matric (E1)	200	(33.33)
Graduates (E2)	233	(38.83)
Post Graduates (E4)	121	(20.17)
Professionally Qualified	46	(7.67)
Total	**600**	**(100.00)**

The majority of the respondents (72.16%) either belong to E1 (up to Matric) or E2 (Graduates). Another 20.17% belongs to E3 (Post Graduates) and only 7.67% belongs to E4 (Professionally Qualified).

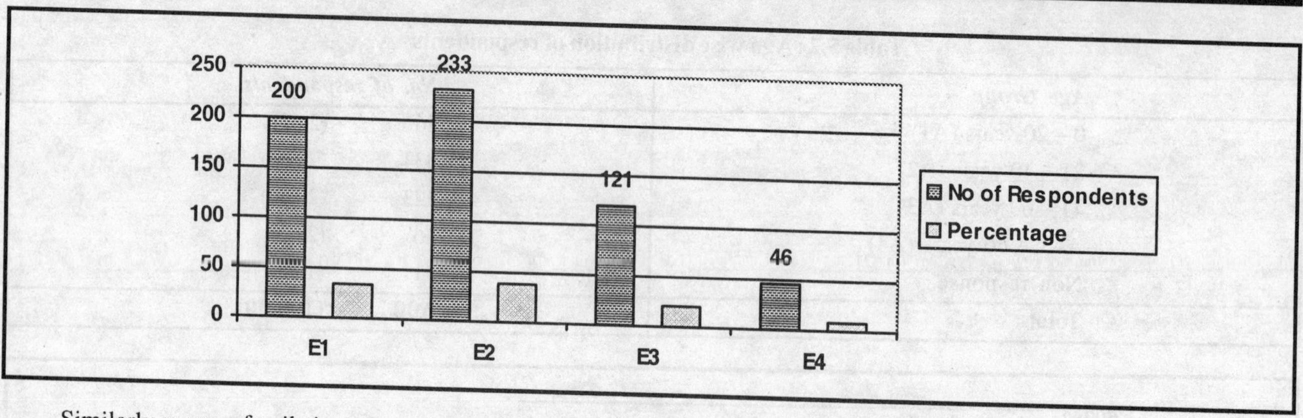

Similarly average family income has been divided into four groups, *viz*., up to ₹ 2000 (11), ₹ 2001 – 4000 (12), ₹ 4001 – 8000 (13) and above ₹ 8000 (14). Income wise distribution of the respondents is given in Table 5.4

Table 5.4 : Income wise distribution of respondents

Income Group	*No.of Respondents*	
Up to ₹ 2000 (11)	201	(33.50)
₹ 2001 – 4000 (12)	270	(45.00)
₹ 4001 – 8000 (13)	107	(17.83)
₹ 8000 and above (14)	22	(3.67)
Total	**600**	**(100.00)**

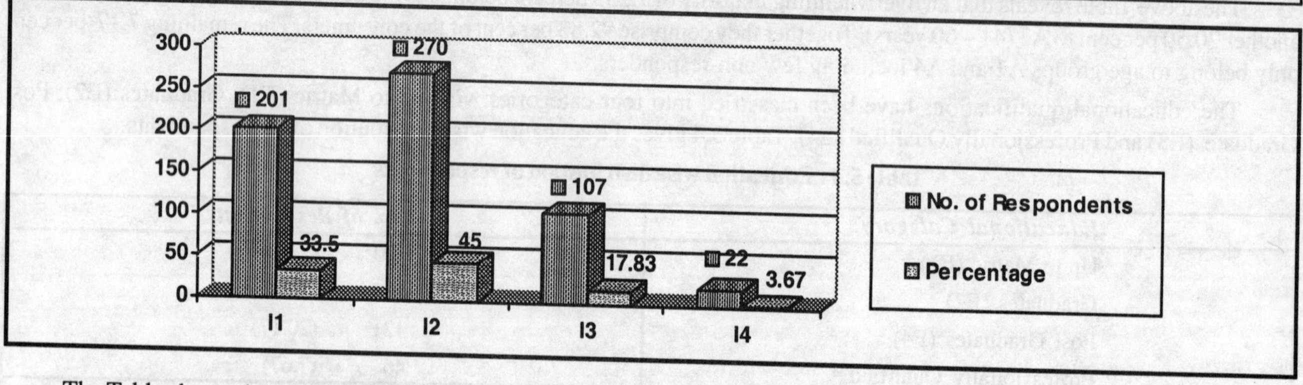

The Table shows that 45.00% of the respondents belong to I2 (₹ 2001 – 4000) where as 33.50% belong to 11 (up to ₹ 2000). About 18% comprise 13 (₹ 4001 – 8000) and only a small quantity of 3.67% belong to 14 (₹ 8000 and above).

Finally, occupation wise distribution of the consumer is tabulated in Table 5.5. for this purpose four classes of occupation have been considered, *viz*., 'Service' (O1), 'Business' (O2), 'Housewives' (O3' and 'Others' (O4). The 'others' include retired personnel, students, research scholars, professional, etc.

Table 5.6 : Occupation wise distribution of respondents

Occupational Class	*No. of Respondents*	
Service (O1)	346	(57.67)
Business (O2)	81	(13.50)
Housewives (O3)	107	(17.83)
Others (O4)	60	(10.00)
Non Response	6	(1.00)
Total	**600**	**(100.00)**

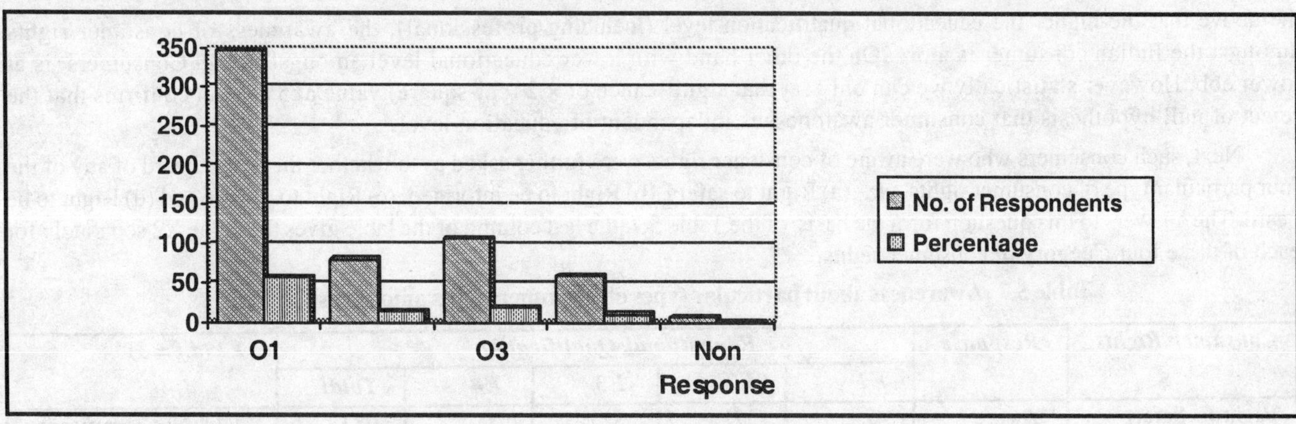

From the above Table it can be concluded that 57.67% of the respondents belong to 'service class. Only a very few belong to the 'business' class. However. About 18% are housewives.

SECTION II

In this section detailed analysis of the opinions expressed by the consumers to the various queries have been studied. The analysis have however been carried out on thebasis of only one attribute, *viz*., educational level since it was felt that this factor is one of the most important which can influence the opinions of the respondents. As stated in Section 1, educational level has been classified in four categories upto matric (E1), graduates (E2), post graduate (E3) and professionally qualified (E4).

Awareness about consumer rights

Firstly, the respondents were asked whether they aware of consumer rights or not. Their responses have been tabulated in Table 5.6.

Table 5.6 : Awareness about consumer rights in general

Response	*Educational Category*				*Total*
	E1	*E2*	*E3*	*E4*	
Aware	55 (27.50)	136 (58.37)	100 (82.64)	37 (80.43)	328 (54.67)
Not Aware	145 (72.50)	97 (41.63)	21 (17.36)	9 (19.57)	272 (45.33)
Total	**200**	**233**	**121**	**46**	**600**

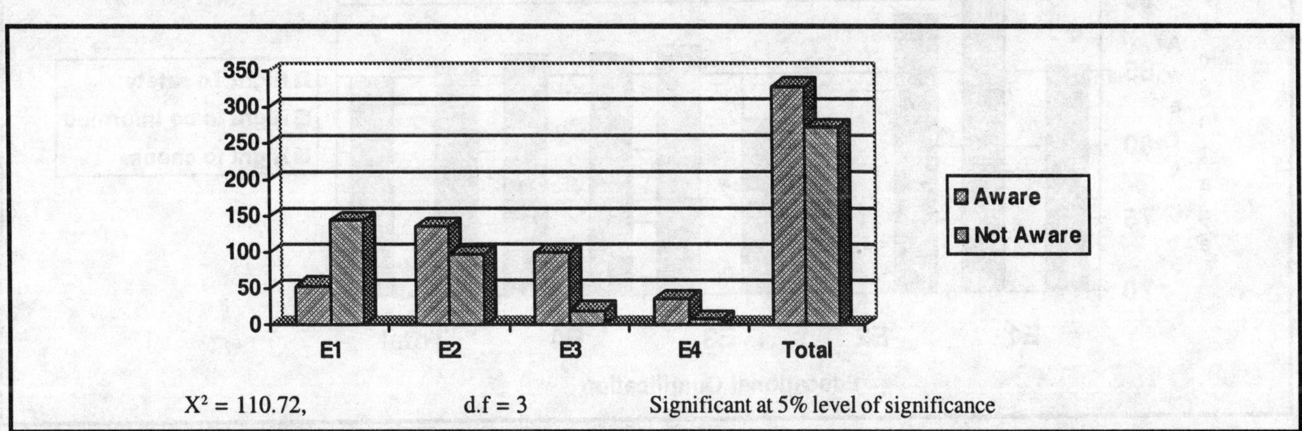

$X^2 = 110.72$, d.f = 3 Significant at 5% level of significance

From the Table we find that out of the total respondents, 54.67% are aware of consumer rights whereas 45.33% are ignorant. Education wise, for post graduates category (E3) is 82.64% belong to the highest followed by 80.43% for professionally qualified (E4) and 58.37% for graduates (E2) categories respectively. The lowest awareness is the up to matric category (E1) which is only 27.50%. looking, otherwise, the majority 72.50% in this category are ignorant of the consumer rights. It is interesting to note from the above that the higher the educational qualification level (including professional), the awareness of consumer rights amongst the Indian consumer is more. On the other hand with lower educational level amongst Indian Consumers is at lower ebb. However statistically we can only sat that significance of × 2 (chi-square) value at 5% level confirms that the reject of null hypothesis that consumer awareness is independent of education level.

Next, such consumers who were aware of consumer rights were further asked as to whether they have heard of any of the four particular type of consumer rights, *viz.,* (a) Right to safety, (b) Right to be informed, (c) Right to choose and (d) Right to be heard. The answers to this question form the basis of the Table 5.7. the last column of the table gives the value X2 separately for each of these four category of consumer rights.

Table 5.7 : Awareness about particular types of consumer rights among respondents.

Consumer Rights	*Response*	*Educational Qualification*					*X2 (d.f = 3)*
		E1	*E2*	*E3*	*E4*	*Total*	
Right to Safety	Aware	47 (85.45)	121 (88.97)	82 (82.00)	32 (86.49)	282 (85.98)	2.34, Not Significant at 5% level
	Not Aware	8 (14.55)	15 (11.03)	18 (18.00)	5 (13.51)	46 (14.02)	
Right to be Informed	Aware	43 (78.18)	114 (83.82)	85 (85.00)	31 (83.78)	273 (83.23)	1.24, Not Significant at 5% level
	Not Aware	12 (21.82)	22 (16.18)	15 (15.00)	6 (16.22)	55 (16.77)	
Right to Choose	Aware	50 (90.91)	109 (80.15)	87 (87.00)	32 (86.49)	278 (84.75)	4.32, Not Significant at 5% level
	Not Aware	5 (9.09)	27 (19.85)	13 (13.00)	5 (13.51)	50 (15.24)	
Right to be Heard	Aware	37 (67.27)	85 (62.50)	60 (60.00)	25 (67.57)	207 (63.11)	1.16, Not Significant at 5% level
	Not Aware	18 (32.73)	51 (37.50)	40 (40.00)	12 (32.43)	121 (36.89)	
	N	55	136	100	37	328	

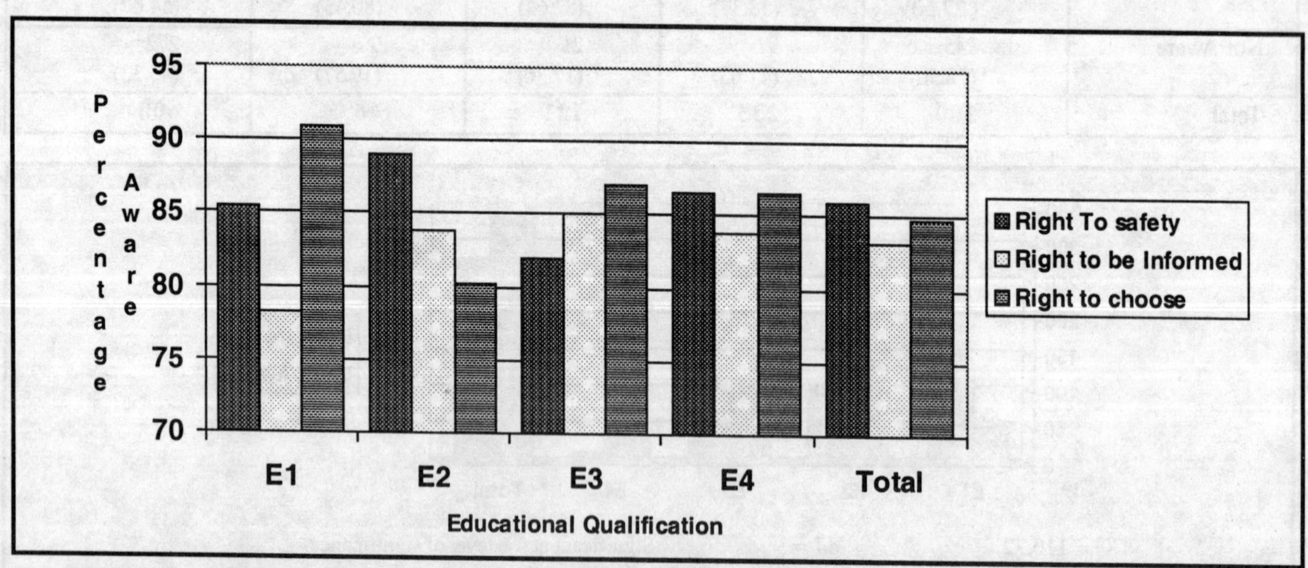

We shall now examine all the four types of consumer rights one by one:

(a) Right to safety: A fairly large section of the total respondents, that is, 85.98% are aware of this consumer rights. Education wise also the percentages are balanced among the various categories of educational level and range from 88.97% for E2 to 82.00% for E3. the percentages for E1 and E4 are 85.45 and 86.82 respectively. X2 values is also not significant at 5% level of significance, thereby confirming that education has no impact on awareness.

(b) Rights to be informed: In this case, the overall percentage of awareness is 83.23, the highest percentage of 85.00 is for E3, followed by 83.82 and 83.78 for E2 and E4 respectively. This shows that here also the awareness is fairly uniform for the various categories of education level. The X2 has been found to be not significant at 5% level.

(c) Right to choose: The overall percentage is 84.76 for this consumer right. Strangely enough the awareness for up to matric individual (E1) is highest, that is, 90.91% the percentage of post graduate (E3) and professionally qualified (E4) and more or less the same, being 87.00 and 86.49 respectively. The lowest percentage came from graduate category. Here, again X2 is not significant at 5% level showing independence of education on awareness.

(d) Right to be heard: Although the degree of awareness in this case is less than the other three consumer rights, it shows marginal variations among the individuals from four educational categories. Out of the total respondents, 63.11% shows awareness. E4 accounts for highest percentage of 67.57, the next highest being 67.27 for E1, marginally less than E4. for E2, it is 62.50%. the lowest percentage of 60.00 is for post graduates (E3). Once again, the value X2 is not significant .

Examining the above analysis critically, it is worthwhile to note that though the general awareness to consumer rights is very much dependent on the educational level (Table 5.6), the awareness of particular type of consumer rights like right to safety, right to be informed, right to choose, and right to be heard among those who have already heard of consumer rights is more or less same irrespective of education level (Table 5.7)

CONSUMERS AWARENESS ABOUT VARIOUS LEGISLATIONS

Various legislations for consumers' protection exists in India. Twentyone such legislations have been listed for the purpose of one study. The respondents were then asked to whether they are aware of these consumer protection legislations. Their responses have been tabulated in Table 5.8

Table 5.8 : Awareness about Consumer Protection Legislation

Consumer Protection Legislation	*Response*	*Educational category*				*Total*	*X2(dif.=3)*
		E1	*E2*	*E3*	*E4*		
I. The Essential Commodities Act, 1945	Aware	16 (8.00)	76 (32.62)	62 (51.24)	35 (76.09)	189 (31.50)	115.49
	Not Aware	184 (92.00)	157 (67.36)	59 (48.76)	11 (23.91)	411 (68.50)	
II. The Monopolies And Restrictive Trade Practices Act, 1969(MRTP)	Aware	10 (5.00)	68 (29.18)	49 (40.50)	28 (60.87)	155 (25.83)	89.75
	Not Aware	190 (95.00)	165 (70.82)	72 (59.50)	18 (39.13)	445 (74.17)	
III. The Prevention of Food Adulteration Act, 1954	Aware	18 (9.00)	94 (40.34)	70 (57.85)	32 (69.57)	214 (35.67)	111.15
	Not Aware	182 (91.00)	139 (59.86)	51 (42.15)	14 (30.43)	386 (64.33)	
IV. The Trade and Merchandise Marks Act, 1958	Aware	7 (3.50)	27 (11.59)	22 (18.18)	15 (32.61)	71 (11.83)	36.96
	Not Aware	193 (96.50)	206 (88.41)	99 (81.82)	31 (67.39)	529 (88.17)	
V. The Sale of Goods Act, 1930	Aware	6 (3.00)	48 (20.60)	29 (23.97)	28 (60.87)	111 (18.50)	89.72
	Not Aware	194 (97.00)	185 (79.40)	92 (76.03)	18 (39.13)	489 (81.50)	
VI. The Hire Purchase Act, 1972	Aware	7 (3.50)	47 (20.17)	32 (26.45)	20 (43.48)	106 (17.67)	56.06
	Not Aware	193 (96.50)	186 (79.83)	89 (73.55)	26 (56.52)	494 (82.33)	

VII. The Packaged Commodities Regulation Order, 1972	Aware	9 (4.50)	19 (8.15)	15 (12.40)	16 (34.78)	59 (9.83)	40.27
	Not Aware	191 (95.50)	214 (91.85)	106 (87.60)	30 (65.22)	541 (90.17)	
VIII. The Drugs and Cosmetics Act, 1940	Aware	15 (7.50)	51 (21.89)	38 (31.40)	25 (54.35)	129 (21.50)	59.67
	Not Aware	185 (92.50)	182 (78.11)	83 (68.60)	21 (45.65)	471 (78.50)	
IX. The Dangerous Drug Act	Aware	12 (6.00)	40 (17.17)	44 (36.36)	19 (41.30)	115 (19.17)	46.80
	Not Aware	188 (94.00)	193 (82.83)	77 (63.64)	27 (58.70)	485 (80.83)	
X. The Drugs and Magic Remedies (Objectionable Advertisement) Act 1954	Aware	8 (4.00)	22 (9.44)	13 (10.74)	13 (28.26)	56 (9.33)	26.44
	Not Aware	192 (96.00)	211 (90.56)	108 (89.26)	33 (71.74)	544 (90.67)	
XI. The Household Electrical Appliances (Quality Control) Order	Aware	10 (5.00)	50 (21.46)	28 (23.14)	25 (54.35)	113 (18.83)	67.75
	Not Aware	190 (95.00)	183 (78.54)	93 (76.86)	21 (45.65)	487 (81.17)	
XII. The Agricultural Products (Grading and Marketing) Act,1937 (AGMARK)	Aware	38 (19.00)	60 (25.75)	36 (29.75)	23 (50.00)	157 (26.17)	19.65
	Not Aware (81.00)	162 (74.25)	173 (70.25)	85 (50.00)	23 (73.83)	443	
XIII. The Fruits Product Order, 1955 (FPO)	Aware	11 (5.50)	36 (15.45)	18 (14.88)	13 (28.76)	78 (13.00)	21.02
	Not Aware	189 (94.50)	197 (84.55)	103 (85.12)	33 (71.74)	522 (87.00)	
XIV. The Standard of Weights and Measures (Packaged Commodities Rules) 1977	Aware	15 (7.50)	91 (39.06)	58 (47.93)	32 (69.57)	196 (32.67)	130.49
	Not Aware	185 (92.50)	142 (60.94)	63 (52.07)	14 (63.04)	404 (67.33)	
XV. The Prevention of Blackmarketing and Maintenance of Supplies of Essential Commodities Act, 1980	Aware	14 (7.00)	74 (31.76)	59 (48.76)	29 (63.04)	176 (29.33)	95.98
	Not Aware	186 (93.00)	159 (68.24)	62 (51.24)	17 (36.96)	424 (70.67)	
XVI. The Paper (Production and Regulation Control) Order, 1979	Aware	2 (1.00)	15 (6.44)	13 (10.74)	9 (19.57)	39 (6.50)	26.49
	Not Aware	198 (99.00)	218 (93.56)	108 (89.26)	37 (80.43)	561 (93.50)	

XVII. The Indian Contract Act, 1972	Aware	8 (4.00)	46 (19.74)	32 (26.45)	27 (58.70)	113 (18.83)	81.23
	Not Aware	192 (96.00)	187 (86.26)	89 (73.55)	19 (41.30)	487 (81.17)	
XVIII. The Indian Standards Institution Act, 1956, ISI	Aware	37 (18.50)	71 (30.47)	66 (54.55)	31 (67.39)	205 (34.17)	67.28
	Not Aware	163 (81.50)	162 (69.53)	55 (45.45)	15 (32.61)	395 (65.83)	
XIX. The Standards of Weights and Measures	Aware	14 (7.00)	68 (29.18)	57 (47.11)	29 (63.04)	168 (28.00)	93.80
	Not Aware	186 (93.00)	165 (70.82)	64 (52.89)	17 (39.96)	432 (72.00)	
XX. Consumer Protection Act,1986	Aware	9 (4.50)	71 (30.47)	57 (44.63)	24 (52.17)	158 (26.33)	81.87
	Not Aware	191 (95.50)	162 (69.53)	67 (55.37)	22 (47.83)	442 (73.67)	
Local Taxes	Aware	53 (26.50)	122 (52.36)	76 (62.81)	33 (71.74)	284 (47.33)	59.78
	Not Aware	147 (73.50)	111 (47.46)	45 (37.19)	13 (28.26)	316 (52.67)	

Note: All X2 values are significant at 5% level of significance

For each of these legislations X2 value has been calculated to test the null hypothesis that ' knowledge of legislation does not depend on educational category'. These X2 values have been shown in the last column of the table. From the table we find that out of total respondents, the overall percentages of awareness of these legislations are quite low. In fact, these mostly vary between 9.33% for the Drugs and Magic Remedies (Objectionable Advertisement) Act 1954 and 35.67% for the Prevention of Food Adulteration Act 1954. There are a few exceptions like the Paper (Production and Regulation Act) Control order, 1979 which has the lowest percentage of 6.50 and local taxes for which the percentage is the highest, that is 47.33. education wise it can be observed from the table that the awareness is maximum for professionally qualified (E4) individuals followed by post graduates and graduates, the minimum being for up to matric qualified. To corroborate these points let us examine the awareness about few legislations individually. For example consider the legislation No. 1 – The Essential Commodities Act,1955, here the highest percentage for awareness is educational category E4 (76.09%) followed by E3 (51.24%) and E2 (32.62%). E1 has the lowest percentage of 8.00. next consider the Act No. 4 – The Trade and Merchandise Act , 1958. Here the trend is also same as that of Act No. 1. the percentages are in descending order of E4, E3, E2 and E1 and these are 32.61, 18.18, 11.59 and 3.50 respectively. In case of Act No. 8 – The Drugs and Cosmetics Act, 1940, the percentage of professionally qualified persons is 54.33 followed by 31.40 and 21.89 per cent for the post graduates and graduates. The percentage of 7.50 is the lowest for up matric level (e1) category. Similarly for Act No. 12- The Agricultural produce (Grading and marketing) Act 1937 (AGMARK) – the highest awareness percentage is again for E4. though there are is marginal difference in percentage between E3 and E2 (4%), the pattern is the same, percentage of E3 being higher than E2. The percentage of E1 is 19.00. Now consider the Act No. 16 – The Paper (Production and Regulation) Control Order, 1979. As mentioned earlier, this has the lowest percentage of awareness that is 6.50 percent. Education wise also only 2% among the under graduates have heard about this Act. Even the highest percentage of awareness is only 19.57 for professionally qualified individuals. This is followed by 10.74 and 6.44 percent for post graduates and graduates respectively. Lastly take the case of Act No. 21 – Local Taxes where the overall percentage is highest that is 47.33. here a very sizeable percent of 71.74 of E4 population have heard of this Act. Among E3 and E2 respondents the percentages are 62.80 and 52.36 respectively who are conversant to this Act. Even among the under graduates, the awareness is fairly good being 26.50 per cent.

Glancing through the remaining acts in this table, we can observe the same pattern of awareness among the individuals of various educational categories. Thus the above analysis shows that higher the educational level, greater is the awareness. Statistical analysis carried out through X2 test show that all X2 values are significant at 5% level. This however, only brings out the tfact that awareness is not independent of the educational levels of the individuals thereby rejecting the null hypothesis.

In the next part, the opinion of the respondents was sought, as to what extent they agree that the various consumers' issues listed in the questionnaire should be included under consumerism. Their responses have been recorded on five different levels of agreement/disagreement, *viz.*,

(a) Strongly agree (SA)
(b) Agree (A)
(c) Neither agree nor disagree (NA/ND)
(d) Disagree (D) and
(e) Strongly Disagree (SD)

Table 5.9 gives the number of individuals and percentages (in parenthesis) in each of these five levels.

Table 5.9 : Respondents Attitude towards the inclusion of specific issues under Consumerism

ISSUE	*LEVEL OF AGREEMENT*				
	Strongly Agree	*Agree*	*Neither Agree Nor Disagree*	*Disagree*	*Strongly Disagree*
I. Information (more informative Advertisement & Clearly written warranty)	402 (67.00)	155 (25.83)	42 (7.00)	1 (0.17)	0 (0.00)
II. Health and safety (testing/evaluation of standards, etc.)	454 (75.67)	96 (16.00)	48 (8.00)	2 (0.33)	0 (0.00)
III. Repair and services (improved servicing of appliances and automobiles)	301 (50.17)	202 (33.67)	89 (14.83)	5 (0.83)	3 (0.50)
IV. Pricing issues (high prices of food and products)	416 (69.33)	106 (17.67)	45 (7.50)	22 (3.67)	11 (1.83)
V. Pollution in the environment (directly air/water)	325 (54.17)	155 (25.83)	89 (14.83)	19 (3.17)	12 (2.00)
VI. Market concentration (lack of competition)	176 (29.33)	184 (30.67)	170 (28.33)	49 (8.17)	21 (3.50)
VII. Product quality (frequent breakdown of product, poor, etc.)	401 (66.83)	123 (20.50)	46 (7.67)	20 (3.33)	10 (1.67)
VIII. Consumer representation (lack of consumer representation)	287 (47.83)	179 (29.83)	104 (17.33)	15 (2.50)	15 (2.50)
IX. Advertisement (deceptive advertisement, obscene)	170 (28.33)	229 (38.17)	126 (21.00)	43 (7.17)	32 (5.33)
X. Legislation (preventive measures required)	297 (49.50)	233 (38.83)	62 (10.33)	8 (1.33)	0 (0.00)

The Table reveals that majority of the respondents agreed that all the issues listed should be considered in the consumer movement. Respondents reaction to each of the issue is analyzed as under

A. Information

Here 92.83% agree that information should be provided by the manufacturers about the various products on the packagings. Process of the products including local taxes should be provided, also expiry date of medicine, etc., be clearly mentioned on the container. The guarantee/warranty should be clearly spelt out and properly explained.

B. Health and Safety

91.67 per cent feel that for better health hygienic products and stringent safety regulations. they are of the opinion that there is lack of testing facilities in India for evaluating the standards/quality of products. There is also need for safety requirements while using the various products in the daily life.

C. Repair and Services

A majority of 83.84% feel that there is need for improved services since backup services that are provided by manufacture's are not up to the mark. The main problems encountered are delay in availability of spare parts, excessive cost, unsatisfactory repairs carried out, etc.

D. Pricing Issues

The analysis shows that 87.00% of the consumers are very much concerned about pricing problems faced in the Indian market. The general view is that the prices of various products/commodities available in the market are too high and there is an inflationary trend which further pushes the prices day by day. So there is need for control and supervision in this aspect by the Government as well as other agencies.

E. Pollution in The Environment

Response patterns show that 80.00% respondents are greatly concerned about pollution in the environment. Water is getting polluted due to discharge of industrial effluents and waste in streams and rivers. Again, there is pollution of air due to gaseous substances given out by automobiles, industrial units like thermal power plant, cement factories, etc. Thus, there is need form prevention and control of air pollution. There is also noise pollution due to road traffic, loud speakers, television at high frequencies which causes harmful effects on the human body. These specific problems should receive serious attention by the business, government and all consumer groups.

F. Market Concentration

The findings of the survey indicate that there is lack of competition in certain areas. This feeling has been conveyed by 60.00% of the consumers. Telephone services, electricity supply, milk supply, Government transport facilities (air, rail, bus) are predominantly supplied by Government undertakings, Municipal Corporations and public services. In such cases monopoly situations are perceived. The majority is of the opinion that competition is needed to ensure their fair price, better quality of services and other improved facilities to the consumers and also free enterprise system should be operated in the interest of the consumers.

G. Product Quality

An over whelming majority of 87.33% have commented on poor product quality. The specific problems encountered by the consumers are of the various nature like faults, breakdowns, mechanical failure, structural defects, and others like decay, rust, etc, of various articles/equipment. Also the performance of the articles are not up to the expected level. Since there is lack of product quality the improvement is needed in this direction by the manufacturers. The realistic statement of public reference have emerged from the data collected which suggests the need for reevaluation of firms product policies to give more satisfaction to the aggrieved consumers, thereby giving weightage to consumerism in India.

H. Consumer Representation

It is important to note that 77.66% of the respondents have agreed that there is lack of consumer representation at various levels, *viz.*, Government, Voluntary Organizations. Safe guarding the rights and the interests of the buyers has been the main thrust of consumerism. So the survey suggest that there should be more participation of the consumers in the decision making process of the voluntary organizations as well as Government agencies.

I. Advertisement

66.50% of the consumers has felt that the advertisements of most of the products are not believable. Most manufacturers' advertisements do not provide reliable information about product quality and performance. So buyers face problems related to false/misleading/deceptive advertisements. Control and supervision by the various government and non government organizations to stop the obscene/misleading advertisements through various media for the welfare of the consumers is very much needed.

J. Legislations

A vast majority of 88.33% is of the opinion that there is need for preventive measures to control various types of cheating, exploitations of the consumers by the business community. Stringent laws are required to control various unscrupulous activities of the traders. Also existing laws should be enforced strictly to check the mischevious activities of the businessmen.

In order to examine the reactions on these issues of consumerism with respect to various educational level the weighted averages for theses categories have been obtained by assigning weights of 2, 1, 0, –1, –2 to

(i) strongly agree

(ii) agree

(iii) neither agree nor disagree

(iv) disagree

(v) strongly disagree, respectively.

These have been shown in the following table, Table 5.10

Table 5.10 : Average Weighted Score for specific issues to be included under consumerism (Education wise Distribution)

ISSUE	Educational Category				TOTAL
	E1	E2	E3	E4	
1. Information	1.43	1.65	1.69	1.83	1.60
2. Health and Safety	1.45	1.75	1.80	1.87	1.67
3. Repair and Services	1.16	1.39	1.41	1.43	1.32
4. Pricing Issues	1.58	1.49	1.34	1.52	1.49
5. Pollution In Environment	1.14	1.26	1.50	1.30	1.27
6. Market Concentration	0.81	0.74	0.59	0.87	0.74
7. Product Quality	1.54	1.48	1.37	1.46	1.48
8. Consumer Representation	1.13	1.17	1.21	1.39	1.18
9. Advertisement	0.66	0.76	0.83	1.11	0.77
10. Legislation	1.25	1.34	1.51	1.61	1.37

The Kendall's coefficient of concordance W=0.839, X2=30.20, d.b=9, significant at 5% level of significance

The table reveals that irrespective of the different educational categories majority of the respondents agreed or strongly agreed regarding the inclusion of listed issues under consumerism as average weighted scores in almost all the cases was more than one except for the issues 'Market Concentration' and "Advertisement'.

In fact, the weighted average scores are nothing but average ratings given to issues to consumerism by the individuals belonging to different educational categories. After assigning ranks to their ratings W statistics has been calculated. W takes values between 0 and 1, W=0 showing no concordance and W=1 showing perfect concordance. The value of W in this case has been found to be 0.839. The significance of W has been tested by X2 Test. X2 comes out to be 30.20 for 9 degrees of freedom which is significant at 5 per cent level of significance. This shows that there is significant agreement among individuals belonging to different educational categories with respect to rankings/ratings of various issues for inclusion under consumerism.

It is quite natural that any consumer, while purchasing a product, will look for some information about the product in the package/containers. Broadly speaking, he/she may like to have information on any one of the various items like

(i) date manufacturing

(ii) price

(iii) quality mark

(iv) name of the manufacturer

(v) date of expiry and

(vi) quality, standard unit or weight

The responses on the individuals on this aspect have been shown in Table 5.11

Table 5.11 : Product information sought on package/container by the respondents

Items on which information sought	*Educational Category*				
	E1	*E2*	*E3*	*E4*	*TOTAL*
Date of Manufacturing	138 (69.00)	212 (90.99)	111 (91.74)	43 (93.48)	504 (84.00)
Price	189 (94.50)	225 (96.57)	114 (94.21)	41 (89.13)	569 (94.93)
Quality Mark	142 (71.00)	195 (83.69)	100 (82.64)	35 (77.38)	472 (78.67)
Name of the Manufacturer	118 (59.00)	174 (74.68)	92 (76.03)	38 (82.61)	422 (70.33)
Date of Expiry	131 (65.50)	214 (91.85)	114 (94.21)	42 (91.30)	501 (83.50)
Quantity, Standard Unit of Weight	170 (85.00)	197 (84.55)	100 (82.64)	39 (84.78)	506 (84.33)
N	200	233	121	46	600

Note: percentages are more than hundred because of multiple choices.

We will now discuss in detail the various items related to information provided on the labels of the container/package of various products.

A. Date of Manufacturing

Out of the total sample,84.00% have stated that they look for the date of manufacturing of the product. 'Professionally Qualified' individuals (E4) have the highest percentage of 93.48. In case of up to matrix E1 only 69.00% look for the information and the rest 31% are not keen to see the available information on the table. The corresponding percentages for graduates and post graduates are of the same order that is 90.99 and 91.74 respectively.

B. Price

The price is an important factor which affect purchase decision and thus a very high percentage of 94.83 of total sample look for it on the labels of packages/containers. The same is true separately for the respondents belonging to categories E1, E2,E3, and E4, the percentages among them varying between 89.13 for E4 to 96.57 for E2.

C. Quality Mark

A vast majority (78.67%) do look for the information regarding quality mark such as ISI, AGMARK, etc., on the labels. Obviously 21.33% do not consider this aspect to be serious enough. Analyzing education wise, 83.69% of the respondents from E2, 82.64% from E3, 77.38% from E4 and 71.00% from E1 category are keen to look for this information. Being less educated 29.00% of the individuals belonging to educational category E1 do not bother about this information. Besides this, sometimes due to inadequate availability of daily necessities and essential commodities, poor consumers are forced to buy whatever article is available in market and are thus exploited by the traders.

D. Name of the Manufacturer

70.37% of the total respondents surveyed seek for this information, the percentage for educational categories vary between 82.61 for E4 to 59.00 for E1. Here also the individuals who do not seem to care for this information mostly belong to E1, their percentage being as high as 41.00.

E. Date of Expiry

This is one of the most important information necessary for any product and 84.33% of the total respondents do look for this information. Among the better educated people, this percentage is even higher *viz.*, 94.21 for E3, 91.85 for E2 and 91.30 for E4. for E1 it 65.50%.

F. Quantity, Standard Unit of Weight

Out of the total 600 individuals, 506 that 84.33% are very much conscious and look for quantity mentioned on the labels of the package and also about the correct weights of the goods purchased. It is interesting to note that the same is uniformly true for each of the educational category, the percentages being between 85.00 for E1 to 82.64 for E3. Curiously, the highest percentage of individuals who seek for this information belong to E1 category.

From the analysis above we may conclude that majority of Indian buyers look for product information before purchasin a product. In order to get some feedback respondents were then asked as to what additional information they would like to have on the labels of the package/containers. Their responses have been summarized and is shown in Table 5.12

Table 5.12 : Additional Product Information required on Package/Containers by Respondents

Information	*Educational Category*				*Total*
	E1	*E2*	*E3*	*E4*	
Instruction for usage/maintenance of products inc., service preferably In local language	5 (2.5)	9 (3.86)	6 (4.96)	3 (6.52)	23 (3.83)
Details regarding safety aspect, warning for harmful effect if any for the users	0 (0.00)	5 (2.15)	8 (6.61)	2 (4.35)	15 (2.50)
N	200	233	121	46	600

From the table we find that responses are quite low, only 3.83% for item 1 and 2.5 % for item 2 among the total sample. Education wise also the scenario appears to be the same. However few salient features may be mentioned as below:

(i) Only 6.52% of the respondents from E4 are of the opinion that product information should contain instructions for usage, maintenance of the product including service provided by the manufacturers of the equipment in printed form in the local language.

(ii) Similarly 6.61% of the respondents belonging to the educational category E3 are of the view that product information should have details regarding safety of the product, handling of the product and warnings may be given to the user for any harmful effects. This will enable the consumers to handle the product in a proper manner avoiding accidents or health hazards problems. Besides these observations on the product information, some people have also commented on the quality of the packages which may be well be taken. They have suggested that packages should be attractive, strong and waterproof and the containers should be safe for handling by the buyers.

CONSUMER COMPLAINTS

In this part we shall discuss the findings regarding the consumer complaints concerning defective products. These have been presented in Tables 5.13, 5.14. and 5.15.

Table 5.13 : Reporting of complaints about defective products

Response	*Educational Category*				*Total*
	E1	*E2*	*E3*	*E4*	
Yes	35 (17.50)	47 (20.17)	50 (41.32)	12 (26.09)	144 (24.00)
No	165 (82.50)	186 (79.63)	71 (58.68)	34 (73.91)	456 (76.00)
N	200	233	121	46	600

X2 =26.52, d.f=3, significant at 5% level of significance

The Table 5.13 show that only 144 respondents out of 600 (24%) have stated that they have made complaints regarding defective products to various authorities. It seems that a vast majority of 76% have not bothered to make any complaints. Of the individuals belonging to post graduate category (E3) the responses for lodging a complaints are quite high, that is 41.32%. for professionally qualified (E4) and graduates (E3_ the percentages are 26.09 nad 20.17. the lowest response have come from the E1 category). In general it appears that lack of reports, complaints regarding defective items to the concerned authorities may be due to lack of courage, lack of knowledge and other reasons. However, X2 values of 26.52 for the 3 degrees of freedom has been found to be significant at 5 % level showing that response depends very much on the education category of the individual.

Thereafter, it is felt that complaints lodged by the individuals may be due to various problems faced by them regarding shortage of quantity, short size, excessive price, poor quality, misleading advertisement, etc. Eleven such categories of problems have been enumerated in the questionnaire. As such those individuals who have made complaints (Table 5.13) have been further asked to classify their complaints according to one or more of these categories of problems. Table 5.14 gives the number of complaints along with their percentage under the eleven categories of problems and for various educational categories.

Table 5.14 : Complaints of defective products by Problem Categories

Problem Category	*Educational Category*				
	E1	*E2*	*E3*	*E4*	*Total*
Measurement/Weight (short weight,size)	1 (2.86)	1 (2.13)	7 (14.00)	1 (8.33)	10 (6.94)
Price (excessive price)	3 (8.57)	5 (10.64)	10 (20.00)	3 (25.00)	21 (14.58)
Quality (adulteration)	18 (51.42)	33 (70.21)	26 (52.00)	3 (25.00)	80 (55.56)
Quantity (shortage)	0 (0.00)	4 (8.51)	2 (4.00)	1 (8.33)	7 (4.86)
Advertising (unethical,deceptive)	1 (2.86)	5 (10.64)	1 (2.00)	1 (8.33)	8 (5.56)
Servicing (non replacement of Items, no settlement of claims, harassments)	6 (17.14)	10 (21.28)	15 (30.00)	6 (50.00)	37 (25.69)
Warranty/Guarantee (defective products, poor service, etc).	1 (2.86)	9 (19.15)	11 (22.00)	2 (16.67)	23 (15.97)
Malpractice and Trade Unfair Means (black marketing)	0 (0.00)	0 (0.00)	2 (4.00)	0 (0.00)	2 (1.39)
Discrimination (differential discounts)	0	0 (0.00)	0 (0.00)	0 (0.00)	0 (0.00)
Health & Safety (spurious drugs,pollution)	0 (0.00)	2 (4.26)	1 (2.00)	0 (0.00)	3 (2.08)
Labelling	0 (0.00)	0 (0.00)	0 (0.00)	0 (0.00)	0 (0.00)
N	35	47	50	12	144

A close examination of the table shows that the complaints from the toltal number of respondents (144 in this case) are mostly about quality (55.65%) and servicing (25.69%), warranty/guarantee (15.97%0 about measurements (6.94%) quantity (4.86%). For quality the complaints have been made to the Departmental stores, local shopkeepers , manufacturers as well as dealers and these relate to refrigerators, musical systems, biscuits, detergent powder, powder milk, auto parts, sewing machine, mixer, grinders, electrical appliances, butter, tube, bread, oils, pickle and also cement. Education wise the responses for this problem category are 70.21% for educational category E2, 52.00% for E3, 51.42% for E1. surprisingly it is only 25.00% for the category E4. In the case of servicing complaints the name of the products on which complaints have been made either to the manufacturers/dealers, agents or departmental stores include fridge, music systems, radio, TV, etc. Some of the names of brands/ manufacturers are Kelvinator, BPL TV, Laxman Sylvania, VIP suitcase, Bata shoes, Nelco, Vespa, Escorts, etc. The maximum percentage of complaints is 50.00 for E4, followed by 30.00% for E3,21.28 for E2 and 17.14 for E1. similarly for problem category of warranty/guarantee the complaints largely relates to TV,fans,water heaters, fridge, watches, and name of the manufacturers include Onida/Belteck/Uptron (TV), Kelvinator/Voltas(fridge), Avanti (mopeds) and Titan (watches). The highest percentage of complaints is 22.00 from E3, next is 19.15 for E2, 16.67% for E4 and the lowest being E1 (2.86%). For price category the complaints are on soaps, oils,toothpaste, grocery items, butter. The prices charged by the shopkeepers are in general on the higher side. Here the percentages of complaints are 25.00, 20.00, 10.64 and 8.57for E4,E3,E2 and E1 respectively. As stated earlier the respondents for other categories are small, e.g., 14% of the respondents of E3 category have complained about short size of products, less weight of edible oils. 10.64 percent of E2 respondents have complained for unethical advertisements in case of Phillips, Hawkins, etc., and 4% for unfair trade practices in case of cigarettes manufactured by ITC.

Next we have further sub divided the number of complaints shown in Table 5.14 in

(i) number solved (S)

(ii) number unsolved (US)

These are given in table 5.15.

Problem Category	*Educational Category*								*Total*	
	E1		*E2*		*E3*		*E4*			
	S	*US*	*S*	*US*	*S*	*US*	*S*	*US*	*S*	*US*
Measurements (short size)	1 (10.00)	0 (0.00)	1 (10.00)	0 (0.00)	3 (30.00)	4 (40.00)	0 (0.00)	1 (10.00)	5 (50.00)	5 (50.00)
Price (excessive price)	1 (4.76)	2 (9.52)	1 (4.76)	4 (19.05)	5 (23.81)	5 (23.81)	2 (9.52)	1 (4.76)	9 (42.86)	12 (57.14)
Quality (adulteration,lack of quality)	11 (13.75)	7 (8.75)	19 (23.75)	14 (17.50)	17 (21.25)	9 (11.25)	2 (2.50)	1 (1.25)	49 (61.25)	31 (38.75)
Quantity (shortage)	0 (0.00)	0 (0.00)	1 (14.29)	3 (42.86)	0 (0.00)	2 (28.57)	1 (14.29)	0 (0.00)	2 (28.57)	5 (71.43)
Advertising (unethical)	0 (0.00)	1 (12.50)	1 (12.50))	4 (50.00)	0 (0.00)	1 (12.50)	1 (12.50)	0 (0.00)	2 (25.00)	6 (75.00)
Servicing (non replacement, harassments, non settlement	3 (8.11)	3 (8.11)	4 (10.81)	6 (16.22)	6 (16.22)	9 (24.32)	5 (13.51)	1 (2.70)	18 (48.65)	19 (51.35)
Warranty/Guarantee (defective products, poor service)	1 (4.35)	0 (0.00)	6 (26.09)	3 (16.04)	8 (34.78)	3 (13.04)	2 (8.70)	0 (0.00)	17 (73.91)	6 (26.09)
Malpractices & Unfair Trade (tie up sales,mistrading)	0 (0.00)	0 (0.00)	0 00)	0 (0.00)	0 (0.00)	2 (8.70)	0 (0.00)	0 (0.00)	0 (0.00)	2 (100.00)
Discrimination (differential discounts)	0 (0.00)	0 (0.00)	0 (0.00)	0 (0.00)	0 (0.00)	0 (0.00)	0 (0.00)	0 (0.00)	0 (0.00)	0 (0.00)
Health/Safety (spurious drugs,pollution)	0 (0.00)	0 (0.00)	1 (33.33)	1 (33.33)	1 (33.33)	0 (0.00)	0 (0.00)	0 (0.00)	2 (66.67)	1 (33.33)
Labelling	0 (0.00)	0 (0.00)	0 (0.00)	0 (0.00)	0 (0.00)	0 (0.00)	0 (0.00)	0 (0.00)	0 (0.00)	0 (0.00)

Note: S $\rightarrow$ Complaints solvedUS Complaints Unsolved

The percentages given in the table have been calculated on the basis of the number of complaints solved/unsolved for various educational categories in each of the problem category divided by the total number of complaints made in that category (as given in last column of table 5.14) multiplied by 100. for example, for category quality the number of cases solved for educational category E3 is 17 and the total number of complaints is 80. thus the percentage of success achieved by E3 is 21.25. Further the last column of Table 5.15 gives the total number of cases solved/unsolved and their percentages. A close look with the findings reveal that highest percentage of success in solving problems is 73.91 in case of warranty/guarantee category. This in turn consists of contribution of 34.78% from E3, 26.09% from E2, 8.70% from E4 and 4.35% from E1. In case of health and safety, total percentage of success is 66.67% contributed equally 33.33% by E2 and E3. 61.25% of cases have been solved for quality in which success achieved by E2 is the maximum (23.75%) followed by 21.25% by E3, 13.75% by E1 and and also 2.50% by E4.

Similarly for measurements out of 50.00% of the cases solved the success achieved by E3 is 30.00% and 10% each for both E2 and E1. for servicing category, 16.22% of successs has been achieved by the respondents of educational categoryE3, 13.51% by E4,10.81% and 8.11% by E2 and E1 respectively out of the total success per cent 48.65. for price category the highest percentage is 23.81 for E3, the next best is 9.52% for E4, the lowest being 4.76% for E1 and E2 both. In case of quantity only E2 and E4 have contributed 14.29% each for the overall success percentage of 28.57%. Lastly the lowest percentage of cases solved is 25.00% in case of advertisement. Out of this only E2 and E4 have contributed 12.50% each the rest of the complaints made by E1, E2 and E3 remained unsolved.

Importance of Various Consumer Issues

In the next section of the questionnaire nine important Consumer Issues have been listed and the respondents were asked to give their opinion as to the degree of importance they attach to each of the nine consumer issues. The findings have been summarized in Tables 5.16 and 5.17 . Let us now examine the impressions of the respondents on each issue separately from Table 5.16.

Table 5.16 : Degree of importance given by the respondents to specific issues of consumerism.

Specific Issues	*Most IMP*	*IMP*	*Neither IMP. Nor IMP*	*Un IMP*	*Most Un IMP*
Information	351 (58.50)	222 (37.00)	26 (4.33)	——	1 (0.17)
Health and Safety	460 (76.67)	102 (17.00)	35 (5.83)	2 (1.67)	1 (0.17)
Standards Repair Services	235 (39.17)	290 (48.33)	64 (10.67)	10 (1.67)	1 (0.17)
Pricing Issues	383 (63.83)	191 (31.83)	23 (3.83)	—	3 (0.50)
Pollution In Environment	321 (53.50)	212 (35.33)	57 (9.50)	7 (1.17)	3 (0.50)
Consumer Representation in Gov.	249 (41.50)	228 (38.00)	113 (18.83)	8 (1.33)	2 (0.33)
Product Quality	456 (76.00)	132 (22.00)	8 (1.33)	3 (0.50)	1 (0.17)
Advertising	106 (17.67)	295 (49.17)	170 (28.33)	27 (4.50)	2 (0.33)
Legislation	238 (39.67)	261 (43.50)	88 (14.67)	12 (2.00)	1 (0.17)

Note: IMP.—>IMPORTANT UNIMP—> UNIMPORTANT

1. Information : Here 95.50% of the total sample believe that information is a vital issue concerning consumerism in India. In fact customers feel that the manufacturers should aim at giving objective information which may enable them to make a choice a amongst products on the basis of their essential characteristics. The information can take the form of a label or to be introduced in the document available to the consumers in a clearly distinguishable manner.

2. Health and Safety : Consumers attitude towards this aspect is positive and 93.67% have stated that health and safety standard is a major issues of consumerism. The products sold should confirm to acceptable safety and health standards, product safety is basic requirement and Government and non Governement agencies should be vigilant that manufacturers and suppliers stick to them.

3. Repair and Services : A large majority of 87.50% of total respondents feel that this aspect of consumerism is very important and relevant.

4. Pricing : A significant section of the population, that is, 95.66% feel that pricing is an important issue. The general feeling is that price of an article vary greatly from one store to another. The price should be uniform everywhere and retail prices including local taxes should be same in all shops.

5. Pollution In The Environment : This is a serious consumer problem which is being encountered. With industrialization, air, water and the general environment is being polluted by dangerous substances posing potential threat to consumers' health and well being. It is pertinent to note that 88.83% feel that this is an important issue.

6. Consumer Representation : A good majority of 79.50% feel the need for more consumer representation in government and voluntary agencies. Consumers have felt that their growing voice and influence will make the consumer movement more fruitful. In fact the social phenomenon started by the consumer movement has helped in the formation of National Consumer Protection parties.

7. Product Quality : This aspect is an important factor concerning consumerism in India. The fact has been aptly reflected in the analysis since 98.00% feel the importance of this vital issue.

8. Advertisement : A fairly large majority (66.84%) have expressed that advertisements can play a vital role in consumerism provided they are not misleading incorrect or unethical.

9. Legislation : Last 83.17% believe that legislation play important role in consumer protection.

In order to further examine whether there is any agreement among the various educational categories in rating the specific issues of consumerism, we have calculated average weighted scores by assigning weights 2, 1,0, –1, –2. to

(a) most important

(b) important

(c) neither important nor unimportant

(d) unimportant

(e) most unimportant

These scores have been shown education wise and by total in Table 5.17 for each of the nine issues of consumerism under consideration.

Table 5.17 : Average weighted scores for specific issues of consumerism as per degree of importance (Education wise distribution)

Specific Issue	*Education Category*				
	E1	*E2*	*E3*	*E4*	*Total*
Information	1.45	1.56	1.59	1.67	1.54
Health and Safety Standards	1.53	1.74	1.81	1.89	1.70
Repair and Services	1.18	1.28	1.29	1.28	1.25
Pricing	1.63	1.58	1.56	1.48	1.59
Pollution in Environment	1.33	1.42	1.51	1.28	1.40
Consumer Representation in Government	1.20	1.21	1.09	1.28	1.19
Product Quality	1.69	1.78	1.69	1.76	1.73
Advertising	0.71	0.84	0.82	0.87	0.79
Legislation	1.19	1.15	1.30	1.26	1.20

The Kendalls' coefficient of concordance (w) =.92

X2 =29.50, d.f=8, significant at 5% level of significance

Examining the average weighted scores for total, we find that the highest rating of 1.73 has been given to product quality, followed by 1.70 to health and safety standards. These values are very near to 2 (Most Important) which is the highest possible score. Similarly all other ratings are above 1(Important) except in the case of advertisement. However in case of educational categories almost the same can trend can be seen. The Kendall's coefficient of concordance W and X2 have been found to 0.92 and 29.50 respectively. The value x2 is significant at 5% level, which indicates that there is strong evidence of concordance among the different educational categories in rating the specific consumer issues.

CONSUMER ATTITUDE TOWARDS CONSUMERISM

In order to determine general attitude on the part of consumers about specific marketing activities 39 statements, covering the various dimensions of consumerism have been listed. The respondents were asked to indicate as to what extent they agree/ disagree with these statements like earlier cases, the choices of levels of agreement have been fixed as

(a) Strongly agree

(b) Agree

(c) Neither agree nor disagree

(d) Disagree

(e) Strongly Disagree

For analysis, these 39 statements have been further categorized under seven groups, *viz.*,

(i) Philosophy of Business

(ii) Product Quality

(iii) Advertising

(iv) Other marketing Activities

(v) Consumerism

(vi) Consumer Responsibilty

(vii) Government Regulations.

The analysis carried out on the above basis has been given in Tables 5.18 – 5.31. for each aspect two tables have been constructed one showing individuals at various level of agreement and the other educational category wise average weighted score.

Table 5.18 : Consumer Attitude towards Philosophy of Business

STATEMENT	*LEVEL OF AGREEMENT*				
	Strongly Agree	*Agree*	*Neither agree nor Disagree*	*Disagree*	*Strongly Disagree*
Most of the manufacturers do not bother about customers	240 (40.00)	176 (29.33)	70 (11.67)	94 (15.67)	20 (3.33)
Most of the manufacturers are more interested in making profit rather than customer satisfaction	297 (49.50)	183 (30.50)	48 (8.00)	58 (9.67)	14 (2.33)
In general manufacturers produce according to the needs of consumers	45 (7.50)	272 (45.33)	115 (19.17)	135 (22.50)	33 (5.50)
Manufacturers perform the job of providing good products at reasonable process	22 (3.67)	96 (16.00)	147 (24.50)	256 (42.67)	79 (13.17)
If a customer gets injured, falls ill while using a defective product, the manufacturer should be made to pay damages	460 (76.67)	117 (19.50)	18 (3.00)	3 (0.50)	2 (0.33)

From the Table 5.18 we now examine all the five statements one by one. A majority of the respondents (69.33%) agreed that most of the manufacturers do not bother about customers. In fact barring a few reputed organizations others are apathetic towards customers. The answer to the second statement suggest that most of the manufacturers are more interested in making money rather than customer satisfaction. This view has been expressed by 80.00% of the sample respondents. It appears that Indian consumers are dissatisfied lot, their interests being neglected by the manufacturers due to want of any sound business policy looking into the consumer interest. 52.83% of the respondents are of the opinion that in general manufacturers produce according to the needs of the consumers. Since 28%, leaving aside 19.17% who are uncertain, have the opposite views, it is clear that opinions expressed for and against are more or less in the ration 2:1 a small minority of 19.67% respondents agreed that manufacturers are providing good products at reasonable rates. An overwhelming 55.84% are of the opinion that manufacturers seldom provide quality goods at reasonable rates. They are more interested in making profits rather than customer satisfaction by serving the customers in providing goods at fair prices. There is no doubt that this is an alarming situation in the Indian market. There is a very little doubt among the majority of the respondents that is 96.16% that if a customer gets injured or falls ill using a product which is defective the manufacturer should be made to pay the damages. A large number of individuals have reported cases of food poisoning, skin rashes, etc., and problems in using soaps, detergents and other cleaning agents. However, only 0.83% of the total sample surveyed which is very small, attribute the cases of these problems to people who do not read or ignore the instructions/warnings contained in the labels/packages of the product.

The Table 5.19 gives the education wise average weighted scores for these statements.

Table 5.19 : Philosophy of Business – Average weighted scores

STATEMENT	*EDUCATIONAL CATEGORY*				
	E1	*E2*	*E3*	*E4*	*TOTAL*
Most of the manufacturers Do not bother about consumers	0.95	1.02	0.52	0.72	0.87
Most of the manufacturer are more interested in making profits rather than customer satisfaction	1.03	1.30	0.56	1.09	1.15
In general manufacturers produce according to the needs of the consumer	–0.07	0.33	0.60	0.57	0.27
Manufacturers perform the job of providing good products at reasonable prices	–0.58	–0.40	–0.49	–0.11	–0.46
If a customer gets injured or falls ill while using a product the manufacturer should be made to pay the damages	1.68	1.74	1.69	1.83	1.72

The Kendall's coefficient of concordance (W)=.89.

X2 =14.20, d.f =4, significant at 5% level of significance

Examining the table we find that majority of the respondents irrespective of the educational category they belonged , agreed or strongly agreed with most of the statements as the average weighted scores are more than one. Only in the case of the statement "manufacturers perform the job of providing goods at reasonable rate" the scores are negative which shows that respondents from all the educational category disagreed with the statement. The value of Kendall's coefficient has been found to 0.89 which is significant at 5% level of significance. This confirms that there is concordance among educational categories E1,E2,E3,and E4 in rating the statements regarding the business philosophy.

The Table 5.20 and 5.21 deal with the second group of statement, that is, on Product Quality.

Table 5.20 : Consumers Attitude towards Product Quality

STATEMENT	*Level of Agreement*				
	Strongly Agree	*Agree*	*Neither Agree nor Disagree*	*Disagree*	*Strongly Disagree*
Quality of most of the products have been improving over the years	32 (5.33)	212 (35.33)	139 (23.17)	166 (27.67)	51 (8.50)
People look for packed and branded products while purchasing	133 (22.17)	314 (52.33)	12 (21.50)	24 (4.00)	0 (0.00)
People look for ISI mark on the package while making a purchase	150 (25.00)	271 (45.17)	127 (21.17)	50 (8.33)	2 (0.33)
The average person is willing to pay higher	150 (25.00)	310 (51.67)	67 (11.17)	60 (10.00)	13 (2.17)

prices for quality products that will ensure health and safety standards					

Regarding the responses to the statements from the above table, it has been revealed that a majority of 40.66% agreed that quality of products manufactured in India are improving with the passage of time. Three-fourth of the respondents agreed that people look for packed and branded products while purchasing a product, since they feel more secure and safe in using these products manufactured by the renowned firms. The third statement is complimentory to the earlier statements and 70.17% of the respondents believed that people look for an ISI/AGMARK/FPO etc., marks on the products/packages/containers including the labels while purchasing a products. This has been the trend of the buying habits of the Indian consumers as they feel that the products confirming to the above marks are quality products and are safe for usage. From the finding of the previous two statements, *viz.*, second and third, it is quite natural to expect that people will not mind in paying a little more with AGMARK, ISI mark, etc. The same feeling has been reflected by the majority (76.67%) in their responses to the statement which says that the average person is willing to pay higher process for quality products that will ensure health and safety standards.

Table 5.21 gives the average weighted scores calculated for the statements on product quality by various educational categories.

Table 5.21 : Product Quality Average Weighted Scores

	Educational Qualification				
STATEMENTS	*E1*	*E2*	*E3*	*E4*	*TOTAL*
Quality of most of the products have been improving over the passage of time.	–0.05	0.00	0.02	0.28	0.01
People look for packed and branded product while purchasing	0.80	0.99	0.96	1.07	0.93
People look for ISI/AGMARK/FPO on packages while purchasing	0.85	0.92	0.75	0.91	0.86
The average person is willing to pay more to ensure health standards and safety	0.87	1.10	0.57	0.54	0.87

The Kendall's coefficient of concordance (W)=.62 x2 =7.5 d.f=3, not significant at 5% level of significance

In Table 5.21 we observe that except the first statement quality of products have been improving over the passage of time the majority of the respondents belonging to various educational categories more or less agree with the rest of the statement. For the first statement the average weighted score are slightly less than zero for E1, nearly zero for E2 and E3 and marginaly above zero for E4. this indicates that majority of the respondents belonging to various educational categories are uncertain about this statement. For the other three statements the score are nearly one for all the educational categories. However the Kendall coefficient of concordance does not come out to significant at 5 % level of significance showing that there is no concurrence among the respondents belonging to various educational categories.

The finding of the third group which pertains to the advertisement have been given in Table 5.22 and 5.23

Table 5.22 : Consumers Attitude toward Advertising

	Level of Agreement				
STATEMENT	*Strongly Agree*	*Agree*	*Neither Agree nor disagree*	*Disagree*	*Strongly Disagree*
Most products advertising is believable	97 (16.17)	191 (31.83)	125 (20.83)	151 (25.17)	36 (6.00)
Advertising often persuades people to buy things they should not buy	126 (21.00)	288 (48.00)	105 (17.50)	73 (12.17)	8 (1.33)
Most advertisements are exaggerative and do not present the true picture of the product	149 (24.83)	265 (44.17)	87 (14.50)	95 (15.83)	4 (0.67)

Advertisements are reliable source of information about the quality and performance of the product	24 (4.00)	226 (37.67)	185 (30.83)	130 (21.67)	35 (5.83)
Advertising is usually for objectionable products and insults intelligence of consumers	24 (4.00)	107 (17.83)	248 (41.33)	200 (33.33)	21 (3.50)
Advertisements make false and misleading claims	46 (7.67)	156 (26.00)	226 (37.67)	161 (26.83)	11 (1.83)
Advertisements have no utility or role to play in society	29 (4.83)	81 (13.50)	107 (17.83)	264 (44.00)	119 (19.83)

From the Table 5.22 it has been revealed that only 48.00% of the respondents expressed their agreement that most product advertising is believable, 20.83% are uncertain about this and 31.37% disagree and feel that advertisements are misleading and deceptive in nature. 69% of the respondents feel that advertising by the manufacturing organizations often persuade people to buy things that they should not buy and most of the advertisements are edaggerative and do not presents the true picture of the products. These respondents have faced some kind of problems concerning incorrect and misleading advertisements. Only 41.67% believed that advertisements are reliable source of information about the quality and performance of the product. Most of the respondents were uncertain (41.33%) or disagreed that advertising is usually for objectionable products and insults the intelligence of the consumers. About one third, that 33.67% of the respondents believe that advertisements make false and misleading claims. The misleading false advertisements in general relate to various products like television, video and some equipment, furniture, cloth and footwears, cosmetics. Lastly majority of the respondents (63.83%) do not agree that advertisements have no role or utility to play in the society. They are of the opinion that some of the advertisements do influence their purchasing decision and the advertisements may provide them vital information such as where the product is manufactured, who has made the product or supplied the services, etc., what composition is to make appropriate decision for the buyers.

Table 5.23 gives the average weighted scores calculated on these statements for the educational categories.

Table 5.23 : Advertising – Average weighted Scores

STATEMENTS	*Educational Categories*				
	E1	*E2*	*E3*	*E4*	*TOTAL*
Most products advertising is believeable	0.39	0.29	0.02	0.3	0.27
Advertising often persuades people to buy things that they should not buy	0.68	0.75	0.78	1.02	0.75
most advertisements are exaggerative and do not present the true picture of products	0.69	0.72	0.91	0.98	0.77
Advertisements are reliable sources of information about the quality and performance of the product	0.15	0.20	0.05	0.11	0.12
Advertising is usually for objectionable products and insults intelligence of customers	–0.02	–0.19	–0.24	–0.14	–0.15
Advertisemensts make false and misleading claims	0.22	0.07	0.03	0.02	0.11
Advertisements have no utility or role to play in society	–0.37	–0.68	–0.84	–0.63	–0.61

The Kendalls coefficients of concordance (W)=.93, $\times 2$ =22.32, d.f = 6, significant at 5% level of significance.

The above table reveals that majority of the respondents belonging to the various educational categories agreed with the statements like advertising persuades people to buy things that they should not buy and most advertisements are exaggerative and do not present the true picture of the products as the average weighted scores are nearer to 1 in these cases. Statements which have negative average scores indicate disagreement among the educational categories. For example the statement advertisements have no utility or role to play in the society have scores approaching to minus one in most cases. Regarding the statements, advertisements are reliable sources of information about the product's quality and performance, advertising is usually for objectionable products and insults intelligence of consumers average weighted scores reveal that most of the respondents in all the educational categories either disagreed or were uncertain about these statements (average weighted scores being negative or approaching towards zero). The Kendall's coefficient of concordance W has been found to significant at % level of significance showing that there is concurrence among the respondents from various educational categories in rating the statements on advertisements.

The next group of questions and other marketing activities has three statements and the results of the analysis are given in Table 5.24 and 5.25.

Table 5.24 : Consumer Attitude towards Other Marketing Activities

STATEMENTS	*Level of Agreement*				
	Strongly Agree	*Agree*	*Neither Agree nor Disagree*	*Disagree*	*Strongly Disagree*
in general the quality of service provided by the manufacturers and dealers are getting better	25 (4.17)	220 (36.67)	150 (25.00)	158 (26.33)	47 (7.83)
generally the product guarantee is backed by the manufacturer	39 (6.50)	218 (36.33)	155 (25.83)	163 (27.17)	25 (4.17)
the contests that manufacturers sponsor to encourage the people to buy their products are usually dishonest	44 (7.33)	160 (26.67)	225 (37.50)	155 (25.83)	16 (2.67)

In response to notion that in general the quality of services provided by the manufacturers and dealers is getting better, 40.84% have expressed their agreement. Due to competitive market, various manufacturers of consumer goods are feeling the need for providing consumer satisfaction, thereby trying to improve upon the quality of services. Still there is dissatisfaction of the general public with the services they get and this has been voted by 34.16% of the respondents. It is apparent that much more has to be done by the manufacturers in improving the situation. The opinion that generally product guarantee is backed by the manufacturers has been expressed by 42.83% of the population. Whereas 31.34% disagree, 25.83 remain indecisive. 34% of the respondents agreed with the statement that the contest that the manufacturers sponsor to encourage people to buy their products are usually dishonest. However, 28.50% do not subscribe to this view. A large majority of 37.50% are unable to give any decision one way or other.

Table 5.25 gives weighted average scores by educational categories regarding other marketing activities.

Table 5.25 : Weighted Average Score – Other Marketing Activities

STATEMENTS	*Educational Activities*				
	E1	*E2*	*E3*	*E4*	*Total*
in general the quality of service provided by the manufacturer and dealers is getting better	-0.07	-0.03	0.17	0.39	0.03
generally the product guarantee is backed by the manufacturer	-0.11	0.06	0.48	0.67	0.14
the contest that manufacturers sponsors to buy the product are usually dishonest	0.25	0.12	-0.14	0.00	0.10

The Kendall's coefficient of concordance (W)=.06, X2 =.48 d.f=2, not significant at 5% level of significance.

Examining the table it can be observed that the responses of the respondents belonging to various educational categories are divided with respect to all the three statements as the average weighted scores are approaching towards zero in almost all the cases. The Kendall's coefficient of concordance has also been found to be not significant at 5% level of sigvificance showing there by that there is no concordance among the educational group in rating these statements on other marketing activities.

We now consider the group of statements which deals with consumerism. This group consists of nine statements and the results of analysis have been shown in Table 5.26 to 5.27

Table 5.26 : Consumer attitude towards consumerism

STATEMENTS	*Level of Agreement*				
	Strongly Agree	*Agree*	*Neither Agree nor Disagree*	*Disagree*	*Strongly Disagree*
manufacturers seem to be more sensitive to consumer complaints as compared to the past	28 (4.67)	191 (31.83)	131 (21.83)	191 (31.83)	59 (9.83)
most business firms make sincere efforts to entertain complaints	26 (4.33)	148 (24.67)	140 (23.33)	218 (36.33)	68 (11.33)
from the consumer viewpoint the procedure followed by most manufacturers and governments in handling complaints are not satisfactory	284 (47.33)	226 (37.67)	67 (11.17)	16 (2.67)	7 (1.17)
consumerism has not been an important factor in changing business practices and procedures	158 (26.33)	206 (34.33)	98 (16.33)	119 (19.83)	19 (3.17)
the exploitation of the consumers by the business firms deserve more attention than it receives	323 (53.83)	222 (37.00)	42 (7.00)	12 (2.00)	1 (0.17)
cheating on weights and measures should be punished severely	445 (74.17)	136 (22.67)	13 (2.17)	5 (0.83)	1 (0.17)
the sorry state of affairs about consumerism is due to lack of consumer education.	221 (36.83)	276 (46.00)	69 (11.50)	29 (4.83)	5 (0.53)
the future of consumerism will be important than it is today	155 (25.83)	321 (53.50)	112 (18.67)	12 (2.00)	0 (0.00)
the future of consumerism will be enduring	115 (19.17)	274 (45.67)	168 (28.00)	42 (7.00)	1 (0.17)

The Table 5.26 reveals that little over one third of the respondents surveyed, that is 36.50% are of the opinion that manufacturers seem to be more sensitive to consumer complaints as compared to the past. This is fairly true as we have seen from the study on industrial organizations given in a subsequent chapter that many Indian companies have started Consumer Service Call in their organizations at the corporate level and also grievances/complaints cell at branch level. Excluding 21.83% who are indecisive, 41,67 % disagree with the view and feel that much has still to be done by the Indian manufacturers to solve the complaints of the Indian buyers. 29% of the respondents agree that most business firm make sincere efforts to entertain consumers complaints. The percentage of disagreement is quite high, that is 47.67 and they feel complaints are not handled in proper manner. A large (85%) are of the opinion that from consumers point of view the procedures by most manufacturers and government in handling complaints and settling grievances are not satisfactory for the consumer. There is total lack of apathy for the consumer. Their voice is not heard, their claims are not settled and grievances are not handled properly. These are quite serious and need improvements on the part of the manufacturers and government organizations. The opinion that consumerism has not been an important factor in changing the business practices and procedures has been shared by 60.66% of the respondents surveyed. It is striking to note that 90.83% of the respondents feel that the exploitation of consumers by the business firms deserves more attention than it receives. Again an overwhelming 96.84% believe that cheating on weights and measures should be severely punished by the appropriate authorities. Over 82.00% of the respondents feel that the sorry state of affairs about consumerism in India is due to lack of consumer education. Due to this business community gets the opportunity to fleece the customers for their benefits. The percentage of respondents who feel that the future of consumerism will be important in India than it is today is as high as 79.33. Lastly 64.84 % of the total respondents surveyed have expressed the opinion that the future of consumerism in India will be enduring. The education wise weighted average score for the statements on consumerism have been shown in Table 5.27.

Table 5.27 : Consumerism Average Weighted Scores

STATEMENTS	Educational categories				
	E1	*E2*	*E3*	*E4*	*TOTAL*
manufacturers seem to be more sensitive to consumer complaints as compared to the past	–0.27	–0.13	0.12	0.20	-0.10
most business firm make sincere efforts to entertain consumer complaints	–0.48	–0.24	–0.05	0.07	-0.26
from the consumer point of view the procedures followed by most manufacturers and government in handling complaints is not satisfactory	1.40	1.27	1.07	1.28	1.27
consumerism has not been an important factor in changing business practices	0.75	0.63	0.36	0.54	0.61
the exploitation of the consumers by the business firms deserved more attention than it receives	1.49	1.46	1.27	1.33	1.42
Cheating on weights and measure should be punished severely	1.73	1.69	1.66	1.72	1.70
The sorry state of affairs about consumerism is due to lack of consumer education	1.17	1.15	1.07	1.04	1.13
The future of consumerism will be important than it is now	0.98	10.3	1.04	1.22	1.03
The future of consumerism will be enduring	0.67	0.77	0.87	0.93	0.77

The Kendall's coefficient of concordance (W)=.98, X2=31.45 d.f=8, significant at 5% level of significance

The Table reveals that majority of the respondents belonging to various educational category agreed strongly or agreed on most of the statements as the average weighted scores are 1 or more than 1. However in case of the statements manufacturers seem to be more sensitive to consumer complaints as compared to before and most business firms make sincere efforts to entertain consumer complaints most of the respondents belonging to different categories disagreed or were uncertain. Average weighted scores being negative or approaching zero, the Kendall's coefficient of concordance (w=.98) has been found to significant at 5%level of significance. This shows that there is fair degree of concurrence among the educational categories in rating the statements on consumerism.

Table 5.28 : Consumer attitude towards consumer responsibilities

STATEMENTS	Level of Agreement				
	Strongly Agree	*Agree*	*Neither Agree nor Disagree*	*Disagree*	*Strongly Disagree*
many of the mistakes consumers make in purchase of products are due to their own carelessness or ignorance	128 (21.33)	219 (36.50)	120 (20.00)	109 (18.17)	24 (4.00)
the problems of consumer are less serious now than before	50 (8.33)	203 (33.83)	145 (24.17)	142 (23.67)	60 (10.00)
consumers often try to take advantage of manufacturers and dealers by making claims that are not justified	41 (6.83)	101 (16.83)	147 (24.50)	217 (36.17)	94 (15.67)
protecting the environment is more important than improving the standard of our living	207 (34.50)	234 (39.00)	111 (18.50)	37 (6.17)	11 (1.83)

The above Table reveals that a majority of the respondents (57.83%) believe that many of the mistakes consumers make in purchase of a product are due to their own carelessness or ignorance. This may be due to lack of knowledge and education, also product information are not provided on most of the package/container. However there is a feeling among the respondents that consumers have some responsibilities and they should exert their rights and fight for their rights. They should make wise buying decisions and try to expose the activities of dishonest traders through various channels available and report the same to consumer authorities. Over 42% of the respondents surveyed think that the problem of consumers are less serious now than they were before. This apprehension by the respondents may be due to the various changes that have taken place in the recent past in the Indian market. Various legislations have been brought out by the government under the pressure of the activist groups to cater to the needs of the consumer interest. Now, there are various government regulation for the manufacturing organizations to produce better quality products. Most of the respondents disagree that consumers often try to take advantage of the manufacturers and dealers by making false claims that are not justified. People are becoming more and more aware about the protection of the environment and in fact is reflected out by the 73.50% respondents who felty that protecting our environment is more important than improving the standard of our living. Due to rapid industrialization development, our environment is getting polluted day by day by various means like noise, air, water etc. and existence of human being is threatened by pollution. So protecting our environment is of the prime importance for the survival of human beings and growth of human being and for the future generation to continue on this planet. It is quite heartening to know from the above analysis that a large majority of the population do realize the danger of environment pollution. However more effort is needed to improve the situation further. The government with the active help and cooperation of all concerned, industries, individuals, etc., must formulate an action plan to protect the environment from various types of pollution.

We now analyse the education wise distribution of the average weighted scores for these statements as given in Table 5.29.

Table 5.29 : Consumer responsibilities – Average weighted scores

STATEMENTS	*Educational categories*				
	E1	*E2*	*E3*	*E4*	*TOTAL*
many of the consumers, mistake in purchasing products are due to their own carelessness or ignorance	0.29	0.65	0.52	1.00	0.53
the problem of consumers are less serious now than they were before	0.10	0.04	0.08	0.26	0.07
consumers often try to take advantages of manufacturers and dealers by making false claims that are not justified	-0.37	-0.39	-0.40	-0.20	-0.52
protection of the environment is more important than improving our standards of living	0.85	1.09	0.91	1.20	0.98

The Kendall's coefficient of concordance (W)=1.00, X2 =12.00, d.f= 3, significant at 5% level of significance.

From the Table it can be seen that respondents belonging to all the educational categories agreed or were uncertain on all the statements except the statement consumers often try to take advantage of the manufacturers or dealers by making claims that are not justified, where most of the respondents from various categories either disagreed or were uncertain. The Kendall's coefficient of concordance W has been found to be equal to 1.00 ahowing perfect concurrence among the educational categories in rating the statements. This has been confirmed by X2 test also.

The last group of statements consists of seven statements which relate to government regulations. The findings on them have been given in Table 5.30 and 5.31

Table 5.30 : Consumer attitude towards government regulations

STATEMENTS	*Level of Agreement*				
	Strongly Agree	*Agree*	*Neither Agree Nor Disagree.*	*Disagree*	*Strongly Disagree*
I feel I am being cheated when it says 'local taxes extra'	178 (29.67)	227 (37.83)	98 (16.33)	91 (15.17)	6 (1.00)
the govt. should test competing brands of products and make	376 (62.67)	197 (32.83)	19 (3.17)	6 (1.00)	2 (0.33)

the results of these tests available to consumer.					
The govt. should set minimum standard of quality for consumer products	393 (65.50)	175 (29.17)	18 (3.00)	8 (1.33)	6 (1.00)
govt. should control food prices	411 (68.50)	157 (26.17)	19 (3.17)	9 (1.50)	4 (0.67)
the govt. should exercise more responsibilities for regulating the advertising, sales,and marketing activities of the manufacturers	308 (51.33)	205 (34.17)	66 (11.00)	19 (3.17)	2 (0.33)
the various consumer protection laws made by the govt. are inadequate in providing consumer protection	299 (49.83)	215 (35.83)	73 (12.17)	12 (2.00)	1 (0.17)
Consumer Protection Act will be helpful in protecting the interest of the consumers	217 (36.17)	286 (47.67)	72 (12.00)	21 (3.50)	4 (0.67)

Examining the statements one by one we find that about two third of the respondents surveyed (67.50%) agree or strongly agree with the statement 'I feel cheated when the package says local taxes extra. The consumers feel the price of the product generally cost more than expected since many of the products state only the basic prices with the extra costs relating to other chargeable taxes which vary from state to state. This creates confusion in the minds of the buyers as to the prices of different products that are sold in the market. To avoid such confusions, government should make it mandatory for the manufacturers to print the price of the product including all taxes for the state. An overwhelming majority of 95.50% is of the opinion that the government should test the competing brands of products and make the results available to the consumers as to help them make a better purchase decision. A vast majority of 94.67% maintains that the government should set minimum standard for quality of consumer products. 94.67% of the respondents surveyed want government should control the food prices in India. Food items are essential commodity for the Indian buyers throughout the length and breadth of the country. Hence the government has a responsibility to control the prices of food items, so that general public may get the essential commodity at a fair price in adequate quantities and also free from adulteration. The government should exercise more responsibility for regulating the advertising, sales and marketing activities of the manufacturers is the view expressed by 85.50% of the respondents. They are of the opinion that the administrative authority should strictly control the business practices of the manufacturers to provide satisfaction to the consumers.

A large majority of 85.66% feels that the various consumer protection legislations made by the government are inadequate in providing protection to consumers. Besides, there is a need for stringent control and action on the part of the administrative authorities to enforce the existing consumer legislation that are available in India to protect the interests of the consumers. Many individuals (83.84%) believe that Consumer Protcction Act will be helpful in protecting and promoting the interests of the consumers' in India. Admittedly this particular legislation will go a long way in fulfilling the expectations of the Indian consumers.

Finally the Table 5.31 gives the average weighted scores for the above statement.

Table 5.31 : Government Regulations—Average weighted Scores

	Educational categories				
STATEMENTS	*E1*	*E2*	*E3*	*E4*	*TOTAL*
I feel I am being cheated when it says 'local taxes extra	1.01	0.71	0.68	0.67	0.80
the government should test competing brands of products and make the results of these tests available to consumer	1.60	1.56	1.57	1.46	1.57

the govt. should set minimum standard of quality for consumer products	1.51	1.61	1.60	1.57	1.57
govt. should control food prices	1.67	1.58	1.62	1.41	1.59
the govt.should exercise more responsibility for regulating the advertising, sales and marketing activities of the manufacturers	1.41	1.30	1.27	1.30	1.33
the various consumer protection laws made by the government are inadequate in providing protection to consumers	1.43	1.32	1.31	1.07	1.33
Consumer Protection Act will be helpful in protecting the interest of the consumer	1.10	1.17	1.12	1.22	1.15

The Kendall's coefficient of concordance (w)=.90, X2=21.64, d.f=6, Significant at 5% level of significsnce.

The Table reveal that majority of the respondents from the various educational category agreed or strongly agreed on all the statements since average weighted score are more than 1 the coefficient of concordance has ben found to be .90 which is significant at 5% level of significance. This shows that concurrence among the educational categories in rating the various statement is quite high.

Lastly the respondents were asked to give their opinion among the various factors or means which may help in strengthening the consumer movement in India. Some of the factors like company action, holding of conference/seminars, mass media, etc., which are relevant in strengthening consumerism in India have been included in the question. The responses in this regard have been recorded in Table 5.32.

Table 5.32 : Consumers responses on strengthening of consumerism in India.

Factors on which Consumer Opinion Sought	*Educational categories*				
	E1	*E2*	*E3*	*E4*	*TOTAL*
Company action	51 (25.50)	77 (33.05)	46 (38.02)	20 (43.48)	194 (32.33)
Holding of Seminars	36 (18.00)	62 (26.61)	43 (35.54)	14 (30.43)	155 (25.83)
Mass Media	112 (56.00)	175 (75.19)	97 (80.17)	33 (71.74)	417 (69.50)
Voluntary Organizations	57 (28.50)	119 (51.07)	65 (53.62)	24 (52.17)	265 (44.17)
Government Action	139 (69.50)	182 (78.11)	101 (83.47)	32 (69.57)	454 (75.67)
Any other	7 (3.50)	14 (6.01)	13 (10.74)	2 (4.35)	36 (6.00)
N	200	233	121	46	600

Analysis of the various means for strengthening the consumer movement in India as suggested by the respondents is as bwlow:

1. Company Action: 32.33% of the respondents surveyed would like to see more company action in consumer matters than at present. They are of the opinion that industrial organizations should become more consumer oriented. They should work together more with government and consumer organizations. Education wise the highest response is 43.48% for E4 and the lowest is 25.50% for E1.

2. Holding of Seminars: The response to this query is poor, only 25.83% of the community have desired more consumer education , that is , informing the consumers of their rights, public awareness campaigns through conferences or seminars. Here the highest response (35.54%) is form the educational category E3 and the lowest (19.00%) is from E1.

3. Mass Media: In this case 69.50% of the respondents feel that consumer education may be provided through mass media like radio and television the percentages for educational category E2, E3 and E4 are all above 70, it is only 56.00% for E1.

4. Voluntary Organizations: 44.17% of the total sample surveyed have desired greater involvement in consumer matters by the voluntary organizations. They expect the voluntary organizations to play appositive part in consumer movement, to assist the consumers to fight for their rights, to conduct more investigations and adopt a stronger watch dog role. Education wise the responses are above 50.00% for all categories except for E1 for which it is quite low (28.50%).

5. Government Action: A very large majority of 76.67% who have responded to this query and would like to see more government involvement in stricter enforcement of existing legislations and mounting more investigations against defaulters. They also expect government's greater control over prices, more price surveillance and more for information concerning governments role for public welfare. Like wise the highest percentage came form educational category E3, the percentage being 83.47. similarly 78.11% have responded from E2. the percentage for E4 and E1 are more or less same that is 69.57 and 69.50 respectively

6. Any Other: The main response under this category have been the action by consumers themselves. The response is very poor and only 6.00% of the respondents surveyed mostly among E3 feel that consumers themselves have a role to play in the strengthening of the consumer movement India. In fact they want that Indian consumers should be more aware of their roles and activities and should participate vigorously through the activist group so as to make a significant contribution towards a powerful consumer movement in India.

In conclusion it may be observed that awareness to consumer rights is more for higher educated individuals. The necessity for including issues like information, health and safety standards, environmental pollution, product quality, etc., under consumerism have been felt by most of the respondents. Consumers irrespective of their educational qualification do look for various information like price, quality, date of expiry, etc., on the package/container while making their purchases. On most of the cases there is concurrence in rating various statements on general consumer issues classified under broad categories like philosophy of business, product quality, advertising, consumer responsibility, etc. For strengthening consumer movement in India the majority respondents feel that government should take some concrete measures to safeguard the interest of the consumers. They also suggested active participation by management and use of of mass media like radio and televison. Surprisingly few consumer have favoured action by consumers themselves in strengthening the consumer movement in India.

Sampling inspection is not a good substitute for 100% inspection

—✦—✦—✦—

Chapter 6

Consumerism and Consumer Movement — An Opinion Survey of Companies in India

This chapter is based on the opinions expressed by the company executives of the Indian industries (small/medium/large scale) concerning consumerism and consumer protection. The classification of industries into small, medium and large scale have been made on the basis of their annual turnover. Those companies whose annual turnover is up to 1 crore have been classified as small scale industry (S), those from 1 crore to 10 crore as medium (M) and over 10 crore as large scale (L). a questionnaire involving various aspects of consumerism and consumer movement was prepared and information was collected from the above categories of industries. In this regard 100 organizations have been surveyed. A simple analysis carried out on the basis of frequencies and percentages an as follows. Figures in parenthesis in all tables represent percentages while witout parenthesis are simple frequencies.

The distribution of 100 companies in different categories of manufacturers have been shown in Table 6.1

Table 6.1 : Distribution of organizations based on Annual Turnover

Category	*Annual Turnover (in rupees)*	*Number*
Small Scale Organizations	up to 1 crore (33.33)	33
Medium Scale Organizations	1 crore to 10 crores (25.00)	25
Large Scale Organizations	Above 10 crores (42.00)	42
Total		100 (100.00)

Out of the hundreds respondents the distribution of three categories of organizations is more or less of the same order, 42% and 33.33% comprise large scale and small scale industries respectively, 25% belong to medium scale industries.

Table 6.2 shows further classification, organizations according to ownership, *viz*., sole ownership, partnership, company proprietory/corporate ltd.

Table 6.2 : Ownership types of organizations

Types of Ownership	*Category of Organizations*			*Total*
	L	*M*	*S*	
Sole Ownership	2 (4.76)	3 (12.00)	1 (3.03)	6 (6.00)
Partnership	—	—	8 (24.24)	8 (8.00)

Company: Corporate ltd.	40 (95.24)	22 (88.00)	24 (72.73)	86 (86.00)
N	42	25	33	100

From the above Table we find that majority belong to the company type of ownership irrespective or category of organizations. Thus 95.24% of the large scale industry, 88% of the medium scale and 72.73% of small scale industry have company form of ownership. For large scale and medium scale there are no partnership type of ownership which is quite normal. For small scale industries, we naturally expect partnership and this has reflected in the analysis of these industries are owned on partnership basis.

Next to ascertain the marketing objective of the companies the respondent organizations were enquired about it. The responses of the organization were as follows.

Table 6.3 : Marketing objective of the companies

Objectives	*Category of Organizations*			*Total*
	L	*M*	*S*	
To remain leader in the market	31 (71.81)	8 (32.00)	5 (15.15)	44 (44.00)
To satisfy the consumer	34 (80.95)	15 (60.00)	19 (57.57)	68 (68.00)
To maintain or increase share in the market	22 (52.38)	9 (36.00)	9 (27.27)	40 (40.00)
To build image as a supplier of quality goods	34 (80.95)	15 (60.00)	22 (66.67)	71 (71.00)
Any other (improvement in sales after service for customer satisfaction)	2 (4.76)	—	—	2 (2.00)
N	42	25	33	100

The Table reveals that the majority of the organizations (71%) try to build their image for supplying quality goods. Further a good number of them want tot satisfy the consumers (68%) and to remain keaders in the market (44%). Few organizations (40%) want to maintain or increase share in the market. With respect to the category of the organizations it has been seen that 80.95% of large scale organizations refer to satisfy their customers or build their image in the market and 73.81% want to remain leader in the market. For medium scale organizations it has been seen that 60% want to satisfy their customers or build their image but only 32% want ot remain leader in the market. For small scale organizations 57.57% want ot satisfy their customers where as 16.67% would like to build their image and only 15.15% want to reamain leader in the market. 52.38% of large scale industries prefer to maintain or increase share in the market the same is true only for 36% and 27.27% of medium and small scale industries respectively.

As regards after sales services, only 4.76% of large scale organizations pay attention in improving such services, but medium and smallscale organizations are little bothered about the customers once the sales procedures are completed. It may be noted that most of the marketing organizations are consumer oriented and further improvement of after sales services are strongly needed for all categories of organizations for the well being of the consumers, thus not only quality products are needed to be supplied but also adequate after sales service should be provided for the greatest satisfaction of the customers.

CONSUMER PROTECTION LEGISLATION APPLICABLE TO VARIOUS FIRMS

The organizations were then asked to indicate the main consumer protection legislations applicable to their firms. Their responses have been tabulated in Table 6.4

Table 6.4 : Consumer protection legislation applicable to various firms.

Consumer Protection Legislations	*Category of Organizations*			*Total*
	L	*M*	*S*	
Standard of Weights and Measures Act 1976. The Standard of Weight and Measures (packaged commodities rules1977)	5 (11.90)	—	1 (3.03)	6 (6.00)

The Essential Commodities Act 1955	2 (4.76)	2 (8.00)	—	4 (4.00)
The Prevention of Food Adulteration Act 1954	5 (11.90)	3 (12.00)	—	8 (8.00)
The Consumer Protection Act 1986	4 (9.52)	2 (8.00)	—	6 (6.00)
The Drugs and Magic Remedies (objectionable advertisement) 1954	3 (7.14)	3 (12.00)	1 (3.03)	7 (7.00)
The Bureau of Indian Standards Act 1986 The Agricultural Products 1937	9 (21.43)	1 (4.00)	4 (12.12)	14 (14.00)
The Monopolies and Restrictive Trade Practices Act 1969	2 (4.76)	—	1 (3.03)	3 (3.00)
Other Shops and Establishment Act	—	—	8 (24.24)	8 (8.00)
Not applicable/ Not mentioned	18 (42.86)	16 (64.00)	20 (60.61)	54 (54.00)
N	42	25	33	100

From the Table it is observed that though most of the org. are aware of one or more of the consumer protection legislations applicable to their firms, e.g. Bureau of Indian Standards Act 1986 (14%), the essential commodities Act 1955 (4%), the Prevention of food adulteration Act 1954(8%), yet a large majority of 54% have not given any comment ahowing lack of knowledge amongst executives aboute these legislations. Even for large scale organizations about 43% could not give their comments. It is quite high figure for these organizations and the situation requires remedial measures. It is felt that menagers of the large organizations who are working in different departments should be given training and education on consumer protection laws for improving the quality of products and proper distribution of the same.

In case of the medium scale and small scale industries the awareness to consumer protection law is even lower than the large scale industries. In fact 64% of the medium scale industries could not name the legislations applicable to their firms. Thus proper training of executives from time to time is necessary for the above two organizations also. Further business executives pay more attention to the legal aspects of marketing. It should be noted that the volume of the consumer problems could be considerably reduced by effective implementations of the consumer protection laws.

Next an analysis of the manufacturers opinion as to how the consumer protection legislations are helpful has been carried out and the results are given in Table 6.5.

Table 6.5 : Manufacturers opinion on how consumer protection laws are helpful

Opinions	*Category of Organizations*			
	L	***M***	***S***	***Total***
To increase the sales	6 (38.09)	2 (8.00)	3 (9.09)	11 (11.00)
To provide customer satisfaction	24 (57.14)	22 (88.00)	12 (36.36)	58 (58.00)
Maintenance and quality improvement	3 (7.14)	1 (4.00)	2 (6.06)	6 (6.00)
Others/not applicable	11 (26.19)	1 (4.00)	17 (51.51)	29 (29.00)
N	42	25	33	100

From the Table we find that more than half of the organizations (58%) are of the opinion that these legislations provide satisfaction to the consumers. Very few organizations (11%) feel that these legislations are helpful in increasing the sales. Similarly a very small number of them (6%) think that legislations are helpful in maintaining andimproving the quality of the products. For large scale industries 57.14% of them feel that these laws provide satisfaction to the customers. The figures for the medium scale and small scale organizations are 88% and 36.36% respectively. Though 38.09% of the large scale industries think that the laws are helpful in increasing the sales, only 8% of medium scale industries and about 9% of small scale industries feel likewise. Similarly 7.14%, 4% and 6.06% of large, medium and small scale industrie respectively feel that these legislations are helpful in maintaining and improving the quality of the products.

The responses of the manufacturers towards consumerism and consumer protection laws in relation to the marketing efforts have been tabulated in Table 6.6

Table 6.6 : Consumerism and consumer protection laws related to marketing efforts

Opinions	*Category of Organizations*			
	L	*M*	*S*	*Total*
An opportunity	28 (66.67)	10 (40.00)	17 (51.51)	55 (55.00)
Obstruction	1 (2.38)	9 (36.00)	5 (15.15)	15 (15.00).
Others	4 (9.52)	2 (8.00)	—	6 (6.00)
No response	9 (21.43)	4 (16.00)	11 (33.33)	24 (24.00)
N	42	25	33	100

From the Table the predominant and consistent view which emerges for all categories of organizations (55%) is that the consumer protection laws are an opportunity to increase their marketing efforts. While only a small minority (15%) feel that these legislations are an obstruction to their marketing efforts, others (24%) have not offered any comments. About 67% , 40% and 52% of the large, medium, and small scale organizations respectively feel that these legislations are an opportunity to their marketing efforts. Only 2.38% of large scale, 36% of medium scale and 15.15% of the small scale industries feel that these legislations are an obstruction to their marketing efforts. No comments have been received in case of 21.43%, 16% and 33.33% of large, medium and small scale organizations respectively. In spite of these observations we find that manufacturing organizations are feeling the impact of comsumerism and trying to adjust the challenging situation ahead of them.

Consumer complaints and grievances

Table 6.7 shows the various modes of communication through which the complaints are received form the consumers.

Table 6.7 : Modes of communication for receiving complaints from consumers

MODES	*Category of Organizations*			
	L	*M*	*S*	*Total*
Through consumers directly	35 (83.33)	13 (52.00)	17 (51.51)	65 (65.00)
Through voluntary organizations/ associations	7 (16.67)	2 (8.00)	4 (12.12)	13 (13.00)
Through dealers/distributors	32 (76.19)	17 (68.00)	13 (39.39)	62 (62.00)
Through government dept.	10 (23.80)	6 (24.00)	2 (6.06)	18 (18.00)
Company's own sales force	5 (11.90)	—	3 (9.09)	8 (8.00)
Media	1 (2.38)	—	—	1 (1.00)
Not applicable/ No response	1 (2.38)	—	1 (3.03)	2 (2.00)
N	42	25	33	100

It is evident from the table that mostly the complaints are received from either through customers directly (65%) or through dealers/distributors (62%). The complaints received through government departments like MRTPC and through voluntary organizations are very few (18% and 13%) respectively. In case of large scale organizations the complaints received directly through consumers are 83.33% whereas 52% consumers of medium scale industries and 51.51% of small scale industries are prepared to send their complaints directly to the organizations. The complaints received through dealers and distributors are quite high, 76.19%, 68% and 39.39% for the large, medium and small scale industries respectively. Through government departments like MRTPC these figures are quite low and are only 23.8%, 24% and 6.06%. about 12% of the complaints for large scale industries and 9% complaints for small scale manufacturers have been received by the firms through their own sales force. This is present trend of consumer complaints to manufacturing organizations. It is interesting to note that company's sales force are the real spokesman of the company. In their area of operation, they come in contact with the genuine customer through the various outlets. In many cases they meet the actual users face to face. If the management of the company utilizes their services properly they can get the feedback for, the rural as well urban customers. The marketing executives can utilize their sales force to build up a good customer relations by solving the consumer grievances on the spot through them and also with the active cooperation of their enlightened dealer and distributors.

The companies receive various types of complaints from the customers relating to the quality of products, replacement of defective products, etc., the kind of general complaints experienced by the organizations are depicted in Table 6.8

Table 6.8 : Distribution of organizations regarding the kind of complaints received

COMPLAINTS	*Category of Organizations*			*Total*
	L	*M*	*S*	
Compensation	7 (16.67)	3 (12.00)	1 (3.03)	11 (11.00)
Refund	8 (19.05)	2 (8.00)	1 (3.03)	11 (11.00)
Replacement	16 (38.09)	6 (24.00)	11 (33.33)	33 (33.33)
Quality	24 (57.14)	10 (40.00)	13 (39.39)	47 (47.00)
Service	8 (19.05)	7 (28.00)	10 (30.30)	25 (25.00)
Warranty/guarantee	5 (11.90)	6 (24.00)	4 (12.12)	15 (15.00)
Advertisements	—	1 (4.0)	—	1 (1.00)
Any other	—	—	—	—
Not applicable/ No response	3 (7.14)	2 (8.00)	—	5 (5.00)
N	42	25	33	100

From the Table it is clear that majority of the complaints received are related to quality of goods, (47%). Next complaints related to replacement (33%), services (25%), guarantees (15%), compensation (11%) and refund (11%) in that descending order. In case of large scale industries 57.14% complaints are for quality whereas 40% and 39.39% of complaints from medium and small scale industries are for the same. The complaints regarding compensation are 16.67% and 12% for large and small scale industries respectively and 3.03% for small scale industries. Complaints related to warranty/guarantee are 24% for medium scale, these are about 12% for both small scale and large scale organizations. The complaints related to refund are 19.05% for large scale but only 8% and 3.03% for medium and small scale industries. The above analysis tends to confirm that high percentage of complaints received by the business organizations irrespective or their category, for necessary action.

The kind of action taken by marketing organizations for handling the consumer grievances have been given in Table 6.9.

Table 6.9 : The ways in which consumer complaints are handled by the organizations

WAYS	*Category of Organizations*			*Total*
	L	*M*	*S*	
Sending them polite letters	19 (45.24)	6 (24.00)	8 (24.24)	33 (33.00)
Replacement of product	33 (78.57)	10 (40.00)	19 (45.24)	62 (62.00)

Compensating	21 (50.00)	6 (24.00)	1 (3.03)	28 (28.00)
Servicing the equipment	10 (23.81)	11 (44.00)	18 (54.54)	39 (39.00)
Personal visit by the company's representatives to the aggrieved perty	6 (14.29)	—	1 (3.03)	7 (7.00)
Non applicable/ No response	1 (2.38)	3 (12.00)	2 (6.06)	6 (6.00)
N	42	25	33	100

It is evident from the Table the organizations have been taking some kind of actions in handling the consumer grievances. The Table reveals that majority of them (62%) have replaced their products. Some 39%, have serviced the equipment. Few of the 33% have sent polite letters in response to the complaints received. Still fewer 28% have compensated. The personal visits by the company's representatives to the aggrieved parties have been in very few occasions, 78.57% have replaced the defective product, 50% by way of compensation and 45.24% by servicing the equipments and ony 14.29% by sending representatives for personally looking into the grievances of the consumers. For medium scale industries 44% have handled the complaints by servicing the equipment, 40% by replacing the products, 24% for both sending polite letters and compensation. None of them have sent any representatives to the aggrieved parties. For small scale organizations 54.54% have serviced the product, 45.24% have replaced theproduct, 24.24% have sent polite letters whereas 3.03% have sent representative to solve the problems at a personal level and another 3.03% have compensated. Also many of the organizations have set up consumer sercice cells in their organizations mainly at the head office and branch office to take prompt actions against the grievances of their customers. However, greater efforts are needed to handle the consumers grievances more effectively.

Ways to provide satisfaction to consumers

The next set of questions that was asked, to all the respondents as to whether they have made any change in their product or its marketing for the customer satisfaction. The responses in this regard have been recorded in the form of the Table 6.10.

Table 6.10 : Changes made by the manufacturers in the product for customer satisfaction

RESPONSES	*Category of Organizations*			
	L	*M*	*S*	*Total*
Yes	15 (35.71)	7 (28.00)	17 (51.52)	39 (39.00)
No	27 (64.29)	18 (72.00)	16 (48.48)	61 (61.00)
N	42	25	33	100

It is observed that from the Table that majority of the respondents (61%) have not made any improvements whereas rest 39% have made changes in their products for the customer's satisfaction. For large scale industries 64.29% have not made any changes. In case of medium scale manufacturers the figures are 72% and 28%. For small scale organizations the above trend is reversed as 52.52% have reported changes made in their product. The above 48.47% have made no such changes. The above analysis reveals that the situation is quite alarming for Indian consumer and Indian industries should come up to serve the customers in a better way. At present their services are much below expectations of their customers. It is important to note that there have been a lot of complaints by the Indian customers who are dissatisfied with the poor quality of the products and improper services. Hence manufacturing concerns have to pay more attention to solve the problem of their customers and handle their grievances promptly, also to make necessary changes and bring in innovations to produced goods as per the needs of the customers so as to stay alive in the competitive business world.

Those organizations which have reported to have made changes/improvements in their products or their marketing, were asked to indicate the kind of changes they have made. The details in this regard are shown in Table 6.11

Table 6.11 : Changes made by organizations in their product or marketing

TYPE OF CHANGES	*Category of Organizations*			
	L	*M*	*S*	*Total*
Producing better quality product	6 (40.00)	4 (57.14)	8 (47.26)	18 (46.15)
Design modification	3 (20.00)	—	2 (11.76)	5 (12.82)
Application of modern technology	3 (20.00)	—	2 (11.76)	5 (12.82)
Improvement in after sale service	4 (26.67)	3 (42.86)	3 (17.65)	10 (25.64)
Improvement in better packaging	1 (6.67)	—	4 (23.53)	5 (12.82)
Setting up consumer grievances cell	6 (40.00)	1 (14.29)	1 (5.88)	8 (20.51)
Introduction of effective distribution system	1 (6.67)	1 (14.29)	1 (5.88)	3 (7.69)
Others	—		3 (17.65)	3 (7.69)
N	15	7	17	39

Percentages are more than 100 because of multiple responses.

From The Table we find that a significant majority of professional organizations (46.15%) actually went ahead to produce better quality products. Only 25.64% in setting up of consumers grievance cell, 12.82% each in modification of design, on application of modern technology and improvement of better packaging. Again a bare 7.69% of the organizations have introduced effective distribution system to resolve the consumers' grievances quickly. For large scale organizations 40% have been producing better quality products, 8% have set up consumer grievances cell and 26.67% have made improvement in after sales services. Again 20% have made design modifications, and 20% have applied modern technology. Only 7% have introduced effective distribution system. For medium scale organizations 57.14% are for providing quality goods, 42.86% have made improvements in after sales service only. 14.29% are for setting up consumer grievance cell and another 14.29% for introduction of effective distribution system. None of them applied design modification or applied modern technology. In case of small scale industries, 47.06% are for providing quality goods, 25.53% for improvement of better packaging, 17.65% for design modification, 11.76% for application of modern technology, 5.88% for setting up of consumer grievances cell and another 5.88% for introduction of effective distribution system. About 18% have made changes which are not covered on any of the earlier types.

Who should be responsible for consumer welfare?

Here we have examined the attitudes of marketing professional to four distinct type of parties in consumer matters, namely

(i) management of the organizations/trade and industry

(ii) government and their agencies

(iii) non government/voluntary organizations and

(iv) the consumer themselves.

Table 6.12 : Manufacturers opinion on who should be responsible for consumer welfare in India

OPINIONS	*Category of Organizations*			
	L	*M*	*S*	*Total*
Management of the company	33 (78.57)	18 (72.00)	22 (66.67)	73 (73.00)
Voluntary organizations	10 (23.81)	5 (20.00)	10 (30.30)	25 (25.00)
Government and their agencies	27 (64.29)	13 (52.00)	10 (30.30)	50 (50.00)

Consumer themselves	4 (9.52)	2 (8.00)	—	6 (6.00)
No response	—	—	2 (6.06)	2 (2.00)
N	42	25	33	100

From the Table it can be concluded that majority of the organizations (73%) would like to see more professionalism in the management of the companies and involvement of the management of the business organizations in the consumer activities. Thus the desire for active participation of the management of trade and industry in the consumer matter is very high. A sizeable majority (50%) felt that the various governmental department and their agencies should play a vital role in the interests of the consumer, specially in the rural and backward areas. As depicted in the Table, active portion of the population (25%) seems to be satisfied with the current involvement non government consumer organizations on consumer matters and feels that they should play a vital role for the consumers protection activities and consumerism welfare in India. Only a small minority (6%) of the respondents feel that the need for involvement of consumer themselves. For large scale industries 78.57% want involvement of the management of the company, 69.29% are for the non government agencies, but only 9.52% are for the consumer themselves. For medium scale organizations these figures are 72%, 52%, 20% and 8% respectively. In case of small scale industries it is 66.67% for management involvement, 30.30% for both government and non government agencies whereas 6% have not responded.

From the above discussion, it is clear that consumer must be more aware, learn how to distinguish needs from wants, should ask for more information and question about prices, availability and quality of goods and services. The consumers should be able to act on their behalf backed up by the confidence of knowledge and learning how to get a fair deal. They must be united to fight against the malpractices of the traders. Only vigilant consumers can save themselves from unscrupulous businessmen. Consumers should protest against the business injustice and should make every endeavour to correct these injustices single handedly or collectively. They should safeguard their own interests and right in an organised manner, *viz.*, to form citizen groups. Together such groups can acquire the strength and influence to make sure that adequate attention is given to consumer interest.

Problem relating to development of consumer movement

We shall be narrate the respondents' opinion regarding the various problems which relate to the development of consumer movement and consumer protection in India.

Table 6.13 : Various problem relating to development of consumerism and consumer protection in India

PROBLEMS	*Category of Organizations*			
	L	*M*	*S*	*Total*
Lack of consumer awareness towards various laws and consumer protection acts	20 (47.62)	6 (24.00)	18 (54.54)	44 (44.00)
Lack of knowledge regarding consumer rights	5 (11.90)	2 (8.00)	2 (6.06)	9 (9.00)
Absence of quality consciousness among consumer	6 (14.28)	7 (28.00)	3 (9.09)	16 (16.00)
Lack of consumer orientation by corporate management	3 (7.14)	2 (8.00)	10 (30.30)	15 (15.00)
No response	6 (14.28)	5 (20.00)	5 (15.15)	16 (16.00)
N	42	25	33	100

From the Table it is seen that majority of the organizations (44%) feel that lack of consumer awareness towards various laws and Consumer Protection Acts is a major factor which retards the development of consumerism or consumer movement in India. 16% of the organizations attribute it to the fact that consumers are not quality conscious, another 9% feel that it is due to lack of knowledge regarding consumer rights. 15% of the organizations are of the opinion that indifference of corporate management towards the consumer is responsible for the slow development of consumerism in India.

For large-scale industries 47.62% feel that lack of awareness towards Consumer Laws and Act is responsible for underdevelopment of consumerism in India. Another 14.28% feel that it is due to the absence of quality consciousness among consumers and yet 11.90% attribute it to the fact that consumer are not aware of their rights. 7.14% feel that the corporate management is indifferent towards consumers. About 14% have not commented. Similarly in case fo medium scale industries 28% feel the lack of quality consciousness among the consumer to be the reason for retarded consumerism in India, 24% attribute to the lack of awareness about consumer protection acts 8% for each the lack of knowledge regarding consumer rights and absence of consumer orientation by the corporate management. A sizeable percentage that is 20 have not sent any comments. For small scale organizations the figures are 54.54% for lack of awareness, 30.30% for corporate management indifference towards consumers and 9.09% for the lack of quality consciousness among consumers and 6.06% for lack of knowledge regarding consumer rights. Apart from this 15% have not responded.

The above discussions reveals that lack of knowledge is a great hindrance for the consumer movement in India. There should be critical awareness amongst the purchases of goods related to the satisfaction quality and services that are available to them at a fair price. But due to lack of knowledge the puzzled and poor consumers are unable to make intelligent purchase decisions. To help them in this matter corporate management should be more consumer oriented and try to guide the consumers in arriving at reasonable purchase decision and also in settling the grievances to their full satisfaction.

Lastly the business executives ideas concerning the strengthening of consumer movement in India have been presented in Table 6.14

Table 6.14 : Ideas for strengthening consumer movement in India

IDEAS	*Category of Organizations*			
	L	*M*	*S*	*Total*
Consumer council should be opened at district levels, quick disposals of consumer grievances by authorities	3 (7.14)	3 (12.00)	3 (9.09)	9 (9.00)
Consumer education through government agencies and voluntary organizations & media	17 (40.48)	18 (72.00)	13 (39.39)	48 (48.00)
Government should be vigilant to implement the consumer protection acts	12 (28.57)	4 (16.00)	5 (15.15)	21 (21.00)
The Government agencies and the voluntary organizations should ensure that prompt supply of essential commodities also peoper services to the consumers	4 (9.52)	—	3 (9.09)	7 (7.00)
No response	10 (23.81)	2 (8.00)	12 (36.36)	24 (24.00)
N	42	25	33	100

The Table reveals that proportionally more organizations (48%) are of the opinion that in order to strengthen the consumer movement, consumers should be educated through the government agencies and voluntary organizations and also through media. Few of them (21%) feel that government and voluntary organizations should exercise vigil for implementation of consumer protection laws. Only a small minority 9% feel that there should be quick disposals of consumer grievances by the authorities and for that purpose councils should be opened at district levels. Another 7% of them wants that the government agencies and voluntary organizations should ensure prompt supply of essential commodities and proper services to the consumer. A sizeable number 24% has not given any comments. For large scale industries 40.48% feel the need for proper consumer education by government and voluntary organizations, 28.57% want the government and voluntary organizations should be vigilant for the implementation of consumer protection laws, ensuring a fair deal from the business community to the dissatisfied consumers especially from the weaker sections. For the medium scale industries 72% feel that consumer education should be through government and voluntary organizations and also through media. Another 16% want vigilance by government and voluntary organizations for implementation of consumer protection laws and only 12% for opening district level councils. For small scale industries these figures are 39.39%,15.15% and 9.09% respectively. However, 36.36% of the respondents have not offered any comments.

In conclusion it may be observed that the present study has helped us in focusing the reactions of the marketing organizations (large/medium/small scale) towards various issues of consumerism and consumer movement in India, *viz.*, awareness of consumer protection laws, handling of consumer complaints, causes for underdevelopment of consumerism India and ways for strengthening it. It has been revealed that most of the organizations irrespective of the category show lack of awareness of consumer protection acts. Proportionally more large scale organizations have handled the consumer complaints successfully by replacing the defective items in majority of cases. Most of the small scale organizations have provided better after sales service. A large number of large and small scale org. attribute lack of consumer awareness regarding various laws and consumer protection acts. As the main reason for under development of consumer movement in India. For strenghtening the movement some of the suggestion made by them are consumer education by government and voluntary organizations and strict vigilance for implementation of various consumer protection laws by government and voluntary organizations.

QUALITY
IS
SIMPLE
NOT EASY,
BUT
WORTH IT!!

To safeguard their interest consumers must check:

In any packaged material, the month & year of manufacture, name & address of the manufacturer, net quantity or weight & Maximum Retail Price (M.R.P), address and telephone number of the consumer grievance redressal cell of the manufacturer. If imported, it must carry the name & address of importer with valid registration, in addition to the above. **Don't pay more than the M.R.P.**

Buy readymade garments verifying sizes in "cm' only. Stickers of "XL", "L", "M", "S" etc don't signify any standard size.

Chapter 7

Voluntary Organisations — Their Role in Consumerism and Consumer Movement in India

Voluntary and non government organizations in India have helped to some extent in educating and creating awareness among the consumers in India. In this chapter their role towards consumerism and consumer movement has been dealt with. Data have been collected on a number of aspects of the consumer movement, viz., motivation to establish these organizations, their area of operation, types of services offered, nature of complaints received, etc., from 38 voluntary organizations through exhaustive questionnaire. For analysis the organizations have been further classified in two categories namely,

(i) organizations in existence for less than 10 years (A)

(ii) organizations in existence for 10 years and above (B).

out of 38 organizations, 15 belong to category A and the rest 23 to category B.

ANALYSIS AND DISCUSSION

Motivations and Objectives of Voluntary Organizations

At the outset we have tried to ascertain the reasons for which have motivated these organizations to establish themselves for the benefit of the customers. Table 7.1 shows the various motivations which have resulted in the formation of these voluntary organizations.

Table 7.1 : Motivation to start the organizations

Motivation	*Category of organizations*		
	A	*B*	*Total*
Rising price	1 (6.67)	1 (4.34)	2 (5.26)
Inferior quality of goods	1 (6.67)	1 (4.34)	2 (5.26)
Unpleasant behaviour of the traders	—	1 (4.34)	1 (2.63)
Creating awareness among people and protect consumer rights	9 (60.00)	18 (78.26)	27 (71.05)
Redressal of complaints	7 (46.67)	3 (13.04)	10 (26.32)
N	15	23	38

Note: Figures as such are frequencies whereas those in parenthesis show percentages in this table and in subsequent Tables.

Even after so many precautions, if a consumer is deceived,

- He should ask the seller to remove the defect or deficiency or to replace the goods.
- If the seller does not respond or if the consumer is not satisfied by the action taken by the seller, move to the Consumer Affairs Dept, Govt of West Bengal or to the Directorate of Consumer Affairs & Fair Business Practices, Govt of West Bengal or to the Directorate of Legal Metrology, Govt of West Bengal or file complaint with the appropriate Consumer Disputes redressal Agency

Consumer Disputes redressal Agencies (Forum/commission) under Consumer Protection Act, 1986.

- Quasi-judicial authority under the statute to redress consumer disputes.
- In West Bengal every district has one district forum (Kolkata & Darjeeling have 2 each) and State Commission, apex body in the state, at Bhabani Bhaban.
- There is National Commission in Delhi, which is the apex body in the country
- District forum will redress consumer disputes for claims up to ₹ 20 lakhs.
- If claim is more than ₹ 20 lakhs but up to ₹ 1 crore, it goes to the state commission.
- If above ₹ 1 crore, it goes to the National Commission.

The above Table reveals that most of the organizations (71.05%) have been started for creating awareness among the consumer and protect their rights. Whereas a few (26.32%) were started to deal with the redressal of complaints from consumers, a small minority (5.26%) of them have been formed to combat the rising prices and another 5.26% to deal with the inferior quality of goods. The same trend can be observed for A and B categories of organizations. For A 60% of them have been formed for creating consumer awareness and protect their rights, 46.47% for redressal of complaints from the customers. These figures are 78.26% and 13.04% respectively for category B of organizations. In general exploitation of consumer has led to the formation and establishment of voluntary organizations in India. These organizations have tried to create public awareness to initiate public discussions in matters of consumer interests.they also have spread education amongst the consumers and tried to resist malpractices like hoarding, black marketing, price rigging by the traders.

Next the respondents were asked about the aims and objectives of their organizations and the results have been summarized in Table 7.2

Table 7.2 : Area of operation of the organizations

Area of Operations	*Category of organizations*		
	A	*B*	*Total*
Local	10 (66.67)	11 (47.83)	21 (55.26)
District	8 (53.33)	9 (39.13)	17 (47.37)
State	8 (53.33)	13 (56.52)	21 (55.26)
Country	7 (46.67)	8 (34.78)	15 (39.47)
Any other	3 (20.00)	5 (21.74)	8 (21.05)
N	15	23	38

From the Table we find that majority of the organizations (55.26%) are working at local level as well as state level. This is followed by organizations working at district level (47.37%) & material level (39.47%). For Acategory organizations majority of the organizations (66.67%) are operating at local level. About 53% are functioning at district level as well as state level. Another 46.67% are working at the national level. In case of category B organizations 56.52% are working at the state level followed by 47.83% at local level, 39.13% at district level and 34.78% at the national level. The analysis also reveals that activists of these organizations are quite widespread and there are sufficient reasons to believe that at all levels the consumers awareness is created and their complaints pursued by these organizations.

Sources of funds

The fund raising activities of these organizations in India have also been evaluated. The main purpose is to find out how these organizations run their activities and meet their expenses. Table 7.3 depicts the main heads under which they raise their funds.

Table 7.3 : Sources of funds for voluntary organizations

Sources	*Category of Organizations*		
	A	*B*	*Total*
Through members	14 (93.33)	19 (82.61)	33 (86.84)
Through government agencies	4 (26.67)	7 (30.43)	11 (28.95)
Foreign aids	1 (6.67)	2 (8.70)	3 (7.89)
Any other (donations grants, etc.)	6 (40.00)	7 (30.43)	13 (34.21)
N	15	23	38

The Table reveals that majority of the organizations (86.64%) raise their funds through regular subscriptions from the members. Over 34% are getting funds from other sources like donations, grants, advertisements for their periodicals. Another 28.95% have been receiving funds from government agencies. A very small minority (7.89%) has been receiving foreign aids. For organizations of below 10 years of age 93.33% are getting funds through regular subscription from members, 40% from other sources, 26.67% from government agencies and only 7% from foreign aids. For organizations of 10 years or more the trend is the same as 82.61% raise funds from memberships subscriptions, 30.43% from both government and other sources whereas only 8.70% through foreign aids. From this it is clear that these organizations mainly depend on the subscriptions from their members, assisted by a small amount from donations and government aids.

Modes of propagating the idea of consumerism

We will now discuss how these consumer associations try to propagate the ideas of consumerism and consumer protection amongst the general public. Table 7.4 summarizes the various modes through which the ideas have been propagated by these associations.

Table 7.4 : Modes used to propagate the ideas of consumerism

Modes	*Category of Organizations*		
	A	*B*	*Total*
Newspaper/TV/radio	11 (73.33)	21 (91.30)	32 (84.21)
Seminars/conferences/exhibition	13 (86.67)	21 (91.300	34 (89.47)
Public meetings/lectures/ group discussion	3 (20.00)	12 (52.17)	15 (39.47)
Publication of literature	6 (40.00)	6 (29.09)	12 (31.58)
N	15	23	38

From the above Table it has been revealed that main modes to propagate the ideas of consumerism have been through seminars/conferences (89.47%) and newspapers/TV/radio (84.21%). Over 39% of the organizations are propagating the ideas through meetings/lectures/personal contacts while 31.58% are doing so through publications of literature. For A category of organizations 86.67% have been propagating their ideas through seminars, educational workshops and arranging exhibitions and creating awareness amongst the consumers. Approximately 73% prefer newspapers, television and radio and another 40% by publishing literature as their modes of propagation. 20% have been propagating the ideas through public meetings, group discussions and personal contacts. Similarly for B category organizations 91.30% have been propagating through both newspaper/ TV/radio and through seminars/conferences, etc., and 52.17% by arranging meetings, discussions and personal contacts and lastly 26.09% through publication of literature.

The respondents were then asked to specify the various seminars/conferences conducted and basic theme of the seminars, etc., during the period of 5 years that from 1987 to 1991. the results have been tabulated in Table 7.5

Table 7.5 : Seminars conducted during 1987-1991 on few basic themes by A and B categories of organizations

Basic themes of the seminar	*Number of organizations conducting seminars*									
	1987		*1988*		*1989*		*1990*		*1991*	
	A	*B*	*A*	*B*	*A*	*B*	*A*	*B*	*A*	*B*
Consumer Protection Act	—	4 (17.39)	—	2 (8.70)	1 (6.67)	4 (17.39)	2 (13.33)	5 (21.74)	—	4 (17.39)
Consumer rights/ consumer education	—	1 (4.35)	2 (13.33)	—	—	—	1 (6.67)	—	1 (6.67)	—
Consumer awareness	4 (26.67)	2 (18.69)	3 (20.00)	4 (17.39)	4 (26.67)	3 (13.04)	2 (13.33)	2 (8.70)	2 (13.33)	3 (13.04)
MRTP Act and other consumer law	—	—	1 (6.67)	—	1 (6.67)	—	—	—	1 (6.67)	—
Prevention of food adulteration of essential commodities	— (4.35)	1	— (8.70)	2	— (8.70)	2	— (4.35)	1	— (4.35)	1

Other	— (30.43)	7	— (21.74)	5 (13.33)	2 (13.04)	3 (33.33)	5 (21.74)	5 (20.00)	3 (34.78)	8
No response	10 (66.67)	12 (52.17)	9 (60.00)	11 (47.83)	8 (53.33)	11 (47.83)	5 (33.33)	12 (52.17)	7 (46.67)	10 (43.48)
N	15	23	15	23	15	23	15	23	15	23

On examining the Table we find that there have been a lot of no response for both categories of the organizations. It varies from 33.33 % to 66.67% for A category and from 43.48% to 52.17% for B category during the period of five years. Thus the information available on the seminars conducted on various themes are not quite sufficient to make any valid conclusion. However seminars on creating consumer awareness have been conducted uniformly during the period. For A category it is 26.67% in 1987 and 1989, 20% in 1988 and 13.33% in 1990 and in1991. For B category it is 18.69% in 1987, 17.39% in 1988, 13.04% in 1989 and in 1991 and 8.70% in 1990. Few seminars ranging between 6.67% to 17.39% have also been conducted on Consumer Protection Act by these organizations. In previous section we have observed that the organisation have been communicating mostly through seminars, conference but surprisingly the response to number of seminars conducted has been rather poor. This probably may be due to the fact that either the organizations are making exaggerated claims about the communicating ideas of consumerism through seminars and conferences or they are not maintaining proper records of the seminars and conferences conducted by them.

The respondents organizations were further asked what type of other programnmes they have been organizing for the education of the consumers in general.

It is observed that a large majority (52.63%) is creating awareness and strengthening consumer movement through meeting and lectures. About 45% of organizations are educating through publication of periodicals, magazines, television and radio talk. Considered separately for A and B categories the trend is almost the same.

These organizations were next asked about their future plan for holding seminars, etc., concerning consumer matter and the topic of the discussions. The responses elicited from them have been shown in Table 7.6

Table 7.6 : Future plans for holding seminars and themes of the seminars

Basic themes of the seminar	*Category of organizations*		
	A	*B*	*Total*
Pollution and environmental programmes	—	1 (4.35)	1 (2.63)
Consumer's day for consumer awareness	1 (6.67)	4 (17.39)	5 (13.16)
Consumer education/Consumer Protection Act/MRTP etc.	7 (46.67)	9 (39.13)	1 (42.11)
Rising prices, handling complaints of consumer	3 (20.00)	2 (8.70)	5 (13.16)
Adulteration/healthcare	—	3 (13.04)	3 (7.89)
No response	4 (26.67)	5 (21.74)	9 (23.68)

The Table reveals that 42.11% of the organizations stated that they would like to hold seminars on consumer education, consumer protection laws, MRTP and other acts. Over 13% have shown intention to hold seminar in consumers day for consumer awareness and another 13.16% for holding seminars on rising prices and complaints of consumers. From 23.68% of the respondents there has been no responses. About 47% respondents belonging to category A organizations would like to hold seminars on consumers, education, etc., however 26.67% have not responded. For B category 39.13% want to hold seminars on consumer education, consumer protection act, MRTP and other acts 17.39% for holding consumer day for creating consumer awareness. However in this case also number of non responses are quite high (21.74%). The above analysis shows that the voluntary organizations are keen to hold seminars on various topics of consumers interest and want to help the consumers in every possible way. Still there is a scope for improvements and it is felt that the voluntary organizations should pursue and act more vigorously to attain their objectives.

As we have seen the voluntary organizations have been playing a major role in consumer education/protection and also giving various services to the consumer in India, therefore the respondents were asked about the specific services rendered to the consumers and members of the organizations. These responses have been shown in Table 7.7.

Table 7.7 : Type of services rendered to the members of the organizations

Type of Services	*Category of Organizations*		*Total*
	A	*B*	
Legal aid	10 (66.67)	13 (56.52)	23 (60.53)
Consumer education	14 (93.33)	20 (86.96)	34 (89.47)
Consumer training programmes	8 (53.33)	16 (69.57)	24 (63.16)
Consumer redressal	11 (73.33)	22 (95.65)	33 (86.84)
Others publication of journal Information booklets	3 (20.00)	5 (21.74)	8 (21.05)
N	15	23	38

It is clear from the Table that a large number of organizations (89.47%) are devoting time energy on consumer education followed by redressal of consumer complaints (86.84%), conducting comsumer training programmes (63.16%) and providing legal assistance to the aggrieved consumers (60.53%). For category A organizations 93.33% are providing consumer education,73.33% are for consumer complaints and 66.67% are for legal aids. Likewise for B category organizations 95.65% of them have been handling consumer complaints for redressal, while 86.96% have been providing consumer education. About 70% have been giving training to the consumers and 56.52% , the legal assistance in the form of fighting public interest litigation cases on a wide range of issues like environment pollution, water supply, supply of gas etc., before the courts. Further about 21% have been providing information on various issues of consumer interests like reporting of cases won in courts by these organizations on behalf of consumer, informative and educative article on the right of consumers through the publication of journals and booklets. The percentages of A and B categories of organizations who are providing information through publication of journal and booklets are 20 and 21.74 respectively.

CONSUMER COMPLAINT CELL

The next important thing which arises for consideration is consumer complaints. The respondents have therefore been asked whether they have any complaints cell in their offices for the welfare of the consumer. The replies obtained through YES/ NO have been reported in Table 7.8

Table 7.8 : Organizations having complaint cell

Responses	*Category of organizations*		*Total*
	A	*B*	
Yes	10 (66.67)	20 (86.96)	30 (78.95)
No	5 (33.33)	3 (13.04)	8 (21.05)
N	15	23	38

It is quite evident from the Table that most of the organizations (78.95%) are having complaint cell in their offices. Similar is the case for A and B catefory of organizations. For A category 66.67% and for B category 89.96% have complaint cell. Although the majority of them are aware of usefulness of maintaining a consumer complaint cell, it must be borne in mind that for proper handling of complaints each and every organizations must have a complaint cell.

In Table 7.9 we have given the ranges in which the no. of compaints have been received by the organizations in a year.

Table 7.9

Ranges (per annum)	*Category of organizations*		
	A	*B*	*Total*
Up to 50	9 (60.00)	10 (42.48)	19 (50.00)
51 – 150	1 (6.67)	3 (13.04)	4 (10.53)
151 – 500	1 (6.67)	4 (17.39)	5 (13.16)
501 and above	2 (13.33)	2 (8.70)	4 (10.53)
No responses	2 (13.33)	4 (17.39)	6 (15.79)
N	15	23	38

Most of the organizations (50%) have received up to 50 complaints in a year. Only 13.16% have received complaints ranging from 151 – 500. Another 10.53% of the organizations have received complaints between 51 -150 and yet another 10.53% from 501 and above. There have been some no responses also (15.79%). For A category 60% have received 50 complaints in a year and this figure is 43.48% for category B organizations. Rest of the few organizations in both categories have received complaints in the higher range.

Further, we have classified the nature of complaints into few broad need on the basis of answers received from the respondents. The distribution of these complaints have been tabulated in Table 7.10

Table 7.10 : Distribution of nature of complaints

Type of Complaints	*Category of organizations*		
	A	*B*	*Total*
Relation to various services like LPG, civic amenities, housing board, poor banking, milk supply quality, public distribution and transport system	7 (46.67)	9 (39.13)	16 (42.10)
Electric supply bill, water supply bill telephone connection bill	4 (26.67)	2 (8.70)	6 (15.79)
Issues relating to consumer protection laws, MRTP Act and other acts	1 (6.67)	1 (4.35)	2 (5.26)
Poor quality of material/household/ products/guarantee/replacement	2 (13.33)	7 (30.43)	9 (23.68)
Others	10 (66.67)	4 (17.390	14 (36.84)
No responses	4 (26.67)	7 (30.43)	11 (28.95)
N	15	23	38

Percentages are more than 100 because of multiple choices.

A majority of the organizations (42.10%) have received complaints relating to various services and of public concerns. These complaints are mainly relating to non availability of LPG, poor services rendered by gas agencies, poor banking services improper milk services, inadequate and insufficient public distribution system. There are complaints also against housing board and their malfunctioning and poor transport facilities. About 24% of the organizations have received complaints about poor quality of materials, household products, non compliance of guarantee etc. In 18.95% of the cases there has not been any response. For A category of organizations 66.67% received complaints such as food adulteration, non refund of scooter deposit, excess charges by auto rickshaw drivers, harassment of railway officials to commuters, repair of roads, shortages in weights and measures, etc., which have been classified as others and do not fall under any of the first four types of complaints given in the above table. However 46.67% have received complaints relating to various civic service. Likewise for B category organizations, 39.13% complaints related to civic services. About 27% of the respondents have not sent any response. Similarly for B category organizations about 30 have not responded.

PROBLEM RELATING TO CONSUMERISM/CONSUMER MOVEMENT

Next the organizations were asked to give their opinion on the various problems relating to consumerism/consumer movement in India. Their reactions have been tabulated in Table 7.11.

Table 7.11

Problems	*Category of Organizations*		
	A	*B*	*Total*
Lack of awareness education	5 (33.33)	11 (47.83)	16 (42.10)
Apathy of government	5 (33.33)	5 (21.74)	10 (26.32)
Poor quality/adulteration/spurious goods/high price/underweight	1 (6.67)	3 (13.04)	4 (10.53)
Lack of fund for consumer movement	3 (20.00)	1 (4.35)	4 (10.53)
Lack of consumer participation	1 (6.67)	4 (17.39)	5 (13.16)
Cumbersome legal procedures	2 (13.33)	—	2 (5.26)
Lack of testing facilities	2 (13.33)	2 (8.70)	4 (10.53)
N	15	23	38

From the Table it seems that 42.10% of the organizations are of the opinion that lack of consumer awareness and consumer education is hindering greatly the consumer movement in India. About 26% feel that government is indifferent towards the problems of the consumer. Another 13.16% attribute lack of consumer participation. Others (10.53) feel there has been a multiple combination of problems faced by the consumer like underweight, adulteration, spurious goods and unreasonable prices. For A category organizations, 33.33% feel lack of consumer awareness and education, 33.33% for government apathy, 20% for lack of funds, 13.33% for cumbersome legal procedures and ineffective laws and another 13.33% for lack of testing facilities. Similarly for B category 47.83% feel the lack of consumer education and awareness, 21.74% for government apathy, 17.39% for lack of consumer participation and 13.04% for poor quality and spurious products. From the responses it has been observed that there is lack of co- ordination and utility among various consumer organizations. It is felt that they should work unitedly for increased awareness and consumer education through meetings, workshops, public hearings and forming advisory committees. They should convince the government to take more interests in consumer problem. Government should also be asked to provide these organizations financial assistance for accomplishing their objectives.

Finally, we will examine the various responses received to the last question regarding the strengthening of consumer movernent in India at three levels, namely,

(a) at the consumer level

(b) at the government level and

(c) at the industrial level.

The basic results for above three cases have been summarised in Table 7.12, 7.13 and 7.14 respectively

Table 7.12

Statements	*Category of organizations*		
	A	*B*	*Total*
Creating awareness about consumer rights, consumer education	9 (60.00)	14 (60.87)	23 (60.52)
Prtocipation in semnar/training programmes, conducted by voluntary organizations	5 (33.33)	—	5 (13.15)
Availing redressal avenues in vogue	4 (26.67)	5 (21.74)	9 (23.68)
No response	—	4 (17.39)	4 (10.98)
N	15	23	38

Most of the organizations (60.52%) stated that consumer movement in India can be strengthened by giving more consumer reducation, bringing in further awareness about consumer rights than at present among the citizens. About 24% have felt that whenever consumers come across a complaint regarding the quality of the product being sub standard they should approach the proper authorities to redress the same. Another 13.15% observed that the consumer should participate in seminars, conferences and training programmes conducted by the voluntary organizations. However nearly 11% have not sent any responses. For A category of organizations 60% are for creating awareness among the consumer, 33.33% for active participation of consumer, 26.67% for availing the existing redressal avenues by the consumers. Whereas for the B category organizations 60.87% are for consumer awareness and education and 21,74% for availing the present redressal avenues. Surprisingly no organization has suggested attending the seminars by the consumers. How- ever no response in this category is about 17%. Table 7.13 depicts the organizations responses regarding the ways for strengthening consumer movement at the government level.

Table 7.13 : Ways for strengthening consumer movement at government level

Statements	*Category of organizations*		
	A	*B*	*Total*
Propagation of ideas on consumer protection through mass media	2 (13.33)	3 (13.04)	5 (13.16)
Setting up district forum in each district	1 (6.67)	1 (4.35)	2 (5.226)
Support and funding of voluntary organizations without any political prejudice	6 (40.00)	9 (39.13)	15 (39.47)
Strengthening of available redressal Instrument for quick and prompt Action on consumer complaints	3 (20.00)	4 (17.39)	7 (18.42)
Strict implementation of consumer Protection acts and other laws For consumer welfare	5 (33.33)	5 (21.74)	10 (26.32)
No response	2 (13.33)	3 (13.04)	5 (13.16)
N	15	23	38

A sizeable majority of the organizations (39.47%) feel tht government should support and provide grants to the various voluntary organizations so that they can accomplish their goals in a better manner. About 26% are of the opinion that consumer protection acts and other laws for the welfare of consumer should be strictly implemented and yet another 18.92% are for streamlining the available redressal instrument so that quick and prompt action can be taken on consumer complaints. In fact government should educate its staff memvers for proper handling of consumer complaints. The same trend is for both the categorie s of organizations when examined separately. For A category of organizations when examined these figures are 40, 33.33, and 20% and for B category these are 39.13, 21.74 and 17.39 recent respective;y. only 13.33% of A category of organizations and 13.04% of B category of organizations want that government should propaget the ideas on sonsumer protection through radio, television and through mass media.

Lastly we will examine the respondents opinion regarding the ways for strengthening consumer movement at industrial/ corporate level. The responses are tabulated in Table 7.14

Table 7.14 : Ways for strengthening consumer movement at industrial level

Statements	*Category of organizations*		
	A	*B*	*Total*
Catering to the needs of the consumers by establishing complaint cell, providing more information on product through publicity/bulletin/leaflets and satisfactory after sales service	6 (40.00)	2 (8.70)	8 (21.05)
Improvement of product quality and product performance	3 (20.00)	2 (8.70)	5 (13.16)
Recognition of consumer rights following government rules and regulations consumer acts and manufacturing goods as per ISI marks etc	6 (40.00)	9 (39.13)	15 (39.47)
Co ordination with the voluntary organizations for solving consumer problems	1 (6.67)	1 (4.35)	2 (5.26)
No response	1 (6.67)	5 (21.74)	6 (15.79)
N	15	23	38

In this Table we have examined that the attitudes of the voluntary organisation towards the trade and industrial establishments, participation in strengthening consumer movement in India. Clearly most of them (39.47%) stated that all companies should recognize the consumer rights, follow government rule and regulations and manufacture goods as per the ISI specifications. Another 21.05% wanted that all companies must have complaint cell to cater to the needs of the consumers, provide more informationof their products through publicity, leaflets, etc. The industry must also give satisfactory after sales service and replace defectice products. A small minority (13.16%) felt that companies should improve their product quality and product performance. In case of A category of organizations 40% are for establishing complaint cell, satisfactory after sale service etc., another 40% for recognition of consumer rights and manufacture of quality goods as per ISI mark AGMARK, etc., and 20% for improving the products quality and performance. For B category of organizations 39.13% are for recognition of consumer rights, following government rules and regulations, etc., but only 8.70% are for bothe establishment of complaint cell, satisfactory after sales service, and for improvement of product quality and product performance. However non response in this category has been quite high as 15.79%.

Summarizing the finding of the present study we may observe that the main objective of the voluntary organizations is consumer welfare and to some extent they are working towards that end by creating awareness among consumers, handling their complaints and giving them legal assistance. According to these organizations the prime reason for slow development of consumerism and consumer, movement in India is lack of consumer awareness and consumer education and they feel that efforts in this direction are needed to be speeded up. But due to financial constraints as most of these organizations are funded by the fees of the members they are unable to do it. Thus they suggest that in order to strengthen the consumer movement government should encourage them and provide financial support. This will help them in carrying out extensive training programmes conducting awareness and also in handling complaints of many more consumers and fighting their cases with legal assistance.

It is a common misconception that the provision of 100% inspection will guarentee 100% perfect goods.

Because it's about your health
they can't ask for more than
the printed price !
JAGO
GRAHAK
JAGO
ALSO REMEMBER
The printed prince on the label now includes all taxes.
Obtain the bill for medicine you bought.
Always check manufacture and expiry dates to
ensure medicine provided to you is safe.
Self Medication is injurious to health, hence
take medicine only on advice of doctors.
Ensure your complaint is heard properly by
its seller and manufacturer.
Seek assistance from the Consumer Forum, if any
complaint is not properly redressed.
For more information log on to
www.nppaindia.nic.in
For filling of complaints
consumers can log on to
www.core.nic.in
For guidance on consumer issues, call:
1800 180 4566
or 1800 11 4000
011-27006500 (12 Lines)
(Normal call charges apply)
Issued in Public interest by:
Department of Pharmaceuticals
Ministry of Chemicals & Fortilizers, Government of India
Shastri Bhawan, New Delhi - 110 001
Website: www.Pharmaceuticals.gov.in
Ministry of consumer Affairs, Food and Public Distribution
Department of consumer Affairs, Government of India
Krishi Bhawan, New Delhi - 110 001
Website : www.fcamin.nic.in

Chapter 8

Research Findings

Consumer satisfaction and consumer protection are main challenging issues to modern day marketing. Consumerism offers business to reexamine its market policies and programmmes for meeting the ever growing need of the consumers. The present study has been undertaken to examine the consumerism and consumer movement in India. The specific objectives of the study are,

1. To trace and document the historical development in consumerism and consumer movement in India.
2. To analyse the consumers opinion regarding consumerism and consumer protection legislation in India.
3. To study the activities of Indian companies in the changed circumstances and observe the reaction of the marketing executives with respect to consumerism.
4. To analyze the working of various types of consumer associations in India regarding consumer movement.
5. To identify the parameters needed to implement consumerism and consumer movement in India.

For the purposes of the study, three opinion surveys on consumer, Indian companies and voluntary organizations have been constituted separately. The consumer opinion survey was conducted on 600 individuals selected from the city of Delhi. They belonged to various educational groups occupational classes and income groups. The survey on companies was based on opinions of 100 companies. The survey on voluntary organizations constituted responses from 38 such organizations. The findings of these surveys are discussed in subsequent sections. Finally suggestions have been made with respect to the roles, the consumer companies and voluntary organisation and government, should play in improving the state of affairs regarding consumerism and consumer movement in India.

A. CONSUMER OPINION SURVEY

In this survey, the individuals were used to asked to give their opinion on consumer protection laws and various other aspects of consumerism. The analysis was carried out after classifying the individuals in to four different categories (a) up to matric (E1) (b) graduates (E2), (c) post graduates (E3) and professionally qualified (E4). A summary of the results are given below:

(a) Consumer Rights: It has been observed that more than half of the respondents are ware of consumer rights in general. Higher the educational level higher is the awareness, a fact confirmed by X^2 chi square test also awareness about four specific consumer rights namely right to fate, right to be informed, right to choose and right to be heard among those who are aware of consumer rights in general is quite high irrespective of their educational level

(b) Consumer Protection Laws: Most of the respondents are not aware of the various consumer protection legislations available in India like the Monopolies and Restrictive Trade Practices Act 1969 (MRTP), the Trade and Merchandise Act 1958, the Packaged Commodities Regulation Order 1975, the Household Electrical Appliances Act, the Fruit Products Order 1955, etc. However a fairly large section of the respondents are aware of the Acts like the Prevention of Food Adulteration Act 1954, Local Taxes etc. It has been observed that non awareness is maximum among the educational category up to matric followed by graduates, post graduates and professionally qualified.

(c) Consumer Issues: It was felt that the consumer issues such as information, health and safety standard, repair and service, pricing issues, pollution in the environment, market concentration, advertisement and legislations are quite important and should be included under consumerism. Opinion on these issues was soughts by using Likert Scale. Average weighted score on ratings were calculated for each of these issue separately for the educational categories. Comparing the ratings we find that there is considerable agreement among the educational categories E1,E2,E3, and E4 regarding the inclusion of these issues under consumer movement. This fact has been further confirmed as the value of Kendall's coefficient of concordance (W statistics) has been found to be significant.

(d) Product Information on Packages/Containers: Any customer would like to have some information about the product he is purchasing. He may seek information on any one of the following aspects like (a) Date of expiry, (b) Date of manufacturing, (c) Price, (d) Quality mark, (e) Name of the manufacturer and (f) Quantity standard unit or weight etc. It has been observed that a vast majority of the respondents irrespective of the educational background do look for this information specially price, date of expiry, date of manufacturing and quantity. Regarding any additional information to be incorporated on the labels of the packages the response was poor and even among those who responded there were no worthwhile suggestion except a few stressing the need for the products to conform to BIS, etc., and few others for giving details regarding the safety aspect and for harmful effect if any for the users.

(e) Complaints About Defective Products: The number of complaints about defective products have been made by some of the respondents. But among those who have made the complaints, the highest number is among the post graduates (E3). This is followed by the professionally qualified (E4) and graduate (E3). The lowest number of complaints have been made by the educational category E1. This may be due to lack of knowledge, education and other means. The value of x^2 has been found to be highly significant confirming that response depend on the educational level of the respondents. A close examination further shows that the complaints are mostly about quality, servicing, warranty, and price. Very few have been made about measurements, advertisements and quantity. Mostly the complaints about quality, servicing, and warranty related to TV, fridge, electrical goods, scooters, shoes etc. Complaints about price were related to bathing soap, Toothpaste, grocery item, butter, edible oil, etc. Examining the remedial measures taken by the manufacturers about the defective items it has been found that they have been able to solve more than half of the cases reported either by repairing or replacing the defective products. Respondents with post graduate qualification E3 have achieved the highest success in getting their problem on the defective items solved by the manufacturers or distributors.

(f) Importance of Consumer Issues: Earlier we have found positive responses from the individuals belonging to different educational categories about the inclusion of certain issues under consumerism. The respondents were also asked to rate the different issues. Looking at the average ratings it has been found that highest rating has been given to Health and Safety Standards both by the education categories E3 and E4. in case of E1 and E2 the highest ratings are for Product quality. Lowest rating of course has been found uniformly for all the educational categories to advertising. The overall picture shows that ratings to these issues by various educational categories are more or less of the same order. Further since the value of Kendall's coefficient of concordance has been found to be highly significant, it confirms that there is evidence of agreement among the different educational categories in rating the consumer issues.

(g) Consumer Attitudes Towards Consumerism and Consumer Movement: 39 statements covering a wide range of problems on consumer movement have been grouped under the following broad classes

(i) Philosophy of business
(ii) Product quality
(iii) Advertising
(iv) Other marketing activities
(v) Consumerism
(vi) Consumer responsibilities
(vii) Government regulations

1. Philosophy of business: A majority of respondents irrespective of the educational category they belong to agreed or strongly agreed with most of the statement regarding business philosophy such as if a customer gets injured or fall ill while using a defective product, the manufacturer should be made to pay the damages; most of the manufacturers do not bother about the consumer; most of the manufacturers are more interested in making profits rather than customer satisfaction. However most of the respondents disagreed with the statement manufacturer perform the job of providing good products at reasonable prices. Kendall's coefficient of concordance W has also confirmed that there is concurrence among the educational categories in rating the statements.

2. Product quality: A majority of the respondents agreed that with the statement people look for packed and branded products as well as ISI mark, etc., on packages while purchasing a product and the average person is willing to pay higher prices for quality products that will ensure health and safety standards. However the respondents were uncertain about the statement that quality of most of the product has been improving over the passage of time. However Kendall's coefficient of concordance has not been found to be significant at 5% level of significance showing that thereby there is no concurrence between these statements.

3. Advertising: Some of the statements on advertising about which a large section of the respondents belonging to different educational categories agreed are: advertising often persuades people to buy things that they should not buy; most advertisements are exaggerative and do not present the true picture of the product quality and performance, etc. Most of the respondents have disagreed with the statement advertisements have no utility or role to play in the society. Kendall's coefficient of concordance has also confirmed that there is concurrence among the respondents in rating these statements.

4. Other marketing activities: The majority of the respondents from different educational categories given divided opinion on the statement like : in general the quality of service provided by the manufacturers is getting better and the contest that manufacturers sponsor to encourage their products to make people their product are usually dishonest. W statistics have shown that there is no concurrence in rating these statement.

5. Consumerism: A large majority of respondents have agreed or strongly agreed with most of the statements on consumerism such as the exploitation of the consumers by the business firms deserves more attention than it receives; cheating on weights and measures should be punished severely; the sorry state of affairs about consumerism is due to lack of consumer education; from consumers viewpoint the procedures followed by, most manufacturers and government in handling complaints and settling grievances are not satisfactory and the future of consumerism will be important that it is today. Kendall's W statistics has also confirmed that there is fair degree of concurrence among the educational categories in rating these statements.

6. Consumer responsibilities: A majority of the respondents agreed that many of the mistakes customers make while purchasing a product are due to their own carelessness or ignorance and protecting the environment is more important than increasing the standard of living. However most of the respondents disagree that consumer often try to take advantage of manufacturers and dealers by making claims that are not justified. High significance of W also show that more or less perfect concurrence among the educational categories in rating these statements.

7. Government regulations: A large majority of the respondents irrespective of their educational categories agreed or stringently agreed on all the statements on government regulations. Some of the statements are, the government should test competing brands of products and make the results of these available to consumer; government should set minimum standards of quality for consumer products; the government should control food price and so on. The coefficient of concordance has been found to be significant showing that education wise rating of these statements is highly concurrent.

(h) Strengthening the Consumer Movements: Lastly the opinion was sought from the respondents for strengthening the consumer movement in India. Few options like company action, holding of seminars, mass media, etc., which are felt relevant in strengthening consumerism in India, were included in the questionnaire and respondents were asked to express their views on them. As far as company action is concerned most of the post graduates felt its necessity but very few of under graduates showed positive response towards it. The responses towards holding seminar for consumer education were rather poor except a sizeable majority of educational category E3 but the use of mass media like television and for the purpose of educating the consumers was favoured by a very high majority of individuals belonging to educational categories E2, E3 and E4 and a fairly high percentage of individuals from E1. Except E1 about half of the respondents from educational categories E2, E3 and E4 desired general involvement of the voluntary organizations on consumer matters, their role in consumer education and assisting consumers to fight their cases. Most of the respondents irrespective of their educational level were unanimous about government's role for public welfare. They expect regular government control over prices, strict enforcement of existing legislations and action against defaulters. Strangely only a few of the respondents felt the necessity that the consumers themselves have a role to play in strengthening the consumer movement in India.

The main findings of the survey can be summarized as follows:

1. Awareness about consumer rights is more among the higher educated individuals, viz., graduate and post graduates.
2. Awareness regarding various governments legislations available in India is rather poor in the various educational categories.
3. All the respondents felt the necessity of including a number of issues like information, health and safety, pollution in environment, product quality, etc., under consumer movement though with a varying degrees of agreement.
4. Most of the respondents irrespective of their educational background, while purchasing any product do look for various informations like price, quality, date of expiry, etc., on the packages/container.

5. Complaints about defective products were made mostly by more educated individuals. They were also able to successfully get remedial measures from the manufacturers, distributors and dealers in majority of the cases.
6. The majority of the respondents irrespective of this educational categories have agreed or strongly agreed with the large number of statement on consumer issues such as quality of most of the products have improved with the passage of time; advertising is often persuading people to buy things which they should not buy; protecting the environment is much more important than increasing our own living standards and the sorry state of affairs about consumerism in India is due to the lack of consumer education. Only in the very few cases they have disagreed namely advertising has no role to play in the society.
7. For strengthening the consumer movement in India most of the respondents felt the necessity of active participation of management of companies, use of mass media like television and radio and role of voluntary organizations for consumer education. A majority of the respondents irrespective of their educational background agreed that government should actively participate in the welfare of the public. Action by consumers themselves have not found favour with most of the respondents. Similarly a few were in the favour of holding seminars and conferences for creating consumer awareness.

B. AN OPINION SURVEY OF COMPANIES IN INDIA

The survey was conducted on hundred Indian companies manufacturing various industrial as well as consumer goods. These companies were classified into three categories on the basis of their annual turn over. Those having annual turnover of Rs. one crore were classified as small scale organizations (S), Rs. 1 crore to Rs. 5 crores as medium scale organizations (M), and over 5 crores as large scale organizations (L). A summary of findings emerging from this survey are given below:

1. Objectives of the Study: A successful majority of the large medium and small scale organizations want to satisfy their customer or build their image in the market. A majority of large scale organizations also prefer to remain leader in the market or prefer to maintain or increase share in the market. Very few medium and small scale industries want to remain leader in the market.

2. Consumer Protection Legislations: Opinion was sought from the companies regarding the applicability of various consumer protection legislations to their organizations. Irrespective of the category of the organizations the awareness about various legislations appears to be very low. However a majority of the large scale organizations are of the view that the legislations provide satisfaction to the consumers. Very few feel that the legislations are helpful in maintaining and improving the quality of the product. Further a large number of large, medium and small scale industries feel that these legislations are an opportunity to their market effort. A negligible section feel that these legislations are a hindrance to their marketing efforts.

3. Complaints and their Handling: Various kinds of complaints such as compensation, refund, replacement, quality, service, etc., have been received mainly through distributors or through customer directly. The complaints received by large scale organizations were higher than those by medium and smalls scale industries. A small number of large scale and medium scale organizations have received complaints from their own sales force. Most of the large scale organizations have tried to handle the complaints by replacing the defective products, compensating, servicing the equipment or by sending their representatives to solve the problems at personal levels. Only a few of the small scale organizations and medium scale organizations have been following the above practice.

4. Improvements Carried Out by Manufacturers for Customer Satisfaction: Majority of the large scale and medium scale organizations have not carried out any changes in their products for the consumer satisfaction. Surprisingly half of the small scale organizations surveyed have made changes. The changes in the products relate to providing better quality products, modification in design providing better after sales service, better packaging and setting up of customer service cells.

5. Responsibility for Consumer Protection Activities and Consumer Welfare in India: Opinion was sought from the respondents as to who should be responsible for the consumer protection activities and consumer welfare in India. In case of large scale organizations majority of them want involvement of the management of the company and the government. Few wants participation of the non government agencies and still a few are for the involvement of consumer themselves. The same trend is observed for medium and small scale industries also though to a lesser extent.

6. Problems in the Development of Consumerism: The respondents were asked to give their views regarding various problems which retard the development of consumerism and consumer movement in India. A sizeable number of the large scale organizations has put the responsibility on the lack of awareness on part of the consumer about the various laws and consumer protections acts followed by few who feel that the consumer are not quality conscious about various products. In case of medium scale organizations most of them feel that the main reason for slow development is due to lack of consumer awareness about various laws and consumer protection acts. For small scale industries the opinion is more or less the same as that in case of large scale organizations except that a sizeable majority feel that the corporate management's indifference towards consumers also contribute to slow growth of consumerism in India.

7. Strengthening of Consumer Movement in India: For strengthening the consumer movement in India, a sizeable number of large and medium scale organizations feel the need of proper consumer education by government and voluntary organizations. Few among the large and small scale organizations also want strict vigilance by government and voluntary organization for implementation of the consumerism protection laws. The observations made by small scale industries are quite identical with the above though to a lesser extent.

The main finding therefore may be summed up as follows:

1. The awareness about consumer protection legislations is rather poor among all categories of organizations. Majority feels that legislations are an opportunity to their marketing efforts.
2. Large scale industries have received more complaints and they have tried to handle then successfully in majority of the cases.
3. For providing greater satisfaction to consumers improvements have been carried out by large scale organizations in respect of improving the product design, providing better after sales service.
4. Mostly large scale organization and to a lesser extent medium and small scale organizations want involvement of company and government organizations for consumer welfare in India.
5. A sizeable number of large and small scale organizations attribute the lack of consumer awareness about various laws and consumer protection acts as the main reason for slow growth of consumerism in India.
6. To strengthen the consumer movement in India the necessity of proper consumer education by government and voluntary organizations have been felt by a large majority of large and medium scale organizations. Small scale organizations also more or less corroborate with this law.

C. VOLUNTARY ORGANIZATIONS – THEIR ROLES IN CONSUMERISM AND CONSUMER MOVEMENT IN INDIA

This survey has been based on opinions of 38 voluntary organizations classified into two categories : organizations in existence for 10 years (A), and organization inexistence for 10 years and above (B). these organizations have been motivated to work for the consumer welfare.

1. Objective of the Organizations: Responding to a specific query on their objective almost all the organizations belonging to A and B have stated their main objective to consumer protection activities, consumer redressal and social welfare. A majority of the A category organizations were working at local as well as district level. Few are working at district and national level. The same is true for B category of organizations. Irrespective of their category most of the organizations are getting their funds through regular subscription from their members. A small proportion of these are getting help from government department and agencies. Still few are getting foreign aids.

2. Propagating the Idea About Consumerism: The main modes of propagating the idea of consumerism by the majority of organizations are through seminars and newspapers, TV, and radio. Some of them are also propagating the idea through meetings/ lectures/personal contacts and publication of literature. Both the categories of organizations have conducted a number of seminars on varied topics related to consumer awareness during a periods of 5 years that is from 1987 to 1991. Some of the topics on which seminars are conducted are consumer protection act, consumer rights, consumer education, MRTP act and other consumer laws. Regarding the future plans a fair proportion of the organization want to conduct seminars on consumer education, few on prices and consumer complaints.

3. Services Rendered by Organizations: It has been seen that voluntary organizations have been playing a major role in providing consumer education. These services rendered by them are varied mainly providing legal aid, conducting seminars programmes and redressal of consumer complaints. Most of the organizations are providing consumer education and a fair majority are handling consumer complaints for redressal and also giving legal aid in the form of fighting public interest litigation cases.

4. Handling of Complaints of Consumers: A vast majority of B category organizations have stated that the existence of complaints in their organizations. Similarly a fair proportion of category A organizations also have complaint cells in their offices. Most of the organizations have been receiving complaints in the range of 0-50 per year. Some of them have received complaints in the higher ranges also. The nature of both A & B category of organizations pertain to various services relating to LPG civic amenities, milk supply and distribution, poor banking services etc. Quite a few of A category have received complaints in electric supply/bill, water supply/bill, telephone connection/bill. Similarly complaints on poor quality of material products have been received though mostly by B category organizations.

5. Problems Relating to Consumerism and Consumer Movement: Opinion was sought on the various problems which are being faced in promoting consumerism and consumer movement being faced in India. While a sizeable section of A category organizations feels that the lack of consumer awareness and government apathy as the hindrance in the development of consumerism and consumer movement, there are a few others who put the blame on the lack of funds, cumbersome legal procedures and lack of testing facilities. In case of B category organizations about half of them feel that a considerable number of attribute to government apathy as the main problem as the main problem in promoting the consumerism and consumer movement.

6. Strengthening the Consumer Movement in India: Finally the respondent were asked to give suggestions regarding the consumer movement in India at three level, *viz.*, (a) Consumer level, (b) Government level and (c) Industrial/Corporate level.

(a) Consumer level: A large majority of the organizations have emphasized the need of creating awareness among consumers about their rights and education. Only a few of the A category organizations want participation of consumers in seminars/training programmes conducted by the voluntary organizations.

(b) Government level: A sizeable majority of the organizations irrespective of their categories feel that voluntary organizations should be supported and given financial aids by government for achieving their goals. Few others want strict implementation of consumer protection acts.

(c) Industrial level: Most of the organizations want that companies should recognize consumer rights, follow governments' rules and regulations and manufacture good as per as ISI specification, AGMARK etc. Most of the A category organizations also feel that all companies must have complaint cell to cater to the needs of the consumers. And provide more information on their products through publicity, leaflets.

The main findings can be summarized as follows:

1. The main objective of the voluntary organizations is consumer welfare. Most of these organizations are funded by their members whereas a few get government aids.
2. They propagate the idea of consumerism through seminars, meetings personal contacts and publications.
3. Most of the organizations provide consumer education, handle consumer complaints and give the legal assistance.
4. Regarding the problems relating to consumer movement in India majority of A category organizations attribute them to the lack of consumer awareness, lack of funds and government apathy. Among B category organizations most of them feel the lack of consumer education and awareness.
5. For strengthening consumerism and consumer movement in India most of the organizations have agreed that more awareness should be created through active participation of consumers in training programmes to be conducted by voluntary organizations. They want that the voluntary organisation should be encouraged and given financial help by government. They also feel that the companies should manufacture goods as per the ISI mark, AGMARK, etc., and establish cell for handling consumer complaints.

We shall now discuss the main findings of above three surveys and try to arrive at certain conclusions. On the basis of these conclusions we shall make some recommendations for improving the state of affairs regarding consumerism and consumer protection.

It has been observed that awareness about consumer rights is not quite widespread among the masses though educated classes are proportionately more aware of their rights. The needs to educate more consumers and create awareness has been stressed by voluntary organizations and they have suggested active participation of consumers in the various programmes organized by the government/voluntary organisation. Not only consumers belonging to the different educational categories but also most of the large, medium and small scale industries have shown lack of knowledge about various consumer laws and consumer protection acts. A vast majority of large, medium and small scale organizations have indicated the necessity of consumer education by voluntary organizations and government departments. In fact voluntary organizations which are in existence for less that 10 years classified as A category and those who have been existence for 10 years and above classified as B category are already propagating the idea of consumerism through training programmes, seminars, meetings, personal contacts and publication of results. These organizations want the support and financial grant from the government to carry our their objective in a better way. There is also a good deal of concurrences about various issues of consumerism among different educational categories of consumers. The under graduates, graduates, post graduates and professionally qualified all agree though to varying degree on the statements like payment of compensation to a consumer who fall ill or injured while using a defective product, average person is willing to pay more which ensures better health and safety standards, advertisements are exaggerative, people look for branded products, government should control food prices etc. Similarly there are certain statements such as advertisement has no role to play in the society, many of the mistakes consumers make while purchasing a product are due to their own carelessness ignorance for which most of them have shown disagreement. It is clear that consumers want good quality product which ensures health and safety standards and they are willing to pay higher prices for it. Though the manufacturing company have indicated that they are carrying out improvements in product design, providing better after sales services for consumer satisfaction yet greater efforts are needed by the companies in this direction. While the manufacturing organizations and voluntary organizations attribute the slow growth of consumerism mainly to poor consumer awareness, the voluntary organizations also put the blame on government apathy, lack of funds, cumbersome legal procedures and lack of testing facilities. Strangely only a few consumer feel the necessity of involving themselves in serving the cause of consumerism and consumer movement in India.

Regarding suggestions for strengthening consumer movement in India consumer feel the necessity of active participation by the companies. They want voluntary organizations to play a major role in educating the consumers, the fact also corroborated by voluntary organizations themselves which want active participation of consumers in their training programmes, meeting, and seminars. More efforts on the part of government in consumer welfare has also been stressed by majority of large, medium, and small scale organizations. Further voluntary organizations want the companies should manufacture quality goods as per as ISI mark which are preferred by most of the consumers. Companies should establish complaint cell for prompt and satisfactory redressal of consumer complaint.

From the above discussion it has been revealed that for improving the state of affairs regarding consumerism and consumer protection; consumers, companies, voluntary organizations and government will have to work in close co operation with each other. Thus the recommendations are made on the basis of the foregoing observation:

RECOMMENDATION

A. Consumers' Responsibilities

1. The Indian consumers should be more vigilant while purchasing a product.
2. They should not accept cheap quality goods which may be have harmful effects.
3. They should buy as far as possible branded products by reputed manufacturers or products with ISI mark, AGMARK, FPO, ISO, etc., the cost may be higher.
4. Consumers should be aware of their rights and assert them withour hesitation.
5. They should be well conversant with the various consumer protection acts and laws available for their benfits. For this they should actively participate in the training programmmes, seminars and conferences being conducted by the voluntary organizations and other agencies to acquaint them with these acts.
6. Consumer should actively involve themselves in the consumer movement by becoming members of the various consumer groups in order to carry on effectively their own battle against unfair services.
7. The terms and conditions of the guarantees should be carefully read and products usage be done as per instructions by the manufacturer.
8. In case of the defective item they should take up their cases with the manufacturers either through consumer groups or through voluntary organizations.

B. Company's Responsibility

1. Companies should not manufacture products of inferior quality and should produce good conforming to the ISI/ISO specifications. They can even set up high standards of their own and manufacture accordingly for the benefit of the consumers.
2. The protection of the consumer interest and their rights should be the main aim of the Indian manufacturers.
3. Companies should adopt fair business practices in order to gain consumer confidence.
4. All types of manufacturers large, medium and small scale should try to improve upon the manufacturing process by adopting modern technology to strive for zero defect in their products.
5. The clauses given in the guarantee card should be accurate and in simple languages so as to avoid any confusion in the minds of the consumers.
6. The advertisements concerning the products should be informative, free from misleading or false or tall claims
7. The manufacturers should provide prompt after sales service. Supply of spares should be ensured through dealer/distributor.

Complaints should be attended to immediately. The replacement of defective item should, be done without any harassment to the customers. The dealers should be instructed accordingly. The manufacturers also should establish consumer grievances cells in their respective organizations for prompt and satisfactory redressal of consumer complaints.

C. Role of Voluntary Organizations

1. The voluntary organizations should organize more training programmes, meetings, lectures to create awareness among the consumer. They should also try to have personal contacts with the consumers.
2. They can have surveillance over the distribution of essential commodities and public distribution system
3. They can act as liaison between government bodies, manufacturing organizations and consumer so as to deal effectively with the grievance of the consumers in close coordination with all the type of institutions mentioned above.
4. These organizations should work in close cooperation with various institutions like Bureau of Indian Standards, Chamber of Commerce, Scientific Establishments, Trade Associations and Regional Testing laboratories and disseminate information to its members and impart education.
5. Besides specific consumer complaints these organizations should take up large issues to promote the interests of the consumers. They could form legal action committees to cater to the needs of the general consumers of their locality.
6. The organizations could establish laboratories with the assistance from the government or by raising funds of their own

D. Government Responsibility

1. Government should establish comprehensive policy to guide their departments to guide their departments in responding to the consumer issues.
2. Government should see that the consumer protection laws and acts are strictly implemented.
3. Existing rules, regulations and control should be simplified so as to encourage higher productivity by the companies.
4. Government should strengthen the public distribution system and maintain adequate supply of essential goods to the fair prices shops. Besides maintaining checks by their own staff. Government organizations should allow surveillance by voluntary organizations on the quality and quantity of the goods supplied to the consumers by the owner of the shops at fair prices.
5. Government should rationalize sales tax and other taxes throughout India and bring uniformity. The local taxes should be made uniform throughout the country so that it can be included in the printed price of packaged commodities thus avoiding over charging by the traders.
6. Quality and effiency of the public services like banks electricity, water, telephone, etc., should be improved.
7. Government should take appropriate action for safety of technical installations and equipment in order to avoid accidents specially in air based transport railways and other organizations.
8. Government should continue to give all possible support including financial assistance to voluntary organizations to carry out their various programmes, viz., conducting training programmes helping consumer in the redressal of their complaints, providing necessary legal assistance to consumers to fight for their rights.
9. Government must set up testing laboratories and can also give financial aid to voluntary organizations for helping them in settling up such facilities.
10. Quick and simple legal procedures should be introduced for settlement of disputes arising in all government or service departments.

The emerging conclusion of this study are pointers to the directions in which the government as well as the management of various companies need to focus their attention. The above conclusions can be taken to be tentative hypothesis for in depth research relating to various dimensions of consumerism and consumer movement.

Some of the areas on which future research can be taken up are consumer attitude towards standards, testing facilities, etc., socio economic parameters on consumer affairs; identification of specific problems faced by the disadvantaged consumers like children, disabled, handicapped; programmes relevant to policy matters on consumers marketing producing good quality goods, etc., and periodic consumer opinion survey to identify and predict underlying consumer issues.

TENDER TV

Some of the suggestions by the NCPCR

- No child should be cast in a role that might distress him or her
- At least 50 per cent of the payment must be in fixed deposits or bonds
- A child can only participate in one TV show at a time and not work for more than one shift every day, with a break every hour
- Children cannot shoot on weekdays
- A parent has to be present with the child during shooting

Children shouldn't be cast in a role that might "distress" them, according to a new set of guidelines on employing child artistes for TV serials, reality shows and commercials.

The National Commission for Protection of Child Rights has also suggested a format for paying child artistes, in a bid to secure their future.

—✦—✦—✦—

PART III
Illuminating Judgements/ Decisions(CPA)

Chapter 1

Landmark Judgements of Supreme Court in India

1. Haryana Urban Development Authority v Raj e Ram [I (2009) CP J 56 (SC)]

Date of Decision: 23.10.2008

Dealing with a batch of cases involving re-allottees of plots who had filed complaints after getting the plots transferred in their names, the Supreme Court held that the re-allottees were not entitled to interest on the amounts deposited on the ground of delay in receiving possession. The Court referred to its decision in *HUDA v Darsh Kumar fill* (2864) *CPJ* 449 (SC)/ and held that the case of re-allottees could not be equated with that of the original allottees who were made to wait for long for possession and thus put to mental agony and harassment. The re-allottees were aware that time for performance was not the essence of the contract and the original allottees had accepted the delay. On facts, the Court noticed dial the re-allottees had taken possession but not paid the full price when they approached the District Forum. The Court relied upon *Ghaziabad Development Authority* u *Balbir Singh* [11 *(2004) CPJ* 12 *(SC)] and Bangalore Development Authority v. Syndicate Bank II/(2007) CPJ* 17 *(SC)].*

2. Punj Lloyd Ltd. v Corporate Risks India Pvt. Ltd. [I (2009) CPJ 10 SC]

Date of Decision: 11.121

The complainant sought compensation from the opposite party insurance broker because of the difference in premium charged by the insurer, ICICI Lombard General Insurance Company Ltd. in place of Oriental Insurance Company, The complaint was dismissed in limine on the ground that it involved complicated questions of fact that could be gone into only by a civil court. The Supreme Court held that merely because a complaint disclosed complicated questions was not a ground for relegating the complainant to a civil court. The Court found that it was difficult to say from the statements in the complaint that it disclosed complicated questions of fact, which could only be gone into by a civil court before bringing the opposite party on record and asking it to file its defence. It was only after the pleadings of both parties were on record that the Commission ought to have formed an opinion. The Court relied upon its decision in *CCI Chambers Cooperative Housing Society Ltd. v Development Credit Bank Ltd. [III (2003) CPJ 9 (SC)]* holding that "...The decisive test is not the complicated nature of questions of fact and law..." but "whether the questions, though complicated they may be, are capable of being determined by summary inquiry." The Court also referred to its decision in *Dr. J.J. Merchant & Others v Shrinath Chaturvedi [III (2002) CPJ 8 (SC)].*

3. Martin F. D' Souza v Mohammad Ishfaq [I (2009) CPJ 32 SC]

Date of Decision: 13.02.2009

Dealing with this medical negligence case, the Court referred to its decisions in several cases" including *Jacob Mathew v State* of *Punjab* & Am *[III (2005) CPJ 9 (SC)],* and also the English case of *Bolam v Friern Hospital Management Committee* [(1957) 1 WLR 5 82] and reiterated that the test in fixing medical negligence was the standard of the ordinary skilled doctor exercising special skill but a doctor need not possess the highest expert skill. The Court noticed that though the medical profession was regarded as noble, it had become a business and many doctors in India had forgotten their Hippocratic Oath. However, the Court went on to observe that the law was a watchdog and not a bloodhound and as long as a doctor performed his duty with reasonable care, he could not be held liable even if the treatment was unsuccessful. It further observed that different doctors had different approaches to treatment and adopting one approach could not, by itself, be a ground for alleging/holding medical negligence. It also observed that courts and consumer for a were not experts in medical science and must not substitute their own views over those of specialists. Finally, the Court passed the direction that whenever a complaint is filed against a doctor or a hospital in consumer for a criminal courts, such for a courts should refer the matter to a competent doctor or committee of doctors who are specialists in the field to which the complaint relates. Only when a report is made that there is *uprima facie* case of medical negligence that the for a criminal court should issue notice.

4. U.T. Chandigarh Administration & Another v Amarjeet Singh & Others [II (2009) CPJ 1 (SC)]

Date of decision: 17.03.2009

This was a batch of cases where the complaints of auction purchasers of plots on existing sites had been allowed on the ground that there was delay in provision of amenities and the Administration was directed to reschedule the recovery of balance instalments of the auction price without charging penal interest for the delayed payment of instalments or ground rent. The Supreme Court distinguished these *cases from Lucknow Development Authority v M.K. Gupta* [III (1993) *CPJ* 7 *(SC)) and Ghaziabad Development Authority v*

Balbir Singh [11 *(2004) CPJ* 12 (SC)] and held that here, plots on existing sites (as opposed to those in a layout proposed to be developed over time) were auctioned, without any statutory requirement or assurance of providing (civic) amenities. Thus, the resultant contracts related to lease/sale of immoveable property. There was no hiring or availing of Services of a developer by the persons bidding at the auction. Further, there was no sale of goods. The complainants were thus not "Consumers" within the meaning of the term in the Consumer Protection Act. Bidders who participated in auctions with open eyes could not refuse to pay the accepted. bid amounts in time on the ground that the plots/sites suffered from disadvantages: or lack of amenities. The Court also did not find any statutory obligation an the Government to provide amenities for plots; sold!/teased- by[1] auction under the Punjab (Development & Regulation) Act, 1952. The' Court relied; upon/referred to its decisions in

Municipal Corporation, *Chandigarh v. Shanti Kunj Investments Pvt. Ltd [2006)4SCC 109]; Sector* 6, *Bahadurgarh Plot Holders Association V State of Haryana* [(1996) *I SCC* 485] *and Secretary, Bhubaneswar Development Authority v Susanta Kumar Mishra* [CA *No. 605/2009]*

5. State Bank of India v B.S. Agricultural Industries (I) [II (2009) CPJ 29 (SC)]

Date of Decision: 2Q.CK

B.S. Agricultural Industries/complainant filed a complaint against the Bank for compensation for not returning take bills when the party did not retire them. The District Forum allowed the complaint. When the ease reached the Supreme' Court, it observed that the District Forum had not considered the issue of limitation despite the Bank having taken a specific plea. The Court referred to S.24A of the Consumer Protection Act, which lays down limitation of 2 years for tiling of complaints. It held that the said provision, was peremptory in nature and required the consumer for a to see, before admitting a complaint, that it had been tiled within limitation. The consumer for a, however, for reasons to be recorded mi writing, may condone the delay in filing the complaint if sufficient cause is shown, It held that as a matter of law, the for a must deal with complaints on merits only it' the complaints had been filed within limitation and if beyond limitation" sufficient cause had been shown and delay condoned. The Court dismissed the complaint as it had been filed beyond limitation.

6. Vikram GreenTech (I) Ltd v New India Assurance Company Ltd. [II (2009) CP J 34 (SC)]

Date of Decision: 01.0

Vikram GreenTech (I) Ltd. (insured) preferred! a complaint that despite the surveyor giving a repent and clarifying that the comprehensive floriculture policy covered all the poly-houses, which had suffered damage in storm/cyclone the insurer had declined the claim. The Supreme Court upheld the order of the National Commission that since the policy clearly mentioned the number of poly houses as six, the claim would be confined to only these.

The Court held that insurance was a species of commercial transactions and an insurance contract must be construed, like any other contract, on its own terms. However, in insurance contracts, there is also a requirement of "ubenrima fide", i.e., utmost good faith on the part of the insured. The four essentials of an, insurance contract are (i) the definition of the risk" (ii) the duration of the risk, (iii) the premium and! (iv) the amount of insurance. The terms of the insurance policy have to be strictly construed the insured cannot claim anything, mare than what is, covered by the policy. A document take the proposal form, is a commercial documents and, being an integral part of the policy, reference to the proposal form may be essential. However, the surveyor's; report cannot aid in construing a policy.

7. C.P. Sreekumar (Dr.) v S. Ramanujam [II (2009) CPJ 48 SC]

Date of Decision: 01.05.2009

The accident-hit respondent/complainant was admitted to the appellants; hospital. When the hip fracture developed to a more serious kind, the appellant decided to perform a hemiarthroplasty instead of internal fixation procedure. The respondent alleged negligence that hemiarthroplasty was not justified and instead, internal fixation procedure should have been adopted Dealing with: the appeal!, the Supreme Court relied upon its decision in *Jacob Mattew v. State of Punjab & Anr. III (2005) CPJ 9; (SC)* and *English Court decision in Bolam v. Friern Hospital Management Committee, (1957) 2 All ER 118 (QBD)* and held That too much suspicion about the negligence of attending doctors and frequent interference by courts was dangerous as it prevented doctors from taking correct decision and ultimately, the patient would be the sufferer. The complain ant has to discharge; the onus of proving medical negligence. The Court found that while there were textbooks which prescribed internal fixation as, the preferred option, there were other textbooks too that recommended hemiarthroplasty and held that the doctor's choice in this case was not so palpably erroneous as to dub it as professional negligence.

8. Nizam Institute of Medical Sciences v Prasanth S. Dhananka & Ors. [II (2009) CPJ 61 (SC)]

Date of Decision: 14.05.2009

After the surgery for excision of tumour, the complainant developed acute paraplegia a with, complete loss, of control over the tower limbs and related complications and this ended in complete paralysis. The National Commission found that there was no written consent on record for the surgery to excise the rumour and that the consent taken for biopsy could: not be construed as implied consent for the main surgery. Dealing with the complainant's appeal for enhancement of compensation, the Supreme Court relied upon *Saimira Kohti v Dr. Prabha Manchanda & Anr.fi (2008) CPJ 56 (SC) II]*, which laid down that a patient's right in regard to his body was inviolable as was his right to decide whether he should undergo a particular treatment, and that additional treatment, which can be given outside the consented procedure, was confined touch treatment as was necessary to meet an emergency. The Court also-concluded that there was negligence since no neuro sturgeon was called in at the time of surgery though the medical literature revealed that in case of tumour in posterior mediastinal, the possibility of extension of tumour into tine foramen and vertebral column must be kept in mind. The Court substantially enhanced the compensation payable to the complainant under the heads of expenses on driver-cum-attendant and nurse, future medical expenses and loss of future earnings and also granted compensation for pain and suffering. The Court commented that a court must not be chary of awarding 'adequate compensation'

National Commission

1. Accounts Officer, Jharkhand State Electricity Board & Another v Answar Ali [II]

(2008) 2CPa 284(NC)- Majority view [III (2008) 3 CPJ322 (NC) - Minority view] Date of Decision; 10.04.2008 (Majority view); 16.04.2008 (Minority view)

On remand from the Supreme Court, the National Commission, by a majority of 2:1, dealt with this batch of revision petitions (the lead case being cited above) and gave a series of findings on the import of various sections of the Electricity Act, 2003 in relation to those of the Consumer Protection Act, 1986:

(i) A consumer of electricity supplied by an Electricity Board, a private company or the Government is a "consumer" under s.2 (1)(0) of the Consumer Protection Act (and also a "consumer" as defined in the Electricity Act - this fact is not noticed in the majority but in the minority view). Hence, a complaint by a consumer alleging any deficiency in the service of supplying electricity is maintainable under the Consumer Protection Act and the Electricity Act does not take away the consumer's right to approach a consumer forum (even in matters relating to assessment of electricity charges made by the assessing authority under s. 126 of the Electricity Act, added, keeping in view 'the contextual import of the majority view).

(ii) This is because, read together, sections 173,174 and 175 of the Electricity Act make it clear that the provisions of the Electricity Act would not have effect insofar as they are inconsistent with the Consumer Protection Act, the Atomic Energy Act and the Railways Act and the Legislature did not intend to bar the jurisdiction of consumer fora. Section 42(8) of the Electricity Act also provides that the remedies conferred on consumers under s.42(5), (6) & (7) of that Act are without prejudice to the rights which a consumer may have apart from the rights conferred upon the consumer by the aforesaid sub-sections.

(iii) Section 145 of the Electricity Act specifically bars the jurisdiction of the civil court to entertain any suit or proceeding in respect of any matter, which an assessing officer referred to in s. 126 or an appellate authority referred to in s. 127 of the Electricity Act or the adjudicating officer appointed under the said Act is empowered to determine. It also provides and that no court or 'other authority' shall grant injunction any in respect of any action taken/to be taken in pursuance of any power conferred by or under the Act. The phrase 'other authority' may include consumer fora. Read with sections 173 and 174, it would, however, imply to the extent there is inconsistency between the Electricity Act and Consumer Protection Act, the provisions of the

Electricity Act would not apply. Therefore, 'other authority' would not include the consumer fora in respect of matters provided for in section 126 of the Electricity Act.

(iv) In view of the Supreme Court's decision in *Kishore Lai v Chairman, ESI Corporation [(2007) 4 SCC 597]* and several other cases, the jurisdiction of consumer fora would not be curtailed unless there is an express provision in another piece of legislation prohibiting them from taking up matters provided for in that legislation. Hence, against an assessment order under s.126 of the Electricity Act, a consumer has the option to either file an appeal under s.127 of the Electricity Act or approach the appropriate consumer forum by filing a complaint. The consumer has to select his remedy. However, before entertaining a complaint in this regard, the consumer forum would direct the consumer to deposit an amount equal to one-third of the assessed amount with the licensee (on the lines of the requirement ins. 127(2)). Finally, the consumer fora would have no jurisdiction to interfere with the initiation of criminal proceedings or the final order passed by the special court constituted under s.153 or the civil liability determined under s-154 of the Electricity Act.

[**Note 1:** The dissenting view, however, held that there was no inconsistency between the provisions of the Consumer Protection Act and those of sections 126 and 127 of the Electricity Act and, therefore, the provisions of sections 173 and 174 of the latter Act need not be invoked in cases under sections 126 and 127 of the said Act. A consumer of electricity can of course approach a consumer forum for complaints of deficiency in supply of electricity but no more. The consumer fora do not have the jurisdiction to deal with complaints relating to assessment of charges for unauthorised use of electricity, tampering of meters, etc., as also over matters that fall in the domain of special courts constituted under the Electricity Act. Note 2: The word "tortuous" used at some places in the majority judgment should be read as "tortious".]

2. Ajay Kalia & Others v Air India Ltd. & Others [II (2009) CPJ 204 (NC)]

Date of Decision: 23.07.2008

The National Commission, while hearing a complaint regarding delay in flight, referred to the Guidelines of Air India dealing with Flight Irregularities and held that the same were required to be made known to the public at large. Air India was directed to display the Guidelines at a prominent place at every airport in the country from where it operates and also publish the summary thereof, in a newspaper.

3. Nipun Nagar v Symbiosis Institute of International Business [I (2009) CPJ 3 (NC)]

Date of Decision: 07.11.2008

The opposite party institute refused to refund the entire fee to the complainant who had surrendered his seat after getting admission to another institute. The National Commission observed that the institute had, in fact, admitted more students than the sanctioned strength and thus suffered no loss. It also relied upon the public notice issued by University Grants Commission providing that Institutions should refund the entire fee, except processing fee of not more than ₹ 1,000/-, to students withdrawing before start of the course, and allowed the complaint.

4. Chief Executive Officer, Zilla Parishad & Others v Sagunabai Navalsing Chavan [I (2009) CPJ 192 (NC)]

Date of Decision: 03.12.2008

The complainant alleged negligence in performing the tubectomy operation by a medical officer of the Zilla Parishad hospital, as thereafter she got pregnant and delivered a child. Relying upon *Indian Medical Association v V.P. ShalJtha & Ors. [III (1995) CPJ 1 (SC)J,* the National Commission held that the complainant was not a consumer under the Consumer Protection Act since the tubectomy was performed free of charge and, in fact, she got an incentive from the Government for undergoing the operation. The Commission also referred to the decision in *State of Punjab v. Shiv Ram & Ors. [IV (2005) CPJ 14 (SC)]* wherein it was observed that there are chances of failure of sterilisation and in certain percentage of cases re-canalisation could take place due to natural causes.

5. Ashok Ramnik Lai Tolat v Gallops Motors Pvt. Ltd. [II (2009) CPJ 63 (NC)]

Date of Decision: 16.12.2008

The complainant averred that he was misled into purchasing the motor vehicle Chevrolet Forester AWD model by the advertisements of M/s General Motors India Pvt. Ltd. that the vehicle was an SUV (sports utility vehicle) when it was a passenger car. The car manufacturer and its dealers referred to the owner's manual, which described the vehicle as a passenger car. In revision petitions filed by both parties, the National Commission held that the motor vehicle was not an SUV and the complainant was misled into believing it to be so on the opposite party's representations. This amounted to an unfair trade practice within s.2(r) of the Consumer Protection Act. Since the complainant had used the vehicle the for 1 year and it had run 14,000 km, the Commission directed ₹ 12.5 lakh out of the purchase price of ₹ 14 lakh to be refunded. The Commission observed that about 260 such vehicles had been sold in India during the relevant year. As the other consumers had not approached the consumer fora, the Commission opined that it would not be desirable to call upon the opposite parties to withdraw all the units. However, the Commission imposed punitive damages of ₹ 25 lakh on the opposite party.

6. Haryana Urban Development Authority v Dr. Maya Vaid [II (2009) CPJ 348 (NC)]

Date of Decision: 19.12.2008

The complainant claimed that the plot allotted to him by HUDA was of odd shape ("shermukhi") and in excess of the applied for area of 300 sq. intrs. He approached the Administrator but his grievance was dismissed without reasons. The District Forum allowed the complaint and held that HUDA could demand price only for a plot of 300 sq. mtrs. and that the plot be re-shaped accordingly. In appeal 'the State Commission also awarded interest @ 12% p.a. on the amount deposited. In revision filed by HUDA, the National Commission held the HUDA was clearly at fault since it had allotted a plot with excess area and odd shape. The Commission held the delay of bearers in redressing the complainant's grievance as unacceptable and rejected the plea of HUDA that after allotting an alternative plot, it should not be made to pay interest on the price to be refunded for the excess area. The Supreme Court decision in *Bangalore Development Authority v Syndicate Bank [II (2007) CPJ 17 (SC)J* was held inapplicable in this case.

7. Life Insurance Corporation of India v Girdhari Lai P. Kesarwani & Another [I (2009) CPJ 228 (NC)]

Date of Decision: 14.01.2009

The National Commission relied upon the decision of the Apex Court in *Harshad & Shah & Anr. v LIC of India & Ors. [III (1997) CPJ 9 (SC)]* wherein it was held that an agent had no authority to accept the premium on behalf of the LIC and that the premium deposited by the agent after the death of the assured deceased would not entitle the claimant to get the amount insured under the policy. *Bhanwar Kanwar v R.K. Gupta & Another [II (2009) CPJ 193 (NC)] Date of Decision: 29.0L2009.*

The complainant alleged before the National Commission that he had been misled by the opposite party's advertisement and representations that the latter could treat the complainant's son (suffering from fits) with ayurvedic medicines. After taking the medicine, the condition of the complainant's son deteriorated. An allopathic doctor opined that the child would not grow as a normal child. Tests revealed that the tablets given by the opposite party were 'Selgin', an allopathic medicine not to be given to children. The Commission found that in the correspondence with the complainant, the opposite party had been representing his medicine as ayurvedic whereas tests revealed it to be allopathic. The Commission also observed that the opposite party had been approaching people by giving advertisements and interviews published in newspapers/magazines and many must have been misled. Holding the opposite party guilty of unfair trade practices, the Commission directed him to pay a compensation of ₹5 lakh and deposit half of this in the Consumer Legal Aid Account.

9. Azizul Haq Khan (Dr. @ Lallan) v Shyamapati & Others [II (2009) CPJ 49 (NC)]

Date of Decision: 11.02.2009

The complainant alleged negligence against a Unani physician holding degree of Fazile-Tibb-O-Jarahat' (B .U.M.S.) that he prescribed some injections and allopathic medicines to her without first advising or requiring her to undergo any prior diagnostic tests. Subsequently, the complainant was admitted to a hospital where she underwent amputation of phalanxes (fingers and toes) of both hands and both feet. She alleged it was a case of drug induced peripheral thromboangitis and dry gangrene and thus, the Unani physician was responsible. In Appeals filed by both parties, the National Commission found that the material on record and medical literature did not support the case of 'drug induced' gangrene. Relying upon the Apex Court ruling in *Dr. Mukhtarchand & Others v State of Punjab [(1998) 7 SCC 5791* and a notification issued by Government of Uttar Pradesh, the Commission held the appellant competent to administer allopathic medicines in Uttar Pradesh. The Commission, however, found that the prescription of the Unani physician did not mention the patient's history of complaints or his clinical diagnosis and yet he prescribed several injections of various kinds. Referring, to medical literature on the injections, the Commission concluded that the Unani physician had no clue of what he was doing - he prescribed a veritable cocktail of allopathic medicines that were meant for diseases as wide-ranging as to include meningitis, scepticaemia, typhoid, etc. Applying the 'Bolam test', the Commission held the Unani physician guilty of medical negligence on four counts, *viz.*: (a) at the time of first examination of the patient, he did not record the prescription properly; (b) the prescription, written even after 6 weeks of treatment, did not reflect any clinical observations, diagnosis, etc.; (c) he failed to diagnose the ailment correctly; and (d) prescribed a wide range of medicines that had all the attributes of an 'overkill'.

10. Bahar Agrochem & Feeds Pvt. Ltd. v Prasad Gurusidappa Prachande & Others [II (2009)

Date of Decision: 12.02.2009

The opposite party contested the jurisdiction of the consumer forum to entertain a complaint regarding damage to crop on account of usage of zymegold, a bio- fertilizer as it involved complex and complicated issues which could not be adjudicated in summary jurisdiction. While dismissing the revision, the National Commission observed that in order to decide as to whether a consumer forum can deal with and decide a matter, it was necessary to see the facts first in each case. No stmitjacket formula could be prescribed. The Commission referred to Supreme Court decisions in *Dr., JJ, Merchant & Ors, v Shrinath Chaturvedi, CCI Chambers Co-operative Housing Society Ltd. v Development Credit Bank Ltd. and Punj Lloyd Ltd., v Corporate Risks India Pvt. Ltd. (supra)* and held that the issues involved in the present case could not be said to be complicated questions of facts or law which could not be decided in consumer proceedings. It held that the consumer fora are competent to deal with such issues and, wherever necessary, cross-examination of witnesses and experts can be permitted.

11. United India Insurance Co. Ltd. v Dipendu Ghosh & Another [II (2009) CP J 3 11 (NC)]

Date of Decision; 20.02.2009

The complainant obtained a 'speeial-peril-poliey' for his godown-cum-manufacturing unit. Due to rains, the complainant suffered losses and lodged a claim with the insurer. The surveyor appointed by the insurer gave a report that the flood did not enter the *factory/godown* but there was moisture in view of water logging, which affected the material lying there resulting in losses. The insurer repudiated the claim on the ground that loss was due to moisture. In revision, the National Commission rejected the contention of the insurer that the loss was not caused 'directly' by 'storm, cyclone, flood and inundation* The Commission referred to the dictionary meaning of 'direct cause' and held that the loss was caused because of inundation and thus would fall within the policy.

12. Head Postmaster, Ponnai, Kerala vV.Ayyapan [1I(2009)CPJ330(NC>]

Date of Decision: 24.04.2009

Ayyapan complained that he could not perform the last religious rites of his dead son because the telegram sent by the hospital reached late, much after his son was buried in the municipal burial ground- The District Forum dismissed the complaint relying upon $.9 of the Indian Telegraph Act which stipulated that" „ „ the Government shall not be responsible for any loss or damage which may occur in consequence of any telegraph officer failing in his duty with respect to receipt, transmission or delivery of any message..."

The State Commission allowed the appeal; The National Commission dismissed the revision filed by the Post Office holding it deficient in service from the material on record. It also held that that the Post Office could not take shelter under s,9 of the Telegraph Act by taking a technical view of the case and public servants must work with some conscience In cases like these.

13. Life Insurance Corporation of India v Kulwant Kumari [II (2009) CP J 317 (NC)]

Date of Decision: 01. 05.2009

Late Kailash Chander got himself insured with the LIC (opposite party) for ₹ 1 lakh on 09,04,2000. Though the policy lapsed because of non-payment of premium, it was later revived, Kailash Chander died on 04,04,2003, LIC repudiated the complainant's claim on the ground that the assured was suffering from diabetes mellitus two years prior to the date of revival of the policy. The consumer fora below allowed the complaint. Dismissing the revision petition filed by the LIC, the National Commission observed that undisputedly the policy was not repudiated on the ground that at the time of taking the Initial policy there was any misrepresentation or intentional concealment of facts. The burden to prove the concealment was on the Insurance Company In terms of s.45 of the Life Insurance Act, 1938. LIC's contention that two years had to be counted from the date of revival of the policy was also rejected as this was contrary to the Supreme Court decision in *MIthoolal Nayak v Life Insurance Corporation of India [AIR 1962 SC 814].*

JCT Limited, one of the leading manufacturers of textiles, is the flagship company of the Thapar Group – one of the largest Indian conglomerates. JCT's textile division was the first industry in India to be accredited with an ISO 9002 certification in 1996.

Landmark Decisions – National Consumer Disputes Redressal Commission

NATIONAL CONSUMER DISPUTES REDRESSAL COMMISSION NEW DELHI

MA NO. 254 OF 2007

IN

FIRST APPEAL NO. 311 OF 2006

(Against the order dated 31.05.2006 In complaint No. SC-30/0V04 of the State Commission, West Bengal)

KOLKATA METROPOLITAN

DEVELOPMENT AUTHORITY

Appellant(s)

VERSUS

BIDHAN NAGAR SOURA V CO-OPERATIVE HOUSING SOCIETY LTD ... Respondent(s)

BEFORE

HON'BLE MR. JUSTICE S.N. KAPOOR, PRESIDING MEMBER MR. B.K.TAIMNI, MEMBER.

For the Appellant : Mr, Anindita Gupta with Mr. S.K. Sharma, Advocate

For the Respondent : Mr. Prabir Basu with Mr. Sanjay Kr, Ghosh, Advocate.

Dated the 7th day of September. 2007.

ORDER

Since the matter is being heard today itself, the application for early hearing is disposed of.

Heard learned counsel for the parties.

It is submitted by learned counsel for the appellant-that valuation given by the valuer about cost of repairs which was required to be made, was on very high side and unrealistic and therefore, she prayed that another valuer should be appointed. We feel that this is highly belated prayer. We have taken note of the fact that the complainant-respondent filed the complaint for removing the defects in the construction of flats at Sourav Abasan at Bidhannagar, Kolkata and sought compensation mental agony etc. in all, ₹ 69.90 lacs and along with cost of ₹ 20,000/-. It appears that State Commission has taken note of the report of Shri Mahitosh Chakraborty, Chartered Engineer & Registered Valuer of Hon'ble: High Court, Kolkata A.G.O.T. (West Bengal), item wise details have been furnished by the Chartered Engineer.

If in this light, the State Commission has accepted the cost of repair of ₹ 18,51,823/- we feel that no exception Pan be taken to it. The State Commission had reduced the compensation to ₹ 2 lacs with cost of ₹ 3,000/-

Learned counsel for the appellant also submits that ₹ 2 Lacs is on very high side. It is submitted on behalf of the respondent that if not all at least 18 complainants had suffered on account of defects, The flats were booked as far back as on 18.12.2002. Lease deed was registered on 29.05.2003, We reduce this compensation from ₹ 2 lacs to ₹ 1 lac payable along with cost of ₹ 10.000/- in all, including the cost of this present appeal as well as cost awarded by the State Commission the appeal is partly accepted by modifying the impugned order in above terms.

Sd/-

(S.N.KAPOOR)

PRESIDING MEMBER

TRUE COPY

ADVOCATE

Service Quality in Banks

State Consumer Disputes Redressal Commission West Bengal BHABANI BHAVAN (GROUND FLOOR) 31, BELVEDERE ROAD, ALIPORE KOLKATA - 700 027

S.C. CASE NO.49/RP/08

DATE OF FILING: 24.6.2008

DATE OF FINAL ORDER: 30.09.2008

PETITIONER

The New India Assurance Co. Ltd. 23, Ganesh Chandra Avenue Kolkata-700013

RESPONDENT

Sunil Kr. Neogi

Samik Kr. Neogi

P-32, Vijoy Nagar, Madhyamgram North 24-Parganas

BEFORE: HON'BLE JUSTICE MR. A. CHAKRABARTI, PRESIDENT

MEMBER	:	Mr. S.N. BASU
MEMBER	:	MRS. S. MAJUMDER
FOR THE PETITIONER	:	Mr. N.R. Mukerjee, Advocate
FOR THE RESPONDENT	:	Mr. Uday Ch. Jha, Advocate
	:	ORDER:

HON'BLE JUSTICE MR. A. CHAKRABARTI, PRESIDENT

This Revisional Application was filed by New India Assurance Company Ltd. challenging the order dated 27.5.2008 whereby the Judgment Debtor/Petitioner was directed to satisfy the decree on or before 27.6.2008 in default steps would be taken as per provisions of law.

Mr. N.R. Mukherjee, the Ld. Advocate for the Judgment Debtor/ Petitioner contended that the Consumer Protection Act as its stands today, does not permit execution of the decree by the Forum as order of the Forum does not enjoy the status of decree of a Civil Court after amendment of the Act in the year 2002. It is contended that as the order sought to be implemented was for payment of money the only course open for its implementation is u/s.25 (3) of the Act. The Forum cannot avail of any other course for execution of its order granting relief of payment of money. The Section 27 of the Act does not empower the Forum to issue warrant of arrest for non-compliance of the final order passed by a Forum and powers u/s.13 (4) of C.P. Act, were referred to. Only in case the attendance in court is directed and still not complied by the Judgment Debtor, Section 27 can be availed of It is argued that the said Section 27 is for imposition of penalty for non-compliance of an order by which Forum gives certain specific directions in course of the proceeding before it and not for execution' of its final order granting monetary relief for which Section 25(3) has been specifically provided.

On behalf of the Decree Holder it is contended by Mr. Uday Chandra Jha, Ld; Advocate that the Consumer Protection Act, 1986 was amended by Consumer Protection (Amendment) Act 2002 amending various Sections out of which Sections 25 and 27 are under consideration presently. In respect of these two Sections amendment indicate that for execution of any order passed in its final judgment by a Forum, old procedure of execution like a Civil Court in respect of its decree, was omitted and instead it was made more effective by amending Section 27 and prescribing a procedure for imposition of penalty for non-compliance of any order passed by a Forum and in respect of such imposition of penalty the Forum/Commission is to exercise power equivalent to First Class Judicial Magistrate in a summary trial. It is stated that the legal fiction created originally in the 1986 Act by treating an order of a Forum/Commission as decree by a Civil court executable in the same manner, was omitted and instead implementation of order was provided by imposition of a penalty u/s.27 exercising powers of a First Class Judicial Magistrate in a summary trial. Reliance was placed on the Judgment in the case of *M/s. Maruti Udyog Ltd.-vs.-Ram Lai reported in 2005(1) Supreme 721, State of Karnataka-vs.- Vishwabarathi House Building Cooperative Society reported in 2003(2) Supreme 578 and Prudential Capital Markets Ltd.-vs.-Dipankar Guha reported in 2007 CT J 1125.*

The Ld. Advocate for the Decree Holder argued that in respect of enforcement of a decree the provisions of Sections 13 and 14 are not be relevant and, therefore the provision of various reliefs, are not to be looked into for interpreting Sections 25 and 27 of the Act. It is argued that the contention of the Judgment Debtor if accepted restricting applicability of Section 27 only in those cases where relief has been granted but no monetary relief is included, the language of the Section 27 has to be violated. The expression "any Order" used in Section 27 does not permit any such restriction. Law is clear that when ordinary meaning can be attributed to a statutory provision, no other word can be read in the said provision.

It is contended that Section 27(2) has a non-obstante clause and therefore limitations of applicability of summary trials on the basis of quantum of penalty cannot be made applicable proceeding u/s.27. Extent of the penalty provided in Section 27 will not restrict its application so far as procedure of a summary trial by a Criminal Court is concerned. It is argued that the expression "complaint" used in Section 27 is not a complaint as defined in Section 2(1) (c) but it is a complaint as used in Section 200 of the Code of Criminal Procedure. Summary trial procedure is applicable both in summons cases and warrant cases and, therefore, the specific reference to power of a First Class Judicial Magistrate and proceeding applicable to a summary trial cannot be read with a restrictive meaning.

Reference was made to the judgment in the case of *State of Karnataka-vs.-Parmjit Singh reported in 2006 (2) Supreme 543*.

On facts it is stated that in the present case after the appeal was dismissed and the order of the Forum had reached a finality, impugned order was passed.

With regard to the general defect as argued by the Judgment Debtor that a wrong person may be arrested in case a company is a Judgment Debtor, it is contended by Decree Holder that in such a case that person is always entitled to bring it to the notice of the Forum concerned to get the wrong corrected. Mere such possibility will not help interpretation of the law.

It is argued that when procedure under Code of Criminal Procedure is made Applicable personal appearance of a judgment debtor is required everyday of hearing before the Forum applying the principles of Section 205 of the Code of the. Criminal Procedure.

Considering the aforesaid it appears that when the law was amended by the Amending Act of 2002, the earlier fiction created making an order of a Forum/Commission a decree of a Civil Court was taken away and instead the procedure and powers of a First Class Judicial Magistrate trying a summary trial was made applicable. It seems that legislature was not satisfied with the application of Civil Courts' lingering procedure of implementation of a decree in respect of execution of an order passed in a summary proceeding under the Consumer Protection Act and, therefore, the quicker proceeding of criminal courts was made applicable for implementation of the order of a Forum/Commission. It is rightly argued by the

Decree Holder that power and procedure of a First Class Judicial Magistrate trying a summary trial were enacted in Section 27 by reference and all the provisions of Cr. P.C. for such trials are to be read in the said Sec.27. The judgment in the case of *P.C. Agarwala-vs-Payment of Wages Inspector reported in 2005(8) scc 104* supports this view.

In this respect the Judgment Debtor's contention is that penalty in C.P. Act being three years, the provisions of summary trial/summons cases cannot be made applicable, But this contention is not acceptable as merely the procedure has been enacted by reference and therefore the quantum/period of penalty has nothing to do in this respect.

So far as the contention of the Judgment Debtor is concerned that Section 27 only deals with reliefs of any nature except monetary relief as in respect of monetary relief Section 25(3) was provided, does not appear to be acceptable. The reason for such conclusion is that Section 27 mentions "any order" and there is no guideline in Section 27 which makes us to read such an expression "any order" with a restrictive meaning. It appears that Section 25(3) gives an option to a Decree Holder to apply under the said provision for recovery of money. Section 27 provides an additional avenue in respect of any order whatsoever and the section itself does not indicate any restrictive application.

The contention of the Judgment Debtor is that C.P. Act does not speak of arrest and Section 13(4) only speaks of enforcing attendance of a defendant or a witness. But Section 13 relating to pending proceedings under this Act cannot be looked into for the purpose of interpreting other provisions of the statute which speak of stages after final judgment. Moreover Sec. 13(4) has a specific purpose which in no way can be looked to for ascertaining scope of Sec.27.

The case of *Patel Roadways Ltd.,-vs-Birla Yamaha Ltd. 2000(2) Supreme 594* referred by Judgment Debtor was decided in different context and is not applicable in the case in hand. The questions considered by the Full Bench of Andhra Pradesh High Court in *Dr. C.v. Ratnam-Vs-Union of India reported in 2002 CT J 421* were considered by the Apex Court in the case of *State of Karnataka-vs-Vishwabarathi House Building Co-op. Society (Supra)* judgments in the both the cases having been written by the Hon'ble Mr. Justice S.B. Sinha. The other judgment referred by the judgment debtor being 2000(3) Supreme 363 *(R.N. Dey-vs-Bhagyabati Pramanick)* having held that contempt proceeding cannot be used for executing decree or implementation of order, also has no application in this case.

With regard to the contention that when an order has been passed against a company, a junior officer of the company cannot be arrested as he does not represent the company, it appears that it is true that in such a case a company is the Judgment Debtor. But when a company violates any order which results in arrest of the violator, Principal Officers of the company are to be held responsible. While finding as who is to be dealt with when a company has committed an offence our Apex Court has followed the Classic statement of Viscount Haldane, Lord Chancellor in *Lennard's Carrying Co. Ltd.-vs-Asiatic Petroleum Co. Ltd. (1915 AC 705)* which is as follows:

"A corporation is an abstraction. It has no mind of its own any more than it lias a body of its own; its active and directing will must consequently be sought in the person of somebody who for some purposes may be called an agent, but who is really the directing mind and will of the corporation, the very ego and centre of the personality of the corporation. That person may be under the direction of the shareholders in general meeting; that person may be the board of directors itself, or it may be, and in some companies it is so, that person has an authority coordinate with the board of directors given to him under the articles of association

Following the said principle the Apex Court in the case of *J.K. Industries-vs.- Chief Inspector of Factories & Boilers 1996(6) SCC 665* held as follows: Where the company owns a factory it is the company which is the occupier, but since company is a legal abstraction without a real mind of its own, it is those[1] who in fact control and determine the management of the company, who are held vicariously liable for Commission of Statutory Offences. The directors of the company are, therefore, tightly called upon to answer the charge, being the directing mind of the company.

Therefore in respect of a company judgment debtor, such persons are to be dealt with for the offence of non-compliance of the order of the Forum/Commission.

The contention of the Judgment Debtor that the restricted use of Section 27 is permissible only when the order of the Forum/ Commission has reached a finality, also is not acceptable as mere filing of an appeal does not amount to stay of the order appealed against. Unless stayed, or set aside a final judgment of a Forum/Commission has to be obeyed by the Judgment Debtor.

With regard to definition of "person" we have considered the provisions of law and particularly Section 2 (m) of C.P Act. But in view of sub-Clause (iv) of Section 2(m) of the C.P. Act and Section 3(42) of General Clauses Act, the position is clear that a person includes a company.

With regard to the further contention of the Judgment Debtor that even in Section 27 a formal conferment of power is required on Forum/Commission to enable it to act as a First Class Magistrate, it appears that language of the said Section 27 makes it clear that by the said statutory provision itself such conferment of power was made on Forum/Commission. A contrary meaning will make the said Section 27 infructuous as the said Act has not prescribed any authority which is empowered to such conferment nor any procedure which makes such conferment possible. The judgment of the Apex Court in the case of *State of Karnataka-vs.- Parmjit Singh*

"Rules of procedure are not by themselves an end but the means to achieve the ends of justice. Rules of procedure are tools forged to achieve justice and are not hurdles to obstruct the pathway to justice. Construction of a rule of procedure which promotes justice and prevents its miscarriage by enabling the Court to do justice in myriad situations, all of which cannot be envisaged, acting within the limits of the permissible construction, must be preferred to that which is rigid and negatives the cause of justice. The reason is obvious. Procedure is meant to subserve and not rule the cause of justice. Where the outcome and fairness of the procedure adopted is not doubted and the essentials of the prescribed procedure have been followed, there is no reason to discard the result simply because certain details which have not prejudicially affected the result have been inadvertently omitted in a particular case. In our view, this appears to be the pragmatic approach which needs to be adopted while construing a purely procedural provision. Otherwise, rules of procedure will become the mistress instead of remaining the handmaid of justice, contrary to the role attributed to it in our legal system."

In so far as the present facts are concerned it appears that application was made by the Decree Holder for compliance of the order by the Judgment Debtor and specific direction was given by the executing Forum and only on non-compliance thereof, impugned order was passed. As regards the officer who is to represent the company, in case a company is found to have committed an offence, its Principal Officers and/or the person carrying on its function are liable as held hereinabove. Contention of the Judgment Debtor that a junior officer who was not even a party to the proceeding cannot be arrested, requires consideration. In such case the concerned officer can approach the Forum/Commission seeking his relief pointing out Principal Officers who are liable on behalf of such Judgment Debtor company.

In view of the above findings the Revision Petition is disposed of without interfering with the impugned order but granting liberty to the petitioner to approach the Forum below indicating the Principal Officers of the Judgment Debtor liable in the matter. No order as to costs.

(S. Majumder)	(S.N. Basu)	(Justice A. Chakrabarty)
MEMBER(L)	MEMBER	PRESIDENT

STATE CONSUMER-DISPUTES REDRESSAL COMMISSION WEST BENGAL
BHABANI BHAVAN(GROUND FLOOR) 31, BELVEDERE ROAD, ALIPORE.
KOLKATA-700027,

S. C. CASE NO, SC-30/0/04 DATED:- 31.05.2006.
APPELLANTS/COMPLAINANTS : BIDHANNAGAR SOURAV HOUSING COOPERATIVE SOCIETY LTD.
RESPONDENTS/O.P.S. KOLKATA METROPOLITAN DEVELOPMENT AUTHORITY
BEFORE:
HON'BLE JUSTICE MEMBER:-S.N.BASU
MEMBER-A.K.RAY
FOR THE PETITIONER/APPELLANT;-
FOR THE RESPONDENT/O.P.S.:-

ORDER

SHRI S. N. BASU, MEMBER

1. This is a compliant filed by Bidhannagar Saurav Housing Co-operative Society having its address at EE -183, Salt Lake, P.S.:- Bidhannagar, Kolkata-700 091 against Kolkata Metropolitan Development Authority represented by ifs Estate Manager, Management & Marketing (Flat), Unnayan Bhaban, Salt Lake, Kolkata 700 091. The fact of the case in brief, are that the complainant is a registered co-operative housing society having its Registration No. 04/KMAM of 2003 with 106 members who are all allottees of 108 ownership flats taken on lease of 999 years from the Opposite Party, Pursuant to the contract with the O.P. separate Lease Deed in respect of each of the 106 flats had been registered with the Additional Registrar of Assurances, Kolkata. The allottees who are all members of the complainant-co-operative Housing Society, are stated to have accepted the possession of the said flats for their living purpose in good faith and without knowing the contents, purport and effect of the clauses of the Lease Deed prepared by the Opposite Party, They further stated that they had put their signatures in the said Lease Deeds in order to enjoy the facilities and amenities attached to the said flats. Since the said Deed of Lease had been prepared as per settled format of the Opposite Party. Allegedly, in the said lease the Opposite Party purposely incorporated a few clauses at Page Nos. 4 & 5 in order to cover up their deficiency in service knowing fully well that the defects would not be otherwise acceptable before any legal forum as these restrictive clauses are against the principles of public. The clauses so incorporated relate to inadmissibility of any complaint regarding the construction of flat, its plan, fixtures and fitting as also the amenities and facilities provided their by the O.P. The complainant cites the decision in *AIR 1994 (SC) 787 Lucknow Development Authority-v.-M,K. Gupta* in this context to contend that through the O.P. is a Development Body, the deficiency very much falls within the purview of COPRA.

2. The case was heard exparte. Though the O.P.- had entered appearance they did not appear in any hearing thereafter. After the allottees had taken possession of the flats several defects were noticed inside the flat. The defects relate to construction of the flat, fixtures and fittings, common place, painting, flooring and drainage. Since the complaint relating to construction of the flat was not entertained by the O.P. despite formal intimation being made about the defects the complainant had engaged an expert engineer-cum-valuer firm, *M/s.* Mohitosh Chakraborty, Chartered Engineer & Registered Valuer of the High Court at Kolkata to identify the defects and work out the financial implication for repairing the defects to make the flats habitable. The said firm filed their report to the complainant Co-operative Society on 26.11.2004 with has also been made an annexure to the affidavit filed by the complainant. The said Engineer-cum-Valuer firm had identified the defects of the flats in several respects, viz, Terrazzo flooring, sewerage system service drain, water-logging in lift-well, waste lines, shutter, marble and kota floor, storing waste slab, water tank of roof, roof tiles, storing floor at ground level, raising of electrical main switch through overhauling of all lifts and painting inside and outside the flat as listed in the said report. The firm had also worked out the financial implication to execute the above works in respect of 106 flats at ₹ 18,51,823.00. The complainant states in the petition that the cause of action had arisen on 18.12.2002 when the possession of different flats were given to the allotees and thereafter on 29.05.2003 and thereafter when the Lease Deeds were given to the allotlees and thereafter on 29.05.2003 and thereafter when the Lease Deeds were registered. The complainant submits that since O.P. is not legally bound, to execute various repair works in view of the said disputed clauses of the Lease Deed, the Commission may issue necessary directions of the O.P. for undertaking necessary repair works as pointed out in the Report submitted by the Chartered Engineer to make the flats habitable, to the allottees and also to pay compensation of ₹ 68.90 lakh, alongwith cost of ₹ 20,000.00.

3. During the hearing the complainant had filed evidence on affidavit affirming the statement in the complaint together with the Report of the Chartered Engineer. They have also filed a copy of the Possession Certificate which states that no repair or rectification work of any defect of the flats or garage shall be undertaken or done by K.M.D.A. after the delivery of possession of the flats is given to the allottee. They have also during hearing the following case laws on which, they relied,) 1997(1) CPR45, (ii) 1996(2) CPR45, (iii) 20C4CTJ 1 (SC), (CP), (iv) 2004 (3) CPR 449. in course of hearing the complainant they had also exhibited before the Commission the Original documents in respect of the Xerox copies filed by them. Complainant has in particular tried on decision in *AIR 1994 SC 787-Lucknow Development Authority-V.-M.K. Gupta*. The landmark decision of the Hon'ble Apex Court has dealt with several issues which were till date undecided and had been the subject matters of litigation. One of the important

issues is whether allottee of a constructed flat/house should be treated as a consumer as sale of such constructed house is generally treated as a consumer as sale of such contracted house is generally treated as property transaction and not 'service and unless the component of 'service' is established, an allottee cannot come within the ambit of C.P. Act. The Hon'ble Apex Court gave a clear decision therein that while the construction of the flat and its transfer falls within the purview of such property transaction any delay in making delivery of the flat/house within the scheduled time or issues relating to defects in the constructions fall within the purview of service, "if the service is defective or it is not what was represented then it would be unfair trade practice as defined in the Act. Any defect in the construction activity would be denial of common comfort and service to consumer. Such disputes or claims are not in respect of immovable as argued but deficiency in rendering-of service of particular standard, quality or grade. Such deficiency or omissions are defined in sub-clause (ii) of Clause ® of section 2 as Unfair Trade Practice. If the builder of a house use substandard material in construction of a building or makes face or misleading representation about the condition of the house then it is denial of the facility or benefit of which a consumer is entitled to claim value under the Act. When the contractor or builder undertakes to erect a house or fiat then it is inherent in it that he shall perform his obligations as agreed to. A flat with a leaking roof or cracking wall or substandard floor is denial of service. Similarly, when a Statutory Authority undertakes to develop land and frame housing scheme on it, while performing statutory duty render service to the society in general and individual in particular. A person who applies for allotment of a building site or for as flat constructed by the Development Authority enters into an agreement with a builder or a contractor is a potential user and nature of transaction is covered in the expression service of any description'. The Apex Court further had observed also that a Government or Semi-Government body or a local authority is as much amenable to the Act as any other private body; rendering similar service. In view of the above decisions of the Hon'ble Apex, Court we find that the allottees of the flats of the O.P. very much fall within the purview of C.P. Act, 1986. The O.P. through its impugned Lease Deed imposed several restrictions on the allottees with the members of the O.P. were obliged to sign even before thoroughly checking the quality of work executed in their flat, but the most curious part of the impugned Lease Deed is that the O.P. brazenly makes itself unaccountable in respect of all the responsibilities regarding executing any further repair or corrective works in the flats even if such defects actually existed to the detriment of the allottees prior to the flats were allotted to them. In such circumstances the present case is conspicuously an instance of, Unfair Trade Practice and falls within the purview of Sub-section ® of Section 2 (1) of the C.P. Act, 1986, and consequently O.P. must take necessary corrective steps to make the flats habitable to the allottees.

5. In consideration of the facts and circumstances contained in the foregoing paragraphs and the prayer of the Society In para-15 read with para -11 of the complaint we are inclined to say that the O.P. has been found negligent on two counts; i) Its deficiency due to failure in taking corrective steps to remove defects in the newly constructed flats, despite being requested to do so repeatedly, and (ii) making restrictive provisions in the Lease Deed which preclude the allottees to obtain any further service from the O.P. after taking possession, of the flats even though such defects existed before the flats were handed over. We are, therefore, inclined to hold that the O.P. has miserably failed to alleviate the genuine sufferings of the allottees due to existence of several defects in the flats constructed by the O.P.

6. The complainant has therefore, come up with the prayer for Issuing direction on the O.P. for (i) setting right the defects in the construction of flats at Sourav Abasan; (ii) compensation for mental agony and harassment caused to the members of the Saurav Abasan for the defects in constructions of the flats for ₹ 68.90 lac and also for payment of cost of ₹ 20,000.00. We have already discussed in there foregoing paragraphs that the defects in the construction were listed out by *M/s.* Mohitosh Chakraborty, Chartered Engineer & Valuer who are also the paneled Engineer's Valuer of the Hon'ble Kolkata High Court. The item wise details have been furnished by the Chartered Engineer and the estimated cost has also been worked out by them on the basis of the current schedule. We are therefore, inclined to say that the total amount of cost of ₹ 18,51,823.00 for removing the defects is admissible in our view. However, regarding the amount of compensation which has been claimed for ₹ 68.90 lac we think that the amount has been calculated very much on the higher side, We accept the position of the Inconvenience harassment, mental agony and even some amount of cost incurred by the members due to a large number of defects obtaining in their flats Considering the entire issue we are of the considered view that an amount of compensation of more or less. ₹ 2,000.00 per. member is a reasonably amount. We also think that the claim for cost of litigation of ₹ 20,000.00 has been shown on the higher side. After taking all the facts and circumstances into consideration it is directed that (a) the O.P., K.M.D.A, represented by its Estate Manager, Management & Marketing (Flat), shall remove the defects as pointed out by the Chartered Engineer firm, *M/s.* Mohitosh Chakraboty in their Report dated 26.11.2004 within a period of 90 days form the date of communication of this Order failing which the O.P. shall pay the above amount of ₹ 18,51,2004.00 to the complainant Co-operative Society for execution of the rectification/works to the buildings by the complainant's own machinery; (b) it is further ordered that he O.P. shall pay compensation of ₹ 2 lacs to the complainant Co-operative Society of the harassment and mental agony suffered by its members and the inconvenience faced by them for living in defectively constructed flats; (c) it is also directed to pay litigation cost of ₹ 3,000.00 to the complainant.

The complaint be allowed *ex parte* with cost.

Sd/-

Member

TRUE COPY

ADVOCATE

NATIONAL CONSUMER DISPUTES REDRESSAL COMMISSION

NEW DELHI

FIRST APPEAL NO. 18 OF 2009

(Against order dated 30/09/08 in SC. Case No. 49/RP/08 of th6

State Commission, West Bengal

NEW INDIA ASSURANCE CO. LTD. & ANR.. ....

Appellant(s)

Vs.

MR. SUNIL NEOGI & ORS ....

Respondent(s)

BEFORE:

HON'BLE MR. JUSTICE R.C. JAIN,

PRESIDING MEMBER

For the Appellants : NEMO

For the Respondents : NEMO

Dated, the 13 day of February. 2009

ORDER

No one appears for the appellant insurance company. The present proceedings purportedly First Appeal has been filed after a delay of 74 days. The First Appeal is mis-conceived because it has been filed against an order passed by the West Bengal State Consumer Disputes Redressal Commission in a revision which was filed before the State Commission against an order passed by the District Forum -in execution proceedings. The First Appeal before this Commission lies only against the orders passed by the State Commission in exercise of its original jurisdiction rather than against the order passed by the State Commission in exercise of its revisional jurisdiction. For this reason and for the reason that there is undue delay of 74 days which has not been explained satisfactorily, this misconceived appeal is dismissed as such.

Sd/-

(R.C.JAIN)

PRESIDING MEMBER

YD/03/Court3

NATIONAL CONSUMER DISPUTES REDRESSAL COMMISSION

NEW DELHI

REVISION PETITION NO. 1678 OF 2005

(Against the order dated 8:3. 2005 in Appeal No. 25 of 2003 of the State Commission, West Bengal)

Bank of Maharasthra.

Head Office at Lok Mangal,

1501, Shivaji Nagar,

Pune and amongst other places a Branch at 31-A, S.P. Mukherjee Road, P.S. Bhowani Pore,

Kolkata ....Petitioner

Vs.

MD. Khurshidul Hassan,

Proprietor *M/s.* Calico India Exports, 38, MELEOD Street, P.S. Parkstreet, Kolkata ....Respondent

BEFORE:

HON'BLE MR. JUSTICE B N P SINGH, PRESIDING MEMBER

HON'BLE DR. P D SHENOY, MEMBER

For the Petitioner : Mr. Ashish Kalia, Advocate

For Respondents : Mr. Rauf Rahim and

Mr. Yadunandan Bansal, Advocates

PRONOUNCED ON 9th July 2009

ORDER

PER DR. P.P. SHENOY, MEMBER

The respondent was the complainant before the District Forum.

2. In the course of business transaction, the complainant received three export orders from a foreign buyer, Western Australia, for supply of coated paperboard printed and printed folders and envelopes. Accordingly he shipped three consignments of the said goods. Pursuant to the aforesaid exports of goods, the complainant submitted all the relevant documents relating to the said three shipments, viz., Invoices, Original Bill of Lading, Bills of Exchange and other necessary documents for the purpose of collection of the proceeds from the foreign buyers through the buyer's Bankers the Commonwealth Bank of Australia Adelaide Street, Fremantle, Western Australia. The said bills were to be collected after 30 days, 75 days and 30 days from the dates of the 1st 2nd and 3rd Bills of Lading respectively.

3. The said three bills were duly credited in the account of the complainant by the Bank of Maharashtra (for short 'the Bank) on 3.11.2000, 1.12.2000 and 20.12.2000 respectively. Subsequently, the complainant carne to learn that the Bank had sent those three bills to the Commonwealth Bank of Australia. The complainant was surprised to learn that the Bank, after purchasing all the three bills resorted to debiting the account of the complainant of the said three Bills with interest thereon, totalling ₹ 13,24,691/-, in total contravention of the Banking norms. It was found that the Bank was not showing any interest in realizing the export proceeds from the foreign buyer through the Commonwealth Bank of Australia. The complainant had made several complaints to the Bank and had also to undertake a trip to Australia, accordingly, the complainant filed a complaint before the State Commission.

4. The complainant claimed refund of ₹ 13,24,691/- apart from travelling expenses, boarding and lodging and legal expenses to the tune of ₹ 7,00,000/- and towards business loss, mental agony, harassment etc. ₹ 52,00,000/- with the total claim of ₹ 72,24,691/- before the State Commission alongwith interest @ 18% p.a.

5. Before the State Commission, the issue of maintainability of the case came up for consideration, i.e., whether the complainant can be considered to be a consumer under the Consumer Protection Act and whether the complainant who had availed services of the Bank for the purpose of collecting its export proceeds from the foreign buyer could be treated as for 'commercial purpose' or not. The State Commission held as follows:-

"The complainant earns profit through his main business, namely export of *various products, but the banking services hired by him from the OP is not used for any activity directly intended to generate profit. In that view of the matter, following the judgment* of *the Apex Consumer Court, we hold that the services availed* of *by the complainant from the OP bank for collection* of *export proceeds is not for commercial purposes, and, hence, he is very much a consumer under the amended C. P. Act. Therefore, the complaint case filed by the complainant is legally maintainable under the C.P. Act".*

6. Aggrieved by the order of the State Commission, the bank has filed this Revision Petition before us.

7. We have heard the learned counsel for the petitioner and the respondent.

8. Section 2(d)(ii) of the Consumer Protection Act, 1986 reads as follows:-

"Consumer" means any person who hires or avails of any services for a consideration which has been paid or promised or partly paid and partly promised, or under any system of deferred payment and includes any beneficiary of such services other than the person who 'hires or avails of the services for consideration paid or promised, or partly paid and partly promised, or under any system of deferred payment, when such services are availed of with the approval of the first mentioned person but does not include a person who avails of such services for any commercial purposes".

Section 2 (g) defines the word 'deficiency' and Section 2(0) defines 'service' which read as under:

2 (g) "deficiency" means any fault, imperfection, shortcoming or inadequacy in the quality, nature and manner of performance which is required to be maintained by or under any law for the time being in force or has been undertaken to be performed by a person in pursuance of a contract or otherwise in relation to any service; 2(0) "service" means service of any description which is made available to potential users and includes, but not limited to, the provision of facilities in connection with banking, financing, insurance, transport, processing, supply of electrical or other energy, board or lodging or both, housing construction, entertainment, amusement or the purveying of news or other information, but does not include the rendering of any service free of charge or under a contract of personal service", (emphasis added)

9. The definition of 'service' under Section 2(0) clearly covers provision of facilities in connection with banking. So the issue to be decided is whether the complainant had availed the services of the Bank for the purpose of collecting its export proceeds from the foreign buyer, would be treated as for 'commercial purpose' or not.

10. It would be beneficial in this connection to go through; some of the important Judgments of the Hon'ble Apex Court and our Commission.

11. In *Laxmi Engineering Works Appellant vs. P.S.G. Industrial Institute, Respondent - AIR 1995 SC 1428,* the Hon'ble Apex Court held as under:-

"So far as the present case is concerned, we must hold (in agreement with the National Commission), having regard to the nature and character of the machine and the material on record that it is not goods which the appellant purchased for use by himself exclusively for the purpose of earning his livelihood by means of self-employment, as explained hereinabove".

12. Sub-section 2(d) has two sub-clauses (i) relating to buyer of goods and (ii) hirer of services. As this Judgment relates to the purchaser of goods, the ratio of this is not applicable to the case under consideration. Accordingly, it will be useful for us to look into the cases relating to hiring and or availing of services. In *Harsolia Motors vs. National Insurance Co. Ltd.-I (2005) CPJ 27 (NC),* this Commission held as under:

"If the goods are purchased for resale or for commercial purpose then such consumer would be excluded from the coverage of Consumer Protection Act, 1986. Such illustration could be that a manufacturer who is producing one product 'A', for such production he may be required to purchase articles, which may be raw-material, then purchase of such articles would be for commercial purpose. As against this, the same manufacturer if he purchases a refrigerator, a television or an air-conditioner for his use at his residence or even in his office, it cannot be held to be for commercial purpose and for this purpose he is entitled to approach the consumer forum under the Act.

Similarly, a hospital which hires the services of a medical practitioner, it would be a commercial purpose. But, if a person avails of such services for his ailment it would be held to be not a commercial purpose.

Further, from the aforesaid discussion, it is apparent that even taking wide meaning of the words 'for any commercial purpose' it would mean that goods purchased or services hired should be used in any activity directly intended to generate profit. Profit, is the main aim of commercial purpose. But, in a case where goods purchased or services hired in an activity which is 'not directly intended to generate profit, it would not be commercial purpose.

In this view of the matter, a person who takes insurance policy to cover the envisaged risk does not take the policy for commercial purpose. Policy is only for indemnification and actual loss. It is not intended to generate profit".

The ratio of this case is applicable to the case on hand.

13. *Geekay Agropack (P) Ltd. vs. State Bank of Mysore & Anr. II (2006) CPJ 204 (NC)* is relevant for our purpose. The short question involved was there any deficiency in service by the State Bank of Mysore (respondent No.1, Exporter's Bank/ Seller's Bank) or the Citibank (respondent No.2, Importer's Bank/ Purchaser's Bank) in not collecting the export proceeds from the consignee, in a case where goods, were to be released by giving 45 days credit facility to the consignee.

14. After hearing the case, this Commission partly allowed the complaint by holding that Respondent nos. 1 and 2 namely State Bank of Mysore and Citibank to be held jointly liable to pay compensation.

15. Aggrieved by the order of the National Commission, Citibank as well as the complainant had filed Civil Appeal before the Hon'ble Apex Court and the Apex Court has observed as under:-

"We have heard learned counsel for the parties. We are of the opinion that the view taken by the National Commission cannot be faulted with and we are in complete agreement with the National Commission that there was a deficiency in service by the Citibank N.A., New York and consequently by the State Bank of Mysore also. Therefore, compensation has been adequately awarded for deficiency in service against both the Banks and it would be open for the State Bank of Mysore to recover the said compensation from the Citibank, N.A, Consequently, there is no reason to interfere with the impugned judgment and order.

The appeal filed by Geekay for not getting adequate compensation for the total amount of loss, it is open for the appellant Geekay to file a civil suit before the appropriate Court which, we are informed has already been filed. The National Commission could have awarded compensation only for the deficiency of service only. The said compensation has been awarded by the National Commission. Therefore, there is no reason to interfere in the appeal filed by Geekay also. In the result, all these appeals are dismissed. No order as to costs insofars proceedings before this Court are concerned".

16. In view of the above Judgment of the Hon'ble Apex Court confirming the Judgment of the National Commission, we have no doubt in our mind that the respondent is a consumer under the Consumer Protection Act and he has not availed banking services from the petitioner for commercial purposes. Therefore, the complainant is entitled to relief if it is found that there is deficiency in service by the petitioner bank. Accordingly, we hereby confirm the Judgment rendered by the State Commission in holding that the complaint case filed by the complainant is legally maintainable under the Consumer Protection Act. Therefore, we dismiss the Revision Petition filed by the petitioner with ₹ 10,000/- costs and remand the matter back to the State Commission for disposal of the case on merits.

17. While issuing notice to the respondent on 11th July, 2005 the National Commission had granted stay of further proceedings before the West Bengal State Commission directing the petitioner Bank to deposit ₹ 5.00 lakhs with the State Commission. Therefore, the State Commission while deciding the matter on merits may keep this fact in view.

Sd/-
(B.N.P. SINGH)
PRESIDING MEMBER

Sd/-
(P.D. SHENOY)
MEMBER

Important Decisions (Govt. of West Bengal)

Government of West Bengal
Office of the Assistant Director,
Consumer Affairs & Fair Business Practices
Durgapur Regional Office
AB-2/9, ADDA, 2nd Administrative Building
City Centre, Durgapur-16

Name of the Complaint & address	Name of the OP & address	Nature of Complaint	Type of Redressal	Date of receipt of the complaint	Date of settlement
1. Snehasish Mukherjee 12, Rabindra Sarani, Rabindra Pally, Dhandabag, PO Amrai, Duragpur, Dist - Burdwan	The Director, Soroj Mohan Institute of Technology Guptipara, Hooghly	Non refund of paid amount in spite of left of the Institute	₹ 40,430/- has been refunded on interference of this office	08.04.09	06.05.09
2. Samiran Dakshit 24/6, Harsha Bardhan Road, A-zone, Durgapur-4	The Chairman, Duragpur Institute of Management & Science Sahid Sukumar Banerjee Sarani, Durgapur-12	-Do-	₹ 66,030/- has been refunded	13.05.09	05.06.09
3. Joy Prakash PandeyStreet No. 33B, Quarter No. 27B, PO-Chittaranjani Dist - Burdwan, Pin-713331, West Bengal	State Bank of India, Chittaranjan Branch, PO-Chittaranjan, Dist - Burdwan, Pin-713331	Without paying money from SBI, ATM, the Bank debited an amount of ₹ 6,000/- from account	Took the case with SBI authority and at last credited the same amount of ₹ 6,000/- in the A/c	21.05.09	13.07.09

4. Sita Bhowmick 6/4, J.N. Das Path, Sail Co-op. Housing Complex, Durgapur-16	Post Master, City Centre P.O., Durgapur-16	Nonpayment of MIS maturity value of ₹ 1,16,200/-	Payment of ₹ 1,16,200/- has been made on logical strong arrangement of this officer	29.05.09	10.06.09
5. G.K. Raha C/o Aloka Saha, Saha Bardi Mission School Road,Bhnupur-722122	Divisional Manager United India Insurance Co. Ltd. DD-15, 3rd Administrative Building, 2nd floor, City Centre, Durgapur-16	Non payment of OPD treatment claim of ₹ 3,512/-	Payment has been made on interference of this office	13.07.09	29.07.09
6. Bijoy Sankar Singh, Madhabpur, PO-Kajora Gram, Dist - Burdwan	The Manager, State Bank of India, Kajora Gram Branch	A cheque for ₹ 1,04,925/- has been misplaced & payment had not been made	On effective approach the SBI has credited the amount of ₹ 1,04,925/-	19.08.09	26.08.09
7. Samapti Dutta, NIT, Durgapur Quarter No. D5 14/B	Durgapur Variety Store, Benachity, Market, Durgapur.	Mislead and sold a defected shirt but not agreed to change	By serious steps and persuasion they took back the shirt and adiusted the value.	25.08.09	02.09.09

Government of West Bengal
Office of the Assistant Director,
Consumer Affairs & Fair Business Practices
Durgapur Regional Office
AB-2/9, ADDA, 2nd Administrative Building
City Centre, Durgapur-16

Name of the Complaint & address	Name of the OP & address	Nature of Complaint	Type of Redressal	Date of receipt of the complaint	Date of settlement
1. Sri Biswabandhu Roy, C/o.- Jaga Bandhu Roy, Gopal math, Punabadu Plot, Durgapur - 713217	Bengal College of Engineering & Technology Sahid S.K. Banerje Sarani Bidhannagar, Dgp-12.	Won- refund of Admission fees in B.C. A. Course ₹ 2,030/-	Got back the money deducting only the cost of dress materials. ₹ (42,030-5,000)= ₹ 37,030/-	15.12.2008	05.01 .09
2. Sri Suvash Mill, Faridpur, P.O. - Palashdiha Durgapur -713208.	The Manager, S.B.I Durgapur Main Branch, Durgapur -713203	Non-credit of RS.15,000/- against Ch. No. 795778 dt. 29.11 .07.	Credited the entire amount with interest.	03.07.08	15.11.08
3. Sri Arnit Chattopadhyay, Tejganj, NatunganJ, Burdwan - 713102.	Deputy General Manager, B.S.N.L. Burdwan.	Non-refund of unspent balance of ₹ 2,100/-	Got back the unspent balance of ₹ 2, 1 00/-	03.04.08	31.12.08
4. Sri Mrininoy Banerjee, Dhandabad, P.O. Ararai Durgapur.	Proprietor, Mullick Infocom, Benachity, Durgapur - 13.	Defective Mobile Set.	Replaced the set with a new one.	12.06.08	31.12.08
5. Sri Tushar Banerjee. Secondary Road, Durgapur - 713204.	Tata Indicom, City Centre, Durgapur - 16	Non-refund of security deposit ofTelephone (P. C.O of ₹ 4,000/-	Got back the security deposit along with interest.	16.10.08	19.11.08
6. Sri Santanu Debnath, Dhandabad, 2/13, Sibtala, Dur Qapur- 7T3203.	Durgapur Transport, Durgapur-01	Lost Textile materials sent through transport.	Got back the cost of the materials in 3 instalments.	20.09.08	23.09.08
7. Sri Debi Chandan Chowdhury Neamatpur, Nayapara, P.O.- Sitarampur , 713359	Sony World, 17, G.T. Road, Asansol.	Non-repairing of Camera (Handycam) within the warranty period.	Repaired the Camera free of cost which charged more than as. ₹ 10,000/-	15.12.08	22.12.08
8. Sri Kingshuk Mukherjee, 6/9, Sepco Township, Durgapur - 05.	The Proprietor, M/s Online Computer & Services, Kalpataru, Durgapur - 16.	Non-refund of Advanced money for buying a Xerox Machine.	Got back the money advanced.	21.07.08.	
9. Sri Subhodh Kr. Mukherjee, Qr. No. 35/60, Harshabardhan Road, 'A' Zone, Durqapur - 04.	Mr. Binoy Panda, D.I.A.M., Rajbandh, Durgapur - 12.	Non- refund of admission fees in B. Tech Course.	Refunded ₹ 29, 075/- vide Cheque No. 626733 dt. 16. 10.08	02.09.08	18.11.08

10. Sri Subrata Kundu, Sreepally, Andal, Pin - 713321.	Manimala Girls' High School, Asansol - 04	Non- refund of admission & other fees in class-XI. Refund claimed due to mal administration of the school,	Refunded the amount deducting only admission fees.	30.07.08.	21.1 0.08
11. Sri Amitayu Das 48/8, Ananda Vihar, Durgapur -04	Mr. Abhijit Roy CCE Beekav Auto Pvt. Ltd, N.H.-2 Chanda More, Asansol-713339	Non repairing of a newly owned Maruti Alto Lx.	Repalred the Car after intervening the problem.	30.01.09	5.02.09
12. Sri K. C.Santra, Vill.- Srikrishnapur, P.O. + G.P. Jotsriram, Dist.-Burdwan.	Station Superintendent, Jamalpur Gr. Electricity Supply, Vill Halara, Jamalpur.	Sending of 'Average' Bills although having Energy Meter in active condition.	Bills have been started to be sent as per actual Meter reading.	19.02.09	17.03.09
13. Sri Santosh Kr. Santra, Vill.- Srikrishnapur, P.O. + G.P .-Jotsriram, Dist.- Burdwan.	Station Superintendent, Jamalpur Gr. Electricity Supply, Vill Halara, Jamalpur.	Sending of Bills for shallow connection in another person is meter no's reading.	Bills have been sent -against the actual owner's meter reading.	19.02.09	1 7.03.09
14. Sri Susanta Kr. Santra, ViII - Srikrishnapur, P.O. + G.P.-Jotsriram, Dist.- Burdwan.	Station Superintendent, Jamalpur Gr. Electricity Supply, Vill- Halara, Jamalpur.	Sending of Average Bills for shallow connection, although having Energy meter in operation	Adjustment Bill will be sent from the coming months.	19.02.09	17.03.09
15. Sri Aniket Das, 5/ 20, Srinagar Pally, Benachity, Durgapur-13,	Sri Bhaskar Saha, Tile Ananda, Benachity, Durgapur - 13.	Although made full payment, Water filter was not supplied.	Filter delivered installed.	12.03.09	27.03.09
16. Sri Biprendu Kr. Chakraborty, MLA, Durgapur.	The Commissioner, EPF assistant Organisation, Durgapur.	No issuance of statement of EPF accounts since 1992 of the employees of St. Michael School, Durgapur.	On continuous effort up dated statements of accounts of 171 employees have been prepared & handed over to employees concerned.	28.11 .08	05.02.09

SUMMARY AND CONCLUSION

As we look back, the three-tier Consumer Fora established under the Consumer Protection Act, 1986 have much to their credit. They have helped generate widespread awareness among citizens of their rights as consumers and accelerated enforcement of those rights as never before. Indeed, the honest and well informed consumer ought to be "the king (or the queen)" in an economically liberal yet well-regulated market, operating in a caring, democrating polity. However, despite our collective contributions to that goal, may I paraphrase Robert Frost and remind us all that we still have many "promises to keep" and many more "miles to go" in this endeavour? And, that we can certainly not afford "to sleep"?

> **Defining Business Purpose and Mission**
>
> "Who is the customer?" is the first and the crucial question in defining purpose and business mission. It is not an easy, let alone an obvious question. How it is being answered determines, in large measure, how the business defines itself. The consumer that is, the ultimate user of a product or service-is always a customer.
>
> ***Peter F. Drucker***

The question arises why people, are so bothered of protecting the interest of consumers only. Having common Socioeconomics, the consumers are the largest economic group in a country's economy, affecting and affected by almost every public and private economic decision. But they are also the only important group whose view are not cared about. The reason is that consumers are the most scattered and unorganized set of people. In an open market economy. The government has minimum interference in economic activities. The producers and suppliers decide the quantity, quality, distribution and price of the goods and services produced, especially, the consumer goods. As a result some profit seeking entrepreneur may adopt such policies and practices that are against the interest of consumers. The producers may produce or offer adulterated, fake or low quality products and sell it at the highest possible price or discriminating price. They may provide the consumer with misleading advertisement or wrong information about the company, deceptive package, exaggeration of claims and false quantity of products. The producers may also show a negligence of services and provides unsatisfactory service/product performance or cause environmental pollution. A wide range of consumer pay their hard earned money to buy several products; but in case they do not get the right value for their money in terms of right quality or quantity of goods and services both or if they are made wrong promises they are supposed to stand against deceit. Quite often, they are unaware of their rights or unable to raise their voice against exploitation. So it is imperative that steps are taken to protect the right of the largest economic entity that is known as consumer. He should surely be saved from any sort of exploitation.

Thanks to the Consumer protection Act, 1986, our country has a vibrant consumer movement today due to the efforts of Government. consumer organizations and the establishment of consumer courts. India is the only country in the world which has exclusive courts for redressal. This has been internationally praised including the developed countries. The consumer protection Act has succeeded in bringing about fair play in the supply of goods and service to a large extent. However, the rapid changes in the consumption pattern of the modern day consumer is bringing new challenges in the consumer movement in the country. The Book focus on the consumer movement in India, Copra(CPA). Its problems and the government's efforts to promote it. It also suggests some steps to be taken for the overcoming lacunae, if any. This is my humble effort for enlighten of consumers and serving the need for awareness also consumer education.

In developed countries, almost every month the consumers notice the announcement of a new victory in the form of a new trading agreement, a new institution. Programmes about consumers affairs, publication in newspapers. TV. Radio and Government media are making the consumer movement official (Basu, 1986).

The consumers are certainly entitled to have certain basic rights such as the right to safety; the right to be informed, the right to choose and the right to be heard. But these rights have limited coverage as large number of consumers are not aware of these rights. At the same time, consumers in India are highly disorganized. Because of these factors, the business community resort to all kinds of unhealthy trade practices such as hoarding, black-marketing, charging *exorbitant* prices, adultearation, supplying sub-standards products, using deceptive and misleading advertisements and so on.

Consumerism and consumer protection has been a neglected aspect in our country. Not much has been conducted on these issues. Verma (1980) made an attempt in studying the regulation of restrictive trade practices but consumerism and other Acts and Regulations related to consumer protection were not covered.

Though consumer regulation is a complex subject, yet it is quite fascinating. Moreover, it contains the diverse disciplines of commerce, economics, law and business administration. It is, therefore, inexplicable as to why it has not so far received adequate attention from research scholars in India. Hardly anu in-depth study on the subjects has so far been undertaken. The issues taken in this study will provide support to the SOCIAL WELFARE aspect in the fields of trade, commerce and socio-economic planning. The findings can be of use to various institutions, universities and organizations connected with Consumer Movement in India and abroad.

It is needless to mention that since enactment of Consumer Protection Act, 1986 the Consumer Affairs Department of this Government is striving to ensure protection of interest and rights of the consumers as envisaged in the said act. By this time several books, booklets, leaflets etc. in different languages have been published under the aegis of this department to promote Consumer Awareness as well as Consumer Education.

Generation of Consumer Awareness is a huge task and it cannot be achieved in a brace of shakes. With the passage of time perpended decisions of the apex court of India, National Consumer Dispute Redressal Commission & State Commissions have rendered many valuable trend-setting findings on a vast ranging subjects involving consumer rights and interests. With a view to percolate such exemplary decisions from such bodies of law for protecting the interest of the consumers in general and to put the legal provisions into practice these endeavour is very much appreciable.

The present publication falls under the first category providing details of C.P. Act and Rules. I do profoundly believe that this will be of great help for the Consumers, VCOs, NGOs, Government Functionaries & the Consumer Activists to promote & protect the interest of consumers. This is obviously a timely exercise and a right step to uphold the theme 'Empowerment of Consumers – Assert Rights, pursue Remedie' as was set by the Government of India on the eve of World Consumer Rights Day, 2007.

Consumer protection

India

Young population

Per cent of population, 2003

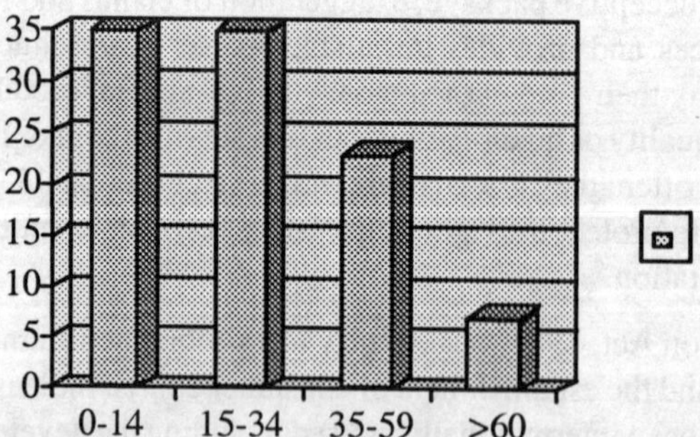

Highest proportion of population below 35 years (70%) in India...

Changing Consumer Demography

- Increasingly affluent, with bulging middle class
- The youngest population in the world
- Increasing literacy levels
- Higher adaptability to technology

- Urbanization is a continuing trend
- Increasing "consumption" mindset in India.

How effective have been the Consumer Courts!

While a lot has been written about delays in disposal cases, the actual statistics speak otherwise. As on 28.02.07, the overall disposal was 90.33% in respect of District For a, 72.31% in respect of state commission and 80.6% in respect of National Commission. On pursing the overall disposal rate, it is clear that the high disposal rate of cases in Consumer Court is a trendsetter for all quasi-judicial organization:

S. No.	Name of Agency	Cases filed since inception	Cases disposed of since inception	Cases pending	% of total disposal
1.	National Commission	45798	36914	8884	80.60%
2.	State Commissions	392978	284154	108824	72.31%
3.	District Forums	2319724	2095320	224404	90.33%
4.	Total	2758500	2416388	342112	87.80%

The Rights of the Consumer guaranteed under section-6 of Consumer Protection Act, 1986:

1. To be protected against the marketing of goods and services which are hazardous to life and property;
2. To be informed about the quality, quantity, potency, purity, standard and price of goods or services, as the case may be so as to protect the consumer against unfair trade practices;
3. To be assured, wherever possible access to a variety of goods and services at competitive prices;
4. To be heard and to be assured that consumer's interests will receive due consideration at appropriate forums;
5. To seek redressal against unfair trade practices or restrictive trade practices or unscrupulous exploitation of consumers; and
6. To consumer education.

Even after so many precautions, if a consumer is deceived,

- He should ask the seller to remove the defect of deficiency or to replace the goods.
- If the seller does not respond or if the consumer is not satisfied by the action taken by the seller, move to the Consumer Affairs Dept, Govt of West Bengal or to the Directorate of Consumer Affairs & Fair Business Practices, Govt of West Bengal or to the Directorate of Legal Metrology, Govt of West Bengal or file complaint with the appropriate Consumer Disputes redressal Agency

Consumer Disputes redressal Agencies (Forum/Commission) under Consumer Protection Act, 1986.

- Quasi-judicial authority under the statute to redress consumer disputes.
- In West Bengal every district has one district forum (Kolkate & Darjeeling have 2 each) and State Commission, apex body in the state, at Bhabani Bhaban.
- There is National Commission in Delhi, which is the apex body in the country
- District forum will redress consumer disputes for claims up to ₹ 20 lakhs.
- If claim is more than ₹ 20 lakhs but up to ₹ 1 crore, it goes to the State Commission.
- If above ₹ 1 crore, it goes to the National Commission.

Fire dampers in AC ducts

Triggered by fire alarms or independent sensors, a set of flaps otherwise in an open position collapses and blocks the flow of air through AC ducts. This prevents smoke or toxic particles from travelling to different parts of the building through the ducts.

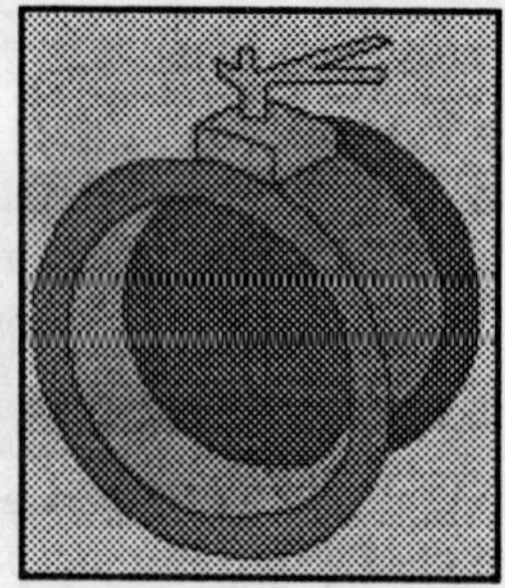

Sprinkler systems

Based on smoke or heat-detection sensors, designed to douse the first flames and keep them from spreading.

Fire-rated doors

Solid wooden doors with fire-retardant paints and special chemical lining at their edges that expand during fire and create a seal that blocks smoke. These doors can withstand a fire for 30 minutes to two hours.

Fire-fighting drills

A crucial human factor that often determines the levels of casualties in a large fire. Security and staff in installations such as hospitals or schools need to know exactly how to handle fire-fighting equipment and respond during fires

Fire alarm

To activate emergency responses and warn people to evacuate or be ready for rescue.

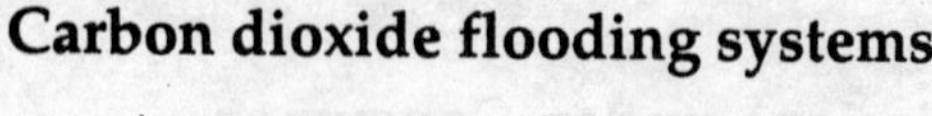

Carbon dioxide flooding systems

A compact system of piping and carbon dioxide cylinders specifically intended to extinguish fires that may arise from electric panels within buildings by flooding the panel housing with carbon dioxide

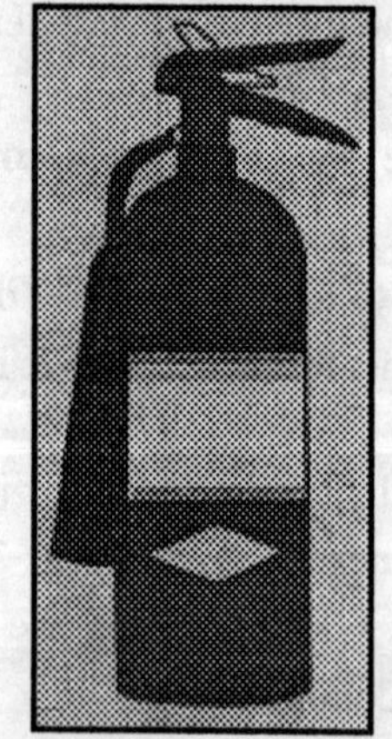

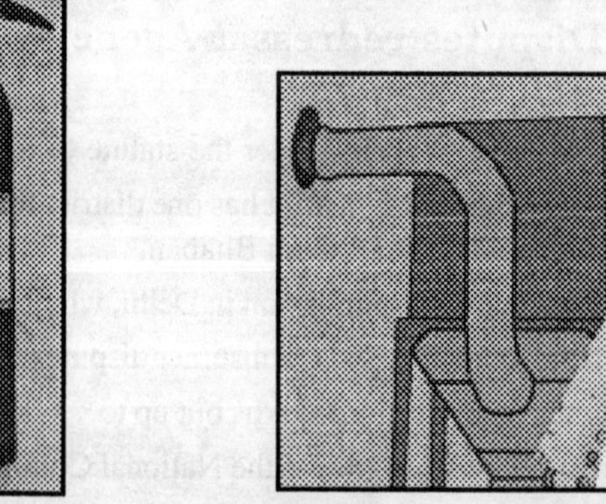

Smoke extraction systems

They use a combination of exhaust fans and exclusive smoke ducts to extract smoke as well as prevent the accumulation of smoke, particularly in corridors, making it possible for people to escape

SAFETY MEASURES TO AVOID FIRE/ACCIDENTS

APPENDICES

APPENDIX I

PART I

CONSUMERISM AND CONSUMER MOVEMENT IN INDIA

Background Data

1. Name and address of the consumer (person who decides to buy the items for house hold)

. . . .

. . . .

. . . .

2. Sex — Male/Female

3. Age — . . . . Years

4. Educational Qualifications
   a. Up to Matric . . . .
   b. Graduate . . . .
   c. Post Graduate . . . .
   d. Any Other (pls specify) . . . .

5. Family's average Income (monthly)
   a. Up to ₹ 2,000/- . . . .
   b. ₹ 2,000 to ₹ 4,000 . . . .
   c. ₹ 4,000 to ₹ 8,000 . . . .
   d. Over Rs. 8000/- . . . .

6. Occupation . . . .

1. Are you aware of consumer rights and consumerism in India:

   Yes . . . .   No . . . .

2. If yes, have you ever heard about the following rights
   a. Right to safety   Yes . . . . .   No . . . . .
   b. Right to be informed   Yes . . . . .   No . . . . .
   c. Right to choose   Yes . . . . .   No . . . . .
   d. Right to be heard   Yes . . . . .   No . . . . .

3. Which of the following government legislation protecting consumers interests are you aware of? Kindly provide the requires information corresponding to each of the legislations: (Kindly tick)

	Consumer Protection Legislations	*Aware*	*Not Aware*	*To which kind of products applicable*
I.	The essential commodities Act 1955	....	......	....
II.	The Monopolies and Restrictive Trade Practices Act 1969	....	......	....
III.	The Prevention of food Adulteration Act 1954		......	....
IV.	The Trade and Merchandise Act 1958	....	......	....
V.	The Sale of Goods Act 1930	....	......	....
VI.	The Hire Purchase Act 1972	....	......	....
VII.	The Packaged Commodities Act 1975	....	......	....
VIII.	The Drugs and Cosmetics Act 1940	....	......	....
IX.	The Dangerous Drug Act	....	......	....
X.	The Drug and Magic Remedies Act 1954	....	......	....
XI.	The Household Electrical Appliance Order	....	......	....
XII.	The Agricultural Produce Act 1937	....	......	....
XIII.	The Fruits Product Order 1955	....	......	....
XIV.	The Standards of Weight and measures Rules 1977	....	......	....
XV.	The prevention of Blackmarketing and Maintanence of supplies Of essential commodities act 1980	....	......	....
XVI.	The paper Production Control Order	....	......	....
XVII.	The Indian Contract Act, 1972	....	......	....
XVIII.	The Indian Standard Institutions act 1956	....	......	....
XIX.	The Standards of Weights and Measure Act	....	......	....
XX.	Consumer Protection Act	....	......	....
XXI.	Local Taxes	....	......	....
XXII.	Any other related to Consumer rights and protection	....	......	....

4. To what extent do you agree that the following issues should be included under consumerism (tick all under the appropriate head)

	Issues	*Strongly Agree*	*Agree*	*NeitherAgree No Disagree*	*Strongly Disagree*
I.	Information	....	......	....	....
II.	Health & Safety	....	......	....	....
III.	Repair & Services	....	......	....	....
IV.	Pricing Issues	....	......	....	....
V.	Pollution In the Environment	....	......	....	....
VI.	Market Concentration	....	......	....	....
VII.	Product Quality	....	......	....	....
VIII.	Consumer Representation	....	......	....	....
IX.	Advertisement	....	......	....	....
X.	Legislation	....	......	....	....
XI.	Others	....	......	....	....

5.

i. While buying a product what information do you look for on the packages containers :

(a) Date of manufacturing . . . .

(b) Price . . . .

(c) Quality . . . .

(d) Name of the manufacturer . . . .

(e) Expiry date . . . .

(f) Quantity, standard unit Or weight . . . .

(g) any other (pl. specify) . . . .

ii. Suggest any other information which should be provided on the container

6.

i. Did you ever complain to anyone about the defective products:

Yes . . . . No . . . .

ii. If yes about which of the following problems categories have you complained, to whom the complaint was made, about which product and manufacturer the complaint was made and what were the results:

Problems	*To whom the complaint was made*	*Name of the product for which the complaint made*	*name of manufacturer*	*Result*
1. Measurements	. . . .	. . . .	. . . .	. . . .
2. Price	. . . .	. . . .	. . . .	. . . .
3. Quality	. . . .	. . . .	. . . .	. . . .
4. Quantity	. . . .	. . . .	. . . .	. . . .
5. Advertising	. . . .	. . . .	. . . .	. . . .
6. Servicing	. . . .	. . . .	. . . .	. . . .
7. Warranty	. . . .	. . . .	. . . .	. . . .
8. Malpractices and unfair trade means	. . . .	. . . .	. . . .	. . . .
9. Discrimination	. . . .	. . . .	. . . .	. . . .
10. Health/Safety	. . . .	. . . .	. . . .	. . . .
11. Labelling	. . . .	. . . .	. . . .	. . . .
12. Other	. . . .	. . . .	. . . .	. . . .

7. Kindly rate the following issues of consumerism in terms of their importance

Specific Issue	*Most Imp.*	*Imp.*	*Neither Imp. Nor Un Imp.*	*Un Imp.*	*Most Un Imp.*
1. Information	. . . . . .	. .	. . . .	. . . . . .	. . . . . .
2. Health/Safety	. . . . . .	. .	. . . .	. . . . . .	. . . . . .
3. Repair/Service	. . . . . .	. .	. . . .	. . . . . .	. . . . . .
4. Pricing Issues	. . . . . .	. .	. . . .	. . . . . .	. . . . . .
5. Pollution in the Environment	. . . . . .	. .	. . . .	. . . . . .	. . . . . .
6. Consumer Representation In Government	. . . . . .	. .	. . . .	. . . . . .	. . . . . .
7. Product Quality	. . . . . .	. .	. . . .	. . . . . .	. . . . . .

8. Advertising	.....	...	....	....	....
9. Legislation	.....		....		....
10. Others	.....	...	....		....

8. Please read the following statements and express your opinion by putting a tick in the space which best indicates how strongly you agree or disagree with each of the statements.

Statement	***Level of agreement***				
	Strongly agree	***Agree***	***Neither Agree Nor Disagree***	***Disagree***	***Strongly Disagree***
1. Most of the manufacturers do not bother about the consumer	.....	.....	....	.....	....
2. Most of the manufacturers are more interested in making profit rather than customer satisfaction	.....	.....	....	.....	....
3. In general manufacturers produce goods according to the needs of the consumer	.....	.....	....	.....	....
4. Manufacturers perform the job of providing good products at fair prices	.....	.....	....	.....	....
5. Quality of most of the products has been improving with the passage of time	.....	.....	....	.....	....
6. Many of the mistakes consumer makes in product purchase are due to their own ignorance	.....	.....	....	.....	....
7. People look for packed and branded products while purchasing	.....	.....	....	.....	....
8. People look for ISi ark while purchasing a product	.....	.....	....	.....	....
9. Most of the products advertising is believeable	.....	.....	....	.....	....
10. Advertising often persuades people to buy thing that they should not buy	.....	.....	....	.....	....
11. Most advertisements are exaggerative and do not present the true picture of the product	.....	.....	....	.....	....
12. Advertisements are reliable sources of information about quality and performance of the product	.....	.....	....	.....	....
13. Advertising is usually for objectionable products	.....	.....	....	.....	....
14. Advertisements make false claims	.....	.....	....	.....	....
15. Advertisements have no utility in society	.....	.....	....	.....	....
16. In general the quality of service provided by the dealers is getting better	.....	.....	....	.....	....

17. Gradually the product warranty is backed by the manufacturer . . . .
18. The constest that manufacturer sponsor to encourage the people to buy their product are usually dishonest . . . .
19. The problems of the consumers are less serious than before . . . .
20. The average person is willing to pay more for quality . . . .
21. I feel I am cheated when it says local taxes extra . . . .
22. Consumers often try to take advantage of the dealers my making injustified claims . . . .
23. Manufacturers seem to be more sensitive to consumer complaints than before . . . .
24. Most nusiness firms make sincere effort to entertain consumer complaints . . . .
25. From the consumer point of view the procedures followed by manufacturers and government in handling complaints are not satisfactory . . . .
26. Protecting the environment is more important than increasing our standard of living . . . .
27. Consumerism has not been animportant factor inchanging business practices and procedures . . . .
28. The exploitation of the consumers by the business firms deserves more attention than it receives . . . .
29. Cheating on weights and measures should be punished . . . .
30. The govt. should test competing brands of products and make the result of these tests available to consumer . . . .
31. If a customer gets ill or injured while using a defective product the manufacturer should be made to pay the damage . . . .
32. The govt. should get minimum standards of quality for consumer products . . . .
33. Govt. should control food price . . . .
34. The govt. should exercise more responsibility for regulating the

advertising sales and marketing activities of the manufacturers . . . .

35. The various consumer protection legislation made by the govt. are inadequate in providing protection to the consumers . . . .
36 Consumer protection act will be helpful in protecting and promoting the interests of the consumers . . . .
37. The sorry state of affairs about consumerism is due to lack of consumer education . . . .
38. The future of consumerism will be important than it is today . . . .
39. The furtue of consumerism will be enduring . . . .

In your opinion the concept of consumerism van be strengthened in India through

(a) Company Action . . . .
(b) Holding of seminars . . . .
(c) Mass Media . . . .
(d) Voluntary organizations . . . .
(e) Govt. Action . . . .
(f) Any other(specify) . . . .

PART II

CONSUMERISM AND CONSUMER PROTECTION IN INDIA AN OPINION SURVEY OF COMPANIES IN INDIA

1. Name of the company/organization

   . . . .

2. Address

   . . . .

   . . . .

3. Form of the organization
   - i. Sole Ownership . . . .
   - ii. Partnership . . . .
   - iii. Company: Proprietory . . . .
   - iv. Any other (specify) . . . .

4. Annual Turnover
   - i. Up to 35 lakh . . . .
   - ii. ₹ 35 lakh to 1 crore . . . .
   - iii. ₹ 1 crore to 5 crore . . . .
   - iv. ₹ 5 crore to 10 crore . . . .
   - v. Above ₹ 10 crore . . . .

1. What are the marketing objectives of your company?
   - i. To remain leader in the market . . . .
   - ii. To satisfy customers . . . .
   - iii. To maintain or increase Share in the market . . . .
   - iv. To build image as a supplier Of quality products . . . .
   - v. Any other (specify) . . . .

2. Mention the main consumer protection legislation applicable to your firm

   . . . .

   . . . .

3. The above mentioned legislation help:
   - i. To increase your sales . . . .
   - ii. To provide customer satisfaction . . . .
   - iii. Any other (specify) . . . .

4. For your marketing efforts consumerism and consumer protection legislations are:
   - i. An opportunity . . . .
   - ii. Obstruction . . . .
   - iii. Any other (specify) . . . .

5. How do you receive complaints from the consumers?
   i. Through consumers directly . . . .
   ii. Through voluntary organization . . . .
   iii. Through dealer . . . .
   iv. The Govt. deptt. (MRTP) . . . .
   v. Any other (specify) . . . .

6. The complaints you generally receive are related to
   i. Compensation . . . .
   ii. Refund . . . .
   iii. Replacement . . . .
   iv. Quality . . . .
   v. Service . . . .
   vi. Guarantee/Warranty . . . .
   vii. Advertisements . . . .
   viii. Any other (specify) . . . .

7. How do you solve consumer problems?
   i. Sending them polite letters . . . .
   ii. Replacement of product . . . .
   iii. By way of compensation . . . .
   iv. Servicing the equipments . . . .
   v. Any other (specify) . . . .

8. Has the company made any changes in the recent past to give the consumers greater satisfaction

   Yes . . . . No . . . .

   If yes, how?

   . . . .

   . . . .

   Give details

   . . . .

   . . . .

9. Who should be responsible for consumers protection and consumer welfare in India?
   i. The management of the company
   ii. Voluntary organizations . . . .
   iii. Govt. Agencies . . . .
   iv. Any other (specify) . . . .

   . . . .

10. In your opinion what are the various problems relating to development of consumerism and consumer movement in India.

    . . . .

    . . . .

11. How can be consumer movement in India be strengthened?

    . . . .

    . . . .

PART III

CONSUMERISM AND CONSUMERM MOVEMENT IN INDIA VOLUNTARY ORGANIZATIONS

1. Name of the organization

. . . .

. . . .

2. Address/Location

. . . .

. . . .

3. Date of incorporation—year of starting the Org.

. . . .

4. What motivated you to start the organization

. . . .

. . . .

. . . .

5. What are the aims and objectives of your organization?
   i. Social Welfare . . . .
   ii. Consumer's Redressal . . . .
   iii. Consumer protection activities . . . .
   iv. Consumer's Education . . . .
   v. Any other (specify) . . . .

   . . . .

6. What is your are of operation?
   i. Local . . . .
   ii. District . . . .
   iii. State . . . .
   iv. Country . . . .
   v. Any other (specify) . . . .

7. How do you raise the funds for your organization?
   i. Through Members . . . .
   ii. Govt. Agencies . . . .
   iii. Foreign Aids . . . .
   iv. Any other (specify) . . . .

8. What sources are you doing to propagate the ideas of your organization?
   i. Newspaper . . . .
   ii. Seminars . . . .
   iii. Any other (specify) . . . .

9. Kindly provide the following information with respect to holding seminars during the last five years on Consumerism/ consumer movement

Year	*Topic*	*Basic Theme*	*Target Participants*
1987.			
1988.			
1989.			
1990.			
1991.			

10. What types of other programmes are you organizing to educate the consumer?

11. What are your perspectives plans about holding of seminars in ear future and basic theme you want to propagate on consumerism and consumer movement?

12. What types of service do you offer to the consumers/members of the organization?
    i. Legal Service
    ii. Consumer Education
    iii. Consumer Training Programmes related to consumer awareness
    iv. Consumer Redressal
    v. Any other (specify)

13. Do you have any complaint cell? Yes . . . . . . No . . . . . .

14. How many cases have you taken or solved so far?

15. In your opinion what are the various problems relating to consumerism/consumer movement in India?

16. What more can be done to strengthen the consumer movement in India?

i. At the consumer level

ii. At the government level

iii. At the Industrial/corporate level

—✦—✦—✦—

APPENDIX II

CONSUMER ISSUES IN THE POWER SECTOR

Introduction

Electricity service industry has long been treated as a natural monopoly. Soon after Independence, the Electricity (Supply) Act of 1948 created State Electricity Boards as State-owned monopoly electricity service providers. Since consumer rights exist only in a competitive market, there was no consumer choice in a monopoly electricity market. Powerful groups of consumers could assert their sectional interests only through the political process. Political and government intervention in the management and operation of the State Electricity Boards eventually took its toll. By the early 'nineties of the last century, State Electricity Boards faced financial and consequent operational collapse due to politically palatable below-cost pricing policies and inefficient performance. While the Boards had an accumulated loss of ₹ 26,000 crores, Governments, Central and State, also did not have resources for funding very large investment required for creating additional generation capacity and renovating and expanding the run-down T&D system. Reform and macro-adjustment of the electricity sector was therefore primarily initiated to attract private sector investment to the sector and any value-addition to the electricity services provided to the consumers was secondary and incidental. Whatever may have been the genesis and motivation of the reforms, the early State Reform Acts of Orissa, Haryana, Andhra Pradesh, Karnataka, etc; and the latest Electricity Act of 2003 incorporated for the first tim a basis and framework for consumer rights in the electricity service industry. The purpose of this Paper is to highlight the issues of major concern to the consumers in the electricity service industry and suggest measures to further empower them so that they act as responsible stakeholders in the development of the industry.

Quality of Service Issues

The electric power industry all over the world is beginning to look at reliability and quality of service as interrelated aspects of utility performance. Utility performance is no longer being considered independently of customer needs and responsibilities. That electricity services have to be managed as commercial rather than as engineering services is a paradigm change that must take place in India as quickly as possible. Sections 57 to 59 of the Electricity Act, 2003, mandate the regulatory commissions to prescribe Quality of Service (QoS) standards to be maintained by the distribution licensees and penalties and compensation to be levied on them for failure to adhere to these standards. Consequent on the notification of the Electricity Act, 2003, most of the State Electricity Regulatory Commissions haye framed regulations laying down Quality of Service standards and penalties to be imposed on the distribution licensees for not adhering to these standards. Three samples of such guaranteed standards laid down by the State Electricity Regulatory Commissions in Andhra Pradesh, Orissa and Tamil Nadu are attached as Annex 'A', 'B' and 'C' respectively. Similar standards prescribed by OFGEM, the U.K power regulator, and the voluntary standards adopted by a U.S power utility are attached as Annex 'D' and 'E' respectively.

The standards obtaining in U.K and U.S.A are far more stringent than the prevailing Indian standards. While it is recognized that very stringent Quality of Service standards comparable to U.K and U.S standards are difficult to adhere to in the present run-down condition of India's distribution utilities and may immediately result in heavy financial outgo in payment of penalties and compensation to the consumers, India's electricity regulation should have laid down a benchmark to be achieved in say 5 years and a roadmap for annual incremental standards from the base year, the resent standards being treated only as the base year standards. Without such a benchmark Quality of Service standards to be achieved within a fixed time frame there will neither be compulsion nor motivation for the distribution licensees to improve standards of service.

The Quality of Service standards discussed above deals with guaranteed standards involving payment of penalties and compensation to the consumers. In respect of Overall Standards of Service, where no payment of penalty or compensation to individual consumers is involved but the overall quality and level of performance of the distribution licensee is judged by the regulator, the Indian regulation does not provide for penalizing the utility in terms of reduction in percentage of return on investment or denying tariff increase asked for by the licensee if the performance of the licensee is below the benchmark standards. The Overall Standards of Service in U.K set by U.K's electricity regulator, OFGEM, and those voluntarily adopted by Pacific Power utility in U.S.A and filed with the relevant State Public Utilities Commissions are in Annex 'F' and 'G' respectively.

Consumers' Right to Information

The average consumer's interface is with the distribution licensee where the license is granted by the State Electricity Regulatory Commissions (SERCs). All SERCs in India have issued regulations on consumers' right to information which relate to (a) notice before entry by the licensee's staff into consumer's premises (b) notice before re-classification of the consumer's category (c) notice before disconnection and (d) notice before outages. These rights to information, limited in nature, by and large meet the irritants, which an average individual consumer might face in its normal dealings with the distribution licensee. SERCs' regulations are however. silent on the consumers' right to information on the macro picture of the licensee's performance in quality of supply system upgradation plans procurement of power and financial management. Consequent on the promulgation of the Right to Information Act, a consumer has now the right to demand such information from the relevant SERC which in turn has to get it from the licensee and supply it to applicant. SERCs may be advised to frame appropriate regulations, in line with the RTI Act makin it obligatory for the distribution licensee to share the above type of information with the consumers.

Tariff Determination and Tariff Issues

Power sector reforms in India have brought the process of tariff determination into the public domain from the closed circuit of decision-making by the State Electricity Board and the political executive of the day. The new process is modelled on the U.S system which has a history of more the than one hundred years of independent regulation and decision-making by the regulator after consultation with all stakeholders. Consumers who are the most affected group as a result of any tariff decision have been brought into the loop along with the licensee and the government who are the other important stake-holders. The revenue requirement of the licensee for the ensuing year and its estimate of revenue likely to accrue on the basis of existing tariffs are notified widely by the SERC and the licensee inviting written comments and objections from consumers, consumer groups and any one wishing to comment. After analyzing the written comments, the SERC holds open hearings to listen to the stakeholders airing their views and debating the issues. These written comments and oral hearings form an important input in the final decision of the SERC on tariffs.

The new process, no doubt, is a paradigm shift in decision-making by involving stake holders and bringing total transparency in transactions but has major deficiencies considering the present stage of evolution of independent regulation in India. In U.S.A, resource-rich consumer groups employing accounting, financial, engineering and management consultants who are able to ferret out relevant and crucial information and analyze them in the light of consumer concerns bridge the information asymmetry between the licensee and the consumer or consumer groups. Consumers in India are either not organized or, when organized, lack domain knowledge and tools to analyze them and marshal arguments based on facts and analysis of facts. For consumers to play their rightful role as vital stake-holders in the electricity service industry it is essential to create a level playing field by empowering them with relevant information on the licensees' entire range of operations. In the present stage of regulatory development, this role can be played by the SERCs who should share the information they have on the licensees' operations without compromising their role as neutral umpires. This will be a transitory provision till Indian consumer groups, like their American counterparts, build up adequate capacity of their own.

Information is not all; making sense of the information is more important. The annual revenue requirement (ARR) of the licensee is the basic document on which tariff is determined. It contains technical, commercial and financial data, which is so complex that it is difficult for a layman to comprehend it. SERCs should direct the licensees to attach a glossary with explanation of technical and financial terms used in the ARR and also give explanatory notes for each proposal.

There are a large number of consumer categories and sub-categories mainly for the purpose of tariff. These categories and sub-categories have been created on the basis of end-use of electricity i.e., Street lighting, hospitals, water supply plant etc, rather than on the basis of cost of supply (costs are to be recovered in tariff). End-use as the basis of categorization creates demand for inclusion in low tariff or subsidized categories, which in turn creates a platform for patronage. Ideally, if the voltage of supply and the associated cost of supply becomes the basis of categorization, there would only be three categories of consumers: (I) consumers getting supply in low tension (LT) (2) consumers getting supply in high tension (HT) and (3) consumers getting supply in extra-high tension (EHT). Any group within these three consumer categories requiring subsidy for any end-use reason like poverty or public purpose or industrial competitiveness should get it from the relevant public authority or private body without proliferating categories for the sake of being eligible for subsidy within the electricity industry. When the cost of energy services for the average consumer is increasing from year to year, it is not fair to burden him further with the cost of low rates or subsidy for numerous special groups of consumers.

Grievance Redressal Mechanism

Consumer grievances or complaints mostly relate to wrong or inflated billing, defective meter and non-replacement of defective meter, timely repairs and disconnection. State Public Utilities Commissions in USA devote considerable time and resources to answer consumer queries and mediate in resolving consumer grievances with the electric utilities. They have well-trained staff to handle consumer concerns. Consumers are encouraged to take up their grievances with the electric utility in the first instance. If the issue is not resolved or the consumer is not satisfied, the grievance can be taken up with the Public Utilities Commission (PUC). An average Public Utilities Commission in U.S.A handles 10,000 to 15,000 consumer complaints in a year.

Though India has adopted U.S regulatory practices, in the matter of grievance redressal, the procedure and practice has been made hierarchical with several layers. The earlier State-level Reform Acts had not created hierarchically statutory institutions of Consumer Grievance Redressal Forum (CGRF) and Ombudsman. If any SERC felt the need for a preliminary sifting of consumer grievances, it created an informal body of senior executives drawn from the utility and the Commission to do so. There was also no next level of Ombudsman. A consumer who, failed to get redress from the utility could approach the SERC, which was responsible to listen to consumer grievances and adjudicate on them. This was entirely in line with the U.S practice where Public Utility Commissions are respected by the consumers for their sympathetic and fast handling of consumer complaints and feared by the regulated utilities for the penalties they can impose and the consequential loss of business reputation.

Right from the beginning of regulatory reform, there was demand from the regulators that dealing with consumer complaints, which would be very large in number in the Indian context in view of the inherited inefficiency of the utilities, would derail them from performing their primary role of regulating electricity industry. They were also of the view that since any consumer including the electricity consumer was entitled to move Consumer Redressal Forums set up under the Consumer Protection Act, 1986, there was no need to provide another additional forum to electricity consumers. The Electricity Act, 2003, has deferred to this view to the extent of totally insulating the SERCs from individual consumer grievances and making CGRF the preliminary forum and Ombudsman the final forum of redress. The only linkage these two institutions have with the SERCs is that they are constituted under the aegis ofthe latter, though the SERCs have no authority to interfere in their decision.

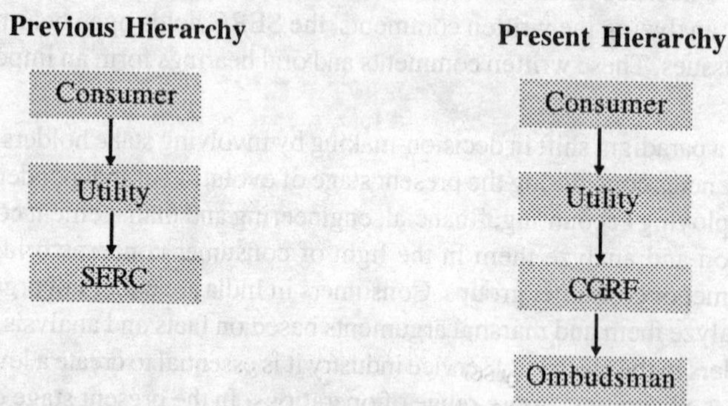

In the banking sector, the Reserve Bank of India has prescribed a simpler procedure of grievance redressal for the bank consumers. If a consumer does not receive reply to his grievance from the bank within one month or he is not satisfied with the reply, he may take up the issue with the Banking Ombudsman of the relevant region. SERCs directly stepping in to deal with consumer grievances would have created greater credibility of the alternate system of governance in the form of independent regulation. Like their U.S counterparts, they would, in most cases, have only played the role of mediating between the consumers and the utility and, would, in fact, have commanded greater deference and attention from the utility in settlement of consumer grievances.

The institutions of CGRF and Ombudsman have been created by the Electricity Act, 2003, after long and careful deliberation. CGRF, which did not exist before the Electricity Act, 2003, as a statutory body, has no parallel or precedent inelectricity regulation abroad nor any similar institution exists in any service sector in India. The almost near-unanimous view of the SERCs is that these new institutions of consumer grievance redressal have performed fairly well during the short period of their existence and their performance and efficacy in creating a new paradigm of customer care may be evaluated after a few years before any corrective action is initiated. Meanwhile, the structure of Complaint Management System should be made compliant to ISO 15700 and certified by the, accredited certifying agency. Only a consumer perception and satisfaction study thereafter will be able to establish whether these two institutions have been able to achieve their objectives.

Strengthening and Improving SERCs

SERCs being relatively new institutions in the power sector with responsibility for oversight on a large range of activities of the sector have to widely disseminate to the consumers and the wider public their charter of duties and responsibilities including their duty of consumer protection and their character as autonomous and impartial bodies. There is still a very widespread perception that SERCs are the same old governmental bodies or subservient to the government and oblivious of consumer interests like most other government bodies. This perception has been further strengthened by appointment of retired bureaucrats, mostly retired Chief.

Secretaries of the States, as Chairpersons of the SERCs in many States. While a large measure of credibility in the appointment of judicial persons, in the appointment of retired bureaucrats, there is a suspicion of reward for past favours and anticipation of future compliance. Therefore, non-governmental professionals with excellent reputation within their peer groups in relevant regulatory areas like power management, economics, finance, accountancy, cost accountancy, legal jurisprudence, customer relations management, management of public systems, etc., should be appointed to the SERCs for the latter to fulfill their mandated function efficiently and also to remove incredulity of the consumers and the wider public about their autonomous and impartial character.

SERCs' personnel for consumer interface have to be strengthened both in terms of manpower and training. The SERCs today have a lone Information Officer/Public Affairs Officer to interact with the consumers. This area of the SERCs needs to be augmented with a larger staff, well trained to respond to consumer concerns if the SERCs have to become more pro-active in consumer care. This consumer interface unit should disseminate regulations, codes and procedures on new connections, metering and billing, disconnection, consumer rights, guaranteed standards of performance, etc.

Consumer education should be actively promoted by the SERCs through seminars for representative bodies of consumers, public notices and sponsored articles in vernacular newspapers, flyers and inserts in newspapers, interactive programmes on radio and TV and audio-visual notices on TV. Chairmen and members of SERCs should travel to as many locations as possible within the State to interact with the consumers, listen to their grievances and suggestions and take quick follow-up action on them. Today, they seem as remote as the government officials of old. An imaginative policy for consumer education should be framed and backed up with sufficient funds.

APPENDIX III

BUREAU OF INDIAN STANDARDS

The Bureau of Indian Standards, the National Standards Body of India, is a Statutory organization under the Bureau of Indian Standards Act, 1986. The Act provides that Bureau is a corporate body and responsible for laying down policy guidelines for BIS. It comprises of members representing the Industries; Consumer Organizations: Scientific & Research Institute & Professional Bodies, Technical Institutions; Central Minister; State Governments & the Members of Parliament. The role and responsibilities of the Bureau primarily include harmonious development of the activity of standardization, product certification and quality systems certification and their promotion.

The Minister in-charge of the Union Ministry of Food and Consumer Affairs, is the President of the Bureau and the Minister of state its Vice-president.

The Executive Committee of the Bureau administers its day to day activities and Director General is its Ex-officio Chairman.

THE FUNCTIONS OF THE BUREAU

The functions of the Bureau are

— Standard Formulation,

— Certification of Products and Quality Systerns,

— Laboratory Management,

— Standards Promotion, and International Co-operation.

STANDARDS FORMULATION

Indian Standards are formulated keeping in view the national priorities, programmes for industrial development, technological needs, export promotion, consumer health, safety, etc. So far over 17,000 standards have been formulated in different technological areas. These standards are evolved based on concensus principle through a network of technical committees comprising representatives from Industry, Research and Development Organizations, Consumers, Testing and Laboratory Experts, Government etc. The Standards formulated fall in the following categories:

— Product Specifications,

— Methods of Test,

— Codes of Practices, Guidelines,etc.

— Terminologies, Glossaries, etc.

— Basic Standards.

The main emphasis of the organization is to:

— *formulate standards expeditiously*

— *review the standards regularly to keep them contemporary in the context of modern technological developments, and*

— *harmonize the standards with international standards or their equivalents for facilitating international trade.*

CERTIFICATION

Product Certification

The product certification scheme is basically voluntary and aims at providing quality, safety and dependability to the ultimate customer. Presence of certification mark known as 'Standard Mark' on a product is an assurance of conformity to the specifications. The conformity is ensured by regular surveillance of the licensee's performance by surprise inspections and testing of samples, drawn both from the factory and the market.

The Act also provides for:-

— *authorizing the foreign manufacturers to use Standard Mark;*

— *bringing articles under compulsory certification on grounds of safety; health, environmental* protection *and energy conservation; and*

— *penalty for spurious marking and misuse of the Mark.*

India is a certifying member of IEC System of Quality Assessment of Electronic Components (IECQ) and IEC System for Conformity Testing to Standards for Safety of Electrical Equipment (IECEE). BIS has major role as National Authorization Institution (NAI) and National Standards Organization (NSO) under IECQ and National Certifying Body (NCB) under IECEE-CB Scheme.

Considering the long experience of BIS in certification, underwriter Laboratories (UL), Canadian Standards Association (CSA) and South African Bureau of Standards (SABS) have authorised BIS to operate their certification scheme in India.

ECO Mark

The Government of India has instituted (February 1991) a scheme to be known as ECO Mark scheme for labelling environment friendly products. This scheme is administered by the Bureau of Indian Standards. The scheme provides for labelling of household and other consumer products which meet certain environmental criteria along with quality requirements prescribed in relevent Indian Standards. Additional requirments for ECO Mark will now form part of the concerned Indian Standard for certification.

For a product to be eligible for the ECO Mark, the product shall conform to the relevant Indian Standard as well as additional requirements incorporated for ensuring environment friendly nature of the product. For this purpose, Mark is a combination of BIS Standard Mark and the ECO

Logo. ISI

Quality Systems Certification

The worldwide movement for quality management systems at the enterprise level as a prerequisite for building competitiveness in the world trade has had impact in India. Its installation and certifications provides a demonstrable and transparent system. BIS is a national agency authorized to operate Quality Systems Certification in India. It has taken following steps:

(a) Adopted ISO 9000 series of International standards as Indian Standards under dual numbering system.

(b) Aligned procedure for operation of Quality Systems Certification based on international criteria and is comparable to any other such systems being operated in the world, and

(c) Awards certificates to enterprises meeting the requirments of IS/ISO 9000 series of standards. Surveillience is maintained by adequate audit system. BIS quality system scheme is accredited by Raad voor Accreditatie (RvA) Netherlands.

EMS Certification

With. the growing concern for environment friendly Industrial activity, ISO 14000 series of standards have been developed. BIS, after adoption of these standards as national standards, has launched Environment Management Systems (EMS) Certification.

HACCP Certification

BIS launched HACCP (Hazard Analysis and Critical Control Points) based on Quality System Certification Scheme as per IS/ISO 9000 : 1994 and as per the rquirements of IS: 15000 standard and also certification separately as per IS : 15000 (equivalent to Codex ALINORM 97/13A)

LABORATORY MANAGEMENT

The Bureau has a chain of laboratories located in different parts of the country for conformity testing of certified products and samples offered by applicants for grant of licence which is an essen-tial feature of BIS Certification System.

To meet the growing volume of testing of samples the laboratory network of the Bureau has been strengthened, streamlined and modernization of BIS Laboratory has been taken up.

Apart from this, the following additional activities are also undertaken by BIS Laboratory:

— *Approval of outside laboratories,*

— *Periodic calibration of instruments and gauges, and*

— *Procurement and characterization of Standard*

Reference Materials.

BIS laboratories play a leading role in research and development of speedy and effective test methods for adoption and for stipulating requirements in Indian Standards.

STANDARDS PROMOTION

A well orchestrated plan exists for improved adoption of Indian Standards by industry, large scale purchasing organizations, statutory bodies and universities. The main emphasis of promotion is on:

— *development of complementary level of standardization, namely company standardization and association level standardization.*

— *effective implementation of standards through sectoral committees, such as steel, food, textiles, information technology automotives and power*

— *state level committees on standardization and quality systems to ensure better implementation of Indian standards*

— *use of Indian standards in legislation*

— *greater interaction with Public and Private Sector Undertakings*

— *basing public purchase on standards and standard marked products*

— *use of standards in educational system*

— *intensified media campaign to create awareness.*

INTERNATIONAL COOPERATION

BIS as founder member of International Organi-zation for Standardization (ISO) continues to take an active part in international standardization. BIS as a member of ISO Council:

— *participates in its policy making bodies like Development Committee (DEVCO), Committee on Conformity Assessment (CASCO), Committee on Information (INfCO) and Committee on Consumer Policy (COPOLCO)*

— *holds Secretarial resposibilities of 5 Technical Committees and 5 Subcommittees and main-tains participation status in 162 Technical Committees.*

BIS is also actively involved in International Electrotechnical Commission (IEC) and has participation status in 37 Technical Committees.

BIS organizes annually International Training Programmes in Standardization and Ouality Systems for Developing Countries So far 590 personnel from 65 countries have been trained under this Programme. In addition specialized training programmes are also organized for personnel from developing countries in specific areas.

BIS AND CONSUMERS

BIS service to consumers and creating quality consciousness among them has almost been a sacrosanct act. Keeping this in view, BIS has:

— *set up Consumer Affairs and Public Grievances Department at Headquarters*

— *nominated Public Grievance Officers at Regional and Branch Offices to deal with consumer complaints against BIS services and Marked products.*

Consumer Affairs and Public Grievances Department also creates awareness among consumers of its rights as enshrined in the Consumer Protection Act, 1986.

BIS SERVICES

BIS has well organized service network. These are:

(a) **Sale outlets:** Indian standards are sold at Headquarters, Regional and Branch Offices and also through selected book sellers. International and foreign standards are also procured and made available to the industry.

(b) **Library Service:** BIS Headquarters has one of the largest Libraries of standards. Besides HQs library facilities exist in regional and branch offices. Membership to the BIS Libraries is open to both individuals and companies. Information centres have been established in industry concentrated areas such as Mysore and Jamshedpur. Efforts are being made to establish more such centres.

(c) **Central Enquiry Service:** The Government of India (Ministry of Commerce) designated BIS as the Central Enquiry Point for India in 1983 under the GATT agreement on Technical Barriers to Trade. BIS provides information on standards, regulations and certification systems of member countries of World Trade Organization (WTO) to Indian export-ers and about India to other member countries. Notifications on proposed standards and regulations received from WTO are disseminated to industry. Similarly the notifications on proposed Indian Standards for which there is no International Standards and in which there is some deviation from the corresponding International Standard are sent to WTO on a regular basis for receiving comments from the mem-ber countries of *WTO.* Besides, it has detailed database of Standards and certification system. Information about BIS Licensees is available on floppy.

(d) **Publications -** BIS brings out standards India and Manakdoot, house magazines, Standards Worldover : Monthly Additions' and Standards Monthly Additions' which serves as basic source of information. In addition, two bulletins Current Published Information on Standardization and EEC Norm Scan, keep the Industry abreast with the latest in the field all over the world.

BIS AND ISO 9000

The ISO 9000 series of Quality Systems Standards brought out in 1987 and subsequently revised in 1994, by International Organization for Standardization (ISO) have made a dramatic impact on business around the world. The standards have become derigueur for doing business in the world market.

INTERNATIONALIZATION OF INDIAN STANDARDS

The ISO 9000 series of standards were published in India by BIS in 1988 and subsequently revised in 1994, as IS/ISO 9000 series of standards (IS/ISO 9001,9002, 9003 etc.) with totally identical text. These have been popularized in industry and service sectors as a prelude to installation of quality management systems.

CREATION OF SEPARATE INFRASTRUCTURE

A seperate independent division of quality systems has been established within BIS for serving as a focal point for operation and coordination of Quality Systems Certification

The Technical committee ISO/TC 176, Quality Management and Quality Assurance, is responsible for formulation of ISO 9000 series of International Standards. BIS, the National Standards Body of India, represents India as participation member on this committee. As the national focal point, BIS, through its Quality Management Sectional Technical Committee MSD 2, liaises with ISO/TC 176, BIS is thus fully abreast with the latest developments in ISO/TC 176 and keeps the industry informed of any developments.

TRAINING OF AUDITORS

The mainstay of quality systems certification is quality of auditors. therefore, training of auditors is essential for effecient and objective assessment of quality systems. As a result of the initial concerted efforts in training of its officers, BIS today has over 175 qualified audiors and certified in training of its officers, BIS today has over 175 qualified auditors and certified quality engineers, for successfully operating and managing the Quality Systems Certification Scheme (QSCS).

CERTIFICATION SCHEME

The Quality Systems Certification Scheme of BIS was launched in September 1991, under the provisions of the Bureau of Indian Standard Act, 1986. The operation of the scheme entails initial assessment and subsequent surveillance of the quality system installed and implemented by the organization for verification of its conformity to the prescribed requirements of the respective quality systems standard. By 1998, BIS has already awarded over four hundred and forty certificates. The field covers a wide range of industries including chemicals, ceramics, cement, automotives, textiles, mechanical, metallurgical, electrical, electronics. BIS Quality Systems Certification Scheme has also made inroads into the service sector, as well as financial and banking sectors.

PRE-CERTIFICATION SERVICES

To apprise the industry and trade about IS/ISO 9000 standards and BIS Quality System Certification, BIS offers the following Pre-Certification Services:

QUALITY SYSTEMS APPRECIATION PROGRAMME

This programme provides guidance on interpretation and appreciation of contents of standards and the steps that industry should take towards starting a quality system programme in the organization.

QUALITY SYSTEMS SURVEY

This is intended for those industries which have already taken steps to implement quality systems and are in the process of conducting an internal audit. In this programme, auditors identify span of coverage of existing system from available documentation and indicate any gaps/overlaps.

TRIAL ASSESSMENT

This assessment is for those industries which have already installed quality systems. It provides and indepth assessment for ascertaining efficacy of implementation of quality systems. It not only brings out nonconformities for taking corrective action but also instills confidence in industries before they apply for certification.

ALL INDIA INFRASTRUCTURE

The Quality Systems Certification Scheme and its Pre-Certification Services are available to enterprises throughout the country. While the policy matters and broad guidelines are laid down at the Headquarters at New Delhi, the pre-certification and certification services, are being provided through 5 Regional Offices located at New Delhi, Bombay, Calcutta, Chandigarh and Madras and 17 Branch Offices in the country.

ACCREDITATION BY RvA, NETHERLANDS,

BIS quality manual and procedures for certification of Quality Systems are in line with internationally accepted criteria. Accreditation of BIS QSCS by Raad voor Accreditatie (RvA), Netherlands, (erstwhile RvC) is a testimony of BIS QSCS operating to internationally accepted criteria. The BIS certification of quality systems thus finds ready acceptance in the world markets.

MEMORANDUM OF UNDERSTANDING WITH OVERSEAS BODIES

The demand for certification of quality systems from a wide cross section of the industry is increasing including export-oriented units. BIS is endeavouring for mutual recognition of its certification scheme with certification bodies in Europe and in other parts of the world. The Memoranda of Understanding (MOU) has been signed with DQS, a leading German quality systems certification body and British Standards Institution Quality Assurance, UK. The MOU would provide Indian enterprises additional facilities of seeking foreign certificates, if required, in addition to the BIS Quality Systems Certificate.

INTERNATIONAL ACCREDITATION SYSTEM

India felt necessary that an international accreditation scheme for certification bodies of quality systems should be evolved. Therefore, BIS initiated a proposal to unify practices of certification bodies around the world at the international level, and the aspect of Quality System assessment recognition is under active deliberation in ISO. It is expected that such, a scheme would emerge in the near future.

CORPORATE QUALITY POLICY

The Bureau of Indian Standards (BIS), the National Standards Body of India, resolves to be the leader in all matters concerning Standardization, Certification and Quality.

In order to attain this, the Bureau would strive:

- To provide efficient timely services.
- To satisfy the customer's needs for quality of goods and services.
- To work and act in such a way that each task, performed as individuals or as corporate entity, leads to excellence and enhances the credibility and image of the Organization.

BIS would achieve these objectives by working in close cooperation with all concerned organizations and by adopting appropriate management systems, motivation and ensuring active participation of all its employees.

SPECIAL FEATURES OF BIS QUALITY SYSTEMS CERTIFICATION SCHEME

1. The National Standards Body (NSB) of a country represents that country in the international forum on Standardization including ISO which has formulated ISO 9000 family of Standards. Bureau of Indian Standards (BIS), is the National Standards Body of India.
2. Being member of ISO, BIS takes part in the deliberations of its Technical Committee ISO/TC 176, Quality System and Quality Assuarance' responsible for formulation of ISO 9000 family of Standards and also in ISO/TC 207 formulating of standards on Environmental Management Systems. As such, it is always abreast of the latest developments in the field. National standards are exact replica of international standards on the subject and are numbered as IS / ISO 9001, 9002 etc. Therefore, ISO 9000 certification given by a NSB, that too a body with vast experience of almost half a century in product certification and quality-related matters besides standardization, has great significance.
3. ISO is not operating any certification scheme. However, it has compiled a Directory of certification bodies worldover and as expected, the name of BIS is included in the Directory.
4. BIS Quality Systems Certification Scheme is accredited by Raad voor Accreditatie (RvA) [earlier known as RvC], Netherlands, for 10 major areas of economy.
5. As a member body of ISO, and otherwise also, BIS is well known the worldover. Many references are received regularly from abroad about organization certified by it and such a list has been provided in reply to such queries for inclusion in the worldwide directory and other information being compiled by some organizations. BIS is the nodal centre for GATT Enquiry in India and receives & provides information to all the signatories of GATT, regularly.
6. BIS has over 175 officers on its rolls who have undergone Lead Assessors Course recognized by IQA, U.K. and many of them are registered with IQA under its IRCA Scheme.
7. BIS has a network of Regional Offices and Branch Offices throughout the country for providing timely and efficient service.
8. BIS is a non-profit organization and as such its quality systems certification and pre-certification services are very cost effective.
9. BIS is the only organization in India which operates Quality System Certification Scheme under an Act of Parliament. Since the operation of the scheme is authorized and regulated under the provision of this Act, the information gathered as a result of quality system certification activity is kept confidential.
10. BIS has already granted more than four hundred and forty certificates under this certification scheme to various organization in accordance with IS/ISO 9001 and IS/ISO 9002, covering wide field of economy, including engineering, textiles, chemical, electrical, electronics, cement, pharmaceutical,food, financial, banking services and wholesale & retail trade.

For more details contact: Director (Quality Systems), Bureau of Indian Standards, Manak Bhawan, 9, Bahadur Shah Zafar Marg, New Delhi - 11 0002 Ph: (011) 323 1842, 323 0131 Fax: (011) 323 4062, 323 9399

OR

any of the Regional/Branch Offices of BIS located at Bombay, Calcutta, Chandigarh, New Delhi and Chennai, Ahmedabad, Jaipur, Bangalore, Bhopal, Bhubaneshwar, Coimbatore, Faridabad, Ghaziabad, Guwahati, Hyderabad, Kanpore, Lucknow, Patna, Thiruvanthpuram, Nagpur, Pune, Rajkot.

QUALITY SYSTEMS CERTIFICATION BY BUREAU OF INDIAN STANDARDS

Benefits to, the certified firm

- The firm with BIS Quality Systems Ceritification licence provides:
  - (i) clear indication of its capabilities;
  - (ii) strong evidence of its committment to quality;
  - (iii) assurance of consistence in quality of product/service with timely delivery;
- Disruptions to routine caused due to multiple assessment by various customers are reduced.
- Firm is forced by itself-self motivated to consider improvement to the system regular audits by BIS
- Reduces the incidence of product failure, in-turn improves credibility of the firm.
- Leads to less material wastage, production down time, rework, etc. through an increase in 'quality know-how' and efficiency.
- Being internationally recognized, the firm's quality will have worldwide acceptance.
- Better choice and monitoring of the firm's supplies.
- Puts all operations on a scientific basis.
- Motivates all employees and ensures their involvement.
- Provides stepping stone to TQM.

BENEFITS TO CUSTOMERS

- Provides assurance and satisfaction that their needs for quality will be met.
- Saves time and money by reducing the need for assessment of their suppliers.
- Reduces incoming inspection costs.
- Work with reduced inventory levels, effecting significant cost reductions.
- Simplifies purchase decisions.
- Creates confidence in their suppliers because of the approval by an independent third party.
- Better service (better and quick complaint redressal).

OPERATING QUALITY SYSTEMS
AS PER QUALITY SYSTEM STANDARDS
LEADS TO
DOING RIGHT THINGS
FIRST TIME
EVERY TIME AND ALWAYS TO
THE CUSTOMER'S SATISFACTION

Historical

Construction programmes are interwoven in a large measure in all sectors of development, be it housing, transport, industry, irrigation, power, agriculture, education or health. Construction, both public and private, accounts for about fifty per cent of the total outlay in any five Year Plan. Half of the total money spent on construction activities is spent on buildings for residential, industrial, commercial, administrative, education, medical, municipal and entertainment uses. It is estimated that about half of the total outlay on buildings would be on housing. It is imperative that for such a large national investment, optimum returns are assured and wastage in construction is avoided.

Soon after the Third Plan, the Planning Commission decided that the whole gamut of operations involved in construction, such as administrative, organizational, financial and technical aspects, be studied in depth. For this study, a Panel of Experts was appointed in 1965 by the Planning Commission and its recommendations are found in the 'Report on Economies in Construction Costs' published in 1968.

These studies led to conclusion that one of the important steps towards achieving economy is through the formulation of a unified building code at the national level, which would rationalize and unify building codes and bye laws of various departments and local bodies respectively and which would reflect the latest trends in building construction activity. For this, it was recommended that a Notional Building Code be prepared to unify the building regulations throughout the country for use by government departments, municipal bodies and other construction agencies. The then Indian Standards Institution (now Bureau of Indian Standards) was entrusted by the Planning Commission with the preparation of the National Building Code. For fulfilling this task a Guiding Committee for the preparation of the Code was set up by the Civil Engineering Division Council of the Indian Standards Institution in 1967. This Committee, in turn, set up 18 specialist panels to prepare the various parts of the Code. The Guiding Committee and its panels were constituted with architects, planners, materials experts, structural, construction, electrical illumination, air-conditioning, acoustics and public health engineers and town planners. These experts were drawn from the Central and State Governments, local bodies, professional institutions and private agencies. The first version of the Code was published in 1970. After the National Building Code of India was published in 1970, a vigorous implementation drive was launched by the Indian Standards Institution to propagate the contents and use of the Code among all concerned in the field of planning, designing and construction activities.

Since the publication in 1970 version of the National Building Code of India, a large number of comments and useful suggestions for modifications and additions to different parts and sections of the Code were received as a result of use of the Code by all concerned, and revision work of building byelaws of some States. Based on the comments and suggestions received the National Building Code of India, 1970 was revised in 1983.

Some of the important changes in 1983 version included: addition of development control rules, requirements for greenbelts and landscaping including norms for plantation of shrubs and trees, special requirements for low income housing; fire safety regulations for high rise buildings; revision of structural design section based on new and revised codes, such as Concrete Codes, Earthquake Code, Masonry Code; addition of outside design conditions for important cities in the country, requirements relating to noise and vibration, air filter, automatic control, energy conservation for air-conditioning; and guidance on the design of water supply system for multi-storeyed buildings.

Thereafter three major amendments were issued to the Code, two in 1987 and the third in 1997. Considering a series of further developments in the field of building construction including the lessons learnt in the aftermath of number of natural calamities like devastating earthquakes and super cyclones witnessed by the country, a Project for comprehensive revision of the Code was taken up under the aegis of National Building Code Sectional Committee, CED 46 of BIS and its 18 expert Panels; involving as many as 400 experts. As a culmination of the Project, the revised Code has been brought out in 2005 as **National Building Code of India 2005** reflecting the state-of-the-art and contemporary applicable international practices. The salient features of this latest revision of the Code are:

(1) Inclusion of a complete philosophy and direction for successfully accomplishing the building projects through Integrated Multidisciplinary Approach right from conceptual stage through planning, designing, construction, operation and maintenance stages.

(2) A series of reforms in building permit process.

(3) Provisions for ensuring and certification of safety of buildings against natural disaster by engineer and structural engineer.

(4) Provision for two stage permit for high rise residential and special buildings.

(5) Provision for periodic renewal certificate of occupied buildings from structural, fire, electrical and health safety point of view.

(6) Provision for empowering engineers and architects for sanctioning plans of residential buildings up to 500 m^2.

(7) Inclusion of detailed town planning norms for various amenities such as educational facilities, medical facilities, distribution services, police, civil defence, fire services, etc.

(8) Revision of parking requirements for metro and mega cities.

(9) Updating of special requirements for low income housing for urban areas

(10) Inclusion of special requirements for low income housing for rural habitat planning.

(11) Inclusion of guidelines for development planning for hilly areas.

(12) Revision of the provisions for buildings and facilities for physically challenged.

(13) Fire safety norms completely revamped through detailed provisions on Fire Prevention, Life Safety and Fire Protection.

(14) Inclusion of new categories of starred hotels, heritage structures and archeological monuments for fire safety provisions.

(15) Substitution of halon based fire extinguishers/fire fighting system.

(16) Promotion to new/innovative building materials/technologies.

(17) Inclusion of latest provisions for earthquake resistant design and construction.

(18) Inclusion of details on multi-disaster prone districts.

(19) Inclusion of new chapter on design and construction using bamboo.

(20) Chapter on prefabricated and composite construction for speedier construction.

(21) Updating of provision of safety in construction.

(22) Complete revision of provision on building and plumbing services in line with applicable international practices.

(23) Provisions on rain water harvesting.

(24) Inclusion of new chapter to cover landscaping needs.

ACTUAL COVERAGE

The National Building Code lays down a set of minimum provisions designed to protect the safety of the public with regard to structural sufficiency, fire safety and health aspects of buildings; so long as these basic requirements are met, the choice of material, methods of design and construction is left to the ingenuity of competent professionals. It covers, *inter alia* the following important aspects:

(a) Integrated approach through multi-disciplinary team work to obtain maximum benefits in terms of quality, timely completion and cost effectiveness by utilizing appropriate knowledge and experience of qualified professionals right from the conceptualization through design, construction and completion stages of a building project and in deed during the entire life cycle.

(b) Administrative provisions which pertain to the efficiency and effective application of the Code defining powers, duties and responsibilities of those concerned;

(c) Requirements to ensure safety from fire and health hazards related to the occupancy and use of buildings;

(d) Stipulations with regard to use of accepted and new building materials from consideration of safety, performance, compatibility, durability and economy;

(e) Design practices for structures as a whole using various materials like reinforced and prestressed concrete, structural steel, timber, bamboo, masonry, etc., and guidelines for design of prefabricated structures and mixed/composite constructions, duly taking into account the various loads, forces and effects including due to natural calamities like earthquake;

(f) Measures to ensure safety of workers and public during construction;

(g) Provisions for safe and efficient design or lighting, ventilation, electrical and allied installations, air conditioning, heating, lift and escalator installations, and acoustics systems;

(h) Provisions with regard to the requirements of water supply, drainage and sanitation including solid waste management and the design of water supply and drainage system in buildings, and safety requirements for the installation of gas supply; and

(i) Requirements regarding landscape planning and design and signs and outdoor display structures with a view to promoting safety and quality of outdoor built environment.

This information is brought out in 11 Parts, details of which are given below:

PART 0 INTEGRATED APPROACH - PREREQUISITE FOR APPLYING PROVISIONS OF THE CODE
PART 1 DEFINITIONS
PART 2 ADMINISTRATION
PART 3 DEVELOPMENT CONTROL RULES AND GENERAL BUILDING REQUIREMENTS
PART 4 FIRE AND LIFE SAFETY
PART 5 Building MATERIALS
PART 6 Structural DESIGN
- Section 1 Loads, Forces and Effects
- Section 2 Soils and Foundations
- Section 3 Timber and Bamboo
  - 3A Timber
  - 3B Bamboo
- Section 4 Masonry
- Section 5 Contrete
  - 5A Plain and Reinfor(ed Con (rete
  - 5B Prestressed Contrete
- Section 6 Steel
- Section 7 Prefabrication, Systems Building and Mixed/ Composite Construction
  - 7 A Prefabriated Concrete
  - 7B Systems Building and Mixed/Composite Construction

PART 7 CONSTRUCTIONAl PRACTICES AND SAFETY
PART 8 BUILDING SERVICES
- Section 1 Lighting and Ventilation
- Section 2 Electrical and Allied Installations
- Section 3 Air conditioning, Heating and Mechanical Ventilation

	Section 4	Acoustics, Sound Insulation and Noise Control
	Section 5	Installation of lifts and Escalators
PART 9	PLUMBING SERVICES	
	Section 1	Water Supply, Drainage and Sanitation (induding Solid Waste Management)
	Section 2	Gas Supply
PART 10	LANDSCAPING, SIGNS AND OUTDOOR DISPLAY STRUCTURES	
	Section 1	Landslape Planning and Design
	Section 2	Signs and Outdoor Display Structures

Theme of the Code

The National Building Code of India is a single document in which, like a network, the information contained in various Indian Standards and other information is woven into a pattern of continuity and cogency with the interdependent requirements of Parts/Sections of the Code carefully analyzed and fitted in to make the whole document a cogent continuous volume. Thus the Code gives all the information required by the architect, engineer, structural engineer, construction engineer, services engineers and other professionals from the early stages of planning to translating the building on to terra firma.

The provisions of the whole Code have been drafted with performance orientation, with a view to giving full freedom to the ingenuity of the architects and engineers. However, in certain cases, these performance oriented clauses have been translated into empirical rules for easy implementation of such provisions.

The whole Code has been built around the four pillars of safety, namely, (i) structural safety, (ii) health safety, (iii) fire safety, and (iv) public safety (encompassing electrical safety and safety during construction). The various provisions of this Code have been specified after checking them against these safety requirements.

This Code strongly emphasizes the importance of preplanning in the construction activity and lays down areas where preplanning would have to be done in a more co-ordinated manner. A continuous thread of preplanning is woven which, in itself, contributes almost two-thirds of economics in construction particularly in building and plumbing services. The need for spaces and areas required for such services is brought out so that the same can be assessed at the planning stage and provided for.

The need for proper planning and coordination among professionals right from conceptualization to completion and subsequently in operation and maintenance, has been conspicuously brought out in Part 0 of this Code.

As this Code is intended to help regulate the building construction activity for the whole country, this would be applicable to municipal corporations, local urban bodies, public works departments and other construction departments and agencies dealing with construction. Therefore, the administrative byelaws and technical provisions, which are required in these regulatory media, are both included in the Code.

The Code as now published represents the present state of knowledge on various aspects of building construction. The process of preparation of the Code has thrown a number of important issues which have been duly dealt with. However, a continuous programme is envisaged by which additional knowledge that is gained through technological evolution, users' views over a period of time pinpointing areas of clarification and coverage and results of research in various connected fields, would be incorporated in the Code from time to time to make it a living document.

Implementation

The National Building Code of India is intended to serve as a model for adoption by PWDs and other construction departments, local bodies and other construction agencies. Existing PWD codes, municipal byelaws and other regulatory media could either be replaced by the National Building Code of India or suitably modified to cater to local conditions in accordance with the provisions of the Code.

In the case of municipalities and other local bodies which are the main agencies to regulate the main building activity within the jurisdiction of the cities and towns, it is the administrative requirements and byelaws provisions for the health safety aspects which should mainly constitute the coverage of their byelaws. Guidelines on all these aspects are included in the National Building Code of India. The information cited above is mainly covered in Parts 2, 3, 4, 5 and 10 of the Code. The other parts of the Code are equally valid and should be referred to in the bye laws.

In the case of Public Works Departments of the States and Centre, MES, Railways and other governmental construction agencies who would regulate the construction within their jurisdiction with the help of their handbooks, codes and specifications of works, it is the information contained in Parts 0, 5,6,7,8 and 9 of the Code which should mainly be used/adopted to modernize their regulatory media. The present PWD specifications and handbooks essentially deal with the materials specifications and the construction procedures for various items of work; these requirements are given in Parts 0, 5 and 7 of the Code. The structural design requirements and procedure for the design and installation of various services, etc, are not covered in detail in the above codes and detailed information on the same is given in Parts 6, 7, 8 and 9 of the Code. Even though the essential contents of the departmental code should be aimed only for the design and construction of the buildings, there are certain planning requirements which should also be included in these codes, which are covered in Parts 3 and 4; depending upon the setup in each department, information from the above parts should be included in their regulations.

In the case of other constructional agencies like public sector projects, the whole Code would be applicable to them and implementation of the complete Code would result in substantial economies along with safety. Similarly the private construction agencies should make full use of the provisions of the Code.

Publication

The Code has been published in one full volume containing all the Parts and Sections. Besides, five separate groups to cater largely to the interest/agency dealing with different aspects of building activity have also been published as follows:

		Price	
		₹	US$
Full Volume (Parts 0 to 10 all sections included)		8700	1740
Group 1 (Parts 0, 2, 3, 4, 5 and Part 10 Sections 1 & 2) For Planning	Building/Development work	2330	470
Group 2 (Part 0 and Part 6 Sections 1 to 7)	For Structural Design	3380	675
Group 3 (Part 0 and Part 7)	For Constructional aspects	830	170
Group 4 (Part 0 and Part 8 Sections 1 to 5)	For Building Services	2180	435
Group 5 (Part 0 and Part 9 Sections 1 & 2)	For Plumbing Services	1060	210

However, while using a particular group, it may be borne in mind that there are other areas of information available in other groups which would require the attention of the same agency even if not directly connected with that phase of work. For example, while Group 1 would mainly help in planning the building schemes, Group 4 and Group 5 also draw the attention from the point of view of preplanning in respect of building and plumbing services.

Bureau of indian standards
Manak Bhavan, 9 Bahadur Shah Zafar Marg, New Delhi-110 002
Website : www.bis.org.in

BIS & Small-scale Industries

It is common knowledge that small-scale sector has contributed to the industrialization of the country to a very large extent and our planners have been ascribing it a place of prominence in our various 5-year plans. Even though small-scale enterprises have come a long way since the plan process began in the country, a proper environment conducive to their harmonious growth and efficient operations to dovetail in overall development of the economy to its desired level needs to be created. BIS has also had a special relationship with the small-scale sector. Right from the inception of Certification Scheme, small-scale units were especially assisted in obtaining certification and concessions were provided to them. Over the years, these concessions have been maintained. With the changing global trade and influx of multinational companies (MNCs) into the country, BIS commitment to small-scale sector has been further strengthened so that they survive the onslaught and contribute to increasing the exports. Standardization, Quality Certification - both Product and System (ISO 9000) are important catalysts for achieving competitiveness.

What BIS Does

BIS is the National Standards Organization (NSO) established as Society in 1947 as Indian Standards Institution and subsequently made a Statutory Body as BIS under the Bureau of Indian Standards (BIS) Act 1986. BIS is engaged in Standards formulation; Certification of products and quality management system of an organization; Training standardization and quality management; Consultancy; Information Services and providing technical help to exporters.

Standardization

National Standards for the country are formulated by BIS and are known as Indian Standards. These standards reflect the State of Art technology and experience of manufacturers, technologists and users, etc. They also provide the basis for organizing production of goods at the economical cost and optimum quality level. These standards are reviewed regularly to keep them current in context of modern technical developments. Presently over 17,000 Indian Standards are in force.

Information Centres

In order to assist the small-scale industries, BIS has established 'Standards Information Centres' in the industrial areas which are away from BIS Branches so that entrepreneurs could get advantage of referring to Indian as well as foreign standards at their doorsteps. Two such centres at Mysore and Jamshedpur are already functioning and the third centre has been established recently at Agra on the request of DCSSI, to cater to large concentration of small enterprises in and around Agra.

BIS Certification Mark

BIS operates a Certification Marks Scheme under the Bureau of Indian Standards Act 1986. The Certification Mark granted under the scheme is known as Standard Mark. This ISI Mark is an assurance of product conformity to the specification under the scheme. A manufacturer is granted licence to use the Standard Mark after assessment of his infrastructure facilities for manufacturing and quality control checks to produce goods of consistent quality as per relevant standard.

The conformity to standards is further ensured by regular surveillance of licensee's performance by surprise inspections and testing of samples drawn both from the factory and the market. Some of the Government organizations and Public Sector Undertakings have taken policy decision to purchase BIS Certified goods only. Financial institutions provide various incentives to the small-scale sector like subsidy for setting up laboratories, rebate in interest rate on loans for joining Certification Scheme, etc. BIS also gives concessions to small-scale manufacturers in the fee payable for certification.

BIS Certification Scheme has helped the Small-Scale Sector to upgrade quality and compete with large-scale sector thereby dispelling the myth that the Small-Scale Sector cannot produce quality products. PVC Pipes, Diesel Engines, Cables & Conductors and Deepwell Handpumps are some of the prime examples of products where large scale sector opted voluntarily for Certification Scheme first but in no time, the Small-Scale Sector has achieved the desired quality levels. Today majority of the manufacturers are from the Small-Scale Sector and holding BIS licence for these products.

ECO Mark

The Ministry of Environment and Forests, Government of India has instituted in February 1991 a scheme known as 'ECO Mark Scheme' for labelling environment friendly products and this scheme is operated by BIS. The scheme provides for labelling of household and other consumer products which meet certain environmental criteria along with quality requirements prescribed in relevant Indian Standards. Additional requirements for ECO Mark now form part of the concerned Indian Standard for Certification. ECO Mark is a combination of BIS Standard Mark and the ECO Logo.

Quality System Certification

BIS was the first agency authorised by Government of India to operate Quality System Certification under the provisions of the Bureau of Indian Standards Act, 1986. BIS has adopted ISO 9000 series of International Standards as Indian Standards under dual numbering system. The operation of the scheme entails initial assessment and subsequent surveillance of the Quality System installed and implemented by the organization for verification of its conformity to prescribed requirement of the respective quality systems standards. BIS Quality Systems Certification Scheme is accredited by Radd voor Accreditatie (RvA) Netherlands.

EMS Certification

With the growing concern for environment friendly industrial activity, ISO 14000 series of standards have been developed. BIS, after adoption of these standards as national standards, has launched Environment Management System (EMS) Certification.

HACCP Certification

BIS launched HACCP (Hazard Analysis and Critical Control Points) based on Quality System Certification Scheme as per the requirements of IS 15000: 1998 standard (equivalent to Codex ALINORM 97/13A).

Advisory Services Relating to BIS Certification and ISO 9000/ISO 14000 Certification

BIS also provides advisory services and the necessary steps required to get licence under BIS Certification and Quality Systems Certification Scheme. Details about test equipment required for testing of product as per relevant Indian Standards would also be provided to entrepreneurs on nominal charges.

ISO 9000/ISO 14000 Certification

To assist the industry, specially small scale manufacturers to adopt quality system standards, BIS provides the following pre-certification services:

Quality System Appreciation Programme

Quality System Survey

Quality System Trial Assessment

Awareness and Training Programmes

Awareness programme on *Standardization and Quality Systems specifically designed for small scale sector is organized all over the country by BIS. In the above programme* a *session* on *'financial Matters' has also been included where the faculty apprises the participants seeking clarifications about various schemes/assistance available for quality upgradation.*

BIS organizes training programmes in a *number of areas, namely Quality System, Company Standardization, Statistical Quality Control and Laboratory Testing.*

Quality Systems Appreciation Programme *- Quality Systems Appreciation Programme provides thorough knowledge of the requirements applicable to IS/ISO 9000 series of standards, the assessment process and procedures and the methodology for installation and operation of applicable quality system standards.*

Company Standardization *- This training programme covers concepts, areas, techniques and organizational aspects of company standardization. The programme is organized at the specific request of* a *company to initiate their managers and supervisors in the concepts and techniques of Company Standardization. BIS also provides consultancy for establishing and strengthening company standardization activity in industry..*

Statistical Quality Control *- The training programme provides detailed information relating to principles and application of SQC with particular emphasis* on *process control and sampling techniques. SQC consultancy services are also provided to industries to tackle various quality problems by the application of SQC techniques. The programme can be conducted for company or group of individual managers belonging to different companies.*

Laboratory Testing *- The training* on *laboratory testing relating to* a *particular product is provided by BIS* on *request of BIS licensees. Such training helps the licensees in streamlining the procedures, improving quality and productivity. Such training may also be provided to aspiring applicants, if they are in sufficient number in* a *particular field.*

Information Services

Technical Enquiry Service *- Technical enquiries from industry, exporters and individuals received through telephone, fax letters and in person, are answered by the professional staff. Enquiries related to the Indian Standards are answered free of cost whereas enquiries about the foreign standards corresponding to Indian Standards taking more than 10 minutes time are charged at the rate of ₹ 250/- per hour.*

ISO Information Network *- BIS exchanges standards and information with other national standards bodies under ISONET Exchange Programme. BIS also disseminates the information received through the ISO Committee* on *Information (INFCO) to the users in India.*

GATT/WTO Enquiry Point *- The Government of India (Ministry of Commerce) designated BIS as the Central Enquiry Point for India in 1983 under the GATT Agreement* on *Technical Barriers to Trade. BIS provides information* on *standards, regulations and certification systems of member countries of World Trade Organization (WTO) to Indian exporters and about India to other member countries. Notifications* on *proposed standards and regulations received from WTO are disseminated to industry. Similarly the notifications* on *proposed Indian Standards for which there is* no *International Standard and in which there is some deviation from the corresponding International Standard are sent to WTO* on a *regular basis for receiving comments from the member countries of WTO.*

Manaksandarbhika *- BIS is maintaining* a *database of bibliographies of foreign standards known as 'Manaksandarbhika'. The information relates to standards published by standards bodies of the world. It has got more than 2.5lakh records about the standards published. Each record contains subject code, country code, designation of the standard and the title. The database is updated every month. This information is provided* on *chargeable basis.*

Buyers' Guide *- Database of manufacturers authorised to use BIS Certification Mark* on *their products is available with* a *user friendly retrieval software* on *floppy diskettes. It gives names and addresses of the manufacturers who are authorised to use BIS Certification Mark* on *their* products, *licence number and validity of the licence held by the manufacturer. The Database is useful for the purchaser, consumer organizations and government departments. It is updated monthly and the updates are available* on *demand to the users. The initial set of floppy diskettes is presently priced at ₹ 1,000/- and monthly update service can be subscribed to* an *annual fee of ₹ 1,000/-.*

Specific Financial Incentives to Small-scale Enterprises

1. **BIS Certification Marking**

   Marking fee concession up to a *maximum* of *₹ 10,000/- depending* on *type of product*

   (This concession is applicable on *the minimum marking fee only).*

2. **IS/ISO 9000 Certification**

   Application fee of ₹ *10,000/-* for small scale industries as against ₹ *15,000/-* for large scale.

   Licence fee of ₹ *40,000/- for small scale industries as against* ₹ *60,000/- for large scale for a period of three years.*

3. **Incentives by Government and Financial Institutions**

   Specific incentives to particular sectors of *the industry are provided by the Government of India, various State governments and financial institutions. These details are available with BIS.*

BIS Single Window for Small-scale Entrepreneurs

BIS provides information and assistance on *all the above aspects through its INFORMAtiON & SSI FACILITATION CELL located at BIS Headquarters at New Delhi. The CELL helps the Entrepreneurs in locating appropriate standards whether for domestic* or *export trade; identifying test equipment or obtaining Certification Mark; helping prospective licensees with training programmes, ISO Awareness and Advisory Services; identifying export markets and the applicable standards and other related information in the field* of *Quality.*

For further details in any of *the above services, please contact :*

Director (Standards Promotion)
Bureau of Indian Standards
Manakalaya, 9 B.S. Zafar Marg, New Delhi - 110002
Tel: 3235069,3239401 Fax: +91 11-3234062,3239382,3239399

"CONSUMER IS THE KING"

REFERENCES

Adulteration of food and other commodities — *Consumer Bulletin*, 18 February 1974, pp.18-19.

Andreasen, Allan R and Best, Arthur, "Consumer complain" – does business responds? – *Harvard Business Review* Vo. 35, July August 1977, pp. 94-104.

Association Bulletin Vo. XI, No. 4, April 1986, p. 180.

Barksdale, Hiram C and darden, William R "Consumer attitudes towards Marketing and Consumerism" – *Journal of Marketing* Vol. 36, October 1972, pp. 28-35.

Ashok R. Patil "Consumer Protection in Educational Services" *University News*, No. 47, No. 19. pp. 1–8

Barksdale, Hiram C, French Warren A , "Response to Consumerism – How change is perceived on both sides" – MSU **Business Topic,** Vol. 23, No.2, 1975 pp. 55-67.

Barnhill, J.A, Barksdale , Hiram C and Perreault William D jr. "Marketing , Consumerism and Government – A comparison of American Canadian Attitudes" – **Journal of Contemporary Business,** Vol. 10 , No. 4, 1981, pp. 59-80.

Basu, Geeta, Consumer Protection – **Consumers' Action Forum News Letter,** January – March, 1986.

Blood, Peter B, "U K Marketers call consumerism both challenge, opportunity", — **Marketing News** Vol 10 , No. 1, July 1976, p. 6.

Buskirk, Richard H and Rothe, James T "Consumerism – An Interpretation" __ **Journal of Marketing** Vol. 34 , October 1970, pp. 61-65.

"Consumer Movement in India" – **Economic Times,** 25th September, 1982.

"Consumer Safety and satisfaction – a key to successful marketing" – **Report on Consumer Action Forum Survey,** Calcutta, May 1987.

Dr. Agarwal V.K., Consumer Protection Law and Practice – Bharat's

Consumer Protection Mannual with practice Manual – **Taxman's** New Delhi.

Demeron, Kenneth, "The Consumer Movement" – **Harvard Business Review,** XVII , 1939, pp. 276-277

Day, Georges' and Akker, david "A guide to Consumerism" —— **Journal of Marketing,** Vol. 34, July 1970 pp. 12-19

Dholakia, Nikhilesh and Bhandari, Labdhari and Khurana, Rakesh , "Consumer protection : Some Policy Issues" — **Economic Times,** 20th November, 1976.

Drucker , Peter, "Speech to the National Association of Manufacturers" – **Marketing News,** 15th October 1969.

Engel, James F., Kollet, David T. and Block Well, Roger D., **Consumer Behaviour** – Dryden Press, Hinsdale Illinos 1973, p. 614

Foxall, Gordon, "Towards a balanced View of consumerism"— **European Journal of Marketing** (UK), Vol. 12, No. 4, 1978, pp. 264-274.

Gaedeke, Ralph M, **Consumerism in the 1980's,** A study of the development of underlying reasons for the Business Relation to Todays' Consumer Protection Movement – University of Washington Press 1969.

Gaedeke, Ralph M, "the Movement for Consumer Protection : A century of mixed accomplishments" – **University of Washington Review** Vol.29 No.3, 1970 pp.31-40.

Gaedeke, Ralph M. and Etcheson, Warren W., **Consumerism Viewpoints form Business Government and the Public Interests,** 1972 – Harper and Row, Publishers 49 East 33rd Street, New Work 10016.

Jenes, Mary, Gardnier , "The Consumer Movement and Marketing" – **Executive Vol.** 4 1978 p.19.

Garg , R.B.L., "The Consumer at bay" **The Financial Express,** 10th February 1981, p. 5.

Greenland , Leo, "Consumerism – Cold War gets Hotter" – **Market Times,** Vol 21, No.1 January/February, 1974, pp. 4 -6.

Greyser, Stephen A and Diamond, Stephen L, "Business is adapting to Consumerism" – **Harvard Business Review,** September/ October 1974

Greyser , Stephen A, "How the American Public Views Consumerism" – **Advertising Quarterly** (UK) No. 54, 1977/78, pp. 28-34.

Gupta, Joyeeta "Consumerism: Emerging Challenges and Opportunities" — **Vikalpa,** Vo. II, No.2 April – June 1986, pp. 149- 158.

Hidayatullah M – **Readers Digest** , India November 1984.

Jacob, Thankama, **A Consumer Guide** – McMillan Company of India. Ltd, 1977.

Jenes, Mary Gardnier, "The Consumer Movement and Marketing" **Executive Vol. 4**, No.3 1978, pp. 16-19.

Kallet Arther and Schlink, F.J, **100,000,000 Guineapigs** – Grosset and Dunlop, New York 1933.

Kangun Norman, Cox, Keith K Higginbotham James and Burton, James "Consumerism and marketing management" – **Journal of Marketing** Vol.39, April 1975 pp.3-10.

Keith Robert J, "The Marketing Revolution" – **Journal of Marketing, American Association,** January 1960 pp.35-38

Kotler, Philip "What Consumerism means for Marketing" – **Harvard Business Review,** May June 1972, pp.48-57

Lamb Ruth de Forest, **American Chambers of Harrors – the Truth about Food and drugs** – Farror and Rinehard, New York 1936

McDaniel, Tsephen W, "Marketing Malpractices : The nedd for marketing quality control" – **M/s South Journal,** Vol. 1 No.4, October ,1981, pp.14-18

Mehta D.S., "Changing face of Indian Consumer" – **Hindustan Times** 2 May, 1992, pp.29.

Narayanan , P.S., "The Beleaguered Consumer" – **The Hindu** 16th July 1979.

Nicholas Frank C, "Weigh Market, Head Critics" – **Marketing News,** Vol II, No. 26 , 30th June 1978m pp. 8-9.

Nicoulaud, Brigitte M.M, "Consumerism and Marketing Management responsibility" – **European Journal of Marketing** (UK) Vol.2, 1987, pp.7-16.

Patel J.S.Km "What Consumerism Means" – **Eastern Economist,** 12th September 1974.

Pesticides Residues – **Financial Express** 28th February 1985

Poduval, P.R, "**Consumerism : Social significance and effectiveness", In Consumer Protection and Legal Control** (Edited by P. Leelakrishnan), Eastern Book Company, Lucknow, 1981, pp. 41-48.

Rayudu, C.S "Consumer Movement in India" – **Indian Journal of Marketing** Vol. 16, no.1 and 2, September – October, 1983 p.23.

Resnik, Alan J. and Hermon, Robert R., "Consumer Complaints and Managerial response:A Holistic approach" – **Journal of Marketing** Vol. 47 1983 pp. 86- 97.

Roy, P.K. and Srivastave K.P., "Public Distribution System in Bihar" – **Yojana** 16th June, 1980, p. 30.

Sengupta S.P., *Commentaries on the Consumer Protection Act.* Kumar Law. pp. 3-43

Seventh Schedule to the Constitution List III Entry 18 – **Government Of India Gazette, Extraordinary Part II,** Section 1, 17th February, 1976.

Shankariah A. Ojha, Ghanshyam Das, and Sadanandam R, "Problems of Public Distribution System" —**Yojana** 16th February 1982, p. 17.

Sheth, J.N. "Cross cultural Influence on Buyer—Seller Interaction Negotiation Proces – **Faculty Working Papers,** University of Illinos September 1980 p. 11.

Siegal, Sidney, **Non-parametric Statistics for the Behavioural Sciences,** McGrawhill, Kigakusha Ltd., Tokyo 1956, pp. 229- 238.

Singh K. Food Adulteration in the State of Jammu and Kashmir – a survey – **Journal of the Indian Law Institute,** Vo. 31,No.1 1989, pp. 91-105.

Singh, Rghbir "Consumer Attitudes towards consumerism – An Explanatory Study" – **Consumer Confrontation,** vol. 10, No.1 jan- Feb 1990, pp.8-11.

Sigh Raghbir "How do consumers perceive Consumerism – An Explanatory Study" – **Management and Labour Studies,** Vol. 15, No.3 July 1990, pp.146-152.

Sinha B.P., *Readings in Kautillyas Aarthasastras* – Agma Prakasan, Delhi 1976, pp. 69-71.

Sixth Five Year Plan 1980 -85 – **Planning Commission Government of India,** 1981 p.81.

Straver, Will "The Consumerist Movement in Europe" – **European Journal of Marketing** (UK) Vol.12, No.4, 1978 pp.316-325.

Sundaram I, Satya, **Consumer Protection in India** – B.R, Publishing Corporation, 1985pp.55-56.

"Ten years of Community Consumer Policy" – EEC Document Brussel, XI/822.1986 – En p.1.

Thomas , T – Speech delivered at the 4th Annual General Meeting of Hindustan Levers Ltd. 1977.

Trade Prctices Commissions, "Survey of Consumer Opinion in Australlia" – **Australian Government Publishing Service**, Canberra , January 1987.

Trivedi B.B. "Economics of Public Distribution Syatem" – **Indian Consumer Cooperator,** March 1979

US Congress, Senate Committee on Government Operation hearings — The Federal Role in Traffic Safety; **89th Congress First Session,** 1965, p.784.

Verma, D.P.S., "Need for consumer protection laws" – **Economic Times** 21st June 1978.

Verma D.P.S "Regulation of restrictive Trade Practices" – Department of Commerce, Delhi University Ph. D Thesis August 1980.

Willbeforce, Lord, Campbell , Alan and Elles Neil The **Law of Restrictive Trade Practices and Monopolies,** Chapter 1 and 2 1966.

Wig, A.R "Making the Consumr aware of Rights – **The Hindustan Times,** 31 August 1986.

Wright R.L.D, Understanding Statistics on Informal Introduction for the Behavioural Sciences—Hard court Brace, Jovanovich, Inc. New York, 1976.

Yogender T.Y., "Case for Consumer Movement"—**Mainstream,** 5th July 1980, p.17.

Zahn Paul, "Mews Advocacy Role will have strong impact on Marketing" – **Advertising Age,** Vol. 48, no. 12, 21st March 1977, p. 24.

FURTHER READING

Legislative Support for Women

Women-specific Legislations

- The Immoral Traffic (Prevention) Act, 1956
- The Dowry Prohibition Act, 1961 (28 of 1961)
- The Indecent Representation of Women (Prohibition) Act, 1986
- The Commission of Sati (Prevention) Act, 1987 (3 of 1988)

Women-related Legislations

- The Guardians and wards Act, 1860 (8 of 1890)
- Indian Penal Code, 1860
- The Christian Marriage Act, 1872 (15 of 1872)
- The Indian Evidence Act, 1872 (yet to be reviewed)
- The Married Women's Property Act, 1874 (3 of 1874)
- The Workmen's Compensation Act, 1923
- The Legal Practitioners (Women) Act, 1923
- The Indian Succession Act, 1925 (39 of 1925)
- The Child Marrige Restraint Act, 1998 (19 of 1929)
- The Payments of Wages Act, 1936
- The Muslim Personal Law (Shariat) Application Act, 1937
- The Factories Act, 1948
- The Minimum Wages Act, 1948
- The Employees' State Insurance Act, 1948
- The Plantation Labour Act, 1951
- The Cinematograph Act, 1952
- The special Marriage Act, 1954
- The Hindu Marriage Act, 1955 (28 of 1989)
- The Hindu Adoptions & Maintenance Act, 1956
- The Hindu Minority & Guardianship Act, 1956
- The Hindu Succession Act, 1956
- The Maternity Benefit Act, 1961 (53 of 1961)
- The Beedi & Cigar Workers (conditions of Employment) Act, 1966
- The Foreign Marriage Act, 1969 (33 of 1969)
- The Indian Divorce Act, 1969 (4 of 1969)
- The Medical Termination of Pregnancy Act, 1971 (34 of 1971)
- Code of Criminal Procedure, 1973
- The Bonded Labour System (Abolition) Act, 1976
- The Equal Remuneration Act, 1976
- The Contract Labour (Regulation & Abolition) Act, 1976
- The Inter-State Migrant Workmen (Regulation of Employment and Conditions of Service) Act, 1979

- The Family Courts Act, 1984
- Juvenile Justice Act, 1986
- The Child Labour (Prohibition & Regulation) Act, 1986
- National Commission for Women Act, 1990 (20 of 1990)
- The Infant Milk Substitutes, Feeding Bottles and Infant Foods (Regulation of Production, Supply and Distribution Act, 1992
- The Pre-natal Diagnostic Technique (Regulation and Prevention of Misuse) Act, 1994

FOR CONSUMERS' INFORMATION

National Consumer Disputes Redressal Commission
Janpath Bhavan, 'A' Wing, 5th Floor, Janpath,
New Delhi - 110 001.
Phone: 23712109, Dy. Registrar: 23358074. Fax: 011 23712456.

State Consumer Disputes Redressal Commission
Bhavani Bhavan, (Ground Floor), Calcutta - 700 027
Phone: 2479-9871

BIBLIOGRAPHY

1. Joel Barker, video – The Power of Vision. Charterhouse Learning.
2. QFD Manual American Supplier Institute, 15041 S. Commerce Drive, Dearborn, Michigan 48120.
3. American Supplier Institute, Quality Systems, Challenge House, Sherwood Drive, Bletchley, Milton Keynes MK3 6DR.
4. American Supplier Institute, Executive Awareness – the methods of Dr Genichi Taguchi.
5. Poka-yoke, Improving Product Quality by Preventing Defects, Nikkan Kogyo Shimbun, Ltd/Factory Magazine. Productivity Press, Cambridge Massachusetts.
6. Measurement Systems Analysis, Reference Manual, AIAG.
7. Introduction to Quality Engineering, Genichi Taguchi, Asian Productivity Organisation.
8. General Motors Ltd and its subsidiaries.
9. Ford Motor Co for the use of FMEA techniques.
10. Conway Quality Inc. in association with like Gallimore & Associates Ltd – Training Course.
11. Shainin Consultants, Inc. – Observing various techniques.
12. BSI – Quality Assurance – Training Course.
13. "How to Eat an Elephant" – book by my friend, John Gilbert.
14. "Demings Road to Continual Improvement" – book by William W. Scherkenbach.
15. "Murphy's Law" – book by Arthur Bloch.
16. "Taguchi Methodology with Total Quality" – book by Graham Wilson & Robert Millar.
17. "Gower Handbook of Quality Management" – book edited by Dennis Lock.
18. "Creating Culture Change: the key to successful Total Quality Management" – book by Philip E. Atkinson.
19. Winning with Quality – book by Rory L. Chase.

I would like to thank all who have influenced my thinking and generally contributed to the development of my thoughts in writing this book.

P.K. Dutta,

Flat No. 204, Block No. B, 2nd Floor

Ganges Shubham, 29/E/1/A

Birpara Lane, Kolkata-30